W9-CMM-400

LEARNING DISABILITIES

Fourth Edition

LEARNING

Basic Concepts, Assessment Prac

DISABILITIES

tices, and Instructional Strategies

Patricia I. Myers
Donald D. Hammill

pro·ed

8700 Shoal Creek Boulevard
Austin, Texas 78758

© 1982, 1990 by Patricia I. Myers and Donald D. Hammill

Portions of this book first appeared in *Methods for Learning Disorders* by Patricia I. Myers and Donald D. Hammill, © 1969, 1976, published by John Wiley and Sons, Inc.

All rights reserved. No part of this book may be reproduced in any form or by any means without the prior written permission of the publisher.

Printed in the United States of America

Library of Congress Cataloging-in-Publication Data

Myers, Patricia I., 1929–
    Learning disabilities: basic concepts, assessment practices, and instructional strategies / Patricia I. Myers, Donald D. Hammill.— 4th ed.
        p. cm.
    Includes bibliographical references.
    ISBN 0-89079-225-9
    1. Learning disabilities. 2. Learning disabled children— Education. 3. Handicapped—Education. I. Hammill, Donald D., 1934–   . II. Title.
LC4704.M93   1990
371.9—dc20   89-29044
                                                         CIP

pro·ed

8700 Shoal Creek Boulevard
Austin, Texas 78758

10 9 8 7 6 5 4 3 2 1   90 91 92 93 94

LC
4704
.M93
.1990

CONTENTS

v

PART II: ASSESSMENT PRACTICES IN LEARNING DISABILITIES

PART III: REMEDIATING SPECIFIC LEARNING DISABILITIES

PART IV: ADJUNCTIVE THERAPIES THAT INFLUENCE INSTRUCTION

PREFACE

The present revision of *Learning Disabilities: Basic Concepts, Assessment Practices, and Instructional Strategies* is the fourth edition of the book published in 1969 under the title *Methods for Learning Disorders*. The field of learning disabilities has made significant progress in those past 20 years. Such progress may be noted in the quantity and quality of research aimed at better defining the specific problems of learning disabled persons, at investigating the cognitive, rather than perceptual, aspects of the problem, and at probing the adult status of learning disabled persons. In addition, the National Joint Committee for Learning Disabilities (NJCLD), composed of representatives from eight influential professional and parent associations, has evolved a common definition of learning disabilities (see Chapter 1).

However, in spite of a commonly accepted organizational definition of learning disabilities, many researchers and practitioners have continued to redefine the problem allowing more and more students with borderline intellectual ability, linguistic and cultural differences, and limited educational opportunity to be labeled learning disabled. The vast majority of public school programs for so-called learning disabled students use the resource room model, which results in students being tutored in the regular curriculum with seldom an emphasis on teaching methodologies aimed at remediation or amelioration of the specific problems presented by the students. Many resource rooms house 12 to 15 students (and sometimes more) at a time, and the students are subjected to the same large group instruction teaching strategies and to the same curriculum as if they were still in the regular classroom. In light of such programming, it is no wonder that the "Regular Education Initiative" (REI) is being supported by so many educators. And it may well be that the students who are being placed today in resource rooms would make just as much progress, given a little additional attention, in the regular classroom as they do in the resource room. But, make no mistake, it is the severely learning disabled student who is again "falling between the cracks" just as in the pre-1970 era.

Our contention is that the NJCLD definition should be adhered to rigorously in diagnosing students with learning disabilities; other academically borderline students should remain in the regular classroom with the curriculum adapted to their instructional levels. Moreover, the entire concept of the resource room placement for severely learning disabled students should be reevaluated. Such a placement might be adequate for the younger student who is presenting specific problems in only one area of learning and who with specialized teaching techniques could master the content of that area. But the severely disabled student, who could be classically diagnosed as having aphasia, dyslexia, dyscalculia, apraxia, and so on, probably would profit greatly from being placed for a year or two in a self-contained classroom in which intensive, specific remedial methodologies are implemented.

We are aware that segregating students in special classes may have detrimental effects on their self-esteem, but those negative effects in no way can be greater than the devastating effects of being in resource rooms for 10 to 12 years and graduating from school still unable to read or otherwise communicate adequately. Many bright learning disabled students are dropping out of school or are graduating today unable to find and hold a job and unable to enter college.

The purpose of *Learning Disabilities: Basic Concepts, Assessment Practices, and Instructional Strategies* is to call attention once again to the student who is severely learning disabled—the student who needs a type of instruction different from what is provided in the regular classroom. Most of the students in learning disability programs today receive a slowed-down, individualized version of the regular curriculum. We contend that this is not appropriate for students with a specific learning disability that is severe enough to disrupt completely their progress in one or more academic areas. Moreover, we contend that many of the methodological approaches discussed in this text still represent the best habilitative techniques developed—whether they were designed in the 1920s, as Grace Fernald's system of teaching reading, or developed in the 1970s, as Laura Lee's program for teaching oral language.

The reader is cautioned to look at each of the methods discussed as being appropriate for students with certain types of learning disabilities. As is true of the regular curriculum, there is no one method that is appropriate for all handicapped students. Selection of the remedial method is dependent upon careful observation and assessment of the student.

The book is intended for a variety of professionals working in the field of learning disabilities. The primary audience is teachers who develop the curriculum and daily lesson plans for students. Another major audience is appraisal personnel who need to be much more knowledgeable about methods, techniques, and programs. Because the book is written for the teacher, there is little formal appraisal information; however, implicit in the description of learning disabled students and remedial programs is a great deal of information that can be used to supplement the appraisal process in a way that leads to the development of individualized education plans.

In short, the book provides any professional in the field of learning disabilities with a comprehensive discussion of the concept of learning disabilities, the range of remedial or habilitative methods developed for learning disabled persons, and a critique of the efficacy of each method. We have tried to be candid but charitable with regard to authors whose work we have reviewed, giving honor where honor is due but not holding out any panaceas. The education of the learning disabled child, youth, and/or adult is a long-term and, sometimes, tedious process, and there are few rose gardens along the way. But teachers who have laboriously and painstakingly taught learning disabled students to conquer the printed word, to speak in clear, connected sentences, or to solve the intricacies of arithmetic computation after those individuals have convinced themselves and others that they can never learn, will be forever "hooked" on the teaching of students with learning disabilities.

PART I

BASIC CONCEPTS IN LEARNING DISABILITIES

Part I presents the overall concept of learning disabilities with particular emphasis on definition and etiology, the history of learning disabilities, and a final chapter on the major types of learning disabilities. The definition of learning disabilities used is that developed by the National Joint Committee on Learning Disabilities and is the only definition espoused by the authors. The reader should give careful attention to the definition, as it is the basis for much of what is discussed in the entire book.

The etiology section in Chapter 1 is brief because we had no intention to present detailed material on anatomy, physiology, or pathology, but it is important as part of the orientation to the rest of the book. It underlines the authors' contention that learning disabilities result from damage to or maldevelopment of the central nervous system and that without credible evidence of such, a diagnosis of learning disability should not be made.

The second chapter recounts the history of learning disabilities from the early 1800s to the present and the efforts of pioneers in the field such as Broca, Wernicke, Orton, Cruickshank, and Kirk. The last chapter in Part I is devoted to a description of the major types of learning disabilities that affect an individual's ability to use oral and written symbols, whether verbal or mathematical, and the ability to reason and conceptualize. In addition, correlates of learning disabilities such as perceptual and motor disorders, while not considered learning disabilities, are discussed.

1

THE CONCEPT OF
LEARNING DISABILITIES

The authors of special education textbooks written before 1965 make no reference at all to the term *learning disabilities*. This is hardly surprising; it was only after that date that learning disabilities began to be accepted as the generic label under which a variety of syndromes affecting learning, language, and communication could be grouped. Before 1965, local, state, and federal education agencies did not officially recognize learning disabled as a category of handicapped individuals, that is, as a defined group of individuals whose special education or other treatment needs could be paid for with public money. As a result, there were few classes for learning disabled children, fewer remedial or habilitation facilities for youths and adults, and almost no college teacher preparation programs in the learning disabilities area. In the past 25 years, however, "learning disabilities" has become a legally constituted category of handicapped students, the use of the term has become pervasive in American education, and the number of students said to have learning disabilities is larger than any other group of handicapped students.

Because interest in learning disabilities has developed so rapidly, many experienced professionals are confused about numerous aspects of this "new" developing field. Particularly confusing are questions like: Who are learning disabled persons? How many cases are there? Why do they have these problems? What are the observable manifestations of their disabilities? From what professional backgrounds and roots has the field grown? It is hoped that the contents of this chapter will help the reader find answers to these and other questions pertaining to learning disabilities.

This chapter provides a basic knowledge of learning disabilities and is not intended to be an all-encompassing presentation. Detailed discussions of the topics considered in this chapter are available from sources cited throughout the text. Specifically, this chapter discusses (a) the definition of learning disabilities, (b) the incidence of learning disabilities, (c) brain dysfunction as a probable cause for these disabilities, (d) the role of environmental factors, and (e) the characteristics associated with learning disabilities.

DEFINING LEARNING DISABILITIES

Few topics pertaining to learning disabilities have evoked as much interest and controversy as those relating to definition of the condition. Beginning in 1962 with Kirk's first effort to define the term and continuing to the present time, professionals, parents, and government agencies have tried to develop a valid and widely accepted definition.

Early Attempts to Define Learning Disabilities

At first, there was no consensus as to which term should be used to describe the condition, much less an agreement on how the term should be defined. In a paper prepared for the Southern Regional Education Board, McDonald (1967) reports the results of a questionnaire to which 35 educators and psychologists working in the general area of learning disabilities gave "twenty-two terms which one or more of them use as an exact synonym for the title 'Children with Learning Disorders'" (p. 1). The collection of terms reflects a wide range of orientations, for example: (a) educational—"remedial education," "educationally handicapped"; (b) medical— "brain injured," "minimal brain dysfunction"; and (c) psycholinguistic—"language disorders," "psycholinguistic disabilities." Some are general terms such as "psychoneurological disorders" and "learning disabilities"; others narrow down to specialized achievement areas such as "problem readers" and "reading disability."

Fortunately, conditions today are much improved because *learning disabilities* has become the term of choice owing greatly to the efforts of Sam Kirk (Wiederholt, 1974). Chalfant (1989) reports that state education agencies are now using only five terms to describe the population in question: learning disabled, learning disabilities, specific learning disabilities, perceptually impaired, and perceptual communication disorders in children. The term appears in the titles of all major periodicals that publish in the area (e.g., *Journal of Learning Disabilities, Learning Disability Quarterly, Learning Disabilities Focus,* and *Learning Disabilities Research*). The term is also a part of the name of most associations that are devoted to the condition, including the Learning Disabilities Association of America, the Council for Learning Disabilities, the Division for Learning Disabilities, and the National Joint Committee on Learning Disabilities.

While the use of *learning disabilities* has become dominant, a commensurate consensus on the definition of that term has been slow to form. A tendency exists for people to define the term idiosyncratically. This leads to a situation where two people may use the same term to describe different populations. It is easy to imagine the problems that spring from such confusion over definition.

This confusion concerning definition is demonstrated by Cruickshank (1972), who has written that after completing his public lectures on learning disability he is often questioned by parents about their particular child,

> who stuttered, who teased the family cat, who could not deal with geometry in the 10th grade but who otherwise was getting along well in school, who had night terrors; who was diagnosed by the family psychiatrist as depressed—all of these under the label of learning disabilities. . . . Parents in their concept of learning disability have talked with me about nail biting, poor eating habits, failure of the child to keep his room neat, unwillingness to take a bath, failure to brush teeth. Teachers have questioned me about disrespectful children, children who will not listen to the adult, children who are sexually precocious, children who are aggressive—all in the belief that there are learning disability children. One parent asked me if the fact that his college-student son wore long hair and he "suspected" lived with a girl outside his dormitory was the result of a learning disability! (p. 382)

Apparently, many professionals and parents have no clear idea about who these people with learning disabilities are. Therefore, a definition of learning disabilities is required that is both broad enough to include all of the diverse conditions subsumed under the label and, at the same time, sufficiently definitive to permit the distinguishing of learning disabilities from other handicapping conditions.

The growing use of the term prompted the development of many definitions, of which those of Kirk and Bateman (1962), Myklebust (1963), Bateman (1964), and the National Advisory Committee on Handicapped Children (1968) were among the most notable. Of these the most influential was decidedly the last one. The definition developed by the National Advisory Committee was included in Public Law 91-230 (Children with Specific Learning Disabilities Act of 1969, The Elementary and Secondary Amendments of 1969) and was changed only slightly when it was incorporated into Public Law 94-142 (The Education of All Handicapped Children Act of 1975). The definition is now known as the U.S. Office of Education (USOE, 1977) definition. This definition as presently found in P.L. 94-142 reads as follows:

> The term "children with specific learning disabilities" means those children who have a disorder in one or more of the basic psychological processes involved in understanding or in using language, spoken or written, which disorder may manifest itself in imperfect ability to listen, think, speak, read, write, spell, or do mathematical calcula-

tions. Such disorders include such conditions as perceptual handicaps, brain injury, minimal brain dysfunction, dyslexia, and developmental aphasia. Such term does not include children who have learning problems which are primarily the result of visual, hearing, or motor handicaps, of mental retardation, of emotional disturbance, or environmental, cultural, or economic disadvantage.

One of the most frequent and consistent criticisms leveled against the field of learning disabilities has been the lack of consensus among professionals concerning a definition of the condition. The 1968 National Advisory Committee's definition enjoyed an acceptance that exceeded all others. Yet even when the definition was institutionalized through the passage of P.L. 94-142, giving it the aura of officiality, there was still widespread dissatisfaction and disagreement regarding the definitional issue.

It must be recalled that the P.L. 94-142 definition was rather well regarded and served the educational community well in many ways, especially by providing a basis for federal and state funding of instructional and related services for school-aged children. In spite of this widespread acceptance, the dissatisfaction continued. The members of the National Joint Committee on Learning Disabilities (NJCLD), a group composed of official representatives from eight organizations,[1] believed strongly that the federal definitions had inherent weaknesses that made them unacceptable as definitions that could be used to delimit a field as broad and complex as that of learning disabilities. The reasons for this belief are given in the following discussions, the contents of which are drawn mostly from *Learning Disabilities: Issues on Definition* (National Joint Committee on Learning Disabilities, 1981) and *A New Definition of Learning Disabilities* (Hammill, Leigh, McNutt, & Larsen, 1981).

Exclusion of Adults. Because learning disabilities may occur in individuals of all ages, the use of the term *children* in the 1968 and P.L. 94-142 definitions is unnecessarily restrictive. Since the enactment of the federal law, a major trend in the field has been the rapid development of interest in adolescents and adults with learning disabilities. This interest is exemplified by the work of Alley and Deshler (1979), Mangrum and Strichart (1988), D. Johnson and Blalock (1987), and Wiederholt (1978a). The significance of this trend is indicated further by recent initiatives of the Learning Disabilities Association of America (previously the Association for Children and Adults with Learning Disabilities) and the Council for Learning Disabilities (previously the Division for Children with Learning Disabilities) to change their names to reflect concern for the entire population of learning disabled individuals.

---

[1]The NJCLD is composed of representatives of the American Speech-Language-Hearing Association (ASHA), the Learning Disabilities Association of America (LDA), the Council for Learning Disabilities (CLD), the Division for Children with Communication Disorders (DCCD), the Division for Learning Disabilities (DLD), the International Reading Association (IRA), the National Association of School Psychologists, and The Orton Dyslexia Society.

Reference to Basic Psychological Processes. The inclusion in the 1968 definition of the phrase "basic psychological processes" generates extensive and possibly needless debate in the field. The original and legitimate intent of that phrase seems to have been to underscore the intrinsic nature of learning disabilities while simultaneously shifting the focus away from what was an unfortunate overemphasis on the neurological biases so predominant in the early days of the field. The 1968 National Advisory Committee recognized the need to differentiate clearly between learning disabilities caused by internal factors, whether psychological or neurological, and other learning problems caused by environmental influences such as poor or insufficient instruction. However, the phrase "basic psychological processes" became closely associated with the "mentalistic process" and "perceptual-motor ability" training programs that evolved from the theoretical models that were popular during the time when the definition was developed and implemented.

The presence of this particular phrase in the definition led to a polarization of professionals into two distinct and often disputing camps—those who advocated the direct instruction of reading, writing, speaking, and so on, and those who advocated the training of certain psychocognitive abilities presumed to underlie or greatly influence proficiency in reading, writing, speaking, and so on. These latter abilities were called processing abilities and included such constructs as memory, perception, sequencing, modality, and closure.

We are not concerned at this point with the relative merits of the two approaches to instruction; that is a curricular and not a definitional issue. What is important to the discussion of definition is that the majority of both groups probably would agree with the original intent of the phrase, namely, that the cause of the learning problem is intrinsic to the affected person. It is the wording of the phrase that has elicited so much unnecessary controversy.

Inclusion of Spelling as a Learning Disability. In the 1968 definition, spelling is listed as a specific disorder. In a statement clarifying the specific areas of achievement to be evaluated, the U.S. Office of Education (1977) acknowledged that although " 'spelling' is listed in the statute, the components of spelling can be assumed under the other seven areas of function. Spelling as a category *per se* has been deleted from the final regulations" (p. 65085), although it remains in the official definition. The redundant inclusion of spelling, which is typically considered to be subsumed under written expression, should be eliminated from any definition.

Inclusion of Obsolete Terms. The definition of learning disabilities certainly is not enhanced by the presence of the list of *conditions* that the term purportedly includes, namely, "perceptual handicaps," "brain injury," "minimal brain dysfunction," "dyslexia," and "developmental aphasia." These terms were included in the 1968 definition in an ill-advised attempt to clarify the definition; in reality they add to the confusion. Historically, these terms have been as difficult to define as has learning disability. Professionals in medicine, psychology, speech pathology, and reading have argued long and bitterly for generations over the precise meanings of these labels.

To include such ill-defined terms in a definition of learning disabilities invites controversy, confusion, and misinterpretation. These are attributes of which we already have an abundance and with which we have lived long enough.

The "Exclusion" Clause.   The wording of the final—that is, the "exclusion"—clause has contributed to the widespread misconception that learning disabilities can occur neither in conjunction with other handicapping conditions nor in the presence of "environmental, cultural, or economic disadvantage." Let us repeat: This is a misinterpretation of the federal definitions and simply is not an accurate conception of the original intent of the definitions. A careful reading of the clause leads to the interpretation that learning disabilities cannot be the direct or primary result of the excluded conditions and situations listed. Presumably, learning disabilities can be secondary or in addition to those conditions and situations. In the hypothetical case of a blind 14-year-old child who lost much of the ability to produce spoken language as a result of a brain tumor, we would have no difficulty in diagnosing and labeling this child as learning disabled. This is a clear-cut case of a multiply handicapped child who is both visually impaired and learning disabled, both conditions being primary and neither being causally related to the other. Any discussion of whether the youngster was disadvantaged in any way would be irrelevant to the question of identification. In summary, the objection to the "exclusion" clause in the federal definitions is directed more toward its ambiguity than to its intention.

The Definition Proposed by the NJCLD

The members of the NJCLD felt that these objections to the federal definitions provided overwhelming justification for a new definition. In 1981, after prolonged discussion and compromise, the representatives of the organizations reached unanimous agreement on a new definition. In 1989, this definition was revised. Their current definition reads as follows:

> Learning disabilities is a general term that refers to a heterogeneous group of disorders manifested by significant difficulties in the acquisition and use of listening, speaking, reading, writing, reasoning, or mathematical abilities. These disorders are intrinsic to the individual, presumed to be due to central nervous system dysfunction, and may occur across the life span. Problems in self-regulatory behaviors, social perception, and social interaction may exist with learning disabilities but do not by themselves constitute a learning disability. Although learning disabilities may occur concomitantly with other handicapping conditions (for example, sensory impairment, mental retardation, serious emotional disturbance) or with extrinsic influences (such as cultural differences, insufficient or inappropriate instruction), they are not the result of those conditions or influences. (National Joint Committee on Learning Disabilities, 1989, p. 1)

Even the best-worded definitions are subject to inadvertent misinterpretation; to avoid this, or at least to minimize it, we will discuss the new definition phrase by phrase. In this way we can express the intention of the NJCLD and our own corroboration of the critical elements in the definition.

"Learning disabilities is a general term"—The committee felt that learning disabilities is a global or generic term under which a variety of specific disorders can be conveniently and reasonably grouped. Most authorities either express or imply allegiance to the idea that learning disabilities are specific in nature. By this they mean that the individual's difficulty is in one or more ability areas but does not encompass all ability areas. For example, a child may have severe problems in reading and yet be quite competent in spoken language; or a youngster's spoken language abilities may be extremely poor, even though his or her intellectual abilities fall within or above the normal range when measured through nonverbal performance tests. Therefore, when Rappaport (1966) writes of "insufficiencies," Ashlock and Stephen (1966) of "gaps," Gallagher (1966) of "imbalances," Kirk and Chalfant (1984) of "intraindividual differences," and Woodcock (1984) of "intracognitive and intraachievement discrepancies," they are all referring to the criterion of specificity in the definition of learning disabilities.

"that refers to a heterogeneous group of disorders"—The concept of disorders that are specific and different in kind, that is, heterogeneous, is reinforced in the second element of the definition. Viewed in this light, learning disabilities is an umbrella term bringing together and encompassing a group of disorders that are manifested in those ability areas detailed by the definition.

"manifested by significant difficulties"—The effects of any one of these disorders on an individual are highly detrimental; that is, their presence handicaps and seriously limits the performance by the individual of some key ability. Because there is evidence that in some public schools learning disabilities is used as a synonym for "mildly handicapped," the NJCLD wanted to emphasize the fact that the presence of learning disabilities can be just as debilitating to an individual as the presence of cerebral palsy, mental retardation, blindness, or any other handicapping condition. The committee's intent in the definition is to place itself squarely in the camp of those professionals who feel that the diagnostic label of learning disabilities should be reserved for those "hard-core" cases of genuinely serious disability.

No mention is made in the definition of "discrepancies" or of expected level of performance because there has been no attempt to make the definition operational. Operationalization is the next step to be taken; but it should be taken by those schools, agencies, and other institutions dealing with learning disabled individuals. Recent attempts by the U.S. Office of Education to develop and establish discrepancy formulas were abandoned, primarily because of negative reactions from the field. The specific arguments against the use of discrepancy formulas are available in the work of Hammill (1976), where it is contended that (a) uncontrollable test reliability problems arise when the results of various tests are combined in a formula, (b) reporting discrepancy in terms of grade levels makes identification of many primary and preschool children impossible because tests for very young children do not use grade equivalents, and (c) the use of existing formulas can result in a ludicrous misdiagnosis of many adolescents.

No matter how the operationalization of the definition is undertaken or by whom it is done, the intent of the NJCLD and most professionals in the field must be kept in the forefront. Every effort must be made to set objective criteria for identification of learning disabled individuals that ensure the identification of only those serious disorders that present themselves as truly handicapping and debilitating to the individual in whom they can be demonstrated.

"in the acquisition and use of listening, speaking, reading, writing, reasoning, or mathematical abilities."—For an individual to be considered learning disabled, the disorder has to result in a serious impairment of one or more of the listed abilities. On this point the NJCLD has reflected the almost total agreement among professionals in the field of learning disabilities. This agreement is based on the fact that all practitioners remediate, teach, or compensate for reading, speaking, arithmetic, or other disabilities as listed, either directly or through attempting to train so-called underlying mentalistic processes (memory, perception, etc.) in the hope that success will generalize to those abilities or will make the child readier to acquire those abilities. Therefore, regardless of their particular orientation to learning disabilities, most professionals in the field would agree that the final goal of instructional efforts is to produce or facilitate more efficient performance in reading, listening, talking, arithmetic, and the other specified abilities. More detailed discussions of these different types of learning disabilities are available in Chapter 3.

"These disorders are intrinsic to the individual,"—This phrase in the definition means that the source of the disorder is to be found within the person who is affected. The disability is not imposed on the individual as a consequence of economic deprivation, poor child-rearing practices, faulty school instruction, societal pressures, and so on. Where present, such factors may complicate the identification of the disorder and may hamper the treatment of it, but they are not considered to be the cause of the learning disability.

"presumed to be due to central nervous system dysfunction,"—Flatly stated, the cause of the learning disability is known or presumed dysfunction in the central nervous system. These dysfunctions may be sequelae of traumatic damage to tissues, inherited factors, biochemical insufficiencies or imbalances, or other similar conditions; but make no mistake, the integrity of the central nervous system in its structure or function is called into question. The phrase is intended to spell out clearly the intent behind the statement that learning disabilities are intrinsic to the individual.

Practically the entire learning disability community, regardless of differing methodological orientations or theoretical frameworks, would probably agree with the positions just expressed. They would certainly adhere to the idea that learning disabilities are fundamentally constitutional in origin (see Adelman, 1979, 1989;

Bryan & Bryan, 1986; Chalfant & Scheffelin, 1969; Cruickshank, 1976; Hallahan & Cruickshank, 1973; Johnson & Myklebust, 1967; Kephart, 1971; Kirk & Gallagher, 1989; Mercer, 1987; Orton, 1937; and Strauss & Lehtinen, 1947; among many, many others).

The NJCLD was quick to point out that in some cases a causal relationship between linguistic or academic problems and central nervous system dysfunction is easy to determine, but that in most cases it is not obvious. For example, the relationship between cause and disability is apparent in cases in which the individual shows a noticeable reduction in language proficiency after experiencing a stroke or brain injury of some sort, that is, in those cases when the onset of the disability is sudden and traumatic. These are acquired disorders, acquired after full language proficiency has been developed. In contrast, the vast majority of learning disabilities are developmental in nature; that is, the problems emerge slowly, and their appearance is manifested only when the child attempts to develop or master some ability area, such as reading. In developmental learning disabilities, attempts to determine the cause of the problem become very difficult, and conclusions are often speculative.

Because of the difficulty in establishing cause and effect relationships between the learning disability and central nervous system dysfunction, the NJCLD agreed that hard evidence of organicity did not have to be present in order to diagnose a person as learning disabled, but that no person should be labeled as learning disabled unless central nervous system dysfunction was the suspected and presumed cause. Certainly, individuals should not be diagnosed as learning disabled if the cause is known or thought to be something other than central nervous system dysfunction.

"and may occur across the life span."—This phrase simply means that learning disabilities can be found in people of all ages. They are not just conditions unique to school-aged populations.

"Problems in self-regulatory behaviors, social perception, and social interaction . . . do not by themselves constitute a learning disability."—The NJCLD recognized that these problems are often seen among persons with learning disabilities and that their presence complicates treatment but maintains that they are not examples of learning disabilities. A pure case of social misperception would not likely be recognized as a learning disability. Instead, the chances are greater that a person who evidenced such a malady would be diagnosed as emotionally disturbed, behavior disordered, or even other health impaired. To consider such problems as being learning disabilities would lead to further diagnostic confusion by blurring the distinction between the learning disability and the emotional disturbance categories.

"Although learning disabilities may occur concomitantly with other handicapping conditions . . . or with extrinsic influences"—This clause means very simply that learning disabilities are found among all kinds and types of people, including those with other major handicapping conditions, those from all racial and ethnic groups, and

those from all levels of economic status. This is not an exclusion clause, but an inclusion clause, recognizing that individuals may be learning disabled and also blind, deaf, and/or mentally retarded; they may be learning disabled and be members of a different culture; or they may be learning disabled and have suffered extreme economic deprivation. There is no need to catalog the multiplicity of combinations that are possible. Suffice it to say that the definition formally recognizes the possibilities of multiply handicapped learning disabled individuals. In fact, learning disabilities have long been noted among persons having the conditions usually listed in exclusion clauses.

Auxter (1971) has documented the presence of learning disabilities in some deaf children. He investigated two groups of auditorially handicapped children who were matched in IQ and chronological age. All the children were free of gross physical defects. The groups differed only in academic performance. He found differences between groups in motor speed, physical fitness, and reaction time, but not in visual perception and balance. Auxter's work interests us because it demonstrates that sensorially impaired children can show marked intraindividual differences that cannot be attributed to either subaverage mental ability or their handicapping condition.

Specific learning disabilities have also been found in considerable numbers among culturally disadvantaged children (Kappelman, Kaplan, & Ganter, 1969). This observation should not surprise anyone, because children from poor, minority, and disadvantaged homes are considered high risk from the moment of their conception. Prenatal care among them is rare, maternal and child nutrition is poor, health care for the infant is absent and/or confounded by the ministrations of "folk doctors," and the prematurity rate is alarmingly high. Who would not expect to find more children with both central nervous system dysfunction and learning disability in this group?

It is true that in schools, administrative decisions are made frequently to label students according to their more debilitating handicap. Thus a mentally retarded learning disabled youth might be classified as mentally retarded for overall programming purposes; but this is done in accordance with local or state policies regarding how students are counted for reimbursements and not in response to the intention of the definition.

"they are not the result of those conditions or influences."—The last element of the definition restates the belief that learning disabilities are different from other handicapping conditions, and although they may coexist in an individual with another handicap, they arise neither from the presence of another handicap nor from extrinsic, environmental influences. Stated more directly, persons may have a learning disability *in addition to* another handicap; but they may not have a learning disability *because* of another handicap.

For example, failure to read print is not a learning disability in children who are totally blind, but their inability to use adequate, age-appropriate syntactic forms when speaking might well be evidence of a learning disability. By the same token, a deaf child who is experiencing difficulty in learning to speak clearly with good articulation does not present an example of a learning disability, only of a learning problem directly resulting from his or her deafness.

A number of teachers will note readily that many, possibly most, of the "learning disabled" students enrolled in their programs do not satisfy either the 1977 USOE or the NJCLD definition. This is because in many school districts all students who are thought to be able to profit from tutoring or remedial education are arbitrarily called learning disabled. As a consequence of such definitional liberality, the learning disability programs have become glutted with underachieving students, culturally different students, and poorly taught students. Often truants and delinquents are also labeled and assigned to learning disability programs.

Of course, some of these individuals are indeed learning disabled, but most are not. A well-trained and experienced teacher armed with regular classroom methods and the knowledge of how to adapt them to meet individual needs will usually be successful in instructing most of the non-learning disabled problem students. These nonhandicapped problem learners are more appropriately called "students with learning and behavior problems." The cause for their difficulties and strategies for overcoming them are not the primary topics of this book. Professionals interested in teaching these nonhandicapped problem students are referred to the books by Hammill and Bartel (1990), Wallace and Kauffman (1986), and Smith (1989) all of which have the same title, *Teaching Students with Learning and Behavior Problems*, and to Mercer and Mercer's (1989) *Teaching Students with Learning Problems*, Polloway, Patton, Payne, and Payne's (1989) *Strategies for Teaching Learners with Special Needs*, Wallace, Cohen, and Polloway's (1987) *Language Arts: Teaching Exceptional Students*, and Wiederholt, Hammill, and Brown's (1983) *The Resource Teacher*. In these works the reader will find an ample supply of assessment and instructional techniques that are most appropriate for use with that large group of students who need assistance but who are not truly learning disabled.

Status of Current LD Definitions

Since 1977, only four definitions of learning disabilities have been seriously proposed: the 1977 USOE definition, the definition of the NJCLD, and two recent contenders by the Association for Children and Adults with Learning Disabilities (now called the Learning Disabilities Association of America) (1986) and the Interagency Committee on Learning Disabilities (1989). It is too early to tell what influence the latter two definitions will have on the field, but certainly those of the USOE and of the NJCLD are the most accepted today.

Hallahan, Kauffman, and Lloyd (1985) suggest that the "official" 1977 USOE definition is the most widely accepted today because it is the one under which federal programs are administered and because it has been adopted by most states. Readers should keep in mind that this definition was developed for the purpose of guiding funding practices associated with federal school legislation. As such, it emphasizes school-aged children and academic subjects. No one ever intended that this definition would serve as a comprehensive theoretical statement about the nature of learn-ing disabilities, would account for all of the learning disabilities that are possible to occur, or would indicate all of the times during life when they might be present. For these reasons, this definition cannot be accepted as *the* learning disabilities definition.

From the start, the NJCLD intended its definition to be comprehensive. It clearly indicates that learning disabilities are constitutionally based disorders that seriously affect an individual's performance in reading, writing, listening, speaking, math, and reasoning. It asserts that these disabilities can coexist with any other handicapping condition or with environmental disadvantage and that learning disabilities can be present at any time during a person's life.

To us, the NJCLD definition is superior to any other that is available. It is likely that the "official" definition will continue to be used for governmental purposes and that the NJCLD definition will be increasingly accepted by professionals. Readers who require a particularly thorough discussion of definitions and definitional issues in learning disabilities are referred to Hammill (1990), who traces the history of the attempt to define learning disabilities, discusses the 11 definitions that have been proposed since 1962, and makes the case for uniting behind the NJCLD definition.

THE INCIDENCE OF LEARNING DISABILITIES

Estimates made by the experts in the field of learning disabilities relative to the inci-dence of the condition in the population have varied widely from 1% to 30%. Actual field studies have yielded findings that are almost as diverse.

The National Advisory Committee on Handicapped Children (1968) estimated that 1% to 3% of school-aged children are learning disabled. The validity of this estimate received some support from Wissink (1972), who surveyed 39 "leaders" in the learn-ing disability area as to their estimates of the incidence of children with learning disabilities in a school population. Half of the respondents estimated the incidence to be 5% or less, though almost a third thought that the incidence was 15% or more. In relation to the incidence of learning disabilities, Adelman (1979) commented recently that "official government-related estimates of LD tend to be 1 to 3 percent, while the most conservative figures from researchers have tended to be around 5 to 6 percent" (pp. 5–6). Gearheart and Gearheart (1989) reported that some parents and physicians believe the figure is as high as 15% to 30%.

Several comprehensive surveys of school populations have been completed in an effort to determine an exact incidence, but they have had little success in estab-lishing a set figure. Meier (1971) found that 15% of 3,000 second graders in eight Rocky Mountain states could be classified as learning disabled. In a study of 2,800 third and fourth graders, Myklebust and Boshes (1969) concluded that only 7% to 8% were learning disabled. After reviewing 21 of these studies, Bryant and McLoughlin (1972) concluded that the incidence of learning disabilities ranged from 3% to 28%, half being above 13%.

While expert opinions and survey findings concerning the incidence of learning disabilities may differ, we know how many students are being served under the learning disability label. Data reported by the U.S. Department of Education for the years 1986–1987 are reproduced in Table 1.1 and Figure 1.1. The percentage of the school enrollment identified as learning disabled is presented in Table 1.1. The number of students being served in special education broken down by area of handicap for the years between 1977 and 1987 is presented in graph form in Figure 1.1.

The conclusions drawn from these data are clear. First, learning disabled students constitute 4.8% of the school enrollment. Second, they are by far the largest category of handicap in that approximately 44% of all handicapped students are classified as learning disabled. Third, the popularity of the learning disability category appears to be increasing though not at the level experienced during the years 1977 to 1983.

Question: What do the results of all these studies and estimates tell us about the incidence of learning disabilities? Answer: Not very much!

When individuals differ on the definition of learning disabilities, they will naturally identify different types of children as learning disabled (LD). Even when they agree on a learning disabilities definition, professionals may use different criteria to qualify students for services under the LD label. In either case, incidence figures will be affected.

TABLE 1.1. Students Receiving Special Education Services, Ages 3–21: 1986–1987 School Year

Handicapping Condition	Percentage of Total School Enrollment*
Learning disabled	4.80
Speech impaired	2.85
Mentally retarded	1.61
Emotionally disturbed	.96
Deaf and hard of hearing	.16
Multihandicapped	.24
Orthopedically handicapped	.14
Other health impaired	.13
Visually handicapped	.07
Deaf-blind	less than .01
Total	10.98

Note. From *To assure the free, appropriate public education of all handicapped children,* U.S. Department of Education, 1988, Tenth Annual Report to Congress on the Implementation of P.L. 94-142, The Education for All Handicapped Children Act.

*The percentages are based on handicapped children ages 3–21 as a percent of total school enrollment for preschool through 12th grade.

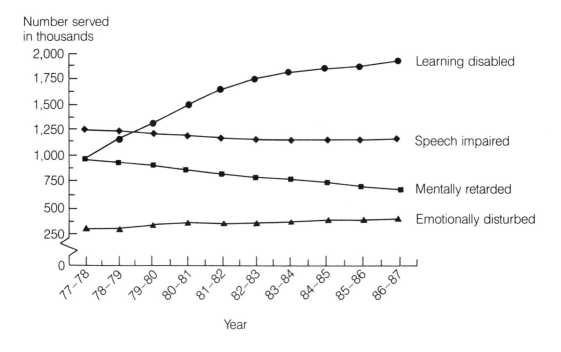

Number served
in thousands

FIGURE 1.1. Children receiving special education services, school years 1977–78 to 1986–87. *Note.* From *Tenth Annual Report to Congress on the Implementation of the Education of the Handicapped Act,* M. Will (Ed.), 1988, Washington, DC: U.S. Department of Education.

Usually, the lack of agreement concerning the incidence of learning disabled children can be traced back to the tendency of school diagnosticians and administrators to classify nonhandicapped problem learners as learning disabled and to the absence of definitive, operational criteria that can be used to distinguish between the two groups. Without specific criteria to serve as guides to case identification, our definitions are much like the United States Constitution in that they are open to an appreciable amount of interpretation. Some professionals are "strict constructionists" and tend to conceive of learning disabilities as including little more than the "hard-core," that is, classically defined clinical types, especially the dyslexic, dysphasic, or Strauss syndrome child. To them a figure of no more than 3% seems reasonable; and these children are more likely to be found in private schools or clinical settings than in public school operations.

Other professionals feel more comfortable with a relaxed, liberal interpretation that includes the underachieving, unmotivated, and poorly taught child, that is, the child with "learning and behavior problems." To them an incidence figure of 15% to 30% seems minimal; for in those urban school districts characterized by large concentrations of minority and economically impoverished people, the figure is reported to be much higher. For example, in the Philadelphia public schools, half of the sixth-grade population reads below the 17th percentile. Though others might consider all these children to be learning disabled, we certainly do not.

Until operationally useful criteria emerge that can be used to identify precisely the children in question, we will have to be content with widely disparate "guesstimates" regarding the incidence of learning disabled children in the school population. Our own opinion is that the number of persons who could satisfy the intent of the definition described in the previous section would be unlikely to exceed 3%.

THE ETIOLOGY OF LEARNING DISABILITIES

Scientific Study of Causes/origins

Most professionals in the field maintain that true learning disabilities, as defined earlier, are the consequence of central nervous system (CNS) damage, dysfunction, or structural anomaly. The CNS is composed of the brain and spinal cord; it serves as a switchboard for the regulation of incoming impulses and outgoing responses as well as for interconnecting neural associations. Since the system operates as a processor of information, inferior performance can seriously inhibit or retard a child's ability to learn or respond. Genetic or developmental variations in CNS structure, biochemical irregularities, and cerebral trauma can cause the brain to function abnormally and can produce those particular disorders in listening, speaking, reading, writing, math, and thinking that we have come to call learning disabilities. Four topics are dealt with in this section: (a) physical evidence of CNS irregularities, (b) conditions that produce CNS irregularities, (c) the effect of CNS irregularities on individuals, and (d) the role of etiology in making educational decisions.

Physical Evidence of CNS Irregularities

The major methods used to determine the presence of CNS irregularities in learning disabled individuals include autopsy, electroencephalography (EEG), computerized tomography (CT), and magnetic resonance imaging (MRI). Examination of the brain upon autopsy is a technique that has been used for many years. During the 1800s, Broca and Wernicke used autopsies to establish the areas of the brain primarily responsible for the expression and reception of spoken language. In the mid-1900s, Penfield and Roberts (1959) more extensively mapped these functions of the brain using electrodes applied to the exposed brains of epileptics during surgery. The physical evidence presented resulted from examination of only dyslexic children and adults. Extrapolating such evidence to other types of learning disabilities presents no problems.

Recently, Geschwind and Galaburda (1987) reported awareness of six cases of intractable dyslexic adults in whom all were discovered to have arteriovenous malformations (AVM) in the left temporoparietal region of the brain. Previously, Mori, Murata, and Hashimoto (1980) likewise reported on series of AVMs in the language areas of the left hemisphere.

Geschwind and Galaburda (1987) concluded from both their own research and detailed review of other studies that brain abnormalities in dyslexia are developmental in nature and can be attributed to alterations in the cerebral cortex and in interconnected subcortical structures as a result of disturbances in fetal development.

Duffy and McAnulty (1985) used the EEG topography mapping technique to study a group of 44 dyslexic boys who had no history of other neurologic disorders, psychiatric problems, or attention deficit disorder. When compared with an age-matched control group, EEG topographic mapping clearly differentiated the dyslexic group from the normal reading group. Not only were expected changes in the left posterior language areas present in the dyslexic children, but abnormalities were also registered in other areas of the brain. This study as well as others conducted by Duffy (1980) seems to indicate that the neurologic deficit in dyslexia is not due to a focal or specifically localized trauma and is not limited to the speech-language areas of the brain.

As discussed above, CNS irregularities have been demonstrated at autopsy and through computerized EEGs, but computerized tomography and magnetic resonance imaging have generally failed to reveal gross brain abnormalities. However, it should be noted that Bigler (1990) reported that some CT/MRI studies have revealed cerebral asymmetries in the brains of dyslexics.

Conditions that Produce CNS Irregularities

A wide variety of conditions are known to cause the brain to malfunction. These conditions—which can occur before, during, or after birth—include trauma, such as head injuries, cerebral hemorrhage, and febrile diseases (Kohn & Dennis, 1974; Pirozzolo & Wittrock, 1982; Witelson, 1985); prenatal developmental anomalies (Galaburda, 1985a; Galaburda & Kemper, 1979; Geschwind & Galaburda, 1987); inherited predispositions (Hinshelwood, 1917; Orton, 1937); and biochemical deficiencies and imbalances (Cravioto, 1973; Green & Perlman, 1971).

With specific reference to brain dysfunction in unborn children or neonates, Eastman stated in 1959 that unfavorable intrauterine environment is associated with at least two-thirds of the cases and that premature birth, physical trauma, Rh factor incompatibilities, and congenital malformations are the prime contributors. To this assertion must be added the body of Geschwind and Galaburda's work done during the 1980s from which they conclude that developmental learning disorders may also result from fetal developmental anomalies such as disorders of neuronal migration, micropolygyria (abnormal convolutions), primitive layering, primitive neurons, and so on.

Most of the conditions mentioned above result in a situation in which the brain cells are deprived of sufficient oxygen. Because of this, they die. When enough neural tissue is affected, the brain will malfunction. The condition of the brain's being deprived of ample oxygen is called *anoxia*. Since oxygen insufficiency is associated directly with most of the previously mentioned causative conditions, anoxia could be considered the primary, that is, actual, cause of most brain dysfunction.

Human cells need oxygen in order to perform the metabolic processes necessary for the maintenance of life. Oxygen is transported to the cells of the body by the hemoglobin contained in the red blood cells; anything that interferes with the circulation of the blood (e.g., strangulation or hemorrhage) or with its capacity for transporting oxygen (high fevers) can cause oxygen deprivation in body tissues.

Toubin (1960) states that of all the tissues in the body, nerve cells are the most vulnerable to anoxia, and other writers (Best & Taylor, 1939) have noted that the neurons of the cerebral cortex undergo irreparable damage if deprived of their blood supply for 5 minutes or longer. The cells of the lower centers of the brain, like those of the medulla oblongata, which control vital life processes of the body, are able to undergo longer periods of oxygen deprivation; some of them remain unaffected after as long as 60 minutes of anoxia. A direct relationship exists between the length of time that the central nervous system is deprived of an adequate oxygen supply and the severity of the brain damage incurred.

Genetic factors cannot be overlooked in any discussion of learning disorders. Rossi (1972) has discussed the possibility that some forms of learning disability appear to be based on constitutional genetic neurochemical dysfunctions. It has long been suggested that many cases of specific reading disability were inherited (Hallgren, 1950; Orton, 1943). Support for these positions is provided by Silver (1971), who, after studying 556 selected children, discovered familial patterns in children with "neurologically-based learning disabilities," that is, children evidencing problems in receiving, processing, storing, retrieving, and expressing information.

Effects of CNS Irregularities

In general, in addition to causing death, brain impairments can adversely affect at least four major areas of human function: motor, mental, emotional, and sensory. These functions and their associated disabling manifestations are outlined in Table 1.2.

With reference to impairments of motor function, cerebral palsy and paralysis would be examples of overt or hard signs. Their existence in a person is strongly suggestive of brain dysfunction. Hyperactivity and clumsiness are soft signs and cannot be taken as conclusive evidence of the presence of organicity. So if a student were cerebral palsied and had cortical blindness, the chances would be great that he or she suffered from brain dysfunction. Evidence would be less supportive of such a diagnosis if the person were merely awkward in movement and demonstrated short attention span, perseveration, and temper tantrums.

This point has been clearly demonstrated by Myklebust and Boshes (1960), who compared the pediatric and neurological status of moderately and severely learning disabled children in public school with control pupils. No differences were found

TABLE 1.2. Manifestations of Cerebral Dysfunction

Areas of Cerebral Function	Possible Overt (Hard Sign) Manifestations	Borderline (Soft Sign) Manifestations
Motor	Cerebral palsy Paralysis	Minor tremor, hyperactivity, perseveration Isolated hyperreflexia Excessive clumsiness

Mental	Mental deficiency
	Specific learning disability:
	   dysphasia, dyslexia,
	   dyscalculia, etc.
		Mild or minimal retardation
		Concrete patterns of thought
		Difficulty in abstraction
		Problems in reading, writing, speech, math, etc.

Emotional	Autism Psychosis	Impulsiveness, distractibility, emotional lability, short attention span, low frustration tolerance, tantrums
Sensory	Cortical blindness or deafness Visual field defects	Impaired memory for shapes or designs Impaired spatial concept Visual or tactile inattention (extinction)

among the groups regarding the 23-item *pediatric* examination, which suggests that the learning disabled population is basically as "healthy" as their peers. The findings pertaining to the *neurological* characteristics of the groups are more interesting. The obvious ("hard") signs of abnormal neurologic functioning—for example, motoric and convulsive involvements—occurred much more frequently in the groups with learning disabilities than in the control group (75% compared to 25%). However, the "soft" signs, such as distractibility, awkwardness, and impaired spatial orientation, occurred in almost equal proportion in the disabled and control groups (53% compared to 47%).

When brain dysfunction is the cause for learning disability, its effects are manifested in three ways:

1. by the loss of an ability,

2. by the inhibition of the development of an ability, and

3. by the interference with the operation of an ability.

Using spoken language as an example, we can say that adults or children who lose their ability to speak after sustaining a cerebral hemorrhage illustrate the first instance; children who are delayed considerably in language development represent the second; and individuals who speak but frequently have difficulty with syntax and/or proper word selection exemplify the third.

Of the three impairments of function the teacher will be most familiar with the last two. Students so affected are likely to be found in the low reading achievement groups and among those referred for speech therapy. While these examples pertain to speech and language, others could be cited that pertain to disorders of reading, spelling, writing, and other academic activities.

The Relationship Among Areas of Brain Dysfunctions

In young children the most common causes of brain disorder, such as anoxia and hereditary factors, are associated with diffuse tissue impairment. This means that the affected cells are usually dispersed across the brain and are not confined to any one area. An obvious consequence of this fact is that many, perhaps most, brain-involved children are multiply handicapped. Therefore, one should not be surprised to learn that all populations of children and adults known to suffer from brain dysfunction include large percentages of people with learning disabilities. Among the motor impaired, Hansen (1963) reported that almost half of the cerebral palsied children he studied had significant difficulty in reading and writing; a third of them also had difficulty in math. Among mentally retarded children, the presence of learning disabilities is fairly common, for example, the Strauss syndrome child (Strauss & Lehtinen, 1947). Regarding sensory impaired children, Myklebust (1964a) has observed that aphasia and dyslexia are fairly common among deaf people. As for emotionally disturbed children, Kauffman (1977) observed that severely emotionally disturbed individuals share many characteristics with the learning disabled population. A few cases of "pure" learning disability, that is, cases without any additional problems in other areas of cerebral function, have been reported, but they are rare indeed.

It should be noted that the terms *learning disabled* and *neurologically impaired* are not at all interchangeable. While almost all learning disabled people possess educational inadequacies as a consequence of assorted brain dysfunctions, it does not necessarily follow that all people who have cerebral dysfunctions are learning disabled. Many cerebral palsied persons, for example, are not educationally or linguistically handicapped in any way, even though they suffer from an apparent brain disability. The same is true of individuals variously described as hyperactive, hyperkinetic, organic, and neurologically handicapped. It is equally true that some learning disability cases exhibit no *other* overt evidence at all of brain dysfunction. By definition, therefore, learning disability is reserved for use as a generic term that represents a collection of language or language-related disabilities that are known or presumed to be caused by brain dysfunction.

The Role of Etiology in Making Educational Decisions

We conclude this discussion of the causes of learning disabilities with the following cautionary statement. For the teacher or the clinician who is not engaged in systematic research, the primary concerns are to handle the correlative symptoms manifested by the children if they are troublesome and to teach the children to read, speak, write, and so on. Whether learning disabilities in an individual case are symptoms that result from brain injury or from developmental delay will not essentially alter the methods of teaching the student. For example, the student who has a reading disorder seemingly marked by inadequate left-right orientation reversals and substitutions may benefit from instructional techniques such as those described by Fernald (1943, 1988). The teacher who is satisfied that the student can learn to read using the Fernald method is not likely to change the approach if neurological examination reveals that the child is or is not brain impaired. A positive diagnosis of brain dysfunction does not dictate any particular teaching method. It is only through an analysis of the student's learning needs and behavior that the teacher can structure an appropriate program of instruction.

Therefore, even though most learning disabilities probably do arise from underlying neurologic disturbances, the educational evaluation of the problem is based on analysis of the individual's present behavior (including both strengths and deficits) and not on past injuries. Isolation of definite or presumed etiologies for the observed disabilities is of only tangential interest and value to the teacher-clinician and plays a minor role in the preparation of instructional programs.

ENVIRONMENTAL FACTORS THAT CONTRIBUTE TO THE SEVERITY OF LEARNING DISABILITIES

While adverse environmental factors are not to be considered the direct causes of learning disabilities, their presence may complicate instruction and lower the chances for success. It is important, therefore, for the professional interested in the complete study of children or adolescents to evaluate their case histories and interview parents and teachers to try to determine the influence of environmental factors on poor school or language performance. This approach is in no way limited to the study of learning disabled students. All students in difficulty are influenced by environmental factors, and in some cases those factors are the source of the problems observed.

There are five factors believed by some professionals to adversely affect a student's learning and sometimes to masquerade as learning disabilities. These factors—insufficient early experience, behavior problems, cultural/linguistic differences, malnutrition, and poor teaching—are discussed in a format that can be used to elicit case history information from parents, teachers, or other involved parties.

Insufficient Early Experience

- Was the child separated from parents, particularly the mother, for lengthy periods during infancy for whatever reason?

- Did the child suffer any lengthy debilitating illnesses during infancy or early childhood?

- Did the child suffer any unusual restraints on mobility during infancy or early childhood?

- Did the child experience any lengthy deprivation of sensory experience during infancy or early childhood, either transient hearing loss due to middle ear infections or reduced visual acuity resulting from infections or allergies?

- Was the child neglected to the point that opportunities for interaction with parents, adults, or other children were severely curtailed?

- Has the family been so mobile as to be considered transient?

Behavior Problems

- Were any of the following difficulties noted during infancy or early childhood?
  Unusual amount of crying
  Poor sleep patterns
  Poor feeding patterns
  Exaggerated restlessness
  Lethargy

- Were any of the following difficulties noted during infancy, early childhood, or prior to identification of the child as learning disabled?
  Temper tantrums
  Hyperactivity
  Poor attention
  Distractibility
  Poor impulse control
  Cruelty to animals or other children
  Lack of friends
  Excessive fighting
  Withdrawal from other persons or social situations

Cultural/Linguistic Differences

- Does the child come from a family that appears not to reflect the values and attitudes of the dominant culture with regard to the following?

  The importance of education
  The desirability of social interaction
  The authority of the law
  Contemporary morality
  The work/success ethic

- Does the child's family speak a language other than English?

- Does the child speak English?

- Is the child more proficient in another language than English?

- Is the child more proficient in a dialect of English than standard English?

Malnutrition

- Has the child suffered from severe malnutrition during infancy or early childhood for any reason, whether economic, disease related, or psychogenically caused?

Poor Teaching or Lack of Educational Opportunity

- Has the child had an excessive number of days absent from school for whatever reason?

- Has the child's education been severely and repeatedly disrupted for whatever reason?

- Does the child's cumulative school record indicate a history of repeated failures without educational intervention?

- Has the child been abused either physically or psychologically by previous teachers?

- Has the child been exposed to instruction by unqualified teachers?

Positive responses to the questions posed above and to many other questions of the same type could indicate that in addition to a learning disability a child may have other significant problems that must be taken into account when developing an instructional program. This is not to say that positive responses to these questions always indicate concomitant problems; some children appear to come through devastating experiences during infancy or early childhood without bearing significant scars. Neither are the questions aimed at uncovering a significant emotional problem; we assume that the child is not emotionally disturbed. We are simply attempting with such questions to discover whether there have been environmental factors in the child's early life that might contribute to the severity of his or her learning disability, or whether there are ongoing factors, such as behavior problems or cultural/linguistic differences, that may influence instruction.

CHARACTERISTICS OF PERSONS WITH LEARNING DISABILITIES

When used in this context, the term *characteristics* refers to those peculiar traits or qualities typically observed in individuals who are known to have learning disabilities. Since the learning disabilities are presumed to be the consequence of brain dysfunction, most people who have attempted to catalog the characteristics associated with learning disabilities have actually recorded the characteristics of persons with brain dysfunction. The most notable of these attempts was made by Clements (1966), who reviewed the literature relating to the observable symptoms caused by "minimal brain dysfunction (MBD)." His list of symptoms still stands today as a prototype of all such listings of pathological behavior arising from MBD. The list, in abbreviated form, is as follows:

1. Disorders of speech and communication
2. Academic problems
3. Disorders of thinking process
4. Impairments of concept formation
5. Test performance that is uneven and unpredictable
6. Impairments of perception
7. Specific neurological indicators
8. Disorders of motor function
9. Various physical characteristics: drooling, enuresis, slow toilet training, and so on
10. Emotional characteristics: impulsiveness, maladjustment, explosiveness, low tolerance for frustration, and so on
11. Sleep characteristics: irregular sleep patterns, abnormally light or deep sleep, body or head rocking, and so on
12. Irregular relationship capacities
13. Variations in physical development
14. Irregularities in social behavior
15. Variations and irregularities in personality
16. Disorders of attention and concentration

The reader will note that brain dysfunction causes a variety of difficulties, only some of which are learning disabilities. For example, the first four items in the list above are definitely representative of specific types of learning disabilities described in detail in Chapter 3. By this we mean that students diagnosed as learning disabled are likely to show noticeable differences in one or more of those four areas. In fact, were this not the case, it would be impossible to diagnose a person as learning disabled. The remaining characteristics on the list are more representative of other constitutionally based handicaps, such as cerebral palsy, mental retardation, physical disability, and sensory impairment.

Since brain dysfunction commonly affects more than one ability area, it is not surprising that an individual with a known learning disability would have problems in other areas as well. To illustrate, young children with spoken language disorders are frequently reported to suffer from perceptual disabilities, awkwardness, and short attention span. In such cases it is important to remember that the learning disability is caused by the brain dysfunction and not by any awkwardness, perceptual problems, or concentration difficulties that might also be present. No doubt the presence of these disorders is frequently associated with learning disabilities and makes the education of the child more difficult; but the disorders are not the cause for the learning disability. They are probably most accurately referred to as "correlates" of learning disabilities. Many of these correlate disorders should be managed instructionally; for example, efforts should be made to make clumsy children less awkward, but it must be kept in mind that only direct training of oral language will result in improvement in oral language and only direct teaching of reading will improve a child's reading ability.

2

A BRIEF LOOK AT THE PAST, PRESENT, AND FUTURE OF THE LEARNING DISABILITIES MOVEMENT

The history of learning disabilities is divided here into three parts. The first part deals with the foundations phase and focuses on the people who contributed to the theoretical basis that preceded, and actually made possible, the formation of the learning disabilities movement. The second part, the early years of the field, deals with events that established learning disabilities as a specific area of study and contributed to its growth during the years 1963 through 1990. The third part provides a brief glimpse into the future.

THE FOUNDATIONS PHASE

The content of this section is based predominantly on Wiederholt's (1974) conceptualization of the history of learning disabilities. The foundations phase begins with the initial observations of Gall (circa 1800) and concludes with the formation of the Association of Children and Adults with Learning Disabilities (now called the Learning Disabilities Association of America) in 1963. Between these two events occurred a steady development in both theoretical positions and treatment practices related to selected problems that were the sequelae of brain disorders. The ideas generated during this period were incorporated en masse into the learning disabilities movement during the 1960s and still form the conceptual core of the field today.

For illustrative purposes, the contributions to theory, assessment, or remediation made by individuals during this phase are classified according to the type of disorder for which they were primarily intended. Thus, the work of a particular theoretician or practitioner could be classified under one of three headings: disorders of spoken language, disorders of written language, or correlative disorders.

A schematic presentation of these contributions is given in Figure 2.1. In this figure, the date after each name refers to the publication of the individual's most noteworthy contribution to learning disabilities. For example, the 1961 date associated with Kirk refers to the publication date of the first edition of the *Illinois Test of Psycholinguistic Abilities* (ITPA).

The early years of the foundations phase (circa 1800 to 1929) are characterized by the formulation of theoretical positions concerning learning disabilities. These speculations were based essentially on the study of adults with acquired brain damage or poststroke patients. The clinical observations of physicians were the primary bases on which these theories were built. Little or no empirical hypothesis testing using controlled research procedures was undertaken during this period.

The systematic investigation of learning disabilities began around 1800 with Gall's examination of adults who had sustained head injuries and, apparently as a result, had lost the capacity to express their feelings and ideas through speech, while experiencing no intellectual privation.

When the current definition of learning disabilities is compared with the observations of Gall, one readily sees that he was studying a condition (aphasia) that, if it occurred in a child rather than in an adult, we today would call a specific language disorder and would categorize further as a learning disability. For additional evidence of this, consider Gall's diagnostic procedures in light of our present-day definition. First, he noted that some of his patients could not speak but could write their thoughts proficiently, thus demonstrating the presence of intraindividual or specific differences. Second, by documenting that the individual had been normal in verbal expression abilities prior to the head injury, he demonstrated that the problem definitely was a consequence of brain involvement (i.e., damage, disorganization, or dysfunction) and that this physical impairment had in some way disrupted the functioning of those particular psychoneurological processes that permitted the accurate transmission of language through speech. Thus, the presence of intrinsic deficits was confirmed. Third, he felt that it was critical to show that the patient's performance was not caused by other conditions, notably mental retardation or deafness.

Unfortunately, Gall's speculations concerning causality led him into phrenology and, as a consequence, into scientific disrepute. But other physicians continued his work in language pathology, for example, Bouillaud, Broca, Jackson, and Wernicke, among many others. They studied, refined, and expanded the earlier theories on

Developmental phase dimension	Type of disorder dimension		
	Disorders of spoken language: (Listening, Speaking)	Disorders of written language: (Reading, Writing)	Correlative disorders: (Perceptual-Motor Processes, Hyperactivity-Distractibility)
Early foundations phase (1800–1929)	Gall 1802 Bouillaud 1825 Broca 1861 Jackson 1864 Bastien 1869 Wernicke 1881 Marie 1906 Head 1926	Dejerine 1887 Hinshelwood 1917	Goldstein 1927
Late foundations phase (1930–1962)	Osgood 1953 Eisenson 1954 Myklebust 1954 Wepman 1960 Kirk 1961 McGinnis 1963 Fitzgerald 1966	Gillingham 1934 Orton 1937 Fernald 1943	Strauss & Werner 1933 Lehtinen 1947 Kephart 1955 Cruickshank 1961 Frostig 1961 Barsch 1962 Getman 1962
Early years of LD movement phase (1963–present)	The field of learning disabilities 1963		

FIGURE 2.1. Individuals whose work contributed to the foundations phase, grouped by disorder type. *Note.* Adapted from "Historical Perspectives on the Education of the Learning Disabled" by J. L. Wiederholt, in *The Second Review of Special Education* (p. 105), L. Mann and D. A. Sabatino (Eds.), 1974, Austin, TX: PRO-ED. Reprinted by permission.

aphasia and attempted to discover the precise areas of the brain that, if damaged, would result in loss of language.

Geschwind (1962) states that Dejerine was one of the first physicians to report a case of "acquired reading disability," that is, an adult who, because of brain damage, had lost the ability to read while retaining his proficiency in understanding and using spoken language. Hinshelwood extended this line of study and was among the first to assert that some kinds of congenital brain defects might cause children to have developmental reading problems, that is, "congenital word blindness," and to speculate about methods by which affected children could be taught to read. Orton disputed many of Hinshelwood's positions and formulated his own theories regarding the causes for and the remediation of those specific reading problems that he called "strephosymbolia." At about the same time, Fernald developed the framework for what would be called the VAKT (visual-auditory-kinesthetic-tactile) approach to remedial reading instruction, a system not too different from that espoused by Orton.

The foundation efforts in the area of the correlative disorders were exemplified by those of Goldstein (1939). He observed that adults who had sustained brain insult frequently developed a variety of additional disordered behaviors, which he termed "catastrophic reactions." Therefore, one of his primary postulations was that cerebral damage rarely caused a specific behavioral disturbance; instead, he believed that such an insult would eventually affect many areas of performance. Strauss and Werner extended these principles to the study of brain damaged mentally retarded children and concentrated their study on a subtype that eventually became known as the Strauss syndrome child, that is, the supposedly brain injured child who evidences perceptual problems, distractibility, disinhibition, perseveration, and other detailed reactions.

During the latter years of the foundations phase (circa 1930 to 1963) a concerted effort was made to translate the theoretical postulates derived previously into remedial practice. The focus of inquiry decidedly shifted from adults to children, and the ideas that had been developed from the study of adults were transferred in total to the study of children with developmental disorders. For the first time, psychologists and a few educators became prominent in the field of learning disabilities. As a consequence of this effort, many tests and training programs were developed that at first were used mostly in isolated clinics, institutions, and private schools, and later in public schools as well.

In the area of disorders of spoken language, numerous tests were developed during the foundations phase, of which those designed by Wepman (*Auditory Discrimination Test*, 1960), Kirk and McCarthy (*Illinois Test of Psycholinguistic Abilities*, 1961), and Eisenson (*Examining for Aphasia*, 1954) represent but a few. Also, many innovations were made in remedial treatment procedures, such as those suggested by Myklebust and by McGinnis. Orton's theorizing stimulated the development of the remedial reading systems of Gillingham and Stillman, both of which emphasized remedial phonics training.

Strauss's ideas on training, which were presented in works coauthored first with Lehtinen (1947) and later with Kephart (1955), contributed greatly to the education of brain injured, perceptually handicapped children. Cruickshank combined Strauss's orientation with Lehtinen's instructional techniques and applied them to teaching the nonretarded, perceptually impaired, hyperactive child. Also, considerably influenced by Strauss, Frostig directed her attention to teaching children who evidenced a variety of educational problems that were usually associated with perceptual deficiencies. Her most visible contributions during this period were the *Developmental Test of Visual Perception* (Frostig, Maslow, Lefever, & Whittlesey, 1964) and the Developmental Program in Visual Perception (Frostig & Horne, 1964). In addition, Getman and Barsch both designed activities for training visual-motor skills in children that became very popular, as did the procedures of Kephart and of Delacato in the area of motor development.

In addition to the Wiederholt (1974) reference, readers who require a more detailed account of the foundations period are referred to the works of Luria (1966), Schuell, Jenkins, and Jimenez-Pabon (1964), and Head (1926) for information concerning disorders of spoken language; Hinshelwood (1917) and Orton (1937, 1989) for disorders of written language; and Hallahan and Cruickshank (1973) for correlative disorders, including the Strauss syndrome.

THE EARLY YEARS OF THE LD MOVEMENT

On April 6, 1963, at a conference sponsored by the Fund for Perceptually Handicapped Children, Samuel Kirk mentioned that he had used the term *learning disabilities* to describe

> a group of children who have disorders in development in skills needed for social interaction. In this group I do not include children who have sensory handicaps such as blindness, or deafness, because we have methods of managing and training the deaf and the blind. I also exclude from this group children who have generalized mental retardation. (1963, p. 3)

That very evening the convention voted to organize itself as the Association for Children with Learning Disabilities (ACLD). In 1989, ACLD changed its name to the Learning Disabilities Association of America (LDA). A national advisory board was selected whose membership represented a broad spectrum of opinions about disorders of spoken and written language and about perceptual-motor performance. The professional diversity of the board members reflected the "integrative" nature that learning disabilities would henceforth exhibit. The field now had a generic name under which the variety of learning disabilities could be classified and an organization of parents and professionals dedicated to the interest of the affected children. One could say with some justification that the field of learning disabilities as an established entity began at this time.

Wiederholt's (1974) historical narrative concludes with the events of 1963. Since then learning disabilities as a field has continued to develop and experience all the growing pains that one would expect of an emerging area. To date these early years have been characterized by five ongoing aspects. First, the interest in learning disabilities led to the founding of new organizations that were devoted specifically to the area. Second, considerable federal and state funds became available. Third, the funds stimulated the rapid expansion of local school programs. Fourth, groups other than physicians and psychologists (e.g., parents, educators, speech pathologists, and researchers) became influential in the movement. Fifth, as more and more professionals with diverse backgrounds joined the learning disabilities movement, serious conflicts erupted over paradigms, diagnostic procedures, and instructional interventions.

The Advent of LD Organizations

All but one of the major organizations that deal exclusively with the interests of people with learning disabilities were formed after 1963. Only The Orton Dyslexia Society was organized before that date, a year generally accepted as marking the beginning of the learning disabilities movement.

The presence of these associations gives the field of learning disabilities its professional and political base and contributes greatly to development of a sense of identity on the part of their members. Through their journals, newsletters, conferences, and social-professional networks, these associations give direction on issues, share information on topics, contribute to the knowledge base of the field, and lobby governmental agents for better services.

Many organizations make important contributions to learning disabilities (e.g., American Speech-Language-Hearing Association, National Association for School Psychologists, International Reading Association), but only five deal exclusively with learning disabilities. These are described briefly below.

Learning Disabilities Association of America (LDA). Founded in 1963 under the name Association for Children with Learning Disabilities, LDA is the largest organized group in learning disabilities. As of 1989, it had 50,000 members enrolled in 48 state and 750 local chapters. Even though the association is concerned primarily with parental issues, many professionals are members. Known to be an effective advocate for its interests, LDA also provides outlets for the exchange of ideas through its annual convention, news briefs, and a new journal, *Learning Disabilities*. (LDA, 4156 Library Road, Pittsburgh, PA 15234)

Council for Learning Disabilities (CLD). In 1968, CLD was formed as a division within the Council for Exceptional Children, an organization composed primarily of professionals who work in colleges and schools in the area of special education and related fields. Originally the group was named the Division for Children with Disabilities. The purpose of the division was to promote the education and general welfare of persons with learning disabilities. In 1978, CLD began publishing a journal, the *Learning Disability Quarterly*, and sponsoring an annual international convention. In 1982, the membership voted to become independent of the Council for Exceptional Children. As an independent association of 4,000 members, the leadership of CLD hopes to attract a large multidisciplinary membership rather than focusing exclusively on educators. (CLD, P.O. Box 40303, Overland Park, KS 66204)

Division for Learning Disabilities (DLD). In 1982, DLD was formed in the Council for Exceptional Children to replace CLD, which had seceded earlier that year. The division grew quickly, and it now has over 13,000 members, numerous state affiliates, and two journals, *Learning Disabilities Focus* and *Learning Disabilities Research*, published on a semiannual basis. (DLD, Council for Exceptional Children, 1920 Association Drive, Reston, VA 22091)

The Orton Dyslexia Society, Inc. (ODS).   The oldest of the learning disabilities organizations, ODS was founded in 1949 and was named in honor of Samuel T. Orton, a noted physician who studied children with diverse language disorders. It maintains both a medical and educational emphasis focused on problems of reading and writing. Its principal periodicals are the *Annals of Dyslexia*, published once a year, and *Perspectives on Dyslexia*, a quarterly newsletter. Present membership is 8,600 organized into local units or societies. (ODS, 724 York Road, Baltimore, MD 21204)

National Joint Committee on Learning Disabilities (NJCLD).   The NJCLD was organized in 1975 to establish greater cooperation among organizations primarily concerned with individuals with learning disabilities. Organizations represented on the committee are the American Speech-Language-Hearing Association, Learning Disabilities Association of America, Council for Learning Disabilities, Division for Children with Communication Disorders, Division for Learning Disabilities, International Reading Association, National Association of School Psychologists, and The Orton Dyslexia Society. The committee provides an interdisciplinary forum for the review of issues, responds to national issues as the need arises, seeks agreement on major problems, and prepares and disseminates statements to clarify topics in the area of learning disabilities. (NJCLD, c/o The Orton Dyslexia Society, 724 York Road, Baltimore, MD 21204)

Summary.   The above described organizations are the professional and political arms of the learning disabilities movement. It is through membership in these associations that teachers, psychologists, parents, and others find a professional identity with learning disabilities. The lobbying efforts of these associations protect existing funding for learning disabilities programs and seek new sources of financial support. The journals, newsletters, and special publications keep those who work in the field aware of new methodologies, proposed legislation, and other issues that affect the field. The presence of these associations has contributed greatly to the consolidation and integration of the many different viewpoints and disciplines that go to make up the field of learning disabilities.

Legislation on Behalf of People with LD

Federal legislation authorizing special programs for handicapped people had existed since the 1960s. Unfortunately, individuals with learning disabilities were not included under these laws. As a result of intense, effective lobbying by interested professionals and parents, federal legislation was finally passed to promote services for individuals with specific learning disabilities. A brief outline of this legislation is provided below.

P.L. 89-10 (The Elementary and Secondary Education Act of 1965). This act was amended in 1969 in order to mandate the federal government to facilitate the development of the learning disabilities field as a separate entity within special education. The amendment (The Children with Specific Learning Disabilities Act of 1969) was widely known as the Yarborough Bill in honor of the Texas senator who sponsored the legislation.

P.L. 94-142 (The Education of All Handicapped Children Act of 1975). This law mandated that school districts provide free and appropriate education to all handicapped children including those with learning disabilities. Bryan and Bryan (1986) summarized the law's major features as follows:

1. Individualized education program (IEP), which requires statement of:
   a. Explicit annual educational goals
   b. Short-term instructional objectives
   c. Dates of initiation and duration of services
   d. Appropriate objective criteria and evaluation procedures

2. Education in the least restrictive environment

3. Parental involvement in decision processes

4. Appeal processes when parents are dissatisfied

5. Use of assessment procedures that are not racially or culturally biased

6. Use of multiple procedures to determine educational programs. (p. 9)

P.L. 98-199 (The Education of the Handicapped Act of 1983). The law reaffirmed the federal role by expanding and including many components in P.L. 94-142 and especially supported better preschool, secondary, and postsecondary programs for handicapped persons as well as special education teacher preparation, early childhood programs, parent training, and information dissemination.

These laws made the rapid growth of learning disabilities programs in the schools possible. But the federal contribution was not limited to just enabling legislation. A number of specific projects were sponsored by the federal government since 1966. Many of these influenced the growth of learning disabilities programs greatly. A few of the more notable projects are discussed next.

1. In 1966 the first of three federally sponsored task force reports was published, *Minimal Brain Dysfunction in Children: Terminology and Identification* (Clements, 1966). It was followed by *Minimal Brain Dysfunction in Children: Educational, Medical, and Health Related Services* (Haring & Miller, 1969) and *Central Processing Dysfunctions in Children: A Review of Research* (Chalfant & Scheffelin, 1969). The reviews of research and statements of position included in these monographs were useful in providing professionals with an informational base on which to conceptualize the field of learning disabilities and to implement services for children.

2. The Advancement Institute for Leadership Personnel in Learning Disabilities, at which 87 teacher-trainers met and discussed problems and issues in preparing

professionals in learning disabilities, did much to stimulate communication and cohesiveness among professionals working in this area. It was one of the first meetings at which individuals from one university had the opportunity to meet their counterparts in other colleges. The final report of this meeting (Kass, 1970) still makes interesting reading because the timely views of the participants on approaches to teacher training and the reflection of the "elder statesmen" (Cruickshank, Frostig, Kephart, Kirk, and Myklebust) on their contributions to learning disabilities are included.

3. Beginning in 1971 and continuing under differing funding guidelines, the Bureau of Education for the Handicapped (now the Office of Special Education and Rehabilitation Services) authorized Child Service Demonstration Projects (CSDPs) throughout the country. These operations were to serve as models in stimulating statewide instructional services to learning disabled children.

4. The Leadership Training Institute in Learning Disabilities (LTI) operated from 1971 to 1975. In addition to providing the CSDPs with technical assistance, the LTI staff collected an appreciable amount of data on then-current school practices in learning disabilities. This was made available in two monographs (Bryant, 1972; Bryant & McLoughlin, 1972).

5. In 1977 the Bureau of Education for the Handicapped shifted its interests from demonstration to research projects. As a result, five multidisciplinary research institutes were funded to address salient questions in the field of learning disabilities. The creation of the institutes was intended to supply a base of empirical evidence in a field overburdened with often conflicting theoretical postulations. Each institute investigated a different area of concern. The Columbia University institute researched "information processing" deficits and their relationship to language comprehension in upper elementary-aged learning disabled students. The Chicago Circle campus of the University of Illinois institute studied language and social skills, reading, and learning/recall problems. The institute at the University of Kansas considered issues relating to the identification and treatment of learning disabled adolescents. The institute at the University of Minnesota investigated identification, assessment, and placement issues. The University of Virginia institute focused on attentional deficits and self-activated learning strategies. A considerable portion of the Winter 1978 issue of the *Learning Disability Quarterly* discusses the purposes and activities of these institutes (see articles by Bryant; Bryan & Eash; Meyen & Deshler; Hallahan; and Ysseldyke, Shinn, & Thurlow). The entire Spring 1983 issue of *Exceptional Education Quarterly* is devoted to the findings of the institutes.

The Rise of LD Services in American Education

Within a relatively few years, learning disabilities which had no official standing under the law before 1969 became the largest area of the handicapped being served in special education. This increase was the direct outgrowth of professional and parental lobbying efforts which led to the passage of legislation that provided funding specifically for learning disabilities.

Between 1977 and 1987, the number of learning disabled children receiving services in the public schools rose unprecedentedly from one to two million (Will, 1987). The number of students with learning disabilities who attended private facilities evidently increased proportionally, because the 13th edition of the *Directory of Facilities and Services for the Learning Disabled* (1989) listed over 500 private schools and clinics.

This increase is not limited to the elementary and secondary schools. On the contrary, postsecondary educational institutions have experienced a similar rise in the enrollment of learning disabled students. In fact, many colleges have established special programs to attract students with learning disabilities. Mangrum and Strichart (1988) offer three major reasons why colleges have initiated these special programs: (a) They feel a social responsibility to the handicapped, (b) declining enrollments are offset by tuition from these groups, and (c) compliance with Section 504 of the Rehabilitation Act of 1973 is mandatory if they are receiving financial assistance from federal sources. This act requires colleges to accommodate persons with "specific learning disabilities." Bursuck, Rose, Cowen, and Yahaya (1989) studied the ways in which postsecondary programs have sought to accommodate students who have learning disabilities and to comply with the law.

Mangrum and Strichart (1988), Nelson and Lignugaris/Kraft (1989), and Siperstein (1988) are good sources for college personnel who want to develop and implement special programs for the learning disabled student. Students will find *Unlocking Potential: College and Other Choices for the Learning Disabled* (Scheiber & Talpers, 1987) and *Lovejoy's College Guide for the Learning Disabled* (Straughn & Colby, 1984) useful in selecting a suitable college.

The sudden appearance of learning disabilities presented serious problems for the American educational system because many administrators had little knowledge about learning disabilities, few teachers had been trained to handle this new category of handicap, and college programs for preparing teachers and other personnel to work with the learning disabled were almost nonexistent. Though the situation is greatly improved today, much remains to be done, especially at the postsecondary level (Parks, Antonoff, Drake, Skiba, & Soberman, 1987).

Infusion of Diverse Interest Groups

Before 1963, physicians and psychologists dominated the field that became known as learning disabilities. This domination ended with the passage of federal legislation supporting special school programs and services for the learning disabled. The law shifted the focus of the learning disabilities movement from the clinic to the classroom and gave parents and educators a major role to play in programming and placement. Soon these new people were joining existing learning disabilities associations or forming new ones. Before long, they were influential in all of these associations and predominant in some. A brief description of the newcomers to the learning disabilities field and their contributions follows.

Parents.   Perhaps the most important group of people to become influential in the learning disabilities movement after 1963 were parents. Parents were the "shock troops" of the field. It was primarily due to their advocacy and insistence that mandating legislation was passed (often over considerable opposition) to help the learning disabled. Their influence is seen in laws which specified that parents would have a role to play in planning programs for their children and spelled out their rights regarding due process.

Individual parents tend to conceptualize the field of learning disabilities in terms of their particular child. In so doing, they often hold distorted ideas as to what the field looks like in general. From time to time, they harbor a not unfounded distrust of professionals who work in the field. They feel that many professionals have not been sufficiently committed to the interests of their children; have failed to make their children better through teaching, medication, or so forth; have belittled their cherished (though nonvalidated) treatments; or have monetary gains as the primary goal in working with their children.

Parents have contributed considerably to the well-being of the learning disabilities field. They represent its heart; they live every day with the consequences of learning disabilities; they have the greatest investment in the field; they have every reason to be impatient, militant, and testy. There would be no field as we know it without them.

Educators.   Of course, individual educators were present during the foundations phase (e.g., Gillingham and Lehtinen), but for the most part their work was associated strongly with that of physicians or psychologists (e.g., Orton and Strauss). With the passage of federal legislation, educators were thrust into playing a central role in learning disabilities. These laws required public schools to provide service for learning disabled people from preschool through college. Students who were previously not served or who were served in private schools, speech therapy clinics, and special university facilities were now to be taught in public schools. As a result, the need for teachers trained to handle learning disabled students was intense.

To meet this need, the federal government stimulated the development of teacher training programs at the college level, and state educational agencies set up special certification endorsements for the LD category. Leigh and Patton (1986) reported that, at the time they wrote, 34 states offered a teaching certification endorsement in "learning disabilities."

Soon a large group of trained teachers existed who identified themselves with the field of learning disabilities. Most of these were new teachers; others were experienced teachers from regular education, speech pathology, and remedial reading who had been retrained specifically in learning disabilities. The great majority of those new teachers were educated in university programs that had only recently been established in colleges of education.

Not surprisingly, most of the professors and instructors associated with these teacher training programs approach theoretical and practical issues in learning disabilities from an educator's point of view rather than from a psychologist's or physician's orientation. Educators tend to rely on the principles of direct instruction (i.e., if the problem is reading, teach the student to read directly by providing experiences with print or exercises involving letters, words, and written discourse). To them, this approach seems more sensible than the off-task techniques associated with process training and traditional instruction methodologies in learning disabilities. Doubtlessly, the influence of educators has done much to loosen the hold that processing training and other instructional fads have had on the field.

Not so beneficial is the educator's tendency to conceptualize learning disabilities in terms of problems of mild to moderate degree, to downplay the role of etiology, to fixate on the school-aged child, and to focus on remediation of specific problems rather than on treatment of the whole child. These ideas as implemented in the schools combined to blur the distinctions between learning disabled students on the one hand and remedial or slow learning students on the other. The fact that these groups are often confused in actual school practice is aptly demonstrated by Ysseldyke, O'Sullivan, Thurlow, and Christenson (1989) and Ysseldyke, Algozzine, Shinn, and McGue (1982).

Speech-Language Pathologists. Professionals trained in speech and language pathology have exerted a consistent influence on the field of learning disabilities since it began. Because of an interest in acquired and developmental aphasia, their concern with spoken and written language disorders is a natural extension. Speech pathologists play a primary role when working with preschool learning disability cases. Many current spokespersons in the learning disabilities movement were originally "speech therapists" (e.g., Myers, Myklebust, D. Johnson, and Hammill).

Unlike educators, speech and language pathologists often have experience with moderate-to-severe organic-based language disability cases. They also have a better than usual grasp of theory related to language disorders. In the early 1960s, the aphasia models of Osgood (1957) and Wepman, Jones, Bock, and Van Pelt (1960) were influential with this group; these models gave way to the transformational grammar theories of Chomsky (1967), which have now been integrated with or supplemented by the modern ideas pertaining to the importance of semantics and pragmatics.

The theoretical ideas generalized among speech and language pathologists and linguists were implemented in two ways. Some professionals attempted to merge the modern ideas about language with the traditional learning disability ideas about mental processes. This resulted in the development of a variety of assessment and intervention techniques loosely referred to as "psycholinguistic" approaches. The authors of these approaches adopted the theories of Osgood and Wepman as their conceptual base. Notable among efforts was the work of Kirk and McCarthy (1961), Kirk, McCarthy, and Kirk (1968), Bush and Giles (1977), and Karnes (1968). Thorough discussions of their approaches are found in Chapter 14.

Most speech pathologists abandoned the psycholinguistic models such as those based on the Osgood paradigm fairly quickly and turned to the transformational grammar theory promulgated by Noam Chomsky. The emphasis in this theory on phonology, syntax, and semantics was much more congenial to the training and orientation of most speech pathologists, and they embraced the tenets of transformational syntax quite readily. During most of the 1970s and well into the 1980s, most speech and language programs focused on the development of grammar and sentence construction/transformation as appropriate areas for language development and/or remediation. However, it should be noted that some leaders in the field, such as Laura Lee, never lost sight of the fact that language must be viewed as a medium for meaningful intercourse between and among individuals.

During the 1980s, a shift toward the holistic area of semantics and away from the atomistic view inherent in grammar occurred, and speech and language therapy became more oriented toward the meaningful aspects of language. Speech pathologists began incorporating elements of pragmatics in their programs; therapy, for the most part, has returned to the development of meaningful discourse.

Probably because of speech pathology's historical interest in aphasia resulting from CNS trauma and because of the amount of research in dichotic listening, the field still maintains an abiding interest in central auditory processing. It is not yet apparent to the observer that this interest has transferred to the therapy conducted by most speech pathologists.

In some clinical and hospital settings, it is more apparent that speech pathologists have been strongly influenced by the recent studies of closed head injuries and have become interested in the cognitive, probably nonlinguistic, problems of such patients. This interest is slowly being manifested in public schools therapy programs, where more and more head injured students are being seen in special education.

Researchers.   To some degree, the work of researchers gives a field its creditability. Without research to help answer questions, a field becomes hopelessly mired down in pointless argument, needless speculation, and unverifiable claims. The availability of a body of relevant research contributes to raising an area of study to a true science.

Because of the intense interest in learning disabilities during the 1970s, large sums of money became available to support research projects, a fact that attracted many first-class investigators to a field where few had existed previously. During the foundations phase and the very early years of the field, most of the theories and practices that were developed had been based on the observations of clinicians studying their patients or students. These ideas and techniques were now to be tested by the relatively rigorous statistical and analytical procedures of objective, trained researchers. Clinical observations continued to be important, especially as a means for generating hypotheses, but acceptance of a premise now depended upon the outcome of substantive research.

Based on the sheer volume of studies published, as well as their quality, one would say that James Ysseldyke, Bob Algozzine, Tanis Bryan, Frank Vellutino, Albert Galaburda, Kenneth Kavale, Daniel Hallahan, Don Deshler, Joseph Jenkins, Joseph Torgesen, Bernice Wong, and Keith Stanovich were among the most prolific authors of controlled, statistical research published between 1970 and 1985 in the field of learning disabilities. Because of the work of these and other researchers, the scientific community has developed an increasing respect for the field of learning disabilities. The presence of so many researchers investigating various aspects of learning disabilities is evidence that the field is progressing and maturing.

Resolution of the Major Paradigm Dispute in LD

In the late 1960s and early 1970s, it was fashionable in learning disabilities circles to advocate a process approach to diagnosis and intervention. This approach was based on the idea that the mind contained certain psychoneurological processes that were required for adequate cognitive development and academic performance. These so-called basic learning processes included the auditory, visual, tactile, motoric, and vocal processes as well as such nonmodality phenomena as feedback, attention, sequencing, closure, and memory. Disorders in these mentalistic, and possibly hypothetial, processes were thought to seriously affect learning. For example, a popular theory was that the reading problems of a learning disabled child (i.e., a dyslexic) might be the result of deficient visual or auditory perceptual development. More extreme advocates of this orientation postulated that difficulty in balance, eye tracking, coordination, or sensory-motor integration in young children might lead to academic problems later in life. The implications for education were that training the processes was important. Some professionals even believed that process training should take precedence over teaching academics directly. The logic was that once the disordered processes were perfected, academic learning could take place normally.

At this time, many process tests were designed and marketed. The results of these tests enabled diagnosticians to identify students who suffered from all kinds of so-called process disorders. Training packages, materials, and curricula for ameliorating the identified process problems were also plentiful. The process orientation in one form or another was pervasive and evidenced in classrooms and clinics by the presence of exercise mats, *Illinois Test of Psycholinguistic Abilities* (ITPA) kits, trampolines, balance beams, parquetry sets, Frostig-Horne worksheets, and other paraphernalia. As a result, many learning disabilities specialists did process training in perception, memory, closure, attention, and modalities while regular and special education teachers did direct remediation in reading, writing, listening, speaking, and math.

To some degree or other, almost all of the pioneers in the learning disabilities movement during the late foundations phase were advocates of some form of process training. These professionals included Kirk, Cruickshank, Myklebust, Barsch, Frostig, Delacato, Ayres, Getman, Kephart, and many others.

Lester Mann was an early dissenter. Given the spirit of the times, Mann and Phillips (1967) courageously voiced an opposing point of view in their article *Fractional Practices in Special Education*. Mann (1971) followed this up with a particularly withering theoretical attack on the process approach entitled *Psychometric Phrenology and the New Faculty Psychology*. In this article, he points out that process approaches are similar to the long discredited "faculty psychology" ideas so prevalent during the 1800s, and that those who use the approach risk fractionalizing both children and the way in which their problems are conceptualized. But Mann's opposition was philosophical, and counterarguments formulated by Barsch (1971), Bortner (1971), Hagin and Silver (1971), and others were cogent and occasionally powerful apologies for then-current attempts to train basic abilities.

In 1972, matters took a different turn. A number of research studies had been published by then, and their results tended to support the arguments originally voiced by Mann. During this period, the research of Hammill and his colleagues, especially Wiederholt, Newcomer, and Larsen, was prominent. Skirting the issue of whether or not the theory of process training had any merit, they concluded that existing research showed clearly that process abilities as measured by existing tests did not particularly relate to cognitive or academic performance and that presently available methods for training processes had failed to produce desired gains in cognitive, academic, or even process abilities.

At first, Hammill's work focused on visual perceptual processing abilities (Goodman & Hammill, 1973; Hammill, 1972; Hammill, Goodman, & Wiederholt, 1974; Hammill & Larsen, 1974b; Larsen & Hammill, 1975; Wiederholt & Hammill, 1971). In 1974, attention was shifted to the study of the processing approach represented by the ITPA and its related training programs (Hammill & Larsen, 1974a; Hammill, Parker, & Newcomer, 1975; Newcomer & Hammill 1975, 1976; Sowell, Parker, Poplin, & Larsen, 1979).

Surprisingly, publication of this research provoked a fire storm in the learning disabilities field. Many professional reputations were at stake, and millions of dollars that were invested by publishing companies in process materials were at risk. Defenders of the ITPA in particular responded with a series of defenses and counterattacks, all of which were followed by rebuttals from Hammill and co-workers.

In these years, Hammill and his colleagues were not alone in asserting the research opposition to process training; they were merely more active in politicizing issues pertaining to such training. After 1972, a steady stream of investigations that were uniformly negative to all aspects of the process orientation were published (Arter & Jenkins, 1977; Kavale & Mattson, 1983; Vellutino, Steger, Moyer, Harding, & Niles, 1977; Ysseldyke, 1973). The challenge to the process orientation raised by the increasing volume of negative investigations was not answered in the research literature by advocates of the processing approach, an omission that eventually proved fatal to their cause.

Almost immediately, the controversy which had begun in the research literature spread to other issues and to other arenas. In particular, the meetings of the Council for Learning Disabilities became a battleground, and to a lesser degree the operations of the Council for Exceptional Children were affected. Many college instructors, teachers, psychologists, and administrators took positions on the basis of the issues and personalities. Certainly, numerous personal relationships were strained or broken during the period of this controversy; others were forged by the struggle. The conflict also had certain generational aspects in that younger professionals who were less identified with traditional, pre-1963 learning disabilities tended to side with the supporters of direct instruction, in opposition to the process-oriented professionals who tended to be older and more established in special education institutions.

The controversy polarized the field, and most professionals more or less identified with one orientation or the other. The political center of the learning disabilities movement practically dissolved in the mid-1970s. As one might expect under these conditions, the professional climate at this time was acrimonious and often personally abusive. No quarter was asked; none given.

By the early 1980s, the "process wars" began to abate. In the schools, process approaches were increasingly replaced with more on-task forms of assessment and instruction. Processing tests, such as the ITPA (Kirk & McCarthy, 1961) and the *Developmental Test of Visual Perception* (Frostig et al., 1964), lost their markets. Books written by the most prominent process advocates ceased to the reprinted. Articles recommending process approaches disappeared from the special education literature. For the moment, the issue of process training is resolved and direct instruction has emerged as the model of choice.

The resolution of this key issue was critical to the survival of the learning disabilities movement. A field based on the mentalistic processing model so prevalent during the 1960s and early 1970s probably would not have lasted. This is especially the case since the vast majority of the relevant research did not support the model, and the younger professionals were committed to other points of view. Learning disabilities needed an approach with a better data base for its foundation; at the time, the principles of direct instruction satisfied this purpose.

The spirited upheaval caused by the processing debate is neither foreign nor harmful to a profession. In fact, it is often a sign of a vibrant, healthy, and emerging life force. Kuhn (1970) points out that such conflicts often break out in an area when the time has come to shift from one paradigm to another. The shifts themselves can be slow and evolutionary or quick and revolutionary as was the case when the learning disabilities community changed its allegiance from a processing model to a direct instruction model.

Readers who are interested in the political ramifications of the processing conflict are referred to Wong (1986), Lieberman (1980), Cruickshank (1985), Kavale and Forness (1985), and Poplin (1989). Of particular interest are the April 1980 issue of the *Journal of Learning Disabilities*, which was devoted entirely to "an alert to the learning disability community," and the reply by the International DCLD (now CLD) Board of Trustees (1980) entitled "A factual response to April's fiction." Though the issue ostensibly being dealt with in this "alert" and "response" pertains to the secession of CLD from CEC, the exchange is really one more episode in the processing controversy. In this case, the editor of the *Journal of Learning Disabilities* had sided with the LD traditionalists, and the DCLD trustees with the challengers. An ironic note is that J. L. Wiederholt, who drafted the DCLD response, is now editor of the *Journal of Learning Disabilities*.

A GLIMPSE INTO THE FUTURE

No doubt an era in the history of learning disabilities has ended or is coming to an end. The heady thrust to establish a field is over because learning disabilities is now deeply entrenched as a specific area of handicaps. Strong associations exist to defend the field; legislation protects and provides for learning disabled persons; programs for teaching students with learning disabilities are present from the preschool through postsecondary years; professionals from many diverse areas have become integrated into the field; and the learning disabilities community has come through its first civil war stronger than ever. Thus, the ground is prepared for the field's future growth.

Writing a history is a scholarly, often creative effort requiring the analysis and structuring of facts and events. Predicting the future, on the other hand, is a risky business that is best left to clairvoyants who can depend upon their crystal balls for insight. It is fairly easy, however, to identify present-day events or ideas that are important and that might exert an influence on the future of learning disabilities. Regrettably, one cannot tell which of these will significantly influence the future or to what extent they will be influential. To us, the following current topics bear watching.

The Regular Education Initiative

The Regular Education Initiative (REI) is a movement stimulated by agents of the government (e.g., Will, 1986) and a group of professionals (e.g., Reynolds, 1988; Wang, Reynolds, & Walberg, 1986). The purpose of the effort is to significantly reduce categorical programming in the schools by integrating handicapped, including learning disabled, students into regular classes. If successful, the numbers of students diagnosed and served under the LD label would be reduced dramatically. Since most of the students served under the REI would have mild problems, those who continued to be labeled LD would have relatively more severe problems. This fact would impact all aspects of learning disabilities greatly.

The success of the REI is by no means a foregone conclusion. Serious questions about how the REI is to be implemented were raised by Daniel Hallahan, James Kauffman, James McKinney, Tanis Bryan, Donald Deshler, Jean Schumaker, Phillip Strain, Melvin Semmel, John Lloyd, Michael Gerber, and other prominent special educators in the January 1988 issue of the *Journal of Learning Disabilities* and by Wiederholt and by Newcomer in the Summer 1989 issue of *Learning Disability Quarterly*. That the REI can be controversial at times is evident in the exchange of ideas between Douglas and Lynn Fuchs and Margaret Wang and Herbert Walberg in the October 1988 issue of *Exceptional Children*. Must reading for all persons interested in this topic is Kauffman's (1989) "The Regular Education Initiative as Reagan-Bush Education Policy: A Trickle-Down Theory of Education of the Hard-to-Teach."

Disagreements Among Advocates of Direct Instruction

A growing disagreement is developing between two wings of the direct instruction movement. Advocates of direct instruction are unanimous in their opposition to process training, and they agree that to obtain improvement in a skill the instructional activities have to approximate those of the skill being taught. Simply put, this means that students learn to read by reading or by instruction in obvious reading skills. Here, however, two polar approaches are possible: holistic (sometimes called constructionist) and atomistic (sometimes called reductionist).

In teaching reading, a holistic (or wholistic) advocate would consider the complete person in planning instruction. This focus on the whole extends to the curriculum as well. For example, the holistically oriented teacher would consider the student's motivation, setting, and needs; immerse the learner in the world of print; lead him or her to discover reading through targeted but relatively free activities; and rarely teach anything less than meaningful units (words or sentences). To this latter point, meaningful words would not be broken down into nonmeaningful phonetic units for the purpose of instruction. Thus, the emphasis is placed on the teaching of wholes—whole person, whole word, whole idea, and so on.

Teachers who have an atomistic approach break everything down to subparts or particulars, teach the parts (often in isolation), and reassemble the parts into wholes at a later time. The emphasis here is on skills and drills. Reading begins by teaching differences among graphemes, sounds associated with graphemes, syllabic units, phonics, and so on. Since the approach is ready-made for reinforcement theory, progress charting, and task analysis, many behaviorists have gravitated to this position.

The two positions have been described in the extreme in order to make the distinction between them easier. In everyday application, however, most successful practitioners probably employ a good mix of each approach and differ only in their emphasis.

Poplin (1988a, 1988b), Reid (1988), and Iano (1986, 1987) provide particularly insightful arguments in favor of holistic positions. Defenses of behavioral principles, cautions against a too hasty acceptance of holistic positions, and outright oppositions to constructionist points of view are found in Kimball and Heron (1988), Forness (1988), Carnine (1987), Lloyd (1987), and Forness and Kavale (1987).

The Reemergence of the Cognitive Information Processing Model

Around 1980, some professionals involved in learning disabilities, mostly psychologists, began to assert a reformed cognitive information processing model. Disillusioned by the field's experience with early operationalizations of the model (i.e., with perceptual-motor and ITPA-like psycholinguistic processing ideas), these individuals began to reformulate the model and reconsider its role in learning disabilities.

Supposedly, the new orientations are different from those proposed by Kephart, Frostig, Cruickshank, Kirk, and others and thereby more promising. At the very least, Swanson (1987) writes that "contemporary information processing theory is far more sophisticated and comprehensive in methodology than that which guided previous work" (pp. 4–5). To be sure, Swanson's (p. 4) model is more elaborate than the one previously offered by Kephart (1971). Torgesen (1986) goes further and points out that early advocates (specifically Kirk, Kephart, and Frostig) had to operate in a "relative conceptual and scientific vacuum" (p. 402). The assumption here is that one reason the early information-processing advocates failed to conclusively establish the model in learning disabilities was that they lacked a complete theoretical and research base.

Like earlier processing theorists and practitioners, Swanson (1987), Wong (1986), Samuels (1987), Torgesen (1986), and Kolligian and Sternberg (1987) believe intensely in the value of converting theory into testable hypothetical constructs. Using both observation of behavior and research findings as a base, they move quickly and confidently from the concrete obvious to the abstract hypothetical. Thus, failure of a child to satisfactorily complete a digit span task might be attributed to a problem in phonological coding (a hypothetical construct, i.e., a thing defined or presumed to exist) in opposition to the obvious conclusion that the child merely has difficulty recalling sequences of digits. The work of the previously listed professionals is replete with examples of hypothetical constructs (e.g., short-term memory, working memory, sensory register, metacomponents) and special vocabulary (e.g., interface, meta-"everything"). These abstractions are then grouped and organized into hypothetical models, paradigms, or schemata which are intended to explain how people think and process information. In stark comparison to the strict behaviorist who is content with the simple stimulus-response (S-R) model, the cognitive information-processing advocate arranges his or her hypothetical constructs to generate a systematic, reasonable explanation of what might go on between the S and the R in an individual's head.

These models can be employed to build assessment devices and training materials which can be validated by research. If the use of the material does develop the abilities tapped by the test and if these abilities can be shown to have relevance, then perhaps the theory underlying both the materials and the test is valid. At the present time, the newest wave of process-oriented professionals have focused on model building and preliminary research. Eventually, they will have to prove the utility of their ideas in the classroom and the clinic through carefully designed and executed research.

Individuals who are inclined toward cognitive information processing are all Platonists. As such, they are naturally inclined to flirt with professional heresy by treating their abstract constructs as if they were real. A professional's mind is a creative thing. It can visualize a large-winged man-eating reptile and define it as a "dragon," but it cannot make the image real. We can conceptualize theoretical models and populate them with apparently reasonable hypothetical constructs, but unless we can prove that a model has utility in practical situations, it remains nothing more than a figment of someone's imagination, a useless mental construction. To their credit,

Kirk, Kephart, and Frostig knew this to be true. They accepted the challenge to show the practical value of their processing ideas and lost. Only the future knows if the latter-day process-inclined professionals can do better.

To date, the interest in learning disabilities has passed through two more or less distinct phases and is possibly well into a third. The third phase is so new that we don't know its characteristics and therefore can have no name for it. Doubtlessly, the passage of time will make "muddy water clear"; someone at a future date will be able to chronicle and analyze the important events, ideas, and personalities that influenced this period. We can assure the reader, however, that in the field of learning disabilities, as in all living organisms, change is inevitable.

3

MAJOR TYPES OF LEARNING DISABILITIES

In both children and adults, learning disabilities may exist in isolation, in combination with other learning disabilities, or in combination with other handicapping conditions such as mental retardation, deafness, blindness, and so on. The key to treating a learning disability is the identification of the particular disability so that a degree of specificity in remediation can be instituted. This chapter deals with descriptions of the following types of learning disabilities and related problems: (a) disorders of spoken language, (b) disorders of written language, (c) disorders of arithmetic, (d) disorders of reasoning, and (e) correlates of learning disabilities. The final section contains a discussion of the correlates of learning disabilities.

DISORDERS OF SPOKEN LANGUAGE (LISTENING AND SPEAKING)

The study of spoken language disorders in children developed from work done in the 19th and early 20th centuries by a variety of professionals (mostly physicians) with adults who had suffered traumatic brain damage. The damage sustained by these individuals often resulted in a condition called *aphasia*, which means loss or impairment of the ability to use language. In addition, aphasic patients have many associated perceptual-motor problems, each of which has its own terminology, such as *agnosia* (the loss of the ability to interpret either visual, auditory, or other sensory stimuli) and *apraxia* (the loss of the ability to execute previously learned motor patterns). For many years, children who were delayed in language development or whose developing language revealed bizarre deviations from the norm were labeled "childhood aphasics," "dysphasics," or any of a variety of other terms.

At one time, Wepman and his associates attempted to relate the five types of adult aphasia that they had empirically established with five developmental stages in language acquisition. A summary of the relationships is given in Table 3.1. It would appear from scanning Table 3.1 that a good bit of benefit could accrue from accepting such a classification system for children's language disorders. However, the terminology used for the types of aphasia has been firmly attached to adult aphasia and has never entered the literature on children's language disorders. The temptation to adopt the classification system in this chapter is strong for two reasons:

1. It avoids the artificial bifurcation of language into receptive and expressive elements. Throughout the development of language the child's ability to comprehend and to express language is a reciprocal process in which one facet complements the other. In children with very severe language disorders it is impossible to separate the receptive and expressive portions of the problem.

2. It follows, at least to a limited degree, the stages of language development and thus can assist in evaluating the language of a young child. Because it includes two prelanguage stages, this classification system would be more useful than some of the other systems for very severely language disordered children.

Without any attempt at developing a taxonomy of oral language disorders, we note that children may exhibit a variety of delays, disorders, or mild deviations in their language development. These disorders may be manifested in poor symbolization, reduced vocabulary, syntactic omissions and deviations, and general language delay. There may be evidence of problems that are specific to input (or comprehension) and to output (or expression). Some children have difficulty with the discrimination of speech sounds; others have problems in producing the motor patterns appropriate for intelligible speech. There are children who are similar to adult aphasics in that they may have difficulty retrieving words that they know and be unable to formulate propositional speech.

We are not the only authors today who do not attempt to classify the spoken language disorders of children. Lee, Koenigsknecht, and Mulhern (1975), who have adopted a grammatic model of development and designed a teaching approach with heavy semantic and pragmatic overtones, do not classify the disabilities of the children they evaluate and treat, except in reference to stages of development. In fact, none of the authors reviewed in Chapter 9 ("Remediating Disabilities of Listening and Speaking") have developed classification systems. Our conclusion is that designing a

TABLE 3.1. Types of Adult Aphasia and Related Developmental Stages

Type of Aphasia	Stage of Language Development
Global	Prelanguage. Characterized by speechlessness.
Jargon	Prelanguage. Characterized by meaningless autistic and echolalic phoneme use.
Pragmatic	Progressive acquisition of comprehension. Characterized by the oral expression of words and neologisms largely unrelated to meaning or below level of comprehension.
Semantic	The beginning use of substantive language progressing through nominal, verbal, and adjectival words. Characterized by one- or two-word groupings as complete expressions.
Syntactic	The use of syntax or grammar in oral expression.

Note. From "Aphasia in Adults" by H. Schuell, in *Human Communication and Its Disorders* (p. 126), 1970, Bethesda, MD: U.S. Department of Health, Education, and Welfare.

taxonomy for spoken language disorders is not an effective exercise at this particular time.

It is worthwhile to describe in some detail the types of problems manifested by children with disorders of spoken language. To iterate, individuals with oral language problems have difficulty in formulating their own language and/or in understanding that of others. Their speech behavior is characterized by malapropisms, unintelligible jabbering, jargon, mutism, regression to or arrest at infantile levels of grammar and vocabulary, telegraphic speech, inappropriate grammar or vocabulary, circumlocutions, and inordinately long pauses. One or several of these abnormalities in any degree of severity may be found in the language disordered child. An example of a child with a developmental language disorder is provided in the following case history.

R. C., a 5-year-old boy, was referred for evaluation because his speech was unintelligible and occasionally he was thought to have trouble understanding the speech of others. In addition, the father reported that when R. C. related an experience, only the main words were used, and even these were frequently presented in an improper sequence.

The Wechsler Preschool and Primary Scale of Intelligence (WPPSI) was administered, and the results indicated that R. C. was of at least average intelligence. The examiner noted that the child seemed to have considerable difficulty understanding some of the directions and was unable to express himself adequately when he did comprehend. R. C. did appreciably better on the performance section of the WPPSI than he did on the verbal part. For these reasons the hypothesis of a specific spoken language disorder was set forth at that time, and additional testing was undertaken.

Even though the audiological evaluation revealed a mild bilateral conductive hearing loss, the loss was not severe enough to account for the child's apparent language difficulties. The findings of the speech and language evaluation were indicative of both auditory receptive and expressive language disorders. The test results revealed (a) a severe articulation disorder, (b) significantly impaired ability to combine two or more grammatic structures, and (c) significantly delayed acquisition of grammatical forms. Also, during the evaluation much evidence of hyperactivity and distractibility was noted by all examiners.

It should be noted that speech impairments such as dysarthria, poor articulation, nasality, and even stuttering also contribute to unintelligibility in that they affect adversely the quality of the vocal output and make it difficult for the listener to understand what the speaker is trying to communicate. However, speech disorders per se are not considered to be language disorders because they do not affect the symbolic quality of the ideas, vocabulary, or grammar being expressed.

Although the terminology of aphasia has been abandoned when one is discussing language disorders in children, the terms are still used to describe acquired language disorders in older individuals. When a person over the age of 7 or 8—that is, a "linguistic adult"—acquires a language problem as a result of brain damage, the problem is still usually referred to as aphasia. Depending on the severity and pervasiveness of the disorder, the term *dysphasia* may be used to describe a lesser degree of impairment. The primary characteristic of aphasia in the older person is the suddenness of onset—a noticeable impairment of language function in an individual who was previously a proficient speaker. In such cases the person generally retains or recovers control over the speech mechanism, that is, the tongue, lips, jaw, and so on, except when it is used for speech. One of the first reported cases of acquired language disorder was described by Gall in the early 1800s.

In consequences of an attack of apoplexy a soldier found it impossible to express in spoken language his feelings and ideas. His face bore no signs of a deranged intellect. His mind (esprit) found the answer to questions addressed to him and he carried out all he was told to do; shown an armchair and asked if he knew what it was, he answered by seating himself in it. He could not articulate on the spot a word pronounced for him to repeat; but a few moments later the word escaped from his lips as if involuntarily. In his embarrassment he pointed to the lower part of his forehead; he showed impatience and indicated by gestures that his impotence of speech came from there. It was not his tongue which was embarrassed; for he moved it with great agility and could pronounce quite well a large number of isolated words. His memory was not at fault, for he signified his anger at being unable to express himself concerning many things which he wished to communicate. It was the faculty of speech alone which was abolished. (Head, 1926, p. 11)

To illustrate that disorders of language resulting from traumatic brain damage are similar in individuals of varying ages, the above passage could easily have been used to describe A. D., an 8-year-old boy who was seen in a speech and hearing clinic following the rupture of a congenital aneurysm in a cerebral artery. Like the soldier, A. D. was unable to formulate spoken language, although his comprehension of language was relatively unimpaired. When he did attempt to speak, his language was marked by numerous anomic errors; that is, he routinely mislabeled objects and had difficulty recalling the correct words. Therapy for this 8-year-old was, in general, no different from that for a mature adult.

DISORDERS OF WRITTEN LANGUAGE (READING AND WRITING)

The specific learning disabilities described in this section include those associated with learning to read, write, and spell. Many children experience difficulty in reaching a minimal level of competence in such basic school subjects, but not all of them suffer from a specific learning disability. Some are inadequately taught throughout their entire school lives; some come from backgrounds that do not prepare or reinforce children for succeeding in school; some lack sufficient motivation; some do not speak standard English well, a particularly serious problem because standard English is the language of instruction in most schools. Even though students affected by these influences do have need for special instruction and frequently are misdiagnosed as "handicapped" and placed in special education programs, especially the learning disability resource program, they are not handicapped in the most precise meaning of the word. Neither are they the population for whom special education services were intended by the federal initiatives or by most state departments of education programs established under the label of learning disability. Though these children frequently are misdiagnosed as learning disabled, they are more appropriately referred to as children with learning and behavior problems.

Youngsters with learning disabilities involving written language are without a doubt the largest group in the learning disabled population. Even when those children with academic insufficiencies who are not learning disabled are removed from the population, the remainder still constitutes the largest subgroup among the learning disabled. These children with reading disabilities are thought to learn differently from other children and are reported to evidence relatively unique characteristics in their subject area performance. The disorders of written language, that is, reading, spelling, and writing, that are found in children and adults are described briefly in this section.

Reading

Many children fail to master fully the reading readiness activities presented in kindergarten and first grade; do poorly in initial reading instruction taught in the first, second, and third grades; are not particularly responsive to most remedial efforts; and graduate or leave school without ever having learned to read with any degree of proficiency. A few of these students are learning disabled, and the following characteristics are presented to aid in distinguishing specific reading disability from other cases of nonreading.

1. The child is of average or better than average intellectual ability as measured by appropriate instruments.

2. General reading ability, that is, word recognition and reading comprehension, is significantly lower than the child's grade placement and mental age would lead one to expect.

3. Even if word recognition is close to expectation, particularly in the primary grades, reading comprehension is significantly delayed. Word recognition may be spuriously high because of remedial efforts that have led to rote memorization of elementary words by the child.

4. Visual and auditory acuity are not impaired.

5. Speech and oral language skills are relatively intact.

6. Listening comprehension is superior to reading comprehension and often is at expectancy level.

7. The child's oral reading is characterized by an inordinate number of letter and word reversals, an inability to make sound-letter associations easily, faulty phonemic blending, poor discrimination of phonemes, inadequate short-term recall for sequences of letters and words, confusion among letters and words, and impaired left-right orientation.

Traditionally, children and adults who manifest many of the above listed characteristics have been diagnosed as having "developmental dyslexia," "strephosymbolia," or "congenital word blindness," terms all having similar connotation. An example of a child with such a disorder is provided by Hinshelwood (1917), an early pioneer in the study of reading disabilities. He described

> a boy, aged 14 years, bright, intelligent, and quick at games and in no way inferior to others of his own age, unless in his inability to learn to read. The greatest difficulty was experienced in teaching the boy his letters, and it was thought that he never would learn them. He had by constant application acquired a knowledge of the letters, but though at school and under tutors for seven years, and in spite of the most persistent efforts, he could only with difficulty spell out words of one syllable. Words written or printed seemed to convey no impression to his mind, and it was only after laboriously spelling them that he was able by the sound of the letters to discover their import. He read figures fluently, and could do simple sums correctly. The boy himself said that he was fond of arithmetic, and found no difficulty with it. The boy's

schoolmaster, who had taught him for some years, said that he would be the smartest boy in school, if the instruction were entirely oral. (pp. 41–42)

Letter-by-letter reading is by no means unusual in students who have severe reading disorders. Another boy, J. N., who received various forms of remedial instruction for the greater part of his school career, never progressed beyond the letter-by-letter stage of reading. Although he was able to complete law school through the utilization of compensatory techniques such as tape recording lectures, using readers, taking examinations orally, and spending extraordinarily long periods of time reading, he has never become a "reader."

Not all cases of reading disability are as severe as the ones just described; naturally, some are quite mild, and the individuals make rapid progress when exposed to remedial programs. As with oral language disorders, however, there are cases of very severe reading disability. These cases are of great interest to the student of learning disabilities, because they often exemplify the types of problems demonstrated by the milder cases and because the symptomatology is so striking in the severe cases that it is easy to pinpoint and study the characteristics of reading disabilities.

Again, as with oral language disorders, some cases of reading disability are acquired rather than developmental. As with acquired spoken language disorders, the critical element in identification of the reading disability is the sudden loss of the ability to read by an individual who was known previously to have been able to read. Geschwind (1962) described Dejerine's patient who was the first reported case of acquired alexia or reading disability.

Dejerine's patient was an extremely intelligent 60-year-old man who, on October 25, 1887, suddenly observed that he could no longer read a single word. . . .

The patient had a visual of 8/10, spoke fluently without errors and understood all spoken speech. Objects were named perfectly, including pictures of technical instruments in a catalogue. He could identify his own morning newspaper by its form but could not read its name. On presentation he could not identify a single letter by name. The only written material he could read was his own name. Writing was correct, both spontaneously and to dictation, but what was written could not be read back. As Dejerine commented, his writing was rather like that of a blind man, larger than normal and with poor orientation of the lines.

Although the reading of isolated letters was impossible, the patient could identify them by name after tracing their contours with his finger if the examiner formed letters by moving the patient's hand through the air, he could name the letters produced in this way. . . .

On January 5, 1892, another cerebral vascular accident left him with paraphrasic speech and incapable of writing. He died at 10 A.M. on the sixteenth of January and an autopsy was performed . . . twenty-four hours after his death. (pp. 117–118)

The results of the autopsy seemed to confirm Dejerine's suspicion that the reading loss was related to previous brain damage.

Writing and Spelling

The ability to express one's ideas in writing is considered by many to be the highest and most complex form of human communication. To write well, the individual must be able to translate his or her thoughts into carefully sequenced words and inscribe those words onto paper using traditional letter forms. Without doubt, the person with learning disabilities involving spoken language or reading will experience great difficulty in writing. It may be trite to say that input precedes and determines the quality of output; but in dealing with the developmental disorders of children the principle must be kept in mind. With the possible exception of those adults who because of brain injury have lost the ability to read, and yet have retained some competence in writing, it is generally true that people who cannot read cannot write or spell.

Johnson and Myklebust (1967) describe three main types of disorders of writing: (a) dysgraphia, (b) recall deficits, and (c) formulative/syntactic deficits. *Dysgraphia* is a disturbance of the ability to learn the appropriate motor patterns for the act of writing. The problem may be so severe that pencil grasp cannot be achieved or may be so mild that the child's writing simply looks immature and awkward. Dysgraphia is a highly specific problem and may occur in the absence of any other learning disabilities.

For example, C. R., a 6-year-old girl with a form of cerebral palsy that affected only her legs, entered school at a rehabilitation hospital in a one-to-one tutorial. Her academic progress in reading, spelling, and areas other than writing was so dramatically accelerated that it appeared to be almost spontaneous. However, after 6 months of instruction she was still unable to write. She could not copy the simplest geometric designs and could not begin to copy her name or single letters. She did not advance beyond copying a simple circle and even distorted this figure. When she was given the opportunity to use a typewriter, it soon became apparent that she was able to formulate written (typed) language and to spell accurately (she could always spell orally). As with other clearly diagnosed dysgraphics, C. R. simply could not translate the read or spoken elements of language into their written equivalents.

Clear-cut cases of dysgraphia are not commonly encountered. They are more frequently found in combination with other types of learning disabilities, and the symptomatology may become confused. One of the best indicators of dysgraphia, whether in isolation or in combination with other difficulties, is the inability of the child to copy what he or she sees, whether it be geometric designs, letters, numbers, or words. In many cases of dysgraphia there are also problems with nonverbal activities such as tying shoelaces, using tools or other instruments, and following a sequence of movements, as in "Simon Says."

Disturbances in writing that are due to recall deficits are attributed by Johnson and Myklebust (1967) to deficits in visual memory. Whether this attribution is correct need not concern us at this point; it is sufficient to say that there are children with writing disabilities whose writing is characterized by the same type of errors as those diagnosed by Johnson and Myklebust as being caused by deficits in "revisualization." Such children are not dysgraphic because it can be demonstrated conclusively that they are able to copy letters, words, and even whole sentences from a model that is presented to them. However, when they are provided with these same models through oral dictation, they may be unable even to write a single letter correctly. There is often little or no pattern to their errors; letters may be written in an apparently random fashion. Many of these same children are able to name the letters of the alphabet when they see them and, depending upon previous instruction, may be able to give the appropriate sound equivalents for each letter. They seem unable to recall what the letters look like and are unable to write them. As with dysgraphia, writing disorders involving recall are often confounded by the presence of other learning disabilities. Many children may also have reading disabilities or oral language deficits. Obviously, the more difficulties the child presents, the more difficult it becomes to determine the scope and characteristics of the writing disorder.

Johnson and Myklebust (1967) discuss a third type of writing disorder, which they call a formulative/syntactic deficit. Children with writing disorders of this type are those who often do quite well in school until they are required to produce written essays, themes, book reports, and so on. Their complaint at that time is, "I know what I want to say; I just can't write it down on paper." This writing disability has two components: formulation and production of written material and the use of proper syntax or grammar in writing. The two components are usually affected simultaneously, although in some students it appears that ideation and production are limited more than syntax, probably because the written production consists of very short uninspired sentences with little opportunity for syntactic complexity. If the syntactic elements of such production are evaluated, the results would show merely an overly simplified, immature, but grammatically correct syntactic structure.

In the absence of traumatic brain damage in an older student or adult it is unlikely that formulative/syntactic writing disorders would appear in isolation in school-aged children. It is much more likely that such disabilities in writing would be accompanied by similar deficits in oral language. In the absence of other specific learning disabilities, one would be cautioned to investigate the previous instruction of the student in writing if a disorder of this type were discovered. Writing is a highly complex process that has appeared only lately in recorded human history, and it is the last form of language to be learned by the school child. It is not difficult to understand how many children may encounter difficulty in becoming proficient in writing unless they are given good instruction. Even if they are, there may be a number of otherwise competent students who do not learn to express themselves well in writing.

DISORDERS OF ARITHMETIC

Mathematics can be regarded as a symbolic language having the practical function of stating spatial and quantitative relationships and the theoretical function of facilitating thinking. As such, mathematical ability is a vital component of an individual's general communication capacity. In comparison to speaking, reading, and writing disorders, however, we know relatively little about either the nature or the types of specific disabilities in mathematics. This apparent lack of concern among professionals working in the field of learning disabilities is difficult to understand, but perhaps attempts will be made in the near future to delineate the aspects of the problem.

Most authorities limit their discussion of specific disabilities in mathematics to distinguishing between problems related to performing the various arithmetic functions or operations, that is, addition, subtraction, multiplication, and division, and problems that seem to be related to the comprehension of the basic concepts that are assumed to underlie mathematical proficiency, for example, one-to-one correspondence, ordering, conservation, and so forth. Johnson and Myklebust (1967), while not really explaining disabilities in mathematics, have prepared a list of specific behaviors that are indicative of arithmetic disability. This list will assist teachers in identifying those students who have specific learning disabilities in arithmetic.

1. Inability to establish a one-to-one correspondence. The number of children in a room cannot be related to the number of seats, nor an estimate made of how many forks to place on a table at which four people are to eat.

2. Inability to count meaningfully. Although numbers can be said in rote fashion, relationship between the symbol and the quantity is not established.

3. Inability to associate the auditory and visual symbols. It is possible to count auditorially but not to identify the numerals visually.

4. Inability to learn both the cardinal and ordinal systems of counting.

5. Inability to visualize clusters of objects within a larger group; each object in a group must always be counted.

6. Inability to grasp the principle of conservation of quantity. Some dyscalculics are not able to comprehend that ten cents is the same whether it consists of two nickels, one dime, or ten pennies, or that a one-pound block of butter is the same as four one-quarter pound sticks.

7. Inability to perform arithmetic operations.

8. Inability to understand the meaning of the process signs. In certain instances the deficiency is related to a perceptual disturbance (inability to distinguish the difference in the plus and multiplication signs). More important is failure to grasp the meaning conveyed by the signs.

9. Inability to understand the arrangement of the numbers on the page. Children learning to read must know that the sequence of letters within a word is significant. Those learning arithmetic must know that a specific arrangement of numbers also has meaning. Because of visual-spatial problems, this factor often interferes with computation abilities.

10. Inability to follow and remember the sequence of steps to be used in various mathematical operations.

11. Inability to understand the principles of measurement.

12. Inability to read maps and graphs.

13. Inability to choose the principles for solving problems in arithmetic reasoning. The dyscalculic can read the words and do the problems if he is given the principle (add, subtract, multiply, etc.) but without assistance he cannot determine which process to use. (p. 252)

DISORDERS OF REASONING (THINKING AND CONCEPTUALIZATION)

In discussing deficits in the reasoning processes there appear to be two key concepts that affect the overall adaptation of the human organism: organization and integration. Beginning at the earliest stage of development, individuals must learn to organize the sensory experiences surrounding them and to project onto those experiences some level of meaningfulness. At the same time children learn to integrate parts into a familiar whole.

Cognitive development has been described by a variety of authors, ranging from Jean Piaget to Donald Hebb, and yet no one has effectively described the reasoning processes to the point where we may speak cogently of specific reasoning disabilities. The end product of conceptualization is a highly developed and organized problem-solving ability. Whether the process begins with attention, followed by discrimination, and so on, or whether it is a bifurcation process of assimilation and accommodation, the result is a competent, reasoning human being.

Children who are poorly organized in their thinking, whose learning is slow and disorderly, and who cannot easily form abstract concepts are more usually labeled mentally retarded than learning disabled. However, we know from studies of brain damaged adults that some of these so-called cognitive processes are fairly discrete, at least in the adult. Therefore, adult aphasics may demonstrate an inability to perform some tasks involving discrimination, memory, body schema, and so on. It may be that the same specific cognitive deficits are present in children with learning disabilities; however, it is more likely that such deficits exist in learning disabled children as developmental lags that are often overcome by late adolescence (Tarver & Maggiore, 1979).

The following list was developed from a number of sources to provide the teacher with at least partial information about cognitive disorders (Flavell & Wohlwill, 1969; Fowler, 1971; Kagan & Kogan, 1970):

1. Concrete behavior characterized by a dependence upon immediate experience as opposed to abstract behavior that transcends any given immediate experience and results in the formation of conceptual categories

2. Poorly differentiated, unstable, and inconsistent generalizations

3. Little differentiation of part-whole relationships

4. Either passive-apathetic (curious aobut nothing) or hyperactive, driven, impulsive (curious about everything) behavior

5. Poor short-term or long-term retention

6. Either a marked lack in persistence or compulsive perseveration

7. Field dependence as opposed to field independence

8. Internally controlled versus externally controlled behavior

9. Rigidity; resistance to change

The information on specific reasoning (thinking) disabilities is sparse, even though the area was deemed significant enough to include it in the "grocery list" of disabilities covered under most definitions of learning disabilities. There is research being done in the area, but as yet it is limited to comparative studies of various isolated cognitive abilities of normal and learning disabled groups. It is hoped that this type of research will lead to a comprehensive explanation of specific thinking disabilities.

CORRELATES OF LEARNING DISABILITIES

The correlates of learning disabilities are defined as those types of impaired attentional, perceptual, behavioral, social, or motor functions that are often seen in learning disabled children and that are classified as learning disabilities by some authors. We do not view the correlates as either indicators or causes of learning disabilities nor as behaviors that should be treated to alleviate learning disabilities. Rather, they are seen as relatively isolated types of behavior that may or may not be amenable to treatment but that should not be treated as if such treatment would "cure" problems the student may be having in speaking, listening, reading, writing, spelling, or mathematical calculation. This is not to say that such behaviors should be disregarded by the family, physician, or teacher.

The correlates are not easy to categorize; but for purposes of discussion in this chapter, we will focus on three particularly troublesome correlates—disorders of attention, disorders of perceptual function, and disorders of motor function. As is obvious from the discussion in Chapter 1, we do not consider these types of disorders to be learning disabilities, but we do realize that learning disabled children may demonstrate such correlated disorders as, for example, attention deficit disorders (with or without hyperactivity), auditory or visual perceptual problems, perceptual-motor problems, or motor coordination disorders. These difficulties can be treated, some with more success than others, but successful treatment of hyperactivity, for example, does not alleviate reading disabilities. If the reading disability is alleviated solely through the successful treatment of hyperactivity, the child probably never had a specific reading disability. On the other hand, it is equally obvious that a learning disabled child who also has an attention deficit disorder or a perceptual deficit will benefit greatly from a treatment program that takes into account both problems.

The use of the term *correlates* may be in itself a misnomer. Correlate is defined by *The American Heritage Dictionary of the English Language* as "either of two correlative entities" that have a "causal complementary, parallel, or reciprocal relation." We could caution the reader not to interpret our use of the term correlate quite so literally. We are merely saying that children with learning disabilities often manifest other disorders that may be classified as perceptual or behavior problems.

Attention Deficit Disorder

For the interested reader, a relatively short, but comprehensive, description of attention deficit disorder (ADD) with or without hyperactivity is given by Shaywitz and Shaywitz (1988). The nature of the problem was formalized in 1980 when the symptoms of the disorder were set forth by the American Psychiatric Association (1980) in the third edition of the *Diagnostic and Statistical Manual of Mental Disorders* (DSM III). According to DSM III, the criteria for the diagnosis of attention disorder deficit with hyperactivity are:

Inattention (at least three of the following):

1. often fails to finish things he/she starts

2. often does not seem to listen

3. easily distracted

4. has difficulty concentrating on schoolwork or other tasks requiring sustained attention

5. has difficulty sticking to a play activity

Impulsivity (at least three of the following):

1. often acts before thinking

2. shifts excessively from one activity to another

3. has difficulty organizing work (this not being due to cognitive impairment)

4. needs a lot of supervision

5. frequently calls out in class

6. has difficulty awaiting turn in games or group situations

Hyperactivity (at least two of the following):

1. runs about or climbs on things excessively

2. has difficulty sitting still or fidgets excessively

3. has difficulty staying seated

4. moves about excessively during sleep

5. is always "on the go" or acts as if "driven by a motor"

DSM III provides for the diagnosis of three subtypes of the disorder: attention deficit disorder with no other factors present (ADDnoH), attention deficit disorder with hyperactivity (ADDH), and attention and impulsivity in older persons who are no longer hyperactive—attention deficit disorder residual type (ADDRT).

Perceptual Disorders

The literature is replete with descriptions of perceptual and perceptual-motor disorders. Chapters 14 and 15 provide descriptions and critiques of several major training programs that were developed to treat such disorders, along with descriptions of the problems. The teacher may use the following list to catalog the primary perceptual disorders:

1. impairments of discrimination, in which the child may be unable to distinguish between two different auditory, visual, or tactile stimuli

2. impaired recognition of common auditory, visual, or tactile stimuli

3. poor time, space, or distance orientation

4. poor body image

5. poor discrimination of figure-ground or part-whole relations

6. poor left-right orientation

7. poor eye-hand coordination

Motor Disorders

The motor disorders described here are exclusive of those disabilities that would lead to a diagnosis of cerebral palsy or some other neuromuscular condition. However, the manifestations of the disorders could be interpreted by some as very minimal signs of such pathological conditions. Some of the motor disabilities are:

1. poor fine or gross motor coordination

2. general clumsiness or awkwardness

3. frequent delayed motor developmental milestones

CONCLUSIONS

This chapter has been devoted to a description of the types of specific learning disabilities categorized as disorders of spoken language, written language, arithmetic, and reasoning. These particular categories were chosen because of their prominence in the definitions of learning disabilities as given in Public Law 94-142 (The Education of All Handicapped Children Act of 1975) and by the National Joint Committee on Learning Disabilities. The nature and etiology of learning disabilities were not discussed, as these topics were covered previously in Chapter 1.

PART II

ASSESSMENT PRACTICES IN LEARNING DISABILITIES

Chapters 4, 5, 6, and 7 contain information about how proper assessments are made in the area of learning disabilities. In the first of these chapters, important elements of a general nature related to the educational evaluation are described briefly. In the next chapter, example procedures that are frequently used to assess specific learning disabilities, especially those involving spoken language, written language, arithmetic, and correlative abilities, are provided. The third of these chapters deals with a supplementary approach to assessment—task analysis—that has the most direct implications for teaching of all assessment procedures. The final chapter in this part provides information that one needs to know in order to move smoothly from assessment to instruction. Included are such topics as the role of the individualized education plan, classroom approaches to instruction, mastery teaching, and teacher competencies.

The purpose of these chapters is to acquaint the reader with a variety of topics and procedures that pertain to the assessment of learning disabilities. To become proficient in the area of evaluation, one needs to study other more detailed sources and to practice the techniques, preferably under supervised conditions. In recent years, several fine, comprehensive books have been published dealing with assessment. In particular, we recommend *Educational Assessment of Learning Problems: Testing for Teaching* (Wallace & Larsen, 1978), *Assessing Special Students* (McLoughlin & Lewis, 1986), and *Assessing the Abilities and Instructional Needs of Students* (Hammill, 1987) for readers who desire practical information on evaluation; and *Assessment in Special and Remedial Education* (Salvia & Ysseldyke, 1988) for those who are interested in the theoretical concepts that underlie good evaluation practices.

4

THE EDUCATIONALLY ORIENTED EVALUATION

In this chapter, several general aspects involved in evaluation, especially the evaluation of school-aged children, are described. These aspects include discussions pertaining to (a) the purposes of evaluating children, (b) the organizational system that directs the appraisal procedures, and (c) the basic methods used in conducting evaluations, specifically in the informal and test-based approaches.

THE PURPOSES OF EVALUATION

The major purposes of the evaluation process as implemented in most schools today are (a) to screen the students to find those who are experiencing more than expected difficulty and, if appropriate, to identify, diagnose, or label them according to handicapping condition (e.g., mentally retarded, emotionally disturbed, learning disabled, etc.) and (b) to obtain information that can be used to plan individual programs for those children who are identified as handicapped. The process is, of course, an extensive and expensive undertaking that generally involves the administration of numerous tests and consumes a large number of hours for examiners and children alike. Because of the multiplicity and subtlety of their difficulties, learning disabled children probably have been the "beneficiaries" of more testing than any other group of handicapped children.

Most teachers and parents would agree that there is a population of children whose physical, mental, or emotional problems are so debilitating that they should be provided with special education services. Most people would agree also that the disabilities presented by many of these children are not generally found within the range of "normal" variation; rather, they are of such a magnitude or kind that the affected children often need educational assistance above and beyond what the typical classroom teacher can be expected to provide. The reader who can agree with these two statements will likely be amenable to the idea that these handicapped children should be identified clearly and that not every child who is having some kind of academic difficulty should be eligible for special education services, least of all under the learning disabilities label.

At some point along the continuum of services provided by the school, there must be a cutoff that dictates which children will be served by special education and which will remain totally the responsibility of the general education program. Obviously, the vast majority of children who have trouble in school will have to stay in regular classes. In any event, the type of assessment that deals with identification is of the utmost importance in states where laws, policies, or traditions make it mandatory that children be classified according to type of handicap before they can qualify for special services.

THE ORGANIZATIONAL STRUCTURE GOVERNING APPRAISAL PRACTICES

Quite naturally, the identification process begins by locating those students in school who are having difficulty and concludes with decisions being made relative to the type of handicap a child may have, if any, and to the setting in which the child can best be taught. Therefore, a comprehensive school appraisal system will account for referral, screening, in-depth assessment (if necessary), placement, and review.

Each school should have one professional staff member designated to receive referrals, collect pertinent data, call referral committee meetings, and be responsible for implementing the committee's decisions. Ideally, these activities should be carried out by the school principal. If the referral committee decides that the child should be referred to special education because the regular education program cannot meet the child's needs, a special education professional staff member should be designated to coordinate the appraisal and placement activities. The principal should serve as a member of the placement committee because, in many respects, the principal is the person ultimately responsible for the instructional programs of all children in the school; however, giving the principal the responsibility for coordinating the appraisal system probably serves no purpose other than creating an additional burden for this person for which he or she may not be prepared.

Once a person has been appointed to coordinate the appraisal and placement process, it becomes his or her duty to determine whether districtwide policies and procedures with reference to the appraisal system are being followed. This districtwide system should be a written plan that specifies each step in the process, details what staffing pattern is to be used, and provides common forms and reporting procedures for completion at each stage.

After the child has been referred, the principal collects information from the classroom teacher, from the pupil's cumulative record, and from the school counselor. These data would include comments from the child's present and former teachers, along with samples of his or her work; results of achievement and other tests given schoolwide; and any other information that has been collected during the child's school career that may be relevant to his or her present difficulty. These data are presented to the placement committee members, who generally make one of two decisions: The student is not a candidate for assessment, or the student appears to be eligible and further data should be collected. In the latter case the child would be referred to special education for appraisal and, probably, placement.

After the assessment has been conducted, the results are presented to the placement committee, which decides at this point whether the child is eligible for special services under the state or district guidelines. Depending on the nature and severity of the problem, the child may be placed in a learning disabilities resource or self-contained class or in the speech and language therapy program. School districts make different decisions about which program should serve which children, but the decisions must be made in such a manner as to preclude some of the jurisdictional problems discussed later in this chapter.

As yet, nothing has been mentioned regarding the composition of the placement committee. Without belaboring the point, it appears that the principal, as chief administrator and instructional leader; the special education teacher, as the person most knowledgeable about handicapped children; the sending teacher, as the professional person most intimately involved with the child; and an appraisal person, as the one most knowledgeable about tests and test results, should form the core of the placement committee. Depending on the kinds of difficulties the child is manifesting, other school personnel should be included, for example, the speech pathologist, the nurse, the counselor, and so on. In selecting personnel for the placement committee, the purpose of the committee should be kept uppermost in mind. It is this group that is charged with the sometimes awesome responsibility of making critical decisions about a child's educational future. The members must be willing to take the time and invest the energy to evaluate meticulously the data available on the child's difficulties, to determine the kinds of educational experiences needed, and to assign the child to the very best instructional arrangement possible. It is in no way sufficient to move the child to a resource room for one period a day just to get him or her out of the teacher's hair or because "it can't hurt." The committee must interpret and analyze the data and provide both the special and regular teachers with an individualized education plan (IEP) for the child, a plan that points to the direction that the teacher is to take with the child. The choice of the phrase "points to" is deliberate; we feel that only individual teachers, and not some committee, can develop an education plan. An education plan must be based soundly in the scope and sequence of a curriculum, must be the result of a task analysis, and must be stated in measurable objectives.

The IEP for any given child must contain annual goals and short-term objectives, as required by P.L. 94-142; but it is the teacher's implementation plan that contains the day-by-day objectives. The IEP itself is simply a summary statement of the detailed plan developed by the teacher.

BASIC METHODS IN EVALUATION

For discussion purposes the various methodologies that are used frequently in assessing the learning disabled have been reduced to two categories: informal and test-based. Each is described briefly next.

Informal Approach to Assessment

The least structured approach to evaluation is informal assessment, which may be conducted by an appraisal person or by a teacher, although probably it is most frequently done by the teacher. Its most distinguishing features are listed below.

1. Informal assessment relies heavily upon interpretation of children's performance observed in natural settings.

2. Informal assessment is more likely to involve criterion-referenced interpretations of behavior than norm-referenced interpretations.

3. Informal assessment is usually used to measure educational tasks.

4. An informal assessment of high quality can be accomplished only by a person who is thoroughly familiar with child development, the content of the areas being investigated, and the child being evaluated.

5. The data obtained from informal assessment procedures are often less reliable and more subject to individual bias than are those resulting from more formal, structured procedures.

Obviously, informal assessment is not standardized, but it supplements information that has been obtained from standardized testing. The emphasis in the informal approach is on careful observation of the child's response rather than on some arbitrary score; on the functional analysis of the child's performance rather than on the child's failures.

Implicit in the concept of informal assessment is the notion of probing the child's performance in the area being investigated. For example, if the child cannot name colors, can he or she select blocks of different colors as the teacher names the colors? If the child cannot do this, can he or she select one after the colors have been named? Probes investigate the amount and kind of assistance that that child needs in order to perform. It is not enough to say, "The child does not know colors."

Informal assessment emphasizes the simultaneous, systematic observation of a child's total behavior while he or she is responding without limiting the teacher's attention to the correctness or incorrectness of the child's responses. While noting whether the child's response is appropriate, the teacher will also observe the way in which the child responds, the fashion in which the child organizes his or her capabilities to meet the requirements of the task. If the responses are careful and considered, the child's learning will be more easily facilitated than if he or she is impulsive or easily distracted.

A great deal of information about children's learning styles can be garnered from informal assessment. Jedrysek, Klapper, Pope, and Wortis (1972) caution the person conducting informal assessments to look at children's total behavior to determine the effectiveness of their learning styles and to obtain clues about teaching strategies that may need to be employed to overcome some nonfacilitating behaviors. Some of the behaviors that should be noted are the following:

Ability to make decisions
Flexibility
Reflectiveness
Checking out one's answers
Control of impulsivity (of quick answers)
Response to concrete elements of situation (in contrast to abstract; for example, literal responses, giving examples)
Ability to shift from one activity or thought to another (in contrast to rigidity)
Knowledge of completion (and finishing at that point, instead of spoiling a completed product by continuing to work on it)
Motivation
Interest
Ability to sustain interest without interruption (a combination of distractibility, attention span, persistence with the task, restlessness, hyperactivity)
Satisfaction with success
Ability to accept assistance (in contrast to inability to do so when frustrated)
Spontaneous, organized approach to task and environment
Curiosity, exploration, questioning
Orderliness
Anxiety (manifested by hesitancy, erasures, excessive self-correction, inability to deal with task)
Sense of humor
Cooperation
Responsiveness (Jedrysek et al., 1972, pp. 6–7)

Informal assessment is not intended as a replacement or substitute for the formal, standardized testing that is conducted during the identification phase of evaluation. It is not even intended as a substitute for the testing that serves as the basis for developing annual goals for the individualized education plan. It is intended to assist the teacher in designing a day-to-day instructional program for the child. It can be conducted simultaneously with task analysis of a content area to determine what the next instructional task should be and how well that task is performed by the child, even how the task should be taught. Task analysis answers the question, "What is the next task?" Informal assessment answers the questions, "How well does the child perform the task?" and "How can I best teach the child the task?"

Test-Based Approach to Assessment

Many appraisers—educational diagnosticians, psychologists, and others—feel that the results of the tests they administer to learning disabled children provide the teacher with a wealth of information that can be used in educational planning. The truth is that the test results really provide only a limited sample of various behaviors that are assumed to have educational relevance. A child's scores on the *Wechsler Intelligence Scale for Children* (Wechsler, 1974), the *Woodcock Reading Mastery Tests* (Woodcock, 1988), the *Test of Language Development* (Newcomer & Hammill, 1988), and the *Peabody Picture Vocabulary Test* (Dunn & Dunn, 1981) provide information that may assist in deciding whether the child may be classified as learning disabled but do not assist the teacher in determining what to teach the child nor where to begin teaching.

Tests serve many different functions; sometimes the results can be used to predict future performance. The items in a test may have no rational relationship to the behavior being predicted, but if the results predict educational achievement, the test may be considered successful.

Most often, tests are used to provide an appraisal of a child's current level of functioning as compared, usually, with other children the same age. If the child is significantly retarded in comparison with age-mates, there is reason to feel concern about the child's performance and prospects. It should be noted that "significantly retarded" is a extraordinarily complicated construct. Variability is the norm in human behavior and development, and all children do not develop at the same rate, nor even in the same sequence in all aspects of development. Norms are convenient abstractions, but they should not be viewed as blueprints for the particulars of development.

It is useful to have some documentation about the performance levels in several areas of a child's development. In fact, such documentation is mandatory in most states before a child can be placed in the special education program. The normative generalizations (also called test results) are also useful when one is counseling with parents or other professionals. But, surely, no competent learning disabilities specialist will use a test score to determine whether the child has a significant learning disability. The test describes a child's performance and allows a comparison with some normative sample of the child's age-mates, but it does not establish the limits of normalcy; that is, it does not presume to define normal behavior. The child's parents, siblings, peers, and teachers do not react to his or her speech, oral language, written language, and so on, in terms of some numerical index. As one small example, a child is not labeled as having an articulation defect simply on the basis of the number of misarticulations produced. The frequency of such errors may be *correlated* with a judgment of abnormality made by a competent clinician, but it is rarely the *basis* for such a judgment.

The information obtained by administering a standardized test is a useful piece of evidence and becomes part of the fabric we assemble in order to understand a child's problem. It may even be used to determine whether the child has a problem, but it does not define the problem. The experienced diagnostician decides that a child may need special education services on the basis of an aggregation of facts and impressions involving the pattern of performance, the child's age and maturity level, the reactions of others to the child, and, ultimately, the diagnostician's own impressions, sharpened by training and experience, of the child's performance. Regardless of state and federal guidelines, the question of whether a child should be placed in special education should be based on the considered, professional judgment of trained appraisal persons, and not on the application of some set of norms.

Tests that describe a child's current status are often referred to as samples of behavior. This is a useful framework, highlighting our interest in test performance as an indicator of the child's nontest behavior. The more completely and adequately samples of everyday behavior, in whatever area is under examination, can be incorporated into a given instrument, the more useful it is. In this way a test serves to provide a representation of the behaviors in question. It is systematic, economical, capable of standardization, and thus quite useful. But there are problems because the test items are only a sample of behaviors represented, and there are obvious difficulties in selecting or devising items that are representative and comprehensive without ending up with an instrument that is far too lengthy.

There is another, more fundamental problem with the idea of a test as a sample. A sample of what? A sample implies a universe or population; theoretically, to sample representatively, one must first describe the population of items involved and then make some selection from this population. However, such description and selection implies, if not requires, that one knows in advance the boundaries of the population. This means that to select a good sample of reading or oral language or arithmetic behaviors, one must first have a firm idea of what reading or oral language or arithmetic is, or at least what one means them to be. That is precisely the problem; universal agreement as to what is meant by reading or any of the other performance areas is conspicuously absent.

Let us examine one area of child behavior—oral language ability—in light of the above discussion. In some tests, language means a mother's report of the child's vocal development, vocabulary development, ability to recognize an object when it is embedded in a field of the objects, digit repetition, morphological endings, and so on and so on. In others, language is assessed in terms of mean length of utterance, the child's age at first word, some measure of egocentrism, or vocabulary recognition.

In the *Illinois Test of Psycholinguistic Abilities* (Kirk et al., 1968), language is defined in terms of Osgood's learning theory and bears little resemblance to Laura Lee's Developmental Sentence Sorting.

Once the concept of language that is buried in the tests above has been identified, there are decisions that must be made. Does the test represent a good way to think of, or define, language? Do the items in the test really reflect the dimensions of language that are suggested in the author's model? Is there a better model or definition of language? It must be kept in mind that the person who uses a standardized test as the basis for determining whether a child is normal in some aspect of development is buying much more than a test kit; he or she is buying the author's conception of that area of development.

A test is a device for sampling some of a child's behavior, not a direct window into the child's mind. Test authors are often careful, assiduous professionals who have given a great deal of thought to how behavior can be described. Their insights are often valuable and should be given serious consideration; however, the test results only contribute to, and cannot be substituted for, an experienced teacher's judgment.

One should use tests creatively, selecting the parts that seem useful, disagreeing with the test author when one's own experience so dictates, and recognizing the fallibility of any instrument, just as personal limitations are acknowledged. Beyond tests there is the professional's knowledge and experience. Ultimately, these are the most powerful resources available.

In recent years, many books have been written that deal with assessing learning disabilities. Of these, one of the best is *Assessing the Abilities and Instructional Needs of Students*, which is edited by Donald Hammill (1987). (We beg the reader's forgiveness for this reference to our own work.) This volume is a collection of chapters on how to assess different ability areas including oral language (by Patricia Myers), reading (by J. L. Wiederholt and Brian R. Bryant), writing (by Stephen C. Larsen), arithmetic (by Herbert Ginsburg), and socioemotional development (by Linda Brown). The evaluation techniques described emphasize informal, nonstandardized methods that can be easily used by teachers, clinicians, and therapists. We recommend this volume to all professionals who are interested in assessing learning disabilities for instructional purposes.

5

EVALUATING SPECIFIC LEARNING DISABILITIES

A primary purpose for evaluating learning disabilities is to determine which ability areas (e.g., spoken language, reading, etc.) are seriously impaired and which specific skills within a defective ability area are in need of attention. For example, having recognized reading as the disability area, attention is directed to identifying if the problem is centered in phonics, word recognition, reading rate, or comprehension. If phonics is found to be the culprit, further evaluation is called for to locate the specific sound-symbol associations or other skills that need training.

In this chapter, information and procedures that are useful in assessing particular types or families of learning disabilities are discussed in sections devoted to assessing spoken language disorders, written language disorders, arithmetic disorders, and behavior that is correlative to specific learning disabilities.

ASSESSMENT OF SPOKEN LANGUAGE DISABILITIES

To assess a child's linguistic efforts, we must know something about linguistics. There is no sense in using a test built on the ideas and theories of Noam Chomsky unless we know something about those ideas. Even if we find a test to be fully adequate as a representation of language, it surely will not be complete. The test will provide some information about probable areas of difficulty, but the teacher will have to follow through, develop additional tasks, and find ways to make observations. If we do not understand the premises that underlie the test, we cannot use it well in any case. When we have acquired such an understanding, we should feel free to make our own tests, to devise our own sampling methods, and to probe in our own ways.

The language development literature now contains numerous examples of the variety of ways in which language data can be collected and analyzed. Researchers like Bloom (1970) and Brown (1973) make extensive and creative use of spontaneous speech protocols to analyze a child's linguistic knowledge. Berko (1958) conducted a classic experimental study of children's acquisition of grammatical morphemes, using a technique that has been replicated by many authors. Slobin and Welsh (1973) suggest that one way to determine a child's underlying grammatical organization is to present a child with sentences that tax the immediate memory and to observe the kinds of "errors" that occur in the child's attempts at imitation. Essentially the same logic underlies the Gray and Ryan (1973) Programmed Conditioning for Language Test. We can also use the language development literature to discover what linguistic categories to expect from children of varying ages and how to interpret the kinds of errors made (Lee, 1974). The point of all this is that the basic language development literature is rich with methods and insights developed initially not as tests, but rather as procedures designed to reveal something about the language skills of normally developing children.

There is no way to disguise or make palatable the fact that oral language disorders are complex. At present, questions about language are at the core of many efforts in behavioral science; and there is no immediate prospect of the major questions, that is, what language is and how it develops, being resolved. We must look to our own experiences, intuitions, and good judgment in devising ways to describe and treat oral language disabilities. Most of us are equipped with intelligence and training to learn and to apply our knowledge; these are the marks of the fully competent professional.

Oral language assessment is discussed here from two vantage points: informal and test-based. Both of these approaches should be employed in conducting a thorough evaluation of a child with spoken language difficulties. The first method is probably the province of the learning disabilities specialists, since the results accruing from it are particularly useful in educational programming. Tests, which are usually designed only for identification purposes, are more appropriately used by an appraisal person.

Informal Assessment

One of the most natural ways of assessing the oral language competency of children is simply to observe, in both structured and unstructured situations, their language production. What sounds simple is in reality highly complex, because good and useful observations are based upon the observer's knowledge of the nature of language and its development. The teacher, as observer, would do well to become familiar with the literature in language, with particular reference to current approaches to child language as given by McNeill (1970), Menyuk (1974), Cazden (1972), Brown (1973), Vogel (1975), Dale (1976), and Bloom and Lahey (1977).

Observation of the child's language should be conducted in both structured and unstructured settings because often the child's full repertoire is not observable in the ordinary unstructured setting. It is therefore necessary to provide some structure so that the child may demonstrate his or her linguistic competence. The checklist provided in Table 5.1 indicates some of the kinds of linguistic behavior that the teacher should take note of and record. The checklist covers only ages 3 through 6, but the essentials of language are normally mastered by the time the child is 6 or 7 years old. After that age, spoken language development consists primarily of increasingly lengthy productions that are more and more complex in terms of added clauses, phrases, and sophisticated vocabulary.

Using a checklist similar to the one in Table 5.1, the teacher can determine specific areas in which a child is having difficulties and can plan instructional activities to develop those areas. Since one should not generalize from a single instance of behavior, observational techniques should be used to determine, for example, whether the child is having problems with using infinitives correctly all or most of the time or just once in a while. If the difficulty is infrequent, the form is probably still developing, and, as a rule, no formal instruction would be undertaken. If, however, the child is 7 years old and seldom uses infinitives correctly, the teacher should develop an instructional objective for teaching the form.

Much information can be gained by observing a child in a natural, unstructured setting, but sometimes the teacher is interested in knowing whether the child has developed certain oral language skills that are not readily observable in the classroom situation unless some structure is imposed. In that case the teacher can use a play situation and ask the child to respond in specific ways. For example, if more information is needed about the child's use of noun and verb inflections, a play situation involving various toys and objects can be arranged. The child can then be asked a series of questions like, "This man has a farm; he is a _____?" "This girl is catching the ball; she is the _____?" "This boy likes to paint; he is a good _____?" Questions should not be difficult or too subtle; all one is doing is trying to find out whether the child can use the *er* inflection for nouns and verbs. If questions become too difficult (e.g., "What do we call a person who lives in the country and raises corn?"), we may be assessing cognitive ability rather than one simple linguistic form.

Test-Based Assessment

Many tests purport to measure some aspect of language. Some are patently screening tests, indicating only whether the child has some kind of oral language difficulty.

TABLE 5.1. A Checklist of Language Performance

	Yes	Sometimes	No
Semantics and Concepts (3–4 years):			
Relates 2 events in sequence	——	——	——
Repeats 3 digits	——	——	——
Names 3 colors	——	——	——
Names 3 shapes	——	——	——
Names 10 body parts	——	——	——
Classifies basic items such as food, clothing, animals, and furniture into categories	——	——	——
Identifies boys and girls	——	——	——
Knows 4 prepositions	——	——	——
Counts to 5 by rote	——	——	——
Identifies big and little when difference is greater than 1	——	——	——
Distinguishes heavy and light when difference is greater than 1 pound	——	——	——
Distinguishes fast and slow	——	——	——
Distinguishes tall and short	——	——	——
Distinguishes up and down	——	——	——
Answers 6 agent questions: What cries? What sleeps?	——	——	——
Recognizes action in pictures	——	——	——
Understands *not*	——	——	——
Gives full names	——	——	——
Uses *I, you, he, she, it, my, mine*	——	——	——
Syntax and Morphology (3–4 years):			
Uses all basic sentence patterns	——	——	——
Uses compound sentences	——	——	——
Uses compound objects	——	——	——
Uses the following transformations:			
a. Got ("I got a book.")	——	——	——
b. Relative clause ("I know what he's doing.")	——	——	——
c. Inversions ("Now I have a kitten." instead of "I have a kitten now.")	——	——	——
Uses the following verb forms:			
a. Plurals, using /s/ and /z/	——	——	——
b. 's possessive	——	——	——
Uses the following verb forms:			
a. Present progressive	——	——	——
b. Past tense with /t/ or /d/	——	——	——
c. Third person singular	——	——	——
d. Future	——	——	——
e. Present	——	——	——
Uses contractions	——	——	——
Uses interrogative reversals	——	——	——
Uses conjunctions *because, if, so*	——	——	——
Contrasts *It is* and *There is*	——	——	——

(Continued)

TABLE 5.1. *(Continued)*

	Yes	Sometimes	No
Semantics and Concepts (4–5 years):			
Repeats 4 digits	——	——	——
Follows 3 commands	——	——	——
Understands *beside, behind, in front of*	——	——	——
Counts to 13 by rote	——	——	——
Counts 10 objects	——	——	——
Gives 3 blocks on request	——	——	——
Distinguishes long and short	——	——	——
Distinguishes weight when difference is less than 1 pound	——	——	——
Differentiates smooth and rough using paper and sandpaper	——	——	——
Can do common opposite analogies	——	——	——
Differentiates concrete experiences: What do you do when you are			
a. sleepy?	——	——	——
b. hungry?	——	——	——
c. cold?	——	——	——
What do you do with			
a. your eyes?	——	——	——
b. your ears?	——	——	——
Defines words by use	——	——	——
Knows right and left hand	——	——	——
Names days of the week	——	——	——
Recognizes obscurities in pictures	——	——	——
Identifies related objects	——	——	——
Identifies picture similarities	——	——	——
Identifies picture differences	——	——	——
Uses *some, many*	——	——	——
Syntax and Morphology (4–5 years):			
Uses noun inflections as *er* in farmer	——	——	——
Uses noun-verb agreement	——	——	——
Uses possessives *his, hers, their*	——	——	——
Uses sentence pattern N + V N_2 + N_3 ("She showed the girl the boy.")	——	——	——
Semantics and Concepts (5–6):			
Names at least 6 items in categories in 1 minute	——	——	——
Understands first, last, and middle	——	——	——
Counts to 30 serially	——	——	——
Counts 13 objects	——	——	——
Understands same and different	——	——	——
Names nickel, dime, and penny	——	——	——
Uses *more, few*	——	——	——
Understands *fourth*	——	——	——

(Continued)

TABLE 5.1. *(Continued)*

	Yes	Sometimes	No
Knows how many fingers on one and on both hands	____	____	____
Conserves size in pictures ("Which is bigger? The cow or the bird?")	____	____	____
Syntax and Morphology (5–6):			
Uses infinitive ("I want to eat the apple.")	____	____	____
Uses singular and plural *be* verb	____	____	____
Uses *because* conjunction	____	____	____
Uses comparative and superlative	____	____	____
Uses *if* and *so* conjunctions	____	____	____
Uses verb inflections (catch/catcher)	____	____	____

Note. Adapted from *Cumulative Assessment of Preschool Performance* (pp. 31–35), experimental edition, by A. K. Bird, L. C. Carr, L. M. Cummins, and P. A. Spanier, 1974, unpublished manuscript.

Others are more sophisticated instruments and provide normative data across several aspects of oral language. A few tests are designed to measure some aspect of language so thoroughly that the results can be used for instructional purposes. Rather than reviewing all of these tests, we have categorized the tests according to their major purpose(s), the elements of language assessed, and the age range for which they are appropriate. The information is presented in Table 5.2. Readers who are interested in more information about the tests will find full bibliographical entries for each under the author's name in the reference list at the back of the book.

The tests listed in Table 5.2 were categorized by us, not by the test authors; therefore, the developers of the tests might easily disagree with the categorization as to whether their tests could be used for instructional purposes or whether they are measures of semantics or syntax or both elements. Using a purely pragmatic base that has evolved from working with language disordered children and from having used almost all of the tests listed, we arrived at our categorization system as one that reflects our personal experiences with tests.

The reader should note that there is seldom a clear-cut distinction between semantic and syntactic elements in most of the tests. Probably Berko's *Exploratory Test of Grammar* is as truly a syntactic test as one is apt to find, but most of the tests confuse to some extent the semantic and syntactic elements. The *Basic Concept Inventory* (Englemann, 1967) appears to be a fairly straightforward measure of semantic-pragmatic function, even though it is called a concept inventory.

Readers should investigate tests with as much thoroughness as they are able to bring to bear. They should look at the reliabilities and validities of instruments, the samples upon which the tests were standardized, and the model or theory of language that underlies the selection of test items. Without such close scrutiny, test users are abandoning themselves in the wilderness.

ASSESSMENT OF WRITTEN LANGUAGE DISABILITIES

The purpose of assessing written language is to determine how well a student can understand and use graphic symbols, that is, written words and sentences. Proficiency is shown in reading and writing, spelling being subsumed under writing. As is the case with spoken language, the two most common approaches to evaluation involve informal techniques and tests.

Informal Assessment

When teachers and diagnosticians want to assess reading abilities by informal means, they generally have the student read aloud, read graded word lists, answer questions about the content of read material, or retell the ideas that were read. In analysis of oral reading, the teacher has the student read short passages and notes mispronunciations, laborious word-by-word reading, and so on. Graded word lists are composed of words grouped according to grade-level difficulty. Students read the words aloud. The point at which they begin to mispronounce the words is a rough indicator of their word recognition level. For assessing reading comprehension informally the teacher can simply have students silently read printed passages and ask them specific or inferential questions about the material they have read. A valuable variation is to have the students retell in their own words the content of the read material. The teacher/diagnostician's observations of a student's reading abilities can be recorded on a checklist similar to that in Figure 5.1.

The informal reading inventory (IRI) procedure is a more elaborate and comprehensive method of evaluating reading. These inventories usually involve oral and silent reading, and result in judgments about the levels at which students will profit from instruction, can read independently, and will likely experience frustration. The inventories can be made by teachers using paragraphs drawn from basal series; they are also available commercially (see, for example, Newcomer, 1986; Silvaroli, 1976).

For individuals who require a particularly thorough analysis of students' reading comprehension and who are willing to make the effort to gain the high level of skill necessary for its administration, the *Reading Miscue Inventory* (Goodman & Burke, 1972) and *Formal Reading Inventory* (Wiederholt, 1985) are recommended. These techniques encourage teachers to make hypotheses about children's comprehension on the basis of the study of their oral reading. In using the technique, children's oral reading is studied for the purpose of collecting information for generating hypotheses about their comprehension abilities. The term *miscue* is used to make the distinction between true errors (reading *horse* for *house*) and more and less meaningfully acceptable word substitutions (reading *road* for *path*).

TABLE 5.2. Tests of Oral Language

Test*	Purpose		Elements		Age Range
	Identification	Instruction	Semantics	Syntax	
Adolescent Language Screening Test (Morgan & Guilford, 1984)	X		X	X	11-0 to 17-11 years
Bankson Language Screening Test–2 (Bankson, 1990)	X		X	X	4-0 to 7-11 years
Carrow Elicited Language Inventory (Carrow-Woolfolk, 1974)	X		X	X	3-0 to 7-11 years
Clark-Madison Test of Oral Language (Clark & Madison, 1986)	X			X	4-0 to 7-11 years
Clinical Evaluation of Language Functions (Wiig, 1987)	X	X	X	X	5-0 to 17-11 years
Denver Developmental Screening Test (Frankenburg et al., 1975)	X		X	X	Birth to 6-0 years
Developmental Sentence Analysis (Lee, 1974)	X	X		X	3-0 to 7-0 years
Exploratory Test of Grammar (Berko, 1958)	X			X	5-0 to 8-0 years
Expressive One-Word Picture Vocabulary Test (Gardner, 1979)	X		X		2-0 to 11-11 years
Illinois Test of Psycholinguistic Abilities (Kirk et al., 1968)	X		X	X	2-6 to 10-0 years
Linguistic Analysis of Speech Samples (Angler et al., 1973)	X	X	X		3-0 to 9-0 years
Peabody Picture Vocabulary Test (Dunn & Dunn, 1981)	X		X		2-6 to 18-0 years

(Continued)

TABLE 5.2. *(Continued)*

Test	Purpose		Elements		Age Range
	Identification	**Instruction**	**Semantics**	**Syntax**	
Receptive-Expressive Emergent Language Scale (Bzoch & League, 1978)	X		X	X	Birth to 3-0 years
Screening Test of Spanish Grammar (Toronto, 1973)	X		X	X	3-0 to 7-0 years
Test for Auditory Comprehension of Language (Carrow-Woolfolk, 1985)	X	X	X	X	3-0 to 7-0 years
Test of Adolescent Language–2 (Hammill et al., 1987)	X		X	X	11-0 to 18-5 years
Test of Early Language Development (Hresko et al., 1981)	X		X	X	2-6 to 7-11 years
Test of Language Development–2 Primary (Newcomer & Hammill, 1988)	X		X	X	4-0 to 8-11 years
Test of Language Development–2 Intermediate (Hammill & Newcomer, 1988)	X		X	X	8-6 to 12-11 years
Test of Word Finding (German, 1986)	X		X		6-6 to 12-11 years
Utah Test of Language Development–3 (Mecham, 1989)	X		X	X	3-0 to 10-11 years
Vocabulary Comprehension Scale (Bangs, 1977)	X	X	X		2-0 to 6-0 years
The Word Test (Jorgensen et al., 1981)	X		X		7-0 to 11-11 years

*These tests were developed specifically for the assessment of oral language abilities. In general, they do not measure perceptual or other cognitive skills.

Teacher _____

School _____

Grade _____

Student _____   Date _____

I.   General

____ points to each word with finger

____ uses thumb as a guide

____ appears tense in reading situation

____ is easily distracted

____ moves head as he reads

____ holds book too close

____ holds book too far away

____ tries to avoid reading

____ is unable to sit still

____ covers one eye when reading

II.   Oral Reading

____ reads in a slow word-by-word manner

____ reads very rapidly and ignores punctuation

____ has difficulty in pronouncing many words

____ adds words

____ omits words

____ spells out words that he doesn't know

____ guesses at unknown words

____ reverses words

____ reverses letters within words

____ stops at the end of each line

Oral Reading (continued)

____ repeats words

____ repeats phrases

____ repeats lines

____ reads in a loud voice

____ reads the pictures instead of the words

III.   Comprehension

____ cannot recall basic facts

____ uses background of experience rather than reading material to answer questions

____ cannot make inferences

____ cannot draw conclusions

____ cannot answer questions pertaining to vocabulary

____ makes guesses

____ gives answers in great detail

IV.   Other Observations

_____

_____

_____

_____

_____

_____

FIGURE 5.1. Teacher-constructed checklist of reading difficulties. *Note.* From "Teaching Children with Reading Problems" by J. E. Boyd and N. R. Bartel, in *Teaching Children with Learning and Behavior Problems*, D. D. Hammill and N. R. Bartel (Eds.), 1978, Boston: Allyn & Bacon. Reprinted by permission.

When writing is the target of the informal evaluation, there is one procedure that is by far preferable—the analysis of children's spontaneously written material, including stories and essays. A student's composition can be evaluated from many different points of view. A glance is all that is necessary to make judgments about legibility and story length; more care is required in conducting a thorough assessment of such factors as proficiency in vocabulary, grammar, syntax, spelling, punctuation, capitalization, and idea expression.

A teacher/diagnostician could have a class or two (or any group of youngsters) write a story on some given topic of interest. After reading 30 or so essays on the same topic the teacher should be quite sensitive to the themes, vocabulary, grammar, and so on, used by most of the children. Departures or deviations from modal responses are likely to be of clinical interest. Compositions that make use of dialogue, humor, philosophic or moral themes, complex story sequences, paragraphs, and imagination tend to be more mature than those that do not. The quality of the vocabulary used can be estimated by consulting graded word lists or by simply noting the number of large words (those with seven or more letters) used in relation to the total number of words in the composition. Analyzing the grammatic character of individual "thought units" or sentences is often used as an estimate of syntactic complexity. Errors in spelling, grammar, punctuation, and capitalization are easy to identify and can be noted for later instruction.

These informal techniques are useful mostly to experienced persons who have worked with youngsters on reading and writing problems long enough to be able to recognize what is and is not clinically significant.

Test-Based Assessment

Many tests of written language are available. Every achievement test battery used in schools contains at least one subtest that measures reading; however, considerably fewer have subtests of written expression abilities. These tests are useful in documenting a student's progress through the school grades; but teacher/diagnosticians will find the results of "diagnostic" tests to be more beneficial in identifying learning disabilities, inventorying specific strengths and weaknesses, and selecting areas for remedial instruction. Compared with achievement tests, diagnostic tests measure a greater variety of skills associated with reading and writing.

The more commonly employed diagnostic tests are presented in Table 5.3. The contents of the table allow one to learn quickly the purpose of each test, the ability constructs measured, and the age range for which the test is appropriate.

ASSESSMENT OF ARITHMETIC DISABILITIES

Individuals who would assess arithmetic abilities should consider at least four clusters of skills, namely, those skills related to prerequisite abilities, computation, reason-

TABLE 5.3. Tests of Written Language (Reading and Writing)

Test	Purpose		Reading			Writing					Age Range
	Identification	Instruction	Phonics	Word Recognition	Comprehension	Ideas	Linguistic	Spelling	Style	Handwriting	
Diagnostic Reading Scales (Spache, 1981)	X	X	X	X	X			X			7-0 to 14-11 years
Diagnostic Spelling Potential Test (Arena, 1982)	X	X						X			7-0 to adult
Diagnostic Spelling Test (Kottmeyer, 1970)		X						X			School-aged
Durrell Analysis of Reading Difficulty (Durrell, 1955)	X	X	X	X	X					X	Nonreader to adult
Gray Oral Reading Test (Wiederholt & Bryant, 1986)	X		X	X	X						7-0 to 17-11 years
Hudson Education Skills Inventory–Reading (Hudson et al., 1989)		X	X	X	X						School-aged
Hudson Education Skills Inventory–Writing (Hudson et al., 1989)		X				X	X	X	X	X	School-aged
Picture Story Language Test (Myklebust, 1965)	X					X	X				7-0 to 17-11 years
Spellmaster Assessment and Teaching System (Greenbaum, 1987)		X						X			7-0 to adult
Stanford Diagnostic Reading Test (Karlsen et al., 1978)	X	X	X	X	X						7-0 to adult
Test of Adolescent Language (Hammill et al., 1987)	X				X		X				11-0 to 18-5 years
Test of Early Reading Ability–2 (Reid et al., 1989)	X	X	X	X	X						3-0 to 7-11 years
Test of Early Written Language (Hresko, 1988)	X					X	X	X	X	X	3-0 to 7-11 years
Test of Legible Handwriting (Larsen & Hammill, 1989)	X	X								X	7-6 to 17-11 years
Test of Reading Comprehension (Brown et al., 1986)	X				X						6-6 to 17-11 years
Test of Written Language–2 (Hammill & Larsen, 1988)	X	X				X	X	X	X		7-0 to 17-11 years
Test of Written Spelling–2 (Larsen & Hammill, 1986)	X	X						X			7-0 to 17-11 years
Woodcock Reading Mastery Tests (Woodcock, 1988)	X		X	X	X						Kindergarten to 17-5 years

ing, and geometry. By prerequisite skills we mean the capacity to master tasks representative of such Piagetian concepts as conservation, constancy, permanence, and so on. Computation skills refer to the ability to add, subtract, multiply, and divide. Reasoning is associated mostly with the solving of story problems. Geometry deals with the measurement of lines, angles, surfaces, and solids and with their relationships to each other. As in all other areas that can be assessed, the evaluation can involve either informal procedures or tests.

Informal Assessment

Bartel (1990a) has outlined a series of activities that have value in assessing the cognitive abilities thought to underlie math proficiency. These activities are summarized in Table 5.4. Such activities are best used when evaluating young children, usually under the age of 7.

The most popular way of informally evaluating computation skills involves error analysis. Authorities have noted that students do not tend to make random mistakes. Instead, their errors seem to follow a fairly consistent pattern. To this point, Howell and Kaplan (1980) state:

> Little information is obtained by simply reporting the number of errors a student makes. The knowledge that "Jenny got five wrong" is not particularly valuable. However, hearing that "Jenny made five multiplication errors and they all involve × 8" could lead you to think that you should teach Jenny her 8's. (p. 245)

In addition to studying the pattern of errors, the teacher may be interested in learning how it is that the student came to make the error. To determine how students reached a wrong answer is often a simple task—just ask them to verbalize the process they use while they are working out a problem. Take the following two examples.

$$
\begin{array}{lclcl}
\text{a.} & 17 & \qquad & \text{b.} & 17 \\
& +5 & & & +5 \\
\hline
& 112 & & & 85
\end{array}
$$

a. Sally verbalizes, "Seven and five are twelve. Put twelve below the line and bring down the one up there by the seven. That makes 112." In this problem, she is using a process to solve the problem that she thinks is correct, a process that is probably applied to all similar problems.

b. Bill verbalizes, "Seven times five is 35. Put the five below the line and hold the three. Five times one is five. Add three to it and put the eight below the line in front of the five. The answer is 85." He has obviously misread the sign and has multiplied instead of added.

TABLE 5.4. Assessment of Prerequisite Cognitive Abilities

Cognitive Ability	Examples of How a Child Demonstrates Ability		
	Orally State	**Demonstrate with Object**	**Match/Select/Other**
Classification			
by function	Can child state why a toy car does not belong in an array of toy furniture?	Can child arrange groups of objects by function (e.g., all transportation by air, land, water)?	Can child match pictures of items that "go with" other items by function (e.g., mitten with hand, boot with foot)?
by color	Can child state why red block does not belong in group with blue blocks?	Can child group objects by color?	Can child match objects by color?
by size	Can child state why large flag does not belong in group of small flags?	Can child arrange objects into groups by size?	Can child select "large" or "small" object in group?
by shape	Can child state why circles do not belong in group of squares?	Can child group objects by shape?	Can child identify several circular-shaped, rectangular-shaped, objects in the room?
by several criteria simultaneously	Can child state differences between prearranged groups of blue squares, red squares, blue circles, red circles?	Can child sort objects on basis of simultaneous criteria of size and function, size and shape, color and shape, etc.?	Can child select which one "does not belong" in array employing two criteria at once?
Seriation			
linear	Can child state basis of linear serial array based on increasing size?	Can child arrange objects in order of increasingly intense color?	Can child select item missing in a serial array?

(Continued)

TABLE 5.4. *(Continued)*

Cognitive Ability	Examples of How a Child Demonstrates Ability		
	Orally State	**Demonstrate with Object**	**Match/Select/Other**
unit	Can child state relationships between sets of 1, 2, 3, 4, etc.?	Can child develop sequence of objects or numerals, based on units in each?	Can child count to 10 or 20? Can child tell which numeral contains more—4 or 6, 3 or 8, etc.?
temporal	Can child state what he or she did first in a simple task, what last?	Can child follow simple directions (e.g., "First put the block in the box; next put the penny beside the tray")?	Is there informal evidence of child's developing temporal sense (e.g., does child know which task is done after recess without being told)?
One-to-One Correspondence	Can the child state the number of pencils that will be required in a group of three children?	Can the child "order" milk for the class lunch based on the number in attendance? Does child know how to distribute the milk when it is received?	Can the child pair boots or mittens with the owner?
Understanding of Spatial Relations	Can the child state which object is over, under, in, or beside with respect to another object?	Can the child match geometric objects to openings into which they fit?	Can the child distinguish between right and left?
Conservation			
of shape	Can the child state if and why a ball of clay is the same mass whether rolled into a ball or into a rope?	Can the child show that a ball of clay can be made into a rope and back into a ball again?	Can the child do same task as to left, except (a) break clay into smaller pieces and put back into a ball and (b) flatten clay like a pancake and put back into ball.
of liquid	Can child state which glass contains more water?	Can child demonstrate equality by pouring more or less water into glasses?	Can child do task at left when water from one glass is poured into several smaller ones?

(Continued)

TABLE 5.4. *(Continued)*

Cognitive Ability	Examples of How a Child Demonstrates Ability		
	Orally State	**Demonstrate with Object**	**Match/Select/Other**
of number	Can child state which now has more blocks?	Can child make equal numbers in these rows?	Can child recognize that the number of pencils is the same whether they are packed in a box or scattered on a desk?

Note. From "Problems in Mathematics Achievement" by N. R. Bartel, in D. D. Hammill and N. R. Bartel (Eds.), *Teaching Children with Learning and Behavior Problems* (p. 184), 1982, Boston: Allyn & Bacon. Reprinted by permission.

The error analysis and verbalizing technique is equally applicable to assessing arithmetic reasoning and geometry skills as well. For readers who wish to know more about error analysis, there are several fine sources, including Ashlock (1986) and Howell and Kaplan (1980).

Test-Based Assessment

Most diagnostic tests measure various aspects of computation and reasoning; some measure readiness and geometry variables as well. As is true of the other tests mentioned in this chapter, the test may be most useful in determining the level of math ability in a student, in identifying students needing special help, and in targeting particular construct areas that require development. For convenience, currently popular math diagnostic tests are listed in Table 5.5 along with mention of their primary purposes, the elements measured, and the age for which they are most appropriate.

ASSESSMENT OF CORRELATIVE DISABILITIES

In Chapter 3 the major types of learning disabilities were discussed, and in this chapter we have provided the reader with some information related to the assessment of those major disability areas. Also in Chapter 3 there was mention of those disability areas that are supposed by some to be correlated with, causal to, or symptomatic of learning disabilities. In general, these correlative disabilities are disorders of perception, motor function, and behavior (e.g., hyperactivity, distractibility, impulsivity, etc.). In the more recent literature a new set of correlative disabilities has been given

TABLE 5.5. Tests of Arithmetic Abilities

Test	Purpose		Elements				Age Range
	Identi-fication	Instruc-tion	Readi-ness	Compu-tation	Reason-ing	Geom-etry	
Diagnostic Test of Arithmetic Strategies (Ginsburg & Mathews, 1984)		X		X			7-0 to 12-11 years
Fountain Valley Teacher Support System in Mathematics (1976)	X	X		X	X	X	Kindergarten to 13-11 years
Hudson Education Skills Inventory–Math (Hudson & Colson, 1989)		X	X	X	X	X	School-aged
KeyMath–Revised (Connolly, 1988)	X			X	X	X	Preschool to 11-11 years
Stanford Diagnostic Mathematics Test (Beatty et al., 1976)	X	X		X	X	X	8-0 to 17-11 years
Test of Early Mathematics Ability (Ginsburg & Baroody, 1990)	X		X	X	X	X	4-0 to 8-11 years
Test of Mathematical Abilities (Brown & McEntire, 1990)	X			X	X		8-0 to 17-11 years

attention, namely, deficits in certain cognitive skills or strategies such as selective attention, recall, and problem-solving techniques. From the viewpoint of the present authors, it is highly questionable whether these rather exotic, and certainly esoteric, disorders have any direct relationship to the identification and remediation of learning disabilities. Such problems routinely occur in individuals with mental retardation, in those with cerebral palsy, and in normal children with no other difficulties.

From the standpoint of definition and from the theoretical and experiential bases we have adopted, there is little need to proceed beyond the assessment of spoken language, written language, and arithmetic. It is in these areas of human function that learning disabilities are manifested, and it is in these areas that the teacher of the learning disabled will undertake to provide remediation and compensatory education.

For these reasons we do not include in this discussion of assessment any reference to techniques, informal or formal, for the evaluation of perceptual, motor, or behavior disorders.

6

THE TASK ANALYTIC APPROACH
TO ASSESSMENT

In addition to the informal assessment procedures and the test-based assessment discussed earlier, there is a third assessment process that transcends these and provides a bridge between evaluation and teaching. This is the process of task analysis, which bears the hallmarks of criterion referencing, sequentiality, and individualization. From the teacher's point of view, the most important reason for any type of evaluation is to collect information that can be used as the basis for planning instructional programs for individual children. This is the teacher's only reason for assessing students. Regarding the task analysis approach, this chapter contains discussions of scope and sequence charts, underlying principles of the approach, methods of accomplishing a task analysis, and an example of an analysis of a specific task.

The task analysis approach is dependent upon the identification of a scope and sequence of major tasks in whatever remedial area is under consideration and upon the identification of the level at which the student is performing. To the teacher, such assessment is an educational evaluation. According to Jedrysek et al.,

> The educational evaluation is a structured testing and educational procedure designed
> to assess the child's present functions and level of achievement in a variety of areas.
> It provides an opportunity to watch the child learn under standardized conditions

and to explore his capacity to master new learning. It seeks to discover the obstacles which may be present in the form of specific deficits. . . . The evaluation provides a curriculum guide for the teacher; the educational profile of the child is a basis for planning the educational program, based on the systematic and detailed information received about the child. (1972, pp. 1–2)

While we might disagree with the actual procedures followed by Jedrysek and his colleagues and with the tasks that they consider important, their statement concerning the purpose of the educational evaluation is more than acceptable.

All too often in the past, individualized education plans have been based almost exclusively on the results of tests. This is indeed unfortunate because of the shortcomings inherent in this approach; for example, many of the tests used have (a) reliabilities that are too low to permit confident statements about individual children's learning, (b) test content that is usually too limited to serve as the basis for program planning, and (c) undemonstrated validity in terms of their educational relevance. In addition, children being evaluated vary markedly in their day-to-day test performance, and so "diagnosis" is hazardous; and the examiner, generally having little direct knowledge about the child's classroom behavior, tends to "diagnose" entirely on "testing room" behavior and so on. Even though we feel that the use of formal, standardized tests has been overemphasized, especially as a source of educationally relevant information, we are not yet ready arbitrarily and willfully to dispense with all formal testing. Instead, we propose that elements of task analysis be combined with formal testing for a comprehensive evaluation program. If this were done, some of the presently unmet needs existing in most school evaluation programs would be largely satisfied.

Before going any further into a discussion of task analysis we must acknowledge that this approach has at least one of the same shortcomings as the standardized test approach: that is, the scope and sequence of tasks that are selected or developed in any particular area reflect, just as concretely as test items, the definition of the area. For example, the brief task analysis of word recognition in oral reading given in Table 6.1 implies that children learn to read by recognizing letters and sounds, associating the two elements, blending them together, and producing a word. Is this a "true" or adequate definition of this early stage of reading? Many professionals would agree that it is adequate; a number of others would reject the conception. There is no final resolution to these theoretical questions, and the teacher must fall back on his or her own experience of what has been successful, always being ready to change the approach and to analyze the task in a completely different way.

SCOPE AND SEQUENCE CHARTS

Task analysis will be discussed as a process—a process that is employed when we attempt to break down, into the smallest possible steps, a particular task that we want to teach a child. For example, we may find that the child needs to learn how to count objects—not rote, serial counting, but actual object counting. The terminal performance objective would state that the child will be able to count any number of objects, up to 10, when presented with a specified number of objects. In doing a task analysis we must first decide what entry behaviors are necessary. For example, if the child is expected to respond orally, then he or she must be able to say all of the number words from *one* through *ten* intelligibly enough to be understood; the child must be able to see or feel the objects so that he or she is able to count them; and there probably are other requisite entry behaviors that could be named. However, the teacher will *not* teach these behaviors at this time. If they are absent, the teacher may have to discard the present task (counting objects orally) and move to an earlier task such as teaching the child how to say the names of numbers, or the teacher may retain the task but change either the response or stimulus mode.

After recognizing the necessary entry behaviors, the teacher begins breaking down the task of counting into its smallest phases. The first phase or step might be related to teaching the child to say the number sequence from 1 to 10 in a serial fashion before moving to teaching one-to-one matching between number symbol (word) and sets of objects. The process of task analysis does not specify what tasks are to be taught; it merely provides a framework in which the tasks may be analyzed and sequenced. The diagram in Figure 6.1 shows the framework to be used.

As the diagram indicates, the tasks to be taught are embedded within a scope and sequence of curriculum. In Figure 6.2 a scope and sequence for language training is presented (Lee, 1974). The reader should be aware that what is presented is only one of many possible scope and sequence outlines for the teaching of language; it in no way represents the whole of language. Instead, the scope and sequence for a particular aspect of language—the acquisition of syntax—is given. Implicit in the outline are semantic elements, but these are not charted directly. The chart presents seven levels of development. These levels do not correspond exactly to age levels; this would be an impossibility because the language development of the individual child is too idiosyncratic with regard to age. One child might have developed all the levels in the chart by age 8; another child by age 10. Also, there is no guarantee that each component in the scope portion of the chart (reading horizontally) develops exactly at, for example, Level 5, as shown. A child might be using the construction "I want you *to come*," which is an early infinitival complement at Level 5, but at the same time be using most other constructions at Level 4. In general, however, most children develop rather uniformly, and there should not be wide variance in their language across levels.

As the reader can see, the scope and sequence chart has two major components: levels of development in which the items are listed vertically down the page, and the areas of the skill to be covered, arranged horizontally. The horizontal aspect is the "scope"; the vertical aspect, the "sequence." It should not be difficult to imagine what a scope and sequence chart for social studies might look like. Across the top of the chart would be placed the areas of content that are to be covered, and down the chart would be found the sequence in which the various areas are to be covered.

TABLE 6.1. Task Analysis of Objective: Word Recognition in Oral Reading

Behavioral Objectives	Item Numbers	Materials	Teacher Directions	Criteria	Alternative Strategies
Given a set of visual stimuli in the form of objects, pictures, letters, and words, the child will attend to the stimuli.	1	Familiar objects, pictures, letters, and words on cards.	"Look at this ___."	The child is able to attend for 30 seconds.	Use behavior modification techniques to increase attention span.
Given a set of 6 cards, each containing a letter of the alphabet, the child will be able to match like letters.	2	Sets of cards containing single letters of the alphabet with at least 3 cards for each letter, lowercase and capitals.	A. Show the child the model and have him or her find one like it. B. Have the child sort the cards.	19/20 correct	A. Move to simpler stimuli— lines, geometric forms, pictures. B. Have child trace the letters. C. Use color cues.
Given a single card containing one letter of the alphabet, the child will be able to provide orally the phonetic equivalent of the letter	3	3 sets of single-phoneme letters in random order, lowercase and capitals.	Show the letter and say its sound. Then, show the letter and ask the child to produce the sound.	19/20 correct for each letter	A. Copy the letter while saying the sound. B. Trace the letter while saying the sound.
Given a set of 6 cards, each containing a single word, the child will be able to match like words.	4	Sets of cards containing single words with at least 3 cards for each word, lowercase and capitals.	Same as in Item 2.	19/20 correct	A. Name words for the child. B. Have the child trace. C. Have the child copy.
Given a set of cards containing single letters and a model card containing a 3-, 4-, or 5-letter sequence, the child will be able to match the single cards to the model card, preserving the sequence.	5	Multiple sets of model cards with 3-, 4-, and 5-letter sequences and sets of single-letter cards; the sequences should form words.	Ask the child to reproduce the sequence from the model.	9/10 correct	A. Copying or tracing. B. Provide names or sounds for the letters. C. Use color cues.

(Continued)

TABLE 6.1 *(Continued)*

Behavioral Objectives	Item Numbers	Materials	Teacher Directions	Criteria	Alternative Strategies
Given the same conditions as above, the child will be able to reproduce the sequence from memory.	6	Same as above.	Show the model for 5 seconds and ask the child to reproduce it.	9/10 correct	Use verbal mediation; have the child name or sound the letters as he or she looks at them.
Given a set of 3-, 4-, or 5-letter sequences, the child will be able to produce corresponding phonemes in the same sequence as the letters.	7	Sets of 3-, 4-, and 5-letter sequences (words).	Ask the child to look at each letter and say each sound in turn. Attempt a smooth beat as with a metronome.	19/20 correct	A. Expose only one letter at a time. B. Point to each letter in turn as its sound is made.
Given 2-letter words, phonetically regular, the child will be able to produce the phonetic equivalents for each sound in such close temporal approximation that the sounds will blend into a word.	8	Set of 2-letter, phonetically regular words.	Model the process for the child very carefully. Ask the child to look at each letter and say the sound as in Item 7, but instead of using a beat, bring the sounds closer and closer together.	9/10 correct	Few alternatives are possible, but the child can run his or her finger smoothly and quickly across the words as he or she says the sounds.
Given the same conditions as above, but with 3-, 4-, and 5-letter words, the child will be able to blend.	9	Sets of 3-, 4-, and 5-letter words.	Same as above.	9/10 correct	Same as above.

A great number of scope and sequence charts are available. They are the curriculum guides provided by many schools. They are also the guides that more and more publishers of commercial materials are designing to accompany programs in reading, math, language arts, social studies, and so on. In fact, when one begins looking, there is a multiplicity of scope and sequence guides available. However, these guides have not been notably successful, and one of the reasons for their lack of

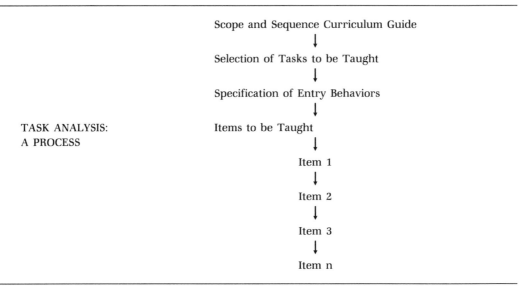

TASK ANALYSIS:
A PROCESS

Scope and Sequence Curriculum Guide
↓
Selection of Tasks to be Taught
↓
Specification of Entry Behaviors
↓
Items to be Taught
↓
Item 1
↓
Item 2
↓
Item 3
↓
Item n

FIGURE 6.1. The framework of task analysis.

effectiveness with children who have learning disabilities is that the tasks specified in the guides have not been broken down so that the teacher is able to teach only one element of the task at a time. It is unfortunate that the tasks usually are stated in broad, global terms, because *all* children with learning disabilities need specific, discrete, and sequential teaching. The children need to know what the *one* thing is that they are attempting to learn.

PRINCIPLES OF TASK ANALYSIS

As the reader is probably aware, all of the principles involved in task analysis, based on a solid scope and sequence guide, are the same as those inherent in the diagnostic teaching process. Several of these principles should be stated—namely, sequentiality, discreteness, and specification of input-output modes and levels of difficulty. Sequentiality, as best can be determined, is one of the most important principles of task analysis. The entire process is predicated upon the "building block" theory of skill learning—that is, that the skills one must acquire in learning a task are to be developed in a sequential order; that one must learn "A" before "B" and "B" before "C." We cannot be exact about this sequence of items for any given task, but it is possible to arrange the items in a logically sequential order before presenting them to children. Tied very closely to the principle of sequentiality is discreteness. The items of a task, arranged in sequence, must be discrete enough that only one element of the task is taught at a time. If the child fails such an item, the teacher then knows exactly what the child is unable to do. The following is an example of an analysis of the task "cutting with scissors":

1. Closes thumb to other fingers of hand

2. Grips and releases with scissors (any position)

3. Grips and releases with scissors held perpendicular to cutting surface

4. Makes short cuts into paper with scissors remaining along vertical plane

5. Cuts through piece of construction paper in straight direction

6. Cuts along drawn line

7. Cuts straight line in two directions (will change direction of paper before changing wrist direction)

8. Cuts out simple patterns—may tear a little

9. Cuts patterns with skillful wrist coordination—little tearing

(Vidaurri, Cano, & Schmidt, 1973, p. 31)

As the reader can see, every effort has been made to make the items as discrete as possible and to arrange them in sequence. Whether this is the proper sequence can be answered only by using the analysis to teach a child to cut with scissors.

A full-blown task analysis should state the input-output modes involved. That is, is a particular step in the analysis relying on an auditory input with an oral output? Or a visual input with motor output? Or on visual input with oral output? This information is valuable because if a child fails a particular item, the teacher could search for alternative modes and perhaps assist the child in achieving success. For example, will the child who fails an item that requires auditory input succeed if visual input is paired with the auditory? If the child is unable to respond orally, can he or she respond if the item response mode is changed from oral to motor?

Another principle in task analysis refers to the level of difficulty of the items. In an item a child may be asked to match letters. In all probability most people would agree that letters are more difficult and complex visual stimuli than are pictures, lines, geometric forms, and so on. Therefore, if the child were unable to match the simplest letters, the teacher could simplify the item by moving back to simpler stimuli like geometric forms, then moving forward to simple, easily distinguished letters, and finally to all letters. On the same item the teacher might use other input modes, incorporating tracing, color cues, auditory stimuli, and so on. However, no more than one variable should be altered at a time. If more than one is altered, the teacher has no way of knowing whether the child succeeded because of a change in the level of difficulty or a change in the input-output modes, or both, and will not know what changes to make the next time a child fails an item.

	Indefinite Pronouns or Noun Modifiers	Personal Pronouns	Main Verbs	Secondary Verbs
1	it, this, that	1st and 2nd person: I, me, my, mine, you, your(s)	A. Uninflected verb: I *see* you. B. Copula, is or 's: *It's* red. C. is + verb + ing: He *is coming*.	
2		3rd person: he, him, his, she, her, hers	A. -s and -ed: *plays, played* B. Irregular past: *ate, saw* C. Copula: *am, are, was, were* D. Auxiliary *am, are, was, were*	Five early-developing infinitives: I wanna *see* (want *to see*) I'm gonna *see* (going *to see*) I gotta *see* (got *to see*) Lem*me* [*to*] *see* (let me [*to*] *see*) Let's [*to*] *play* (let us [us *to*] *play*)
3	A. no, some, more, all, lot(s), one(s), two (etc.), other(s), another B. something, somebody, someone	A. Plurals: we us, our(s), they, them, their B. these, those		Noncomplementing infinitives: I stopped *to play*. I'm afraid *to look*. It's hard *to do* that.
4	nothing, nobody, none, no one		A. can, will, may + verb: *may* go B. Obligatory do + verb: *don't* go C. Emphatic do + verb: I *do* see.	Participle, present or past: I see a boy *running*. I found the toy *broken*.
5		Reflectives: myself, yourself, himself, herself, itself, themselves		A. Early infinitival complements with differing subjects in kernels: I want you *to come*. Let him [*to*] *see*. B. Later infinitival complements: I had *to go*. I told him *to go*. I tried *to go*. He ought *to go*. C. Obligatory deletions: Make it [*to*] *go*. I'd better [*to*] *go*. D. Infinitive with *Wh*-word: I know what *to get*. I know how *to do* it.
6		A. *Wh*-pronouns: who, which, whose, whom, what, that, how many, how much I know *who* came. That's *what* I said. B. *Wh*-word + infinitive: I know *what* to do. I know *who(m)* to take.	A. could, would, should, might + verb: *might come, could be* B. Obligatory does, did + verb C. Emphatic does, did + verb	

FIGURE 6.2. An abbreviated scope and sequence of language training specific to the area of syntax. *Note.* From *Developmental Sentence Analysis* by L. Lee, 1974, Evanston, IL: Northwestern University Press. Reprinted by permission.

FIGURE 6.2. *(Continued)*

Indefinite Pronouns or Noun Modifiers	Personal Pronouns	Main Verbs	Secondary Verbs

7   A. any, anything, anybody, anyone
 B. every, everything, everybody, everyone
 C. both, few, many, each, several, most, least, much, next, first, last, second (etc.)
	(his) own, one, oneself, whichever, whoever, whatever
	    Take *whatever* you like.
		A. Passive with *get*, any tense Passive with *be*, any tense
		 B. must, shall + verb: must come
		 C. have + verb + en: *I've eaten*
		 D. have got: *I've got* it.
			Passive infinitival complement:
			   With *get*: I have *to get dressed*.
			   I don't want *to get hurt*.
			   With *be*: I want *to be pulled*.
			   It's going *to be locked*.

PERFORMING A TASK ANALYSIS

The principles stated above were incorporated into Table 6.1, which shows a complete task analysis of a particular task that is common to many reading programs. Note that only *one* task is presented: the child's oral response to single, phonetically regular words. Obviously, there is a great deal more to reading than this single task, and, in fact, not all reading scope and sequence charts would even include this task. That is a choice the teacher must make, depending on orientation to reading instruction and interpretation of the child's needs.

In the analysis presented in Table 6.1, six components are included; these are listed across the horizontal axis of the chart. The first is a behavioral objective which should include four aspects, namely, the audience, the behavior, the condition, and the degree. These four aspects are described by Merrill and Goodman (1972) as follows:

1. *The audience.* In the case of the task analysis shown in Table 6.1, the audience is the child; in all cases the audience is that individual to whom the objective is addressed.

2. *The behavior.* The behavior is always designated by a verb with an object which describes an observable action on the part of the learner.

3. *The conditions.* The conditions refer to the limitations that are placed on the learner, or on the materials, or on the equipment used by the learner when he or she is being evaluated.

4. *The degree.* The degree is the minimal performance level at which the learner proves that the objective has been mastered. Often, this aspect is designated the criterion; in any event, it is the standard for mastery.

In the second column of the chart is the item number, which is simply a convenience for referring to the behavioral objective. The third component refers to the materials needed by the teacher for the item. Again, this is a convenience so that the teacher may gather needed materials before teaching the item.

The fourth component is the teacher directions. In reality, the teacher directions are part of the behavioral objective because they specify further the conditions under which the behavior occurs. Some authors with a puristic approach to writing behavioral objectives would say that all of the first five components belong in the objective. It has been broken down here for ease in presentation. The criterion for success is given in the fifth component. The criteria could be given in terms of time spans and, in item number 1, in number of consecutive successes, or in number of correct responses out of some designated total.

The sixth component is termed alternative strategies and presents some of the more obvious teaching alternatives for each item. It is under this component that the teacher could note the variations in input-output modes or levels of difficulty that are to be introduced if a child fails an item under the conditions imposed in the first four components.

Accomplishing a task analysis appears to be a time-consuming and laborious job, but there are at least two points to commend it. First, after the task analysis has been completed, it does not have to be done over and over for each child. The child may be unique and will have to be taught in accordance with his or her own pace and learning style, but the content to be taught does not vary. If we look again at the scope and sequence chart for language training in Figure 6.2, it becomes apparent that every child in some way must go through all of the areas on this chart if he or she is to have good language performance. How the child is to be taught does not change that. So once a task analysis is completed, it is finished, except for modifications the teacher makes when it seems that items have been omitted or misarranged. Second, the process of task analysis allows teachers to know *what* they want to teach, *where* they want to begin, *when* they have succeeded, and *what* the next item should be.

A SAMPLE ANALYSIS

In conclusion and to illustrate further the use of task analysis as a ongoing assessment procedure, let us suppose that a child is having difficulty with *Wh*-pronouns as found in the sample scope and sequence chart shown in Figure 6.2. Ervin-Tripp (1975) found that *Wh*-questions seem to develop in the following sequence: "where," "what," "whose," "who," "why," "how," and "when." In this study the task was to answer a brief question immediately following a sentence in a story. Comprehension required to answer *Wh*-questions obviously relies heavily upon preexisting cognitive skills as well as on immediate decoding of the question itself. The following abbreviated set of tasks serves both as assessment questions and as a sequence for instruction:

The Student Will

1. answer *Wh*-questions of one type asked by the teacher about immediately observable objects/pictures/actions (four of five responses in correct category, but not necessarily correct information).

2. answer *Wh*-questions of one type asked by the teacher about immediately observable objects/pictures/actions (four of five responses in correct category and with correct information).

3. answer *Wh*-questions of mixed types asked by the teacher about immediately observable objects/pictures/actions (four of five responses in correct category).

4. answer *Wh*-questions of mixed types when the question is embedded in a sentence, for example, "Tell me who _____?" "Will you tell us where _____?" (four of five responses about immediately observable stimuli).

5. answer mixed *Wh*-questions asked by someone other than the teacher about immediately observable stimuli (four of five responses). (Nelson, 1979, p. 103)

As the reader can see, a sequence of activities like those given above can easily be used to determine the child's present level of functioning with regard to acquisition of *Wh*-questions; such would be an assessment procedure. Once the level of functioning is established—for example, the child can answer *Wh*-questions of one type but not of all types—the sequence can be used for instructional purposes to begin teaching at the appropriate level.

Task analysis is, therefore, both an assessment and an instructional technique. However, it is too time-consuming to be used as part of a formal evaluation battery and should be left to the teacher to be used as part of the ongoing test-teach-test process.

7

FROM EVALUATION
TO INSTRUCTION

This chapter deals with information that the teacher needs to implement an educational program for persons with learning disabilities. Topics included are (a) the role of individual educational planning, (b) a description of the settings in which a student can receive the needed instruction, (c) some mention of jurisdictional problems that might arise between the teacher of learning disabled children and other school staff, (d) a critique of teaching systems that are generally used in the regular classroom and that are often adapted for use with mildly to moderately learning disabled students, (e) a brief mention of mastery teaching, and (f) a listing of teacher competencies.

THE ROLE OF INDIVIDUAL EDUCATIONAL PLANNING

When the regulations for Public Law 94-142 (*Federal Register*, 1977) were published, there seemed to be a general assumption accompanying the regulations that teachers do not plan the individual education experiences of their handicapped students. It is unlikely that anyone ever prepared a document like the individualized education plan (IEP) prior to the advent of P.L. 94-142, but many teachers over the years have developed individual plans for their students complete with long-range goals and daily lesson plans. While not attempting to deal with the bureaucratic jargon and the mix of statutory, compliance, and educational elements in the IEP, we will discuss the importance of individual educational planning.

In moving from the evaluation of a student to the implementation of his or her individual education, the preparation of an educational plan is a critical bridge. It is a bridge that must be constructed carefully by all of those professionals who have played a role in the identification and assessment process and who will continue to play a role in the implementation of the student's educational program. In addition to the school professionals, the student's parents and, where appropriate, the student should be involved in the process. Even the most vociferous critics of the IEP seem to agree that the regulations governing its development have contributed at least one very positive element to the education of handicapped students, and that is the involvement of parents. Even if and when the regulations are removed, it is doubtful that school personnel will return to the times when parents were not actively involved in their children's education.

When we consider individual educational planning for handicapped students, let us keep uppermost in our thoughts that these are children and youth for whom the regular classroom, regular curricula, and regular teaching methods have provided little other than failure. If we work from that premise, it is obvious that when the student is placed in the special education program, there must be alterations in the classroom setting, the curricula and materials to be used, and/or the teaching methods and techniques to be employed. The basic questions to be answered in a student's individual plan, therefore, are:

1. What is the appropriate instructional setting?

2. What is the appropriate curriculum?

3. What are the appropriate instructional techniques?

No one professional person can answer all of these questions; they must be addressed by appraisal personnel who have a great deal of information about the student's present level of performance, by administrators who know the range and availability of instructional settings and related services, by teachers and supervisors who know curriculum and instructional methodology, and by parents who know more about the student and their expectations for him or her than anyone else.

In the individual educational planning process the following steps, at least, should be considered:

What are the student's major disabilities? Does the child have only a severe reading disability or problems in a number of disability areas? Once this question has been answered, the professionals and parents should agree upon the setting of long-term goals. These goals should be fairly discrete in nature, although not necessarily measurable. One such goal could be "To improve spoken vocabulary and syntax."

After the long-term goals are written, the short-term objectives are developed; these should be measurable. If the long-term goal is to improve spoken vocabulary and syntax, a short-term objective might be "J. T. will increase his spoken syntax to include the production of verbs in the regular past tense at a level of 86% accuracy." Built into such a statement is the evaluation criterion, and through periodic checking the teacher can determine how well the instruction is facilitating achievement of the objective.

Once the long-term goals and short-term objectives have been developed, a decision can be made as to the instructional setting in which the goals and objectives can be achieved. If the student has numerous problems and if several goals have been developed, he or she is probably best placed in a special class. If only one goal has been written, it is probable that the student can reach that goal through instruction in a resource room where he or she receives remedial assistance on a daily basis. Other instructional arrangements are often available to learning disabled students, but the decision as to which arrangement or setting is appropriate should be dictated in large part by the problems a particular student is having and the goals and objectives that are developed for his or her education.

At this point the professionals, not the parents, should recommend appropriate curricula, materials, and teaching methods that would appear to facilitate the goals and objectives set for the student. The task of writing daily lesson plans, while a part of the overall planning process, would be the province of only the teacher. The teacher would have some information, although probably incomplete, about the student's present level of functioning with regard to the goals and would have an exact objective toward which to work. The teacher would also have recommendations that he or she would have helped to formulate about appropriate methods and materials, and it would be incumbent upon the teacher to develop daily or weekly subobjectives that represent the small steps toward the objectives.

The process of individual educational planning, when viewed in this manner rather than through the prism of federal regulations, is not a burdensome task, nor would it require a great deal of paperwork—the bane of those who operate under numerous state and federal guidelines. It is a sad illusion, however, to think that the education of handicapped students can proceed in a systematic, efficient fashion without a fairly high degree of planning. Saddest of all is the illusion that *only* handicapped students need individual educational planning. Thousands, if not tens of thousands, of nonhandicapped students in our schools would profit from the implementation of such planning.

INSTRUCTIONAL SETTINGS

For the most part, children with learning disabilities receive their special instruction in one of three situations—in the regular class, the resource room, or the special class. As no two learning disabled children have precisely the same needs or characteristics, no one situation can possibly be best for all affected children. This being the case, today's school administrators have tended to provide at least these three options. In general, the regular class can accommodate the mild-to-moderate cases, the resource room is designed to handle the moderately involved youngsters, and the special class is reserved for the moderately to severely impaired pupils.

Administratively, the types of options provided are affected by the percentage of pupils that the district or school is committed to serve. As a general rule, if 1% to 2% of the school enrollment at the elementary level is estimated to be learning disabled, special classes are likely to be the placement of choice because only the severest cases will be identified. If the commitment is to serve 2% to 5% of the scholastics, both resource rooms and special classes will be needed, the former being implemented in the greater number. If more than 5% of the pupils are to be served, the teacher consultation component will be required in addition to resource rooms and special classes.

The Special Class

Of the three options the special class teacher is responsible for the fewest number of children, usually 5 to 15 depending upon the severity of their problems. On the average, children served in this setting are younger than those enrolled in other situations. Severe language disorders predominate and are complicated by so-called behavior disorders such as hyperactivity, distractibility, emotional lability, and so on. Both hard and soft signs of neurological dysfunction are common. As the children grow older, the associated symptomatology, that is, the "behavioral pathology," tends to dissipate, and the children often become candidates for regular class or resource placement.

The teacher in this setting will assess each pupil, will prepare individualized instructional plans, and will likely use the programs described in this book, either as suggested by their authors or in adapted form. The severity of the problems indicates that the children will have to have at least some one-to-one teaching in addition to small-group work. A child may or may not be partially integrated with regular pupils, for example, in art, gym, lunch, recess, and so on. As soon as the child is able to tolerate, and be tolerated by, the regular classroom on a more or less full-time basis, he or she should be transferred to the regular class and have individual needs met by the resource or consulting teacher.

The Resource Room

Children attend the resource room on a regularly scheduled basis for specific skill training. The child may come from either the regular or the special class. Here, as in the special class, the teacher is primarily responsible for assessing the problem, planning the intervention, and implementing the program.

In many geographic areas this operation may be called a "learning disability" resource room, but in practice, it may be open to all children in the school who evidence problems of any kind and may be used as a vehicle for "mainstreaming" mentally retarded, disturbed, and other mildly handicapped children. We are not too concerned if this is the case, as long as children who are in fact learning disabled receive the appropriate services.

The implementation and management of resource rooms present many problems related to scheduling, grading, public relations with the other school staff, and so on, that are more or less unique to that setting. The reader who is interested in using this particular model in the schools would find the work of Hawisher and Calhoun (1978), Wiederholt (1974), Hammill (1972), Cohen (1982), and Wiederholt, Hammill, and Brown (1983) useful.

The Regular Class

Of all the settings where a child can receive special help, the regular class is definitely the most practical and economically desirable. In fact, the vast majority of pupils who experience difficulty in school, including the child with mild learning disabilities, have their problems ameliorated by the regular classroom teacher. There remain, however, many youngsters who are enrolled in regular classes who have specific problems that their teachers simply lack the experience and/or training to handle. No doubt some of these children, but by no means all, have mild learning disabilities. With information and a little skill, the regular teacher is quite capable of managing successfully most of these pupils.

Recognizing that the number of these pupils is of such a magnitude that resource rooms and special classes are simply not economically feasible, many schools have established teacher-consultant services. The role of the teacher-consultant, sometimes called a "helping teacher," is to aid regular classroom teachers, to accommodate handicapped learners, to individualize instruction, to assess individual pupil needs, to select appropriate intervention strategies and materials, and in general to manage the class more effectively. Even though the consultants may from time to time teach children for demonstration purposes, they are not generally responsible for providing direct services to their children; effect on children's learning is manifested through the mediating influence of the regular teacher. Discussions of this service arrangement are available from Heron and Harris (1987); West, Idol, and Cannon (1989); Idol (1983); and Wiederholt, Hammill, and Brown (1983).

JURISDICTIONAL PROBLEMS WITHIN THE SCHOOL

In an effort to provide services to handicapped children and to other pupils with school-related problems, the schools have set up over the years a multitude of special programs. These include (a) self-contained classes and resource rooms for handicapped pupils, notably those who are retarded, disturbed, blind, and so on; (b) remedial reading and math services; (c) special stimulation and enrichment programs for children from low socioeconomic backgrounds; (d) psychological, counseling, and guidance services; and (e) speech therapy programs, among many other variations. Most of these programs were operational in the schools long before the movement on behalf of learning disabled children was fully under way.

In those days learning disabled children in the schools were provided services only if they manifested a specific problem that came under the province of one of the then-available specialists. It was a common occurrence for a child to be enrolled simultaneously in speech therapy and in remedial reading and for the two specialists to be completely unaware of the fact that they were sharing a pupil. A child might be identified and tested by the speech pathologist for delayed speech in kindergarten, be dismissed from that program at the end of second grade, and be enrolled into remedial reading during the third grade without anyone in the school recognizing that this pupil had been learning disabled throughout his or her entire school tenure. Children with motor problems received no formal attention at all, unless they were cerebral palsied, postpolio, or the like; and the services were rarely provided to the youngster who had the misfortune to suffer from a severe difficulty in arithmetic.

During this time, a pupil who was both disruptive in class and poor in reading often would end up in a class for disturbed children; a child whose reading was inadequate and IQ was low could be enrolled, and frequently was, into a class for educable retarded students. While the remedial reading teacher and the speech therapist administered their own criterion-referenced measures to diagnose and identify children, all other testing, diagnosis, and assessment procedures, even those pertaining to educational variables, were conducted by the school psychologist, guidance personnel, or the educational diagnostician.

The judicious use of persuasion applied by parents and professionals organized on behalf of children with specific learning disabilities resulted in the implementation by public schools of services specifically for these children. Naturally, the duties performed by the learning disabilities specialist often are similar to and sometimes the same as those that have been traditionally performed by other school personnel. For the most part the jurisdictional problems, that is, the who's-to-do-what-to-whom questions, exist between the learning disabilities specialist and (a) those who up to now have been exclusively responsible for conducting educational assessments, for example, the school psychologist and the educational diagnostician; (b) those who have been providing remedial reading and arithmetic services; and (c) those who have been managing the speech and language problems of children.

Jurisdiction over Assessment

In the early learning disabilities programs the common practice was for the psychologist and educational diagnostician to evaluate each pupil, diagnose the specific instructional or process needs, and write a detailed prescription which the learning disability teacher implemented in the classroom. Today, however, because of the disenchantment with standardized testing, the availability and use of educationally oriented informal tests, and an increase in assessment skills, teachers of learning disabled children are moving steadily in the direction of doing most of their own educational evaluation and prescription writing. Where the teacher does the bulk of his or her own assessment, the psychologist and diagnostician assume a consultative role.

We view this movement toward increased teacher independence regarding assessment as desirable, especially if it is confined to measuring educational variables and utilizes criterion approaches or diagnostic teaching rather than standardized tests. It could be argued, of course, that at this time most teachers do not have the essential training to do their own assessment reports and that until they do, other school staff should be responsible for examining the children and planning the instructional program. The assumption here is that it is possible for someone other than a teacher to assess adequately the pupils' needs in reading, writing, spelling, arithmetic, language, and behavior. Even if a proper report were prepared (e.g., one that provided such detailed suggestions as, "The pupil is ready to learn the following blends— /sl/, /bl/, and /kl/" or, "The pupil's manuscript illegibilities are associated with the letters *a*, *e*, *r*, and *t*," it would be "cold" after a week of remedial work. Since there would be little or no chance of securing another prescription within the immediate future, it is more expeditious to train the special teacher to engage effectively in assessment activities. The actual "diagnosing" of a child as learning disabled or non-learning disabled is by law in most states the primary responsibility of the school psychologist. We believe that it would be unwise and unnecessary for the special teacher to administer, much less interpret, noneducational tests such as the WISC batteries, the revised Stanford-Binet, and the Rorschach. We can think of no reason, however, why teachers should not, if they find them helpful and if they are willing to obtain the rather minimal amount of training required, administer and interpret tests of academic achievement such as the *KeyMath* (Connolly, 1988), the *Peabody Individual Achievement Test* (Dunn & Markwardt, 1970), the *Peabody Picture Vocabulary Test,* (Dunn & Dunn, 1981), the *Diagnostic Achievement Battery* (Newcomer & Curtis, 1984), and the *Test of Mathematical Abilities* (Brown & McEntire, 1990).

Jurisdiction over Remedial Education

The situation existing among the programs in remedial reading, math, and learning disabilities is also a subject of some dispute at the present time. In those districts where the learning disabilities program has a "process" orientation and the remedial classes have a "content" orientation, the lines between the two service arrangements can be drawn clearly. The learning disabilities specialist does perceptual-motor and psycholinguistic training, while others do remedial reading and arithmetic. If reading and math are taught at all to learning disabled children, the pupils also have associated process deficits. Fortunately, such a limited focus is not representative of learning disabilities programs in the nation. In fact, in most of the referrals for learning disabilities service the precipitating complaint is poor reading (Kirk & Elkins, 1975), rather than process difficulty; a major element in most special class and resource room curricula is the teaching or remediating of reading, math, and language skills.

Regarding reading, Hartman and Hartman (1973), among others, have attempted to distinguish between two types of problems—the one that is best managed by the learning disabilities specialist and the one that is best handled by the remedial reading person. Theoretically, it may be possible to make such a distinction; but practically, it probably does not matter. In today's schools, an intellectually normal 12-year-old youngster reading at the first-grade level could be enrolled in either a remedial reading or a learning disabilities program. The instructional intervention or the compensatory program designed for this child will more than likely be similar regardless of the job description of the professional who planned it.

It seems to us that at the present time persons trained in reading and in math have a better grasp of assessment and remediation principles associated with those skills than do most individuals trained in learning disabilities. However, as individuals, they often lack a sufficiently broad background in behavior management, handicapped children in general, other areas of academic performance, and language. Basic competence in these areas makes the learning disabilities specialist more able to deal with the multifaceted nature of a child with school problems. In any event there appears to be a pronounced trend in the schools toward grouping all remedial services under the learning disabilities rubric. This is exemplified by the rapid development of learning disabilities programs across the nation. This development is of such magnitude that it is obvious that school administrations are committed to serving considerably more than the 1% or 2% of hard-core cases. As they increase the percentage of children to be served under the learning disabilities umbrella, they simultaneously aggravate the existing jurisdictional problems existing between learning disabilities and remedial reading and math.

At this time we know of no equitable way to settle this difficulty. In the long run the problem probably will be resolved by (a) arbitrary agreements between local program directors; (b) specific guidelines established by state department of education personnel; (c) a serious reduction in state or federal support funds for either remedial or learning disabilities programs, an event that would encourage school administrators to reclassify the defunded program in order to continue to qualify for money; and, (d) if the differences between the two programs are not drawn distinctly and the curricula continue to be much the same, the eventuality of merging their efforts to some extent, thus minimizing or eliminating the problems of jurisdiction.

Jurisdiction over Speech and Language Development

The main area of contention with the speech therapy program concerns the area of language remediation and development. Unlike the learning disabilities specialist, the professionals who are associated with speech and hearing disorders have had a long and enduring interest in the area of language remediation traceable through the work of Myklebust, Barry, McGinnis, Wepman, and Eisenson, among others. During the 1960s the learning disabilities specialists were associated primarily with perceptual-motor training, some remedial reading, and the management of the symptoms described by Strauss, Lehtinen, and Cruickshank. Many of them, however, soon accepted Kirk's adaptation of the Osgood model, the ITPA, and the related training programs. With this acceptance their interest in language began. Today, many language-oriented learning disabilities specialists have studied intently the theories of Chomsky, McNeill, Menyuk, Lee, Piaget, Carrow, and others, and are anxious to apply their principles to education.

The speech pathologist has had and undoubtedly will continue to have a greater interest in the areas of stuttering, cleft palate, voice disorders, dysarthria, acquired aphasia, and severe articulatory disorders than any other professional. Learning disabilities specialists, per se, do not have the training to assume a primary role in working on these kinds of problems, and it is not anticipated that they ever shall. At this time the speech pathologist's ascendancy in the area of speech and language development is undisputed with regard to training and the utilization of his or her services. However, as learning disabilities specialists become more interested in language development and disorders and as they turn away from a perceptual-motor or remedial education orientation, it is likely that they will become more and more indistinguishable from speech pathologists as far as their role in language remediation is concerned. An added factor is the present emphasis on early childhood education for the handicapped, an area in which learning disabilities specialists have been poorly trained compared with speech pathologists, but an area that is receiving increased attention in most learning disabilities training programs. The conclusion is that except for certain expressive "speech" problems as noted in the beginning of this paragraph, speech pathologists and learning disabilities specialists are experiencing a blurring of the lines that have separated their roles.

We will not attempt to resolve the problems inherent in the role conflict between speech pathologists and learning disabilities specialists, but we would like to raise at least four cautions to those who are in administrative positions and are trying to deal with the difficulty. First, the uppermost concern should be that the communicatively disordered child receive the services he or she needs, regardless of which professional person offers that service. If in one case the best qualified person is a speech pathologist, that person should provide the service; if in another case the learning disabilities specialist possesses the necessary competencies, she or he should be the one to serve the child. It is incumbent upon the administrator who is making assignments, and it should be mandatory, to utilize staff in those areas where they are competent, not where they happen to be certified or simply available. We are committed to the philosophy that *poor service is probably worse than no service.*

Second, if learning disabilities specialists are to assume more responsibility for working with children who are language delayed, the college programs must offer the necessary training, both in course work and practicum. Too many programs are still devoted to training in the areas of perceptual-motor problems, reading disorders, and "process deficits" without providing training in normal language development, basic linguistics, language pathology, and language remediation.

The third caution is related to comprehensive staff utilization. Most speech pathologists do not want to be relegated arbitrarily to working only with "speech" problems, usually articulation disorders. It is wasteful of resources and poor management to force masters-level, certified speech pathologists into underemployment simply because they have chosen to work in the public schools. If they are not permitted to perform the services for which they are qualified, the jurisdictional problems will never be resolved.

Fourth, speech should not, because it cannot, be separated from language. Language is a universe of which phonology, the study of speech sounds, is a subset. The reader may have wondered why, when speech was referred to in preceding paragraphs, the word was enclosed in quotation marks; it is because speech and language are inseparable, and speech by itself is an anomaly. There is an impressive body of literature which indicates that children with many types of speech disorders —stuttering, cleft palate, articulation problems—also have language problems that must be dealt with concurrently.

Perhaps the cautions raised above serve only to cloud and complicate the problem of jurisdiction, but the problem itself is cloudy and complicated. The answers cannot be simplistic, or the resolution to the problem will serve only to make matters worse. Readers who would like a frank discussion of jurisdiction problems as seen through the eyes of professionals from different disciplines are referred to a series of articles by Sartain (1976) representing the reading specialist; Larsen (1976) the learning disabilities specialist; and Stick (1976) the speech pathologist. The series is concluded by Wallace (1976), who makes the case for an interdisciplinary approach to providing comprehensive services for learning disabled students.

CLASSROOM APPROACHES TO INSTRUCTION

One of the first steps any special education teacher should take before designing a remedial program for a child is to become thoroughly familiar with the instructional systems used by the regular teachers in the school in which he or she is teaching. This is particularly true when dealing with learning disabled children because so often their needs, particularly if their problems are mild to moderate in severity, can be managed successfully by adapting traditional classroom methods or by reteaching the very basal series that provided such an obstacle when introduced in the regular classroom. Also, it must be kept in mind that these systems are integral to the classroom into which the child must eventually fit who is to be returned full-time to the regular program.

Classroom Approaches to Reading

Most teachers of learning disabled children will have had some experience with the basal and language experience approaches to reading, as these are widely used in the schools today and ample exposure to them is frequently provided as part of a teacher preparation program. Several other approaches, however, probably deserve some mention.

Since the publication of Flesch's (1955) book, *Why Johnny Can't Read*, great interest and controversy have been generated among educators as to the appropriate method of reading instruction. The extent of the interest has been demonstrated in the proliferation of reading methods; the controversy may be followed in most educational journals, where numerous studies have been published, each indicating that one method is superior to another or that there is no significant difference among methods. The majority of the approaches devised within the past 35 years are intended for use in the regular classroom and not in the classroom for children with specific learning disorders. Intention, however, often differs from application, and we have found that many of these approaches to reading instruction are being used in special classes for children with learning disabilities. Several popular reading programs that were developed since 1955 are described by Bartel (1990a) in Table 7.1, Classroom Reading Approaches.

Classroom Approaches to Written Composition

Programs designed to teach composition in regular classes are generally composed of sequenced lessons, systematic activities, teacher manuals, and student workbooks. Usually they incorporate many informal activities that teach punctuation and capitalization; vocabulary, word usage, and grammar; and sentence and paragraph construction.

An example is Englemann and Silbert's (1983) *Expressive Writing* program that was designed for beginning writers who read at or above the third-grade level. The core of the program is 50 forty-five-minute lessons, each of which provides for practice in mechanics (punctuation and capitalization), sentence writing, paragraph writing, and editing. The teacher presents a lesson using instructions found in the *Teacher Presentation Book* (a teacher's manual); the students execute the lesson in space provided in their *Student Workbook*.

Consider Lesson 29 as an example. The lesson has four parts, each dealing with a different skill: editing run-ons, editing *was* to *did*, introducing sequence in paragraphs, and writing a paragraph that reports on an event.

1. Editing run-ons. Students are given a series of run-on sentences to correct. For example, "A girl bought an old bike from a friend and the bike had rust on its handlebars and wheels and the girl and her friend fixed up the bike."

TABLE 7.1. Classroom Reading Approaches

Type of Approach	Where Available	Advantages/Disadvantages/ Special Comments
Complete Basals. These usually consist of reading texts, teacher's manual, and supplementary materials such as workbooks. They are often sequenced in a series from K to Grade 6 or 8. The instructional approach is one of introducing a controlled sight vocabulary coupled with an analytic phonics emphasis.	Holt Basic Reading Ginn 720 Series American Book Company Readers Scott, Foresman Reading Houghton Mifflin Reading Program Macmillan Series E Lippincott Basic Reading Pathfinder (Allyn & Bacon)	1. Basals lend themselves well to the three-reading-group arrangement; less well to individualizing. 2. Content usually designed for the "typical" child; often not appealing to inner-city or rural children. 3. Basals are generally well sequenced and comprehensive; attend to most aspects of developmental reading. 4. Most have complete pupil packets of supplementary materials, saving teacher searching time. 5. Basals are sufficiently detailed and integrated that successful use is possible for a teacher lacking in confidence or experience.

Synthetic Phonics Basals. Similar to above in some ways, but emphasis is on mastering component phonics skills, then putting together into words.	Open Court Reading Program
	Lippincott's Basic Reader Series
	Reading Mastery I–VI
	    (formerly DISTAR)
	Swirl Community Skills Program
	    (SW Regional Laboratory)
		1. Same as above.
		2. Evidence is that a synthetic approach to word attack is rarely utilized by good readers.

Linguistic Phonemic Approaches. Vocabulary that is used is highly controlled and conforms to the sound patterns of English (e.g., *Nan, Dan, man, fan, ran,* etc.). Most programs contain children's texts, teacher's manual, and supplementary materials.	Let's Read (Bloomfield)
	SRA Basic Reading Series
	Merrill Linguistic Readers
	Programmed Reading
	    (Webster, McGraw-Hill)
	SRA Lift-Off to Reading
	Palo Alto Program (Harcourt,
	    Brace, Jovanovich)
		1. Content and usage in stories (especially early ones) sometimes contrived because of controlled vocabulary.
		2. Same as for Complete Basals.

(Continued)

TABLE 7.1. *(Continued)*

Type of Approach	Where Available	Advantages/Disadvantages/ Special Comments
Individualized Reading. Each child reads materials of own choice and at own rate. Word recognition and comprehension skills are taught as individual children need them. Monitoring of progress is done through individual teacher conferences. Careful record-keeping is necessary.	Trade books of many different types, topics, and levels	1. Children are interested in content. 2. Individualized reading promotes good habits of selection of reading materials. 3. An extensive collection of books is needed for students to make choices. 4. Teacher needs comprehensive knowledge of reading skills to make sure all are covered. 5. Required record-keeping can be cumbersome.
Diagnostic-Prescriptive Programs. These consist of entry-testing and exit-testing of skills related to specific skills. Students who pass entry test go on to other needed areas. Reading objectives fully stated.	*Print* Wisconsin Design for Reading Skill (National Computer Systems) Fountain Valley Reading Support System (Richard Zweig) Ransom Program (Addison-Wesley) *Nonprint, Computer-Assisted* Stanford University CAI Project Harcourt Brace CAI Remedial Reading Program	1. Skills are usually well sequenced. 2. Pupils work at own pace. 3. Learning may be boring, repetitive, or mechanistic. 4. Programs provide for ongoing assessment and feedback. 5. Programs deemphasize the language basis of reading (interaction and communication with other people). 6. Only those skills that lend themselves to the format are taught.
Language Experience Approach. This approach is based on teacher's recording of child's narrated experiences. These stories become basis for reading. May be based on level of group or individual child. Stories are collected and made into a "book."	Teacher-made materials	1. Relationship to child's experience is explicit. 2. Approach firmly establishes reading as a language/communicative act. 3. Approach provides no systematic skill development (left up to the teacher to improvise). 4. Approach can reinforce only at child's existing level, rather than pushing him or her on. 5. Usage is highly adaptable to pupils with unique needs and backgrounds.

Note. From "Teaching Students Who Have Reading Problems" by N. R. Bartel in D. D. Hammill and N. R. Bartel (Eds.), *Teaching Students with Learning and Behavior Problems*, 1990, Boston: Allyn & Bacon. Reprinted by permission.

2. Changing *was* to *did*. Students are asked to rewrite a passage so that all the sentences tell what a person or thing did, not what a person or thing was doing. For example, "One boy was falling down" is changed to, "One boy fell down."

3. Introducing sequence in paragraphs. Students are shown a series of related pictures that depict a story. A paragraph accompanying the pictures tells the story depicted. Each element in the story is read aloud in sequence and associated with the picture.

4. Writing a paragraph that reports an event. Students are shown four story-related pictures about a rodeo and a box containing 14 printed words related to the rodeo theme. Students are asked to write a paragraph that reports what happened. They are directed in composing their paragraph, for example, they are told to indent, to start with "The cowboy," to tell what he did in the picture, and so on.

At the end of the lesson, students are given the opportunity to self-evaluate aspects of their work. Other lessons vary in content but are similar in format to this one.

Classroom Approaches to Spelling

Most of the spelling series that are developed for general classroom use adhere to the idea that English spelling is sufficiently rule-governed to justify a basic linguistic approach. In fact, Hammill, Larsen, and McNutt (1977) observed that the authors of the three most popular spelling series—*Silver Burdett Spelling* (1986); *The Riverside Spelling* (Wallace, Taylor, Fay, Kvcera, & Gonzalez, 1988); and *Basic Goals in Spelling* (Kottmeyer & Claus, 1988)—all built their programs on linguistic theories. *Silver Burdett Spelling* serves as an example.

The words for each unit in the *Silver Burdett Spelling* (1986) series are divided into basic lists and enrichment lists that are topical or thematic in organization. The basic words constitute approximately 90% of the words most students use in their daily writing, with each group or list focusing on one particular spelling pattern. The patterns generally are phonological (e.g., short *a* words) or morphological (e.g., prefixes that mean "not"). In addition to providing general spelling lessons, *Silver Burdett Spelling* integrates many skills from a language arts curriculum (e.g., dictionary skills) and contains various enrichment or extension activities for the more able student.

Classroom Approaches to Arithmetic

Although arithmetic difficulties apparently occur less frequently than reading problems, the teacher of learning disabled children still must be knowledgeable about the basic approaches used in regular classes to teach this subject. Teachers of learning disabled students should know thoroughly the basal math texts that are used by the regular class teachers in their schools. However, they will find more useful the special instructional math kits that supplement these texts. Since these kits provide sequenced exercises, diagnostic tests, and record sheets and since they allow for self-pacing, self-teaching, and individualization, such kits are most desirable for use with the learning disabled students. Bartel (1990b) has summarized 10 of the most common in Table 7.2.

TABLE 7.2. Summary Descriptions of Instructional Math Kits

Title and Grade Level (Publisher)	Comments
Basic Computation Skills Series 1, 2, 3 (Holt, Rinehart)	Self-administered diagnostic tests prescribing work on Study-Do sheets. Record sheets, teacher's guide.
Diagnosis: An Instructional Aid (Science Research Associates)	Survey and diagnostic tests (probes), prescription guides, remediation activities. Management system for teaching pupil progress.
DISTAR: Arithmetic I, Arithmetic II (K–2) (Science Research Associates)	Direct instructional method. Teacher's and pupils' books. Take-home workbooks.
Foundations for Math: Basic Math Skill Development (Teaching Resources)	Skill development emphasized.
Fundamentals Underlying Numbers (Teaching Resources)	
Individualized Math System (Rev.) (1–8) (Ginn)	"Program" consists of reusable laminated pages. Pre- and posttests, prescriptive tests.
Math: An Activity Approach (6–9) (Science Research Associates)	Individualized. 188 games and activities from whole numbers through statistics. New skills, review of old skills. Application.
Math—Series 300 to 800 (3–8) (Educational Progress)	Individuals work at own rate and level. Concepts and skill sequence based on most widely used texts. Activity cards. Audiotapes. Student record-keeping.
Project MATH (K–6) (Educational Development Corp.)	Multiple-option curriculum. Interactive units based on teacher/learner input/output.
Skill Modes in Math (4–Adult) (Science Research Associates)	Self-diagnosis. Self-teaching. Student activity and practice cards, record books.

Note. From "Problems in Mathematics Achievement" by N. R. Bartel, in D. D. Hammill and N. R. Bartel (Eds.), *Teaching Students with Learning and Behavior Problems*, 1990, Boston: Allyn & Bacon. Reprinted by permission.

Classroom Approaches to Language Development

In recent years, many language development programs designed expressly for classroom use have become available. The development of these programs seems to have corresponded to the increasing commitment made by the American public to the early education of children from low socioeconomic backgrounds. Without doubt the two most popular classroom approaches are the Peabody Language Development Kits (PLDK) and the DISTAR Language Program.

The Peabody Language Development Kits.   Dunn and Smith and their colleagues (Dunn, Dunn, & Smith, 1981; Dunn, Horton, & Smith, 1981; Dunn, Smith, & Dunn, 1981; Dunn, Smith, Smith, & Dunn, 1982) have prepared this series of kits to stimulate spoken language, to heighten verbal intelligence, and as a consequence to influence positive school achievement. They did not intend that the kits be used to train specific psycholinguistic skill deficits; instead, they hoped that their use would increase general, overall verbal ability in groups of children. The rationale for this program is based squarely on aspects of Osgood's and Guilford's models. Because of this, PLDK could be considered to be a second cousin to the remedial approaches advocated by Kirk and Kirk; Minskoff, Wiseman, and Minskoff; and Bush and Giles, which are discussed in detail in Chapter 14 of this book.

The program, which can accommodate children ranging in mental age from 3 to 9½ years, is divided into four kits, each of which has 180 daily lessons. For the younger children an extensive use is made of tactile and visual stimuli and the language of labels. Also, every effort is made to stimulate grammatic structure and logical thinking. The emphasis of the lessons becomes increasingly more conceptual; and at the 7½ to 9½ age level ideas, concept formation, and creativity are stressed predominantly.

Of all the programs used in the regular classroom that are discussed in this chapter, the PLDK has been studied the most thoroughly. To their credit, the authors of the PLDK themselves conducted quite a number of these efficacy studies before making the program available to the public (Dunn & Mueller, 1966, 1967; Dunn, Nitzman, Pochanart, & Bransky, 1968; Mueller & Dunn, 1967; Smith, 1962). The findings of these and 11 additional investigations were reviewed by Hammill and Larsen (1974a), who concluded that of all the verbal abilities studied—for example, the ability to recognize verbal absurdities, to form verbal abstractions, to use proper grammar, to recall a series of spoken digits, and to use speech to convey ideas—only the last one, unquestionably a critical skill, seemed to be developed successfully by the PLDK.

The DISTAR Language Program.   This three-kit system, which was developed by Englemann and Osborn (I, 1976; II, 1977; III, 1973), is very popular. It is a highly structured program; in fact, the 160 lessons in each kit are so programmed that they must be presented strictly in the prearranged order and in a prescribed manner. Because of this and particular requirements concerning teacher behavior in using the program, some training of teachers is desirable before implementing DISTAR.

The assumptions that the rules of language can be externally imposed through drill and that they should be imposed as directly and quickly as possible form the basis for the program. There is no attempt to justify the lessons in terms of Osgood, Guilford, Chomsky, and so on. Instead, the activities are designed to serve pragmatic ends. For example, Language I focuses on teaching the child the language of instruction, that is, the language used by the teacher in the classroom. Language II emphasizes the teaching of skills that children need to analyze language and to describe the qualities and relationships they see in the world immediately around them. Language III concentrates on the mechanics of language, sentence structure, and effective communication.

DISTAR is appropriate for preschool- and elementary-aged pupils, and groups may be formed according to performance levels. Lessons are presented for 30 minutes daily, and children who perform well are rewarded with reinforcing take-home activities. While the material included in DISTAR is reasonably good and its sequence is excellent, many teachers object to what they consider its "excessive" structure and dependence on rote drill. Whether their opinions represent a differing philosophy of education, a teaching style that is incompatible with the nature of the program, or a feeling that the lessons are boring to teach and therefore tedious, we cannot say.

MASTERY TEACHING

Regardless of the curriculum selected for teaching and regardless of whether specialized methods will be used, Hunter (1984) has identified a number of teaching techniques that she believes "are applicable to all disciplines, all learners, all methodologies and all teaching styles and personalities" (p. vii). These techniques were identified after extensive research involving the observation of many successful teachers. Many of them are techniques intuitively used by good teachers, but Hunter labeled them and tried to explain the psychological theory behind their success.

Rather than delving into Hunter's research and theoretical explications, mastery teaching is presented in terms of the Model for Effective Teaching (Texas Education Agency, 1985), which may be seen in Figure 7.1. As the reader can see, the model is divided into two major sections, planning and teaching, and is presented in the form of a flow chart leading the reader sequentially from one step to the next. Starting at the far left of the figure, one initiates the lesson cycle by establishing the curriculum and selecting an objective and ends by selecting a new objective from the curriculum. The following sections explain each successive step in the lesson cycle.

It should be kept in mind that Hunter's (1984) research was done on students in a regular classroom of probably 20 to 30 students and that the techniques she developed and systematized are *group* techniques. The teachers of learning disabled students must remember that their students are often widely disparate in their learning abilities and styles and that they often cannot be taught as a group. In no way does this critique denigrate Hunter's contributions, but it does serve as a reminder

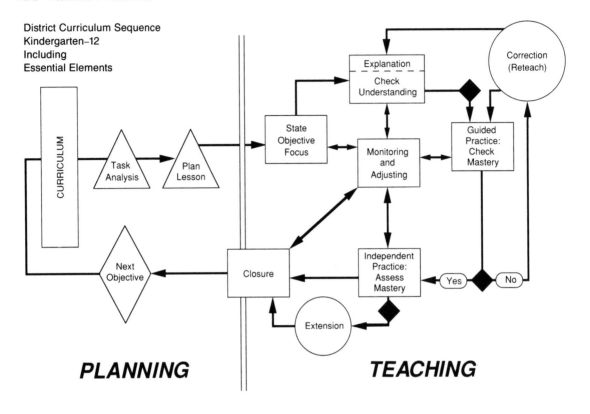

District Curriculum Sequence
Kindergarten–12
Including
Essential Elements

FIGURE 7.1. Model for Effective Teaching: The Lesson Cycle. *Note.* From *A Manual for Instructional Leadership Training,* 1985, Austin, TX: Texas Education Agency. Reprinted by permission.

to teachers of learning disabled students that they must redouble their monitoring efforts and attend closely to the individual students rather than to the group.

Curriculum

Often the curriculum is not selected or developed by the teacher; it is usually district- or even state-mandated. However, the preselection of a curriculum still provides the teacher of learning disabled students with all of the latitude needed to provide effective remediation. Care must be taken to ensure that the curriculum is entered at the appropriate level of instruction; entry points should be provided in the individualized education plan (IEP). The IEP will inform the teacher what grade level is appropriate for the individual student and what prerequisite skills the student possesses.

After the entry point has been selected, the teacher must formulate an objective for the student, an objective that specifies the learning behavior of the student. The student's expected behavior must be specific, observable, and open to validation. Performance cannot be such that students are able to guess, bluff, or simply be lucky in achieving success. Following some of Hunter's (1984) examples, instructional objectives could be similar to the following, which all begin with "The Learner will" (T.L.w.):

T.L.w. *write* ALL NUMERALS 1 THROUGH 10.

T.L.w. *name* THE LETTERS OF THE ALPHABET.

T.L.w. *match* SOUNDS OF /b/, /p/, AND /m/ TO WRITTEN LETTERS.

Task Analysis

Once the decisions regarding the content of the lesson and the instructional objective have been made, the teacher must analyze the task to determine whether the student possesses the skills prerequisite to achieving the objective. If the students do not have those skills, they must be taught or the objective must be changed. A fuller explanation of task analysis may be found in Chapter 6.

Plan Lesson

The third step in the lesson cycle is planning the lesson, which includes deciding what materials, if any, are needed, how the steps of the lesson will be presented, and what kind of performance will be acceptable. Most teachers plan their lessons and seldom "wing it."

State Objective Focus

At this step in the lesson cycle we move from planning to teaching. Students should be told what they are expected to learn from a lesson, and the focus of the objective should be stated clearly (e.g., "Today we are going to learn all of the number combinations that add to 10"). If the focus is stated, students will be aware of relevant material presented and will not be guessing as to "what will be on the test." Teachers may sometimes "bird walk," as Hunter terms tangential digressions, and if students are focused on the objective they will recognize such diversions. With learning disabled students it may be necessary to state the focus several times during a lesson.

Explanation—Check Understanding

The lesson begins in earnest with this step. The teacher explains the lesson, giving numerous examples and using as many concrete materials as appropriate. All during the explanation of the task the teacher checks for understanding on the part of the students, calling on them for feedback.

Monitoring and Adjusting

As the teacher calls upon students for responses to check their level of understanding, he or she will monitor their progress and make adjustments in the lesson as needed. Sometimes the task will be too easy and the teacher must be prepared to extend the objective. In other cases students may simply not be ready for the task and the teacher will drop down to a lower level of instruction. It is vital that the teacher-student relationship be a dynamic one, with the teacher constantly aware of each student's output and ready to adjust at all times.

Guided Practice—Check Mastery

During this step of the lesson cycle, according to Hunter (1984), the teacher will lead the students through the behavior specified in the objective. He or she may guide the group through each step in initial practice, monitor various responses of the group as a whole, infer understanding through the responses of single students, or monitor brief written responses. Unless the teacher has a very small group of students working on the same objective, Hunter's suggestions for guided practice may not work well with learning disabled students. It is not a good idea to rely on group responses to indicate that every student understands the lesson or to rely on a single student's response as indicative of all students' level of understanding.

Independent Practice—Assess Mastery

After Guided Practice the reader will note that there is a yes-no choice point on the flow chart. If the teacher is satisfied that the student understands the lesson, independent practice is initiated. The student will be allowed to perform the task without the teacher's intervention, and mastery will be assessed upon completion. Some accelerated students may go to independent practice straight from the explanation of the lesson without participating in guided practice. However, if the teacher feels that the guided practice for some students was unsatisfactory, he or she may reteach the lesson.

Correction (Reteach)

Sometimes the lesson is at the appropriate level, but more instruction using different materials and examples is necessary before some students are able to proceed to independent practice. In this case the teacher may go back to the beginning of the lesson with these students (while others work independently) and reteach the lesson, paying special attention to the students' understanding at each step.

Closure

At the end of each lesson, the teacher should quickly summarize the main points of the lesson, restating the focus of the objective and telling the students what they have learned.

Extension

Basic or essential skills are taught using the steps outlined above, and many learning disabled students never move beyond these skills in their special classes. As they progress through their remedial programs and return to the regular classroom, they can be taught to extend their thinking beyond the knowledge, comprehension, or application level. Hunter advocates using Bloom's (1956) taxonomy of cognitive skills to elicit higher levels of thinking.

COMPETENCIES FOR TEACHERS

In 1977 the Council for Learning Disabilities (CLD) began a project to identify the competencies that professionals who work in the field should have. In commenting on the competencies the then-CLD president Stephen C. Larsen (1978) expressed the hope that their availability would enhance the quality of services provided to learning disabled persons.

The task was assigned to a committee chaired by Phyllis Newcomer and including Judith Wilson, Patricia Magee, and Linda Brown. It was they who formulated the formats and procedures necessary to survey the CLD membership for information concerning the generation of competency statements. In 1978, after 2 years of compilation and study, the report, *Competencies for Teachers of Learning Disabled Children and Youth*, was completed and distributed to the CLD members.

Since the problems and needs of learning disabled people are many and complex, one is not surprised to learn that the competencies necessary to teach them are equally many and complex. The CLD document is too long to be duplicated here; but a summary of the competencies in oral language, reading, written expression, spelling, mathematics, cognition, behavioral management, counseling and consulting, career/vocational education, educational operations, and historical-theoretical perspectives is provided in Figure 7.2. This outline is taken from an article by Newcomer (1978) in which the activities of her committee are described in detail.

Oral Language

I. General Knowledge

The teacher:
understands the association learning, linguistically oriented, and cognitive theories of language.

II. Assessment

can administer and interpret standardized language tests in the areas of phonology, semantics, morphology, and syntax.

III. Instruction

can select and use appropriate commercial developmental materials and programs.

Reading

I. General Knowledge
  A. Developmental Reading
  B. Specialized Reading
    1. Corrective Reading

    2. Remedial Reading

The teacher:
understands basic theories related to the field of reading.

understands that corrective reading instruction is a system for planning and delivering classroom instruction to students who experience minor deficiencies in the elements of developmental reading.
understands that remedial reading instruction is a system for delivering intensive individualized instruction to students who have major reading problems in word recognition, comprehension, and fluency.

II. Assessment
  A. Screening

  B. Evaluation

  C. Diagnosis

  D. Formative/Summative

has knowledge of the appropriate instruments and techniques for general screening for reading.
has knowledge for the appropriate instruments and techniques for specific assessment of the students' level of reading achievement and the areas that warrant specific attention.
can select and administer formal and informal diagnostic instruments for specific skills related to reading.
can develop and use tests to monitor students' ongoing and final level of mastery.

III. Instruction
  A. Corrective Reading

  B. Remedial Reading

can plan and implement instruction for minor problems associated with gaps or deficiencies in the developmental reading process.
can plan and implement intensive individualized instruction in the skill areas associated with remedial reading.

Written Expression

I. General Knowledge

The teacher:
recognizes written expression as a method of conveying ideas or meanings.

II. Assessment

can administer and interpret standardized achievement tests of written expression.

III. Instruction

can plan and implement an instructional program incorporating the basic components for writing:
  purpose of composition
  comparison and contrasting of skills
  organization of ideas
  types of prose (e.g., narrative, descriptive, expository, argumentation, poetry)

FIGURE 7.2. A summary of the CLD competency statements. *Note.* From "Competencies for Professionals in Learning Disabilities" by P. L. Newcomer, 1978, *Learning Disability Quarterly, 1,* pp. 73–76. Reprinted by permission.

FIGURE 7.2. *(Continued)*

Spelling

I. General Knowledge	*The teacher:*
	understands the nature and rules of English orthography.
II. Assessment	can administer and interpret the spelling sections of standardized achievement tests.
III. Instruction	can teach spelling skills using a planned sequence of activities.

Mathematics

I. General Knowledge	*The teacher:*
A. Number Theory	understands all the concepts involved in numeration and counting.
B. Addition and Subtraction	understands the computation process involved in adding and subtracting whole numbers.
C. Multiplication and Division	understands the computational process involved in solving multiplication and division problems.
D. Fractions, Decimals, and Percentage	understands all the operations involved in adding, subtracting, multiplying, and dividing fractions, decimal numbers, and numbers expressed as percentages.
E. Geometry	understands simple common plane geometric figures (e.g., circle, square).
F. Measurement	understands all concepts involved in measurement of time, linear planes, weight, liquids, and temperature.
G. Money	understands the U.S. monetary system.
H. Verbal Problem Solving	understands the variables that contribute to difficulty in verbal problem solving (e.g., reading level, level of syntactic complexity, distractors, etc.).
II. Assessment	can administer and interpet the mathematics portion of standardized group achievement tests.
III. Instruction	can teach a specific mathematical skill by developing and following a planned sequence of activities.

Cognition

I. General Knowledge	*The teacher:*
A. Nature of Thought	understands various theories regarding thought and process of thinking.
B. Piagetian Theories	understands the implications of a stage theory such as Piaget's and can compare it with age theories.
C. Association Theory	understands the implications of association theory and can analyze learning situations into stimulus and response components.
D. Information Processing Theories	understands the implications of information processing theory as a model of human intelligence.
E. Gestalt Theories	understands theories that view learning wholistically and can analyze: discovery learning perceptual arousal creative or original responses

FIGURE 7.2. *(Continued)*

F. Theories of Intelligence	understands Q-factor theory, "g," and special abilities.
II. Assessment	
A. Formal	can administer and interpret standardized tests of intelligence.
B. Informal	can devise tasks that reveal children's skills at problem solving, inferential thinking, and concept development.
III. Instruction	can incorporate information regarding cognitive development into general instructional programming.

Behavioral Management

I. General Knowledge	*The teacher:*
	understands general theoretical positions related to:
	theories of learning
	theories of personality and psychopathology
	child development (normal and atypical)
II. Assessment	can define target behaviors.
III. Instruction	can use remedial instructional procedures to modify behavior.

Counseling and Consulting

I. Consulting with Teachers and Administrators	*The teacher:*
	must have knowledge about working with exceptional children in school settings involving handicapped and nonhandicapped students.
II. Counseling and Consulting with Parents	can establish and maintain rapport with parents.
III. Counseling and Consulting with Children	must establish and maintain rapport with children.

Career/Vocational Education

I. General Knowledge	*The teacher:*
A. Knowledge of Individual Characteristics	is aware that each individual has unique patterns of abilities and limitations that affect career/vocational decisions.
B. Knowledge of Career and Occupational Opportunities	has comprehensive knowledge of a wide variety of occupational families.
II. Assessment	can administer and interpret standardized vocational/career interest and aptitude tests.
III. Instruction	will provide information pertaining to a wide variety of career opportunities.

Educational Operations

I. Assessment	*The teacher:*
	is able to establish rapport during assessment.
II. Materials	can determine student needs to be met by curricula.
III. A/V	can identify and select media appropriate for stated instructional objectives.

FIGURE 7.2. *(Continued)*

| IV. Environment | can identify variables that influence learning in the school and classroom environment. |
| V. Instruction | can plan and implement a sequential remedial program for a student. |

Historical-Theoretical Perspectives

I. History of Learning Disabilities	*The teacher:* can identify early contributors to the field of learning disabilities.
II. Program Models	can explain various program models used to deliver services to learning disabled children.
III. Professional Organizations	is aware of various professional organizations in learning disabilities.

The validity of the CLD teacher competencies has been supported in at least one investigation. Freeman and Becker (1979) studied the opinions about the competencies of a large sample of Illinois school teachers and administrators. They found that their sample rated all 11 competency areas positively (ranging from an average importance rating for the Historical-Theoretical Perspective cluster to a high importance rating for the Consulting and Counseling and Reading clusters).

These competencies have the potential of being very influential in the field of learning disabilities. They may guide the selection of curricular content included in teacher education programs at all levels. They may in time influence the requirements for teacher certification in the various states. They may serve as criteria for hiring teachers. And finally, with modification, they may even provide the basis for national issuing of credentials by a professional organization.

In another study of this topic, Hudson, Morsink, Branscum, and Boone (1987) analyzed the competencies listed by researchers, individual authors, and associations. Unlike the CLD competencies that emphasized skills necessary to teach content areas (e.g., oral language, reading, writing, mathematics), their competencies focused on school management skills (e.g., planning lessons, selecting materials, conducting evaluations, choosing strategies, etc.). Individuals interested in a comprehensive set of teacher competencies should read both the Newcomer (1978) and the Hudson et al. sources.

PART III

REMEDIATING SPECIFIC LEARNING DISABILITIES

The eight chapters that make up Part III of this book are devoted to descriptions of methods that were developed primarily for use with populations with learning disabilities. The instructional methods described in the latter part of Chapter 7 were developed for general classroom use and are not necessarily intended for handicapped learners. Of course, the methods can be, and frequently are, adapted for remedial or developmental use with a variety of pupils having learning problems, most particularly those with mild-to-moderate learning disabilities. Unlike those programs, the teaching or treatment systems presented in the remaining chapters of this book were designed especially for or have been adopted for use with moderately to severely learning disabled populations.

The casual observer who visits a class for learning disabled pupils in an average school may not see the teacher implementing any of these remedial systems, because in all likelihood the children or youths in those classes do not represent the population of moderately to severely learning disabled individuals. Rather, the classes are composed for the most part of mildly learning disabled and nonhandicapped problem learners for whom the methods described in the preceding chapter should work quite well. In fact, these are often students who could remain in the regular classroom with no specialized instruction if the regular curriculum were adapted to their needs and if the regular teacher implemented the principles of individualized instruction.

The time has come to return to identifying more rigorously those students who should be called learning disabled and to implementing the highly structured, systematized type of remediation described in the remainder of this book. For the most part these systems are best employed on an individual or small group basis with those students who evidence moderate-to-severe difficulty in mastering their particular learning disabilities. Implementation of the systems requires close observation of the student's performance, a consistency in the "test-teach-test" approach, and an attitude toward the student that has sometimes been characterized as "clinical." These precepts presently are not being followed in most schools, perhaps because the students who are being placed in the learning disabilities programs do not really require the types of structure, systems, analysis, and observation that are inherent in the specialized methods.

8

COMPREHENSIVE SYSTEMS FOR REMEDIATING LEARNING DISABILITIES

The authors of the three teaching systems described in this chapter—Johnson and Myklebust, Barry, and McGinnis—attempt to develop a wide variety of basic language abilities, including listening, speaking, reading, writing, and math. Because the approaches are so encompassing, we refer to them as comprehensive training programs.

The approaches described in this chapter were developed originally for use with youngsters diagnosed as aphasic, a condition characterized by language deficit emanating from underlying brain pathology. These three systems are similar, although Barry's techniques seem more appropriate for use with younger children, while McGinnis's approach is better suited for use with older children and adolescents. Johnson and Myklebust contribute a comprehensive theory of language development as well as a collection of training techniques that are suitable for use with most preschool- and school-aged youngsters. The reader should recognize that these systems employ numerous activities for training visual and auditory correlates, but the primary purpose of these activities is to facilitate the development of spoken and written language and math rather than perceptual-motor ability. The following case history describes a child for whom these programs might be suitable.

K. C., a 4-year-old boy, was referred for evaluation because his speech was unintelligible and occasionally he was thought to have trouble understanding the speech of others. In addition, the father reported that when K. C. related an experience, only the main words were used and even these were frequently presented in an improper sequence.

The Revised Stanford-Binet *and the* Columbia Mental Maturity Scale *were administered, and the results indicated that K. C. was of at least average intelligence. The examiner noted that the child seemed to have considerable difficulty comprehending some of the directions and was unable to express himself adequately when he did understand. The hypothesis of an auditory receptive language problem was set forth at that time, and additional testing was undertaken.*

Even though the audiological evaluation revealed a mild bilateral conductive hearing loss, its presence was not so severe as to account for the child's apparent language difficulty. The findings of the speech and language evaluation were indicative of both auditory receptive and expressive language disorder, characterized by (a) poor articulation and syntax, (b) low scores on the subtests of the Test of Language Development *(TOLD), and (c) a significantly low score on the* Peabody Picture Vocabulary Test. *Conversely, comparable strength was noted on all tests that involved the visual and/or motor abilities, for example, the* Bender. *During the evaluation much evidence of hyperactivity and distractibility was noted by all persons involved.*

K. C. was placed in a preschool class, and because of his age the techniques suggested by Barry were prescribed. This approach was supplemented by standard articulation therapy. Near the end of the year, K. C. underwent surgery and suffered unexpected complications. When he returned to school, significant regression had occurred, and the Barry program continued for longer than would be expected otherwise. After 2 years in the preschool he was promoted to an ungraded primary class where the program was organized according to the McGinnis principles. At dismissal, K. C. was still somewhat hyperactive and distractible but easily controlled. His articulation problem was corrected, and his language showed marked improvement with both verbal expression and comprehension adequate for his age. He was recommended for regular first-grade placement. Although no problems are anticipated, should K. C. have academic difficulty, techniques suggested by Johnson and Myklebust for problems in specific areas would be recommended on a supportive tutoring basis.

MYKLEBUST AND JOHNSON: A PSYCHONEUROLOGICAL APPROACH

Helmer R. Myklebust is best known for his work in diagnosis and remediation of language problems of children who evidence deafness (1947, 1954, 1964a) and/or aphasia (1952, 1955, 1957a). Drawing upon his knowledge of speech and language pathology, he expanded his earlier concepts into a comprehensive theory of learning disorders (Myklebust, 1964b, 1968; Myklebust & Boshes, 1960). Since Myklebust's early work in auditory disorders considerably influenced the development of his theory of language and of "psychoneurological learning disorder," frequent reference is made to it in this section. For more than 40 years his research and training activities have been directed toward the development of a frame of reference, the formulation of a series of educational principles, and the perfection of effective remedial techniques for use with learning disabled children. Doris J. Johnson was Dr. Myklebust's student at Northwestern University. Upon graduation she remained at university and is presently professor and head of the Program in Learning Disabilities within the Department of Communication Sciences and Disorders.

Basic Psychoneurological and Developmental Concepts

Semiautonomous Systems. Myklebust accepts as a starting point the concept of semiautonomous systems within the brain that underlie and control the processes of learning. Such a concept hypothesizes semi-independent systems within the brain that may function almost independently of each other, complement one another, or function in a completely interrelated manner. For example, the auditory system may function independently of the visual or other systems as in the acquisition of spoken language. Learning that occurs through the utilization of basically only one system is referred to by Myklebust as intraneurosensory learning. In addition, he speaks of interneurosensory learning, which implies a dependent relationship between two systems and integrative learning, "which utilizes all these systems functioning simultaneously" (Johnson & Myklebust, 1967, p. 26).

As Myklebust notes, probably no learning is completely and purely intraneurosensory; however, a single system may be of such primary importance in the learning of certain elements that for all purposes it functions relatively independently. As in the example given earlier, mastery of spoken words is intraneurosensory learning using primarily the auditory system. Hence, it can be seen that brain dysfunction could impair one system and leave the others relatively intact.

Although there are few examples of strictly intraneurosensory learning, Myklebust says that interneurosensory learning, which occurs when two or more systems function together, is quite common. To account for interneurosensory learning, he introduces the construct of a transducer system within the brain, which acts as a mechanism for translating information from one system to the others. Myklebust cites dyslexia and apraxia as examples of disorders that arise from deficits in the transducing mechanism.

Integrative learning occurs when all semiautonomous systems function as a unit. In many respects the integrative function appears to invest the individual's experience with meaning and therefore seems analogous to the process Myklebust calls "inner language" and to the representational mediation hypothesis of Osgood. Integrative learning includes the acquisition of meaning and the ability to conceptualize.

Myklebust postulates as a corollary the concept of overloading, which implies that information received through one sensory modality may interfere with the integration of simultaneous information received through other modalities. Many children with learning disorders can process information from only one sensory avenue at a time and, according to Myklebust, cannot profit from a multisensory approach to remediation. This concept is obviously important in evaluation of the child in that the data obtained may preclude the use of multisensory techniques.

Psychoneurological Integrities for Learning. Adequate functioning of the peripheral and central nervous systems as well as psychological integrity is considered essential for normal language development (Johnson & Myklebust, 1967). A variety of difficulties may arise when performance in one or more of the necessary integrities is less than optimal. Such problems cannot always be classified as specific learning disabilities in the context used by Myklebust. There is no doubt, however, that suboptimal functioning of any area will result in decreased learning.

When the integrity of the peripheral nervous system is impaired, some sensory limitations will probably ensue. The resultant deafness or blindness can impede language development. For example, before one can acquire adequate speech in a normal manner one must hear and understand one's own speech as well as that of others; deafness disrupts this essential monitoring process. Myklebust does not consider sensory impairment an example of psychoneurological learning disability.

The central nervous system (CNS) must be intact, or psychoneurological learning disabilities are likely to occur. Such disorders may affect speech, reading, writing, arithmetic, and nonverbal performance. Myklebust suggests four specific categories of problems that arise primarily from CNS dysfunction and adversely influence learning.

1. Perceptual disturbance: Inability to identify, discriminate, and interpret sensation. Often seen clinically as poor recognition of everyday experience sensorially.

2. Disturbance of imagery: Inability to call to mind common experiences although they have been perceived. Seen as deficiencies in auditorization and visualization.

3. Disorders of symbolic processes: Inability to acquire facility to represent experience symbolically. Seen as aphasia, dyslexia, dysgraphia, and dyscalculia, and as language disorders.

4. Conceptualizing disturbances: Inability to generalize and categorize experience. Seen as a deficiency in grouping ideas that have a logical relationship—concreteness. (1964b, p. 359)

When one is considering the integrity of the CNS as related to learning disabilities, both intellectual and motor capacities must be examined. Measured intellectual ability on either verbal or nonverbal tests at some specified level is necessary for efficient learning. The child with limited intellectual capacity reveals an overwhelming lack of CNS integrity. Adequate motor capacity is also dependent on the intactness of the CNS. Poor motor performance ranges from crippling conditions such as cerebral palsy to clumsiness and poor coordination exhibited by many children with a learning disability.

A child needs to have integrity not only of the peripheral and central nervous system but of the psychodynamic processes as well. Myklebust (1957b) believes that three basic psychological processes must be intact: identification, internalization, and assimilation. The first is the recognition of and identification with the human voice. Babbling is the first lingual manifestation of identification. Some relationship between defective babbling and language disorders has been mentioned by Myklebust, who pointed out that hearing impaired and receptive aphasic children evidence deviant babbling patterns. Internalization is the second psychological process that must be intact. This process relates the child's experience to the symbols that represent and communicate that experience. Internalization follows identification, but the periods of development overlap and progress simultaneously. Some children who tend to repeat what they hear (echolalic behavior) may have achieved identification but cannot associate experiences, and the echolalia may result from their attempt to integrate their experience. If a child finds language threatening instead of pleasurable or if a child does not identify with the human voice, internalization may be impeded or precluded altogether, and language development may be disturbed. The third required psychological process is assimilation. As identification and internalization develop, experiences become related to one another, that is, assimilation occurs. Through assimilation, abstraction ability becomes possible.

These three processes evolve in a maturational order: identification precedes internalization; internalization precedes assimilation. Necessarily, babbling precedes the understanding of verbal symbols; and a basic verbal competence is essential before echolalia can evidence its negative role. Thus certain psychodynamic factors are seen to exert an influence on language development. Disturbances of these processes can interfere with normal language development and may cause autism or schizophrenia.

Normal Language Development

Definition of Language. Language is defined by Myklebust (1955) as symbolic behavior; it includes the ability to abstract, to attach meaning to words, and to use these words as symbols for thought and for the expression of ideas, objects, and feelings. Myklebust (1964a) hypothesizes five levels of abstraction: sensation, perception, imagery, symbolization, and conceptualization. The individual levels are viewed as overlapping, developmental stages directly related to experience, rather than as mutually exclusive categories. Speech and language, while closely associated, are not considered synonymous. Language is the more inclusive term and is the vehicle for humans' symbolic behavior, a faculty that differentiates them from other forms of life (Myklebust, 1954).

Developmental Hierarchy of Language. In 1964, Myklebust published a graphic description of his theory for the acquisition of language in which five developmentally related levels of verbal behavior are presented (Figure 8.1). The first level is acquisition of meaning or inner language. Next, auditory symbols and experience are

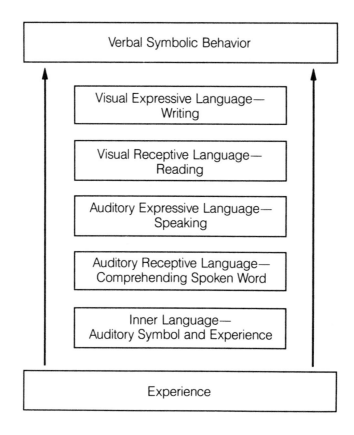

FIGURE 8.1. The developmental hierarchy of man's language system. *Note.* From *The Psychology of Deafness* (p. 232) by H. R. Myklebust, 1964, New York: Grune & Stratton. Reprinted by permission.

associated, resulting in the child's comprehension of spoken words, a process that contributes to the development of auditory receptive language. Auditory expressive language is evidenced in speech. Comprehension of printed words or reading (visual receptive language) is followed by expression of printed words in writing (visual expressive language).

The language processes consist of several receptive-expressive modes, of which the more important are auditory-verbal and visual language. The relationship between the auditory-verbal and the visual language modes is viewed as hierarchical in nature and emerges in a sequential pattern. For example, reading skills are mastered by superimposing visual symbols on the already established auditory language base, and the written form assumes knowledge of the read form (Myklebust, 1964a).

Inner Language.   Inner language is the first aspect of language to develop, emerging at approximately 6 months of age. The behavior initially is characterized by formation of simple concepts that may be evidenced in the child's play activities, such as demonstrating knowledge of simple relationships between objects. At a later stage of development, the child can understand more complex relationships and plays with toys in a meaningful fashion, for example, appropriately arranging furniture in a doll house. In its most complex form, inner language permits the transformation of experience into verbal or nonverbal symbols.

Receptive Language.   Only after inner language has developed to an unspecified degree can the receptive aspect of language emerge. At about 8 months of age children begin to indicate partial understanding of what is said to them. Children respond properly to their names, several substantives, and simple commands. By the end of approximately 4 years of age, children have mastered the acquisition of auditory language, and thereafter the receptive processes provide an elaboration of the verbal system. It should be noted that once inner and receptive language have emerged, there is a reciprocal relationship between the two; development of inner language beyond the simple concept formation phase becomes dependent upon comprehension, and receptive language, to be meaningful, must rely on integrative, inner processes.

Expressive Language.   The last aspect of language to appear is expression, which, according to Myklebust, develops after the acquisition of meaningful units of experience and establishment of comprehension. The child's expressive language, which emerges at around 1 year of age, reflects to a great extent the status and adequacy of the child's receptive abilities.

Psychoneurological Learning Disabilities

Definition and Etiology.   Dissatisfaction with the terms in general use, notably "brain damage" and "learning disorder," prompted Myklebust to select a different label, "psychoneurological learning disability," which he suggests encompasses adequately the behavioral and the physiological parameters involved in the problems exhibited by these children. According to Myklebust and Boshes (1960), children with psychoneurological learning disability often evidence minor awkwardness, certain behavior disturbances, and difficulties in reading, writing, arithmetic, and speaking, all of which are inferred to be the result of brain dysfunction. Irrespective of age of onset or cause, the term refers to all aberrations of behavior in learning that have a neurological base; the disorder is viewed as a behavioral deviation rather than an incapacity to learn. Myklebust's strongly stated position that learning disabilities are invariably caused by neurological dysfunction is consistent with the definitions of learning disability discussed in the first chapter of this book.

Whereas some writers and researchers in the field do not attempt to establish a relationship between learning disabilities and brain dysfunction, Myklebust makes this association one of the hallmarks of his concept of psychoneurological learning disabilities. Even though objective findings of a disturbance in brain function may be lacking and the disabled learner may appear neurologically intact, evidence of the brain dysfunction can be presumed on the basis of behavioral signs (Johnson & Myklebust, 1967; Myklebust, 1968). But he feels that most dysfunctions can be demonstrated neurologically, and when diagnostic techniques become more precise and sophisticated, most learning disabilities will reveal, at the very best, minimal neurological signs. Within this framework, psychoneurological learning disability indicates that the disorder is in the behavior and is attributable to neurological causation. Of interest here is the circular reasoning inherent in this aspect of the concept, inasmuch as one of the fundamental criteria for diagnosis and classification frequently must be made on an inferential basis.

Types of Psychoneurological Learning Disabilities. Failure to master skills in any of the semiautonomous learning systems or at any level within the developmental hierarchy will result in a corresponding disability, which in turn reduces the probability of success at higher levels. For example, no child talks until he or she understands speech, nor does a child learn to read normally unless he or she first has acquired oral language. Further, since written language is the expressive side of read language, the child who cannot read is unable to write. Myklebust (Johnson & Myklebust, 1967) speaks of five general groups of learning disorders: disorders of auditory language, disorders of reading, disorders of written language, disorders of arithmetic, and nonverbal disorders of learning.

DISORDERS OF AUDITORY LANGUAGE. Auditory symbolic language disorder usually is detected when the child is 2 to 4 years of age. This disability is more handicapping than a speech problem because normal symbolic language development is prevented. Originally, three types were recognized by Myklebust (1955): receptive, expressive, and mixed. More recently, Johnson and Myklebust (1967) speak of generalized deficits in auditory learning, disorders of auditory receptive language, and disorders of auditory expressive language.

The child with a generalized problem "hears" but interprets neither speech nor environmental sounds. Since visual and tactile modalities are relatively intact, the child may be identified, mistakenly, as deaf. The receptive form affects the ability to comprehend auditory symbols and has serious detrimental influences on language development. Such children are distinguished from deaf children by their apparent mastery of nonverbal-social or environmental sounds. Frequently, the condition is referred to as receptive aphasia, sensory aphasia, auditory verbal agnosia, or word deafness.

In the expressive form, symbolic communication is disrupted, even though the meaning of the symbols is understood. Three common types of expressive disabilities are emphasized. In the first, the problem relates to "reauditorization" and word selection (anomia). An affected child may comprehend words but may be unable to recall them for spontaneous expression. The speech of a young child who experiences difficulty in word recall is characterized by a disproportionate number of circum-locutions, delayed responses, gestures, nonverbal sounds, and word associations (the substitution of a word from within the same category as the word being sought, e.g., *knife* for *fork*). The older child may resort to written expression as a means of communication and generally prefers silent reading to oral reading. In the second type of auditory expressive deficit, the difficulty centers on inability to effect the motor habits necessary for speech rather than on problems of word retrieval or memory (dyspraxia). The third type is characterized by the presence of defective syntax. An affected child can communicate adequately when single words or short phrases are required but does not exhibit the organization necessary to master complete sentences, as evidenced by unexpected errors in word order, verb tenses, and other syntactical infractions.

DISORDERS OF READING.   When a child enters school and begins learning to read, dyslexia may be recognized as a problem. Dyslexia is an inability to read normally as a result of damage to the brain. Such an impairment may be considered highly disruptive to the language process and debilitating to the total language development of the child. Dyslexia is commonly found in combination with other inadequacies, notably impairments in memory, memory for sequence, left-right orientation, time orientation, body image, spelling and writing, dyscalculia, motor disturbances, and perceptual disorders. However, dyslexia does not result from mental retardation, sensory impairment, emotional problems, or inadequate teaching. All facets of child-hood dyslexia are not necessarily present in a given child; generally, however, these symptoms characterize children having this type of language disability. Other terms used to describe this condition include word blindness, developmental dyslexia, and strephosymbolia.

Two common forms of dyslexia—visual and auditory—are identified by Myklebust. Some, but not all, types of visual disturbance result in visual dyslexia. An affected child has difficulty visually mastering whole words as well as the letters and syllables of individual words and would be expected to learn reading most easily using a phonic approach. Characteristics of reading problems associated with visual dyslexia follow:

1. Confusion of similar words and letters

2. Slow word recognition

3. Frequent letter reversals (*b* for *d*).

4. Letter inversion tendencies (*u* for *n*)

5. Difficulty following and retaining visual sequences

6. Concomitant visual memory disorders

7. Inferior drawings

8. Problems with visual analysis (puzzles)

9. Better at auditory tasks than visual tasks

10. Tendency to avoid games that require visual integration skills

In auditory dyslexia the child is likely to have visual strength, and the whole-word approach to reading will be comparatively easy. This child's difficulties center on phonetic word attack skills, reauditorizing phonemes and words, and sound blending.

DISORDERS OF WRITTEN LANGUAGE. Written language is considered by Myklebust (1965) to be the culminating verbal achievement of humankind, necessarily requiring the establishment of all of the preceding levels of abilities. The normal development of written language presumes the integrity of the sensory and motor processes. Oral and written expression are dependent on the adequacy of the receptive functions. Disorders of the written form include dysgraphia, deficits in revisualization, and disorders of formulation and syntax.

In dysgraphia the child can read and speak but cannot initiate the motor patterns when necessary for expression through writing. He or she cannot even copy letters, words, or numbers. The difficulty is essentially one of visual-motor integration rather than ideation, although it may accompany an ideation problem. Dysgraphia is viewed by Myklebust as a type of apraxia involving the visual-motor system.

In deficits of revisualization, the problem is basically one of visual memory. The child speaks, reads, and copies but cannot revisualize words or letters. As a result the child does not write spontaneously or from dictation. In disorders of formulation and syntax the problem involves ideation; the child can read, spell, copy, and express himself or herself well vocally but is unable to put his or her ideas onto paper. Though difficulties in syntax can exist in isolation, they frequently accompany disorders in ideation and are characterized by word omissions, distorted word order, and improper verb and pronoun usage, word endings, and punctuation.

DISORDERS OF ARITHMETIC. Johnson and Myklebust (1967) state that humans developed the spoken and written symbol systems to express thoughts and feelings; but for the expression of certain ideas, namely, quantity, size, and order, the number system was developed and perfected. As is true of language in general, this system has an inner, receptive, and expressive form. Whereas poor mathematics ability may result from inferior instruction or subaverage mental ability, dyscalculia is associated with a certain type of neurological dysfunction that interferes with quantitative thinking. Two types of arithmetical inadequacy are suggested—those related to other language disorders and those related to disturbances in quantitative thinking.

Children with an auditory receptive language disorder will probably do poorly in arithmetic in school, not because they fail to comprehend the principles involved in calculation but because they have difficulty understanding (a) the teacher's oral discussion of those principles, (b) story problems when they are read aloud, or (c) spoken instructions. The presence of reading disorder places these children at a disadvantage in reading story problems, while dysgraphia may interfere with their ability to write the answers.

Disturbances in quantitative thinking (dyscalculia) involve comprehension of the mathematical principles themselves. The child can read and write but cannot calculate. This condition often is characterized by (a) deficient visual-spatial organization and nonverbal integration, (b) extraordinary auditory abilities, (c) excellence in reading vocabulary and syllabication skills, (d) disturbance in body image, (e) poor visual-motor integration (apraxia), (f) no clear distinction between right and left, (g) low social maturity, and (h) considerably higher scores on standardized tests on verbal tasks than on nonverbal tasks.

NONVERBAL DISORDERS OF LEARNING.   Johnson and Myklebust (1967) recognize that not all psychoneurological learning disabilities are verbal. Some youngsters fail to understand many aspects of their environment such as time, space, size, direction, or self-perception. Such a child is categorized as follows:

> [The child has] a deficiency in social perception, meaning that he has an inability which precludes acquiring the significance of basic nonverbal aspects of daily living, though his verbal level of intelligence falls within or above the average. There are many such children but they are largely unrecognized since test procedures for identifying them, as well as procedures for educational remediation, have been slow in developing. (1967, p. 272)

A variety of diverse skills are represented under nonverbal disorders of learning. Specific types, discussed in detail by Johnson and Myklebust (1967), include problems in gesturing, motor learning, body image, spatial orientation, right-left orientation, social imperception, distractibility, perseveration, and disinhibition.

In addition to being in itself a legitimate form of communication, a gesture often supplements vocal expression. Subsequently, inadequate use of gestures can affect the total communication process of a child. As with other communication skills, inadequacy may result from impairment of either the comprehension or the use of gestures, and occasionally both aspects are involved.

Some children exhibit considerable difficulty in the acquisition of nonverbal motor patterns, such as learning to cut with scissors, jump rope, and comb hair. Such disorders must result from deficits in learning rather than from actual paralysis. Other children may evidence distortions in body image (self-perception or body consciousness). In these cases, the children usually do not know the names of the parts of their bodies or the relationships among the parts. Children with poor body image are likely to suffer also from difficulties involving spatial orientation. Since they cannot position themselves in the spatial world, the children often bump into things, get lost, and make errors in judging distance. Right-left disorientation is another frequently noted nonverbal learning disability that often occurs side by side with poor imagery and spatial orientation. Affected children are not aware of the right-left concept and therefore experience problems in following directions, for example, directions that involve paper-and-pencil routines. In addition, learning disabled children often have trouble in social situations. Such difficulty is not necessarily the result of autism or severe emotional disturbance, because the child wants to fit in but lacks sufficient social understanding and skill to achieve this goal. Attempts to cope frequently are misjudged and rewarded with punishment.

When present, distractibility, perseveration, and disinhibition complicate the entire remedial undertaking. The distractible child does not or cannot attend sufficiently to environmental events, and instead attention is directed fleetingly to all events without respect for their relevancy. In the case of a perseverative child, attention persists beyond the time required, making it difficult for the child to shift his or her attention, although a shift may be desirable. The child exhibiting disinhibition is unable to hold on to or to control ideation processes. An idea can be held or attended to for but a short time before the mind shifts randomly to another internal event.

Remediation of Psychoneurological Learning Disabilities.

Because the brain is composed of systems that sometimes function semi-independently, supplementarily, and in conjunction with other systems, a strong case is made by Myklebust (1964b) for the acquisition of an accurate, differential diagnosis for children with psychoneurological learning disorders. In fact, the planning of an educational program for a child with a learning disability begins with the comprehensive diagnostic study, and such a study is viewed as an essential factor in remediation. Therefore, appraisal of the brain's capacity to receive, categorize, and integrate information as well as of the intactness of the auditory, visual, motor, and tactile modes is undertaken. In many cases the total evaluation will include clinical teaching in order to acquire the additional information that makes possible the alteration of training programs and the verification of test data.

The fundamental principles that guide the remediation of psychoneurological learning disorders are presented by Johnson and Myklebust (1967) in their book *Learning Disabilities: Educational Principles and Practices*. Briefly stated, these considerations are as follows:

1. Teaching must be individualized.
2. Teaching according to readiness in a balanced program is essential.
3. Teaching must be as close to the level of involvement as possible.
4. Input precedes output as a basis for classification or grouping.
5. Teaching should be to the tolerance level, avoiding overloading in particular.
6. Multisensory stimulation should be used.
7. Deficits should be raised without undue stimulation or demand on the disability itself.
8. Teaching to the integrities is necessary but has limitations.
9. Training in perception should be provided when needed.

10. Important variables such as attention, rate, proximity, and size are to be controlled as needed.

11. Both the verbal and nonverbal areas of experience are to be developed.

12. The approach should be guided by both behavioral criteria and psychoneurological considerations.

Through application of these principles to clinical teaching, a set of specific methods and techniques was developed. These techniques are recommended for use with children who have disorders in auditory language, reading, written language, arithmetic, and nonverbal learning.

REMEDIATION OF AUDITORY LANGUAGE DISORDERS. Appropriate training activities are suggested for generalized, receptive, and expressive auditory language disorders. The goal of training children with generalized auditory language deficits is to teach them to understand the meaning of environmental sounds and of speech; the need for simultaneous matching of sounds and experience is emphasized. Learning is facilitated by the availability of an optimal instructional setting that is free of distracting noise and that is provided with visual materials. After the child is aware of sound, as opposed to no sound, noise-producing toys such as bells, drums, and horns are presented for exploration. Localization of sound is taught through activities that require the child to respond to noises made to the right or left and that require the child to follow the sound of a whistle blown by the teacher while walking around the room. During these activities the child is blindfolded. Sound discrimination is facilitated through the matching of noisemaking toys with the sound each makes. One exercise used to develop auditory memory requires that the child imitate a pattern of hand claps—first one, then two, then three, and so on.

Auditory receptive language disorders affect the child's ability to understand speech but do not involve the comprehension of nonverbal sounds. Since these children can hear, the primary goal of training is the development of understanding of what is heard. The teacher should remember to begin training early, to provide sufficient input before expecting acceptable output, to structure material into meaningful units, to present the spoken word and the associated experience simultaneously, to use much repetition, to select a vocabulary that is meaningful to the child, and to present the parts of speech beginning with sounds, then nouns, verbs, adjectives, and prepositions.

Children with auditory expressive language disorders usually understand speech adequately but experience difficulty when using spoken words. There are three common forms, involving reauditorization, auditory-motor integration, and syntax. Problems in reauditorization are characterized by inability to recall words or word-finding difficulty, and the aim of training is to facilitate the spontaneous recall of words. To achieve this goal, sentence completion exercises are used in conjunction with picture cues. In addition, such word associations as "bread and butter" and "needles and pins" are taught. Children with auditory-motor integration problems are unable to say words (apractic), and the goal of education is to develop voluntary repetition and meaningful oral communication. The child is made aware of the sounds he or she already can produce before new ones are introduced. The use of mirrors to see oneself talk or watching others talk helps develop a motor plan for speech. Our children experience difficulty in formulating sentences. They hear and understand but speak in single words or brief phrases and manifest problems in syntax and organization. The objective of educational intervention is to "develop a correct, natural, spontaneous flow of language" (Johnson & Myklebust, 1967, p. 136). One suggested approach is to teach the structure of the language using techniques similar to the audiolingual methods of teaching foreign language. In addition, meaningful sentences are spoken, and the child internalizes the various sentence patterns. Suggested exercises include scrambled sentences, where the child puts the words into a proper sequence, and incomplete sentences, where the child supplies a suitable word to complete a sentence.

REMEDIATION OF READING DISORDERS.   In teaching reading, the printed word generally is associated with a spoken word, which in turn is based upon a concept. For example, the child already has a highly developed impression of cat before ever using the spoken word *cat*. Later, the child associates *cat* with its printed form—cat. Subsequently, the youngster who cannot integrate meaningful experiences or cannot learn through the visual or auditory channels is likely to develop a reading problem. The major objective of training, therefore, is to promote the integration of experience, the spoken word, and the printed word. Since the nature of the dyslexia varies from child to child, precise training procedures are based on the study of each case. Johnson and Myklebust (1967) discuss remedial activities for two common forms of dyslexia—visual and auditory dyslexia.

The visual dyslexic has difficulty in the association of printed words with their meaning, so a phonetic approach is recommended if the auditory modality is intact. Involved in this approach is the teaching of isolated sounds and their eventual blending into words. Initially, several consonants are selected that differ markedly in both sound and appearance (*m, t, s*). The letters are printed on cards that are flashed before the child. At the same time the teacher says the letter's *sound*, not the letter's *name*. Then the child is encouraged to say the sound. Next the pupil is requested to think of words beginning with the sound under discussion. After several consonants have been mastered, the activity is altered, and the child is asked to pick from the group of flash cards the one that goes with a particular sound voiced by the instructor. Sound blends are introduced next, as are long vowels, simple sentences, paragraphs, and stories. Myklebust points out that these activities are related highly to those offered by Gillingham and Stillman (see the discussion of the reading systems included in this book). While teaching this child to read through auditory strengths, the teacher is also responsible for improving visual deficits. A variety of visually oriented matching activities are recommended, including the matching of pictures and printed words, pictures and outline drawings, and objects and drawn outlines, among others. Eventually, the child learns that words have their own configuration, for example, where ⌐⌐⌐, home ⌐⌐⌐, kitten ⌐⌐⌐.

In teaching children with auditory dyslexia to read, a whole-word approach is emphasized during the early stage of instruction. The first words to be taught are drawn exclusively from the child's speaking vocabulary and differ in both their auditory and visual forms. Whole printed words are matched with objects and experience. For example, in teaching nouns a card is presented to the child with the word *shoe* on the left and a picture of a shoe on the right; this facilitates the development of the association. For verbs, the child jumps and is presented with the printed word *jump.* The activities progress in complexity, and adjectives, prepositions, short phrases, and sentences are introduced. The teacher also seeks to improve the child's auditory deficits.

REMEDIATION OF WRITTEN LANGUAGE DISORDERS. Johnson and Myklebust (1967) have postulated three major forms of written language disorders and have offered remedial suggestions for each. In dysgraphia, a problem of visual-motor integration, affected children must acquire adequate visual and kinesthetic patterns if writing is to be mastered. Initially, the child watches the instructor draw several vertical lines on the blackboard; however, no attempt is made at this time to have the child reproduce the figure. While the child is blindfolded, his or her index finger is guided repeatedly over the drawn figure until he or she can follow the pattern unassisted. The blindfold is removed, and the child is encouraged to coordinate the visual and the motor tasks by reproducing the figure. Additional drawings are presented, but the visual, kinesthetic, and combination progression is maintained. Reinforcement techniques are suggested and include the use of stencils (templates), dot-to-dot figures, and tracing with copy paper. Success with these activities indicates that the child is ready to learn manuscript letters and numbers. Each letter to be taught is analyzed thoroughly; thus the child recognizes, for example, that the letter *b* is composed of a line and a semicircle. To aid in the beginning stages of letter formulation, practice letters written in dotted lines are provided, and the child connects the dots. Arrows are superimposed on these figures to illustrate the direction to be followed in completing the letters. Attention must be directed toward spacing and erasure habits, for they can render the writing difficult to read.

In training children in visual memory (revisualization), special care is devoted to the selection of materials. Words are printed in larger type than usual and may be in color in order to strengthen the visual impression. The use of a pocket flashlight as a pointer as well as many verbal instructions tends to facilitate attention, which is so necessary in remediating memory deficits. Auditory and tactile reinforcements are recommended as aids in improving recall; for example, spelling words can be learned through tracing them several times. Numerous activities are suggested to help develop partial recall; one of them has the child complete partially drawn pictures from memory, and another one asks the child to make a circle into as many pictures as possible (e.g., a sun, a face).

The initial objective in training disorders of formulation and syntax is to make the youngsters aware of their errors in writing. This is accomplished to some extent by having them listen to the teacher read aloud sentences they have written. Since these children usually are intact auditorially, they can hear the errors. Later, they read their own work aloud and monitor the errors. The teacher can construct sentences and stories that contain a variety of mistakes, and the pupil is encouraged to locate as many as possible. To encourage abstraction in writing, the child is given specific and detailed instructions as to what is to be written; outlines and key words are used also. Johnson and Myklebust (1967) provide a number of exercises and ideas that are helpful in developing formulation and syntax.

REMEDIATION OF ARITHMETIC DISORDERS. The acquisition of skill in the use of quantitative relationships is the goal of teaching dyscalculic children. Often training must begin at a basic nonverbal level, and the principles of quantity, order, size, space, and distance must be taught. In general, the development of these concepts is facilitated by the use of concrete materials and considerable auditory verbalization.

The reasoning processes required for early quantitative thinking are based to a considerable extent on visual perception; thus, puzzles, pegboards, form boards, and jigsaw puzzles are helpful for those dyscalculic children who manifest associated problems in form perception. An adequate grasp of size and length is possibly related to such mathematical concepts as perimeters and areas. One exercise offered to develop this skill requires the child to grade four circles made of felt according to size, beginning with the largest and concluding with the smallest. One-to-one relationships are taught with various matching exercises that stress one-to-one correspondence; for example, a series of paper dolls is placed in a row, and the child is encouraged to draw one hat for each figure. One technique among others offered by which a child may be taught to count requires motor responses such as stringing beads or touching pegs as he or she counts aloud. Having acquired a concept of quantity and the skill to count aloud, the child must learn that numbers refer to visual symbols; the number quantity of three, therefore, can be represented by a spoken word, by 3, or by a written word without altering the basic concept. All suitable activities (number lines, number stepping blocks, etc.) use visual symbols.

The ideas of Piaget (1953) regarding the assessment of conservation of quantity are considered important, and familiar Piagetian tasks are recommended. In one activity reported, the child was requested to fill a cup of water and to pour the contents into a glass; next the child was asked to fill the cup again and to pour the water into a flat bowl; when asked to comment about the amounts in each container, the child maintained that the glass contained more water. To develop conservation, concrete materials that can be manipulated are suggested, notably Cuisenaire rods and toys frequently associated with Montessori schools. Another problem related to dyscalculia is the inability to recognize quickly the number of objects in a group. In one training activity a plate with small groups of dots is flashed using tachistoscopic procedures, and the child matches the flashed form with a like form on an answer sheet. In addition, children may need to be taught the language of arithmetic—the meaning of signs, the arrangement of numbers, the sequence of steps for calculation, and problem solving.

REMEDIATION OF NONVERBAL DISORDERS OF LEARNING.   The use of realistic pictures and photographs is fundamental to the assessment and remediation of nonverbal disorders of learning. In the selection of suitable pictures, consideration must be made of their size, color, and background. In general, pictures larger than 4 × 10 inches are avoided, realistically colored pictures are preferred, and the best backgrounds are devoid of confusing shadings and clutter. Exercises are prepared that entail the matching of real objects with their pictures, pictures of objects with their drawn outlines, and other combinations.

In teaching nonverbal motor learnings such as buttoning, typing, and cutting, each act is reduced to its basic movement patterns. For example, when children are taught to skip, they are instructed how to stand first on one foot and then on the other foot; they watch themselves in a mirror to obtain a visual image of the activity; they listen to the sounds made by others while skipping to obtain the auditory pattern; and, finally, they are encouraged to try the activity themselves. Rope jumping, cutting with scissors, and other skills are taught in a similar manner. Some children lack sufficient body image and need special training. One suggested exercise requires that the child lie down on a sheet of wrapping paper while the teacher draws the child's outline. The child then observes the completed drawing and discusses its parts with the teacher. Later, the facial features, fingernails, and other details are added. Work with mirrors and body puzzles are also helpful in the perfection of body image.

Since learning disabled children tend to be highly distractible, the room should be free of excessive visual stimulation and noise. Cupboards are covered; floors are muted with rugs or tile; and rubber tips are placed on the legs of furniture. To control perseveration, which often accompanies distractibility and which may be the by-product of fatigue, the period of instruction should be structured to provide for rest periods and frequent breaks in routine. Toys that stimulate perseveration are removed from the situation as soon as they are recognized as such. Disinhibition in children is managed by the establishment of daily routines, which aid them in mastering desired patterns of behavior. Techniques useful in the management of hyperactivity include teaching an affected child to walk down the hall with hands in pockets, which discourages the child from touching everything along the way, or to walk down the hall following a pattern marked on the floor, which keeps the child from popping in and out of adjacent classrooms. Youngsters who lose control of themselves and exhibit euphoric laughter, excessive gross motor activity, or other disruptive behavior are removed from the cause or scene of the overstimulation and placed in a small, quiet environment, possibly another room or a part of the classroom, until control is restored. Additional remedial suggestions, exercises, and techniques are offered by Johnson and Myklebust (1967) for training or developing gestures, right-left orientation, spatial orientation, and social perception.

Many of Myklebust's latter writings promote an understanding of his concept of psychoneurological learning disabilities. From this frame of reference he has evolved criteria for diagnosis and classification of learning disabilities in children, as well as appropriate remedial approaches. While he continues to stress the importance of the auditory language system, Myklebust emphasizes the reciprocal relationships of visual, auditory, and graphic channels in verbal and nonverbal learning.

BARRY: TEACHING THE YOUNG APHASIC CHILD

For some years, Hortense Barry taught children with communication disorders in an experimental classroom. Her book *The Young Aphasic Child: Evaluation and Training* is a compilation of pertinent, practical information, procedures, techniques, and materials found to be of value when used with such children. Much of the information included in the book is derived from Barry's own teaching experience, though she points out that many of her ideas are taken from other sources. An eclectic approach, therefore, is implied by Barry in dealing with aphasic children; she feels that "no one specific method, no one set of tools, no one simple approach is or can be the solution to so complex a problem" (1988, p. 3). Barry's book was originally published by the Volta Bureau in 1961. During the early 1980s, it ceased being printed. In 1988, PRO-ED reissued the book as part of its Classics Series.

Orientation

Barry describes aphasia as "the inability to use and/or understand spoken language as a result of defect or damage in the central nervous system" (1988, p. 6). Two main types of aphasia are cited: receptive aphasia (sensory or auditory), in which the child lacks understanding of spoken language, and expressive aphasia (motor or verbal), in which speech is understood but the child does not talk normally. The most common diagnosis is that of mixed aphasia, in which the child demonstrates characteristics of both receptive and expressive aphasia. In addition to these two types there are two less frequently seen conditions: central aphasia, in which the inner language functioning is disturbed, and global aphasia, in which there apparently is no inner, receptive, or expressive language function.

Barry's approach is based on principles set forth by Myklebust: the concept of inner, receptive, and expressive language and the need for presenting language in the same sequence in which normal children are presumed to acquire it. First, training in inner language is given to help the child relate better to the environment. Symbolic toys help familiarize the child meaningfully with his or her environment. Until the child learns to manipulate toys successfully, no attempt is made to teach receptive or expressive language.

Then receptive training, or the "feeding-in process," is begun, and finally, after the child has begun to structure his or her own auditory world, expressive language training is given. No expressive language is demanded during the training for receptive language, although Barry states that many children spontaneously begin to give back some of the language to which they have been continuously exposed.

Evaluation

Before aphasia can be diagnosed, other causes for the lack of normal verbal communication must be ruled out. Peripheral hearing loss, mental retardation, and severe emotional disturbance must be eliminated as primary problems before the diagnosis of aphasia is tenable. It is important to note that children admitted to Barry's class for aphasics had average intelligence, which was shown through clinical or teacher impressions rather than by formal psychological tests.

In the absence of a team of experts or in the presence of conflicting opinions, Barry suggests that six areas of the child's behavior should be explored by the teacher. The areas to be evaluated include (a) the case history, (b) hearing, (c) language, (d) psychomotor function, (e) emotional and social adjustment, and (f) motor abilities.

The first step in the teacher's evaluation of the child is the taking of a history. This should include pertinent information on pregnancy, delivery, family (siblings, handedness, speech or hearing disorders), motor development (when the child sat up, walked, etc.), illnesses, social development (toilet training, feeding, dressing, sleeping habits, eating habits, behavior), communication, and education. The history is primarily the parent's impression of the child.

The next step is a hearing evaluation with the interest concentrated on auditory perception and memory rather than acuity. The child is tested for awareness of sound, voice, and speech and then for discrimination of sound, voice, and speech patterns. Auditory perception and auditory memory also are tested.

Step three is a language evaluation in which inner, receptive, and expressive language are tested individually, and always in the stated order. Familiar toy objects such as small figures and furniture are used in these tests rather than pictures, since pictures themselves are symbols.

In step four psychomotor functioning, which includes figure-ground, visual-motor, body image, and spatial relationship functioning, is evaluated.

The fifth area investigated is that of the child's emotional and social adjustment; and the final step is an evaluation of motor abilities including gross motor skills, fine motor skills, and speech motor control.

Barry (1955a, 1955b) compiled a list of characteristic behaviors in speech, language, reading, and writing that are associated with aphasic children. Use of the list could contribute to the informal teacher evaluation. After careful review of the entire evaluation, if the teacher is still unable to reach a definite conclusion upon which to plan suitable therapy or training, he or she proceeds with "diagnostic teaching," a combination of continued evaluation and therapy.

Training

Three important considerations in the training of aphasic children are (a) the physical setup, (b) corrective therapy for psychomotor dysfunctions and impaired functions, and (c) the development of language and skills related to language.

The Physical Setup.   The number of pupils in the special class should be limited; the physical environment should be uncluttered and free from distractions. Pupils are seated apart from one another, and highly distractible children are assigned seats that face a wall with their backs to all activity. Attempt is made to teach children to work without direct supervision on assigned tasks so that the teacher may have the opportunity to give the pupils additional individual help. The materials are selected carefully and should be simple and easy to handle. Any pictures used in these classes need to be free from unnecessary details. All materials should be filed when not in use in order to maintain the uncluttered appearance of the classroom.

Barry (1988, pp. 19–25) outlines a sample day complete with time allotments and structured teaching activities that can be used. This highly structured day, which begins at 9:00 in the morning and ends at 3:00 in the afternoon, is planned with routines and time limits that are carefully observed and that provide the pupil with needed security. Explicit directions are given in simple, direct language. The child is taught step by step where to put things, when to take turns, and how to walk quietly. All this is accomplished in a kind but firm manner. This approach helps the children, whose perceptions may be unstable, to order their world and to integrate their experiences. Specifically, the day's activities include training in visual perception, reading and number readiness, auditory perception, language, and writing; there is time out for snack, outdoor play, lunch, and rest.

Corrective Therapy for Psychomotor Dysfunctioning and Impaired Perceptions.

The child who cannot control or integrate his or her behavior needs firm and deliberate procedures. For this reason, structure is the key to teaching aphasic children. Barry (1988) divides the training of the impaired functions into four areas and suggests possible activities for each area. Areas to be trained are (a) impaired body image, (b) impaired perceptions, (c) figure-ground disturbance and spatial disorganization, and (d) motor disabilities, in the order listed.

TRAINING IMPAIRED BODY IMAGE.   If the child's body image (awareness of self as an entity separate from others) is impaired, Barry stresses the need for training in that area before attempting further training.

A number of highly structured procedures are proposed. The child is helped to model a human figure from clay (calling it a boy, a girl, or a daddy). The location of the eyes, nose, mouth, and arms is pointed out. The pupil is taught to make a life-sized outline of another child lying on a large piece of paper on the floor; the pupil then cuts it out and is encouraged to draw parts of the body. Development of adequate body image is facilitated further by having the child look at himself or herself in a mirror. The use of stuffed animals permits the child to feel parts of the body and to discuss the body while dressing the figure. Other suitable procedures can be found in Barry's (1988) book.

TRAINING IMPAIRED PERCEPTIONS.   Once the child perceives the body and its parts realistically, training can proceed to the remediation of impaired perceptions. After visual perception training, children should be able to form visual relationships, to make visual contact with objects, to look where they want to look, and to change focus both in direction and distance at will. They must be able to organize and synthesize visual fields and to translate into movement what they see. Specific techniques that are helpful in developing visual perceptions include the child's participation in matching and sorting activities that make use of different colors, forms, and objects; the copying of simple forms; and coloring, cutting, and pasting tasks.

Occasionally a child needs tactile perception training. Activities are designed to develop the child's ability to discriminate and recognize forms, textures, and objects by touch alone. An initial task might require the child, with eyes closed, to feel one block and to place it with other blocks having different shapes. The child then looks at all the blocks and identifies the one that had been felt. This procedure is varied for use with other tactile stimuli, for example, distinguishing among cans filled with sand, soap flakes, flour.

Training of auditory perception and memory is often necessary. After training in this function the child should have developed both awareness and discrimination among sound stimuli and symbols. Training proceeds from gross to finer sounds and finally to the sounds of voice and speech. The child must have intensive practice relating motor responses to auditory stimuli. In teaching awareness of sounds, children are encouraged to raise their hands or jump when they hear a musical instrument, the jingling of coins, or spoken nonsense syllables. In teaching discrimination among sounds, children are taught to select from a group of instruments the one that was sounded behind them (discrimination between loud and soft sounds is developed at this time). Discrimination among speech sounds may be taught by requiring the child to associate the syllables *moo* and *baa* with the pictures of a cow and a sheep. This task is increased in difficulty as the child succeeds to one-syllable words, to two-syllable words, and so on. In teaching auditory memory, cards are prepared with short and long vertical lines to represent high-low or loud-soft patterns (visual clues) produced by the teacher. The child selects the proper card to match the sounds. Imitation of rhythms and nonsense syllables is used to give practice in memory.

TRAINING FOR FIGURE-GROUND DISTURBANCE AND SPATIAL DISORGANIZATION.   After training in figure-ground discrimination and spatial orientation, the child's fluctuating impressions tend to become stabilized. Having auditory figure-ground disturbance, the child attends to all sounds equally and therefore must be trained to listen and to control the sound background. Auditory figure-ground disturbance may be improved by using the suggestions for training awareness and discrimination against a background of soft music. If visual figure-ground disturbance is present, the child must learn to bring the foreground sharply into focus. Training is designed to help the child attend to the foreground stimulus without being overly aware of the background. The teacher gives practice in finding differences, making a whole from parts, discrimination of figure from ground. This latter is accomplished by use of a cardboard stencil placed over white paper, both tacked onto a board. The child colors within the stencil; as the child becomes more skillful, the stencil is removed and the child colors within an outline. To gain spatial orientation, the child is trained to find a reference point and to use judgment in spatial matters. Training consists of finding the top, bottom, sides, and back; of learning up, down, over, under, in, bigger, heavier, and so on, in concrete situations. The teacher may employ the color cone, the three-hole form board, cut-out forms of different colors to be matched to identical forms pasted on a board, designs of many kinds for the child to copy, puzzles, and sequencing activities involving gradations of color, size, weight, and so on.

TRAINING IN MOTOR SKILLS. The final section on impaired functions discussed by Barry deals with the training of motor skills. Once again the training begins with gross motor abilities (moving and stopping), proceeds to the fine motor skills (using the fingers), and then progresses to speech motor skills. In training gross motor skills, all practice in moving and stopping is encouraged. Running, skipping, hopping, throwing, kicking, walking up and down stairs, and walking within prescribed limits are suggested activities. In training fine motor skills, activities such as picking up small objects and dropping them into holes or slots, buttoning, stringing beads, folding, and cutting are useful. In training speech motor skills, relaxation exercises such as dropping the head forward and rotating it slowly or babbling and yawning are employed first. Other activities include having the child (a) breathe in and out through the nose, or breathe in through the nose and out through the mouth, or blow a ping-pong ball across a table; (b) imitate or sing nonsense syllables or digits to improve voice production; (c) use articulation exercises such as chewing, with and without voice, raising and lowering the jaw, protruding the tongue and moving it from side to side and up and down, and protruding the lips.

Training Language and Related Skills.

Language training usually is started at the same time as, and coordinated with, perception and motor training. In normal language development, inner language begins to function at about 8 months of age, receptive language at from 8 to 13 months, and expressive language from 13 months on. In training language disabilities this same order is followed, but training is begun at the level at which the child is impaired.

In training inner language the child is helped to relate better to environment, to "make believe," to use past experience, and to integrate. Until the child can do this, receptive and expressive language training are not attempted. Specifically, inner language is developed by manipulation of and play with objects representing items in the child's daily experience until he or she can make relationships in a meaningful way.

The techniques for training receptive language are described by Barry (1960) as a "feeding-in or pouring-in" process. The use of basic color words is suggested as a beginning point, and 2-inch solid color blocks are used. Red, blue, and yellow are taught first. The color name is given again and again. "This is red, red. See, it's the same as your tie, red. Let's find something else red." Rather than following this example, the teaching might be more effective if instances of red and not-red are presented. The teacher encourages eye-to-eye contact, sits very close to the child in order to focus visual attention, and uses a hearing tube to focus auditory attention. The teacher speaks in a low, clear voice, using much repetition, until the child is able to respond by pointing to the correct block. After several colors have been taught, the teacher removes the visual clue by sitting behind the child, who must now listen attentively to the auditory stimulus. If the child who has difficulty with auditory patterns is at least 5 years old, the printed form of the word may be given. However, if the child's behavior appears disturbed, caution must be exercised in using the multisensory approach. In this event the auditory channel should be emphasized. Toy furniture and figures are presented with much conversation regarding their use. These activities are repeated until the child knows the names of a great many things. Action words are then introduced, with prepositional phrases following these. No expressive language is demanded of the child during this training, though. Most likely the child will begin to imitate spontaneously.

In expressive language training, "any vocalizations that are meaningful to the child are accepted by the teacher and are used as a basis of communication" (Barry, 1988, p. 45). Nouns, verbs, and prepositions are presented in the same order as for receptive language. The pronoun *I* is encouraged early, and the child is helped to relate his or her experiences. "What did you do?" "What is this?" "Where is Mommy?" Speech is encouraged and corrections are made casually. As the child progresses, more parts of speech are used. For structure, the Fitzgerald Key is used, and accuracy is demanded. Words that have been learned are kept on charts according to "who," "where," "what," "what color," and "how many." These charts are used for reference by the children learning to read and write.

Aphasic children's difficulty in learning to read is part of their general impairment in perception and behavior. Many of the techniques mentioned previously as training for impaired functions are devices used in reading readiness programs. Many of the approaches used in remedial reading programs are adaptable in teaching reading to aphasic children.

In teaching writing, the child first must be proficient in the handling of crayons and pencils. Specially lined paper is used, and there is much structuring in all writing. The child is required to follow dots and to stay within limits. For beginning writing, boxes for each letter may be added to the lined paper. Manuscript is used, and cursive writing is not introduced until the child is ready for the adjustment required.

Number concepts are taught in about the same manner as they are taught to a normal child; however, it takes the aphasic child longer to master each step, so more practice is given. Concrete materials are used extensively. Individual bead boards are used so that the child can touch each bead while counting. The child learns the written symbol and the printed form of the number words and then matches these with the configuration.

The key word in Barry's corrective therapy is "structuring," which means putting things in order, teaching limits and sequence, clarifying, simplifying, concretizing, bringing the foreground sharply into focus, and blocking out nonessentials. Structuring is the performance of a simple activity in deliberate, sequential steps in response to deliberate, sequential commands, and it involves using every technique, device, or trick that will help the child to hear, see, and understand better. Since Barry employs structuring primarily as a device to facilitate the development of language in children who generally experience deficits in that ability, her system is discussed along with the system of McGinnis.

McGINNIS: THE ASSOCIATION METHOD

Mildred A. McGinnis taught elementary school for several years and in 1916 joined the staff at Central Institute for the Deaf in St. Louis, Missouri. Two years later she was named director of the Speech and Correction Division and held that post until she retired in 1963. Also, in 1963, the Volta Bureau published her most influential work, *Aphasic Children*, which dealt with the education of children with organic-based language disorders. (This book was reprinted by PRO-ED in 1988 as part of its Classics Series.) She was awarded a Fulbright grant to lecture in countries around the world in 1964, one of many lecture tours she made. After McGinnis's death, Silverman (1967) wrote, "Courage, staying power and salty Hibernian wit are all part of her rich legacy to CID. But the heart of the legacy is her persistent commitment to the task of bringing the precious skill of communication by speech to whom nature denied it."

McGinnis (1964) reports that there are nonlanguage children with multiple handicaps who respond adequately to the Association Method, if the primary problem is aphasia. The child who is predominantly aphasic, but who also has a hearing loss, for example, does not learn effectively by educational methods for the deaf. Similarly, the child whose predominant problem is severe emotional disturbance, and whose secondary problem is aphasia, does not respond adequately to the Association Method until the emotional disturbance has been resolved, in part or wholly.

McGinnis (1988) referred to language delayed children as types of aphasics; namely, expressive or motor aphasics and receptive or sensory aphasics. The children with expressive or motor aphasia are those with combinations of motor aphasia and normal intelligence, motor aphasia and above normal intelligence, motor aphasia and mild mental retardation, motor aphasia and secondary cerebral palsy, and retardation. The second type of child McGinnis refers to is the sensory aphasic who responds well to the Association Method. These children she described as having predominantly sensory aphasia with scribble speech, scribble speech with intelligible words, sensory aphasia and echolalia, and the silent child.

Prall (1964) reports that the role of aphasia in childhood psychosis and autism was little appreciated until McGinnis and others began working in the field of aphasia. In childhood psychosis one of the primary symptoms is lack of speech development; it is important, therefore, to have a clear differential diagnosis and an appropriate method to help the child acquire language in order to help him or her with the secondary problems.

McGinnis (1988) reports that the method used in teaching aphasic children is called the Association Method because it develops and associates systematically each of the several specific skills that must be coordinated for the development of ability to understand and to use oral communication. The development and organization of the sequence of steps and procedures that constitute the Association Method were completed shortly after World War I and have been applied in the teaching of aphasic children at Central Institute for the Deaf in St. Louis since that time.

There are six essential differences between the Association Method and the approach commonly used with deaf children:

1. There is no formal lipreading of what the child cannot say.

2. There are no voice-building exercises disassociated with words.

3. Nouns are presented sound by sound in the initial stages.

4. The written form accompanies every sound that is taught.

5. The acoustic and lipreading steps are given after, not before, the child can say the nouns and associate them with the objects they symbolize.

6. When sounds and nouns are learned, recall is expected without constant prompting by the teacher.

The educational objective is to prepare aphasic children for entrance into regular schools as near their appropriate age and grade level as possible. Although the Association Method emphasizes the development of speech and language, the overall program provides for teaching academic subjects as well.

The method initially stresses the mechanics of speech more than the ideas to be expressed or understood through spoken language. McGinnis's observations of the children classified as receptive aphasics led her to believe that their problem is more an inability to communicate verbally about their daily experiences than a lack of understanding of their experiences. Therefore, the Association Method's approach to teaching emphasizes the development of skill in the use of the tools of communication enabling the child to speak about his or her experiences and to interpret the speech of others.

McGinnis utilizes the simple-to-complex approach in teaching speech and language to the child. Simple speech acts are taught first and then combined and built into acts requiring more complex expression and understanding. The Association Method is based upon five major principles:

1. Words are taught by a phonetic or elemental approach.

2. Each sound is learned through emphasis on precise articulation production.

3. The correct articulation of each sound is associated with its corresponding letter symbol written in cursive script.

4. Expression is used as the foundation or starting point in building language.

5. Systematic sensorimotor association is utilized.

The child in therapy is first taught to produce each sound and to associate it with the written letter symbol for the sound. Sounds are taught using the Northampton-Yale sound designations. Supporters of the Association Method believe it is easier to hold a child's attention on an individual speech sound than on sentences, phrases, or words. The child has a much simpler task on which to concentrate when learning to produce single sounds and is able to achieve some success, which helps to motivate him or her to continue trying for speech and language improvement. By teaching the child how to produce a sound accurately and by providing the sound's corresponding visual symbol, a frame of reference is established that the child can use in the retention and recall of the language being taught. The later associations of speaking and writing (expressive skills) with reading, lipreading, and hearing (receptive skills) are built on the initial association of articulation placement and letter symbols.

Before sound combinations are made, formulating a complete word, the child says each sound in the word separately. At this stage it is important to teach the child to produce sequences of sounds that make up words. At first the child's speech will appear rather stilted; however, after time and practice, smooth articulation occurs without the loss of accuracy in the production of individual speech sounds. McGinnis stresses that production of words precedes any attempt to establish recognition of the meanings of words.

She states that children with receptive aphasia are not expected to understand any word until they have first produced the word for themselves (McGinnis, Kleffner, & Goldstein, 1956). As the child progresses from learning of single speech units (sounds) to more complex speech units (words), the principle of systematic association of motor skills and capacities is more fully utilized. This principle can best be illustrated by the advocated method of teaching nouns in the following sequential steps:

1. The child looks at the written noun word and produces each sound contained in the word in the sequence in which it is written.

2. The child matches the *picture* or the *object* represented by this word to the written form of the word.

3. The technique of simultaneous talking and writing is employed as the child writes the word and articulates each sound as he or she writes the letter(s) for it.

4. After the teacher says the word aloud (first broken into sequence of separate sounds and then blended into a word unit), the child repeats the same procedure and then matches the *object* or *picture* to the written form of the word. This process is repeated three times by the child:

    a. After the teacher says the word.

    b. As the child identifies the picture or object named by the word.

    c. As the child identifies the written form of the word.

5. The teacher presents pictures representing the nouns already taught, and the child must say the name of the object from memory without the aid of lipreading, auditory stimulus, or written form.

    Not all of the vocabulary and language children learn must be taught in a formal manner. Once they have gained some skills in the use of language, they develop increasing ability to acquire new vocabulary and language in an incidental fashion.

    There are primarily two types of programs representing the basic language and speech curriculum the child is expected to complete over a period of time—the vertical and horizontal programs. The vertical program represents the total sequence of items that a child will be expected to learn. The horizontal program represents the daily class program and consists of items from the vertical program.

Vertical Program

1. Contains the sequence of items to be taught.

2. Is divided into three units of language in which progress is measured not by grades but by language units.

3. Before advancement from one unit to the next, the child must be proficient at using independently all structured language forms within the unit presently under study.

Horizontal Program

1. Consists of items taken from the vertical program and carried out in a daily program in the classroom.

2. Items are presented early in the program and then discontinued after having been mastered by the child.

3. The teacher concentrates on those items in which the child needs the most attention; included should be items necessary to prepare the child for grade work in geography, arithmetic, and other subjects.

    In addition to the two basic language programs, correlative programs are employed to reinforce material previously presented. The correlative programs consist of:

1. Attention-getting exercises

2. Exercises leading to writing

3. General tongue exercises, which are gradually replaced by specific exercises for the development of individual speech sounds

4. Number work

5. Multiplication tables

6. Calendar work

7. Specific and special teaching approaches for the motor aphasic child

McGinnis's (1988) training manual is thorough and presents a concise and detailed description of the method and how it should be implemented. There are many useful and important teaching techniques that could be applied in one way or another to all children having language difficulties.

In the manual, McGinnis states that there are several stages or levels a child must complete if the program is to be considered successful. The initial step is the presentation of Attention Activities. The aim of these activities is to teach habits of attention and exact response, and to train the children to do independent seatwork, which replaces free-play periods as the program progresses. The attention-getting exercises are first presented to the group, with each child performing individually while classmates observe.

The second level of the program is synonymous with the vertical program and is composed of three language units. Children must learn all the language forms in one unit and be able to use them independently before they can move on to the next unit.

First Unit of Language

In the first language unit the child begins to take the first steps in the acquisition of oral language. Formal teaching is directed toward the child's learning 50 nouns. At the same time other activities help prepare the child for orderly learning and memory.

Interspersed with formal instruction on individual sound production are short play periods. These periods help the child to adjust during the first few weeks in school and also help to distinguish between work and play. Attention-getting exercises are used with the instruction to help the child learn to concentrate. Drawing strings on balloons and imitating tongue movements are some of the exercises that are suggested.

The teacher writes each child's name on a card and then assists the child in learning to respond to his or her name. Simple commands necessary for class management are placed on a chart, and the child is again taught to respond.

Individual sounds are developed by articulation practice and association with the written symbols on the chalkboard. Beginning books are made for each child to keep a record of the sounds learned. Cross-drills and practice in lipreading and acoustic association add further to the child's sound development.

When nouns are introduced, the same procedures used for individual sound development are followed. For further clarification, pictures and objects are used along with strip charts on which the nouns that have been taught are recorded. When the proper number of nouns are learned, the child is ready for the second unit of language. The following activities make up the first language unit:

1. Attention-getting exercises

2. Single-sound development

3. The combination of sounds into nouns

4. The association of meaning with nouns

5. Writing-readiness exercises and writing of nouns

6. Lipreading and auditory training with individual sounds and then in word combinations as nouns

7. Association of the meaning of commands that relate to daily class routine from both written and oral stimulation

Second Unit of Language

In the second unit the teaching of language is begun. Simple sentences are introduced and a question chart is made. The chart is important because its items are guides for progressing through the second unit of language. An example chart is provided in Figure 8.2.

Articles and pronouns are presented. Animal stories are developed by the class through the gradual addition of descriptive sentences. Through use of animal stories, new vocabulary is introduced, memory span is increased, and numbers and adjectives are introduced.

Personal description stories are developed. Prepositions are taught by using concrete examples, first with pictures, then with actual objects. Teaching the present progressive of verbs is begun by writing a sentence describing an action. The child then reads and copies the sentence until articulation and memory of sentence structure are mastered.

The second unit progresses through the following steps:

1. Simple sentences are introduced:
   a. I see _____.
   b. This is _____.
   c. I want _____.
   With the exception of the pronoun *I*, capital letters are not used at this time. The articles *a* and *an* and the adjective *some* are added to the nouns.

QUESTIONS

What do you see?   I see   a _____.
an _____.
some _____ s.

What is this?   This is   a _____.
an _____.

Who is this?   This is my   _____.
_____.

What do you want?   I want   a _____.
an _____.
some _____ s.

is _____ _____? The _____ _____ blue.
What color   red.
are _____ _____? _____'s _____ s are brown.

How many _____ s has a _____? A _____ has   1 _____.
2
3 _____ s.
4

How many _____ s do you see? I see   1 _____.
2
3 _____ s.
4

fly?
Can a _____ hop?   Yes, a _____ can _____.
swim?   No, a _____ cannot _____.

FIGURE 8.2. A sample question chart.

2. Questions are introduced after each sentence is taught. A basic question chart is made using the following questions:
    a. What do you see?
    b. What is this?
    c. What do you want?

3. The pronoun *my* is introduced with the question, "What is this?" when the child is asked about pictures of parents and siblings.

4. Description stories describing animals and requiring the memory of four sentences are introduced at this point. After description stories progress to eight sentences, the teacher includes descriptions of inanimate objects such as toys, bicycles, and cars. Description stories serve as a teaching experience for the development of new vocabulary, adjectives, and number concepts. New nouns and adjectives are recorded on strip charts, and the noun charts should record both the singular and plural form.

5. Numbers are introduced as the first description stories about animals are begun. A number chart is made, and addition facts are begun. The question "How many _____ has a _____?" is added to the question chart. Characteristics of animals promote the question, "Can a _____ fly, swim, climb, etc.?" which is added to the chart.

6. Having the children describe one another provides a medium for teaching the uses and concepts of the pronouns *he, she, his, her,* and *your.* These pronouns are not recorded on a chart.

7. The prepositions *in, on,* and *under* are introduced by the question, "Where is _____?" This question is added to the chart.

8. No new language concepts are taught at this stage. Roundup stories are used, and the teacher "rounds up" all the language concepts the children have learned and applies them to the description of pictures. Pictures of rooms, places, and scenes may be used in this exercise.

9. The cross-drill is continued. New vocabulary is taught by writing the new words and then asking the child to pronounce each individual sound and blend the sounds into syllables.

10. The present progressive form of verbs is introduced. Pictures portraying activities of the action verbs are used in teaching this verb form. The question, "What is the _____ doing?" is added to the chart.

11. The preceding program is supplemented by the introduction of incidental language. The children learn to say the commands recorded on the chart when they are conducting a lesson and to make oral requests that have been recorded on the chart.

12. Calendar work is begun.

Third Unit of Language

After the development of language concepts on a concrete level in units one and two, Language Unit Three introduces concepts of tense and language forms that are more complex. The items taught in this unit are presented in the following sequence:

1. The past tense of the verb is taught, and verb charts are made.

2. Partitives are taught.

3. The past tense of the verb is applied to events other than those occurring in the classroom.

4. Experience stories are developed.

5. Imagination stories are developed.

6. The future tense is introduced.

7. The use of textbooks is begun.

8. Comparisons, categories, and materials are introduced.

9. Language forms as suggested in textbooks are developed.

10. Idioms are explained, and direct and indirect conversation is taught.

When the child has completed the third unit of language, he or she may be ready for regular class placement. The child's future educational program should be determined, however, by a team composed of the teacher, the psychoeducational diagnosticians, medical personnel, and the child's parents. Since the child usually will have a residue of language confusion, he or she undoubtedly will need clinical assistance during the transition period from the special program to the regular classroom.

The approach taken by McGinnis is essentially the same for children who have receptive, expressive, or mixed language disorders. The key word in the preceding statement probably is *language,* and the children best able to benefit from the Association Method are those who are delayed in the acquisition and development of vocal language skills, whether the skills be receptive or expressive. Such children would have difficulty with the graphic symbol system, but their overriding disabilities are in the auditory-vocal areas, inability to comprehend oral language, poor understanding of the language code, deficits in the ability to associate input signals with appropriate output patterns, and an inability to formulate and express intentions or ideas in vocal language.

9

REMEDIATING DISABILITIES OF LISTENING AND SPEAKING

As the reader is probably aware, most professionals in the field of learning disabilities were first influenced by research and concepts from the fields of neurophysiology and learning theory. In particular, they drew heavily on the theories and models presented by Orton, Strauss, and Osgood. This tradition continues today, but many teachers and clinicians who work with nonverbal or language delayed children have found the constructs developed by psychologists and neurologists to be inadequate in developing programs for teaching these children. Within the past years, many specialists in language disorders have turned their interest toward another tradition, that of linguistics.

Between 1960 and 1975 much of the linguistic research that was embraced by professionals working in language disorders had been promulgated by such authors as Braine (1963), McNeill (1970), and Menyuk (1971). These people were influenced in turn by Noam Chomsky (1957, 1965), the originator of transformational grammar. As a result of Chomsky's preeminence in the field of linguistics, his followers placed an unusually heavy emphasis upon grammar and morphology, both in language acquisition and in language usage. The area of semantics, including pragmatics, did not fall into disgrace; the situation was more insidious than that. For years the entire area was virtually ignored, while children's language was viewed and researched as if there were little meaningful, spontaneous conversation produced by the children.

The scene is quite different today. While no one is discounting the importance of syntax, professionals are placing an increasing emphasis on the role of cognition and pragmatics in language acquisition and in the treatment of children's language disorders. In 1970, Bloom recorded the various communicative intents of children performing at the single-word level of language development, and a few years later, Bates (1976) originated the term *pragmatics* and defined it as the rules for the use of language in context. In addition to the work of numerous other authors, these early investigators in the field of pragmatics signaled the dramatic changes that have occurred in the remediation of oral language disorders. This particular period also has witnessed such a regeneration of interest in the cognitive aspects of language development that it would be warranted to say that no clinician today would treat a child with language disorders unless the therapy program had both syntactic/semantic and cognitive/pragmatic aspects.

The developmental linguists have a great deal to tell us regarding the sequence in which children normally acquire certain linguistic constructions. From their work we are obtaining better and more lucid conceptions of the acquisition and development process. In working with the language disordered child, many clinicians feel that the acquisition model has proved to be of far greater assistance than the psycholinguistic models proposed by some psychologists, such as Osgood.

The remedial systems covered in this chapter in general reflect some aspects of both the syntactic/transformational grammar tradition and the semantic/pragmatic orientation. Gray and Ryan's program (1973) is presented as the ultimate in a syntactic program. In fact, Gray and Ryan go so far as to state that a semantically incorrect response is to be reinforced if the targeted syntactic structure is correct. The other three systems covered in this chapter, those of Laura Lee (1974), Jacqueline C. M. Strong (1983), and Fitzgerald (1966) and Pugh (1947), deal with syntactic structures, but the context of teaching is always meaningful and purposeful. In particular, Lee mentions the rebirth of interest in the semantic aspects of language, and Strong emphasizes the cognitive/pragmatic aspects of her program.

At the beginning of most of the chapters dealing with remedial systems we have provided the reader with a brief case history to give some insight into the type of problems for which the system(s) was developed. Rather than adhere rigidly to a predetermined format, we prefer to present at this point a definition/description of the nonverbal child for whom the systems in this chapter would be appropriate. The definition is that given by Gray and Ryan (1973).

A more apt definition of a nonlanguage child is a nonperformer of the verbal-linguistic code. He most generally has some type of nonverbal language which may be grammatical under special rules of gesture language. A distinctive trait about the child is that, despite growing up in a verbal-linguistic environment, he fails to perform verbally himself. The complaint is that all code sending and confirmation of reception is nonverbal—or if verbal, it violates syntactic rules of usage. Specifically, the verbal-linguistic performance of the child is not appropriate. It makes no difference what label is assigned to the fact of nonperformance (autistic, receptive aphasic, dysphasic, language delayed, brain damaged, etc.), the teaching job is still the same. The language teacher must *change* the child's code sending *performance*. (p. 6)

This definition appears to discount the obvious differences among children who are autistic, aphasic, hard of hearing, and so on. However, if the teacher/therapist's task is to alter the language of the child, we believe that certain assumptions must be made. The first is that most children learn in the same way, that is, that the psychological principles underlying stimulus-response conditioning do not change with the etiology of a child's disorder or with the label assigned. Second, we believe that within the present limitations regarding knowledge about language acquisition and development, programs for teaching language to nonverbal children should contain the same content regardless of the etiology or label an individual child carries.

The definition is not intended to disregard the obvious individual differences among children that may *directly* affect their language learning ability in a teaching situation. The hard-of-hearing child will need amplification that is not necessary for the hearing child; the highly distractible, hyperactive, or "brain damaged" child may need extensive modification of behavior before he or she is able to respond to the teaching situation. By the same token, a 4-year-old child will probably need smaller furniture than a 6-year-old child. The teacher must respond to the individual differences among children that are critical to success in the teaching situation, but "to indiscriminantly respond to all observable differences is to invite failure" (Gray & Ryan, 1973, p. 6).

STRONG: LANGUAGE FACILITATION

The tools and procedures of *Language Facilitation* were developed by Jacqueline M. Cimorell Strong (1983) while she was a doctoral student at Pennsylvania State University. The program itself was developed and expanded during her tenure at the University of North Carolina at Greensboro where she trains both undergraduate and graduate students in the rationale, procedures, and implementation of the program. *Language Facilitation* is based foremost upon Piagetian principles, particularly the premise that sensorimotor experiences are the means through which young children learn language, but also embedded in the program are many of the principles of pragmatic language behavior. As Strong (1983) says, "Due to the cognitively oriented nature of the program, pragmatic ingredients have always been informally included" (p. vii). The program is discussed under the major topics (a) rationale, (b) communicative competence, (c) behavioral goals, (d) lesson plans, and (e) record-keeping. Finally, the program is analyzed briefly.

Rationale

Language Facilitation is based squarely upon the "Piagetian premise that play in the form of object manipulation, motoric involvement, and direct experience (with various activities, concepts, and skills) is the channel through which children *naturally* learn language" (Strong, 1983, p. 7).

> The general sequence in the implementation of therapeutic techniques is 1) to motorically involve the child(ren) in an activity that encourages interaction with objects (including the persons in the group) and events; 2) to linguistically mark the child(ren)'s actions; 3) to ask the appropriate probe question(s) depending upon the response(s) to be elicited from the child(ren); 4) to prompt a response from the child(ren) if necessary; 5) to provide the child(ren) with some form of reinforcement; 6) to expand the child(ren)'s abbreviated utterances; and/or 7) to comment upon the child(ren)'s utterance in relation to what is happening in the environment. (Strong, 1983, pp. 9–10)

Included in the program are a number of techniques, as referred to above, that researchers have found mothers use in early interaction with their infants and young children. These are motoric involvement, linguistic marking, probe questions, prompting, expansion, and commenting.

Motoric Involvement.   According to Strong (1983), this technique is based on the principle that language will develop out of experience and experimentation, a principle derived from Piaget (1952) who stated that cognition is sensorimotor action that has become internalized and that language is a symbol system for cognition. The technique of motoric involvement entails the use of therapeutic environments that permit children to become involved through a playful mode while they interact with objects and events. Strong believes that the relationship between the child's play/ motoric involvement and his or her conceptual/language development is a critical factor for teachers and clinicians to understand and implement.

Linguistic Marking.   The use of this technique allows the clinician to provide language delayed children with an auditory model of their experiences. The clinician tells the child what the child is doing as he or she bounces a ball, climbs on a chair, and so on, thereby encoding into language the verbal representation of the child's present activity. By pairing the motor and verbal representations, a firm association between the two is created, and children are able to interpret the verbal representation, which they may not have previously understood, in terms of their own sensorimotor representation, which they understand well.

Probe Questions.   If the clinician wishes to elicit particular responses, probe questions must be asked. It is possible to elicit a variety of responses, and the clinician should remember that the questions must be selected carefully so that the appropriate response is elicited. The question will usually predetermine the particular linguistic form(s), semantic relation(s), and often the communicative intent that is elicited. Questions such as "What are you doing? (eating, wearing)" can be used to elicit progressive verbing responses. *Where?* questions will usually elicit locative (prepositional) responses. *What did?* questions can be used to elicit past tense responses. Other types of questions will elicit other responses.

Prompting. With many young language delayed children all responses will probably have to be elicited in the initial stages of therapy. After linguistic marked probe questions are posed, the clinician will have to provide the proper response. This is not only a traditional technique but one that rests upon a sound empiric base as a vehicle for facilitating conversational turn-taking and lexical and syntactic/semantic development. As Strong (1983) reports, the appropriate interpretation of elicited imitation tasks may not always be clear, but it appears that clinical techniques that include context may be a way of making elicited imitation tasks congruous with normal speech acts.

Expansion. By using the technique of expansion, the clinician elaborates upon the child's abbreviated utterance and thereby provides him or her with the complete, grammatical auditory input of the intended utterance. For example, the child may be engaged in an activity such as throwing a ball. The clinician asks, "What are you doing?" and the child responds, "Throwing." At that point the clinician expands the child's response into, "Yes, you are throwing the ball." According to McNeill (1970), such expansions reflect the surface structure that expresses the deep structure (the meaning) that the child intended.

Commenting. The technique of commenting bears some resemblance to expansion, but a clinician's comments on a child's responses go beyond the presumed deep structure of the child's utterance and provide additional, related information. Using the same example as given under Expansion above, the clinician could not only expand the child's telegraphic utterance but could also add a comment such as, "See how far you throw the ball." The comment is related to the context and bears a semantic relation to the child's response.

Communicative Competence

Language Facilitation includes strategies for the development and remediation of linguistic structure (i.e., morphologic and syntactic structures), but there is also great emphasis on the social utility of language. Social utility refers to the *use* of language in the everyday world in which one communicates to make things happen. The term *pragmatics*, as first used by Bates (1976), is used to denote how language is used to communicate and is defined as the rules for the use of language in context. Strong (1983) states that "children must learn the rules of social interaction as they pertain to both linguistic and extralinguistic codes" (p. 11).

In discussing pragmatics, Strong (1983) reviews a number of taxonomies of communicative intents, but Hopper and Naremore's (1978) identification of five aspects of situational context seems to be the most profitable in terms of oral language development and remediation. These aspects are (a) the people present, (b) what has been said before, (c) the topic being discussed, (d) the communication goal, and (e) the time and place of communication. Each aspect is discussed briefly.

The People Present.   Everyone knows that the composition of a group in which communication is occurring will influence the communication acts of everyone present. We communicate quite differently in a business meeting, a family reunion, or a tête-à-tête. Children who are brought into the clinical situation for the first time and encounter adults who may seem strange and frightening may be misdiagnosed as language delayed when they simply will not communicate in that situation.

The Message Context.   If the emphasis in therapy is on syntax, the message of the communication can easily be overlooked. "All too often, clinicians have been interested in eliciting correct grammatical constructions from the child with little or no attention paid to how the utterance plays off what has previously been said" (Strong, 1983, p. 20). When there is very little practice in meaningful communication during therapy, the clinician should not be surprised when there is little carryover of proper linguistic usage to other environments.

The Content Context.   What are the clinician and child going to talk about in therapy? This is important because the topic of discussion will often determine what the child will say. The stimulus materials often dictate the content of communication, and as Lee (1974) points out, the materials should differ from child to child depending upon the child's intellectual level, interests, and severity of handicap. The clinician should remember that some children interact better with objects that can be manipulated rather than the standard pictures of the therapy room.

The Task Context.   The fourth aspect of the situational context deals with the speaker's intent or what objectives he or she is trying to attain through communication. Again, when the emphasis in therapy is upon syntax, this aspect suffers. Strong (1983) cites an example of how the task context can be overlooked when the clinician is attending only to correct grammatical structures. She says that a child may use interrogative reversal questions with the intent of seeking information (e.g., "Is Daddy going to the store?") but not with the intention of making a request (e.g., "Will you give me a cookie?"). If one looks only for correct form, one would believe that the child has full command of interrogative reversals.

The Surrounding Physical Context.   Strong (1983) points out that the fifth aspect of situational context, the surrounding physical context, does not dictate the topic of conversation although it may mistakenly be thought to do so. In some cases, the physical context can be made the topic of conversation, but conversing in a park as opposed to a house does not predetermine what the content is going to be. Likewise, conversing in a therapy room, a highly artificial physical context, may be a poor substitute for conversing in more real-life surroundings. Clinicians should strive to get out of the therapy room into other physical contexts, ensuring the likelihood that the child will internalize the linguistic forms and constructions that he or she is practicing.

Planning Behavioral Goals

As a vehicle for documenting accountability, Strong (1983) provides a number of examples of final goals in the areas of syntax, semantics, and pragmatics for children with oral language problems. Along with the final goals, a series of subgoals leading to the desired behavior are presented. The specific activities are listed later in the lesson plans. In writing final goals, Strong adheres to the principles of writing behavioral objectives designed by Mager (1962), who stated that each objective must have three discrete parts, as follows:

1. a precise statement of the desired behavior to be elicited;

2. a statement of the conditions under which the behavior would be elicited; and

3. a statement regarding the criterion for success (i.e., the level at which success is attained, 9 out of 10 trials completed successfully, 80% mastery, etc.). Referring to the literature on operant conditioning, Strong has accepted a success criterion of 80%.

An example of one final goal, a pragmatic goal, is shown below.

> *Final Goal:* In response to appropriate situations (approaching and leaving people), the child(ren) will demontrate *greeting* and *closing* behaviors in the form of *hi/hello + name of individual and good-by + name of individual* with 80% accuracy.
>
> *Subgoal 1:* In response to the appropriate contextual situations, the child will be prompted to use greeting and closing behaviors on a gestural basis (waving) with 80% accuracy.
>
> *Subgoal 2:* Same as Subgoal 1, except the prompt is eliminated and the child is expected to respond to the situation on a spontaneous basis.
>
> *Subgoal 3:* In response to appropriate contextual situations, the child will be prompted to use greeting and closing behaviors at the single-word verbal level (*hi, hello, bye, bye-bye, good-by*) with 80% accuracy.
>
> *Subgoal 4:* Same as Subgoal 3, except the prompt is eliminated and the child is expected to respond to the situation on a spontaneous basis.
>
> *Subgoal 5:* In response to appropriate contextual situations, the child will be prompted to use greeting and closing behaviors in the form of *hi/hello + name of individual* and *good-by + name of individual* with 80% accuracy.
>
> *Subgoal 6:* Same as Subgoal 5, except the prompt is eliminated and the child is expected to respond to the situation on a spontaneous basis. (Strong, 1983, p. 25)

At each subgoal level children may be engaged in a variety of activities that place them in the proper context or in proper relationship to objects. For example, if one wishes to teach locatives (prepositions) such as *over, under, in,* and so on, the children should be placed in the appropriate spatial relationship to objects. Such activities thereby become linguistically marked. Responses are elicited by asking appropriate probe questions when children are at the imitative level of language, and the clinician will follow each response with a comment or an expansion of the response. Reinforcement should occur on a continuous basis in the form of either natural consequences or verbal praise unless the criterion for the final goal has been reached. Thereafter, reinforcement should still occur but on an intermittent schedule.

It should be noted that the subgoals must be tailored to the individual child. If the child is already at the single-word stage of development, no subgoals below or at that level are needed. Subgoals would be formulated to teach the child more adultlike forms of language behavior than the form presently being used.

The Lesson Plans

The *Language Facilitation* program presents 35 detailed lesson plans ranging in topics from body parts to household chores to various holidays. The first lesson plan, "The Farm," is presented in very great detail to demonstrate exactly how plans are to be implemented, the flexibility of the plans, and how each can be tailored to fit the needs of many different children functioning at different levels of syntactic/semantic development and communicative competence.

Each lesson plan has three major parts, as follows: (a) materials needed; (b) possible objectives, both syntactic/semantic and pragmatic; and (c) a variety of specific activities. Syntactic/semantic objectives are included for each lesson, but because there is a limited number of communicative functions, the reader will note some redundancy in the pragmatic objectives. The activities presented reflect the previously discussed activities associated with linguistic markings, probe questions, prompts, expansions, and comments.

As the clinician becomes more familiar with the lesson plans, it would be quite easy either to expand and extend the ones presented or to develop additional ones. In Figure 9.1, Lesson Plan 26, "Picnic," is presented to illustrate the layout and progression of the lesson plans.

Record-Keeping

The last section of *Language Facilitation* (Strong, 1983) provides information on data collection and calculation. A separate tally form is presented for each syntactic/ semantic structure and communicative function written into the lesson plans with the exception of locatives, action verbs, negatives, and adverbs. A common tally form can be used to record these elicitations and for other more advanced forms.

It would be desirable to tally *all* of the children's responses during a therapy session but for obvious reasons, that is not feasible. Strong (1983) provides some suggestions for coping with the problem of tallying as many responses as possible.

1. Focus on only one linguistic form or function per activity. Even though an activity may afford the clinician the opportunity to elicit several linguistic forms . . .

or functions . . . it may not be possible to keep track of all of these responses using on-the-spot tallying procedures. . . .

2. Focus on only one child per activity. . . .

3. Tape-record (audio or video) the clinical session, and at a later time, score all or a portion of the responses elicited. . . . A drawback to this suggestion, however, is that unless the session is videotaped, it probably will not be feasible to adequately tally all of the communicative functions because vital contextual information will be lost.

4. Use a clipboard to keep recording forms in place during tallying. (pp. 123–124)

The Sample Record-Keeping Form (Figure 9.2) that follows was developed by Strong (1983) and represents the tallying procedure for a hypothetical group of five children who are focusing on the verb form and the answer function. The "X" notation made on the form indicates the level of response that is expected from each child (e.g., for Chris, the level is imitative two-word sentences, while for Cherie, the level is multiword utterances). The computed averages shown on the form indicate that three of the children have either met or surpassed the 80% criterion level of success. Lower criterion levels such as 70% indicate the approximation of mastery, while even lower levels such as 50% reflect performance occurring at the level of chance.

Analysis of Language Facilitation

Language Facilitation is a well-designed program that almost any clinician would be able to use without extensive training or further reading. Strong (1983) has reviewed the research literature in the field, and the lesson plans she has developed for the program reflect the current state of the art. There has been no published investigation of the efficacy of the program, and its validity at present rests upon its presentation.

Strong (1983) reports that the program has been used in the clinics at Pennsylvania State University and the University of North Carolina at Greensboro and has met with considerable success. She indicates that parents are pleased with the results of the program, and that student clinicians express feelings of confidence, competence, and fulfillment when using the program. She also reports that the program has been used with children who are language delayed as a result of childhood aphasia, mental retardation, hearing impairments, and autism, all of which indicates that the applications of the program are varied. In addition, Strong (1983) presents some anecdotal information regarding the success of the program when used with individual children.

COUGHRAN AND LILES: DEVELOPMENTAL SYNTAX PROGRAM

The *Developmental Syntax Program* (DSP) was developed by Lila Coughran and Betty Z. Liles (1979) during the time they were employed by the Harry Jersig Speech and

LESSON PLAN 26

Theme: Picnic

Materials Needed: a basket, a blanket, bread, peanut butter and jelly, a knife, juice, water, a pitcher, cups, napkins, chairs in a row (like a bus), a ball, rocks for hopscotch, and a stick to draw squares

Possible Objectives

Syntactic/Semantic
1. All those stated previously can be used.
2. In response to *Who?* and interrogative probe questions, the children will use the indefinite pronouns *someone* and *no one* in the semantic-grammatical constructions *Agent + Auxiliary/Copula, Agent + Action,* and *Agent + (Auxiliary) + Action + Object* with 80% accuracy.

Pragmatic
1. All those stated previously can be used.
2. The children will be instructed to think of their favorite picnic activity. They will be told to draw a picture of this activity to show why it is their favorite. The children will take turns showing their pictures to the others in the group and *giving reasons* why they like the activity, with 80% accuracy.

Activities

1. **Activity: Greeting the Children**

2. **Activity: Introduction to Topic**
   The children will be asked if they have ever been on a picnic and, if so, what kinds of food they ate and what other activities they performed. Then they will be shown pictures to help them identify these various food items and activities. They will be told that they are going to prepare for a picnic.

3. **Activity: Preparing to Go on a Picnic**
   a. *Making* peanut butter *and* jelly sandwiches—*opening* the bread
      (1) Linguistic mark: "Someone is opening the bread" or "No one is opening the bread."
      (2) Probe questions

	One-word response	Two-word response	Multiword response
Who is opening the bread?	Someone/no one	Someone is/no one is	Someone/no one is opening the bread
Is someone opening the bread?	Someone/no one	Someone is/no one is	Someone/no one is opening the bread
Is anyone opening the bread?	Someone/no one	Someone is/no one is	Someone/no one is opening the bread

   (3) Prompts
      (a) One-word responses: "Say *someone*" or "Say *no one*"
      (b) Two-word responses: "Say *someone is*" or "Say *no one is*"
      (c) Multiword responses: "Say *someone is opening the bread*" or "Say *no one is opening the bread.*"

FIGURE 9.1. Sample lesson plan. *Note.* From *Language Facilitation: A Complete Cognitive Therapy Program* (pp. 97–100) by J. M. C. Strong, 1983, Austin, TX: PRO-ED. Reprinted by permission.

FIGURE 9.1. *(Continued)*

          (4) Expansion: "Someone is opening the bread" or "No one is opening the bread."
          (5) Comment: "The bread smells fresh when it is just opened."
    b. *Spreading* the peanut butter
    c. *Spreading* the jelly
    d. *Putting* the slices together
    e. *Cutting* the sandwich
    f. *Wrapping* the sandwich
    g. *Making* juice—*pouring* the juice
    h. *Stirring* the juice
    i. *Covering* the juice
    j. *Packing* the basket—*putting in* the cups
    k. *Putting in* the napkins
    l. *Putting in* the sandwiches
    m. *Putting in* the juice
    n. *Closing* the basket

NOTE: If the children are permitted to leave the building, the public school clinician can conduct any of the picnic activities outside. Otherwise, they will have to be performed in the therapy room.

4. Activity: Carrying the Blanket to the Bus
    a. *Walking* to the bus
    b. *Holding* the blanket
    c. *Dropping* the blanket

5. Activity: Carrying the Blanket to the Bus
    a. *Walking* to the bus
    b. *Holding* the basket
    c. *Opening* the basket
    d. *Closing* the basket

6. Activity: Riding the Bus to the Park
    a. *Getting on* the bus
    b. *Sitting on* the bus
    c. *Singing* a bus song:
        The wheels on the bus go 'round and 'round.
        The wipers on the bus go swish, swish, swish.
        The driver on the bus says "Sit right down,"
        The people on the bus go up and down.

7. Activity: Having a Picnic at the Park (Snack Time)
    a. *Spreading* the blanket
    b. *Handing out* the food
        (1) *Opening* the basket
        (2) *Looking inside* the basket
        (3) *Getting out* the food
    c. *Pouring* the juice
    d. *Drinking* the juice
    e. *Eating* the sandwich

FIGURE 9.1. *(Continued)*

8. *Activity: Packing the Basket to Take Back (Cleaning Up)*
a. *Putting* the trash *in* the basket
b. *Putting* the leftover juice *in* the basket

9. *Activity: Games to Play at the Park After Snack Time*
a. *Playing* ball
    (1) *Throwing* the ball
    (2) *Catching* the ball
    (3) *Passing* the ball
    (4) *Rolling* the ball
    (5) *Bouncing* the ball
    (6) *Hitting* the ball
    (7) *Kicking* the ball
b. Follow the Leader
    (1) *Running in* circles
    (2) *Raising* hands
    (3) *Kicking up* heels
    (4) *Swaying* left *and* right
    (5) *Pretending* to be different things
c. Simon Says
    (1) *Jumping up and down*
    (2) *Rolling over*
    (3) *Standing* straight
    (4) *Sitting down*
    (5) *Twisting your* body
    (6) *Shaking your* leg
d. Hide and Seek
    (1) *Peeking through your* fingers
    (2) *Counting* to ten
    (3) *Running*
    (4) *Hiding behind, under, inside, above* _____
    (5) *Finding your* friend
    (6) *Chasing your* friend
    (7) *Falling down*
e. Tag
    (1) *Chasing* each other
    (2) *Tagging* each other
    (3) *Calling "you're* it"
f. Hopscotch
    (1) *Drawing* squares *in* the dirt
    (2) *Gathering* rocks
    (3) *Tossing* rocks *in* the squares
    (4) *Hopping inside* the blocks
    (5) *Turning around in* the air
    (6) *Taking our* time

FIGURE 9.1. *(Continued)*

    g. Ring Around the Rosies
        (1) *Holding* hands
        (2) *Moving in* a circle
        (3) *Moving* to the left
        (4) *Moving* to the right
        (5) *Singing:*
            Ring around the rosies
            A pocket full of posies
            Red bird, bluebird, squat!
        (6) *Squatting down*
        (7) *Sitting on* the ground
        (8) *Standing up*
    h. Ring Toss
        (1) *Throwing* the rings
        (2) *Hitting* the sticks
        (3) *Making* the rings go *onto* the stick
        (4) *Counting* the rings *on* the stick
    i. Duck Duck Goose
        (1) *Running around in* circles
        (2) *Touching someone's* head
        (3) *Chasing* friend *around* the circle
        (4) *Tagging* friend
        (5) *Sitting down in* circle again

10. *Activity: Departing from the Children*

Hearing Center, an affiliate of Our Lady of the Lake University in San Antonio, Texas. Liles, who is presently associated with the Department of Speech Pathology and Audiology at the University of Connecticut, was instrumental in developing the rationale on which the program is based; Coughran, the principal author of the program, presently is serving as director of Court Appointed Special Advocates of Travis County, Texas.

    The DSP was developed to meet the following objectives:

1. To establish a sequentially structured method of eliciting the correct production of syntax construction.

2. To utilize a programmed method of instruction with children whose basic language concepts and comprehension are adequate but who have difficulty using the correct sequence of syntactic structures in connected speech.

3. To effect carryover and generalization of these linguistic constructions into the conversational speech of children.

Sample Record Keeping Form. Verbs

Names	Function	Imitation			Spontaneous		
		Verb	Agt[a] + Verb; Verb + Obj; Verb + Adv	Agt + (Aux) + Verb + (Obj) + (Adv) + (Loc Phrase)	Verb	Agt + Verb; Verb + Obj; Verb + Adv	Agt + (Aux) + Verb + (Obj) + (Adv) + (Loc Phrase)
Chris	Ans[b]		X 卌 卌				
	Reply						
	Com						
	Ack						
	SCDR						
	Rep		100%				
Cherie	Ans	|||		X 卌			
	Reply						
	Com						
	Ack						
	SCDR						
	Rep			50%			
Bobby	Ans				X 卌 卌		
	Reply				|||		
	Com						

[a] Agt, agent; Obj, object; Adv, adverb; Aux, auxiliary; Loc, locative.
[b] Ans, answering; Reply, replying; Com, commenting; Ack, acknowledging; SCDR, suggesting, commanding, demanding, requesting; Rep, repeating.

FIGURE 9.2. Sample record-keeping form. *Note.* From *Language Facilitation: A Complete Cognitive Therapy Program* (pp. 126–127) by J. M. C. Strong, 1983, Austin, TX: PRO-ED. Reprinted by permission.

FIGURE 9.2. (Continued)

	Ack				
	SCDR				
	Rep	90%			
	Ans	I	II	X 卌 II	
	Reply				
	Com				
Michele	Ack				
	SCDR				
	Rep		70%		
	Ans		II		
	Reply	III			
	Com	III		X 卌 III	
Frankie	Ack				
	SCDR				
	Rep		80%		

Program design and construction were based on Coughran's observation and assessment of language delayed/disordered children in the clinical setting. She selected the eight most frequent syntactic errors made by the children and initially developed eight programs. Later, three additional programs were developed to complement and extend the original ones. The programs presently available in the DSP are:

1. Articles

2. Personal pronouns

3. Possessive pronouns

4. Adjectives

5. Verbs *is* and *are*

6. Verbs *has* and *have*

7. Past tense of regular and irregular verbs

8. Plurality

9. Negation

10. Interrogation

11. Conjunctions

The Coughran-Liles program, hereafter referred to as DSP, bears many resemblances to the program developed by Gray and Ryan (1973) and discussed later in this chapter. The DSP, however, has distinct advantages over the Gray and Ryan program for the public school speech-language pathologist. It is much less complex and more easily implemented in a public school setting. There is no necessity for lengthy training of therapists as there would be with the Gray-Ryan program, and furthermore, the DSP is more economical, both in initial capital outlay and in operation costs. In comparison with the Gray-Ryan program, however, the DSP is not as well programmed and has not been field-tested as has the Gray-Ryan. The DSP is presented and reviewed because it is theoretically sound and because it is easily implemented in the public school setting without lengthy inservice training or great expense. In 1975, the American Speech and Hearing Association produced a telecourse, "The Management of Language Disorders: Clinical Applications of Linguistic Concepts," which included a 1-hour videotape and written materials on the DSP. It is doubtful after the lapse of time since publication that field research will be undertaken by the authors.

Overview of the DSP

As mentioned above there are presently 11 programs in the DSP covering a variety of syntactic/lexical structures. Even though each individual program is devoted primarily to teaching a specific structure, the previously learned structures are embedded in successive programs for review and carryover purposes.

Included in the DSP are 16 sets of pictures and 13 story posters that serve as the stimulus materials for the programs. All pictorial material consists of well-done, simple black-and-white line drawings. Other materials could be added by the therapist—particularly real objects for younger children—but it is unlikely that additional materials would be needed for more than a few situations. In addition to the pictures, DSP Therapy Record forms are included in the kit.

In general, each program consists of three phases—Ear Training, Production and Carryover, and Generalization to a Different Context—with a number of steps/ techniques under each phase.

During Phase A—the ear-training phase—of each program, children first learn to recognize the correct form of the construction being taught. They learn to identify instances when the structure is present in phrases and in sentences and then to recognize when errors in usage occur. Finally, they learn to discriminate between correct usage and examples of their incorrect usage. The general methods used in the ear-training phase are the same as those developed for articulation therapy by Powers (1957).

Phase B—Production and Carryover—involves three different techniques. Initially, children are required to repeat a phrase or sentence and then to produce the same correct structure spontaneously through the use of stimulus pictures. Next, a question-and-answer interaction (ascribed to Bereiter & Englemann, 1966) is used. In this technique, one part of a sentence is produced by the therapist first in its correct form and then incorrectly in a question form. The child learns to correct the error in his or her response. Coughran believes that this technique is a key factor in modifying children's ability to manipulate syntactic structures. An example of the technique follows:

Clinician: Do you see *his* bike?
Child: Yes, I see *his* bike.
Clinician: Do you see *him* bike?
Child: No, I see *his* bike.

The third technique in Phase B is carryover training. Once a skill has been established, it is necessary that the skill be carried over into new situations; to accomplish this, the story posters are used, as well as any other materials the therapist may have available. Daily carryover training will be implemented until the child is emitting 90% to 100% correct responses for several days in a row. Thereafter, the therapist will periodically monitor the child's production of previously learned correct responses.

The third phase of training—Generalization to a Different Context (Phase C)—involves eliciting the child's response to a series of questions designed to provide additional structured exposure to the syntactic construction being taught. In addition to these three phases of each program, a number of follow-up activities are suggested for use by teachers and parents to aid in the reinforcement of correct usage in the classroom and at home.

General Procedures for Implementation of the DSP

The general procedures set forth by Coughran include pretesting, program selection, principles of reinforcement, and suggestions for the use of the DSP Therapy Record.

Pretesting. Before implementing the DSP, Coughran suggests that children be screened to determine auditory verbal competency and recommends the use of such standardized tests as the *Test for Auditory Comprehension of Language* (Carrow-Woolfolk, 1985) or the *Peabody Picture Vocabulary Test* (Dunn & Dunn, 1981). After the initial screening is completed, a 50- to 75-utterance linguistic sample should be obtained and analyzed to determine the syntactic errors being produced. Some examples of the types of errors that would make a child eligible for the therapy are given below.

Articles
(a) Omissions
    "I see ball."
(b) Substitutions
    "I see some ball."
(c) Transpositions
    "I see ball a."

Pronouns
(a) Omissions
    "See ball."
(b) Substitutions
    "Me see ball."
(c) Transpositions
    "See ball me."

To obtain baseline information, the therapist should quantify the percentage of correct usage for the total required occurrences.

Program Selection. The 11 programs in the DSP present remedial techniques for the most common syntactic errors of children. After children have been pretested, the therapist should choose the appropriate program at the lowest level to remediate specific errors and then administer the program in sequential order. For example, if the therapist feels that a particular child's most common errors involve the production of verbs, he or she should begin with Program V, making sure that there are no gross errors in Programs I through IV because Coughran states that reinforcement of syntactic usage is cumulative.

Reinforcement. Coughran considers reinforcement as essential to the successful implementation of the DSP. She suggests a variety of reinforcers, both primary and secondary, and recommends that therapists ask parents and teachers for suggestions as to what would be particularly reinforcing for a specific child. Three types of reinforcement are discussed as follows:

1. *Positive.* One reinforcement is given for each correct response. Primary or tangible reinforcers should be faded as soon as possible, being replaced with verbal praise. Ultimately, the child should be able to maintain correct usage with only intermittent reinforcement.

2. *Response-Cost.* In this type of reinforcement, a reward is given for each correct response, but one reward is removed each time the child makes an incorrect response.

3. *Negative.* Initially, a specific number of reinforcing tokens are given to the child, but each time he or she makes an error, one token is removed.

Coughran recommends that the therapist reinforce responses to the specific program that is being administered, but that other errors be ignored unless the errors are specific to a program previously administered. Types of reinforcement and reinforcement schedules should be maintained once they are initiated, but obviously should be altered if the child is not making progress.

The DSP Therapy Record. Provided in the DSP is a therapy record form as shown in Figure 9.3. The form enables the therapist to record the date of the session, the phase and step of the program completed or in progress, the performance level achieved by the child (e.g., 8/10) at the termination of the session, the amount of time spent, the type of reinforcer used and the reinforcement schedule, and any comments.

Steps in Program Administration

Coughran discusses seven general steps in the administration of the DSP. These steps are applicable to all 11 programs and should be followed for each.

Step 1: Preparing for the Session. The therapist locates the appropriate program and step, assembles the required stimulus pictures and story posters as indicated at the beginning of the program, and prepares the needed reinforcers, if any.

Step 2: Preconditioning for Ear Training (Phase A). Throughout the DSP, children are asked to raise their hands in response to the correct stimulus. In the

DEVELOPMENTAL SYNTAX PROGRAM THERAPY RECORD

Student Information

Student's Name _____ Date _____ Sex _____

Birthdate _____ Grade _____ Age _____

School/Clinic _____

Clinician/Teacher _____

session	date	phase	step	criterion	time	reinforcer	comments
1	____	____	____	_____	____	_____	_____
2	____	____	____	_____	____	_____	_____
3	____	____	____	_____	____	_____	_____
4	____	____	____	_____	____	_____	_____
5	____	____	____	_____	____	_____	_____

FIGURE 9.3. DSP therapy record. *Note.* From *Developmental Syntax Program* by L. Coughran and B. Liles, 1979, Allen, TX: DLM/Teaching Resources. Reprinted by permission.

initial stages of therapy, it may be necessary to teach this type of response. In pre-conditioning activities, children may be asked to raise their hands when they hear a bell, an animal sound, and their names. Very young children can be conditioned through the use of concrete objects, teaching them to drop a block in a box whenever they hear the target sound.

Step 3: Preparing for Ear Training (Phase A) and Production and Carryover (Phase B). If necessary, children must be taught to comprehend the concepts "right" and "wrong," because throughout the program they must continually indicate that the therapist's or their own responses are correct or incorrect. The therapist must be sure the child understands these concepts before proceeding. With very young children, or those with limited comprehension, the therapist may use different words, such as, "Does this sound okay, or does it sound funny?" or, "Is this grown-up talk or baby talk?"

Step 4: Presenting the Stimulus Pictures. The therapist is seated facing the child across a small table. The stack of pictures should be placed in front of the child according to any instructions given in the program. The pictures are then removed one by one toward the therapist and placed face down after they have been used.

Step 5: Defining the Criterion Level. Each step of each program has a criterion for mastery or success; for example, 10 correct responses out of 10 consecutive responses. If the child's attention span is too short to obtain 10/10 consecutive responses, the criterion level may be lowered to 5/5 consecutive responses.

Step 6: Reinforcing Correct Responses. The therapist places the number of reinforcers needed to reach the criterion level (10 for 10/10) on the table in front of him or her. In this way, the therapist can keep track of the number of consecutive correct responses made by the child. If the child makes four correct responses and then misses the fifth, all of the reinforcers are removed and the process is begun again. Coughran suggests strongly that no verbal corrections be made, although severely impaired children may need modeling and verbal corrections to reach mastery.

Step 7: Setting Time Limits. Coughran's experience with the DSP indicates that 7½ minutes per session is a good average time limit for most children. Obviously, the therapist must make individual judgments for each child because of differing attention spans and learning curves.

An Example of the DSP: Program III—Possessive Pronouns

Program III covers the four possessive pronouns *his*, *hers*, *its*, and *my*. The therapist first checks to determine whether the child understands the concept of gender by asking him or her to sort the picture cards (Sets 2, 3, and 4) into three stacks representing males, females, and objects. These are the stimulus cards that are used in the bombardment step of the program; a few of the picture cards are shown in Figure 9.4.

Ear Training (Phase A). The program begins with Ear Training (Phase A). There are seven steps as follows.

STEP 1: BOMBARDMENT. The child is instructed to listen but to not respond. While displaying picture cards of males and of singular and plural nouns, the therapist says, "We are going to give these things (picture of nouns) to these people (pictures of males). I want you to listen for 'his,'" and then proceeds to produce phrases such as *his* ball, *his* chair, and so on. No suggestions are given as to how long this procedure is used, but it would appear that only a very short period of time would be devoted to this activity.

STEP 2: RECOGNITION IN PHRASES. Still using picture cards, the therapist says, "Raise your hand when you hear me say 'his.'" The therapist then produces a number of

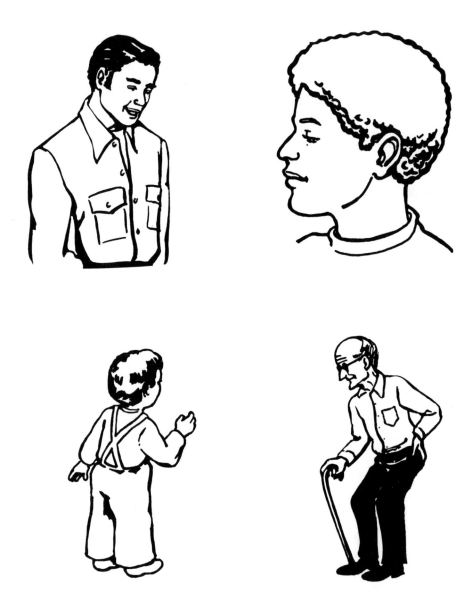

FIGURE 9.4. Picture stimulus cards from Set 4. *Note.* From *Developmental Syntax Program* by L. Coughran and B. Liles, 1979, Allen, TX: DLM/Teaching Resources. Reprinted by permission.

correct and incorrect stimuli, such as *his* ball, *him* shoe, *her* shoe, *my* chair, *his* chair, and so on. After criterion (10/10) has been reached, the step is repeated using only verbal stimuli—no pictures. Step 2 is completed when the child reaches criterion on the second part.

STEP 3: DISCRIMINATION BETWEEN PHRASES. The therapist extends his or her closed hands or two blocks and says, "Choose the hand/block that says 'his.'" While indicating one hand/block, the therapist says, "*his* shoe," and while indicating the other hand/block, says, "baby's bike." The child responds by choosing the hand/block that the therapist associated with the pronoun *his*. A number of such paired phrases are presented until criterion is reached.

STEP 4: RECOGNITION IN SENTENCES. The technique used in this step is identical to that in Step 2 except that sentences, rather than phrases, are produced by the therapist.

STEP 5: DISCRIMINATION BETWEEN SENTENCES. Displaying picture cards, the therapist says sentences such as, "I see *his* bike" and, "I see the girl's bike." The child is asked to choose the hand or block that says *his*. Numbers of sentence pairs are presented in this fashion; in each case, the child is supposed to identify the sentence that contains the pronoun *his*.

STEP 6: RECOGNITION OF ERROR. Cards depicting nouns are placed at the child's right hand, and cards depicting males are placed at the left. The therapist says, "Tell me whether I say it right or wrong," and points to a picture of a male while saying "his" and to a picture of the noun while saying the name of the noun. Stimulus sentences are, "I see him bike," "I see *his* bike," and so on. The child responds by indicating whether the sentence is correct or incorrect.

STEP 7: DISCRIMINATION BETWEEN CHILD'S ERROR AND CORRECT FORM. Asking the child to "Choose the hand/block that says it right," the therapist uses the child's specific error in producing pairs of correct and incorrect statements such as, "I see him bike/ I see *his* bike."

Production and Carryover (Phase B). After the seven steps in Ear Training—Phase A have been successfully completed, the child moves to Production and Carryover—Phase B. The method used by Coughran in Phase B is that developed by Garrett (1969). It should be noted that the Garrett methods were developed to remediate articulation disorders, but as in many areas of remediation, it has been found that a routine developed for one type of disorder has utility when generalized to other types of disorders. There are six steps given by Coughran for Program III under Production and Carryover. They are as follows:

STEP 1: IMITATION OF PHRASES. Designated picture cards are placed in front of the child—one set depicting males and another depicting nouns. The child is asked to imitate the therapist's production of phrases such as "*his* ball," "*his* coat," "*his* chair," and so on.

STEP 2: SPONTANEOUS PRODUCTION OF PHRASES.   This step repeats Step 1 above except that no model is given; the child is instructed to respond as the therapist points to pictures and says, "Now you say it by yourself." It is hoped that the child will respond with the same phrases produced by the therapist in Step 1.

STEP 3: IMITATION OF SENTENCES.   This is a repetition of Step 1; the therapist uses sentences instead of phrases.

STEP 4: SPONTANEOUS PRODUCTION OF SENTENCES.   This step is administered in the same fashion as Step 2 except that the child produces sentences instead of phrases.

STEP 5: ERROR CORRECTION.   The therapist, pointing to picture cards, says to the child, "I'm going to ask you some questions. If I say the sentence right, answer it the same way I say it. If I say the sentence wrong, answer it right." The therapist should vocally emphasize the underlined word.

Therapist: Do you see *his* bike?
Child: Yes, I see *his* bike.
Therapist: Do you see *him* bike?
Child: No, I see *his* bike.
Therapist: Do you see *her* bike?
Child: No, I see *his* bike.

STEP 6: CARRYOVER.   A story poster, such as the one shown in Figure 9.5, is used to elicit target structures from the child on a spontaneous basis. The procedure is repeated over several weeks, using a variety of story posters, to monitor the child's continued correct production of *his*. The therapist displays the poster and says, "Whose are all these things?" The child should respond with, "That is *his* bike," and other appropriate sentences, based on items displayed in the poster.

Generalization to a Different Context (Phase C).   Program III is recycled at this point to teach the child other possessive pronouns such as *her, its,* and *my*. When the additional pronouns have been learned, Generalization to a Different Context—Phase C is begun. This phase is optional and is much less rigorously controlled. The child is instructed as follows:

Therapist: Answer my question in a whole sentence. Do you see *his* bike?
Child: Yes, I see *his* bike.
Therapist: Is it *his*?
Child: Yes, it is *his*.
Therapist: Is it *hers/hims*?
Child: No, it is *his*.

STORY POSTER 4

Copyright © 1974, 1979 by Harry Jersig Speech and Hearing Center

FIGURE 9.5. Story poster. 1979. *Note.* From *Developmental Syntax Program* by L. Coughran and B. Liles, 1979, Allen, TX: DLM/Teaching Resources. Reprinted by permission. Copyright 1974, 1979 by Harry Jersig Speech and Hearing Center.

All of the interaction above should be focused around one picture presentation. Other pictures would be used for *hers*, *its*, and *my*. Coughran notes that the objective possessive for *its* is artificial, and the therapist should not use the question, "Is it *its?*"

Summary

As stated at the beginning of this section, the *Developmental Syntax Program* (Coughran & Liles, 1979) is similar in objectives to the Gray-Ryan language program. The elements of programmed instruction are present in both, although less well defined and delineated in the DSP, and both employ the principles of reinforcement theory. The Gray-Ryan program is probably the better program, but the DSP has distinct advantages. It is easier to implement, and it is economical when compared with the Gray-Ryan. There are no serious observable flaws in the DSP; however, it does need to be field-tested, and it probably should be more comprehensive.

LEE: INTERACTIVE LANGUAGE DEVELOPMENT TEACHING

The assessment and teaching procedures known as *Developmental Sentence Analysis* and *Interactive Language Development Teaching*, respectively, were developed over a 10-year period from about 1965 to 1975 by Laura Lee, her colleagues, and her students at the Northwestern University Speech and Language Clinic. These are clinical procedures designed for teaching grammatical structure to children who have significant language delay or language disorders. Following the presentation of the rationale underlying the approach are descriptions of the *Developmental Sentence Types*, the *Developmental Sentence Scoring*, and *Interactive Language Development Teaching*. The last part of the section deals with an appraisal of the approach.

Rationale for Lee's Approach

As Lee (1974) states, her approach to the evaluation of children's syntactic development and to teaching draws heavily upon the work of psycholinguists such as Roger Brown, Lois Bloom, David McNeill, Paula Menyuk, and others. In addition, she has been influenced by the highly creative and original work of Noam Chomsky. However, in spite of this emphasis on grammar and syntax, Lee has managed to retain her clinician's good common sense. When her teaching approach is examined, it becomes apparent that she is dealing with meaningful language embodying semantic concepts and not just rote drill or imitation of syntactic structures. In fact, she refers to the increasing emphasis in psycholinguistic research on the semantic basis of syntax rather than on the grammatical rules for word order and morphological forms. She draws heavily at this point from Lois Bloom, Roger Brown, and others who are increasingly interested in that part of language known as semantics and pragmatics.

Lee's developmental model is exemplified by the *Developmental Sentence Scoring* chart shown in Figure 9.6. The figure reveals two rather deceptively simple aspects of language development: (a) that with increasing age more and more mature grammatical forms (personal pronouns, main verbs, conjunctions, etc.) appear in the child's language and (b) that as children grow older, they become increasingly competent at combining more types of these grammatical forms into a single sentence. The *Developmental Sentence Scoring* chart as a model of language acquisition has gone through several versions as a result of statistical analyses done primarily by Koenigsknecht and Lee (Lee 1971b). As the chart now stands, it is the model upon which *Developmental Sentence Scoring* and *Interactive Sentence Development Teaching* rest. The reader who is interested in determining where the teaching method "came from" and what direction the approach will take would do well to spend some time inspecting Figure 9.6.

Developmental Sentence Analysis

Developmental Sentence Analysis, Lee's method of assessment, consists of two parts: (a) the *Developmental Sentence Types* (DST) and (b) the *Developmental Sentence Scoring* (DSS). Both of these are useful in classifying and evaluating children's spoken sentences. In many respects they are age-related, or they may be related to the severity of the child's problem. The DST is actually a chart that helps the teacher classify children's spoken word combinations when the word combinations are *incomplete* subject-predicate sentences, that is, sentence fragments. Such word combinations would occur very early in the normal child's language development or would reflect a severe delay in an older child. The DST procedure is appropriate for the normally developing child who is under 3 years of age or for the older child who is not producing subject-predicate sentences. The DSS is a procedure used for the evaluation of grammatical structure in *complete* sentences; therefore, it can be used with older children whose language delay is not severe.

Developmental Sentence Types. The proper use of the DST and the DSS require that the teacher or clinician obtain a rather large recorded sample of the child's spoken language. For the DST the sample should contain at least 100 utterances for analysis. If this many utterances cannot be obtained, the child is probably so severely delayed in language development that the DST is not a suitable procedure to use. In that case, teaching would begin with vocabulary development, teaching the child to name simple objects and actions. However, Lee (1974) states that if a child commands 30 or 40 content words, he or she can begin to combine them. In addition to a corpus of 100 utterances, there are additional requirements, namely, that the sample must be a block of consecutive, not randomly recorded, utterances; all of the utterances must be different, not repetitive; and all unintelligible or echoed (imitated) utterances must be excluded from the corpus.

In analyzing the corpus the teacher or clinician will find some pre-sentence utterances that are actually only stereotypical words and that contribute artificially to

Score	Indefinite Pronouns/Noun Modifiers	Personal Pronouns	Main Verbs	Secondary Verbs	Negatives	Conjunctions	Interrogative Reversals	Wh-Questions
1	it, this, that	1st and 2nd person: I, me, my, mine, you, your(s)	A. Uninflected verb: I see you. B. Copula, is or 's: It's red. C. is + verb + ing: He is coming.		it, this, that + copula or auxiliary is, 's, + not: It's not mine. This is not a dog. That is not moving.		Reversal of copula: Isn't it red? Were they there?	
2		3rd person: he, him, his, she, her, hers	A. -s and -ed: plays, played B. Irregular past: ate, saw C. Copula: am, are, was, were D. Auxiliary am, are, was, were	Five early-developing infinitives: I wanna see (want to see) I'm gonna see (going to see) I gotta see (got to see) Lemme [to] see (let me [to] see) Let's [to] play (let [us to] play)				A. who, what, what + noun: Who am I? What is he eating? What book are you reading? B. where, how many, how much, what ... do, what ... for Where did it go? How much do you want? What is he doing? What is a hammer for?
3	A. no, some, more, all, lot(s), one(s), two (etc.), other(s), another B. something, somebody, someone	A. Plurals: we, us, our(s), they, them, their B. these, those		noncomplementing infinitives: I stopped to play. I'm afraid to look. It's hard to do that.		and		
4	nothing, nobody, none, no one		A. can, will, may + verb: may go B. Obligatory do + verb: don't go C. Emphatic do + verb: I do see.	Participle, present or past: I see a boy running. I found the toy broken.	can't, don't		Reversal of auxiliary be: Is he coming? Isn't he coming? Was he going? Wasn't he going?	

FIGURE 9.6. Developmental Sentence Scoring chart. *Note.* From *Interactive Language Development* (pp. 4–5) by L. Lee, R. Koenigsknecht, and S. T. Mulhern, 1975, Evanston, IL: Northwestern University Press. Reprinted by permission.

FIGURE 9.6. (Continued)

Score	Indefinite Pronouns Noun Modifiers	Personal Pronouns	Main Verbs	Secondary Verbs	Negatives	Conjunctions	Interrogative Reversals	Wh-Questions
5		Reflexives: myself, yourself, himself, herself, itself, themselves		A. Early infinitival complements with differing subjects in kernels: I want you *to come.* Let him *[to] see.* B. Later infinitival complements: I had *to go.* I told him *to go.* I tried *to go.* He ought *to go.* C. Obligatory deletions: Make it *[to] go.* I'd better *[to] go.* D. Infinitive with *Wh*-word: I know what *to get.* I know how *to do it.*	isn't, won't	A. but B. so, and so, so that C. or, if		when, how, how + adjective *When shall I come?* *How do you do it?* *How big is it?*
6		A. *Wh*-pronouns: who, which, whose, whom, what, that, how many, how much I know *who* came. That's *what* I said. B. *Wh*-word + infinitive. I know *what to* do. I know *who(m)* to take.	A. could, would, should, might + verb: *might come, could be* B. Obligatory does, did + verb C. Emphatic does, did + verb			because	A. Obligatory do, does, did: *Do they run? Does it bite? Didn't it hurt?* B. Reversal of modal: *Can you play? Won't it hurt? Shall I sit down?* C. Tag question: It's fun, *isn't it?* It isn't fun, *is it?*	

FIGURE 9.6. *(Continued)*

Score	Indefinite Pronouns Noun Modifiers	Personal Pronouns	Main Verbs	Secondary Verbs	Negatives	Conjunctions	Interrogative Reversals	Wh-Questions
7	A. any, anything, any-body, anyone B. every, everything, everybody, everyone C. both, few, many, each, several, most, least, much, next, first, last, second (etc.)	(his) own, one, oneself, whichever, whoever, whatever Take *whatever* you like.	A. Passive with *get,* any tense Passive with *be,* any tense B. must, shall + verb: *must come* have ÷ verb + en: I've eaten. C. have ÷ verb + en: I've eaten. D. have got: I've got it.	Passive infinitival complement: With *get:* I have *to get dressed.* I don't want *to get hurt.* With *be:* I want *to be pulled.* It's going *to be locked.*	All other negatives: A. Uncontracted negatives: I *cannot* go. He has *not* gone. B. Pronoun-auxiliary or pronoun-copula contraction: I'm *not* coming. He's *not* here. C. Auxiliary-negative or copula-negative contraction: He *wasn't* going. He *hasn't* been seen. It *couldn't* be mine. They *aren't* big.			why, what if, how come, how about + gerund *Why* are you crying? *What if* I won't do it? *How come* he is crying? *How about* coming with me?
8			A. have been + verb + ing had been + verb + ing B. modal + have + verb + en: *may have eaten* C. modal + be + verb + ing: *could be playing* D. Other auxiliary combinations: *should have been sleeping*	Gerund: *Swinging* is fun. I like *fishing.* He started *laughing.*		A. where, when, how, while, whether (or not), till, until, unless, since, before, after, for, as, as + adjective + as, as if, like, that, than I know *where* you are. Don't come *till* I call. B. Obligatory deletions: I run faster *than* you [run]. I'm *as* big *as* a man [is big]. It looks *like* a dog [looks]. C. Elliptical deletions (score 0): That's *why* [I took it]. I know *how* [I can do it]. D. *Wh*-words + infinitive: I know *how* to do it. I know *where* to go.	A. Reversal of aux-iliary have: *Has* he seen you? B. Reversal with two or three auxiliaries: *Has* he been eating? *Couldn't* he have waited? *Could* he have been crying? *Wouldn't* he have been going?	whose, which, which + noun *Whose* car is that? *Which* book do you want?

the length of the utterances. When the child produces these forms, they are counted only once so that it will not appear that the child has a greater command of the language than is really the case. The forms that are to be counted only once are interjections, nouns that are used in direct address, question markers ("Over here, *okay?*"), imperative interjections ("*Look*, here a doggie"), and sentence tags ("Over here, *I think.*").

A number of rules are given by Lee for separating sentences for both DST and DSS evaluation. These will not be covered here because of the detail that is necessary for completing this rather tedious task; however, the interested reader may secure more information from Lee's (1966, 1971a, 1971b) writing on the subject. A few rules will be given under the discussion of the DSS.

Once the language sample has been reduced to its best form, according to the rules provided by Lee, the teacher or clinician compares the child's utterances with the chart shown in Figure 9.7. Inspection of that chart will reveal that it encompasses two dimensions: the horizontal and vertical classifications.

The horizontal classification reflects to some extent the increasing length of utterances in the child's early language development. There is no separation of three-word constructions from six-word constructions, but it is apparent that the longer an utterance is, the more complex it is likely to be. The earlier version of the DST (Lee, 1966) included complete sentences, but since the DSS was developed to assess complete sentences, the chart shown in Figure 9.7 was revised by Lee (1974) to include only pre-sentences.

The vertical classification in the DST chart is used to determine whether a child is developing a variety of sentence types in his or her grammatical rules. Many language delayed children will develop only one stereotyped sentence form, and the DST can be used to determine whether this is the case. The vertical columns of the DST chart show 10 different kinds of sentences that have different semantic contents or messages. The titles of these 10 categories are printed in capital letters in Figure 9.7. Five of these sentence types are appropriate for analyzing single-word utterances (see the first tier in Figure 9.7), and five are used for analyzing two-word combinations and longer constructions (see the second and third tiers). Since the five vertical columns are considered as continuous throughout all horizontal rows, only the five classifications in the first tier are described below.

1. *The noun phrase.* The first column of the DST chart shows the development of the noun phrase, single nouns at the one-word level, and much more highly elaborated noun phrases at the construction level. The noun phrase, as the reader will note from the chart, never becomes a sentence; it must be incorporated into other sentence types.

2. *The designative sentence.* The second column shows the development of the sentence type that is merely the naming, identification, or pointing out of a subject of conversation. It is apparent that many of these designative constructions begin with words such as *here, there, that,* and so on, and may be said to designate a topic of conversation.

	NOUN			DESIGNATOR
SINGLE WORDS	car truck cookie	Daddy Mommy girl	kitty-cat Santa Claus hot dog	here, there this, that it

	Basic sentence elaborations:
	  Plural: *books, cars, men*
				Basic sentence elaborations:
				  Plural: *those, these*

	Basic sentence modifications:
	  Pronoun: *me, something, nobody*
	  Question: *book? car? truck (right?)*
				Basic sentence modifications:
				  Question: *this? that? here? there?*

	NOUN ELABORATION	DESIGNATIVE ELABORATION

TWO-WORD COMBINATIONS	Noun phrase
	  Article: *a car, the truck*
	  Possessive: *Daddy car, Billy truck*
	  Quantifier: *more car, other truck, two boy*
	  Adjective: *big car, dirty truck, red shoe*
	  Attributive: *baby bear, police car*
	
	Basic sentence elaborations:
	  Plural: *the cars, more trucks*
	  Additive: *car truck, Mommy Daddy*
	  Adverb: *now car, truck too, car again*
	  Subject-object: *doggie bone, Daddy ball*
	  Subject-locative: *car garage, Mommy window*
	
	Basic sentence modifications:
	  Pronoun: *this one, my truck, her cookie*
	  Negative: *not car, not truck, not this*
	  Question: *a car? another truck (OK?)*
	  Wh-question: *what car? which one?*
	  Conjunction: *and car, and truck, and this*
		Designator + noun
		  here car, there truck, this car, that truck, it car, it truck
		
		Basic sentence elaborations:
		  Plural: *these cars, there trucks*
		  Adverb: (*that again* = noun + adverb)
		    (*there now, here again* = fragments)
		
		Basic sentence modifications:
		  Pronoun: *here something, there one*
		  Negative: (*not this* = noun + negative) (*not here,
		    not there* = fragments)
		  Question: *that truck? this car (right?)*
		  Wh-question: *what this? what that?*
		  Conjunction: (*and this* = noun + conj.)
		    (*and here, and there* = fragments)

CONSTRUCTIONS	Noun phrase
	  my big car, some more truck, a red box
	Noun phrase + prepositional phrase
	  the car in front, the spot on the floor
	Quantifier + prepositional phrase
	  all of them, some of the other cars
	
	Basic sentence elaborations:
	  Plural: *some other cars*
	  Adverb: *now the car, the other truck too*
	  Additive: *the car the truck*
	  Subject-object: *the doggie another bone*
	  Subject-locative: *the car the garage*
	
	Basic sentence modifications:
	  Pronoun: *his other truck, all of mine*
	  Negative: *not the car, not that one*
	  Question: *the other car? the boy too (huh?)*
	  Wh-question: *what big car? which other one? how much
	    milk? how many cookies? how about that one?
	    what about me?*
	  Conjunction: *and the car, car and truck*
		Designator + noun phrase
		  here another car, there a truck
		  this a red car, that my truck
		  it a big car, it my truck
		
		Basic sentence elaborations:
		  Plural: *here some cars, these big cars*
		  Adverb: *there car too, here car now*
		  Additive: *there Mommy Daddy*
		
		Basic sentence modifications:
		  Pronoun: *that somebody car, here his car*
		  Negative: *that not car, this not a truck*
		  Question: *that a car? this a car (right?)*
		  Wh-question: *who that boy? what that one?*
		  Conjunction: *here a car and truck*

FIGURE 9.7. Developmental Sentence Types chart. *Note.* From *Developmental Sentence Analysis* (pp. 86–87) by L. Lee, 1974, Evanston, IL: Northwestern University Press. Reprinted by permission.

FIGURE 9.7. *(Continued)*

DESCRIPTIVE ITEM	VERB	VOCABULARY ITEM

big, pretty, broken, fixed
one, two, more
one, off, up
Basic sentence elaborations: None
Basic sentence modifications:
  Pronoun: *my, his*
  Question: *red? big (huh?)*
	sleep, eat, walk, fall
	(*look, lookit, wait, stop* = imperative
	  sentence)
	Basic sentence elaborations:
	  Verb elaboration: *going, fell*
	Basic sentence modifications:
	  Negative: *can't, won't*
	  (*don't* = imperative sentence)
	  Question: *see? eat (OK?)*
		yes, no, OK, sh, hey, hi
		bye-bye, night-night, oh-oh
		Basic sentence elaborations:
		  Adverb: *again, now, too*
		Basic sentence modifications
		  Question: *huh? right? OK?*
		  Wh-question: *what? who? where?*
		    when? how? why?
		  Conjunction: *because*

PREDICTIVE ELABORATION	VERBAL ELABORATION	FRAGMENTS

Noun + descriptive item
  car broken, truck dirty, light off,
  TV on, car there, truck here
 	
Basic sentence elaborations:
  Plural: *cars here, lights on*
 	
Basic sentence modifications:
  Pronoun: *that pretty, it big, something*
    here, another on
  Question: *car broken? it gone (right?)*
  Wh-question: *where car? what here?*
    who there?
	Verb + object: *hit ball*
	Verb + locative: *sit chair*
	Verb + particle: *fall down*
	(Noun + verb = sentence: *baby sleep,*
	  that go, it fall)
	
	Basic sentence elaborations:
	  Verb elaboration: *saw car*
	  Plural: *eat cookies, see cars*
	  Adverb: *eat now, fall too*
	
	Basic sentence modifications:
	  Pronoun: *see it, find one*
	  Negative: *not fall, can't go*
	  Question: *see it? go home?*
	  Wh-question: *where go? what take?*
	    what find? (who go? what come? =
	    sentence)
	  Conjunction: *and sleeping*
	  Infinitive: *wanna go, gonna go*
		Basic sentence elaborations:
		  Prepositional phrase: *for Daddy, in car*
		  Plural: *on chairs, in cars*
		  Adverb: *too big, all gone, up now,*
		    here again, right here, over there
		
		Basic sentence modifications:
		  Pronoun: *to you, in it*
		  Negative: *not big, not here*
		  Question: *in here? all gone (huh?)*
		  Conjunction: *and big, but dirty,*
		    and here

Noun phrase + descriptive item: *the car*
  broken, a truck dirty, this light off, the
  TV on, other car there, a truck here,
  car in garage, hat on head, Spot a good
  dog, Tom bad boy
 	
Basic sentence elaborations:
  Plural: *all cars broken*
  Adverb: *light off now, car here too,*
    truck too dirty
  Double locator: *car over there*
 	
Basic sentence modifications:
  Pronoun: *he bad boy, it off now*
  Negative: *this not broken*
  Question: *it off now? car over*
    there (huh?)
  Wh-question: *where that one? who in*
    car? what color car? what in here?
  Conjunction: *car and truck here*
	Verb + object: *eat the cookie*
	Verb + locative: *put the table*
	Verb + particle + noun: *take off hat,*
	  turn on light
	(Noun phrase + verb = sentence: *the car*
	  go, a boy eat)
	
	Basic sentence elaborations:
	  Verb elaboration: *goes in barn*
	  Adverb: *see car now, go in too*
	
	Basic sentence modifications:
	  Pronoun: *want it now*
	  Negative: *not fall down*
	  Question: *see that one? eat more*
	    cookies (OK?)
	  Wh-question: *where put car? what*
	    take out? what find here?
	    what doing to car?
	  Conjunction: *and find car*
	  Infinitive: *wanna see it, gonna go*
	    home, gotta find it
		Words in series:
		  1, 2, 3, 4, etc.
		  dog, cow, pig, etc.
		
		Basic sentence elaborations:
		  Prepositional phrase: *in the car,*
		    for the boy
		  Plural: *on the chairs*
		  Adverb: *in car too, back over there*
		
		Basic sentence modifications:
		  Pronoun: *on my head*
		  Negative: *not in it*
		  Question: *in here too? in the*
		    car (right?)
		  Conjunction: *and for me*

3. *The predicative sentence.* The third column of the DST chart shows the predicative sentence, a sentence that names the topic and then "predicates" something about it. As Lee (1974) notes, there is something anomalous in talking about a predicative sentence, since all sentences must have a subject and a predicate. The term *predicative sentence* was used in the earlier version of the DST and is perpetuated.

4. *Subject-verb sentences.* In the fourth column of the chart the development of the subject-verb sentence is traced. In this dimension the verb is always a lexical word (content word), not a linking verb or copula, such as *is*.

5. *Fragments.* The last column of the chart is used for the classification of utterances that contain neither a subject nor a verb but are only appendages to the three main sentence types, the designative, the predicative, and the subject-verb. Prepositional phrases appear to be the most frequent fragments as shown in the chart.

Unlike the DSS, which is discussed later, no overall score is provided for the DST. However, there are data available from a normative study of the DST that can be used by the teacher or clinician to determine a child's level of performance. Information regarding mean number of utterances is available at each DST level for children 2-0 through 2-11 years as well as for the percentage of utterances in each of the five sentence types for the normative group. These are very rough norms based on the responses of 40 normally developing children divided into 3-month age groups from 2-0 through 2-11 years old. Figure 9.8 is reproduced from Lee (1974) to provide the reader with a graphic representation of a DST chart for a child who is developing language normally.

The reader should note that Lee advises clinicians to avoid rigidity in their use of the DST; the method is intended to be used as a clinical instrument. And she encourages users to modify, enlarge, or simplify the procedures. She is not overly concerned about the lack of normative data, nor does she appear to feel that there is a great necessity for providing such data. Instead, she emphasizes the need for a systematic clinical method for assessing a child's development of grammatical forms in spontaneous speech and feels that the DST provides just such a vehicle.

Developmental Sentence Scoring. There have been three versions of *Developmental Sentence Scoring* (DSS), but only the last (Lee, 1974) will be discussed here. The current DSS chart, which has already been introduced in this discussion (see Figure 9.6), is sometimes known as the Reweighted DSS, referring to the changes made in scoring as a result of statistical analyses of the first two versions. The content of DSS will be reviewed in this section, but no attempt will be made to recapitulate the scoring of the instrument, as this is a very detailed and time-consuming task. The interested reader may refer to Lee (1974).

The DSS is a developmental sequence of grammatical forms arranged in eight categories: indefinite pronouns, personal pronouns, main verbs, secondary verbs, negatives, conjunctions, interrogatives, and *Wh*-questions. The developmental order shown in Figure 9.6 progresses in each category in a vertical fashion from earliest to later development. The developmental order was originally hypothesized as a result

DST Chart of C. F., Age 2-5, a Normally Developing Child

Name: C. F.
(a normally developing child)

CA: 2-5

Single words: 16
Two-word combinations: 22
Constructions: 27
Sentences: 35

	Noun	Designator	Descriptive Item	Verb	Vocabulary Items
SINGLE WORDS	chair Sam table Mom doggie Teddy soup Susie		down	 fell see?	no yeah oh oh-oh OK

	Noun Phrase	Designative	Predicative	Verbal	Fragments
TWO-WORD COMBINATIONS	the girl broken chair a chair broke(n) man a boy dirty doggie a towel toys airplane and baby	here chair	Daddy up radio on Sambo noisy shoes off	eat dinner draw boy find toys eating dinner no fit wanna read	 in there in pool

	Noun Phrase	Designative	Predicative	Verbal	Fragments
CONSTRUCTIONS	a teeny doggie Mommy Teddy Bear now my couch now my chair the dog pool the little one a bike and car	here baby table	a table in there the baby there the radio on good the dinner (rev.) and Daddy away too and girl away too where that one?	find a chair sit on the floor here fall boom-boom out bed eat dinner morning get up in morning have for dinner morning drinking the water found a chair goes in it put baby in there and go night-night go bed and go to sleep	 all broken more

FIGURE 9.8. DST chart of a normally developing child. *Note.* From *Developmental Sentence Analysis* (p. 121) by L. Lee, 1974, Evanston, IL: Northwestern University Press. Reprinted by permission.

of published research in the field and observation of children in the Northwestern University Speech and Language Clinic. The order was later confirmed through statistical analyses by Koenigsknecht and Lee (Lee, 1971b). The scores assigned to various grammatic structures were arrived at finally through the use of the reciprocal averages technique.

To obtain a language sample for the DSS, the examiner can show the child toys or pictures and record the child's verbal responses or telling of a familiar story. The main idea in getting a language sample is to keep the child interested and talking. If during the sample-taking session the clinician discovers that the child is producing incomplete sentences more than 50% of the time, the DSS should not be continued. Instead, the DST could be undertaken.

The corpus for the DSS must contain 50 complete sentences. A sentence is judged to be complete if it contains a noun and a verb in the subject-predicate combination. A sentence need not be grammatically correct to be included in the corpus; it need only meet the subject-predicate criterion. Many examples of questionable sentences that are to be judged as acceptable are given in Lee's (1974) book—for example, two-word subject-predicate sentences, two-word *Wh*-questions, and others.

As with the *Developmental Sentence Types*, the corpus for the DSS must be a block of consecutive utterances. All of the sentences must be different from each other. If more than 50 sentences are produced by the child, only the last 50 are used for scoring purposes.

As was stated previously, only complete sentences are suitable for DSS; therefore, sentences must be separated for DSS analysis into complete and incomplete categories. Many of the same rules for separating sentences for the DST also apply to the DSS. Interjections and nouns in direct address are not counted for DSS, so they need not be separated out. Question markers and imperative interjections such as *look* and *lookit* and sentence tags such as *you know* or *I guess* are separated and given sentence status.

The most important decisions about sentence separations for the DSS revolve around the conjunction *and*. Many children fall into the habit of starting every sentence with *and* or of speaking in run-on sentences connected by *and*. Lee gives a number of rules for separating sentences involving *and* and other conjunctions and for separating pre-sentences from sentences. Figure 9.9 presents a hypothetical corpus to illustrate DSS scoring.

Combination of DST Classification and DSS Evaluation.   Whenever the clinician combines the DST and DSS procedures, making a thorough examination of both pre-sentences and sentences in the child's language sample, the technique is called *Developmental Sentence Analysis*, a term used to indicate that both procedures have been done. *Developmental Sentence Analysis* would appear to be useful only for those children who are in a transition stage between using pre-sentences and producing a fair number of complete sentences. It would not be appropriate for the child who is producing no sentences, in which case only the DST would be used. The technique would not be useful for the child who is producing very little conversation that cannot be scored by the DSS procedure. In that case, use of the DST would be a waste of both the clinician's and the child's time.

For the child who is in transition between pre-sentences and complete sentences, *Developmental Sentence Analysis* will give the clinician a greater amount of information about the child's developmental level in language acquisition. Lee (1974) notes that the DSS score should be considered as a tentative estimate if the child's language sample consists of fewer than 50 complete sentences; however, the information gained from the DSS procedure will aid the clinician in informally assessing the state of sentence development at which the child is performing.

Hypothetical Corpus of 30 Sentences Illustrating Developmental Sentence Scoring

Name: Recording date:
              Birth date:

	Indef. Pro.	Pers. Pro.	Main. Verb	Sec. Verb	Neg.	Conj.	Inter. Rev.	Wh-Q	Sent. Point	Total
1. Boy eat.			—						0	0
2. Boy eat cookie.			—						0	0
3. The boy is eating a cookie.			1						1	2
4. The boys are eating cookies.			2						1	3
5. They ate them.		3,3	2						1	9
6. They didn't eat them.		3,3	6		7				1	20
7. Didn't they eat them?		3,3	6		7		6		1	26
8. Why didn't they eat them?		3,3	6		7		6	7	1	33
9. Why didn't they?		3	inc.		7		6	7	1	24
10. All the cookies were eaten.	3		7						1	11
11. I want to eat some cookies.	3	1	1	2					1	8
12. I want to find some cookies.	3	1,2	1	5					1	13
13. I tried to find some cookies.	3	1	2	5					1	12
14. Could you find them?		1,3	6				6		1	17
15. You couldn't find them, could you?		1,3	6		7		6		1	24
16. Nobody knows where to find them.	4	3	2	5		8			1	23
17. Who knows where she keeps them?		2,3	2,2			8		2	1	20
18. I looked but I couldn't find them.		1,1,3	2,6		7	5			1	26
19. I like eating cookies.		1	1	8					1	11
20. Nobody told me that I shouldn't eat them.	4	1,1,3	2,6		7	8			1	33
21. I only ate a few.	7	1	2						1	11
22. Somebody else must have eaten all the rest.	3,3		8						1	15
23. Let's eat some more.	3,3		1	2					1	10
24. Mommy said, "Don't eat those cookies."		3	2,4		4				1	14
25. That isn't what she said.	1	6,2	1,2		5				1	18
26. Him can't have some.	—	—	4		4				0	8
27. What you eating?		1	—				—	2	0	3
28. Her don't gots any.	7	—	—		—				0	7
29. Mommy find out.			—						0	0
30. You want to get spanked?		1	—	7			—		0	8

CA:
DSS: 13.63

FIGURE 9.9. Developmental sentence scoring of a hypothetical corpus. *Note.* From *Developmental Sentence Analysis* (p. 164) by L. Lee, 1974, Evanston, IL: Northwestern University Press. Reprinted by permission.

Interactive Language Development Teaching

Interactive Language Development Teaching (ILDT) was developed concurrently with *Developmental Sentence Analysis* at the Northwestern University Speech and Language Clinic by Lee and her colleagues. It is a teaching technique based on the developmental model of grammar described in *Developmental Sentence Analysis* (Lee, 1974). The method consists of 62 sample lessons designed for use with small groups of three to six children in a 50-minute session. Modifications of all parts of the technique can be made from group size to session length. However, Lee, Koenigsknecht, and Mulhern (1975) recommend a regular schedule of activities for each session.

If a 50-minute session is the standard, it should begin with a 3- to 5-minute period devoted to settling the children down and preparing them to listen. A calendar activity has been found to be useful for this period. The story presentation follows, and it takes about 30 to 35 minutes. Each lesson revolves around a different story, which the clinician may have written and which serves as the vehicle for the presentation and teaching of language structures. After about 30 minutes of concentrated work, a break is recommended. For a session shorter than 50 minutes the period could end at this point. If the session is to last 50 minutes, the remainder of the time can be used to put away the materials, relax, get a drink, and then engage in a group activity. The children are encouraged to verbalize during the group activity, and as each lesson is recorded and transcribed, the clinician can determine whether the structures being taught in the lesson are being spontaneously produced during the group activity.

The teaching technique was developed for children aged 3 to 6 who are of normal intellectual ability and who have normal sensitivity. Lee et al. (1975) feel that modifications of the method can be used with almost any type of child who is demonstrating language delay regardless of handicapping condition. It should be noted that one of the constraints placed on the use of the DST would necessarily have to apply also to the use of the ILDT; namely, that any child who is nonverbal or who is producing only a limited number of single words would not be a candidate for this approach.

Readers who are particularly interested in the approach to assessment and teaching described in this section should note that two very good 16mm films are available from the Northwestern University Film Library. The first, *Developmental Sentence Scoring: A Demonstration Film*, shows the taking of a language sample and the analysis technique. The companion is *Developmental Language Teaching: A Demonstration Film*, which shows the administration of a language lesson to various groups of children, using the interactive approach. Both films were produced by Koenigsknecht, Mulhern, and Lee.

The Stories. Sixty-two sample stories are given by Lee et al. (1975), and a part of one lesson will be later given as an example. The authors do not feel that the sample stories are to be used as a workbook; they are intended only as examples. Teachers and clinicians are encouraged to write their own stories, provided that certain criteria are met.

The goals of the lessons should be derived from the *Developmental Sentence Analysis* of the child's spontaneous language sample, and any one lesson should not contain more than four or five of the possible structures that would be developmentally appropriate for the child. The following are guidelines for writing new stories.

1. The story topic should be one that is within the child's experience. New information and unfamiliar ideas should be avoided when the goal of the lesson is language development; struggling with content and grammar at the same time is too great a burden.

2. Sufficient narrative should be provided to keep the child's attention. For young, severely delayed children the factors of poor attention and poor receptive skills must be kept in mind, and stories for them should be shorter than those written for older, more advanced children. However, the stories should be long enough to provide a story line; drill is not used in this approach.

3. Adequate buildup of semantic content for the target structures should be provided. One of the major goals in ILDT is the presentation of language in a meaningful context rather than as a series of imitative drills. To achieve this goal, careful attention must be given to the content of the story so that enough information is provided before asking the child a question about the story. A number of examples are presented by Lee et al. (1975) to demonstrate this criterion.

4. New structures are presented as receptive tasks before they are to be elicited as targets. This guideline is particularly useful for the composition of stories for Level II lessons.

5. Frequent review of previously introduced structures should be provided to stabilize the use of the structures.

6. There should be clarification of the concepts underlying the contentive vocabulary; that is, attention should be given to lexical nouns, verbs, and adjectives included in the stories.

7. An effort should be made to include questions that elicit creative thinking. Again, this guideline is more appropriate for Level II lessons. The example given refers to a story about a funny car with a funny name. After the story is read to the children, they are asked, "What is the name of the car?" There is no target response, and it is hoped that the children will supply a variety of "funny" names.

Presenting the Stories. The format for each story includes a column for the teacher's narrative, followed by a question, and a column for the target response that the teacher is trying to elicit. Below is shown an example of this format taken from Level I, Lesson 17: "Going to the Airport" (Lee et al., 1975, p. 136).

Narrative	Target Response	Sentence Point	DSS Total
Here is Bobby.			
Look, he's in bed.			
He is sleeping. See?			
Bobby is in bed.	2 1		
Where is he?	He is in bed.	1	4

The columns for Sentence Point and DSS Total refer to the scoring value of the target response. "He is in bed." Two points are given for the personal pronoun *he*; one point for the connecting word (the copula) *is*; one point for the complete sentence; and the total is 4 points. The child would receive only the number of points appropriate for his or her approximation of the target response, any value from 0 to 4.

All children in the group hear the same story, but the clinician treats each child individually when the child responds to questions. The children will progress at different rates, and the clinician must select and modify the questions asked of each child.

A small room with a circular or V-shaped table, chairs, and a flannel board are the only resources needed to present the lessons. The prepared stories are read to the children in as natural a conversational pattern as possible. As the story is read aloud to the children, flannel board cutouts, toys, puppets, and other objects are presented for illustrative purposes.

The focal point of the lesson is the eliciting of the target responses, and the children are called upon in random order to answer the stimulus question. The same question is often asked of more than one child. If the child is not able to produce the target response as given in the lesson, the clinician engages in an interchange with the child, trying to elicit the appropriate response. Some of the interchange techniques given by Lee et al. (1975) are as follows.

1. Imitation of a complete model

2. Imitation of a reduced model

3. Expansion requests, as, "Tell me more," "Tell me the whole thing."

4. Repetition requests, as, "What did you say?"

5. Repetition of error, using an interrogative inflection, as, "He *go* to the store?"

6. Self-correction request, as, "Is that answer right?"

7. Rephrased question

All of these techniques, which are described more fully with examples in the cited text, are aimed at bringing the child closer to the desired response.

Evaluation of Pupil Progress. Children are evaluated in several ways to determine whether they are making progress. Their performance during the teaching sessions is one aspect to be evaluated, but it is important to assess the children in other situations. The standard evaluation method is the DSS procedure, which Lee et al. (1975) report can be given at intervals of 4 months. The DSS provides an assessment of the children's progress using nonteaching materials in conversation. In Figure 9.10 the norms for DSS (Reweighted) are shown. By plotting a child's successive scores on the chart a continuous record of progress can be displayed. Such a record will demonstrate progress and provide evidence of the effectiveness of the teaching.

The ILDT Lessons. There are 62 sample lessons provided by Lee et al. (1975), showing the types of themes and the language-structure combinations included. As was stated before, these lessons are not to be used as a workbook. Some stories can be omitted for some children; more stories will have to be written for other children.

The lessons are divided into two levels. The first level is focused on the acquisition of basic sentence structure and those early grammatical forms that are used by children who are developing language at a normal rate and in a typical fashion. The second level of lessons is devoted to the later developing grammatical forms and to the combination of several grammatical structures within a single sentence.

The main purpose of the lessons is to teach grammatical structure, but incorporated within the lessons are underlying concepts and vocabulary. To delineate the latter, the items are listed at the beginning of each lesson, along with suggested materials. The best way to describe a lesson to the reader is simply to present a part of one. Figure 9.11 shows the first part of Level I: Lesson 4, "Going to the Store." As the reader can see, the lesson is prefaced with preliminary information for the clinician: the concepts, vocabulary, and materials for the lesson, the elicited structures that receive primary and secondary emphasis in the lesson, and the DSS value of the elicited structures.

Below the preliminary information is the story with the narrative (e.g., "This is Bobby. He's a little boy. He is four years old."), a question ("How old is he?"), the target response, the sentence point, and the DSS value of the target response. The first target response in this lesson is "He is four years old." A child who produces the exact response receives 2 points for the personal pronoun *he*; 1 point for the copula; 3 points for the noun modifier *four*; and 1 point for producing a complete sentence. If the child does not respond with the target response, the clinician initiates one or more of the interchange techniques described above. With the final response, the child receives whatever score the DSS would indicate. There is, of course, the possibility that the child could produce a response better than the target and receive a higher score than that indicated on the lesson. If this occurred frequently, one would suspect that the lesson is too easy for the child and that he or she should be working at a higher level. The opposite of this is also true; a child who consistently misses the target is probably trying to work at too high a level. The clinician must constantly be aware of these level factors and should try to group the children so that as a group they can work together on one lesson with only minimal variations in their performance. There will always be differences in the levels at which children are performing even though they are in the same group. Because

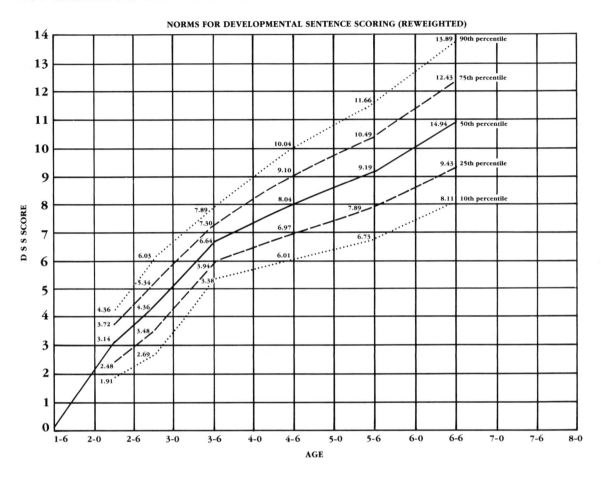

FIGURE 9.10. Norms for the DSS. *Note.* From *Interactive Language Development* (p. 25) by L. Lee, R. Koenigsknecht, and S. T. Mulhern, 1975, Evanston, IL: Northwestern University Press. Reprinted by permission.

of this the clinician must be ready to adapt the questioning and the target response as needed.

To give the reader some indication of the higher levels of language structure that are included in the sample lessons, an excerpt of Level II: Lesson 25, "Picking up Uncle Bill at the Airport," is shown in Figure 9.12. The narrative preceding the question in this lesson is much longer than that in the preceding example, and the total DSS value of the target response is much higher.

LEVEL I: LESSON 4

CONCEPTS	ELICITED STRUCTURES	DSS VALUE
helping, buying, traffic safety	Primary emphasis	
	indefinite pronoun—*some*	3
	personal pronoun—*he*	2
VOCABULARY	main verb—copular *is*	1
milk, store, money,	—uninflected	1
street, corner, across,	—*is . . . -ing*	1
stoplight, red/green, stop/go		
	Secondary emphasis	
FLANNEL-BOARD	indefinite pronoun—*it, this*	1
MATERIALS	personal pronoun—*I*	1
paper figures: Mommy,	conjunction—*and*	3
Timmy, Bobby, storekeeper		
paper cutouts:		
refrigerator, dollar		
bill, street, stoplight,		
car, store front, milk		
carton, paper sack		

GOING TO THE STORE

NARRATIVE	TARGET RESPONSE	SENTENCE POINT	DSS TOTAL
This is Bobby.			
He's a little boy.			
He is four years old.	2 1 3	1	7
How old is he?	He is four years old.		
This boy is Timmy.			
He's not a little boy.			
He is Bobby's big brother.	2 1	1	4
Who is Timmy?	He is Bobby's big brother.		
Here is their mommy.			
Mommy is in the kitchen.			
She's making dinner.			
Oh, oh! Something is wrong!	3	—	
Mommy's looking for some milk.	For some milk.		3
	2 1 3		
What's Mommy looking for?	She's looking for some milk.	1	7

FIGURE 9.11. Beginning of Level I: Lesson 4. *Note.* From *Interactive Language Development* (p. 70) by L. Lee, R. Koenigsknecht, and S. T. Mulhern, 1975, Evanston, IL: Northwestern University Press. Reprinted by permission.

NARRATIVE	TARGET RESPONSE	SENTENCE POINT	DSS TOTAL
Let's eat if you are hungry.			
Let's eat at the restaurant if you are hungry.	1 2	1	12
What does Daddy say?	Let's eat at the restaurant		
	5 1 2		
	if you are hungry.		
Uncle Bill says:			
Good. I am hungry.			
Now they are at the restaurant.			
They are sitting at a table.			
Karen says:			
I want a hamburger so I can eat it.			
I want a hamburger.			
I want a hamburger so I can eat it.	1 1 5	1	14
What does Karen say?	I want a hamburger so		
	1 4 1		
	I can eat it.		
Mommy says:			
I want a hot dog so I can eat it.			
Daddy says:			
I want a hot dog so I can eat it.			
Uncle Bill says:			
I want a hot dog so I can eat it.			
They all want hot dogs so they can eat them.			
Why do they want hot dogs?	3 3 1 5	1	23
	They all want hot dogs so		
	3 4 3		
	they can eat them.		
Everybody is eating lunch.			
They are hungry, so they are eating lunch.			
They are all eating lunch.			
They are hungry, so they are eating lunch.	3 2 5 3	1	16
Why are they eating lunch?	They are hungry, so they		
	2		
	are eating lunch.		
Karen says:			
I like the airport.			
I like eating here.			
I like eating at the airport.	1 1 8	1	11
What does Karen say?	I like eating at the airport.		

FIGURE 9.12. Excerpt from Level II: Lesson 25. *Note.* From *Interactive Language Development* (p. 363) by L. Lee, R. Koenigsknecht, and S. T. Mulhern, 1975, Evanston, IL: Northwestern University Press. Reprinted by permission.

Appraisal of the ILDT Approach

Little research related to the interactive approach to teaching language delayed children has been undertaken. Among the few existing studies is that of Lee et al. (1975), who report the results of a 3-year investigation of their developmental model of grammar (as exemplified by the DST and DSS) and attempt to determine the effects of ILDT. A few investigations are reported in the literature on the assessment procedures, but apparently there are no particularly definitive studies on either *Developmental Sentence Analysis* or the associated teaching approach.

Because the research on the ILDT is so sparse, the study reported by Lee et al. (1975) will be reviewed in this section. The interactive teaching procedures were used by 75 clinicians with 25 children over a 3-year period at the Northwestern University Speech and Language Clinic. The sample group had a mean age of 4 years and 4 months at the beginning of the study. They were of normal intellectual ability. Their hearing was normal, and they had no general neuromuscular problems. All had severe expressive language problems. As measured by the DSS, the mean delay in grammatical development was 21 months.

Twenty-three pretest and posttest measures were administered to the group. For all measures the means of the differences between pretreatment and posttreatment scores were analyzed for statistical significance. It should be noted that not all 25 children started and ended the program at the same time. Rather, the mean duration for treatment was 8 months.

With the exception of the Visual Sequential Memory subtest of the *Illinois Test of Psycholinguistic Abilities*, on which the children scored in the normal range on both pretests and posttests, the comparisons between the other 22 pretreatment and posttreatment measures revealed that the group made significant gains on all. Yet it is somewhat difficult to credit the teaching technique with the gains, because the children were growing older. Without a control group it is almost impossible to accept uncritically the results of this study. The most charitable thing that can be said of the results is that the treatment program in no way seemed to hinder the children's progress and may have facilitated their language development. This approach is indeed promising, and this promise deserves a complete experimental evaluation. It is hoped that the research needed to establish conclusively the value of Lee's techniques will be undertaken soon.

FITZGERALD: STRUCTURED LINGUISTIC APPROACH

No subject is more dependent upon structure and sequence than the English language. The meaningfulness of any sentence is related directly to the order or sequence of words within it. The system devised by Edith Fitzgerald, modified by Pugh (1947), and exemplified by the commercial program the *Fokes Sentence Builder*, is a highly structured, predominantly visual method for teaching the sequence of English to children with severe auditory and language problems. Although originally developed for use with deaf and hard-of-hearing children, the method is recommended for those children with adequate hearing who might profit from such an approach. The procedures can facilitate the mastery of the sequence of the language in children with language delay. Therefore, the criterion for selection of this system is: Does the child exhibit inadequate syntax in oral or written language? The Fitzgerald-Pugh system can be used in conjunction with any of the other methods discussed, although it is probably more closely related to the language development and linguistic systems than to the others.

A concern with the educational needs of deaf children were expressed in Fitzgerald's early work (1912, 1918). She concluded that their need for language was great and that its development had to be emphasized in their training. Since she felt that insufficient practice was the basis for most language problems, the use of meaningful drill was suggested as an essential means for teaching language arts. Therefore, practice and more practice were necessary to perfect language. Expectedly, drill became an important aspect of the Fitzgerald method of teaching "straight language." Although drills are emphasized in her method, one should not think that Fitzgerald advocated an unnatural or mechanical approach to language acquisition, for she strongly cautioned teachers against the development of a merely memorized language. Drill is a part of the method, but mechanical learning is to be avoided.

The culmination of Fitzgerald's work is the book *Straight Language for the Deaf*, which was published originally in 1926 and which subsequently has undergone several revisions and a dozen printings. The steady, continuous demand for her book demonstrates the staying power of Fitzgerald's contribution; the book, now 56 years old, still is widely used. *Straight Language for the Deaf* is actually an instructional manual dealing with three general areas: (a) nongrammatical aspects of language and expressions; (b) grammatical aspects of language such as the use of various parts of speech (pronouns, verbs, etc.); and (c) a presentation of the Fitzgerald Key. Our discussion includes Fitzgerald's ideas regarding nongrammatical aspects of language and a description of the Fitzgerald Key. We feel that the grammatical aspects of language are better covered in a discussion of the Key rather than in a separate section.

A list of guiding principles for teachers can be extracted from Fitzgerald's work and should be reviewed before proceeding with discussion of her system. It is noteworthy that many of the points she stresses are applicable to education in general. The list provides the reader with an understanding of her basic attitude toward instruction and is indicative of the spirit with which the Key is to be used. The guiding principles follow.

1. The teacher should be familiar with the work that comes just before and immediately after the particular grade level she or he expects to teach.

2. The teacher must not be so eager for the child to speak that the essential background for speech is ignored. Such ignorance leads to and encourages parrot-talk rather than language based on understanding.

3. The child's mental picture must be clear or the language used may become a jumble of memorized words that are meaningless to the child.

4. When a child attempts to express himself or herself orally, the teacher must be sure that the child has acquired the language to fit the mental concept.

5. The child must be given the chance to absorb knowledge. When he or she exhibits interest, present the child with materials and knowledge to satisfy his or her need.

6. The child must realize the connection between language use and language understanding. Children are never expected to use words they do not understand.

7. When possible, provide the child with the opportunity to discover and correct his or her own mistakes.

8. Have the child attempt what can be expected. Progress at the child's speed and level.

9. Do not abbreviate. The child cannot be expected to spell words correctly unless they are written out.

10. Insist upon neatness, paragraphing, correct punctuation, respect for margins, and sequence of both time and thought.

11. Be definite in your approach.

12. Learning should be meaningful; all possible mechanical repetition is to be strictly avoided.

Teaching Nongrammatical Aspects of Language

Probably the most interesting and pertinent aspects of nongrammatical language training discussed by Fitzgerald relate to suggestions for teaching children about the calendar, weather, commands, and expressions. Calendar work begins early in the program as a nonlanguage activity and is continued throughout the child's schooling. As children gain facility in language, their concepts regarding the calendar and weather become progressively more complex. At the same time, Fitzgerald warns against practicing calendar work so frequently that it becomes monotonous. Teaching the calendar aids in developing concepts of (a) morning and afternoon; (b) time sequence (dials are set for recess, dismissal, etc.); (c) adverbs, for example, "all day," "again," "several times," and "for a little while," so that they are recognized as "How Often" or "How Long" rather than "When"; and (d) acquaintance with the names of the days and months.

A sample calendar should be drawn on a board (chalkboard, tag board, or bulletin board) that is large enough to include appropriate pictures to designate the month. Fitzgerald is explicit in describing the calendar and where it should be placed in the classroom:

It should be remembered that the day grows old from left to right; therefore, the calendar should be on a south board, and for any changes in the weather during the day, the calendar square (3" × 3") should be divided vertically rather than horizontally. (Fitzgerald, 1966, p. 7)

By placing the calendar on a south board, the east-west progression of the sun during the day is implicitly stated, and at a later time in the program the direction names (east-west-north-south) are taught. Dividing the day with a vertical line to set off morning from afternoon emphasizes the left-right progression of the calendar, and no other marking off or crossing out of the days is permitted.

Another chart headed "Yesterday Was" and "Today Is" is used to emphasize the sequence of time. The teacher is cautioned not to point to a row of figures on the calendar and call it a week. If the teacher does point, the pupil may always think of a week as invariably starting with Sunday. "Tomorrow" is later added; then follows "Last" Sunday afternoon, "Next" Saturday morning, and so on.

Oral reports on the weather begin as soon as possible, but care should be taken in using the terms *warm* and *cold* until concrete facts are available to substantiate these comparative adjectives. The thermometer is a good source for concrete data; therefore, it should be introduced as soon as is feasible. When the child is ready, an exercise called My Day is used in a manner similar to the calendar work and correlates recall, connected language, and written and oral expression.

Regarding the teaching of commands and expressions, Fitzgerald stresses several basic points. When commands are first taught, the child should not have to pretend to carry out the teacher's directions. If commanded, "Comb your hair," the child should be provided with a comb. Only after the child learns the meaning of some actual commands is he or she requested to "make believe." The phrase "I played" is used to express pretense. Fitzgerald notes that when a command calls for two or more things to be done in sequence, one must watch for any tendency to carry out the first part and then return to the starting place before taking the next step.

To teach expressions such as "Thank you," and "You are welcome," the phrases are printed on charts placed in the room so that they can be referred to when the occasion arises. The cards bearing the expressions are moved from time to time so that the child will not associate them with position rather than the printed form. "Good-bye" and "Good morning" are initially placed near the door. Activities pertaining to commands and expressions as well as calendar work are continued through intermediate and upper grades.

The Fitzgerald Key

This section provides readers with a limited knowledge of the Key, some understanding of its use, and an idea for whom the system might be appropriate. It is important to note again that no attempt should be made to implement any method presented in this book without first consulting the original sources. And in the case of the Key, a visit to a local educational facility for the deaf, where the key can be seen in use, would be beneficial.

A highly structured visual system of language instruction for deaf children is presented in *Straight Language for the Deaf* (Fitzgerald, 1966). Fitzgerald maintains that deaf children need a visual guide to follow in structuring sentences because they frequently are unable to hear their errors in construction. The deaf child uses the visual cues to compensate for inadequate hearing sense. Fitzgerald's system encourages compensation through headings that describe the content and provide the sequence necessary for the development of verbal language. These ordered headings comprise a sentence pattern, and the pattern of headings is the Fitzgerald Key. This method probably is suitable for hearing children who also experience difficulty in monitoring their verbalization and who necessarily would profit from the visual reinforcement inherent in the Key.

The Key is written in yellow washable paint across the top of the most prominent blackboard in the classroom. At first only two headings are used (Who:, What:); later, additional headings are introduced (Whose:, How many:, What kind of:, Color:, Whom:, What:). The Key becomes increasingly more complex as the child develops proficiency and as the child's needs dictate. But the Key is used for all grades and for all subjects. The key words are arranged in the order that corresponds to their use in the English language. Fitzgerald's rationale for this approach follows:

> Understanding precedes use. We draw a line between the understanding of language and the use of language, but we insist that visualization and understanding of language go hand in hand as the child proceeds to acquire language. We have proven to our satisfaction that classification of words and thoughts (under key-words and the few symbols we use) and the understanding that follows hasten, to say the least, the child's grasp of and spontaneous use of English. (Fitzgerald, 1966, p. 4)

The Key is supplemented by several symbols used to identify some parts of speech. The symbols are:

With regard to the objections occasionally raised against the use of symbols, Fitzgerald defends her use of them in the following passage:

> We have found that the children sense the difference between these parts of speech more easily when their symbols are used than when verb, adjective, etc., are introduced in conjunction with the key-words, which key-words present definite *thoughts*. The teacher always uses the names of the parts of speech when referring to the symbols. (Fitzgerald, 1966, p. 21)

The average width for each group of headings painted on the blackboard is 16 inches. Usually, they are made wider for younger children and are reduced gradually toward the average. The depth of each group of headings is always 6 inches, which permits four lines 1½ inches apart and allows space to accommodate the four key words in the fifth space. (A cursory look at the headings in Figure 9.13 indicates that the fifth space is occupied by How far:, How often:, How long:, and How much:. The 6-inch depth is required so that they will all fit within the allotted space.) Symbols that represent parts of speech are placed below the space set aside for the key words. The Why: of the fifth space is dropped 1½ inches below the lowest of the other key words, or 7½ inches from the top of the key. Eventually, the Key is transferred from the blackboard to paper when the child is ready.

Fitzgerald offers a number of considerations regarding the use of the Key:

1. The Key helps in phrasing.

2. Suggested command: Say it with the Key.

3. See that children point to the correct key-word.

Who: Whose: What:	What: ( ) Whom:	Whom: Whose: What:	Where:	From: For: With: How:	How far: How often: How long: How much: Why:	When:
The Americans took		the fort		from the British.		
Early took		the ball	from the baby.			
Jack picked up		the pencils		for Miss Blocker.		
I bought		some oranges		for Miss Tinnin.		
I bought		some material for a blouse.				
Melvin went			to the store		for some bread.	
Doyle went			to the doctor's	with Miss Kramer		yesterday.
Mr. Saylor went			to Bastrop	in Mr. Brace's car.		
We saw		Mr. Saylor	in Mr. Brace's car.			
The boys walked					ten miles Saturday afternoon.	
We go			to rhythm		twice a week.	
I love		Mother			very much.	
Hayden likes		apple pie			better than ice cream.	
Miss Creath went			to the beauty parlor			Saturday
					to get a shampoo and	
Myra was crying					a set.	this morning
					because she was lonesome.	

FIGURE 9.13. Example of use of the Fitzgerald Key at the primary level.

4. See that they point to the side to show modifiers. In "Weldon has blue eyes," the pointer is placed to the left of What for *blue* and then directly under What for *eyes*.

5. Do not write connected language in the Key when it is being worked out. Follow the Key as a pattern.

6. Do not help the child with what he wants to say and then have him place the statement in the Key. Let him work it out for himself.

7. Have the child face the class as he points to the Key.

8. Add to the Key as fast as the children can visualize the thoughts back of the key-words—but no faster. (Fitzgerald, 1966, p. 62)

In *Straight Language*, Fitzgerald immediately classifies new vocabulary under certain headings. Two of the earliest headings apply to nouns; Who: for humans; and What: for nouns applying to animals and to inanimate objects. For young children, Fitzgerald tells teachers to hold up familiar objects or pictures, say their names aloud in order to capitalize on any auditory skills that may be present, and place them under the headings Who: or What:. An example exercise is provided below:

Who:	What:

Place these words (or objects or pictures) under the proper heading.

top	ball	mother
boy	car	dog
baby	spoon	cat

After the children have grasped this concept, new categories are added to the Key, such as How many:, What color:, Where:, and Whose:. This collection of headings is referred to as the Primary Key. An example is provided below:

Whose:	Who: What:		How many: What:	What kind of:	Color:	Whom: What:
		=				
	I	see	a	big	red	ball
	Tommy	made	a		green	car

The child can master the use of the Primary Key without knowing how to speak. As children progress in silent reading, they will begin gradually to sense the meanings behind the key words.

Soon after words under these headings are introduced, rules for their order in noun phrases are presented. The first rules are:

How many:	What:	
How many:	What color:	What:

Thus the sequence, or order, of the language is acquired. An example of this rule might be:

How many:	What:	
five	dogs	
How many:	What color:	What:
five	brown	dogs

Later, as the children master the Whose: category heading, they learn that the possessive nouns and the possessive pronouns replace the How many: category, rather than precede it. The rule is:

	Whose:	What:	
not			
	Whose:	How many:	What:

Example:

	Whose:	What:	
	Tom's	coat	
not			
	Whose:	How many:	What:
	Tom's	one	coat

As their vocabulary grows, the children learn "qualifying adjectives," which include words such as *large, pretty, new, beautiful, old,* and *interesting.* These words are referred to by the teacher as adjectives. Since there is no appropriate key word, they are classified under the adjective symbol ⊓ . A new rule for noun-phrase order is now required.

How many: ⊓ : What color: What:

Using the symbol = for verbs, the teacher can build sentences like the following under these headings:

Who: What:	=	How many:	What color:		Whom: What:	Where:
I	see	three	big	blue	balls.	
Bob	ran					to school.
John	bought	a	little		car.	

Additional examples at the primary level are included in the completed primary worksheet presented as Figure 9.13. The Key becomes increasingly complex as the pupil progresses; traditional terms such as subject, indirect object, and direct object are added to the Key. Advanced headings and demonstration of their use are offered in Figure 9.14.

Fitzgerald used the Key until it was no longer needed by the child. The method was not used in isolation but rather was incorporated into the teaching of other academic subjects. The following outline gives the sequence used in teaching vocabulary to children.

A. Words are classified.
    1. Who: is introduced—using real people, then pictures and finally just words.
    2. What: is introduced in the same manner as Who:.
    3. How many:
        a. Teach the symbols and number words of cardinal numbers.
        b. The words *a, the, some, many* are taught.

Subject: Verb:	Indirect: Object:	Direct Object:	Where:	From: For: With: How:	How far: How often: How long: How much: Why:	When:
Betty wrote		what she did in the sewing room yesterday.	on the chalkboard			just now
Miss Compton asked	me	why I did not go to Dallas Easter.				this morning
Frank stayed			in the hospital		until the doctor came.	yesterday
Elbert was	too sleepy to study.					last night
Elbert was	so sleepy that he could not study.					last night
Dan ran				so fast that I could not keep up.		

FIGURE 9.14. Example of use of the Fitzgerald Key at an advanced level.

    4. What color:
      a. Colors are learned.
      b. In describing, How many: always precedes What color:, for example, Three red balls.
    5. Verbs, adjectives, pronouns, connectives, and infinitives are classified.
      a. Drill verbs—*see, saw, have, has*, etc.
      b. Nondrill verbs.
      c. After mastery of a few nouns, verbs should be added to form phrases and sentences.
    6. Who: and Whose:. Possessives of nouns are taught before possessives of pronouns.
    7. Where:, When:, How long:, How often:, Why:, and so on. These are introduced as the children are ready for them.
  B. Further classification of words or phrases.
    1. Unclassified lists are written horizontally.
    2. Classified lists are written vertically.
  C. Obtain original lists from children. Omit How:.
  D. Classify words and phrases according to key words and symbols (written).
    1. Always maintain the order of the Key.
    2. Teach the articles *a, an, the*.
  E. Plurals of What: and Who:
    1. Those with the simple *s* ending (*balls, apples*).
    2. Those that don't change (*deer, sheep*).
    3. Unusual plural forms (*men, women*).
    4. Plurals that require changes in letters (*babies, knives*).
  F. Analyze words in context (and phrases), for example, John opened the *box* (What:). John walked *into the box* (Where:).
  G. Classify all new vocabulary on the blackboard using the Key.
  H. Require that second- and third-grade students keep a vocabulary book as outlined by the teacher.

A Linguistic Analysis of Fitzgerald's Noun Phrase

A method testing the adequacy of Fitzgerald's plan for teaching language would be to evaluate the structures taught in the Key in terms of the concepts of descriptive linguistics. Fitzgerald's work appeared too early to have been influenced greatly by modern transformational linguistic theories. She derived much of her method for presenting grammatical facts from her own observation of normal language and of the difficulties encountered in the language of deaf people. It should be noted that such direct observation of normal language is the method generally advocated by linguists themselves, so it is not surprising that Fitzgerald's work parallels the work of some linguists rather closely.

Although many aspects of Fitzgerald's work can be evaluated in terms of structural linguistic concepts, only one is analyzed in this section—the elements of the noun phrase. It should be noted, however, that transformational-generative grammar, as explained by Chomsky (1957), offers promise of being able to alter the Fitzgerald system so that it would be more flexible and so that it would make English seem more logical to individuals who have trouble understanding the intricacies of this complex language. Since transformational-generative grammars still need refining by the linguists, our analysis is oriented toward structural grammar, which has been more thoroughly studied.

A description of the order of modifiers in noun phrases, which bears striking similarity to Fitzgerald's presentation, is that of the structural linguist Hill (1958). The following is his sample noun phrase illustrating the order of noun modifiers in English:

VI	V	IV	III	II	I	N
All	the	ten	fine	old	stone	houses

As one may observe, Hill's Class I consists of the modifiers that occur nearest to the noun being modified. Class II includes modifiers twice removed from the noun, and so on. Figure 9.15 demonstrates the relationship between the sequences given by Fitzgerald and Hill. The linearity of the relationship indicates close, although not perfect, agreement.

A further illustration of this relationship is provided by Figure 9.16. Hill's sample phrase was amended to read, "All the ten fine grey stone houses," and his order of modification was plotted against the sequential order of Fitzgerald's categories. The resultant matrix once again reveals the high degree of similarity.

The authors feel the analysis indicates that Fitzgerald's system of rules for the order of modifiers in noun phrases bears up well under evaluation on a structural linguistic basis. The linguistic system does allow for some sentences that Fitzgerald's system could not produce, but it also allows some nongrammatical sentences that Fitzgerald would not permit.

The Fokes Sentence Builder Program

The *Fokes Sentence Builder* (Fokes, 1976) is decribed by its author as a comprehensive language program for young children that is to be used as a supplement to regularly scheduled teaching in language development. It is based on the Fitzgerald Key but has been slightly modified to account for the developmental sequence that has been observed in children's language acquisition.

The Sentence Builder is a picture key using a visual display. Fokes believes that the visual display plus the teacher-presented auditory stimulus plus the manipulative activity involved in arranging the pictures are mutually reinforcing. The program is discussed in this section under three subheadings: (a) prerequisite skills, (b) description of materials, and (c) the lessons.

Hill's Classes of Noun Modifiers

	VI	Vb	Va	IV	III	II	I
Whose:	"all" "both" "half"		articles				
		Possessive nouns	Possessive pronouns				
How Many:				Numerals and numerical phrases			
⌐ Qualifying Adjectives					"True" adjectives: *beautiful*	Size: Shape	Noun adjectives: *wood, wooden*
What Color:						Colors	

(left axis label: Fitzgerald's Sequence of Categories)

FIGURE 9.15. A comparison of the order of noun modifiers according to Fitzgerald and Hill.

Hill's Classes of Noun Modifiers

	VI	V	IV	III	II	I	N
How Many:	All		the	ten			
⌐					fine		stone
What Color:						grey	
What:							houses

(left axis label: Fitzgerald's Categories)

FIGURE 9.16. An example of the Fitzgerald Key—structural-linguistic relationship.

Prerequisite Skills. Five prerequisites are given by Fokes before the program is to be implemented. First, the child should be able to combine at least two or three words into a meaningful utterance. Thus the program is inappropriate for nonverbal children.

Second, the child must be able to interact with the teacher or therapist. A child who is unable to relate to the person or to the materials of the program because of emotional or behavioral disorders may find the program frustrating and ineffective.

The third prerequisite is related to the child's attention span. Since the lessons are designed for 20- to 30-minute periods, the child must be able to attend for a considerable period of time. It is not necessary to require the child to sit still and work for the entire 30 minutes, but he or she should be able to work for at least two 15-minute periods with a very short break between them.

Fourth, the child should be able to attend to and respond to visual stimuli, that is, the pictured items. Fifth, the child should have a knowledge of the concepts represented by the pictures used in the program. The Sentence Builder teaches sentence structure, *not concepts*; and if the program is to be effective the child must already know the concepts. Fokes attributes the child's failure to profit from the program as being the result of not meeting the above prerequisites. She cautions the user to examine each youngster carefully to determine whether he or she has the prerequisite skills before the program is begun.

Description of the Materials. The materials in the Sentence Builder kit consist of 200 picture cards divided into five boxes labeled WHO, WHAT, IS DOING, WHICH, and WHERE; a Sentence Line on which sentences are to be constructed by placing the picture cards in sequence; 45 Sentence Markers; 15 Sentence Inserts; one question-mark card; and a teacher's guide.

The five boxes are color-coded, each representing a different grammatical category of words. The pictures in the boxes are black-and-white, realistic drawings. WHO cards show people of different ages and occupations, WHAT cards are pictures of common animals and objects, IS DOING cards are of the human figure involved in an action, WHICH cards illustrate adjectives, but not color or quantity, and the WHERE cards have an X or an arrow to indicate a particular position or location.

The Sentence Markers are used to identify the type of sentence that is being constructed; only one marker is allowed per sentence. Therefore, only one type of sentence may be constructed at a time. The Sentence Markers are abbreviations that represent different sentence types, for example, H is the marker for a declarative sentence with the main verb *to have* in the present tense. The same sentence in the past tense would be represented by the marker P_H. Q is the sentence marker for a question, N for a negative sentence, and so on.

The Sentence Inserts are triangular cards with words printed on them. These are used in constructing sentences that contain, for the most part, troublesome auxiliary verbs such as *can, will, could, did,* and so on, which cannot be pictured.

The question-mark card is provided to denote the question construction; it is not a punctuation mark.

The Lessons. The teacher's guide presents complete instructions for conducting 38 lessons: 19 on building declarative sentences, 13 on building questions, and 6 on building negative sentences. The instructions tell the teacher or therapist which Sentence Markers, Inserts, and boxes of pictures are needed. For example, in Building Declarative Sentences—Lesson One: Sentences with *ing* Verbs (WHO + IS DOING + WHAT), the teacher is instructed to use Sentence Marker 1, designating the declarative sentence in the present tense with *ing* verbs; the *is* and *the* Inserts; and the boxes for WHO, IS DOING, and WHAT cards. One card is selected from each box by either the teacher or the child and is placed on the sentence line as shown in Figure 9.17. The teacher says the sentence while gliding a hand from left to right across the pictures. The child is asked to say the sentence, also moving a hand across the sentence line. After some practice with the basic sentence, one picture at a time is changed, altering the sentence to read as shown in Figure 9.17. The same procedure is followed with each successive sentence: The teacher says the sentence first, then the child says it.

In many of the lessons there are suggestions for modifications that can be made for children who are severely or moderately delayed in language development or for children with little or no delay. In general, the lessons are clearly presented and are easily completed by the teacher. There are difficulties with the 45 Sentence Markers; it would take quite a bit of time to learn all of the abbreviations.

The children are not expected to learn the sentence types nor the abbreviations associated with them; they are for the teacher to learn. A complete record should be kept for each child, noting the sentence types and the grammatical elements that are incorrectly used. The Sentence Markers become a handy device for recording the errors of a child who is having difficulty constructing N_p sentences—that is, negative sentences with *ed* verbs—or F_2 sentences—that is, declarative sentences with the future tense of *to be* as the main verb.

1	WHO	IS DOING	WHAT

The boy	is eating	the banana.
The man	is eating	the banana.
The man	is eating	soup.
The baby	is eating	soup.
The baby	is spilling	soup.

FIGURE 9.17. Representation of Lesson One, expanded lesson. *Note.* From *Fokes Sentence Builder* (p. 17) by J. Fokes, 1976, Allen, TX: DLM/Teaching Resources. Reprinted by permission.

The *Fokes Sentence Builder* is a systematic, logical application of the Fitzgerald Key in packaged form that was long overdue when it was published. It seems to be appealing to teachers and clinicians, who use it without difficulty and, having once mastered the system, can easily extend it well beyond the materials provided in the kit.

GRAY AND RYAN: PROGRAMMED CONDITIONING FOR LANGUAGE

Programmed Conditioning for Language (PCL) is a system and set of materials developed at the Behavioral Sciences Institute in Monterey, California, by a number of staff members. Predominant among the developers of PCL are Burl Gray and Bruce Ryan. Gray, after receiving his PhD in speech pathology from Southern Illinois University, began a career in research, concentrating on the application of behavior modification procedures to problems in human communication. He has published numerous works in the areas of language, reading, stuttering, hearing, voice, and articulation. Gray is presently general manager of Aeroterra, Inc., in Los Angeles. Ryan received his PhD in speech pathology from the University of Pittsburgh and has worked in the public schools as an elementary teacher and as a speech pathologist. After teaching at the University of Oregon and Eastern Oregon College, he went to the Behavioral Sciences Institute, where he was a research associate in speech pathology. Dr. Ryan is currently on the faculty of the Speech and Hearing Department at California State University at Long Beach. His work and publications are devoted primarily to the use of programmed procedures in speech and language training.

Language Content of PCL

Programmed Conditioning for Language is a procedure that has been developed to teach oral language to nonverbal children. The emphasis is on oral language responses. Although we may refer to the four components of language—the phonologic, the morphologic, the syntactic, and the semantic—PCL focuses on one element: grammar. However, because grammar is composed of words with meaning (the semantic component) and because those words are composed of sounds (the phonologic component), it is impossible to teach grammar in isolation. By focusing on grammar, PCL attempts to teach all components of spoken language simultaneously. Grammar in itself is interpreted as a basic set of rules that permits the speaker to generate novel sentences. The speaker need not verbalize these rules, but the language performance will reflect knowledge of them.

The recent work of numerous linguists and psycholinguists was taken by Gray and his associates as their starting point for determining the content of the programs making up PCL. The task set for them was twofold: (a) the selection of those grammatical forms that are most important in the development of language and (b) the sequencing of the forms for teaching purposes.

Selection of Forms. In selecting the forms for inclusion in PCL, Gray and Ryan state that ideally the process should make provision for inclusion of (a) a cross section of the different forms that are necessary for speaking the language, (b) those frequently occurring forms that are common in the language, and (c) the basic forms that the speaker can use as building blocks for learning additional, sometimes more difficult, forms. The work of the linguists was used to select a cross section of necessary forms. Table 9.1 represents the results of the cross section and includes many of the basic classes of grammatical structure.

To determine the frequency of occurrence of the selected forms, Gray and Ryan turned to the work of Berger that contained samples of spoken conversational English. It must be noted, however, that although the forms used in the PCL all have high frequency of occurrence, there is little information on specific grammatical forms, and much research is needed in this area.

The selection of appropriate basic forms was the most difficult task facing the developers of PCL, since all of the fundamental forms have not yet been identified. Gray and Ryan compromised by selecting forms that can be used to formulate quite complex sentences and that lead to other forms of sentences. The results of the selection process are shown in Figure 9.18.

TABLE 9.1. List of Grammatical Forms with Examples Used in the Programs

Form	Example
1 Nouns	Boy
2 Indefinite pronouns	That
3 Personal pronouns	I
4 Main verbs	Is
5 Secondary verbs	Want to *see*
6 Negatives	Not
7 Conjunctions	And
8 Interrogative reversals	Is it red?
9 *Wh*-questions	What is it?
10 Prepositions	In
11 Adjectives	Blue
12 Possessives	His
13 Adverbs	Fast

Note. From *A Language Program for the Nonlanguage Child* (p. 72) by B. B. Gray and B. Ryan, 1973, Champaign, IL: Research Press. Reprinted by permission.

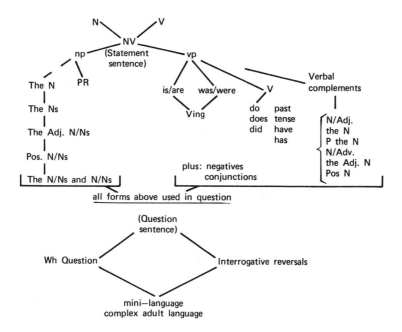

FIGURE 9.18. A tree diagram listing the various language forms in the language programs and their possible combinations. *Note.* From *A Language Program for the Nonlanguage Child* (p. 73) by B. B. Gray and B. Ryan, 1973, Champaign, IL: Research Press. Reprinted by permission.

One may observe from this illustration that if a noun (N) is taught and then a verb (V) is taught, we have a nucleus sentence (NV) when the two are combined. These forms, the noun and the verb, can be expanded into noun phrases (NP) and verb phrases (VP), respectively. They can be used in the question form as well as the declarative. When other forms (the adjectives, pronouns, adverbs, and negatives) are added into the basic NP-VP paradigm, many complex sentences can be generated. The authors state that "these forms appear to be enough to give the child a mini-language and the accompanying rules for more complex forms" (Gray & Ryan, 1973, p. 73).

Sequence of Forms. According to Gray and Ryan, it is important to teach the forms in an appropriate sequence. What is appropriate is not really easy to determine. As was mentioned earlier in this chapter, it would appear that the development sequence, to the extent that it is known, would be the most appropriate sequence. This is the choice of most teachers and therapists. Gray and Ryan have elected, however, to sequence the forms according to their teaching value. They state, "When a child has learned form 1, the next logical form is one which combines form 1 with another form, form 2, and so on until we have 'chained' together all the forms which seem to fit with one another" (1973, p. 73). This is a sound programming technique, although the result may sometimes violate the so-called "natural" order. It is an arbitrary program technology approach to developing a teaching sequence, the results of which can be seen in Table 9.2, which gives the entire curriculum of PCL.

The first program, as shown in Table 9.2, is "Identification of Nouns," the only program in which the child is required to make a nonverbal response. In Program 2, "Naming Nouns," the child is taught a core vocabulary of nouns that he or she can speak. The third program, "In/On," illustrates the programming strategy of PCL rather well. Prepositions do not occur in normal development immediately after a child has learned to say single nouns, but they are important to PCL because they will be needed for Program 4, "Is," and all the way throughout. At later stages, after

---

TABLE 9.2. Language Curriculum

A *Core*
   1 Identification of nouns
   2 Naming nouns
   3 In/on
   4 Is
   5 Is verbing
   6 Is interrogative
   7 What is
   8 He/she/it
   9 I am
  10 Singular noun present tense
  11 Plural nouns present tense
  12 Cumulative plural/singular present tense
  13 The

B *Secondary*
  14 Plural nouns are
  15 Are interrogative
  16 What are
  17 You/they/we
  18 Cumulative pronouns
  19 Cumulative is/are/am
  20 Cumulative is/are/am interrogative

  21 Cumulative what is/are/am
  22 Cumulative noun/pronoun/verb/verbing
  23 Singular and plural past tense (t and d)

C *Optional*
  24 Was/were
  25 Was/were interrogative
  26 What was/were
  27 Does/do
  28 Did
  29 Do/does/did interrogative
  30 What is/are doing
  31 What do/does/did
  32 Negatives not
  33 Conjunction and
  34 Infinitive to
  35 Future tense to
  36 Future tense will
  37 Perfect tense has/have
  38 Adjectives
  39 Possessives
  40 This/that/a
  41 Articulation

Note. From *A Language Program for the Nonlanguage Child* (p. 27) by B. B. Gray and B. Ryan, 1973, Champaign, IL: Research Press. Reprinted by permission.

Program 8, the teacher can run the "In/On" program again, substituting other preposi-tions such as *by* and *to*. Program 4, "Is," teaches the first sentences in the program. The chid responds, for example, with sentences such as, "The dog is black" and, "The boy is on the floor." In Program 5, "Is Verbing," both "verbing" and adverbs are intro-duced, and the child learns models such as, "The boy is running" and, "The dog is running fast." "Is Interrogative" and "What Is" are taught in Programs 6 and 7, respec-tively. Here the question forms of "Is" and "Is Verbing" are introduced following the presentation of "Is" and "Is Verbing" in what the authors state is not a natural sequence but is a logical programming sequence. Program 8 teaches the pronouns "He/She/It" to go with "Is" and "Is Verbing" and to be combined with noun/adjective, noun/adverb, and preposition/noun complements. "I am" is taught in Program 9.

Program 10, "Singular Noun, Present Tense," is devoted to "S Verbs" or subject plus verb, such as, "The boy runs, the dog barks." Only regular verbs are included because the frequency of occurrence of the irregular verbs is quite low except for some forms like *do, does, did*. Program 11, "Plural Nouns, Present Tense," is placed after "Singular Nouns, Present Tense" simply because research on PCL indicated that children performed better following such a sequence; no other logic was employed. Program 12, "Cumulative Plural/Singular Present Tense," is the first of the cumulative programs in which new forms are presented together. Only after the child has reached Program 13, "The," is the article *the* presented. Gray and Ryan reported that in earlier versions of PCL an attempt had been made to introduce *the* near the beginning of the program, but it appeared that it presented too much of a "grammatic/syntactic overload." By the time Program 13 is reached, the child has a fairly good command of language and is able to master *the* without difficulty. In fact, some children will already be using it, and the presentation of Program 13 simply reinforces their acquisition of the article. The remainder of the programs require mastery of *the*.

The first 13 programs represent the "core" curriculum, one or more of which most nonverbal children need. The authors state that the children complete the remaining programs quite rapidly once the first 13 have been taught. Some, in fact, do not even need the other programs that follow.

The next series of programs, 14 through 23, constitutes the secondary group. The auxiliary verb *are* is introduced, first with plural nouns and then in two ques-tion forms, in Programs 14 through 16. The question forms used are the "are inter-rogative," as in "Are the balls blue?" and the "what are," as in "What are the balls?" Program 17 introduces "You/They/We." The next five programs, 18 through 22, do not introduce any new forms; instead, they are cumulative programs for review of previously taught forms in conjunction with one another. The last of the secondary group of programs is 23, which teaches the basic past tense forms, both singular and plural. Gray and Ryan state that Programs 14 through 17 and 23 are particularly useful out of this secondary group.

The third group is termed optional and is composed of programs that teach "Was/Were" (24 through 26), "Do/Does/Did" (27 through 31), "Negatives" (32), "Con-junction and" (33), "Infinitive to" (34), "Future tense to" (35), "Future tense will" (36),

"Perfect tense has/have" (37), "Adjectives" (38), "Possessives" (39), "This/That/A" (40), and last, the articulation program (41). The programs in the optional group do not form a clear sequence because they represent the cross section of forms to which most children generalize. They are necessary forms, but they do not have to be taught in any particular sequence.

These 41 programs represent the entire curriculum of PCL as it presently stands; undoubtedly new programs will be written and old ones will be revised. The changes will not be as drastic as they have been in the past, which is probably why the authors felt confident enough in the status of the program to publish it.

The Delivery System

The delivery system is programmed conditioning that implies the incorporation of basic principles of conditioning such as stimulus, response, and consequence. In addition, Gray and Fygetakis (1968) identified six additional variables that they felt were critical to the successful implementation of Programmed Conditioning for Language. These are model, reinforcement, schedule, criterion, stimulus mode, response mode, and complexity. A discussion of each variable, including the three principles named first, follows.

Response. This variable refers to the desired response to be made by the child. The response may appear in either of two modalities, oral and nonoral, and the evaluation of the response is critical to the success of each program. Initially, short, easy responses are elicited and are only gradually increased in length and complexity. In any program such as PCL the response must be clearly defined and described so that the teacher can reliably determine its presence or absence.

Stimulus. The stimulus is the class of events that precedes the response and that sets the stage for the occurrence of the response. Stimuli in PCL are visual and/or auditory and take the form of pictures and verbal utterances by the teacher. The teacher's verbalization tells the child what grammatical form the child is to learn, and the pictures give the child semantic information about the words used.

Reinforcer. In general terms the reinforcer describes the consequence that is to be used. Tokens, such as plastic chips, beans, and stars, are often given to the child in return for correct responses. Later he or she may exchange some predetermined number of tokens for a toy. Another form of reinforcer, the word "Good," is produced by the teacher after each of the child's responses; it is paired with the token and given at the same time so that eventually the social reinforcer will supplant the token.

Criterion. The criterion refers to the standard of performance of the child. It is a description of the child's behavior and enables the teacher to determine when to move the child ahead in the program. A criterion of 10 successively correct responses is commonly used for each step in the program when three or more children are grouped. If the child is working alone in the program, the criterion is generally doubled to 20 successively correct responses.

Reinforcement Schedule.   When a new skill is being taught the frequency of reinforcement is usually very high—a token for each correct response. As the child learns the skill, however, the amount of token reinforcement is faded out, that is, fewer tokens per number of correct responses are given. The schedule of giving reinforcers diminishes from one for each correct response to one for every other response (50%). Finally, no tokens are given, but the reinforcer "Good" or some other positive comment is continued throughout the program. Note that social reinforcement is delivered on a 100% schedule all through the program; only the token reinforcement is faded.

Response Mode.   Another variable taken into consideration is the response mode, oral and nonoral, that is required of the child. Since PCL is an oral language program, the oral response mode is usually employed.

Stimulus Mode.   There are a variety of stimulus modes that could be used in programming; the ones selected for PCL are the visual and auditory. The visual stimuli are things such as pictures and objects. The auditory stimuli consist of verbal utterances.

   Stimulus and response modes have been combined in PCL to generate different types of oral language behavior. The interrelationships between the modes are shown in Table 9.3.

   The reader can see that the lowest level of behavior would require the production of a nonoral response to a visual stimulus (the bottom of Table 9.3), and the highest level would require an oral response in the absence of any obvious stimulus. This particular concept of sequencing from lowest to highest level of oral language behavior was used in designing the sequence of the program so that the child could move from easy steps to more difficult ones.

Model.   The child needs to know exactly what response to produce—what to say—and the model variable refers to the special kinds of stimuli that assist the child. The model variable is the more familiar "prompt." The model is the part of the stimulus that the child is expected to be able to reproduce or produce at any given step in the program. Therefore, the stimulus is the final target for the child. The models are gradually faded so that the "parroting" element is gradually eliminated. As the child moves through the steps, he or she must "remember" what is supposed to be said without prompting. Gray and Ryan explain the five different models used in PCL as shown in Table 9.4.

   As an example of how the stimulus and the model are related, we can hypothesize the steps shown in Table 9.5.

TABLE 9.3. Interrelationships Between Stimulus and Response Modes

Stimulus Mode		Response Mode	
Visual	Auditory	Oral	Nonoral
—	—	Oral	—
Visual	—	Oral	—
—	Auditory	Oral	—
Visual	Auditory	Oral	—
—	Auditory	—	Nonoral
Visual	Auditory	—	Nonoral
Visual	—	—	Nonoral

Note. From *A Language Program for the Nonlanguage Child* (p. 21) by B. B. Gray and B. Ryan, 1973, Champaign, IL: Research Press. Reprinted by permission.

TABLE 9.4. Models Used in PCL

Models	Explanation
IC: Immediate Complete	The child is given the entire model of what to say just before he or she is to say it.
DC: Delayed Complete	The child is given the entire model, but it must be "held" briefly before the child says the response.
IT: Immediate Truncated	The child is given only a portion of what to say in the model immediately before he or she says it.
DT: Delayed Truncated	The child is given only a portion of what to say in a model, and it must be "held" briefly.
N: No Model	The child is given no model of what to say.

Note. From *A Language Program for the Nonlanguage Child* (p. 22) by B. B. Gray and B. Ryan, 1973, Champaign, IL: Research Press. Reprinted by permission.

Complexity. The last of the program variables is complexity, which refers to the relationship between the number of units in the stimulus and the number of units in the response. If the model is one unit long and the response consists of one unit, the complexity is 1-1. When the model is two units long and the response is also two units, the complexity is described as 2-2. However, the model may consist of one unit and the response of four units with a corresponding complexity of 1-4. The

TABLE 9.5. An Example of How the PCL Stimulus and Model Are Related

Stimulus	Model	Expected Response
Picture is shown and "The dog is black" is said	"is" (IC)	"is"
next,		
Picture is shown and "The dog is black" is said	"dog is black" (IC)	"dog is black"
next,		
Picture is shown and "The dog is black" is said	"dog" (IT)	"The dog is black."

programmer uses the complexity variable to evaluate the ease or difficulty of a step or the sequence selected.

Ancillary Language Training Procedures

The language programs and the delivery system are the core of PCL. In addition, however, there are ancillary procedures that are important to the success of the total program. These are evaluation, measurement of language performance, recording data, the teaching setting, and parent carryover. Only evaluation and the parent carryover procedures are discussed here, as the other areas are not unique to PCL.

Initial Evaluation.   The first step in implementing PCL is selecting the children who need spoken language training. Gray and Ryan state that the recommended testing is quite standard but is aimed at answering only one question, "Does the child have an oral, expressive, language deficit?"

A child who does manifest a grammatical-syntactical deficit for his or her age is considered a candidate for the language training programs. The initial diagnosis must be confirmed and a decision made as to whether PCL would be beneficial. To these ends the Programmed Conditioning for Language Test (PCLT) is administered.

PCLT.   The Programmed Conditioning for Language Test, or PCLT, is a test developed to measure the parameters of language encompassed by the curriculum of PCL. Obviously, it is a test that is unique and peculiar to the programs of PCL.

The PCLT is administered in imitation form, indicating the authors' acceptance of Lee and Menyuk's findings that children will repeat only what they can process. Two scores are derived from the test: the Program Score, which indicates the number of programs (or grammatical forms) that the child has already acquired, and the Adequacy Score, which reflects the child's use of certain grammatical forms, even though they may not be correct. The teacher may use the Program Score to select the specific language training programs the child needs. The Adequacy Score is a type of composite score that gives an estimate of the child's overall expressive grammatic/syntactic language performance.

A pilot study involving 17 four-year-olds and 18 five-year-olds with normal language development provides some minimal normative data for the PCLT. Of interest were the findings that the 5-year-old children scored higher than the 4-year-olds and that, apparently, the normal 5-year-old can produce the syntactic/grammatic forms included in the PCLT. Another small study using the PCLT with "linguistically divergent" children revealed that the older nonverbal children scored lower than the younger, normal speaking children. Gray and Ryan concluded that the "PCLT does measure grammatical-syntactical ability and that it differentiates between normal speaking children and nonlanguage children" (1973, p. 86).

The basic purpose of the PCLT, however, is to assist the teacher in selecting the programs needed by the child and to give her or him information as to where to place the child in the curriculum. The authors report that during the time that the PCLT has been used, it has placed children accurately except for echolalic and bilingual children. Such children are highly skilled in imitation and score spuriously high on the test when actually their day-to-day expressive language is deficient, whether due to a language disorder or to the language barrier.

Criterion Tests.   After the initial testing and the administration of the PCLT the examiner would know whether the child is eligible for language training, which language programs are needed, and which program the child should begin first. In order to determine at what point within a specific training program the child should begin, a criterion test is administered. The questions on the criterion test are of two types: (a) *Wh*-questions such as, "What color is the ball?" and (b) choice questions such as, "Is the ball red or blue?" The teacher or examiner uses pictures or objects as referents for the questions. The questions reflect the forms taught in the various programs. If a child scores 80% or better on the preprogram criterion test, he or she does not need that program and moves to the next one. A child with a score below 80% is put through the program. When a program is completed by the child, the criterion test is given again; if the child scores below 80%, he or she is recycled through the latter portions of that program.

The entire evaluation process has been summarized by Gray and Ryan and is shown in Table 9.6. Beginning with initial testing, the administration of the PCLT, and going through the carryover procedures used in the total program, the child's mastery of language is assessed at each point. Parent carryover is an integral part of PCL and represents a structured attempt to involve parents in the language training of the child.

Parent Involvement.   Following each program after number 1, the symbols IHC may be found. These stand for the command, "Initiate Home Carryover," and are a signal to the teacher that it is time to engage the parents in carryover activities.

TABLE 9.6. Measurement Procedures and Use of Results

Test	Results Indicate
1 Evaluation	Need for Language Training
2 PCLT	Which Program
3 Criterion Test	Pre- and Postmeasure of Program
4 Placement	Where to Start in a Program
5 Show and Tell	
School	Carryover of Language
Home	

Note. From *A Language Program for the Nonlanguage Child* (p. 82) by B. B. Gray and B. Ryan, 1973, Champaign, IL: Research Press. Reprinted by permission.

The parents are given a form that provides instructions on what to do, what kinds of responses are expected, dates, times, and a score sheet.

> Let us assume that a child has completed the "Is" (No. 4) program. Examples of the language constructions, "Boy is old," "Girl is in house," are written on the IHC form so that the parents may know exactly what the child can do. They are further instructed to find pictures in magazines or catalogues and go through them asking questions, such as "Is the car new or old?", "Where is the dog?" These are the same forms of questions which were on the language programs. (Gray & Ryan, 1973, p. 106)

The parents carry out activities such as those described above for 8 days within a 2-week period, marking responses as correct or incorrect and giving only the social reinforcer "Good." They spend only 5 to 10 minutes a day on the carryover activities. At the end of the 2-week period the IHC form is returned, and because parents vary in their ability to complete the activities, they may be requested to do additional or different activities.

The authors note that this small amount of home training has produced adequate transfer of training as observed and reported by the mothers. It should be emphasized that the child is already able to produce the responses that the parents are attempting to elicit; this is not a training program but a carryover, or transfer, program.

Appraisal of Programmed Conditioning for Language

Research on PCL has been conducted for the most part by Gray, Ryan, and their associates at the Behavioral Sciences Institute, although all of the training has not been done at that facility. Some data are available for six types of children: nonlanguage, or linguistically divergent; autistic, trainable mentally retarded; deaf; hard of hearing; and non-English speaking. The data are uneven for the groups; some are reported in terms of performance on criterion tests, such as the *Northwestern Syntax Screening Test* (Lee, 1971a) or some other objective measure; some are reported in terms of program accuracy and average number of responses to completion of the program. The authors state that the "data presented should not be taken as proof of anything" (Gray & Ryan, 1973, p. 106). Rather, the data are to be viewed as a report of one group's experience in using Programmed Conditioning for Language.

The Prime Sample. The most extensive data collection was carried out using a group of 43 children who received training at the Children's House, Behavioral Sciences Institute. This population was kept as close as possible to the traditional label of *dysphasic*. They were hyperactive, normally intelligent children, ranging in age from 3 to 7 years with an average entering age of 4.7 years. They had no gross overriding characteristics such as cerebral palsy or hearing loss, but they may have had some organic brain dysfunction. All of them were non–language-using children.

The data were collected over a 4-year period, but at no time were there more than 14 children enrolled in the program, 7 in each of two classes. There was a constant mixing of "new" and "old" children, with some completing the program before others were enrolled. Each separate report may then be on a different number of subjects, the number of subjects reported simply being the number of children enrolled at a given time or the number being monitored at the time.

During the 4-year period the total number of responses recorded for all children was 288,000; the program run time was 2,160 hours. The children spent a total of 20,160 student hours in language programming and language-related activities such as "Show and Tell" and the home carryover program. As a group, the children responded to the programs with an accuracy percent of 89.9 and required an average of 794 responses to complete an entire program. In a group situation (no more than 7 children) the average time spent in a given program was 3.7 hours. It should be noted that the earlier programs showed lower accuracy rates and required longer to complete.

The average child in PCL was reported to have an accuracy score on the precriterion test for a program of 22% with a posttest score of 93%. This is a substantial gain, even though it is less than that for some individual programs. The authors also presented pretest and posttest scores on the PCLT given at a 1-year interval. The increase in response accuracy on the PCLT for 10 children was 55 percentage points gained in 61 hours of programming per child. The difference between scores was statistically significant beyond the $p = .01$ level. It should be noted that the posttest score was not a terminal score but merely that score obtained after 1 year in the program.

It cannot be denied that there was some kind of change in the children's performance, but the authors note that the change could be attributed to the passage of time and the children's maturation. No control group was available. In an attempt to resolve the problem, 14 children from the sample with a mean age of 5.0 years were pretested and posttested on the *Northwestern Syntax Screening Test* (Lee, 1971a) over a 7-month period. The change in their NSST scores was compared to the change that was reported for normal children on the norms of the NSST for a 6-month period. The PCL children showed a gain of 4.5 points on the NSST, while the normal children gained 1.0 points. The two groups, although the same age, were operating at quite different levels on the NSST, but the PCL children showed a gain four times as great as that of the normal children. The authors summarize their research on the effects of training the prime sample as follows:

> To summarize our experience with the prime population (Children's House) we may conclude that (1) the language programs ran efficiently and resulted in target acquisition, (2) the children demonstrated transfer of training from one form to another, and (3) generalization of language was evidenced in the home setting. (Gray & Ryan, 1973, p. 145)

Other Samples. Programmed Conditioning for Language has been used with several clinical populations other than the one housed at the Behavioral Sciences Institute, and the results of the investigations are presented by Gray and Ryan (1973). Bradfield used PCL with 14 autistic children, ranging in age from 6.0 to 11.5 years, and found that the number of verbal responses increased significantly, beyond the $p = .01$ level. Again, however, there was no control group available, and the results were not uniformly significant. For example, the effect of the program on echolalic behavior was uneven; a few children's echolalia even increased.

The data available from other studies using PCL are also scanty. Seventeen trainable mentally retarded children have been through the program, and the authors state that the results are "promising," but little evidence is given. Deaf and hard-of-hearing children have been trained by altering the program to use either Cued Speech or Seeing Essential English (the SEE method). As with the samples described above, experience in PCL has been limited, and the results are not conclusive in any way.

One other group of children with whom PCL has been used were Spanish-speaking children learning English as a second language. Results from two separate projects are reported, and the pooled data indicate that the children's NSST scores increased significantly, beyond the $p = .01$ level.

As the reader can determine, the evidence related to PCL is still tenuous, and in fairness to Gray and Ryan it should be noted that they make the same statement regarding the present status of the research. It seems to us, however, that it is equally fair to state that the program is promising, most particularly for the nonverbal child who is similar to that described by Gray and Ryan in their "prime" sample.

10

REMEDIATING DISABILITIES OF
READING AND WRITING

Among school-aged children and adults, disorders of written language are the most common form of specific learning disability. While many methods have been developed to remediate these disabilities, the three systems described in this chapter have retained popularity over the years. The techniques offered by Gillingham and Stillman; by Kirk, Kirk, and Minskoff; and by Fernald were all designed specifically for use with individuals who evidenced moderate-to-severe problems in reading, writing, and spelling. A typical child who would most likely profit from their use is described below.

S. T., age 8½ years, was referred because of persistent, severe reading and spelling difficulties. He was in the third grade and was receiving remedial reading instruction (of an unspecified nature). Reversals in oral reading and written spelling were reported by his teacher. She also noted that he had trouble recalling sight words. S. T.'s developmental and medical histories were unremarkable, although his father was reported to be a "slow reader."

Results of the psychological evaluation indicated that S. T. was within the bright to normal range of intelligence. The only problem apparent on the tests was on the WISC-R

Block Design, where he tended to reverse the order of stimuli presented and to become confused. His Bender protocol was slightly below average but, in the main, adequate. His articulation and hearing were within normal limits, as were his vocabulary comprehension, sentence length and syntax, and speech-sound discrimination. It was found that S. T. was reading and spelling at the first-grade level and that his sound-letter associations were fairly good. However, he was unable to use a systematic phonics approach to reading or spelling.

This child is typical of the pupil for whom remedial reading instruction is often prescribed. The severity of this problem suggests that instruction should be remedial rather than developmental. More than likely, S. T. would be having no difficulty with reading if the only instruction necessary was of the developmental, basal reader type. It is just as unlikely that he will profit from turning to a first-grade primer and laboring his way through the basal reader series. Instead, S. T. is a prime candidate for one of the remedial systems described in this chapter, and he would probably benefit most from the methods of Gillingham and Stillman, which are summarized in the chapter.

CURRENT THEORIES ABOUT READING

Before continuing, it would probably be useful to position the three methods about to be discussed in terms of current theories about the acquisition of reading. After reviewing a number of definitions of reading, Wiederholt and Bryant (1987) conclude that "the precise use of the term *reading* means comprehending words, sentences, paragraphs, and/or entire tests" (p. 37). Many theories exist that purport to explain how it is that people learn to read. Among these, the most popular today are the bottom-up (Laberge & Samuels, 1974), the top-down (F. Smith, 1979), and the interactive (Rumelhart, 1977) models.

Advocates of bottom-up models believe written language is so dependent upon oral language that reading is essentially the translation of printed symbols into their oral counterparts. When the translation is done properly, students will recognize the word because they use it in their speech. Thus, a child sounds out the graphemes *c a t*, says them fast (i.e., blends them into the word /cat/), and recognizes that this particular compilation of letters means the familiar spoken word /cat/. Such explanations of reading are called decoding or code-cracking models and are based on the theory that reading comprehension is facilitated by automatic phonic analysis of printed material.

In contrast, top-down models emphasize the cognitive or holistic, rather than the phonic, aspects of written language. Advocates of these models assert that comprehension of printed matter involves far more than phonic analysis and suggest that readers project personal meaning onto print, that reading is an intellectual and motivational constructive process, and that meaning precedes and often does not include the identification of individual letters or words.

The majority of authorities today tactfully espouse the validity of the interactive model, a theory that accounts for the salient aspects of the other two models. Advocates of this theory point out that top-down and bottom-up processing seem to occur simultaneously and that adequate comprehension requires the integration of both graphophonemic and "conceptoholistic" information.

In terms of the remedial reading methods described in this chapter, those of Gillingham and Stillman and of Kirk, Kirk, and Minskoff seem to be based primarily on a bottom-up model in that they emphasize decoding, sound blending, sound-symbol association, and the teaching of phonically regular vocabularies. Fernald's approach suggests adherence to a top-down model because children are taught words they want to learn (e.g., *hippopotamus*). In a bottom-up model, they are taught phonetically regular words (e.g., *hat*). When using Fernald's approach, words are never broken down into their phonic parts.

GILLINGHAM AND STILLMAN: THE ALPHABETIC METHOD

The Alphabetic Method of Anna Gillingham and Bessie Stillman was a direct outgrowth of Gillingham's association with Samuel T. Orton. For a clear understanding of the method it is necessary to review the pertinent theories of Orton so that the reader may understand the rationale upon which the method is based. Following a discussion of Orton's theories is a brief but comprehensive description of the Alphabetic Method and an appraisal of the theory and the method.

Samuel T. Orton's Theory

Orton was born in Columbus, Ohio, in 1879 and died in 1948. He earned an MD degree from the University of Pennsylvania. In 1925, he formulated his theory of disability as a physiological variant, not a defect, of normal learning. To him, language disabilities required careful diagnostic study and individually planned educational treatment, the latter based on systematic teaching with simultaneous training and reinforcement in all of the sensory modalities. Orton's most influential contribution was the book *Reading, Writing, and Speech Problems in Children* published in 1937 by W. W. Norton. In 1989, this book was reissued as part of PRO-ED's Classics Series under a special arrangement with the Orton Dyslexia Society. In addition to the book, the recent edition also includes 15 of Orton's most representative articles and a complete listing of his published works.

Orton, a neuropathologist, spent the early part of his career studying the effect of brain injury on spoken and written language functions in adults. Like the earlier researchers, he found the left hemisphere of the brain to be "dominant" in the normal execution of reading and other language abilities. Orton is unique, however, in that his work eventually carried him beyond the bonds of medicine and came to represent what Satz (1976) called "a scholarly attempt to bridge the disciplines of education and psychology" (p. 273). Our purposes here do not require a detailed discussion of how that bridge came to be built, but a brief overview of its development should facilitate understanding of Orton's theory and of the instructional methods to which it gave rise.

It is important to note, first of all, that Orton's theory was fully consistent with conceptions about cerebral dominance that were well accepted during his time. Most researchers felt that the neural processes underlying reading, linguistic, and cognitive functions were largely localized in the left cerebral hemisphere. Certainly, the cerebral dominance theory would serve to explain the consistency with which Orton and his predecessors found left-hemisphere damage in their adult patients to be accompanied by alexic and/or aphasic symptoms. However, when Orton shifted his attention from the study of adults with acquired brain damage to children with developmental language disorders, the situation became more complicated and, for remedial purposes, more hopeful. Perhaps Orton's positions are best outlined in his book *Reading, Writing, and Speech Problems in Children* (1937, 1989), an essential reference for readers wanting a more detailed review of Orton's theories.

Of particular interest to Orton were reading problems in children, disorders that had traditionally been ascribed to what Hinshelwood (1917) called "congenital word blindness." As he studied a number of such cases, Orton began to discern a common pattern of characteristics, the most distinctive being (a) frequent reversals in the reading of letter and word configurations, such as calling /b/ for /d/ or /was/ for /saw/; (b) left-right directional confusion, accompanied by (and, in the strict Ortonian view, caused by) mixed or confused dominance of hand, eye, or foot; and (c) surprising facility in mirror-reading or mirror-writing, tasks that would be quite difficult even for normal children. Thus "classic" Ortonian cases would tend to sight with their right eyes, write with their left hands, kick balls equally well with either foot, and read (if they read at all) the reverse of what they saw on the page. It was in his attempt to explain the etiology behind this syndrome that Orton's theory began to take shape; and with it, significantly, took shape the notion that not all reading disabled children were fated to a lifetime of "congenital word blindness."

In a recent review of the literature on cerebral dominance and reading disability, Satz noted that

> Orton's greatest contribution lies in his distinction between the acquired disorders of reading, seen in adults following unilateral injury to the left hemisphere, and those specific disorders of reading seen in children with no demonstrable pathology of the CNS. (1976, p. 274)

In cases of acquired reading disorders among adult patients, Orton postulated a pathological defect or lesion that led to the impairment or loss of reading skills. Such a pathological defect, whether "acquired" at birth or through later brain injury, is not functionally unlike Hinshelwood's "congenital word blindness." Among the children he studied, however, Orton differentiated a second and unique type of disorder, one that seemed to stem from physiological-development factors rather than from pathological brain damage. It was this second type of disorder that formed the basis of Orton's theory about specific reading disability in children. Orton outlined the essence of his theory in a 1928 paper:

> In skeleton, then, my theory of the obstacle to the acquisition of reading in children of normal intelligence which results in the varying grades of reading disability is a failure to establish the physiological habit of working exclusively from the engrams of one hemisphere. As a result there is incomplete elision of one set of antitropic engrams and there results confusion as to the direction of reading which serves as an impediment to facile associative linkage with the auditory engrams, which during the learning years at least, carry the meaning. (p. 96)

As the above passage indicates, the left hemisphere plays a "dominant" role in Orton's explanation of early reading. Indeed, according to this theory, the establishment of left-hemisphere dominance is considered the sine qua non of reading acquisition. Children who are delayed or deficient in the establishment of such dominance would be considered as neuropsychologically unprepared to learn to read. As they tried to read graphic symbols, they would experience what Orton called "strephosymbolia" (literally, "twisted symbols"), presumably the result of inter-hemispheric competition in the processing of printed matter. In other words, since the left hemisphere had failed to establish its dominance over the right, images in the right hemisphere of such children would likely be as salient as those projected to the left hemisphere. In the "mind's eye" of these children, the directionality of letters would be a meaningless referent; the graphic symbols on the printed page would appear to be "twisted" and capricious rather than orderly and predictable. In the absence of a clear and consistent directional orientation, the fact that the letter *b* points to the right while *d* points to the left would be meaningless to such children. Until or unless they had developed the "physiological habit of working exclusively" from the left cerebral hemisphere, they would in all probability neither know nor care how to read nor which was the "right" hand to use in writing. Small wonder then, according to Orton, that children in such a state of hemispheric irresolution would find reading from a mirror essentially as easy as reading directly from the page.

The unique aspect of strephosymbolia, of course, is the fact that it suggests the possibility of remediation (or "untwisting")—a much stronger possibility than in cases of reading disorders resulting from inherited causes or acquired brain damage. Perhaps it is these implications for remediation that explain why Orton's neurological investigations were among the first that led directly from theory into educational practice. For if, as Orton contended, the problem was in the failure to establish hemispheric dominance, the solution would seem self-evident. Simply engage the child in activities designed to involve and thereby strengthen left-hemisphere functioning, and in time the prerequisite cerebral dominance would be established. With the attainment of such dominance the "symptoms" of its absence would theoretically disappear. The key question for remedial instructors is quite clear: What sort of activities will serve to foster and promote cerebral dominance? Though it may have been Orton who first posed the question, it was his protégés Gillingham and Stillman who developed the answer in terms of a comprehensive instructional methodology.

While the method developed by Gillingham and Stillman appears at first glance to be complex, the basically simply theme of hemispheric dominance runs throughout the various procedures and activities it recommends. The basic features of their instructional methods have been summarized by J. Orton as follows:

> Their common conceptual background can usually be seen in their introduction of the kinesthetic element to reinforce the visual-auditory language associations and to establish left-to-right habits of progression. Their phonetic approach is generally the same: teaching the phonic units in isolation but giving special training in blending; introducing consonants and the short sounds of the vowels first and building three-letter words with them for reading and spelling; programming the material in easy, orderly, cumulative steps. (1966, p. 144)

The "common conceptual background" of the Gillingham-Stillman and related approaches lies, of course, in their fealty to Orton's neuropsychological assertions about the causes of reading disability. Once the reader (and teacher) is familiar with Orton's assumptions, it becomes possible to discern the logical links between his neuropsychological theory and the educational practice of Gillingham and Stillman. For example, the fact that the program focuses (particularly in its early stages) on forming grapheme-phoneme associations can be seen as an attempt to avoid the dangers of strephosymbolic "symbol-twisting," which is likely to occur in early reading, and the gradual introduction of printed material as an attempt to promote "facile associative linkages" with these already established "auditory engrams." The other features of the method such as encouragement in the use of the "dominant" hand, training of a left-to-right directional orientation, and presentation of tasks in an orderly, sequential manner can all be seen as steps leading toward the same basic goal, which is to establish clear and consistent dominance of the right hand, of the right eye—and most important—of the left brain hemisphere.

The Alphabetic Method

With her friend Bessie Stillman, Anna Gillingham taught at the Ethical Culture Schools in New York City. She served as mathematics teacher, principal of the Open Air Department, and—in the 1920s—school psychologist, one of the first so designated in this country. She participated in the first use of the Binet intelligence scale for the identification of gifted children.

Growing aware of bright children with reading and related language problems, Gillingham took a leave of absence from the Ethical Culture Schools to become a

Research Fellow under Orton at the Neurological Institute, Columbia-Presbyterian Medical Center, New York. She worked closely with Orton and Stillman to devise and refine teaching techniques for children with specific language disabilities.

In 1936, Gillingham and Stillman went to the Punahou Elementary School in Honolulu, Hawaii, to set up and put into operation their program. Other schools became interested, and many established similar programs. Both women returned to New York, where they continued to work together until Stillman's death in 1947. Gillingham visited schools to observe and supervise her method and saw her work spread. She revised her training manual several times (it is presently in its seventh edition) and remained actively involved in her work until 1960, when almost total blindness curtailed her activities. She died in 1964.

Gillingham and Stillman base their work on Orton's theory of incomplete hemispheric dominance as discussed in the preceding section. They state that

> he believed that records on that side of the brain not usually in control of language— records usually ignored—are always present and may sometimes assert themselves. Records made on the two hemispheres, according to him, are in reverse patterns, and so the obtrusion of one from the wrong side would account for the "reversals"; collision of two from opposite sides would produce complete confusion. (1970, p. 16)

Gillingham reports that such reversals and confusions are frequently seen as characteristics of children who exhibit specific learning disabilities and cites examples.

> In the visual field, for example, the word *go* may be read *og*, *was*, may be called *saw*. A well-educated woman glanced at *eat* and read it *tea*. In the auditory field one may hear *loop* called *pool*. A five-year-old, driving by a pasture in which were black-and-white cattle, remarked. "Those are *Steinhols*." A little boy wearied with a prolonged ordeal asked querulously, How *last* will it *long*, Daddy?" In the kinesthetic field the same cause probably underlies the much-talked-of mirror writing. (Gillingham & Stillman, 1970, p. 16)

She explains this phenomenon, as would Orton, by saying that the evolution or development of the language function has not achieved completion and is still subject to variations. "The degree to which the language function of an individual is controlled by one hemisphere determines the degree of language or disability in that individual" (Gillingham & Stillman, 1970, p. 16).

The Gillingham method is geared toward those children in the third through sixth grades who

1. are of normal or superior intelligence;
2. have normal sensory acuity (visual and auditory);
3. have the tendency to reverse letters or words and to mirror write;
4. have difficulty in pronunciation; and

5. have been unable to acquire reading and spelling skills by "ordinary school methods," that is, "sight word methods, even when these are later reinforced by functional, incidental, intrinsic, or analytical phonics, or by tracing procedures." (Gillingham & Stillman, 1970, p. 17)

In contrast to sight-word procedures in which words are first recognized by the child as ideograms and then broken down by the teacher into letter sounds through functional phonics, Gillingham's alphabetic approach proceeds from teaching the sounds of the letters to building these letter sounds into words, like bricks in a wall. The technique aims to establish close associations among visual, auditory, and kinesthetic records in the brain.

In order to use the technique effectively, Gillingham emphatically stresses two points:

1. The remedial pupil should do no reading or spelling except with the remedial teacher. The schedule should ensure that the child is out of the classroom when the rest of the class is having reading and spelling.

2. The steps of the procedure should be followed rigidly, since they are a "series of logical sequences, the omission of any one of which will jeopardize the complete success of the procedure" (Gillingham & Stillman, 1970, p. 42). To use the technique effectively, Gillingham stresses that one must "begin at the beginning" (Gillingham & Stillman, 1970, p. 43).

Gillingham's approach makes use of six basic combinations of the visual, auditory, and kinesthetic modalities. Although she recommends occasional use of tactile stimuli through finger-tracing, the procedure is not necessary to her word-learning program. Tracing, as she incorporates it, involves kinesthetic rather than tactile stimuli. The six basic patterns for integration of fundamental associations are these:

V-A—Translation of visual symbols into sound, vocalized or not.

A-V—Translation of auditory symbols into visual image.

A-K—Translation of auditory symbols into muscle response, for speech and writing.

K-A—Movement of a passive hand by another to produce a letter form, in order to lead to the naming or sounding of the letter.

V-K—Translation of visual symbol into muscular action of speech and writing.

K-V—The muscular "feel" of the speaking or writing of a letter, in order to lead to association with the appearance of that letter.

Gillingham's methods for effecting the associations mentioned above involve the use of very specific materials and techniques, as well as the dedication of a skillful teacher whose background includes several years of successful classroom experience, thorough familiarity with English phonics (plus—by inference—speech production understanding), and an awareness of the neurological hypotheses of Orton. Her guide (which first appeared in 1934) is thoroughly detailed and divides the instructional program into three sections:

1. General preparation of the child before the actual program is begun. The evolution of written language is explained, as are the reasons for which the child is having difficulty with reading and spelling.

2. Reading and spelling with phonetic words.

3. Words phonetic for reading but not for spelling.

General Preparations. In this section, Gillingham and Stillman cover a number of points that they have subsumed under the general rubric of preliminary considerations. These points include a very brief defense of Orton's theories, several case histories, and a description of the character traits and training needed by the remedial teacher. The major points regarding the teacher seem to focus around the need for training in the evolution of language, which includes the theoretical constructs developed by Orton, and the need for a "sympathetic" attitude. However, they are quick to point out that the teacher must be experienced in teaching, a firm disciplinarian, and dedicated to remedial teaching as a professional career.

A fairly lengthy exposition is provided as an "explanation to the pupil." In this, Gillingham and Stillman review the historical evolution of written language, covering picture writing as used by early American Indians; pictographs, represented by Egyptian hieroglyphs; ideograms, shown by the earliest form of Chinese calligraphy; and alphabetic writing.

The authors also stress the need to prepare the pupil for remedial instruction by explaining the nature of the reading disability to the child. He or she may not be able to follow the theory as presented but will at least know that there is an acceptable reason for the inability to read. The child will know that he or she is not dumb, is not at fault, and is not abnormal.

Reading and Spelling with Phonic Words. The sequence followed in this section is that of introduction of letters, words, and sentences.

LETTERS. Each new phonogram is introduced by a key word and is taught by the following processes, which involve the visual, auditory, and kinesthetic linkages.

Association I. This association consists of two parts—association of the visual symbol with the name of the letter, and association of the visual symbol with the sound of the letter; also the association of the feel of the child's speech organs in producing the name or sound of the letter as he hears himself say it. Association I is V-A and A-K. Part b is the basis of oral reading.

Part a. The card is exposed and the name of the letter spoken by the teacher and repeated by the pupil.

Part b. As soon as the name has really been mastered, the sound is made by the teacher and repeated by the pupil. It is here that most emphasis must be placed if the case is primarily one of speech defect. The card is exposed, the implied question being, "What does this letter (or phonogram) say?" and the pupil gives it sound.

Association II. The teacher makes the sound represented by the letter (or phonogram), the face of the card not being seen by the pupil, and says "Tell me the name of the letter that has this sound." Sound to name is A-A, and is essentially oral spelling.

Association III. The letter is carefully made by the teacher and then its form, orientation, etc., explained. It is then traced by the pupil over the teacher's lines, then copied, written from memory, and finally written again with eyes averted while the teacher watches closely. This association is V-K and K-V. . . . Now, the teacher makes the sound, saying, "Write the letter that has this sound." This association is A-K, and is the basis of written spelling. (Gillingham & Stillman, 1970, p. 41)

In addition to the drills described above, there are other associations that Gillingham and Stillman consider basic. If children do not have them, they should be taught through the exercises below:

1. The most basic requirement of all is that the child should be taught the names of each letter, or the letters in each phonogram. This is done by showing the card and teaching the child to say the name.

2. If the child's production of sounds is faulty, there will have to be practice in echo speech, i.e., the teacher will produce the sound for the child to imitate. . . .

3. When the name of the phonogram has been acquired, and correct sounds of speech have been found to be largely dependable, the following drill will be found to be a useful reinforcement: the teacher says the names of various phonograms, and the child responds with the related sound or sound which he has learned.

4. Before he is asked to write there must be whatever practice is necessary in tracing, copying, and writing from memory to dictation, this last being sometimes carried out with the child's eyes averted. Except in tracing and copying, the teacher dictates the name of the phonogram. In all instances the child says the name of the letter as he writes it. This is called "S.O.S." (simultaneous oral spelling). (Gillingham & Stillman, 1970, p. 41)

In the teaching of letters, Gillingham makes two points that should be noted.

1. *Drill Cards.* Consonants are printed on white cards, and the vowels are printed on salmon-colored cards in order to facilitate recognition of distinction between vowel and consonant sounds. Drills with the preceding associations are continued in almost daily practice.

2. *First Group of Letters.* These first phonograms are taught as having only one sound:

a	apple	j	jam
b	boy	k	kite
f	fun	m	man
h	hat	p	pan
i	it	t	top

WORDS. After the 10 letters in the first group of phonograms are fairly well known with all associations, blending them together into words is begun. Words such as the following are printed on small yellow cards and placed in the child's box of phonetic words: *hat, bat, mat, him, tap, at, hip, if, fat, hit, Jim, bib, pat, pit, bit, fib, kit, jab, it.*

1. *Reading.* First certain drill cards that form a word are laid out on the table. The pupil is asked to give in succession the sounds of these letters, repeating the series of sounds again and again with increasing speed and smoothness; if necessary, the child is helped to recognize the word he or she is saying. Then the yellow word cards are exposed one by one by the teacher and read as rapidly as possible by the pupil. Those cards read correctly are laid in one pile, and those read incorrectly in another. However, no attempt for correction or self-correction is made at this point.

2. *Spelling.* A few days after blending is begun, the analysis of words into their component sounds is initiated. The procedure followed is referred to as the "Four-Point Program":

   The teacher says a word then says the word again very slowly, sound by sound. As the child recognizes each sound, its corresponding letter is placed on the table until the word is completed. The teacher says the word again. After the teacher pronounces the word, the child (a) repeats it; (b) names the letters; (c) writes, naming each letter while forming it; and (d) reads the word he or she has written. At this point it should become routine to have the child correct his or her own reading and spelling errors.

   After spelling is begun, the following program for daily lessons is suggested:

   All white and salmon cards so far taught . . . (Assn. I).

   Practice in Association II for these same phonograms.

   Practice in Association III for these same phonograms, sometimes traced, sometimes written to dictation, (sometimes eyes averted), always S.O.S.

   Drill words for reading.

   Drill words for spelling and writing. (Gillingham & Stillman, 1970, p. 54)

Words are selected from the word box, and the Four-Point Program is followed, the idea being to see how many words can be spelled in this way correctly in succession.

As the above daily program is continued, new letters are presented, one or two a day in the following order:

g	go	s	sat
o	olive	sh	ship
r	rat	d	dog
l	lamp	w	wind
n	nut	wh	whittle
th	this	y	yes
u	umbrella	v	van
ch	chin	z	zebra
e	elephant		

Words for each letter are added to the word box for Drill, and a reading graph is charted.

3. *Spelling Rule 1.* After the preceding phonograms have been learned by the pupil, the following spelling rule is introduced: Words of one syllable ending in *f, l,* or *s* after one vowel usually end in double *f,* double *l,* or double *s.* Words in which this rule is applied are written on yellow cards and placed in the word box. As soon as these words have become fairly familiar to the pupil, they are shuffled in with the other cards for reading, graphs, and the Four-Point Program.

STORIES. After the pupil can read and write any phonetic three-letter word, words are combined into sentences and stories. Some of the stories are stapled into small books, and others are printed on tag board. The stories do not have for their purpose entertainment or literary content, but rather they are steps in the development of skill.

1. *Reading Procedures.* The pupil reads a sentence silently; a child who has difficulty with a particular word may ask for help, which usually consists of helping him or her sound out the word. When ready, the pupil reads the sentence out loud. All nonphonetic words in the story are supplied for the pupil by the teacher.

2. *Dictation.* The same stories are used as dictation exercises. Nonphonetic words (words underscored in the story) are written on paper and copied by the pupil. No word is repeated in the exercise, since one of the present goals is to increase the child's auditory span.

Examples of Group I stories containing unequivocal consonants, plain vowels, and Rule 1 are shown in Table 10.1.

3. *Consonant Blends.* Consonant blends are introduced at this point, and words containing blends are shuffled into the pack of phonetic words for daily reading,

TABLE 10.1. Examples of Group I Stories

FAT SAM

Fat Sam had *a* bat.	Sam hit *Ann.*
Fat Sam at bat.	Then *Ann* hit Sam.
Fat Sam sat on *the* mat.	Sam ran *and Ann* ran.
The rat sat on *the* mat.	Ann had a tan *mitten.*
The rat sat on Sam.	This is Ann's tan *mitten.*
Sam ran and *the* rat ran.	Ann *lost* it.
This *is* Thin Ann.	Sam got *the mitten.*
Fat Sam met *Thin Ann.*	Sam *sent the mitten to Ann.*

Note. From *Remedial Training for Children with Specific Disability in Reading, Spelling and Penmanship* (7th ed., p. 60) by A. Gillingham and B. Stillman, 1970, Cambridge, MA: Educators Publishing Service. Reprinted by permission.

frequent graphing, and for spelling in the Four-Point Program. Group II stories containing previously learned phonograms, Rule 1, and consonant blends are then introduced.

4. *Spelling Rule 2.* After introduction of consonant blends, the following spelling rule is introduced: The sounds of all the vowels are changed by a silent *e* on the end of the word. The change in pronunciation is indicated by placing a bar over each of the words. Thus the long vowels are introduced in this particular context. Words ending in silent *e* are typed in a long list of similar words, and the pupil reads the list rapidly. They also are printed on yellow cards and shuffled in with the pack of phonetic words for reading and spelling. Group III stories containing previously learned phonograms and rules, and words with the final *e* are introduced.

   At this point in the program, the schedule of lesson topics consists of:
   a. Daily Review of Drill Cards.
   b. Graphing of Phonetic Words—probably once a week.
   c. Spelling—Four-Point Program—twice a week.
   d. Dictation—twice a week.
   e. Reading whatever Little Stories are now available.

5. *Syllable Concept.* Drill cards, graphing of words read, spelling by the Four-Point Program, and reading of Little Stories continue steadily in daily routine, in addition to exercises three or four times a week to develop the syllable concepts, as follows:
   a. The child is taught to recognize nonsense syllables that are printed on orange cards.
   b. The child is asked to read real words of more than one syllable printed with syllables apart.

    c. Words are typed with syllables far apart, and these syllables are then cut out. Words are then built out of their component parts.

6. *Accent.* The pupil is required to place the accent on each syllable in succession and decide which trial produces a word he or she recognizes.

Words Phonetic for Reading but Not for Spelling. Up to this time, words taught have been purely phonetic, that is, each phonogram has had only one sound and each sound has been represented by only one symbol. Only one possible pronunciation or spelling for the words has been given. Ambiguities in the English language are now introduced. With this introduction of ambiguity the remedial teacher should give the pupil some understanding of the history of language growth and the fact that words change as they pass from country to country and from century to century.

    "From the day when a second sound is introduced for a phonogram or a second spelling for a sound, there will be a radical change in procedure" (Gillingham & Stillman, 1970, p. 79). Association I with the white and salmon cards is constantly reviewed, new cards are added, and some of the familiar phonogram cards acquire new responses. Associations II and III are not applied to any of the new phonograms or responses, and none of the words following each phonogram are to be spelled. The practice words following the new phonograms are typed on the blue cards. The Four-Point Program for phonetic words should be continued every few days. Spelling of words containing phonograms for which more than one sound is possible is presented gradually as a thought process by means of the introduction of Rules and Generalizations. The pupil begins to keep a notebook divided into sections labeled Tests, Rules, Generalizations, Learned Words, and Dictation.

1. *Tests*
   a. Ordinary spelling tests: Words are pronounced by the teacher and written by the pupil in columns, S.O.S.
   b. Labeling tests: In a second column the pupil indicates the reason for spelling a word as he or she has written it by listing the corresponding rule or by indicating if the word is phonetic or a learned word.

2. *Rules.* Rules are gradually added to those previously taught. Each rule is developed, applied, and in time memorized.

3. *Generalizations.* Phonograms having the same sound are assembled.

4. *Learned Words.* Although there are very few words learned as ideograms, such words as the following are learned in this way: *were, has, have, does, goes, come.* They are studied by S.O.S. and are recorded in the notebook, as they are essential in the construction of dictation exercises.

5. *Dictation.* All dictation exercises are filed under this section. The sequence of presentation is essentially the same as that of the previous section: presentation of letters, words, and practice in reading stories containing words in which

previously presented phonograms are recognized and rules and generalization are applied. Exercises for development of the Syllable Concept and Dictionary Technique are included as incidental projects in lessons of a few minutes each while the introduction of new phonograms is proceeding.

Diphthongs are introduced to the pupil as they occur in the book chosen as a basis for the work at this point. The pupil is to read the books being studied in the room of the remedial teacher only. Each diphthong is typed at the top of a strip of tag board followed by practice words which the pupil gradually learns to read.

A series of readers is now selected for study:

> Ideally, the matter presented to be read by the pupil from now on should contain only words which the pupil has never seen before but which fall under headings already mastered. . . . The pupil studies the first sentence, very soon a paragraph or page, and is told in advance any word for which he is not responsible. He asks for help on any word that he does not know. The help given demands quick thought by the teacher. (Gillingham & Stillman, 1970, p. 113)

No guessing of a word from the context of the sentence is allowed.

Toward the end of the period of building up reading skills by the acquisition of phonograms, drill is begun on sight words the teacher has previously told to the student.

Gradually, books selected by the teacher may be given to the pupil for reading at home. Children are encouraged to read all that they can of the material in use in the classroom and to select their own books for reading enjoyment.

Evaluation of progress is an ongoing procedure with the alert teacher constantly aware of a child's level of development and degree of facility in a number of separate but related series of skills. Gillingham has developed a phonics proficiency scale, which provides a more systematic, though unstandardized, measure. It provides an assessment of mastery of words phonetic for reading and spelling, words phonetic for spelling only, and multiple spellings and is presented along with the development of teaching procedures.

In addition to the procedures outlined above, Gillingham makes other pertinent comments regarding difficulties children may have with spelling and handwriting and offers specific suggestions. She notes that the majority of children who have difficulty with reading are poor spellers even after they master the skill of reading. The basis of the remedial spelling program is a strong foundation in phonics. After that is acquired, work is begun in establishing good oral spelling through ear training. Exercises are used so that consonant and vowel sounds, rhyming words, and different word endings may be heard. Nonphonetic words are taught through nonsense tricks and jingles, drill, and general spelling rules. For example, amusing rhymes may help the child to learn the spelling of difficult words.

Advice to Mice

Don't nibble spice
Sugared rice
Is twice as nice
For little mice.
        (Gillingham & Stillman, 1970, p. 185)

Much dictionary work is to be done. As skill in dictionary work increases, the child is encouraged to look up words. The child is also encouraged to trace, copy, and write to dictation. The goal of the spelling remediation process is to enable children to express themselves independently in writing. From word sequences the child should progress to short sentences. It is important that the child's ideas are expressed by written symbols. The teacher should write the symbols first; the child should rewrite them later. Gradually, the child should progress to writing compositions.

To remedy handwriting problems, Gillingham feels that the teacher must first determine which hand is to be used. Then the position of the paper and the hand is practiced repeatedly. Exercises such as freehand loops follow. Proper slant is developed through these exercises. Kinesthetic training is stressed. Lines, circles, and squares are drawn while the student's eyes are closed. Letters are analyzed as to their proportions, straight lines, and curves.

Using the blackboard as a model, the child works daily on various letters. Drill is strongly advised until the child has mentally matched each letter with its form. Either cursive or manuscript writing may be taught in this manner, but according to Gillingham, cursive writing is much easier for the child with confused dominance because there is less of a change for reversals.

An Appraisal of the Orton-Gillingham-Stillman Approach

There are clearly discernible links between Orton's neuropsychological theory and the instructional methodology developed by Gillingham and Stillman. Thus any appraisal of the Gillingham and Stillman teaching method would have to include an evaluation of its underlying theory as well. It is hardly surprising that Orton's premises have generated a considerable amount of discussion, both pro and con. This controversy is by no means settled, and it seems advisable to undertake at least a short examination of the issues that form the bases of the debate. This section is concluded with a brief review of the research dealing with the efficacy of the Alphabet Method of instruction.

Orton's Theory of Cerebral Dominance.   When discussing the validity of Orton's postulations, the primary question to consider is whether and to what extent the notion of cerebral dominance (i.e., of left-hemisphere dominance for language functions, including reading) is supported by neuropsychological research. A corollary to this question concerns the scientific basis for Orton's assumption of a close correlation between eye-hand preference and cerebral dominance, since this presumption underlies both diagnosis and remediation in the Orton model.

The answer to the first question is strongly affirmative, if not unequivocally so. A wealth of studies (Benton, 1965; Caramazza, Gordon, Zurif, & DeLuca, 1976; Dimond & Beaumont, 1974; Geschwind, 1970; Goldstein, 1948b; Milner, 1971; Penfield & Roberts, 1959) have been conducted with brain injured adults, and all of the studies substantiate the relationship between left-hemisphere damage and the subsequent impairment of verbal and analytical cognitive abilities. While these more recent studies have moved away from the original "strict localization" theory whereby the left hemisphere was felt to be the exclusive province of language abilities, they nonetheless do not question the "dominance" of that hemisphere for such functions, at least where adults are concerned. A similar conclusion emerges from the work of Levy (1969) and Gazzaniga (1970) with "split-brain" patients—that is, individuals in whom the corpus callosum connecting the two hemispheres has been surgically severed, most commonly for the purpose of controlling epileptic seizures. Selective presentation of stimuli to the two sides of such "split" brains has shown the left hemisphere to be superior to the right in tasks involving verbal, sequential, and analytical processing.

For an extensive review of the rich and fascinating research in this area the reader is referred to the work of Bogen (1969) and Kinsbourne and Smith (1974). It should be noted, however, that these studies involved adult subjects, that is, individuals in whom language function was already firmly established before they experienced brain damage. Reitan's (1964) studies of hemispheric function in children, the group with whom the Gillingham program is often used, have been less supportive.

Orton did more than simply postulate the prepotency of the left hemisphere for reading. A second premise, and one that formed the basis of remedial instruction, held that mixed or confused motor or ocular dominance was indicative of unestablished hemispheric dominance at the neurological level. Given this premise, it would indeed make sense to train children in the use of a dominant (right) hand and eye, to discourage ambilaterality, and to train a sequential, left-to-right directional orientation. Certainly, Orton had grounds for working under such a premise, for there was a relatively higher incidence of such fixed motor-ocular dominance among the children he studied. Indeed, even more recent investigations (Vernon, 1971) have reported a higher incidence of left-handedness or mixed-handedness among deficient readers. Moreover, Benton, McCann, and Larsen (1965) report having based a remedial program for 150 reading disabled children on this premise; dominance on one (usually the right) hand was encouraged, and mixed eye-hand dominance was "corrected" by occluding the eye contralateral (opposite) to the dominant hand.[1] Of children thus treated, 87% improved, according to the report. While these few studies tend to support Orton's theory, they cannot be taken as confirmation of the superior

---

[1]A note on dominance: Each hemisphere controls functions on the opposite side of the body. Thus a "normal" case would be one in which the left hemisphere (and thus the right eye, ear, hand, and foot) would be "dominant."

efficacy of "laterality training" methods or of the rationale behind such methods. On the contrary, we find that the bulk of recent research tends more to question than to confirm the neuropsychological underpinnings and instructional efficacy of the Orton model.

The past several years have seen an extensive and largely critical assessment of Orton's theory and its instructional implications. In the field of neuropsychological research, serious questions have been raised as to the validity of the notion of cerebral dominance itself; in the field of education, research has come to question whether instructional methods derived from a cerebral dominance model are any more effective than other methods. We shall consider each of these in turn.

Is Orton's Theory Valid? In the area of neuropsychological research, increasing attention is being paid to the capacities of what Nebes (1975) called the "minor" hemisphere. More and more empirical support is being gathered for the intuitively appealing proposition that "two hemispheres are better than one" (Kershner, 1975, p. 278). Even in the area of language abilities—traditionally considered the province of the left hemisphere—several studies (Adair, 1976; Caramazza et al., 1976; Dwyer, 1976) suggest that the "minor" hemisphere might well play a more important role in the development of normal language capacities than was once imagined. At the very least, such studies highlight our currently limited knowledge about the role of the right hemisphere in language abilities. Thus there has evolved, in contra-distinction to the cerebral dominance model, the "hemisphericity" model of brain function, according to which the development of language abilities is felt to involve the active and coordinated participation of *both* cerebral hemispheres. A review of neurological research by Yeni-Komshian, Isenberg, and Goldberg (1975) indicates clearly that the cerebral dominance model on which Orton based his theory is beginning to lose its "dominance," and a model postulating hemispheric interaction rather than hemispheric dominance is beginning to take its place.

Specifically with reference to reading, the cerebral dominance model is also coming under increasing fire. The criticism derives largely from a number of questions that are left unanswered by the Orton model. For example, neurological research has shown that girls tend to show more nondominance in hemispheric functioning than boys. This being the case, why is it that girls comprise a significantly smaller percentage of the reading disabled population among children? The Orton model likewise fails to explain the findings of a recent study by Bakker (1973), which suggest that, particularly in the early stages of the learning-to-read process, it is hemispheric bilaterality—rather than hemispheric dominance—that appears to be optimally conducive to the acquisition of reading skills. Additional disturbing (at least to Orton's advocates) findings have emerged from studies by Belmont and Birch (1965) and Coleman and Deutsch (1964), which show that the relationship between reading disability and handedness or eyedness is at best equivocal. Indeed, after recently reviewing the most current work on the topic, Yeni-Komshian et al. (1975) conclude that neither eye nor hand dominance can be considered a reliable index of cerebral dominance.

Are Teaching Methods Effective? What of the effectiveness of instructional methods based on Orton's theories, especially the ones pertaining to cerebral dominance? Here, too, the assumptions underlying Orton's neuropsychological model of reading disability have come increasingly under question. Given the paucity of efficacy studies, the few that have been performed are generally consistent with the conclusion that there is no evidence to show that the Orton-Gillingham method has any greater effect than any other method. A study by Silberberg, Iverson, and Goins (1973) substantiates this conclusion. They posed the question, "Which remedial reading method works best?" Subjects in the study consisted of four groups of third-grade children classified as remedial readers (IQ of 90 or above, and at least 1 year below grade level in reading). The groups were instructed during the course of the school year by four different methods: (a) the visual emphasis approach (Frostig & Dolch), (b) the auditory-phonic approach (Lippincott Readers), (c) the kinesthetic approach (Fernald), and (d) the Orton-Gillingham approach. Although all four approaches brought about short-term gains on normative measures of reading performance, a 6-month follow-up showed that for all methods the short-term improvement in reading was transitory. In fairness, one should mention that Gillingham says that it takes 2 years of daily instruction to realize success.

The Gillingham program has been critically evaluated by Dechant (1964), who feels that the lack of meaningful activities renders the system unacceptable as a total reading program, and by Gates (1947), who offers the following disadvantages associated with the program:

1. Rigidity of procedures,

2. Forfeit of interest because of the lack of real reading,

3. Delay of meaningful material,

4. Tendency to develop labored reading with a great deal of lip movement. (pp. 495–496)

Gates (1947) also points out that the children with whom this program would be used as a remedial technique often are caught up in small detail. Strang, McCullough, and Traxler (1967) feel that if a child can learn from the whole-word method, it would be unfortunate to deny him or her the opportunity.

With specific reference to Orton's theory, none of his basic assumptions—(a) that establishment of cerebral dominance is a prerequisite for acquisition of early reading skills, (b) that eyedness and/or handedness constitutes a reliable indicant of such dominance, and (c) that instructional methods based on his theories will be more effective than other methods—has received definitive research support. At present, the most that can be concluded is that the methods inspired by Orton's theory, most noticeably the Gillingham-Stillman method, can be effective if they are used by an effective teacher.

KIRK, KIRK, AND MINSKOFF: PHONIC REMEDIAL READING DRILLS

Another system developed to teach phonetic reading to children needing remedial assistance was first made available in 1936 as the Hegge-Kirk *Remedial Reading Drills*. These drills were updated in 1970 by Hegge, Kirk, and Kirk. The most recent version of the manual and drills is available as the *Phonic Remedial Reading Drills* by Samuel A. Kirk, Winifred Kirk, and Esther Minskoff (1985). The underlying rationale and the principles involved in the system do not appear to have changed greatly over the years.

As in the Gillingham and Stillman method, a set of characteristics, which may be used to identify children for whom the drills would be most effective, is set forth in the text. Specifically, the authors state that the drills are most beneficial when used with children who are 7½ years or older, have sufficient mental ability to learn to read, understand second-grade material when it is read aloud to them, evidence a discrepancy between grade expectancy and actual grade performance, have adequate sight and hearing, and are motivated to learn to read.

Unlike Gillingham and Stillman's methods, which are based on the neurological theories of Orton, the *Phonic Remedial Reading Drills* are based on several psycho-educational learning principles that are built into the program and that are used in presenting the material to the child. In all, the drills incorporate 14 basic principles of which only five examples are mentioned here: (a) Only one response is required for each visual symbol (e.g., the letter *a* is taught only as the short *a* in *man*; (b) the lessons (i.e., drills) are sequenced from easy to difficult; (c) repetition is used frequently; (d) nonphonetic words are taught as wholes; and (e) no rules are taught. Detailed instructions are provided for using the lessons and deal specifically with how to integrate sound discrimination, sound blending, and sound-symbol association exercises into the program.

The program itself is composed of 77 lessons divided into six parts. Part I (9 lessons) presents single letters to be associated with single sounds. Part II (22 lessons) presents two- and three-letter sequences that have a single sound. In Part III (11 lessons), previously learned symbols are lumped into larger grapheme units. In Part IV (16 lessons), new configurations are presented. In Part V (6 lessons), exceptions to sounds previously taught are dealt with. Part VI (13 lessons) is concerned with the grammatic understanding of plurals, possessives, past tense, present progressive, and so on. Lesson 4 from Part I is offered as an example of the drills provided (see Figure 10.1). All the lessons have the same format (i.e., focus on a particular letter or letter grouping, provide lists of appropriate words for drill, and conclude with some contextual material for the child to read).

The authors offer a number of suggestions regarding the proper use of their materials and, in fact, make recommendations that extend beyond the drills. These suggestions include the following:

1. Prepare the child with prerequisite discrimination, sound-blending, and sound-symbol association skills, as well as some short vowels and common consonants.

2. Always begin with the first lesson.

3. Require that the child sound each letter "out loud."

4. Stress accuracy, not speed.

5. Praise often.

6. Review lessons frequently.

7. Require the child to attend to task.

8. Teach nonphonetic words as wholes.

9. Avoid teaching phonic rules.

10. Teach nonphonetic words by the grapho-vocal methods.

11. At first, use books that rely heavily on phonically regular vocabularies.

Flesch (1955), among others, was favorably impressed with the Hegge, Kirk, and Kirk system and suggested that even though it was designed as a remedial method, it could be used profitably with 5-year-old beginning readers. However, for several reasons, Kirk and Kirk (1956) maintained that this would be a misuse of the drills. They stated that most young children are perceptually capable of dealing with whole words and should be given the opportunity to do so. They also indicated that reading is not simply the memorization of specific sounds that accompany particular letters of the alphabet, and thus the system should not be used as the only method for teaching reading. Furthermore, as sound blending is critical to the system and mastery of the drills, beginning readers who are deficient in such skills would encounter much confusion and resultant failure when taught by these methods. While agreeing that phonics should play an important role in developing reading, they doubted whether "all children should begin reading by drilling on the sounds of letters" (Kirk & Kirk, 1956, p. 106). Doubtless, Kirk, Kirk, and Minskoff would feel that the same opinion holds for those who would use their new program with children other than those specified.

FERNALD: THE MULTISENSORY/LANGUAGE EXPERIENCE APPROACH

As is the case with the other two systems described in this chapter, the techniques of Grace Fernald were developed for the purpose of teaching children who are severely disabled in reading. However, her techniques differ drastically from the other approaches in several important respects. For example, the systems developed by both Gillingham and Stillman and Hegge, Kirk, and Kirk concentrate to a great extent, if not exclusively, on the breaking down of a word into smaller phonic parts. These components are learned and then synthesized into a whole word. The authors of these programs admit that comprehension should be given consideration, but it

Lesson 4

i

sit	fit	hit	bit	kit
him	rim	dim	Tim	Jim
hid	lid	did	kid	rid
win	tin	sin	fin	bin
will	fill	pill	till	hill

hit	him	hid	hip
sin	sit	sip	six
rib	rim	rip	rig
pig	pin	pit	pig

rig	lid	tin	rim	fit
sip	pig	rib	sit	hit
him	sin	lip	pin	hid
fix	pig	hip	six	fill
in	tip	rim	dig	zip

kit	Bill	fin	nip	dim	it	miss
Tim	rid	lip	sin	hit	hip	if
dip	win	Jim	pig	zip	him	fit
dig	big	fill	rib	six	bit	in
kid	six	tip	rim	sit	bid	fib

FIGURE 10.1. Example of material provided in the *Phonic Remedial Reading Drills. Note.* From *Phonic Remedial Reading Drills* (pp. 29–30) by S. A. Kirk, W. Kirk, and E. Minskoff, 1985, Novato, CA: Academic Therapy Publications. Reprinted by permission.

The Pig Got Hit

A kid had a fat pig.

The pig got hit.

A cab hit the pig.

The cab hit the pig in the rib.

The cab did not kill the pig.

---

is not given a place of importance. In the Fernald approach, the role of whole-word comprehension is pervasive. For example, words are not broken down into their phonic components, and only words already in the child's spoken language are taught. Phonemic, graphemic, and tracing activities are used simultaneously in teaching as reinforcers. Because of this, the Fernald approach can best be described as a system combining elements of language experience and multisensory procedures.

Fernald (1943, 1988) presented both her theories and intervention strategies in the book *Remedial Techniques in Basic School Subjects*. In the first edition, Fernald described her methods and documented their application with case histories on more than 60 "word-blind" students and with numerous other cases of less extreme disability. Over the years, her techniques have remained popular and even today may constitute, in their pure or altered form, the most widely used approach for teaching severely impaired readers.

Fernald's original 1943 book is no longer available. Fortunately, however, a new edition has been prepared by Lorna Idol, *Remedial Techniques in Basic School Subjects* (1988). In this new edition, Fernald's positions are retained intact. Some extraneous material has been deleted, and the pictures have been reshot to present a more up-to-date appearance. In her Foreword and in her introductions to each chapter, Idol (1988) relates Fernald's ideas to current positions about instruction and theories in reading. The contents of the new version set Fernald squarely in the 1980s and should contribute to a renewal of interest in her approach in those who may have mistakenly believed that Fernald's techniques were of only historical interest.

Rationale for the Fernald Method

In 1921 the Clinic School was established at the University of California. For several years before that, a reading project had been in progress with total disability cases. The project included an idiot, an imbecile, a moron, a "word-blind" student, several very poor spellers, a student of extreme mental instability, two students of superior intelligence, an epileptic, a spastic, and a stutterer. Success with these cases brought demand for further experimentation, and a new program was set up in a room of the school.

Included in the new program were children of normal intelligence, most of whom had extreme reading disability. The children were grouped according to type of difficulty, and they attended classes from 9:00 in the morning until 3:00 in the afternoon for 8 months of the year. Complete records were kept. The parents were required to give consent for their child to remain in the program until the remedial work was completed and the child was ready to return to the regular classroom. The aim of the Clinic School program was the development of diagnostic, remedial, and preventive techniques that would help the individual adjust to his or her environment. From this early work the present program was established in the psychology department of the University of California.

Fernald maintains that in order to make satisfactory adjustment to the environment a child needs successful experiences. School, which a child is forced to attend, makes serious demands for continuous readjustment. Unless the child masters the fundamental subjects of reading, writing, spelling, and arithmetic, he or she will find no success in school and future vocational success will be limited. A child may fail to learn because of retarded mental development; a child may have superior intelligence and fail because of conditions that interfere with the learning process. Individuals with normal or superior intelligence can overcome or compensate for emotional disabilities, poor physical adjustment, and difficulties in school subjects if proper diagnosis and adequate treatment are employed.

Whenever possible, the application of remedial techniques should be used before a child has met failure. After the child has experienced extreme failure, negative emotional reactions become part of the remedial problem. Constant failure in class activities often creates in the child a chronic state of emotional instability. Every child has an innate desire to learn, but constant failure results in negative reactions of hate or fear related to the learning situation.

Fernald's case histories show that most children with learning problems had *no emotional upset before entering school.* The school is usually a child's first experience with a group, and repeated failure to achieve may arouse and condition emotions to such an extent that the mention of reading and writing will send the child into a paroxysm of fear or rage or will arouse sullen negative responses. The child may withdraw, assume a fearful or antagonistic attitude toward the group, or compensate for failure by bullying or showing off. Fernald's case histories frequently describe the "solitary child" and the "bombastic child."

Fernald calls the two general methods of handling cases of emotional maladjustment the Analytical Method and the Reconditioning Method. The Analytical Method seeks to discover all the factors that contributed to the individual's emotional problem and then focus on the patient's attention upon the factors involved in his or her particular ideas. Expressing the ideas supposedly relieves the blocking and gives the individual a chance to start constructive voluntary activities that will reduce frustration.

The Reconditioning Method, which Fernald prefers, is the opposite of the Analytical Method. Reconditioning first requires an environment in which stimuli that gave rise to the emotion that is to be modified are avoided. Second, a substitute stimulus that is connected with a positive emotion is provided. After the pattern has been well established, the event that needs reconditioning is introduced. Reconditioning is completed when the event arouses the desired emotional reaction to the substitute stimulus. Reconditioning directs the individual's attention away from everything connected with the undesirable emotional reaction. The information in the case history is used to avoid arousing the undesirable reaction.

The method used at the Clinic School permitted the child to start on the first day with a learning activity that would result in successful learning. No one sympathized or called attention to things the child did not know. The child found out that he or she was capable of learning any word, regardless of its length or complexity. Once the learning process was established, an emotional transformation took place. The child's expression, attitude, and conduct usually improved as the remedial work progressed.

Care was taken to avoid the following conditions because they are emotionally loaded:

1. Extreme pressure upon the child to learn to please the family.
2. Sending the child back into the classroom too soon and forcing him or her to use a method that would reestablish the negative emotional learning block.
3. Putting the child back into the regular classroom and expecting the child to use a method that would cause him or her to feel embarrassed or conspicuous because of a learning procedure that was different from that of the other children.

Exposing the child to situations that would set up negative emotional responses during the early stages of learning was suspected of resulting in an emotional reversal more intense than the original one. Such exposure carried the added disadvantage of negative conditioning of the new technique, which would make it more difficult to reinstate the method. For the child's protection, he or she was not sent back into the regular classroom until sufficient skills had been developed to permit competition with pupils of the child's own age and intelligence level.

Fernald developed a kinesthetic remedial reading method designed to instruct individuals with extreme reading difficulty. Any person with normal or better intelligence was accepted in the program, and in most cases the students learned to read within a few months to 2 years. Although the method has elicited some criticism and skepticism, Fernald continued her work and left the controversy to others. Her experience suggested that every child with a reading disability, from extreme nonreaders to those with a partial disability, could succeed by this method. In addition to improved reading ability, she found that the method also raised the level of spelling and composition in the students with whom she worked.

In Fernald's opinion, cases of reading disability may be divided into two groups: (a) those with partial disability and (b) those with total, or extreme, disability. Fernald first used her tracing method with cases of extreme disability who had attended school regularly and who had no physical or mental subnormalities that could explain their inability to read. Later, she worked with partial disability cases and discovered that they also could be successfully taught by the tracing method. The partial disability cases often were more hampered than the extreme cases because of bad habits that tended to interfere with the learning process.

In the course of her work at the Clinic School, Fernald found that the tracing method produced satisfactory results when used with both total and partial reading disability cases. The general method, as opposed to the techniques, consisted of determining the developmental level of the child through the use of an intelligence test, an achievement test, and a diagnostic reading test.

Evaluation was followed by remedial treatment designed to increase the child's reading ability to a point commensurate with his or her intellectual level and expected educational level. In partial disability cases, three types of difficulty were found:

1. The inability to recognize certain commonly used words.

2. Labored, word-by-word reading.

3. Failure to comprehend content of what is read.

Constant failure with common words tends to attract the reader's attention to the unknown word and to cause the reader to block or panic. Repeated negative conditioning toward the printed page sets the negative emotional response. Slow, laborious, word-by-word reading causes a student to lose track of the unit as a whole, and he or she therefore fails to understand the content of the printed page.

Steps in Using the Fernald Method

The remedial method suggested by Fernald allows each child to learn in the manner to which he or she is best suited. Even children with sensory defects as well as those who learn by visual methods soon adapted to conditions of the remedial program. The stages of the hand-kinesthetic approach are as follows:

1. The discovery of a method by which the child can learn to write correctly.

2. The motivation of such writing.

3. The reading by the child of the printed copy.

4. The extensive reading of other compositions.

Stage One.   In stage one the child is allowed to select a word he or she *wants to learn*, regardless of its length. The word is written for the child with crayon in plain, chalkboard-sized script or print. The child traces the word with a finger and says each part of the word while tracing it. The process is repeated until the child can write the word without looking at the copy. The pupil is allowed as much time as necessary.

The word is written on a scrap of paper first, and then it is incorporated into a story that the child composes. The story is typed, and the child reads the printed story to the teacher. The child places the word or words that have been learned by tracing in a word file. This file is arranged alphabetically, and the child learns the alphabet incidentally. The practice is excellent training for later learning how to use the dictionary as well as for learning the letters of the alphabet. In cases of extreme disability, every word used in the first composition may have to be learned by tracing. Usually, the child soon gains sufficient skill and progresses into the second stage.

Pertinent points relative to stage one are as follows:

1. Direct finger contact in tracing. Fernald notes that the child may use one or two fingers in tracing. She found, however, that learning takes places more rapidly when the child uses direct finger contact in tracing rather than a pencil or stylus.
    2. Writing the traced word from memory. Fernald emphasizes the point that the child should never copy the words that he or she has traced. Looking back and forth between copy and the word being written tends to break the word into fragmentary, meaningless units. In copying, Fernald feels that the flow of the hand in writing is interrupted, and the eyes move back and forth instead of fixing as they should upon the word being written. Fernald contends that the habit of copying words seriously impedes correct writing or spelling, and even interferes with the recognition of words already written.

3. Writing words as units. The word must be learned and written as a whole rather than by sounds or syllables. If a child is unsuccessful in attempting to write a word after tracing it, the incorrect form is removed from view. The child begins the tracing process anew and again attempts to write the word as a whole. Erasing or correcting single words, letters, or syllables is *not* permitted, since Fernald feels strongly that such procedures break up the word into a jumbled, meaningless entity that does not represent the correct form of the word.

4. Using words in context. By always using the words in context, the child experiences them in meaningful groups, which helps to give exact meaning to all of the words.

The child usually has a speaking vocabulary large enough to express those things that are of interest to the child. A child who has a limited vocabulary should start learning to write and read words that he or she already uses in speech.

Stage Two.   Tracing is no longer necessary in stage two of the remedial work. The child has developed sufficient skill to learn words by looking at the word in script, saying the word over while looking at it, and then writing the word without copying. The child continues to write freely and to read the printed copy of his or her work. Writing becomes easier, and stories become longer and more interesting. The child is allowed to write on any subject that interests him or her.

The important connection between stages one and two is that the child continues to vocalize the word being learned. The individual must establish the connection between the sound of a word and its form so that visual stimulation will immediately stimulate a vocal recall. Vocalization of the word should be natural and not a stilted or distorted sounding out of letters or syllables, which results in the loss of the word as a whole. The sounds of individual letters are never produced separately and are never overemphasized. In a longer word such as *important*, the student says *im* while tracing the first syllable, *por* while tracing the second syllable, and *tant* while finishing the word. In writing the word the child again pronounces each syllable while writing it. After a little practice, the two activities—writing and speaking—seem to occur simultaneously without effort.

Fernald suggests no arbitrary limit for the length of the tracing period, because the student usually stops tracing gradually. A decrease in the number of tracings needed to learn a new word is observed first; then a few short words are learned without tracing. Eventually, tracing is no longer necessary. The average tracing period is from 2 to 8 months.

Material should not be simplified to a point below the intelligence level of the child, in terms of either vocabulary range or complexity of subject matter. According to Fernald, students are more highly motivated when reading and writing somewhat difficult material that they can understand than when confronted with material that is below their mental level. Once children discover that they have acquired a technique by which even long and difficult words can be learned, they take delight in learning. Actually, the longer and more difficult words are easier to recognize on later presentation. When tracing is no longer necessary, the teacher can substitute a small word box file for the larger word box. The words now are written in ordinary-sized script.

Stage Three.   The child learns directly from the printed word in stage three. The child looks at the word and is able to write the word without vocalizing or copying. In this stage, books are presented; the student is permitted to read from them and is told the word he or she does not know. When the child is through reading, the new words are reviewed, and the words are then written from recall. A check is made later to determine whether the words have been retained.

Stage Four. The fourth stage begins when the student can generalize and make out new words from their resemblance to known words. The student's interest in reading increases with reading skill. Fernald states that the student is *never read to* either at home or at school until he or she has achieved normal reading skill. However, she does not object to reading to the student after normal reading skill has been developed, because by this time the student prefers to read by himself or herself. Usually, the student finds that to be faster, easier, and more pleasant.

In reading scientific or other difficult material the student is encouraged to glance over a paragraph seeking words he or she does not know. These new words are learned before the student reads so that the paragraph is read as a unit. At first, the new words are retained better if the student pronounces the word while writing it. The student repeats the words, turns the paper over, and rewrites the word. Eventually, the child gains enough skill to retain the word and its meaning if the word is identified for him or her. The teacher records the word for later review to determine whether words learned in this manner are being retained.

The four stages described make up the instructional method designed by Fernald for use with cases of total or partial reading disability. During each stage of the method a child is continually evaluated in an effort to discover whether he or she retains the words learned. If the retention rate decreases, the teacher returns the pupil to an earlier stage of learning.

In discussing the phonics approach to teaching reading, Fernald comments that the child should never sound out words and that the teacher should never sound out words for the child except in those rare cases when the child, due to previous training, wants to sound out a word. Then the child is allowed to sound out a word if he or she does it before reading. Many people believe that phonics must be taught if a student is to develop the ability to recognize new words from their similarity to words that have been experienced in other combinations. As a matter of fact, Fernald says that the student will come to understand word combinations after the development of a varied reading background. After several years of extensive reading, the average individual develops a complex a perceptive background and larger reading vocabulary than either spoken or written vocabulary.

The amount of reading instruction needed to bring a child with a reading disorder to an optimal reading level depends upon the individual and upon the educational age desired. The younger child is ready to return to regular classes when the reading achievement level of the regular class group is reached. The older child should remain in the remedial group until he or she can recognize new words, has established an adequate reading vocabulary, and has developed the necessary conceptual background. Many failures occur because the individual does not have the wealth of reading experience necessary for intelligent, rapid reading. Sufficient skill must be achieved before the student can read with speed and comprehension materials suitable to the student's age and intellect.

Certain bodily adjustments are necessary along with other skills, in order to acquire the particular coordination that characterizes the reading process. Fernald discusses some of the conditions that may affect reading such as farsightedness, nearsightedness, astigmatism, muscle imbalance, aniseikonia, and lack of visual acuity. She states that poor eye coordination is not the reason a child fails to learn to read; some people with monocular vision, nystagmus, and spastic imbalance learn to read with a fair degree of speed and comprehension provided the eye can provide a clear retinal image. Most good readers, however, develop the ability to move across each line of print with a series of sweeps and fixations. Rapid readers make few fixations and only occasional regressions while reading familiar material. A slow reader makes many stops with many regressions.

Appraisal of the Fernald Method

Fernald's remedial reading method is mentioned in most texts on the teaching of reading; thus the method is recognized by most authorities on reading. Smith and Carrigan (1959) say that Fernald's "hand-kinesthetic" technique provides all the conditions known to be essential to learning. The child tells a story (ensures motivation and maximum meaning). The teacher writes each word to be learned. The child traces and pronounces the word aloud (behaviors that demand maximum attention and also provide multiple sensory input). The child writes the word independently and checks its correctness. Thus reward is immediate (fulfillment of expectancy).

Johnson, Darley, and Spriestersbach (1963) state that Fernald recommends supplementing the visual and auditory stimuli with a kinesthetic stimulus to increase the comparative intensity of the task at hand and to apply the psychological principle of reinforcement. The method ensures active attention, presents the material in an orderly sequential manner, and reinforces, reteaches, and reviews until a word is established thoroughly. The method is applicable to the development of the initial sight vocabulary. When the child has established reading skill, the method may be dropped.

Fernald's approach may be supported theoretically by reference to certain neurophysiological concepts advocated by Rood (1962) and Ayres (1964). The actual tactile sensation and the kinesthetic act of moving send neural impressions to the brain. Roods says that every little muscle spindle and every surface hair that is activated by the least movement will create an afferent or sensory stimulus pattern in the brain. In this way, body image and mental alertness are dependent upon the proprioceptive stimuli. The afferent stimulus can be either high threshold (less discriminating) or low threshold (more specific), depending upon the type of fibers activated. The high-threshold fibers are primitive and unmyelinated, and they terminate in the reticular formation of the midbrain. the low-threshold fibers are myelinated, fast, and selective and are collaterals into the reticular formation. According to Rood, if a low-threshold stimulus pathway is used first, it is then readied for a speedier transmission of immediate succeeding stimuli along the same pathway. It may be that the act of tracing a word several times prepares the mental coordinates for an important message and then follows through on a selective avenue of approach. Thus the auditory and visual pathways are being activated in the same manner as the child sees and says the word while tracing it.

Ayres (1964) also builds on an exploration of the two cutaneous systems functioning in humans. The protective or spinothalmic system is the more primitive and serves the purpose of arousing and alerting the central nervous system. The protective system, composed of unmyelinated, high-threshold fibers, is activated by light touch or pain. Superimposed upon this system is the discriminating system, which differentiates between various tactile sensations. Composed of myelinated, low-threshold, selective fibers, it is activated by pressure. Inhibition of the protective system is achieved by stimulation of the discriminative system. Ayres suggests that tactile discrimination might counteract to some extent the hyperactivity believed to be caused by the action of the protective system. This would account for Fernald's successes with children exhibiting a hyperactive, impulsive behavior pattern. As the child traces over the word, the protective system is subdued by the pressure of tracing. When the protective system is inhibited, the child may attend to the task at hand because he or she is no longer oversensitive to the tactile influences in the surroundings.

In addition to the lofty and highly speculative theoretical support offered by Ayres and Rood and to the subjective anecdotal reports from "successful" practitioners of the VAKT approach, advocates of the Fernald method of training can point to some research literature that seems to substantiate their enthusiasm. An early experiment was performed by Berman (1930), who found that the addition of a kinesthetic-tactual stimulus to visual and auditory stimuli led to improvements in the recognition of nonsense syllables and geometric shapes among 9-year-old partially reading disabled children; retention, on the other hand, did not seem to be aided by the method. Loudon and Arthur (1940) report dramatic success in using the method with an extreme case of reading disability, though the lack of tight experimental control and the use of but one subject limit generalization of their findings. A study by Pulliam and his associates (1945) suggested that recall of new vocabulary words was enhanced by the tactile tracing of such words. Finally, a study by Roberts and Coleman (1958) with children from the Clinical School at the University of California at Los Angeles examined and found support for the following hypotheses: (a) that below normal readers will also be below normal in perceptual (or visual?) acuity; (b) that sub-par readers will learn less well when taught by a "purely" visual method; and (c) that they will learn better when kinesthetic elements are added to the curriculum.

It should be recognized, however, that the results of these uncontrolled studies provide only very tenuous support for the Fernald technique, particularly in light of contrary findings reported in other, better controlled studies. An early investigation by Burt and Lewis (1946) found the kinesthetic method to be no more effective than alphabetic, visual, and phonic approaches—a finding quite similar to that of the previously cited study by Silberberg et al. (1973). Furthermore, an investigation by Ofman and Shaevitz (1963) suggests that the distinctive feature of the "kinesthetic method" may have no more to do with its effect on attention than on reading per se. This, of course, is practically moot if the result of the training is in fact increased reading proficiency.

In short, the jury is still out on the relative efficacy of the Fernald approach and will likely remain so until a body of comprehensive and experimentally rigorous studies has been conducted. The method can and does work, but is unclear exactly why. It is likewise unclear whether other methods might not work just as well.

CONCLUSIONS

Only three systems of teaching reading to disabled readers have been presented in this chapter. There is no intent to review all of the various reading programs available to the teacher of children with specific learning disabilities. Instead, the authors have selected a very few systems that are used widely with learning disabled children and that were developed for such children. We could easily have included Bannatyne's (1966) *Psycholinguistic Color System*, Mazurkiewicz and Tanzer's (1966) initial teaching alphabet approach, Gattegno's (1962) *Words in Color*, Spalding and Spalding's (1986) *The Writing Road to Reading*, Woodcock and Clark's (1969) *Peabody Rebus Reading Program*, Englemann and Bruner's (1988) *Reading Mastery Program* (formerly DISTAR), as well as a host of others. They were omitted for two reasons: (a) They were not specifically developed for children with severe reading disorders, (b) some of them are only of historical interest since they are out of print and no longer available, and (c) space limitations required that lines be drawn and specific selections made. This chapter is not intended as a short course in remedial reading, and persons interested in obtaining information about a number of reading systems are referred to the comprehensive texts, *Approaches to Beginning Reading* by Aukerman (1971) and *Teaching Reading to Slow and Disabled Learners* by S. Kirk, Klieban, and Lerner (1978) or Bartel's (1990a) chapter in *Teaching Students with Learning and Behavior Problems*.

11

TEACHING ACADEMICS TO
HYPERACTIVE-DISTRACTIBLE CHILDREN

If the education of dyslexic children began, for all practical purposes, with the work of Samuel Orton and Grace Fernald, then it may be said that the education of most other children with learning disabilities drew most heavily in its earlier days upon the work of Strauss and Lehtinen, particularly as given in their text *Psychopathology and Education of the Brain-Injured Child* (1947, 1989). Following them, Cruickshank and his colleagues, Bentzen, Ratzeburg, and Tannhauser, were instrumental in promoting the concept of "minimal brain injury" as the etiology of many learning disorders in children and, in addition, compiled a set of techniques for working with brain injured children in the book *A Teaching Method for Brain-Injured and Hyperactive Children* (1961). The rationale behind the methods presented by Lehtinen and Cruickshank, as well as summaries of their techniques, is given in this chapter dealing with methods for teaching hyperactive-distractible children. In general, these approaches emphasize cross-modality stimulation in most training activities. The emphasized tasks use auditory, visual, kinesthetic, and tactile inputs in varying combinations, which permit the child to capitalize on all areas of strength while, it is hoped, improving areas of deficit at the same time.

What happens in the brain as the various sensory channels send their messages in a coordinated, simultaneous manner? Hebb (1949) says that there are interconnections of the neural cells in the brain, which possibly form connections in patterns. Parts of the patterns can be excited by more than one type of input, because of the interweaving of the pattern elements. Thus if an auditory input that usually occurs with a visual input happens to enter without the visual input, part of the pattern of the two could be excited by the single input. Consequently, a "set" could consist of forming a word through visual, auditory, and kinesthetic channels, which could eventually be excited by the input of just one channel.

This chapter surveys the multisensory systems of Strauss and Lehtinen and of Cruickshank, who are concerned with both preschool- and school-aged children and who stress the importance of the perceptual buildup as a prerequisite for academic success. The case history that follows describes a child for whom many teachers would recommend a multisensory approach such as that of Strauss and Lehtinen or of Cruickshank.

The public school coordinator of special education referred S. M. for evaluation because of first-grade failure associated with difficulty in attention and memory. The parents supported the complaints raised by the coordinator and added that S. M. had acquired a considerably negative attitude toward school that was evidenced by his (a) poor attendance, (b) inadequate peer relationships, (c) dislike of or inability to do homework, (d) excessive hyperactivity, and (e) possible psychosomatic episodes probably induced to avoid school. In fact, S. M. missed the first 3 weeks of school because of "stomachaches." By Christmas he had finally adapted to school, but the family moved in April, and a change of schools was required.

Results of the WISC suggested that S. M. was of at least low average intelligence. His performance on the individual subtests, however, ranged from scaled score 2 to 14 and indicated the presence of strengths and deficits on both the Verbal and Performance scales. The findings from the ITPA were suggestive of a generalized psycholinguistic problem. Although above CA in Visual Reception, he scored substantially below CA on all the other subtests (including the visual-motor ones). No modality preference was evident; strengths and weaknesses were apparent in both auditory-vocal and visual-motor channels. Deficiencies at the Representational as well as the Automatic levels of language were noted. In speech he was found to have poor discrimination of speech sounds and articulation ability while demonstrating adequate syntax and sentence length. A neurological examination revealed evidence of central nervous system dysfunction.

Due to S. M.'s youth and apparent multiple perceptual difficulties, a perceptual buildup program was recommended, following Lehtinen-Cruickshank precepts. He was referred for placement in a classroom for children with learning disabilities. Should he develop trouble learning to read and should his cross-modality problem persist, the Fernald method would be an appropriate instructional approach.

STRAUSS AND LEHTINEN: EDUCATING THE BRAIN INJURED CHILD

In 1947, when A. A. Strauss and Laura Lehtinen published *Psychopathology and Education of the Brain-Injured Child*, few educators recognized the existence of the minimally brain injured child. Only a few years before, in 1941, Gesell had proposed the idea of the minimally brain damaged child, and little research had been done in this area. Thus Lehtinen was among the pioneers in the education of these children. As the educational director of the Cove School for Brain-Injured Children in Racine, Wisconsin, she worked with Strauss, the president of the school, to evolve a means of teaching these children. Lehtinen has developed not so much a specific method as a teaching procedure based on Strauss's research and on his theory of cortical damage. The fact that her pioneering efforts have not become outmoded attests to their validity.

In order to make the fullest use of the procedures Lehtinen describes, it is necessary to understand the theories on which they are based. The questions Strauss worked to answer were concerned with how the brain continues to function when portions of it are impaired or even destroyed, and to what extent it functions normally after injury and to what extent pathologically.

Strauss's Concept of Cortical Function

Alfred A. Strauss was born in Karlsruhe, Germany, in 1897. After receiving his medical degree from the University of Heidelberg in 1922 and 5 additional years of training in psychiatry and neurology, he entered private practice, at the same time working as a research associate at the University Psychiatric Clinic. He later served as director of the outpatient department of the clinic; as associate professor of neuropsychiatry; and as consultant to the City of Heidelberg, the school board, and the municipal children's home. In 1933 Strauss left Germany. He became visiting professor at the University of Barcelona and helped to establish that city's first municipal child guidance clinic and its first private child guidance clinic.

In 1937 Strauss came to the United States to serve as research psychiatrist at the Wayne County School at Northville, Michigan, and from 1943 to 1946 he served as its director of child care. Three years later he founded the Cove School at Racine, Wisconsin, a residential institution that was to gain international recognition for its pioneering work with brain injured children. In 1950 a day unit of the Cove School was established at Evanston, Illinois. Strauss served as president of the Cove School until his death in 1957.

Strauss made major contributions to both diagnosis and education of brain injured children: He developed tests for diagnosing brain injury in children and specified the differences between the brain injured mentally retarded child and the familial mentally retarded child. His best-known studies concerned children without intellectual deficit who showed characteristics of brain injury in learning and behavior; these studies resulted in the first systematic description of a new clinical syndrome, the minimally brain injured child. His 1947 book, *Psychopathology and Education of the Brain-Injured Child*, coauthored with Laura E. Lehtinen, was a bible for many of the school programs for minimally brain injured children that were begun in the 1950s. Dr. Strauss died in Chicago on October 27, 1957.

In his studies, Strauss used three frames of reference: the ontogenetic (development of the individual), the phylogenetic (development of the species), and the comparative (development across species). Since these approaches are familiar ones, it is not necessary to describe them. Instead, the most interesting aspect of Strauss's theory is his concept of cortical functioning. Because his concept is not based on commonly accepted theory, one finds Strauss, in the first volume of this work (Strauss & Lehtinen, 1947, 1989), cautiously disagreeing with the belief of older clinicians that disordered functions result from injury in localized cortical areas. In the second volume of the series (Strauss & Kephart, 1955, 1989), his rejection of this once commonly accepted theory of point-for-point localization at the cortical level is strong and specific. Today, rigid localization of function is considered untenable by most authorities.

The clearest description of Strauss's concept of brain functioning appears in the later volume. He visualizes the cortex as a vast network of interconnecting fiber paths by means of which impulses travel in interconnecting chains or loops. These chains are so intricately interconnected that an impulse can move freely not only from one chain to another but to any number of chains. The cortex is never at rest. The chains of neurons are always activated and functioning, so that when a new stimulus enters the cortex, it meets an already functioning activity, and the cortex tries to fit the new stimulus into the ongoing activity; if it cannot, a rapid repatterning of activity must take place, and the new stimulus sets into activity a new pattern of chains. Thus the activity of the cortex becomes activity within activity, and the new stimulus travels in a chain with a complex pattern of connecting chains all under action at the same time. From this complex integration of simultaneous activity a single impression fuses, and a concept results.

A pattern of activity that develops in the cortex leaves a trace that influences patterns developed in the future. Therefore, the activity of the cortex is affected not only by the energy entering at a given moment, but also by energy patterns of the past, which have left their trace; it is affected further by the pattern of an activity developed in response to a particular stimulus.

A new stimulus entering the cortex meets simultaneously both the chains currently in action and the influence of chains developed in the past. The new pattern that emerges is an interweaving of past and present activity. This interweaving must be consistent, and the total activity must remain pertinent to the stimulating situation. If not, behavior becomes bizarre and inappropriate. Thus the sometimes strange and unpredictable behavior of brain injured children is explained.

Disagreeing with the theory of point-for-point localization, Strauss believes that a particular stimulus does not have to enter a specific point in the cortex. A neuron can enter into any one of a number of chains, its activity being altered according to the chain. Depending on the orientation of the cerebrum, the same neuron might, 5 minutes later, enter an entirely different chain, generating a pattern differing completely from the one it would have made on the earlier entrance. It might enter a long chain with many interconnecting loops or a short chain with few. Believing that most of the cortex is concerned with general rather than specific activity, Strauss explains the localized areas that have been found in the cortex as areas where a large number of chains all related to certain behavior converge. For example, Broca's area represents a convergence of chains associated with the motor aspects of speech. Strauss feels that localization of specialized functions in the cortex is not acceptable but localization of such generalized centers of convergence is.

In spite of Strauss's rejection of localization of brain function, he says that the effect of brain damage is determined by location of the lesion rather than by its extent. Comparatively minor damage to brain tissue can cause serious disturbance if the damage is close to a convergence center. Here one small unit of damage can cause major interference, for it disrupts a great number of complex, interlocking patterns. Conversely, if the damage is in an area removed from a specific convergence point, the same-sized unit of damage will create far less disturbance, since there are fewer patterns to receive interference. In either case there will always be general, overall disturbance because of the interweaving of the chains.

In this phase of his work, Strauss concerns himself only with the forebrain (the new brain and the old brain, or the telencephalon and the diencephalon), in which impairment produces the specific disturbances characteristic of brain injured children; the disturbances described by Strauss do not follow the destruction of nerve tissue below the level of the midbrain. Injuries found below the midbrain produce neurological signs but not the disorders found in injuries to the higher centers of the brain.

In general terms, Strauss lists these disturbances as distractibility, perceptual disturbances, thinking disorders, and behavior disorders. He delineates the difficult child now categorized as "hyperactive," and his description of the characteristic disorders of this child has become the familiar "Strauss syndrome."

Strauss interprets the strong psychomotor disturbances, which are so prominent a part of the behavior of brain injured children, through Cannon's theory that emotion is a function of the thalamus and that thalamic processes are a source of affective experiences. The subcortical neurons do not require cortical direction in order to be released into action but can be discharged directly, precipitately, and intensely. This uncontrolled release of powerful impulses results in the intense and disinhibited behavior of the brain damaged child. Strauss believes that this explosive release of thalamic energies in emotion can be controlled by cortical process, so that with the increased functioning of the higher mental processes the brain injured child can learn to control hyperactivity and drivenness. From this neurophysiological viewpoint, Strauss and Lehtinen received their notions regarding education and their optimism in the belief that methods can be developed to relieve the perceptual and conceptual disturbances of brain injured children, thereby lessening the behavioral disorders attendant upon the former disabilities.

At the time Strauss and Lehtinen began their work, the "quiet" brain damaged child had not come to attention; the term *brain injured child* connoted only the hyperactive, distractible, driven child. It was with these difficult children that they worked, searching for ways to help them tolerate the classroom situation, to learn to control themselves, and to advance academically. Although the hypoactive child does not need these behavioral controls, the teaching procedures are equally applicable to such a child.

Lehtinen's Educational Principles

Laura Lehtinen received a BS degree in special education from Wayne State University and a PhD in psychology from Northwestern University. For several years she taught an experimental class for exogenous mentally handicapped children in the research department at the Wayne County Training School. It was here that she began to gather many of the insights and experience that led to her contributions to *Psychopathology and Education of the Brain-Injured Child* (1947, 1989).

Subsequently, with Strauss, she cofounded the Cove School and served as its clinical director until 1984. She is presently clinical director emeritus of the Cove School and director of the Cove Foundation, which has a threefold purpose: to develop instructional materials for learning disabled students; to conduct research in learning disabilities; and to foster understanding of learning disability by professionals, parents, and the lay public.

Lehtinen bases her methods of educational treatment on Strauss's clinical and psychological findings; on her own observation of the effect of general disturbance on attention, perception, and behavior; and on the effect of general disturbances of particular perceptual fields upon the learning of special academic skills. She finds the brain injured child, with a different mental organization and characteristic disorders in perception, concept formation, and behavior, to be abnormally responsive to the stimuli of his or her environment. Such a child's reactibility is beyond his or her control, and in a situation of constant stimulation, such as that of a regular classroom, the child can react only in an undirected, disinhibited manner. Many of the child's educational and emotional problems are the result of organic restlessness and distractibility. The child's behavior interferes with group adjustment and learning, and this interference, in turn, leads to repeated failures, producing emotional problems and further poor behavior.

Even with an understanding teacher who is able to make individual adjustments, the hyperactive child can be helped little in a regular classroom. This child must have an environment tailored to his or her needs. In seeking the best means of helping this child, Lehtinen extends her efforts in two directions: manipulating and controlling the environment and teaching the child to exercise voluntary control.

To achieve the environment she considers optimal, Lehtinen keeps the class group small—12 should be the maximum number—and uses a large classroom so that each child can be seated at a distance from the others. The room is devoid of all visually stimulating material, the windows covered, the teacher's clothing plain and unornamented. If necessary, Lehtinen places the children facing the wall or uses screens around them. She divests the children's materials of all but the barest essentials, even cutting away the borders of pictures and using covers over reading material to expose only a small area at a time.

In such a structured environment many of the children are able for the first time to meet academic requirements adequately. With the decrease in distractibility and hyperactivity, ability to perform in a learning situation increases. The interaction of external control and learning is reciprocal. As control is imposed, learning takes place; and with learning, greater control is possible. Direction of the child's behavior must eventually come from within the child. As the organic disturbance lessens, the protections are gradually removed—the child's desk is placed in the class group, pictures and bulletin boards make their appearance in the classroom, and so on.

Having manipulated the situation to achieve behavior control, Lehtinen proceeds with teaching methods based on the child's disabilities. She believes that the approach should be an attack on the organic disturbances rather than a psychotherapeutic approach to relieve emotional conflicts or an approach of stimulation intended to increase interest and motivation. She disagrees with the theory that a child should be developed in the areas of his or her strength so as to have a better sense of achievement. On the contrary, she stresses work in, and development of, the areas of weakness.

Lehtinen points out that in teaching brain injured children the problem presented by the young brain injured child who is just beginning his or her academic experience should be differentiated from the problem of teaching the older child who has been in school several years. The theoretical approach is the same for both, but the method differs. The younger child is taught with various readiness materials; the method for the older child is essentially remedial. Here Lehtinen makes an important point: Even though many of the techniques employed with the older groups are similar to standard remedial techniques, the orientation to the problem is different. Greater emphasis is placed upon the correction of the disability.

Educational Materials

Lehtinen plans her lessons to include motor activities—sorting, cutting, printing or writing, manipulating counters and gadgets. She uses instructional materials or devices constructed according to the knowledge of the particular disturbances of the child, and she inserts a word of caution in regard to these materials: The materials and devices should not be confused with the method; the materials are simply the vehicle through which the method is implemented and are static devices unless the teacher is familiar with the method.

Lehtinen uses many different kinds of teaching materials. For arithmetic there are number wheels, counting boards, "take-away" boxes, various counting devices, number cards, the abacus. For reading she uses word and letter cards, letter puzzles, and slotted covers to expose only one word or a sentence at a time. She does not often use pictures because even in a simple picture there can be distracting details. Commercially prepared workbooks, their pages loaded with distractions, are not suitable for the brain injured child. However, they are valuable source books and can be presented to the child if the pages are cut up and rearranged into simpler form with the unessential, distracting details eliminated.

As described by Lehtinen, the materials can be constructed by the teacher and, in many instances, by the children. In fact, she feels that it is particularly important for the children to construct their materials, for in measuring, cutting, pasting, and the like, they are occupied motorically and at the same time are gaining some insight into how the materials are made and how they will be used. In this fashion, among others, the materials are considered self-tutoring.

These teaching materials are *not* examples of games used to increase motivation or to teach through play. They are materials constructed to present the essential elements of a skill or process so the child can gain insight into it.

Since these instructional materials are constructed to meet the particular needs of a particular child or group of children and vary accordingly, Lehtinen's description of them is not detailed here. It is perhaps more profitable to follow the course she herself stresses—proceed from the underlying principles to whatever method and materials are indicated for a given child.

Arithmetic.   Four general principles underlying arithmetic instruction for brain injured children are specified by Lehtinen:

1. Number concept, based originally upon organized perceptual experiences, depends upon the relationships of objects in space and the resulting development of a number scheme.

2. Development of such a scheme is the outgrowth of ability to organize; it is a semiabstract structure evolved from the understanding of relationships, of parts to parts and parts to the whole.

3. This visuospatial scheme will be abstracted from its perceptual concrete origins when relationships are grasped and meanings understood. This implies the need for perceptual experiences (concrete or semiconcrete) until such organization occurs.

4. For the child with organic disturbances, it may often be necessary to develop special material and techniques of instruction based on our knowledge of such disturbances. (Strauss & Lehtinen, 1989, p. 152)

One must remember that according to Lehtinen the brain injured child lacks the abilities of the normal child to discover spontaneously the significant relationships of the number system. Thus, although the brain injured child usually has little difficulty in learning arithmetical processes, he or she encounters extreme difficulty in understanding the meaning behind the processes. Long before "modern math" made its appearance, Lehtinen was using methods that stressed meaning and relationships. She aims at developing a pattern of visual spatial organization with emphasis upon the relatedness of parts of the pattern. Effort should be directed also toward aiding the child in structuring his or her pattern or organization as completely and normally as possible.

She cautions that habituation through drill should be the last step of the brain injured child's learning of arithmetic skills. Many people feel that if material is practiced often enough and in varying contexts, it will be learned and understood; the natural technique for accomplishing such learning is drill. However, if exposed to excessive drill, the brain injured child may rely upon rote memorization without comprehension, as may any child.

Reading. Approaching the teaching of reading from the standpoint that reading, even when silent, is primarily auditory, Lehtinen lays down the following principles:

1. In the auditory perceptual area as well as in the area of visual perception and behavior, the general disturbances of distractibility, disinhibition, erraticism, and perseveration are evident.

2. . . . Individuals whose imagery is predominantly visual will have difficulty making auditory images.

3. The disturbance of spatial organization apparent in the visual field is, in many instances, a factor productive of disturbance in the auditory field as well. (Strauss & Lehtinen, 1989, p. 173)

The beginning of phonetic instruction is entirely oral. It is not until the child can discriminate the sounds and reproduce them in isolation that symbols are used. After the child has developed fairly adequate auditory discrimination, the letter should be presented as the visual symbol for the sound, and writing should be correlated with this association. At this point, Lehtinen finds it beneficial to assign a color to each vowel sound and to teach an association between color and sound. She stresses an analytical rather than a global method of making a response to the whole word. The child's attention is drawn to the visual and auditory parts of a word, and the child builds words from copy. The words are written on paper, letter by letter, using a stamping set, or they are built from letter cards. The child may copy the completed words, emphasizing certain letters or parts of letters through the use of color, or may write them on the chalkboard.

Writing. Closely allied to reading, the teaching of writing to brain injured children has two underlying principles that direct its aims.

1. Writing is a valuable and effective means of developing visuomotor perception, a psychological function in which we know the brain-injured child is outstandingly handicapped.

2. It is an important adjunct to learning to read, partly through its stimulating and organizing effect upon the visual perception of words and partly through the additional kinesthetic factors involved. (Strauss & Lehtinen, 1989, p. 154)

Using cursive writing and appropriately lined paper, Lehtinen begins writing instruction with the teaching of single letters in isolation. She does this because brain injured children with perceptual disturbances who attempt to structuralize a whole word in order to execute the correct visual-motor patterns find the task exceedingly difficult. The first letter taught is *m* because the abductor movements of the arm (those that proceed outward from the body) develop earlier than the adductor movements (those moving inward across the body). The next easiest letters are the pointed ones, *i, u, w, t,* and *s*. Usually, *e* and *l* come next, though this sequence may vary. The most difficult letters are *a, o, d, c,* and *g,* which combine two movements. The order of the remaining letters depends on the child. The seldom used *x* and *q* are taught last.

The child whose perception of letter forms is weak must be given special help, since this child may confuse the similar forms. The child who perseverates will not be able at first to make letters with movements opposed to the one just mastered. This child can be helped by writing with a stylus on modeling clay rolled out in a pan. The child who has a good deal of motor disturbance can be helped by wrapping the pencil in modeling clay, thus enlarging the area that is grasped. It is important that writing be taught together with reading, its reverse activity. In reading, a visual symbol is translated into an auditory-verbal one; and in writing, an auditory-verbal symbol is translated back to the visual symbol.

In teaching academic skills the brain injured child's particular disabilities must always be kept in mind. Many of these children have poor work habits stemming from their organic disturbances. Others are overmeticulous, and the slightest deviation from the child's standard must be corrected over and over again. The performance of these children is extremely variable. Bright and capable one day, a child may be inert and sluggish the next; a skill or bit of knowledge apparently mastered today may be totally forgotten tomorrow; or the usually good-humored child may become irritable. Bad weather, a very minor yet exciting occurrence (e.g., a skinned knee, hurt feelings, playground stimulation), all are reflected in school work.

In conclusion, Lehtinen says that the teacher of brain injured children must be a therapist; the aim is habilitation. Specifically, in the role as therapist the teacher must

1. observe behavior precisely and continuously,
2. be cognizant of each child's personality and organic disturbances,
3. analyze specific learning disabilities and prescribe appropriate remedial procedures, and
4. analyze behavior disturbances and devise preventative environmental controls.

Thus for the teacher of the brain injured child there is no one specific method, but rather an analytical approach based on understanding of the child and the child's problems.

In considering Lehtinen's teaching procedures, two points should be made. First, both Strauss and Lehtinen believe that emphasis should be placed on the area of the child's weakness rather than on building up the child's strengths, but there is other evidence that when the child's strengths are neglected in favor of remediating weaknesses, the strengths may deteriorate. Second, later studies have shown that brain injured children are perhaps not so highly stimulated by visual stimuli as Strauss and Lehtinen maintain. Dunn (1967) warns that we should look at contrasting research in several areas, including the Strauss and Lehtinen theory that an excess of incoming stimuli causes hyperactivity. Other authors, he reports, feel that hyperactivity is rather an attempt to increase stimulation. Gardner, Cromwell, and Foshee (1959) report that hyperactivity is decreased with increased visual stimulation. Spradlin, Cromwell, and Foshee (1960) state that the increased auditory stimulation of tapes being played had no effect on the activity level of organic, familial, hyperactive, or hypoactive mentally retarded children. Burnette (1962) found no significant difference in the speed with which a list of words was learned in a regular and in a nonstimulating classroom. If these results are accurate, the barren classroom may be more harmful than good.

Other researchers, Semmel (1960) and Zigler (1962), question whether disinhibited, uncontrolled behavior is more common in brain injured children than in other children of similar mental ability. Dunn (1967) reports that others have not found significant differences in concept formation between brain injured and familial mentally retarded children. Frey (1960) tested Lehtinen's techniques in reading and found that they appear to be helpful for Strauss syndrome children.

The teaching procedures are perceptive and flexible, thus escaping the criticism that must be leveled at the rigid methods—that an inflexible teaching procedure cannot meet the extreme variety of problems presented by the very diverse individuals in a brain damaged class. However, it is important to note that the techniques developed by Lehtinen were devised with a particular type of child in mind: the hyperactive, distractible, brain injured child described by Strauss. The child with Strauss syndrome usually displays marked perceptual and conceptual disorders and may differ significantly in many ways from the child who is only dyslexic or the child who, in Myklebust's terms, is an auditory aphasic. Many of the behavioral controls and highly structured perceptual-training procedures would not be applicable to children who do not exhibit signs of Strauss syndrome. Keeping in mind the type of child with whom Lehtinen worked, one may conclude that her methods are rational, well developed, and efficient.

CRUICKSHANK: THE MONTGOMERY–SYRACUSE UNIVERSITY DEMONSTRATION PROJECT

Before Cruickshank et al.'s (1961) study, *A Teaching Method for Brain-Injured Hyperactive Children,* much research had been done in developing effective grouping and instructional techniques for children with central nervous system disorders, and satisfactory results were associated with some of the research. Such has not been the case, however, for children *without* a diagnosis of brain injury, whom Cruickshank described as hyperactive underachievers with emotional disturbance. These children "were not responding adequately to existing methods of classroom instructional programs, and there remained an urgent need to explore the basic causes of their learning disabilities" (Cruickshank et al., 1961, p. 3).

Many methods, techniques, and approaches have been developed in different disciplines in order to meet the needs of emotionally disturbed children with or without brain damage. According to Daley (1962), the first approach is designed to help the child and parents through individual or group psychotherapy because of the belief that until the emotional problems are resolved, the child cannot organize his or her energy into learning activities. In the next approach, behavior is treated as a symptom of, or associated with, the frustration of failure resulting from specific learning disabilities. This approach is based on the assumption that if teaching techniques, grouping criteria, and instructional guides can be developed that provide the children with a continuously reinforced experience in the mastery of learning, then the child will benefit from goal-directed teaching and achieve some social and academic success. The Montgomery County–Syracuse University Study and Teacher Demonstration, conducted by William M. Cruickshank, utilized both approaches to meet the needs of a large number of children who were referred to as hyperactive, acting out, and emotionally disturbed.

The purpose of this section is to review the characteristics of the children in question, discuss the principles underlying the project, study in detail the teaching method, and give a critical review of the principles employed in the utilization of the program.

Characteristics of Brain Injured and Hyperactive Children

Cruickshank states that the brain injured child displays certain characteristics, and the following usually are included: distractibility, motor disinhibition, dissociation, disturbance of figure-ground relationships, perseveration, and absence of a well-developed self-concept and body image. He contends that the first four of these characteristics are a variation of distractibility and that perseveration and body image are separate entities.

Distractibility is described as "the lack of that cortical control which permits prolonged attention to the task and negative adaptation to the unessential" (Cruickshank et al., 1961, pp. 4–5). He feels that distractibility is the chief characteristic of these children, and under the characteristic of distractibility he places motor disinhibition, which he describes as "the failure of the child to refrain from response to any stimuli which produce a motor activity" (p. 5). Dissociation, or the inability to see things as a whole, also is hypothesized as part of distractibility. The entity has been considered an important factor in the adjustment and learning of the brain injured child.

Figure-ground disturbance also appears to be related to distractibility or hyper-activity. Cruickshank feels that relating all of these entities to distractibility or hyper-activity is important in considering the total problem of the learning situation for the child. He believes that perseveration impedes learning and describes it as the inability to shift with ease from one psychological activity to another. Finally, the ideas of self-concept and body image are considered important in the learning abil-ity of these children. Without an adequate self-concept the learning experience would be quite difficult. Cruickshank assumes that once the children's problems are recog-nized, an effective educational program geared to the specific disability of the child will facilitate educational achievement.

Children who exhibited the preceding characteristics were considered for the original study. Some children who did not exhibit evidence of brain injury were included. These children were also hyperactive and indistinguishable from the children with signs of brain injury. The children were between the chronological ages of 6-11 and 10-11. They had mental ages not less than 4-8 and intelligence quo-tients not less than 50. All of the children were having difficulties in school. Several of them could not adjust to the discipline and structure of the classroom situation.

The Approach to Education

A multidisciplinary diagnostic evaluation was done on each child, developmental and environmental data were collected, and case histories were prepared. The diagnostic team was somewhat reluctant to agree on a diagnosis of brain injury, even though the neurologist and pediatrician did support the fact. The diagnostic and clinical data, however, helped Cruickshank describe the children in terms of behavior and language learning disorders. On the basis of the diagnostic data, 40 candidates were separated into two diagnostic groups: (a) those children with clinically diagnosed neurological and medical evidence of brain injury and (b) those children whose case histories demonstrated psychological behavior and learning disabilities typical of brain injured children. The children were then placed in four groups matched by chronological age, mental age, instructional level, degree of hyperactivity and perseveration, and previous experience in special classes. Two groups of 10 each out of the original 40 were designated as experimental, and 2 were designated control.

Cruickshank believes that the educational program for normal children is com-pletely unsatisfactory for these children. An educational environment designed to meet the needs of the children and to teach directly to the disability is considered the best approach. The plan of education, therefore, involved Cruickshank's modifica-tion of Strauss and Lehtinen's concepts of education for brain injured children and was based upon four essential principles comprising a good teaching environment:

1. The reduction of unessential visual and auditory environmental stimuli.

2. The reduction of environmental space.

3. The establishment of a highly structured daily program.

4. The increase of the stimulus value of the instructional materials themselves.

Further, the program involved the extensive and concentrated use of color in the teaching techniques and materials for all areas, since Strauss and Kephart reported that "color perception and responsiveness to color remain intact in spite of the severest disturbances of perceptual and general integration" (Cruickshank et al., 1961, p. 166).

Finally, the program involved many suggestions and detailed teaching techniques borrowed from Montessori to improve visual-motor perception and incorporated Kirk's principles with regard to reading readiness, although all suggestions were modified to meet the needs of the program and of the children.

In discussing the first principle of teaching, Cruickshank describes the normal classroom as one in which many stimuli are present to attract the child, to create an awareness of environment, and to motivate the child to the appropriate activity. He states that this type of setting is not appropriate for the brain injured child because this child is unable to adapt to the negative or unessential stimuli that create for him or her an undesirable learning situation. He suggests, as does Lehtinen, that the room be completely void of extraneous materials. The colors of the walls, woodwork, and furniture should match the floor; the windows should be opaque; the room should be sound-treated; and the number of children should be below normal registration of the elementary classroom. Because of this decrease in all visual and auditory stimuli, the child will be placed in a position where socially positive conditioning is likely to take place.

Relative to the second floor, Cruickshank believes that with such reduction of space, stimuli also are reduced. He suggests that the place where learning activities take place should be reduced to the smallest practical area; in fact, a small cubicle should be constructed for each child. The cubicles should be the same color as other structures in the room, and the child's desk should face the back wall. The cubicle should contain nothing but the child's desk and chair, and all teaching materials must be kept out of sight. Under these conditions the nonstimulating classroom exists. Further controls include restriction of the number of visitors and reduction of all unnecessary auditory and visual stimuli. Later research, including a study by Rost (1967), indicates that there is no evidence that it is beneficial for a "brain injured" or hyperactive child to spend all study time in a separate booth or cubicle.

In his discussion of the third principle, Cruickshank states that these children have never had genuine success in socially approved activities. He notes that their lives have been filled with failure and confused responses that have led others to label them as management and behavior problems. Therefore, the new educational program should be based on success but must be completely teacher-oriented with little or no opportunity for pupil choice. The teacher must command all available material regarding achievement levels and abilities of the child.

The structured program includes specific activities to be initiated at specific times. Each single assignment during the day should be checked by the teacher, and the child should not be allowed to discontinue work until the task is correctly completed. Such a practice should introduce into the classroom learning situation a rigid order of sequential procedures in work organization, which increases the child's sense of responsibility for order and cleanliness. The learning tasks must be within the learning capacity, frustration level, and attention span of the child. This structured situation should continue until the child is functioning with success in most of the activities. After this has been accomplished, the teacher may begin to present the child with opportunities for making choices between activities.

The fourth factor of increased stimulus value of teaching materials was chosen because it was hypothesized that "if hyperactive children are distracted to stimuli, then their attention can be drawn to stimuli which are purposefully organized and specifically placed within their visual field" (Cruickshank et al., 1961, p. 20). Therefore, Cruickshank suggests using material that is intensified in its visual and tactual fields.

As each child enters the program, the teacher tests the child to discover his or her learning needs in visual perception, visual motor and fine motor control, language ability, and number ability. The teacher, in planning a program of instruction, should "begin with work where the child is able to succeed, be sure the child understands what is expected of him, be consistent, use the child's strengths to correct his weaknesses, observe carefully and remember that progress comes slowly" (Cruickshank et al., 1961, p. 146). It is important that the teacher structure tasks so that the child succeeds with each activity. If the child becomes frustrated, the teacher must be close by to help analyze the problem.

In the beginning of instruction, most of the child's work will be on the perceptual level; it will include the use of blocks, stencils, pegboards, color cubes, and puzzles. As the child learns to do more kinds of work, the teacher plans a program that includes many areas—perceptual training, writing, arithmetic, and reading. Two kinds of instructional plans are organized: one for individual lessons that are ready when the child enters the room and a second for group plans in which the children are all organized together for strengthening peer relationships and personal worth.

Teaching Methods

The specific methods Cruickshank recommends for teaching various subjects are discussed next. As has been stated, all lessons are structured highly, incorporating a multisensory approach. He begins by stating that most of the children are inadequate in visual discrimination; therefore, the teacher must develop elementary tasks so that the child may succeed in perceiving whole objects. He suggests that the teacher use color in teaching the children, because color perception reportedly remains intact. Beginning with sorting forms, both paper and block forms and colors, the teacher moves gradually to puzzles, stencils, and pegboards. Sorting and matching of colors, pictures, letters, and numbers also help the child coordinate eyes and hands. More effective eye-hand coordination can be accomplished by having the child cut cardboard in straight lines and gradually progress to cutting out geometric forms.

An auditory training program should be provided for those children who have difficulty distinguishing sounds. Instruction begins with listening exercises requiring the child to listen and account for gross sounds, contrasting sounds, and discrimination of sounds. Slowly, the teacher moves to more abstract tasks in which the children are required to listen to poetry or familiar rhymes and fill in missing parts.

Developing the tactual percept is approached by using sandpaper numbers; teaching the distinction between soft and hard, smooth and rough; recognition of wooden forms by feeling; and writing with the finger.

A child's need for motor training can be discovered by the teacher while observing each child in his or her particular setting. Cruickshank notes that the program of physical activity does not begin until all of the children have made an adjustment to the structured classroom and have begun to succeed in the learning situation. Useful activities and materials are the jumping board, balance beam, walking blocks, jumping rope, throwing and catching, and relay games.

In teaching writing, the developmental kinesthetic approach is recommended, as the senses of touch and motion help the child fix the sound and shape of letters. Only cursive writing is taught because it emphasizes left-to-right progression, the letters are connected in a whole word thus forming a gestalt, and it helps the child's disorganized movement fall into a coherent pattern. "The first letters to be taught are those requiring motions which develop earliest in the child—those moving away from the body" (Cruickshank et al., 1961, p. 197). The pointed letters come next, followed by *a, o, d, c,* and *g,* which require first forward then backward motion.

The teaching of arithmetic is concrete and practical. Number concepts begin with matching patterns and colors, end to end, and independent matching. In introducing numbers the teacher should begin with number symbols and number names. Moving gradually toward the abstract, the child learns addition, subtraction, telling time, multiplication, and, finally, division.

Reading is taught last because the other subjects are thought of as prerequisites to the ability to read. Cruickshank lists the following factors described by Kirk as prerequisites for reading readiness:

1. A mental age of 6 years or more

2. Adequate language development

3. Memory for sentences and ideas

4. Visual memory and visual discrimination

5. Auditory memory and auditory discrimination

6. Correct enunciation and pronunciation

7. Motor ability

8. Visual maturity

9. Motivation

The approach to teaching reading begins with the basic tools necessary for reading and builds on these to attain a reading level. The teacher begins with visual motor training for hand preference, moves slowly through matching of letters, and then introduces whole words. At the same time, auditory perception training is given with training for imitating sounds and correction of deviant sounds. Having successfully mastered these tasks, the child then learns initial consonants by finding pictures with the sound, writing the sound, and saying it with each presentation. After each initial consonant sound is learned, the child proceeds to learning the final consonants and continues with the same techniques used for learning initial consonants. Vowels are introduced after a few consonants are learned. The short *i* is introduced first because it is the easiest to write. The child then learns to build word families with consonants and vowels. Sight words are next introduced along with color words, number words, and the words needed to follow simple directions.

Evaluation of the Project Study

At the end of the academic year the children in the study were reevaluated. The results indicated that all of the children made some gain in their ability to differentiate figure from background and that the experimental group demonstrated more pronounced growth in social maturity. The average increase in academic achievement for the four groups was 2.5 years. It was found that the neurological and EEG data were of the least value of any information received. This was because the study was educational in design and such information was not considered significant enough to bear on the educational program. Cruickshank felt that the organized multidisciplinary approach to underachieving emotionally disturbed children resulted in the understanding and successful teaching of the children, which enabled them to achieve both academically and socially.

The results of the study appear to be quite remarkable in that these children improved so quickly. At first glance it would seem from the study that this method of teaching and diagnosing the brain injured child is the best approach. Several studies of these same children 3 years later, however, show quite different results. Bentzen and Petersen (1962) compared the neurological and EEG findings of Cohn with the clinical data of the experiment. The purpose was to determine whether Cohn's neurological and EEG findings would have predicted which children made the most progress, which made the least, and which made a modest gain. There was no correlation. After 3 years, only six children in the study had been transferred out of the project and into a regular-age grade public school classroom. Of the children who neurologically appeared to have the least chance of profiting from the specialized teaching experience, one was scheduled for residential care, and the others made less than 6 months' progress. Bentzen and Petersen contend that the reason these children did not succeed was "that there was a poverty of language development and lack of integration of the classroom learning experience into a useful, productive mode of life" (1962, p. 140). They further explored the validity of this study by stating that maybe the teachers were too concerned with the performance of a specific task and not enough with the comprehension of a given learning experience.

The report of the study left Lovitt (1989) wanting to know more. He was especially curious about the nature of the control program because students enrolled there did as well as those in the experimental program. Also, he wondered why the researchers "didn't break out their data as to children who were brain injured and those who were not" (p. 22).

Hewett (1964) suggests that the teacher should provide a hierarchy of educational tasks for children with learning disorders. In this way the child will be given tasks to perform at different levels of learning. He feels that an effective program depends on the establishment of a point of *meaningful* contact between the child and the teacher. In his hierarchy he presents an "order task" level that is very similar to the whole Cruickshank program. However, this one level is only a single point on the hierarchy where the teacher can have meaningful contact with the child. The educational program should not be static but should change from day to day, with the teacher increasing control as necessary until the child has progressed to the "achievement task" level. Hewett, while agreeing with Cruickshank on the "order task" level, quickly goes on to other levels of meaningful functioning, which Cruickshank fails to do.

The authors feel that Cruickshank's procedures, which are modifications of principles and techniques developed by Strauss and Lehtinen, are appropriate for some children, probably the same type of children for whom Strauss and Lehtinen provided their methods. It appears that the advantages and disadvantages of the two systems are essentially the same. One may speculate that a combined program of procedures taken from Strauss and Lehtinen, Cruickshank, and Hewett might reveal results quite different from those obtained from the Cruickshank study alone. In such a program, children would approach academic and social learning through a hierarchy of experiences extending upward through the level of meaningfulness, thereby gaining the ability to structure their needs and cope with their environment by relating to themselves, their environment, and other persons in a meaningful fashion.

12

REMEDIATING MATH DISABILITIES

Educators who are searching for special math methods geared specifically to children with disabilities are likely to find that 'rithmetic is not simply the last of the "three R's," but is the least as well. This is not to imply that there is any dearth of instructional programs in math; on the contrary, countless methods and materials await teachers who wish to persuade their students that $2 + 2 = 4$. Unfortunately, relatively few of the instructional resources are tailored explicitly for students who have difficulty in mastering basic quantitative skills and concepts. Compared with disorders of language, reading, and writing, those of mathematics have received relatively scant attention from the theorists and practitioners of special education. Indeed, we must concur with V. Brown, who noted, "Instruction in mathematics for the child labelled as learning disabled has been an area about which little has been written except that, 'Little has been written . . .'" (1975, p. 476).

This situation is more than a little anomalous. While precise figures are unavailable, there is no question that there exist a great number of children who experience learning problems in mathematics. And as Bartel (1990a) has pointed out, such children are every bit as handicapped as children who cannot read. There are both practical and emotional costs to such a handicap. Outside the school, routine tasks such as planning purchases or balancing checkbooks become difficult, if not impossible, to perform. Inside the school the handicap seems to evoke particularly high levels of frustration and anxiety.

On the other side of the desk there is likewise no question that mathematics is an area of concern—if not anxiety—for teachers of learning disabled children. Cawley (1976) reports findings from two surveys indicating that special education teachers devote well over an hour a day of instructional time to mathematics. Thus there is no doubt that learning disorders in the "third R" do exist and that teachers (and children) have been forced to deal with them. That they have not received more specific guidance in their efforts is in large part a function of our concepts of mathematics and mathematics instruction. Let us turn now to a brief consideration of how these concepts have developed.

CONCEPTUAL UNDERPINNINGS OF MATH INSTRUCTION

At least until this century, traditional notions of mathematics instruction suggested a picture of children packed onto hard-backed benches, dutifully plugging away at their "sums." It was a picture in which rote memorization, mechanical computation, and selective attention to computational produce rather than cognitive operation constituted the dominant leitmotifs. More recently, attention has shifted from the study of mathematical products (i.e., answers) to the study of cognitive systems by which such answers are arrived at. The origins of this shift in emphasis can be traced back to the thinking of Brownell, who proposed a "meaning theory" for teachers of arithmetic: "This theory makes meaning, the fact that children shall see sense in what they learn, the central issue in arithmetic instruction" (1935, p. 19). Brownell thus called for an instructional reorganization in the mathematics classroom, the major goal of which was to make instruction less a challenge to students' memory and more a challenge to their intelligence.

Implicit in this stress on meaning and intelligence, of course, is the necessity of understanding how such intelligence develops. Consequently, it is no accident that the work of cognitive developmental psychologists—most notably Piaget—has had such a profound impact on contemporary models of mathematics instruction. While it is beyond the scope of the current text to provide a comprehensive description of Piaget's work in this area, readers are referred to Copeland's (1974) extensive treatment of the nature of Piagetian theory and its instructional implications for the teaching of mathematics. For present purposes it shall suffice simply to review briefly how Piaget's conception of cognitive development came to have "meaningful" implications for instruction in the field.

According to Piaget, there exists a direct relationship between the logical structures underlying mathematical operations and the logical structures underlying cognitive development. Put most simply, the course of such cognitive development runs from the concrete to the progressively more abstract, from the experiential to the hypothetical. One-year-old children in the first, or sensorimotor, stage of cognitive development are almost entirely stimulus-bound. This means that it is not until the subsequent state of preoperational thinking that they become capable of representational thinking—of holding images in their mind of objects or events not directly before them. But as the term *preoperational* implies, children are not yet capable of performing the "operations" or mental activities underlying cognitive operations—including mathematical operations. They have not yet grasped the principle of conservation, the fact that certain qualities such as volume and number remain constant or "invariant" regardless of the physical configurations in which they are represented. Around the age of 6 or 7 children reach the age of concrete operations. At this stage they can understand that one row of 10 beads is equal to another row of 10 beads regardless of the lengths of the two rows, since in either case the number property of the rows is "conserved." They likewise become aware of the "reversibility" of certain operations, including those dealing with number, of the fact that if 2 + 3 = 5, then 5 − 3 = 2. However, at this third stage, children's logical thinking is still rooted in concrete objects and things. It is only at the fourth stage of formal operational thinking, beginning at age 11 or 12, that they become capable of abstract, hypothetical thinking, that is, of performing mental operations based on symbols that are independent of concrete referents in the physical world.

Piaget was aware of the educational implications of his model of cognitive development. In a 1953 paper on the development of children's mathematical concepts, he noted, "It is a great mistake to suppose that a child acquires the notion of number and other mathematical concepts just from teaching. On the contrary to a remarkable degree, he develops them himself, independently and spontaneously" (p. 74). In other words, children lay the foundation for mathematical operations in the same manner as those for other cognitive operations—through active, physical manipulation and exploration interacting with a maturing neurological system. These foundations are laid less through inculcation than through a process of discovery and maturation. Thus to Piaget, "teaching means creating situations where structures can be discovered; it does not mean transmitting structures which may be assimilated at nothing other than a verbal level" (Duckworth, 1967, p. 317). Consequently, Piaget would characterize rote drill work as merely verbal learning, at best, with inadequate or nonexistent grounding in concrete, physical experience. The American psychologist Bruner (1963) conceptualized cognitive development in a manner similar to that of Piaget, positing a three-stage model of development moving from the enactive to the iconic (pictorial) and to the symbolic level of cognition. While Bruner's terminology differs somewhat from Piaget's, as does his belief in the extent to which development can be accelerated by instruction, both theorists hold to the same basic progression from concrete to abstract as a function of cognitive development.

The influence of Piaget and Bruner is very much evident in contemporary approaches to mathematics instruction. Indeed, many current approaches reflect an explicitly developmental orientation, in which instruction is geared toward children's levels of cognitive development and in which mathematical concepts are firmly grounded in concrete experience. Some of these approaches might be categorized as diagnostic, in that there is a somewhat stronger emphasis on remediation, and systematic diagnosis is seen as a fundamental prerequisite for successful remedial efforts. But as we shall see, both developmental and diagnostic approaches have a similar orientation toward a "meaning theory" of mathematics, and toward the developmental sequences through which such meaning is apprehended. Though few if any of these approaches have been designed specifically for children with learning disabilities in mathematics, many of their features are nonetheless relevant to the needs of such children.

CONTEMPORARY INSTRUCTIONAL PRACTICES IN REMEDIAL MATH

When confronted with students who have difficulties in math, teachers are likely to pursue one of two courses of action, especially with mild-to-moderate cases. First, they may choose a regular class math program and "plug" the student in at the appropriate "instructional" level. The idea here is that once a student's functional level is matched with a commensurate instructional level, math learning can begin. Second, the teacher may undertake a detailed analysis of the student's errors to identify the specific kinds of problems or "processes" that are problematic and prescribe a specific remedial regimen.

Those who are concerned with the learning disabled student have long recognized that "plugging the student in" to the available instructional program *may* be appropriate for students who have merely missed some of the recommended instruction along the way. When there are learning disabilities, however, the program itself not only may be inappropriate—it may also be a primary contributing factor to the problems the student experiences or presents. Such programs rarely consider the many variables that must be taken into account for a student with a learning disability, for example, the language of instruction.

Although many of the programs found in regular classrooms refer vaguely to contemporary ideas about mathematics instruction, the very nature of the programs themselves makes it difficult to see the "ideas" made into reality. Such programs are geared toward "covering pages" and toward skills practice. They are further based upon large group procedures that do not encourage individualization. Finally, they do not provide alternative approaches to instruction for the student who did not understand via the single approach used to present material.

The remedially oriented practitioner who wishes to consider the many instructional variables incorporated into modern theories of mathematics instruction must turn elsewhere. One source is in the operationalizing of contemporary ideas through programs of the British Infant School and through commercially available programs such as Project Math (Cawley et al., 1976). The other means lies in the diagnostic *procedures* that are used by persons such as Ashlock (1986), Ginsburg (1987), and Reisman (1977), as well as others. This section discusses both developmental programs and remedial procedures.

Developmentally Relevant Instructional Programs

These kinds of math programs are frequently found in regular classrooms, and most readers will be familiar with one or more of them. They are the highly sequenced approaches that are used to teach math to most school-aged children in the United States. In regard to remedial instruction, teachers of youngsters having difficulties in math will first try to adapt these developmental methods in an effort to design an appropriate program for a child.

V. Brown notes in her 1975 review of contemporary instructional programs that the British differ from their American counterparts in their relatively lesser emphasis on workbooks and worksheets and relatively greater utilization of activities and materials drawn from the everyday environment. The influence of Piaget is strongly felt in the British programs, as instruction is closely and explicitly geared toward children's cognitive and linguistic developmental levels, rather than toward age- or grade-level norms.

One of the best-known and most lucid expositions of the British approach can be found in *Primary Mathematics Today* by Williams and Shuard (1970), which provides a comprehensive set of guidelines for devising a mathematics curriculum in accordance with Piagetian models of children's cognitive development. The authors both acknowledge and reflect "new thinking" (p. 1) about mathematics instruction and ascribe such new thinking to the joining together of several factors: (a) the advent of manipulative materials and apparatus (Cuisenaire rods, Dienes Blocks, etc.), which allow children on their own to experience and experiment with operations, sets, relationships, and other structural substrates of mathematical thinking; (b) a shift in the nature of the work done from memorized arithmetic skills to the description and recording of "experiments" through graphs and other means; and (c) the availability and technological sophistication of computers and calculators, which has helped to shift the focus from the computation of correct answers to the selection of correct strategies and the understanding of the principles underlying them.

Williams and Shuard reiterate a familiar critique of traditional instruction, noting that "systematization without a basis of ideas springing from experience has been a feature of much mathematics education in the past" (1970, p. 1). This is not to imply that their own approach is inimical to systematization.

> However, all mathematics starts for children from encounters with the world, and with the exploration of its behavior. Abstraction and generalization are late stages in a process which starts with handling, doing, and talking. This process cannot be completed, and a child cannot grow to full mathematical maturity, unless both aspects, the real and the abstract, have been explored and knitted into one whole. (Williams & Shuard, 1970, p. 449)

The overall plan of *Primary Mathematics Today* follows this development theme, interweaving concrete experiences with progressively more abstract ideas. Thus the early section of the book deals with "first discoveries" of topics such as representation, patterns, comparisons, classifications, foundations of measurement, and discovery of quantity. These then provide the foundation for more abstract mathematical operations.

Developmentally based programs can be found on this side of the Atlantic as well. As its title implies, *Children Discover Arithmetic* by Stern and Stern (1971) subscribes to the Piagetian model of "discovery learning" rather than to a more drill-oriented behaviorist model. The authors organize mathematical content in a hierarchical structure corresponding to levels of cognitive development and provide suggestions for appropriate materials, activities, and techniques for instruction at each level. These are in turn operationalized into specific behavioral outcomes at each level. Again, extensive use of manipulative materials constitutes a major feature of the early levels of instruction.

Another valuable resource of practitioners of a developmental approach is *The Fabric of Mathematics* by Laycock and Watson (1975). The authors stress the importance of mathematical understanding underlying the use of arithmetical "tools." The scope of their book encompasses five major sections or "threads" of mathematics: number, numeration, measurement, geometry, and sets and logic. Behavioral objectives are provided for each of these "threads" and are organized according to a five-level developmental hierarchy ranging from the presymbolic to the abstract (junior high) level. Appropriate manipulative materials, games, and activities for each of the five levels are also included, as well as audiovisual aids and references for both children and teachers.

Remedial Approaches to Mathematics Instruction

A number of current approaches to instruction, while taking into account students' cognitive development levels, pay relatively greater attention to remedial considerations than do the developmental approaches discussed above. One such approach is the method of "diagnostic-prescriptive teaching" developed by Glennon and Wilson (1972). Glennon and Wilson characterize systematic diagnosis and carefully prescribed teaching as a "rifle approach" alternative to the "shotgun approach" too often taken in mathematics instruction. Their approach is geared to the needs of slow learners who have been "victims of a drill-oriented program of instruction" (p. 283), although it would seem equally applicable to other sorts of students. They define diagnostic-prescriptive teaching as "a careful effort to reteach successfully what was not well taught or well learned during the initial teaching" (p. 283). In this effort they suggest paying close attention to both curriculum and method variables, and they posit a three-dimensional instructional model in which content, types of learning (Gagne, 1970), and behavioral indicators of mastery (Bloom, 1956) are systematically integrated. Diagnostic procedures include the use of individualized criterion-referenced assessments to supplement norm-referenced measures in the concrete and pictorial modes as well as in the symbolic mode, and analysis of process variables.

A closely related method is the "diagnostic teaching" approach of Reisman (1977, 1978) and Reisman and Kauffman (1980), which likewise integrates diagnostic and developmental considerations. "Unless the teacher is able to analyze the relation or task to be learned into its prerequisite parts, he will not know at what level the child's learning has terminated. *The meshing of the steps of the learning hierarchy into the developmental level at which the child is performing is the heart of diagnostic teaching"* (Reisman, 1978, p. 3). Reisman's approach is geared toward mathematics learners at the elementary level and is based on a diagnostic teaching cycle consisting of five interrelated operations:

1. *identifying* the child's strengths and weaknesses in arithmetic,

2. *hypothesizing* possible reasons for these strengths and weaknesses,

3. *formulating behavioral objectives* as the guiding structure for enriching strengths or remediating weaknesses,

4. devising and using *corrective remedial procedures* when necessary, and

5. *evaluating continuously* all phases of the diagnostic cycle to monitor progress and provide the basis for possible revisions.

For those who would adopt her approach, Reisman provides a developmentally based mathematical skills assessment inventory and methods for diagnosis in the affective domain. Both her approach and that of Glennon and Wilson stress the importance of developmental factors in proper diagnosis, as well as the dynamic interplay among curricular, methodological, and learner characteristics.

Closely akin to the diagnostic teaching methods discussed are methods based on analysis of errors in computation. Perhaps the best-known exemplar of this approach is Ashlock (1986), who provides a semiprogrammed approach for the diagnosis of error patterns in computation. Ashlock contends that proponents of the "back to basics" and of the "discovery" schools of thought have created a false dichotomy in which mathematical concepts versus computational skill, or teaching for understanding versus drill, are erroneously seen in either/or terms. In fact, contends Ashlock, computation and concepts are integrally related. Patterns of wrong answers, like those of right answers, are based on concepts that are learned. "Children's mathematical ideas and computational procedures may be correct or erroneous, but the *process* of abstracting those ideas and procedures is basically the same" (Ashlock, 1986, p. 4). Mere drill, without analysis of the procedures underlying computation, is likely to consolidate and reinforce mistakes rather than to remediate erroneous procedures.

Ashlock provides comprehensive guidelines for diagnosing and remediating— one might say "unlearning"—such error patterns. For diagnosis he suggests four basic principles: (a) Be accepting, (b) collect data—do not instruct, (c) be thorough, and (d) look for patterns. Once such patterns have been ascertained, the second or remedial phase of instruction can begin. Ashlock provides numerous examples of such error patterns by which teachers can gain "hands-on" experience in honing their diagnostic and remedial skills and in helping students arrive at appropriate algorithms for problem solving, which he considers the single most important factor in successful math performance. He also provides some general guidelines for remedial instruction of math underachievers. The major emphasis in these guidelines, which are presented below, is on allowing the child to experience success rather than failure and on focusing on cognitive and affective process variables rather than on simple computational drill. Ashlock's (1986) guidelines for diagnosis are as follows:

1. *Encourage self-appraisal by the child.* From the beginning, involve him in the evaluation process. Let the child help set the goals of instruction.

2. *Gear instruction to underlying concepts and procedures the child knows.* Corrective instruction should build on a child's strengths; it should consider what the child is ready to learn. Typically, children need a thorough understanding of subordinate mathematical concepts before they can be expected to integrate them into more complex ideas.

3. *Make sure the child has the goals of instruction clearly in mind.* Take care to ensure that he knows the behavior that is needed on his part, for the child needs to know where he is headed. He needs to know where he is headed eventually ("I'll be able to subtract and get the right answers"), but he also needs to know where he is headed immediately ("I'll soon be able to rename a number many different ways").

4. *Protect and strengthen the child's self-image.* A child who has met repeated failure needs to believe that he is a valued person and is capable of eventually acquiring the needed skill. This does not mean that instruction should be avoided. On the contrary, as Ginsburg notes, "In some cases, helping children to improve their schoolwork may do more for their emotional health than well-meaning attempts to analyze and treat their emotional disturbances directly."

5. *Personalize corrective instruction.* Even when children meet in groups for instruction, individuals must be assessed and corrective programs must be planned for *individuals.* Some individual tutoring may be required.

6. *Base corrective instruction on your diagnosis.* Take into account the patterns you observed while collecting data. What strengths can you build upon?

7. *Structure instruction in a sequence of small steps.* A large task may overwhelm a child. However, when instruction is based upon a carefully determined sequence of smaller steps that lead to the larger task, the child can focus on more immediately attainable goals. He can also be helped to see that the immediate goals lead along a path going in the desired direction.

8. *Choose instructional procedures that differ from the way the child was previously taught.* The old procedures are often associated with fear and failure by the child; something new is needed.

9. *Use a great variety of instructional procedures and activities.* Variety is necessary for adequate concept development. A child forms an idea or concept from many experiences embodying that idea; he perceives the concept as that which is common to all of the varied experiences.

10. *Encourage a child to use aids as long as they are of value.* Peer group pressure often keeps a child from using an aid even when the teacher places such aids on a table. The use of aids needs to be encouraged actively. At times a child needs to be encouraged to try thinking a process through with just paper and pencil, but by and large children give up aids when they feel safe without them. After all, the use of aids is time-consuming.

11. *Let the child choose from materials available.* Whenever possible, the child should be permitted to select a game or activity from materials which are available and which lead toward the goals of instruction. Identify activities for which the child has needed prerequisite skills and which lead to the goals of instruction; then let the child have some choice in deciding what he will do.

12. *Have the child explain his use of materials.* Have him show how and explain why he uses the materials as he does.

13. *Let the child state his understanding of a concept in his own language.* Do not always require the terminology of textbooks. It may be appropriate to say, for example, "Mathematicians have a special name for that idea, but I rather like your name for it!"

14. *Move toward symbols gradually.* Move from manipulatives to two-dimensional representations and visualizations to the use of symbols. Carefully raise the level of the child's thinking.

15. *Emphasize ideas that help the child organize what he learns.* Children often assume that the concept or procedure they learn applies only to the specific task they are involved in at the time. Tie new learnings in with what a child already knows. When so organized, new learnings can be more easily retrieved from a child's memory as the need arises; also, they can be more readily applied in new contexts. Stress ideas such as multiple names for a number, commutativity, identity elements, and inverse relations.

16. *Stress the ability to estimate.* A child who makes errors in computation will become more accurate as he is able to determine the reasonableness of his answers. . . .

17. *Emphasize careful penmanship and proper alignment of digits.* A child must be able to read his own work and tell the value assigned to each place where a digit is written. Columns can also be labeled if appropriate.

18. *Make sure the child understands the process before assigning practice.* We have known for some time that, in general, drill reinforces and makes more efficient that which a child *actually* practices. In other words, if a child counts on his fingers to find a sum, drill will only tend to help him count on his fingers more efficiently. He may find sums more quickly, but he is apt to continue any immature procedure he is using. You stand forewarned against the use of extensive practice activities at a time when they merely reinforce processes which are developmental. Drill for mastery should come when the actual process being practiced is an efficient process. Admittedly, it is not always easy to determine what process is actually being practiced. By looking for patterns of errors and by conducting data-gathering interviews in an atmosphere in which a child's failures are accepted, you can usually learn enough to decide if a child is ready for more extensive practice.

19. *Select practice activities which provide immediate confirmation.* When looking for games and drill activities to strengthen skills, choose those activities which let the child know immediately if the answer is correct. Many games, manipulative devices, programmed material, and teacher-made devices provide such reinforcement.

20. *Spread practice time over several short periods.* A given amount of time spent in drill activities is usually more fruitful if distributed over short periods. A short series of examples (perhaps five to eight) is usually adequate to observe any error pattern. Longer series tend to reinforce erroneous procedures. If a correct procedure *is* being used, then frequent practice with a limited number of examples is more fruitful than occasional practice with a large number of examples.

21. *Provide the child with a means to observe any progress.* Charts and graphs kept by the child often serve this function. (Ashlock, 1986, pp. 16–18)

There is, then, no shortage of instructional programs and/or methodologies from which to choose, and most of those reviewed share a similar developmental orientation in which the scope and sequence of instruction are geared toward the cognitive level at which the child is operating. In both the developmental and the diagnostic-remedial approaches discussed, the emphasis is on planned discovery and understanding rather than on drill and computation; and the focus is on the means by which children move from the concrete, manipulative level to more abstract levels of mathematical operations. But as we noted earlier, few if any of these programs have been designed specifically for learning disabled children. At least part of the reason for this may lie in the developmental focus of the programs themselves; for if the growth of mathematical competence is seen as a function of cognitive development, then learning problems in math would tend to be viewed as developmental lags or deficits to be "outgrown" than as specific disabilities to be remediated. Another factor is the problem of imprecision and variability in current definitions of what constitutes a mathematical learning disability.

Many teachers may be familiar with another mathematics curriculum that is often used with students who have mild learning disabilities, namely, DISTAR Arithmetic (Englemann & Carnine, 1972, 1976, 1990). DISTAR is composed of three levels and is based on a direct instruction model in which complex tasks are broken down into component skills. The skills are taught using behavioral principles, and students learn how to combine the component skills into more complex behaviors (Silbert, Carnine, & Stein, 1990). Not only is the "what" of math instruction covered in the curriculum, but the "how" of instruction is an integral part of the program which uses unison responding, immediate feedback, error correction procedures, and frequent reinforcement. In general, DISTAR Arithmetic shares much in common with all programs developed by Englemann.

Although the effectiveness of DISTAR Arithmetic, as studied by Abt Associates (1976), indicates that it is effective with young culturally disadvantaged children, there is little evidence that it is efficacious when used with children who have significant learning disabilities. In fact, Suydam and Osborne (1977) felt that the program went to extreme lengths to control the environment, and Reid and Hresko (1981) questioned its heavy dependence on teaching computation while neglecting underlying concepts.

Another approach that may be used in math instruction is the Direct-Skills Model, discussed by Blankenship and Lilly (1981), which has its basis in behavioral psychology and is variously known as applied behavior analysis (see Chapter 17), responsive teaching (Hall & Van Houten, 1983), or data-based instruction (Lilly, 1979). These approaches were developed by people who were not interested in the etiology of learning disabilities, the detailed description of the learning disability, nor the possibility that learning disabled children learn differently from their nonhandicapped peers. They adopted the policy of "what you see is what you get"—if the child is unable to do arithmetic, focus on the specific behavior of concern, avoid categorical labels, emphasize functional competency-based assessment, use specific instructional objectives, and collect continuous data. If the child does not achieve an instructional objective, the inadequacy lies in the program, not the child. These direct-skills approaches do not specify the content of what is to be taught in math or in any other subject. Usually instruction is based on the student's regular classroom textbook.

A current noncontent specific approach being used to remediate math deficits in learning disabled students is "strategy training" (for a more complete discussion of this approach, see Chapter 16). With regard to math instruction, Goldman (1986) hypothesizes that because learning disabled students apparently lack self-monitoring and organizational skills, they need strategy training in four activity categories described by Garofalo and Lester (1985). These are:

1. Orientation—behavior used to arrive at the understanding of the problem. Orientation involves attaining a representation of the problem as well as calling upon a variety of comprehension and information analysis strategies such as recognizing familiarity of the task, difficulty level, and success likelihood.

2. Organization—establishing a plan for the solution of the task, including the identification of goals and activities.

3. Execution—the most commonly recognized mathematical activity (i.e., computation). Included are such activities as monitoring progress.

4. Verification—evaluation of the other three activities.

In this chapter two major approaches to the remediation of disabilities in math are discussed, namely, *Project Math*, developed by Cawley, Goodstein, Fitzmaurice, Sedlak, and Althans (1976), and the Bley-Thornton approach (Bley & Thornton, 1981). The reader should note that *Project Math*, which was developed at the University of Connecticut, is no longer commercially available. The principles and structure underlying the program are believed to have strong validity and to provide the teacher with a remedial orientation to math instruction that is not found in most nonremedial commercial programs. Therefore, the program is included in the chapter. Because no comprehensive programs using a strategy approach to math remediation exist at the present, only some principles of remediation as given by Goldman (1989) are presented later in the chapter.

CAWLEY: PROJECT MATH, A COMPREHENSIVE DEVELOPMENTAL/REMEDIAL SYSTEM

This section is devoted to consideration of a mathematics instruction program that was developed expressly for students with specific learning disabilities. It is called *Project Math* and was developed by John Cawley and his colleagues (1976) at the University of Connecticut. *Project Math* is similar in many respects to remedial programs described above, but its authors have been considerably more explicit about the applicability of the program to the special needs of children who have difficulty learning mathematics. While it is not the only mathematics program geared specifically toward this target group, it is the most comprehensive. And while it is no longer available commercially, the rationale upon which it is based has not been faulted.

Project Math: History and Rationale

For the purposes of developing his own model, Cawley adopts a conception of learning disabilities that is consistent with the Learning Disabilities Act of 1969 and that places the existence of a basic disorder in one or more of the basic psychological processes involved in understanding or using spoken or written language. In the case of mathematics, such disabilities are viewed by Cawley as two-dimensional: They can relate specifically either to difficulties in mathematics per se or to children whose mathematical abilities are relatively intact but who have disabilities in other areas (e.g., reading) that impair their mathematics performance.

Thus Cawley's conception does not so much resolve the definitional problems surrounding mathematical learning disabilities as it supersedes them, by claiming equivalence both to "specific" mathematical disorders and to mathematical deficiencies caused by or related to disabilities in other areas. This is consistent with the position of his colleague Goodstein (1975), who contends that the logical structure of mathematics is universal in nature and thus that the term "mathematics for the handicapped" is somewhat misleading. The key issue is not the development of a special mathematics for use with handicapped children, but rather how this universally logical structure is to be taught. The difference, then, is less one of content than of the methodology and sequencing of instruction. This position assumes, of course, that there is widespread agreement about the content of the "universally logical structure," which there is not.

Because of such thinking, we see in Cawley's model a shift from the "content revolution" of the 1960s and early 1970s to "a new revolution—a methodology revolution" (Cawley, Fitzmaurice, Shaw, Kahn, & Bates, 1979, p. 28). In a 1972 paper, Cawley and Vitello presented the basic rationale for the development of such a model. They cited the need "to make special education *special*" (p. 101) and to do so by emphasizing process as well as product. They noted that most special education programs placed excessive emphasis on teaching symbolic operations to children who had inadequate foundations in the concrete, manipulative realm and that too much attention in such programs was paid to achievement and not enough to learning. An alternative model, they proposed, would give careful consideration to the level and nature of the learner's cognitive abilities. It would enable (or force) learners to break out of their rote, mechanical "computational set" and to grasp the principles underlying mathematical operations. It would provide multiple options, with reference both to the use of alternative, but not preferred, modalities of learning and to methods of problem solving, and would focus on enhancing the affective as well as the cognitive growth of the learner. Such was the rationale behind the development of *Project Math*. We shall turn now to an investigation of the program itself and of the extent to which it has realized its purposes.

Project Math: Goals and Organization

The Foreword to the Administrative Guide for *Project Math* indicates that a mathematics program for children with special educational needs must be capable of three things: (a) It must provide the child with wide ranges of experiences with mathematics; (b) it must be able to minimize the effects of inadequately developed skills and abilities on mathematics performance; and (c) it must use experience with mathematics to enhance affective as well as cognitive growth and give a balanced emphasis to the development of skills, concepts, and social growth. From these considerations are drawn the specific goals of *Project Math*:

1. provide the teacher with a number of instructional options, so that handicaps to learning might be circumvented;
2. enhance the learner's chances for success in a mathematics program;
3. provide the learner with a substantial mathematics curriculum designed to facilitate his use of mathematics in daily life;
4. maximize the instructor's opportunities for individualizing instruction;
5. provide a framework in which mathematics content can be used as a tool for enhancing the development of the total child—socially and emotionally as well as academically;
6. provide a supplement to the regular mathematics program for those not-so-handicapped learners for whom such a supplement may be desirable. (Cawley et al., 1976, Administrative Guide, p. 1)

The program is organized into four developmental levels, differentiated according to the mathmatics content covered. For each of the four levels, a Multiple Option Curriculum has been designed, which includes the following major components: Instructional Guides (and learner activity books), Mathematics Concept Inventory, and Verbal Problem Solving. Also included are class and individual progress records and a set of manipulative materials. We shall examine these major components in greater detail.

Instructional Guides. Instructional Guides are the heart of the *Project Math* curriculum. They provide directed activities in six major fields or "strands" of mathematics: geometry, sets, patterns, numbers, measurement, and fractions. Each strand contains a developmental sequence of mathematics concepts beginning at the concrete, manipulative level and progressing to more abstract, symbolic levels. These different strands are interwoven in the sequence of intruction followed by the Instructional Guides. A sample Instructional Guide for Level I is presented in Figure 12.1.

Each Instructional Guide is coded according to level, strand, and sequence. The sample guide in Figure 12.1 is identified as being appropriate for instruction at Level I. In the upper right-hand corner the "N" indicates that the lesson deals with the Numbers strand and that this particular guide is the 141st (of a total of 358 guides) provided at Level I. "Area" denotes a specific topic within each strand, and "Concept" identifies the specific skill or understanding dealt with in the Instructional Guide. Thus the sample Instructional Guide is a numbers guide dealing with the area of ordinal numbers, and more specifically, with the concepts of First and Last.

A key element in each Instructional Guide is the "Interactive Unit," which provides for a combination of teacher input and learner output. These input-output combinations are derived from an instructional model known as the Interactive Unit (Cawley & Vitello, 1972), the major purpose of which is to provide instructional options for the teacher—as well as learning options for the student—by using different combinations of modalities of stimuli and learner responses. The Interactive Unit is graphically presented in Figure 12.2.

There are four basic modalities hypothesized in the Unit: (a) the *Present* mode, which includes showing the child nonsymbolic displays such as the arrangement of materials, pictures, or pictorial activity sheets; (b) the *Construct* mode, which refers to physical manipulation (piling, arranging, moving, etc.) of pictures or objects; (c) the *State* mode, which relies on oral discourse; and (d) the *Graphic Symbolic* mode, which uses written or drawn symbolic materials. A fifth mode, the *Identify* mode, is also hypothesized. It allows for multiple choice and requires only nonverbal responses (e.g., pointing) by the learner.

In all there are 16 possible varieties of instructor-learner interaction (see Figure 12.2), enabling the teacher to select alternative learning combinations for individual students. There are a number of advantages to having multiple options for interaction. For one thing they enable the instructor to circumvent difficulties in other areas (e.g., reading) that may impede mathematics performance. Thus a poor reader could still attain mathematical understanding by working primarily in the Present,

LEVEL 1   **N141**

PROJECT MATH INSTRUCTIONAL GUIDE

STRAND	Numbers	INPUT	OUTPUT
AREA	Ordinal Numbers		
CONCEPT	First and Last		

BEHAVIORAL OBJECTIVE	INSTRUCTOR	LEARNER
	Presents pictures of sets.	Identifies members in first and last positions.

ACTIVITIES

1. **First and Last.** Set up an arrangement such as the following on a flannel board or chalk ledge.

Ask the learner to identify, by pointing, the ordinal position of each figure from first to last in each row, starting from the store. Then change the store front from one side to the other and ask the learner, "Now, which one is first? Last?" Vary this with pictures of boats, houses, barns, and so forth. Discuss the relationship between direction and position with the learners. Then given the learners activity sheets N141.1 and N141.2. They are to look at the arrow in each row, mark a line under the first item in each row, and circle the last item in each row. Be sure to explain how the arrow determines the direction of each line.

MATERIALS

Flash cards with figures (direction cards), houses, barns, boats, etc.
There should be two flash cards the same except for direction.

SUPPLEMENTAL ACTIVITIES N141: a, b, c, d.

EVALUATION

Present a row of objects with an arrow showing direction under the row of objects. Ask the learner to point to the first object in the row and pick up the last figure.

©1976 Educational Sciences Inc.

FIGURE 12.1. Sample Instructional Guide. *Note.* From *Project Math: A Program of the Mainstream Series* Administrative Guide (p. 3) by J. Cawley, H. Goodstein, A. Fitzmaurice, R. Sedlak, and V. Althans, 1976, Wallingford, CT: Educational Services. Reprinted by permission.

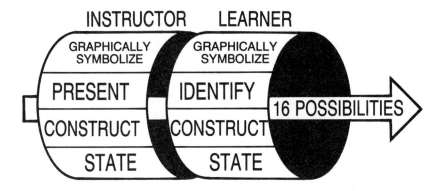

FIGURE 12.2. The Interactive Unit. *Note.* From *Project Math: A Program of the Mainstream Series* Administrative Guide (p. 5) by J. Cawley, H. Goodstein, A. Fitzmaurice, R. Sedlak, and V. Althans, 1976, Wallingford, CT: Educational Services. Reprinted by permission.

Identify, and Construct modes and avoiding reading, that is, the Graphic Symbolic mode. It should be noted, however, that the modes are not considered to be hierarchical or fixed, and instructors are limited only by their imagination in the combinations that can be employed. Another advantage is the potential for affective and social growth inherent in some of the interactive combinations. In the Construct/ Construct combination, for example, the instructor and students are brought into close contact with one another, and the group must necessarily work as a unit— sharing, explaining, demonstrating, and so on. Conversely, some combinations lend themselves ideally to independent work; as, for example, when the instructor "graphically symbolizes" a problem and the student works at "graphically symbolizing" the solution. Finally, the provision of input-output combinations allows for consideration of developmental characteristics. In the sample guide in Figure 12.1, for example, the student is simply expected to discriminantly identify from stimulus material presented by the teacher; only at a more advanced level would the student be expected or required to demonstrate mastery of the same concept in a more abstract (Graphic Symbolic) mode.

Each Instructional Guide also includes an activities section, which outlines the procedure to be followed during instruction and gives a description of materials to be used during instruction. These activities and materials are meant to be suggestive rather than prescriptive. Teachers are encouraged to use their own creativity in the selection and sequencing of Instructional Guides and in devising variations on the themes presented in individual guides. Finally, each guide provides for evaluation of the extent to which mastery of the behavioral objective has been attained. In cases when additional reinforcement or instruction seems advisable, supplemental activities are also suggested. Such supplemental activities provide opportunities for social and affective as well as cognitive enrichment.

In summary, the Instructional Guides provide a rich alternative to a lockstep curriculum approach. At Level I alone the 358 guides and related materials provide for over 2,000 basic experiences with mathematics. These possibilities underscore the wisdom of the old adage that there is more than one way to skin cats—or, in this case, to count them.

Assessment: The Mathematics Concept Inventory. Cawley has developed the Mathematics Concept Inventory, which enables the instructor to assess the status of individual students in terms of what they understand and what they can do relative to the major concepts contained in the program. The inventory is criterion referenced in the sense that it is based on the scope and sequence of the program and serves two major purposes: (a) as a screening device for placing children in the program and (b) as a mastery assessment device to evaluate student progress after a particular sequence of instruction. The Inventory for Level I, for example, is composed of 58 items, each of which corresponds to the core of a concept as taught in a sequence of Instructional Guides in the program. Items that children fail or on which they evidence difficulty are keyed to the sequence of Instructional Guides pertaining to the concept(s) reflected in the item. The teacher has great flexibility in determining where to begin assessment. Inventory results can be used not only to devise individualized instructional programs, but also to determine class instructional groupings.

Verbal Problem Solving. Too frequently, note Cawley et al. (1979), "word" problems have simply been computational exercises or examples "dressed up" in prose. The Verbal Problem Solving component represents an attempt to go beyond or beneath computation and focus on the cognitive strategies that underlie problem solving. This component was designed to be used either in coordination with the entire multiple-option curriculum or as a supplemental program in Verbal Problem Solving (VPS) alone. The VPS component is divided into four levels, which parallel those used in the other components of *Project Math*. The focus at Levels I and II is on the use of attractive picture manipulatives to mediate orally presented verbal problems. It is not necessary that the child be able to read, nor is the major goal the computation of corrent answers. Rather, the purpose at the first two levels is to facilitate the process of problem solving, that is, to focus the student's attention on the information that is relevant and necessary for problem solving. At Levels III and IV the child is introduced to written problem solving, but only the habits of noting relevant informaton and identifying appropriate processes have been established. Vocabulary and grammatical complexity are gradually increased, and problems presented are designed to be analogous to "real life" experiences of students.

The emphasis in verbal problem solving, then, is on what Cawley has termed " 'functional mathematics' . . . that component of mathematics which is applied directly to social, vocational, and leisure activities. It is generally viewed as those activities that are associated with daily living'" (1976, p. 2).

Instruction proceeds in cycles, and the complexity of the problem-solving activities increases systematically with each successive cycle. Each verbal problem features three elements: a stem, which transmits the structure of the problem; an option box, which displays the four choices of sets to be displayed; and an answer oval, which displays the four correct answers to the four optional statements of the problem. The teacher is also provided with a "script" to guide presentation of the problem.

Diagnostic/evaluation codes are also provided for each verbal problem; these describe the problem along four dimensions: (a) the set characteristics of the problem (whether or not categorization is involved); (b) the presence of distracting sets of object cards, containing information extraneous to problem solution and requiring the student to abandon the "computational set" mentioned earlier; (c) the use of an indefinite quantifier (e.g., *some*) for teacher presentation; and (d) the arithmetical operation involved in the problem. The focus of such diagnosis and evaluation, particularly at the early levels, is on thinking rather than computational skills.

> Remember, the primary objective of the VPS component is to train children to attend to the information processing requirements of the verbal problems. With this objective in mind, it is suggested that errors involving miscounting or other incorrect arithmetic operation application are of less concern diagnostically than errors that involve incorrect attention to the relevent information necessary to solve the problem. In other words, *process* is more important than product for children at this level of development. (Cawley et al., 1976, p. 16)

The program encourages teachers to devise alternatives to the problems provided and to use the story mats, object cards, and other VPS materials for enrichment of language and reading activities. Since verbal problem solving involves a combination of cognitive and linguistic skills, teachers can and should make every effort to expand instruction in these related areas. In addition, many of the problem-solving activities are designed in such a way as to foster affective development and social skills by requiring cooperative group efforts.

Strands of Project Math. Instruction within *Project Math* is sequenced in an interrelated fashion across six major areas or strands of mathematics: geometry, sets, patterns, measurement, numbers, and fractions. The foundations for the Geometry strand are laid by the introduction of basic topological concepts: order constancy, basic two- and three-dimensional shapes, lines and paths, similarities, and vocabulary development of basic topological terms such as *inside, outside, on,* and *next to.* Instruction in the Sets strand leads the child from simple classification tasks (e.g., sorting objects according to size or color) to operations involving superordinate sets. The focus in the Patterns strand is on the recognition and understanding of systematic patterns of relationships, which serve to develop readiness for quantitative processing tasks.

Inclusion of a Measurement strand reflects Cawley's belief in the importance of a "functional mathematics" of relevance and value to the tasks of everyday living. Too frequently, measurement tasks are found only as "enrichment" adjuncts to standard mathematics curricula; but in *Project Math* the development of measurement concepts involving height, temperature, time, speed, and distance is integral because they are socially "functional" components of the instructional program.

The basic concepts in the Numbers strand include cardinal property and place value, and they provide the basis for the operations of addition and subtraction. Rather than rote memory, this strand emphasizes understanding of the concepts involved.

The Fractions strand, finally, extends the learner's concept of numbers to include those that represent parts of a group or parts of a whole thing. In laying the foundation for understanding of part-whole relationships, learners begin at the level of enactive experience, for example, examining parts of the body, parts of a flower, or parts of a house, and then noting the interrelationships among these parts as well as the relationship of each part to the whole. Such understanding is then reinforced by working with materials that can be blended or mixed together.

New Directions: A Curriculum Design for Upper Grades

Inspired by their initial success with *Project Math*, Cawley and his associates have more recently been involved in the development of a curriculum (Multi-Modal Math) designed for use at upper grade levels, that is, sixth through secondary but not including math found in college preparatory courses (Cawley et al., 1976; Cawley, Fitzmaurice, Shaw, Kahn, & Bates, 1978a, 1978b). A representation of the basic instructional design for the program is depicted in Figure 12.3.

As can be seen, Multi-Modal Math, A Program for Children in The Upper Grades with Handicaps to Learning and Achievement, shares many features with *Project Math*. As before, initial screening is accomplished via administration of a criterion-referenced Concepts and Skills assessment, Sets of Instructional Guides constitute the basis for instruction. Likewise included is the Interactive Unit model, providing for 16 different combinations of teacher-learner interaction utilizing the basic Construct, Present, Identify, State, and Graphic Symbolic modes.

However, there are also some refinements and modifications of the original *Project Math* model. Only four of the original six strands (Numbers, Fractions, Geometry, and Measurement) are included in the curriculum content at the upper grade levels; this is presumably because the strands of Sets and Patterns would already have been mastered. Additionally, the content range of each strand has been extended. Illustrative of this is the range of activities in Fractions, which now include items through the three basic components of percent (e.g., "What is ____% of a given number?; ____ is what % of ____?; and, ____ is ____ % of what number?"). In addition, each strand is dealt with separately, rather than being presented in an intermingled sequence as they were in the original model. This change in format came about as the result of a 1977–78 field test, which indicated the need to attack specific prob-

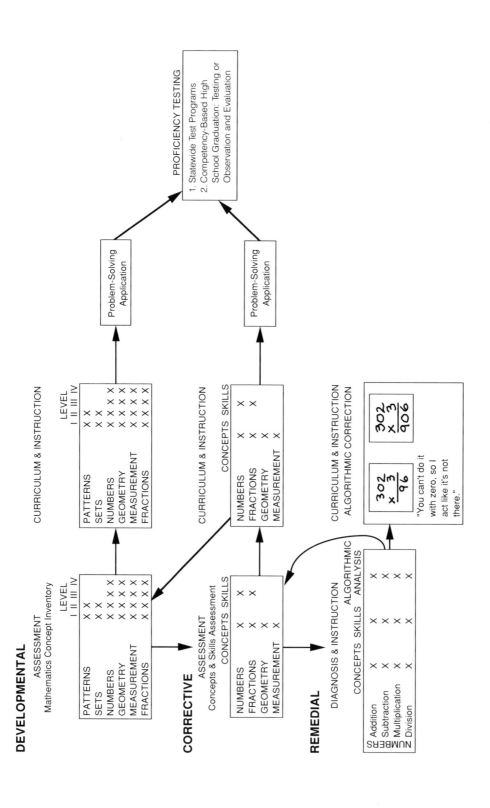

FIGURE 12.3. Comprehensive math model. *Note.* From *Project Math: A Program of the Mainstream Series* (p. 10) by J. Cawley, H. Goodstein, A. Fitzmaurice, R. Sedlak, and V. Althans, 1976, Wallingford, CT: Educational Services. Reprinted by permission.

lems at higher grade levels rather than focusing on the student's overall developmental mathematics performance. Thus, notes Cawley, "there is a contrast between the developmental orientation of *Project Math* and the remedial (corrective) orientation of our current efforts" (Cawley, Fitzmaurice, Shaw, Kahn, & Bates, 1979, p. 41). In both cases, however, assessment is conducted in terms of the individual's current level of functioning relative to proficiency areas, rather than with reference to normative grade-equivalent standards.

As might be expected, finally, the curriculum design proposed for the upper grade levels attaches great importance to the cognitive and affective value of divergent problem-solving activities. Too often, Cawley feels, problems have been "nothing more than computation examples surrounded by words," and obtaining answers has involved "nothing more than 'turning the crank' for the student" (Cawley et al., 1979, p. 26). For Cawley the proper focus should be on the cognitive and information-processing strategies underlying effective problem solving, and such activities can and should be related to academic topics and skills other than mathematics alone. In his view, "problem solving offers a unique opportunity to integrate a host of learner needs into a cohesive activity. Rather than excluding problem solving, programs should emphasize this topic in order to meet the needs of the learning disabled" (Cawley et al., 1979, p. 41).

Programming for Severe Cases

Mathematics has always been viewed as the proper orientation to programming for learning disabled children. Arithmetic, although an important component of mathematics, is simply too limited an approach to the whole child. For this reason the development of programs has always been conducted as a cooperative effort between special educators and mathematics educators. Individuals such as Cawley represented the special education sector, and individuals such as Anne M. Fitzmaurice and Robert Shaw represented the mathematics sector. In all their years of working together this group, by its own admission, has yet to come to grips with the problems of children whom they refer to as "remedial" or "severely disabled." These children are described as *dyscalculic*, a term interpreted by Cawley, Fitzmaurice, and Shaw to mean truly *severely disabled*. For this group it seems that an alternative approach to diagnosis and treatment is desired.

The approaches to the truly severely disabled child necessitate an intensive interaction between child and examiner and child and remedial specialist. As such, diagnosis and instruction are viewed as interrelated and are generally undertaken simultaneously. One approach to the establishment of the diagnostic perspective, the Clinical Mathematics Interview (CMI), is described in Figure 12.4.

As is evident, the CMI model involves a triad of diagnostic considerations. Attention is paid to the *mode* in which instruction is carried out, the mathematical *content* involved in the problem, and the *algorithm* (or algorithms) by which the student attempts to solve the problem. Thus the model not only incorporates features of

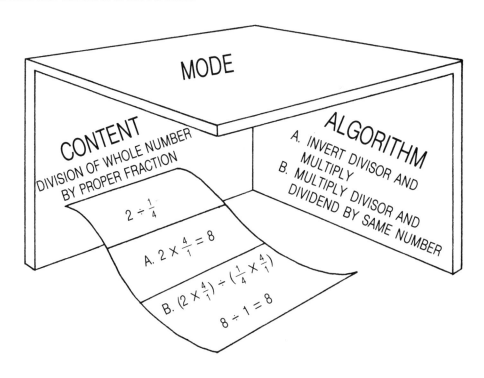

FIGURE 12.4. The Clinical Mathematics Interview model. *Note.* From *Project Math: A Program of the Mainstream Series* (p. 37) by J. Cawley, H. Goodstein, A. Fitzmaurice, R. Sedlak, and V. Althans, 1976, Wallingford, CT: Educational Services. Reprinted by permission.

Ashlock's error analysis but, in addition, takes into account the different modalities of teacher-learner interaction. On the basis of this content × algorithm × modality diagnostic methodology, appropriate remedial modules are designed, providing the teacher with an intensified unit of instruction that will attack a specific problem in great detail, primarily by means of a highly segmented analysis of the content coupled with a task analysis by mode. In reality it is likely to be the algorithmic analysis that provides the most meaningful information relative to the child. One interesting facet of the algorithmic problem is that children who demonstrate faulty algorithms with paper-and-pencil tasks usually are unable to perform these same faulty algorithms with three-dimensional materials. For this reason (see Figure 12.5), the format for dealing with the severely disabled child is a combination of multimodal instruction across given sets of content. This is the next area of mathematical problems among the learning disabled that Cawley and associates plan to embark on.

Appraisal of Project Math

It should be evident that *Project Math* represents the most ambitious and comprehensive effort yet to "meet the needs of the learning disabled" in the field of mathematics instruction. It has done so, moreover, by adopting many of the major features of other contemporary modes of mathematics instruction: a firm conceptual grounding in basic tenets of cognitive developmental psychology; an orientation toward meaning and understanding and away from rote computation, with a corollary emphasis on process rather than product; solid grounding in the "real life" bases and applicability of mathematics; a multidimensional approach to diagnosis and assessment; systematic sequencing of instruction progressing from the concrete to the abstract; and attention to the social and affective variables affecting learning in mathematics and other subjects. In short, Cawley and his associates have kept well abreast of current thinking about mathematics instruction and have made great strides in applying this thinking specifically to the needs of children with learning problems in mathematics.

Unfortunately, there has been little or no research investigating the effectiveness of *Project Math* (or of other approaches, for that matter). The major evaluation effort of *Project Math* undertaken to date has been done by the developers of the program itself. Cawley and his associates (1976) report the results of a 1972–73 field test of the *Project Math* Instructional Guides. Learning outcomes of this instruction were rated as resulting in mastery 63% of the time; in a positive learning experience (but short of mastery) 31% of the time; and in failure experiences for participating children 6% of the time. Additional and more recent evaluations of the project have also been conducted and have resulted in revisions and modifications of the original model. However, these more recent evaluations have been of a formative nature. Hard, summative data on program impact have yet to be disseminated.

Cawley is among the first to point out that the evaluation results available at present, while encouraging, cannot be considered conclusive. The project does appear to work with reference to its own performance criteria, but yet to be answered is the question of how well the program works in comparison to other approaches that also have to demonstrate their own value. The theoretical rationale for such a program seems quite compelling, but only rigorous comparative research can demonstrate whether the results it achieves in the classroom are equally compelling.

THE BLEY-THORNTON APPROACH

Nancy S. Bley, a research and curriculum specialist with the Park Century School in Santa Monica, California, and Carol A. Thornton, an associate professor in the Department of Mathematics at Illinois State University, Normal, developed and published a detailed set of techniques aimed at the remediation of math deficits in *Teaching Mathematics to the Learning Disabled* (1989). Their book cannot be considered

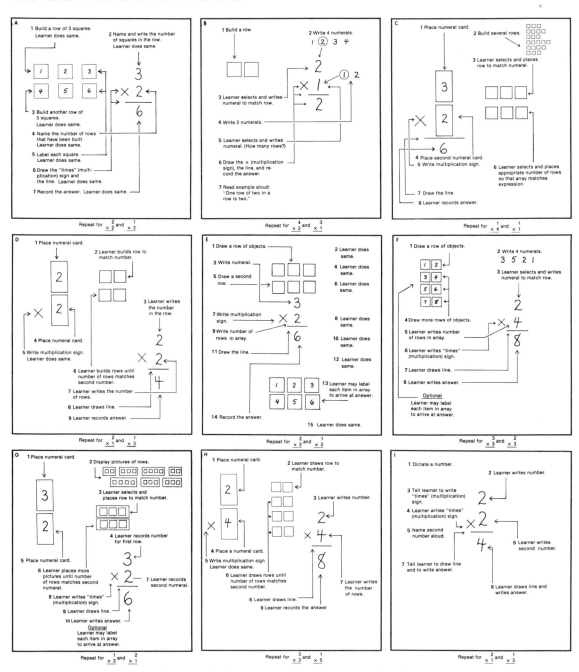

FIGURE 12.5. Module: Diagnostic instruction activity. *Note.* From *Project Math: A Program of the Mainstream Series* by J. Cawley, H. Goodstein, A. Fitzmaurice, R. Sedlak, and V. Althans, 1976, Wallingford, CT: Educational Services. Reprinted by permission.

FIGURE 12.5. *(Continued)*

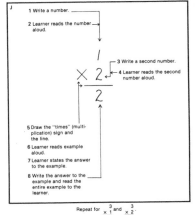

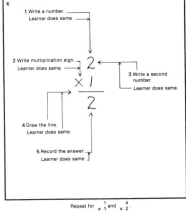

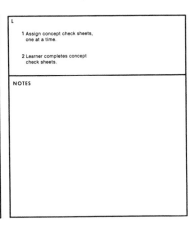

a comprehensive math curriculum, but it does address both the content (the "what" is to be taught) and the specific techniques for teaching the content to learning disabled students.

Bley and Thornton (1989) describe learning disabilities as process deficits and give numerous examples of visual and/or auditory perceptual, memory, and integration deficits in learning disabled students who are performing poorly in math. Interestingly, the techniques they present for remediating math disabilities are not aimed at process remediation but are criterion oriented with regard to the math task to be taught. As such, the techniques are appropriate whatever the teacher's philosophical orientation may be.

General Techniques for Teaching

After a short discussion of various presumed process deficits, Bley and Thornton present 10 general techniques for teaching math to learning disabled students. These techniques, which are excellent for most students, are:

1. Use visual and manipulative materials for illustrative purposes when new and important concepts are introduced. While this is a good technique to use rou-

tinely, it is particularly important when teaching learning disabled students who may have difficulty understanding and retaining abstract verbal material.

2. Use a variety of visual cuing techniques, such as drawing a box around each math problem to be worked, underlining important items, using circles to isolate the problem number from the problem itself, and so on.

3. Assign only a few problems at one time and significantly reduce the amount of required copying from the textbook or chalkboard.

4. Use color coding as a specific visual cue. This is a time-honored technique that can serve to emphasize important items, isolate parts of problems, assist in learning sequenced steps in problem solving, and identify starting and stopping points, among others. The main caution with regard to color coding is to be sure that the student has adequate color discrimination.

5. Alter, adjust, or reinforce the standard textbook presentation whenever necessary. This technique is aimed specifically at the regular math class teacher or the resource teacher who is using a standard textbook. Bley and Thornton (1989) particularly suggest that fractions probably should be introduced before decimals, as the former are more "concrete," and in spite of the fact that newer math textbooks are introducing the decimal system first.

6. Permit students to finger trace or to use tactile/kinesthetic cues. Although Bley and Thornton do not particularly stress a multisensory approach, some of their techniques involve tactile cuing.

7. Capitalize as much as possible on patterns in problem solving and on other associations to assist students in understanding and retaining new material. One of the best known of such techniques is the "one more than" idea. For example, if $6 + 6 = 12$, then $6 + 7$ must equal 13 because 7 is *one more than* 6 and 13 is *one more than* 12.

8. Use a variety of auditory cues to reinforce visual materials. Sometimes, Bley and Thornton suggest, it may be helpful for students simply to close their eyes and listen, thereby blocking out competing visual distractions.

9. Supply students with a variety of sample problems and charts to which they may refer in solving problems. This is another well-respected and time-honored technique. One of the present authors carefully keeps a small, dog-eared chart showing the solution to percentage problems.

10. Sequence instruction in small steps, following one upon another, and provide for frequent practice and review.

None of the general techniques described above is unique to the Bley-Thornton approach; most of them have been used by special education teachers for years.

However, inclusion of the techniques by Bley and Thornton as general principles of instruction place the authors squarely in the tradition of remedial and special education.

Organization of the Bley-Thornton Program

Bley and Thornton's (1989) book is divided into eight major instructional sections with emphasis on the topics that commonly cause difficulty in teaching learning disabled students. The areas covered are early numbers, money and time, basic operations and facts, whole-number computation, decimals, fractions, "hard-to-learn" upper grade topics, and problem solving. Discussions of each area follow.

The Early Learning Program.   In beginning math instruction teachers focus on the numbers 1 to 10, then two-, three-, and higher digit numbers. All through the initial stages, emphasis is upon using objects to exemplify the meanings of numbers. At the point when children can read and write numbers, comparison and sequencing tasks are introduced. Bley and Thornton (1989) assume that teachers know the standard procedures and sequences for developing these preliminary skills, and they focus on areas within early number learning that have proved most troublesome for learning disabled students:

1. recognizing sight groups

2. writing numerals 0 to 10

3. naming the number after a given number

4. counting on

5. writing two-digit numbers

6. counting and skip-counting—two-digit numbers

7. reading and writing larger numbers

8. comparing large numbers

Within each of the eight sections above, Bley and Thornton (1989) provide the reader with an explication of the problem area, examples of typical learning disabilities that affect mastery, a more detailed background and description of the task, and a variety of suggested sequences and activities. They also provide the teacher with many graphic illustrations to accompany the activities. To illustrate the format used throughout the manual a detailed description of the section "Writing Numerals 0 to 10" is given.

Bley and Thornton (1989) state that problems occurring in the area of writing numerals 0 to 10 may be number reversals, disorientations, and other misconfigurations. Typical learning disabilities that may cause difficulties are poor visual discrimination, spatial organization, and/or visual-motor integration. With regard to the background of the area, the authors state that there are two prerequisites to the skill:

1. the ability to count out the correct number of objects corresponding to each numeral being written

2. the ability to control the motor activities necessary to write the numerals

Two preliminary activities for writing may be tracing and finger play. Tracing may include having children use a finger or wet sponge to trace over large numerals written on a chalkboard, guiding the child's hand as he or she traces and giving verbal cues such as "Down," "Around," "The 6 curls up," and so on. Finger play could include having children write numerals in damp sand; tracing large patterns of various materials with their fingers while their eyes are first closed, then open; or teaching them to make numerals such as 4 and 5 using only one stroke.

The sequence and activities and exercises suggested by Bley and Thornton for teaching children to write the numerals 0 to 10 are as follows:

1. *Stencil in.* Children are given stencils to use in writing given numerals. A green dot is placed on the stencil to indicate where the child should begin writing. For the numeral 6, the loop is outlined in red on the stencil to distinguish it from the 9.

2. *Get the feel.* If children confuse two numerals, such as 6 and 9, it may be helpful to have them use stencils for each. Green dots are used to distinguish the different starting points, and the children are asked to name each numeral as they trace it. However, additional color and verbal cuing should be used for one of the numerals. Tracing textured numerals formed from sandpaper or felt is often helpful in assisting children to "get the feel" of writing numerals correctly.

3. *Count and trace.* For children who confuse two numerals, such as 6 and 9, teach them to count and complete the numeral to show how many objects are represented, as shown in Figure 12.6. If necessary, green dots can be used to show starting places. For children who make mirror images of given numerals, activity sheets, such as that shown in Figure 12.7, may be used. In the first three numerals shown, the upper part of the 3 is colored green; in succeeding items, solid then dotted lines are used. Tracing and verbal cuing may accompany the activity, as needed.

4. *You do.* At this point, children begin to write independently on paper the "problem" numerals. Green dots can still be used sparingly to indicate starting points. The children should follow the sequence of counting the objects and tracing the solid numeral. Eventually, numerical patterns are given only at the top of the worksheet (Figure 12.8).

Money and Time.   Before entering school, most children can identify a penny, a nickel, and a dime. Also, most preschoolers have some concept of time, and some

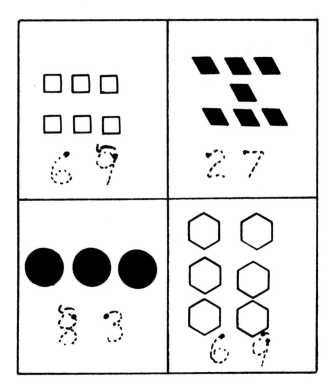

FIGURE 12.6. Count and trace. *Note.* From *Teaching Mathematics to the Learning Disabled* (p. 43) by N. S. Bley and C. A. Thornton, 1989, Austin, TX: PRO-ED.

may even be able to tell time on the hour. As children learn to handle larger amounts of money and to tell time more accurately, the vocabulary involved increases in quantity and complexity and greater demands are placed on the children's language skills. The activities suggested by Bley and Thornton (1989) for teaching money and time include language enhancement throughout all sections. Five topics in teaching money are presented:

1. coin discrimination

2. counting money amounts to $1.00 (using a quarter for any amounts over $.25, rather than other coin substitutes)

3. counting money amounts to $1.00 (using coin substitutes for the quarter for amounts over $.25)

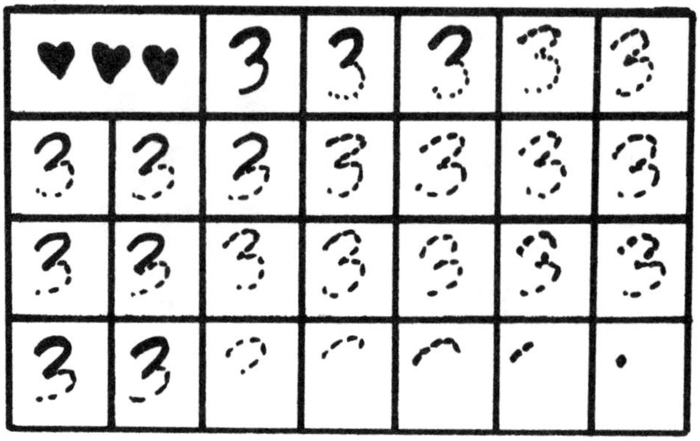

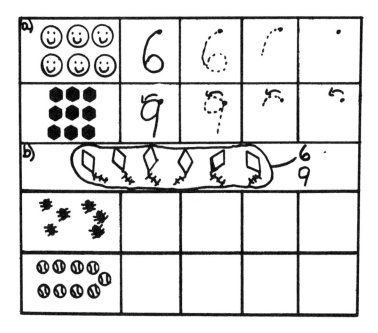

FIGURE 12.7. Count and trace. *Note.* From *Teaching Mathematics to the Learning Disabled* (p. 43) by N. S. Bley and C. A. Thornton, 1989, Austin, TX: PRO-ED.

FIGURE 12.8. You do. *Note.* From *Teaching Mathematics to the Learning Disabled* (p. 46) by N. S. Bley and C. A. Thornton, 1989, Austin, TX: PRO-ED.

4. paying for items and getting change

5. writing money amounts greater than $1.00

The last part of this section deals with time, and Bley and Thornton cover five topics:

1. reading clock times

2. reading and writing clock times

3. naming the correct hour

4. understanding different ways of telling time (15 minutes until 3:00 versus 2:45)

5. understanding and using temporal expressions ("We'll go in 5 minutes," "10 minutes ago," "You are early," "You are late," etc.)

No detailed description of the problems learning disabled children face in the area of learning money and time nor of the suggested teaching sequence and activities is given here. Instruction follows the same format as that described in the section above on writing numerals 0 to 10.

The Four Basic Operations.   Much of elementary school math education is about little more than adding, subtracting, multiplying, and dividing—the four basic operations. This is understandable because the operations are vital to the rest of mathematics since they are involved in all other aspects. Children's success in learning the operations rests on their understanding of each operation and their mastery of the basic arithmetic facts. In this section of their book, Bley and Thornton (1989) focus on 10 critical topics:

1. building concepts for the four operations

2. tracking for basic facts (memorizing)

3. addition facts: models and strategies

4. using subtraction strategies

5. teen minuends

6. comparison subtraction

7. multiplication facts: models, patterns, and strategies

8. "families" to help with subtraction and division

9. zero

10. using a hand calculator

Bley and Thornton's (1989) initial approach is to provide many oral and manipulative activities to build a strong conceptual framework for each operation. In addition a number of techniques for helping learning disabled students memorize the basic arithmetic facts are given. Also, the authors state again and again that many learning disabled students need a structured program that emphasizes the practical applications of the mathematics they are learning.

Whole-Number Computation.   In the preceding section Bley and Thornton's (1989) approach to teaching whole-number operations was discussed. In the section of their text dealing with whole-number computation, the purposes are to assist students in extending and applying concepts they know to more complicated whole-number computations and to highlight some of the difficulties learning disabled students encounter. In particular some of the problems students may have with whole-number computation are:

1. inability to deal with abstract concepts

2. poor memory

3. inability to differentiate among symbols

4. poor associative skills, such as consistently associating the correct symbol (+) with correct process (addition)

After students have learned to associate the correct symbol with the correct process, they still must determine the proper sequence of procedures necessary to solve a problem. For example, in the process of subtracting 19 from 45, it is necessary to subtract, add, subtract, and subtract in sequence, but the entire process is called subtraction. Many students, not only those who are learning disabled, have difficulty learning the correct sequences in whole-number computation, and often specific techniques, such as those described by Bley and Thornton (1989), must be implemented in teaching these critical sequences.

Many of the activities suggested by Bley and Thornton (1989) provide opportunities for students to experience success, because the procedures are highly structured and sequenced. A variety of multisensory practices are employed, and an effort is made to work only with arithmetic facts the students already know, thereby eliminating a source of possible confusion. The areas of whole-number computation covered are:

1. General difficulties
   • controlling for unknown facts
   • basic facts: transfer to larger problems
   • interpreting the printed word or sign for an operation

2. Addition of whole numbers
   - multiples of 10
   - adding other multiples of 10 to a two-digit number
   - one- and two-digit addends
   - regrouping for addition
   - column addition

3. Subtraction of whole numbers
   - two- and three-digit subtraction with regrouping
   - zero in subtraction

4. Multiplication of whole numbers
   - multiples of 10
   - beyond one-digit multipliers
   - regrouping in multiplication

5. Division of whole numbers
   - beginning long division
   - beginning long division: special help
   - five basic steps in division: the sequence
   - longer division computations
   - problems within problems: recognizing and solving the subtraction part of division

As the reader may note, Bley and Thornton (1989) leave little to chance in teaching whole-number computation. They have outlined a rigorous sequence of instruction and provide the teacher with numerous activities to ensure success.

Decimals.   Today many math textbooks introduce decimals before fractions, and Bley and Thornton (1989) also discuss this area first. However, they are quick to point out that the teacher may want to introduce fractions first when teaching learning disabled students, because fractions are more concrete than decimals, more familiar, and more easily understood. The advantages of introducing decimals first are that most calculators and microcomputers express parts in decimal notation, and it is proper to use decimals in metric measurement. In general, introduce decimals first, but if students have inordinate difficulties in understanding and using them, quickly introduce fractions. The approaches used for teaching decimals to learning disabled students are:

1. naming and writing decimals

2. comparing decimals

3. rounding decimals

4. adding and subtracting decimals

5. multiplying decimals

6. dividing decimals

The authors make two additional noteworthy points. First, it is important that students, particularly those with learning disabilities, have strong decimal concepts. It is not difficult to teach the basic operations on decimals, but the ability to add, subtract, multiply, or divide decimals becomes nothing more than a splinter skill if students do not really understand what decimals represent. Second, after students are able to understand and carry out simple decimal computations, there is little to be gained from having them compute longer and longer strings of decimals. The calculator is a more convenient and accurate instrument for computation of long decimals and should be introduced as soon as appropriate.

Fractions. Fractions can be very simple and concrete concepts. Everyone is familiar with the idea of *half*, and the concepts of ⅓, ¼, ⅔, and so on, can be demonstrated easily through concrete materials. However, perceptual and language requirements for learning fractions may prove troublesome to many learning disabled children. For example, if the teacher asks a student to "identify a third of the class," the child may have difficulty associating a number with the words "of the class." Likewise, even though the teacher may use a pie chart to illustrate two-fifths of a circle and two-fifths of a pentagon, the child who has trouble with multiple meanings may not be able to solve the problem because the equal parts of the two shapes are different sizes.

Because of perceptual and/or language difficulties, learning disabled students may need more concrete examples and manipulative materials than their nonhandicapped peers before they can understand and use fractions. The sequence for teaching fractions, according to Bley and Thornton (1989), is:

1. instruction in general areas of difficulty
   * spatial organization problems involving fractions
   * sequencing the computation processes
   * vocabulary specific to fractions
   * recognizing number patterns to facilitate the transition concrete aids to symbolic representations

2. writing fractions

3. using a ruler

4. fraction number lines

5. quotients, improper fractions, and mixed numbers

6. equivalent fractions

7. reducing fractions

8. finding common denominators; comparing, adding, and subtracting fractions

9. regrouping in subtraction

10. multiplying fractions

11. dividing fractions

"Hard-to-Learn" Upper Grade Topics. Bley and Thornton (1989) deal with some of the upper grade math topics that are particularly difficult for learning disabled students. This section should be especially useful to teachers who have learning disabled students in higher grades and who are seeking specific techniques for helping them. In this section the authors discuss:

1. ratio

2. proportion

3. percent

4. integers

5. exponents

Each of these topics involves the transfer of lower level concepts and skills to new types of learning. For learning disabled students such transfer is difficult and probably cannot be achieved unless the abstract aspects of the new tasks are made as concrete as possible. Bley and Thornton (1989) deal with the hard-to-learn topics from the vantage of how learning disabilities may affect students' ability to understand, retain, and apply these topics. In a number of instances, the sequence of instruction suggested differs from that commonly used by teachers. In general, Bley and Thornton's emphasis is upon directly relating new material to previously learned concepts and skills.

Summary

The Bley and Thornton (1989) methods for teaching math to learning disabled students is a highly commonsense approach emphasizing a conceptual foundation, multisensory techniques, strong structure, and a variety of easily implemented activities. Teachers who are instructing learning disabled students with problems in math would do well to look carefully at this approach.

REMEDIATING NONVERBAL PROBLEMS ASSOCIATED WITH LEARNING DISABILITIES

Erin D. Bigler

The initial concept of learning disabilities focused on verbal learning deficits. As learning disabilities research broadened, it became evident that many children so classified had problems that extended beyond verbal-language deficits and included a variety of nonverbal impairments in emotional and social development (Critchley, 1970). In fact, some early researchers (see Connolly, 1971) and clinicians attributed learning disabilities to primary emotional problems. However, as knowledge increased about brain-behavioral relationships, it became evident that the concomitant expression of learning disabilities and problems in social-emotional development shared similar neurologic substrates. This relationship between learning and emotion is a very complex, interactive process, because neurologic factors not only affect the internal regulation of emotion (i.e., direct brain control over emotional expression) but the processing of environmental cues and external emotional stimuli (i.e., the input side of emotional regulation). Also, emotional maturity and neurologic maturation are linked directly (Bigler, 1988). In some cases, a learning disability is a manifestation of a developmental lag in brain maturation which also impedes and slows emotional maturity.

All of these factors suggest that the learning disabled child is more likely to display problems in emotional control, self-regulation, and social perception. This chapter reviews the perspective that these emotional and behavioral correlates of learning disability stem, in part, from similar neurologic factors. The topics addressed in this chapter include discussion of the relationship between learning disabilities and (a) depression, (b) attentional deficits and hyperactivity, (c) impulsivity, and (d) visual spatial deficits. Before these topics can be addressed, a brief overview of brain anatomy along with the interaction among brain dysfunction, learning disability, and emotional dysfunction is in order.

RELATIONSHIP OF BRAIN ANATOMY TO LEARNING AND EMOTIONAL DYSFUNCTION

Before abnormal brain states can be discussed, a brief review of normal brain anatomy is necessary. This is followed by a discussion of abnormal brain states in relation to learning disabilities and emotional dysfunction.

Normal Brain Anatomy Related to Learning and Emotional Behavior

Even though our current understanding is far from complete, there are some well-known brain-behavior correlates in regulating emotion (see Figure 13.1) (Heilman, Bowers, & Valenstein, 1985; Ross, 1985; Sachar, 1981). The frontal lobes are the largest of the four lobes of the brain and have much to do with regulating temperament, impulse control, social appropriateness, motivation, and goal-directed behaviors. The temporal lobes, situated behind and slightly beneath the frontal lobes, are critical emotional regulatory centers, along with housing important memory and language centers. The parietal lobes, particularly the right parietal region, play critical roles in visual-spatial processing and self-awareness. The occipital lobes appear to play little of a direct role in regulating emotion, other than the transfer of visual information which may contain important visual cues necessary for integration of an emotional reaction (i.e., perceiving a visual threat). Also, a neuroanatomical system—the limbic system—that is critical for integrating more primitive emotions such as sexual drive, appetitive behaviors (eating, drinking), and aggression is found deep within the frontal, temporal, and parietal lobes. In a very basic sense the frontal, temporal, and parietal lobe regions regulate the cognitive aspects of emotional function and govern the more primitive impulses generated at the limbic system level. Thus, if damage occurs to one of the lobes, emotional function may be ineffectively regulated and various inappropriate behaviors displayed which, in turn, will be poorly modulated or controlled. Similarly, overactivity at more primitive brain sites (i.e., limbic system level) may override cortical control with the end result being aberrant emotional behavior.

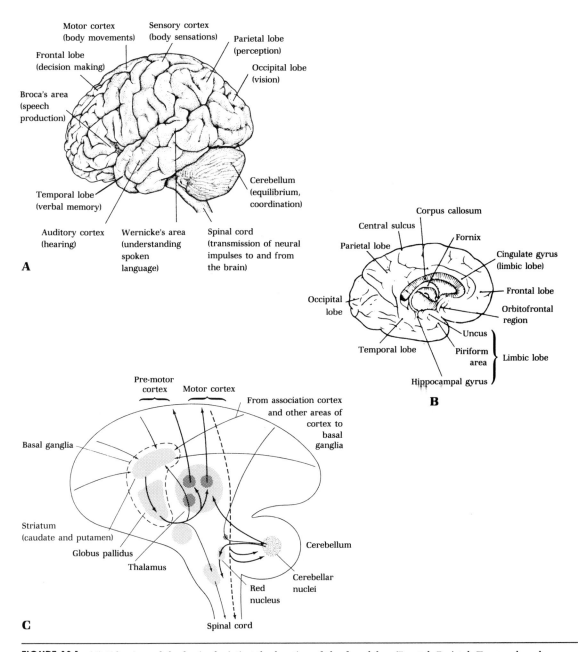

FIGURE 13.1. (A) Side view of the brain depicting the location of the four lobes (Frontal, Parietal, Temporal, and Occipital) along with some areas of function. (B) Mid-sagittal view depicting the position of various limbic structures in the brain in relationship to the four lobes of the brain. (C) The major motor centers of the brain.

Abnormal Brain Function, Learning Disability, and Emotional Dysfunction

Although not fully warranted, dyslexia often has been thought of as the prototype of all learning disorders and certainly is the area that has received the greatest amount of research and clinical interest. Thus, it is fitting first to discuss the research that has examined the relationship among dyslexia, brain dysfunction, self-regulatory behaviors, and emotion.

We long have known that dyslexic children, as a group, display a higher incidence of problems with impulse control, hyperkinesis, attention, social adjustment, and overall emotional adjustment (Rutter, 1982, 1983). As implied in the introduction, early speculation as to the genesis of these problems in the dyslexic individual tended to focus on psychological adjustment issues (Weinberg, Rutman, Sullivan, Penick, & Dietz, 1973). For example, Critchley (1970) stated, "Developmental dyslexics and indeed all children with difficulty in learning to read, tend quite early to develop neurotic reactions" (p. 97).

That this is so is understandable, because learning disabled children often struggle with self-esteem issues as they compare their labored academic achievements with the seemingly effortless achievements of their non–learning disabled peers (Adamson, 1979; Connolly, 1971; Critchley, 1970; Hunt & Cohen, 1984). Often learning disabled children have avoidance reactions to certain learning or school situations because of their learning disabilities. Such situations may tax coping abilities and result in overanxiousness. Additionally, depression may develop in learning disabled children who are experiencing such adjustment problems.

Teachers or parents often misperceive a child's learning problems as an "emotional block." This may add further stress on the teacher-pupil or parent-child relationship and enhance the child's self-perception of failure, all of which impacts negatively on emotional adjustment.

Thus, without impugning any connection between the neurobiological factors regulating learning and emotion, the learning disabled child is emotionally vulnerable. Added to this is the reality of the 20th-, soon to be 21st-, century emphasis on learning and technology and the focus on educational achievement and success . . . a difficult emotional climate for the "normal" learner to navigate and an even more difficult one for the learning disordered individual.

Undoubtedly, emotional reactions occur as the child encounters school failure, and emotional factors certainly disrupt learning abilities. However, the underlying factors governing emotional dysfunction in the learning disabled individual may have a more specific neurologic basis in that the neurologic factors responsible for the learning disorder also may impact emotional regulation. The research linking neurologic deficits, emotional problems, and learning disabilities is discussed below.

Recent postmortem studies of the brains of dyslexic children who died of a nonneurologic illness or accidental death have demonstrated a variety of microscopic brain abnormalities (see Galaburda, 1985b, 1989; Galaburda, Sherman, Rosen, Aboitiz, & Geschwind, 1985). Although many of the abnormalities tended to congregate in expected language areas (i.e., temporal cortex), some abnormalities existed in brain regions traditionally thought to be nonlanguage related, including abnormalities in limbic system structures. Perhaps in some learning disabled individuals abnormal brain development coexists in areas critical to language and emotional function.

Further support for this speculation comes from the work of Duffy and colleagues (see Duffy & McAnulty, 1985) using a different technique—brain electrical activity mapping (BEAM). This is a very sophisticated computer-assisted brain wave [i.e., electroencephalography (EEG)] analysis. This research demonstrated abnormal brain function in regions other than traditional language areas in dyslexic boys, including frontal and right parietal regions. Again, frontal abnormalities may impact impulse control, social maturation, and emotional regulation, and right parietal lobe irregularities may disrupt appropriate development in areas of self- and social perception.

Neuropsychological research also implicates neurologic dysfunction that exceeds language system boundaries in learning disabled children (Rourke, Bakker, Fisk, & Strang, 1983). For example, most neuropsychological studies that have examined reading disabled individuals find at least a subgroup that demonstrate a variety of deficits (usually in the form of perceptual-motor and other cognitive deficits) in addition to their reading disability (Nussbaum & Bigler, 1986; Rourke et al., 1983). This research further supports the role of nonspecific neurologic factors in some learning disabled individuals, and it may be that such individuals are at greatest risk for concomitant emotional disturbance (Nussbaum, Bigler, & Kocke, 1987). For example, Spreen (1989) has demonstrated a direct correspondence among the degree of neurologic involvement, learning disability, and the development of emotional problems. In his longitudinal study from age 10 to 25, those learning disabled children whose learning deficits were associated with "hard" neurological signs (i.e., hemiplegia) were more likely at age 25 to be emotionally dependent, disorganized, and to display poor social interactive skills than matched individuals with no learning problems. Children with minimal or only "soft" neurological signs in association with learning disabilities or those with no associated neurological findings also differed on these measures from normal controls, but not to the extent of the "brain damaged" group. Rutter (1982) has demonstrated similar findings.

Other lines of research have implicated a developmental lag in nervous system maturation (see reviews by Duane, 1989; Rutter, 1983) as the basis for learning disabilities, and this may apply to emotional regulation as well. For example, the frontal lobes, the regions most important for the regulation of emotion, pass through various anatomic developmental stages (mainly myelination and neuronal interconnectiveness) that, in turn, permit the expression of more and more complex behaviors including complex cognition, regulation of attention, and emotional control. For example, Passlar, Isaac, and Hynd (1985) have demonstrated in non–learning disabled children that by "age 10, the ability to inhibit attention to irrelevant stimuli and perseveratory responses was fairly complete, with mastery evident by age 12" (p. 349). However, some nonverbal abilities attributed to frontal lobe functioning were still not mastered by age 12 (see Becker, Isaac, & Hynd, 1987; Welsh & Pennington, 1988). This developmental staging also applies to integration of information between the two hemispheres. For example, Liederman, Merola, and Hoffman (1986) demonstrated that there was little interhemispheric integration of information presented to only one body side from ages 0 to 3.5 years. However, from 3.5 to 10 years there was increasing hemispheric integration which after age 10 approached an adult level. Since much of emotional maturation is dependent on controlling impulse and attending to environmental cues, developmental lag in such frontal lobe or interhemispheric systems may impact emotional regulation, likely resulting in emotional immaturity and failure to match age-appropriate emotional responses to one's environment.

The origin of these abnormalities in many cases is related to the sheer complexity of embryological brain development, where the brain at different gestational stages is growing at a rate of 250,000 new cells per minute (Cowan, 1979). Perhaps this rapid development results in spontaneous errors, and if they occur in critical language areas or emotional regulatory centers, then various forms of learning disability and/or emotional dysfunction result (Hynd & Semrud-Clikeman, 1989). In other cases, the brain damaging effect that produces the learning disorder is more direct (e.g., traumatic birth injury) (Taylor, 1987; Towbin, 1978).

From these various lines of clinical research it is apparent that in some learning disabled individuals there may be significant overlap between neurologic subsystems that regulate both learning and emotion. This also suggests that in examining emotional problems in the learning disabled population, we should not be too quick to label them as "adjustment" problems or simply psychological reactions in response to learning disability, because there may be a biological predisposition for emotional dysregulation in some learning disabled individuals.

DEPRESSION AND LEARNING DISABILITIES

Human emotion varies as a result of a variety of factors. In response to situational stress, perceived failure, tragic personal events (e.g., death of a loved one), or any number of other life events, one may experience transient feelings of depression. This change in mood may persist until coping mechanisms result in emotional stabilization. Yet, in situations where chronic stress persists without resolution, coping mechanisms may not be sufficient to return mood to normal. This is the situation that many learning disabled children face. However, it would be a mistake to characterize the depressive features experienced by learning disabled children as simply related to stress factors, as there may be very important biologic factors that predispose the learning disabled child to depression.

There are many emotional problems that may be associated with learning disabilities (e.g., anxiety disorders, school phobia, etc.). Depression is the one that has been most frequently cited and most thoroughly studied. Hence, this section focuses only on depression. First, an overview is presented followed by a discussion of treatment/intervention techniques.

Overview

Several lines of research with dyslexic children have focused on a greater incidence of depression in such individuals (Mokros, Poznanski, & Merrick, 1989). As discussed above, certainly learning disabled children have to adapt psychologically to their disabilities, and the effectiveness of their adaptation likely is related to the degree of emotional maladjustment expressed. Notwithstanding the pure psychosocial factors, research is accumulating that suggests that a more direct biologic basis may exist between neurologic dysfunction and depression.

Kurt Goldstein (1948a, 1948b) was the first to note that damage to the left side of the brain often resulted in a greater incidence of depression than observed in individuals with damage to the right side of the brain. He used the term *catastrophic reaction* to describe this type of depression in the brain injured individual and believed that this catastrophic reaction was related to the individual's inability to cope with the effects of physical *and* cognitive impairment. These findings, to a certain degree, have been corroborated by others (see Heilman et al., 1985; Ross, 1985; Sachar, 1981), and current speculation is that such lateralized damage may not only impact important regulatory brain centers but also disrupt certain brain neurotransmitters. The neurotransmitter hypothesis has been supported by recent clinical research that has demonstrated amelioration of depression in patients who suffered left hemisphere damage and a catastrophic depressive reaction by successfully treating them with antidepressant medication (Robinson & Szetela, 1981; Robinson, Kubos, Starr, Rao, & Price, 1984; Starkstein & Robinson, 1989).

This research suggests the presence of some relationship between left hemisphere dysfunction that mediates a verbal learning disability and concomitantly predisposes the individual to depression. This is a speculative statement at this point, but one that merits consideration. The right hemisphere also plays a role in emotional regulation, and, in fact, some researchers believe that at some level it plays the more important role because much of emotional experience cannot be processed or characterized by language (Bruder et al., 1989; Nass & Koch, 1987). Some have found (Cullum & Bigler, 1988) that it may be just as likely for individuals with either left or right hemisphere brain damage to display depressive symptoms on psychological tests. However, it is likely that qualitative differences exist between the type and degree of depression expressed by right and left brain damaged individuals. In contrast to what Goldstein labeled a catastrophic reaction associated with left hemisphere dysfunction, right hemisphere dysfunction may have a direct impact on mood regulation. This has implications for children with learning disabilities and suggests that regardless of whether the dysfunction involves the left, right, or both cerebral hemispheres, learning disordered individuals may be at greater risk for developing depressive symptoms.

Treatment/Intervention

All learning disabled children, indeed all children, need positive feedback and support that counters their feelings of inadequacy, being "dumb" or "stupid." This often is achieved by simple statements (e.g., "You always try so hard") and actions by understanding parents and teachers who are sensitive to the feedback they give children. For example, in the dyslexic child the emphasis should be on what the child has accomplished, not on what is lacking. As illustrated in Figure 13.2, the emphasis that this teacher has used is entirely negative and demoralizing to the child. The same information could have been conveyed in a very positive fashion.

If emotional problems increase in severity, whether they be related to learning deficits or not, the child may need further help beyond the support and structure of home and school. Professional counseling, psychotherapy, or psychiatric inter-

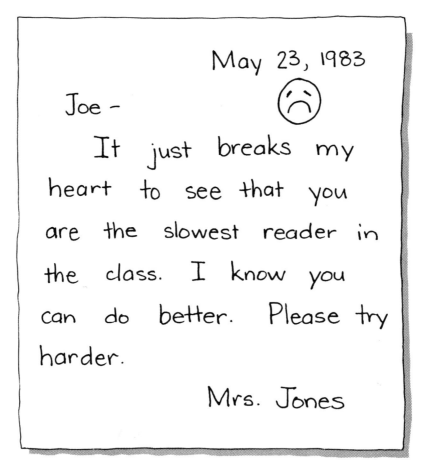

FIGURE 13.2. Copy of an actual note sent home with a dyslexic boy who was not making progress in school. Note the negative tone and the potential for damaging self-esteem. Although the teacher is attempting to "shame" the child to elevate motivation, such negative feedback rarely provides any positive source of motivation for the learning disabled child.

vention may be necessary. Whether such services are available through or at school will vary with each school district, but each will have at least some psychological services available. There are always public-supported as well as private mental health services.

If depression in the learning disabled individual evolves to the point that psychotherapy is instituted, then the individual whose depression is related to primary adjustment problems typically will exhibit a favorable response to counseling alone. Much of this therapy should be directed at preserving self-esteem and enhancing coping mechanisms. Stress and performance anxiety problems often are a part of the clinical picture in working with such children and need to be addressed as well. A number of suggested methods for dealing with self-esteem and stress issues follow.

1. Positive self-esteem emerges from a supportive, stable environment at both home and school. The parents and teachers of learning disabled children should work to establish a home or classroom setting that focuses on positive feedback rather than putting an undue emphasis on the disability. The positive feedback given to the child needs to be realistic and not fabricated. Most learning disabled children will have a variety of strengths, sometimes outstanding abilities, outside the domain of their learning disability. These areas of strength can be a focus for positive feedback and should be used as an example to children that they have "strengths" and "weaknesses" just like everyone. Emphasis should be on the whole child not just on a particular disability or weakness that the child may have in a specified area. Children should be able to acknowledge the disability but not see the disability as the center point of their existence nor believe they are failures because of the disability. In this context, it is often helpful to use examples of famous people who have had learning disabilities (e.g., Greg Louganis, the 1988 Olympic diver, who is dyslexic) but who did not allow the learning problems to keep them from pursuing their talents in other areas. These examples also help the child to realize that a disability in one area does not mean that there will be disabilities in all areas.

2. Grades are a major source of stress for the learning disabled child. If the child's self-concept is too dependent on external feedback, then academic failure may lead to problems with self-esteem. When feasible, grades should be de-emphasized, and an emphasis on effort and willingness to "try" substituted. For the teacher, innovative grading procedures where the grade is not the focal point of indicating progress or lack thereof may be helpful. Parents should avoid using reward/punishment systems based solely on grades.

3. It is very important for teachers and parents to have a realistic appraisal of the child's actual ability level. Goals should not be set that are too demanding or that may set up the child for failure. It is often best to start new tasks at levels where the learning disabled child can succeed. Self-confidence typically builds on successful experiences. Parents and teachers need to monitor their expectations for the child and make sure that they are neither overtly nor covertly communicating to the child disappointment in the child's inability to perform at a certain level.

4. Children with no learning disabilities receive many positive rewards as a result of academic success. These external signs of success (e.g., best reader, winner of a spelling bee, etc.) usually are not available to the learning disabled child. As an alternative, parents, teachers, and therapists need to seek out ways to provide tangible, outward signs of success for the learning disabled child. This could be achieved through hobbies, athletics, or church/community programs (e.g., Boy/Girl Scouts). For example, a learning disabled child may have a particular athletic talent. Any awards, trophies, or pictures that are acquired during competition or play should be prominently displayed in the child's room and/or in highly visible areas of the house. Often, learning disabled children who succeed in areas outside of school will be able to focus a sense of identity in association with that success or talent. Such a focus on success outside school may sustain the child in the school setting.

5. Learning disabled children experiencing emotional problems need some feedback to know that their problems often are typical reactions in individuals with learning problems. These children need to have some outlet for expressing feelings and opinions about what they are experiencing. Learning disabled children often have phases during which they may be experiencing significant adjustment problems and not fully understand the emotional reaction they are experiencing. This is particularly true in late childhood and early adolescence. Although it is very important to develop appropriate channels for emotional expression, fostering such a situation may be quite difficult, particularly in late childhood and early adolescence. Sometimes it is best for the learning disabled child to have peer feedback if this can be done in a constructive and supportive way. Frequently this is facilitated by working within a group of children who have learning disabilities, and such a situation is usually less threatening to the learning disabled child. The setting has to be one that is quite structured and adult controlled, however, to ensure that there is not a focus on negative feedback and negative emotions. Many times this requires the skill of a school counselor or psychotherapist. It is important to keep the learning disabled children from feeling too isolated or alienated to discuss their problems. Refraining from discussing underlying emotional problems often leads to emotional isolation and withdrawal, and children often harbor many negative thoughts and feelings about themselves.

6. Learning disabled children often become anxious in situations in which they have to perform. This is particularly a problem with learning disabled children who are experiencing problems with self-esteem. Such children are often not risk takers and will avoid social contact for fear of embarrassment. The children may need specific desensitization and stress-management programs. Other learning disabled children may not require such an elaborate treatment program, but all children can benefit from learning strategies that permit a better coping with stress. Often, children who are experiencing significant levels of stress will be prone to display depressive symptoms and will have problems concentrating and focusing atten-

tion; all of these factors may have a negative impact on performance level as well. Thus, a very vicious downward spiral may be encountered wherein the anxiety feeds self-doubt and perpetuates a lack of trying, which in turn affects the ability to perform. This overanxiousness results in the child avoiding tasks that require performance in social situations. Again, the best treatment often comes through positive learning experiences and building self-confidence through mastery of certain tasks and abilities.

7. Although essentially a home-related activity, raising animals can be a positive self-esteem exercise for many learning disabled children. Raising and caring for animals often promotes a sense of mastery and control. Having such positive experiences may allow the child to generalize such feelings into other areas.

In some children where the level of depression persists, medication, particularly antidepressants, may be helpful. Such children should meet the criteria for various types of depression as established by the American Psychiatric Association (see Figure 13.3). The biologic factors co-mediating learning disability and emotional dysfunction implicate biologic predisposition toward depression in some individuals in which medication will serve as either an adjunct to counseling/psychotherapy or as the primary means of psychiatric treatment (McGuire & Sylvester, 1989). Along these lines it should be noted that antidepressant medications, in addition to treating depressive symptomatology, may be effective in treating hyperactivity, impulsivity, and nocturnal enuresis in some children (McGuire & Sylvester, 1989).

ATTENTION DEFICIT–HYPERACTIVITY DISORDER

The clinical concept of hyperactivity has engendered considerable debate and disagreement over the past three decades (Nussbaum & Bigler, 1990). Since hyperactivity was a well-known manifestation of certain types of neurologic disorder or brain injury, it was initially equated with the concept of "minimal brain dysfunction" (MBD) and associated diagnostic labels: minimal brain injury, minor cerebral dysfunction, and so on (Rie & Rie, 1980). Controversy surrounded these labels because clinical consensus on how to establish the diagnosis was lacking. Based on the neurologic tests of the day (circa 1950s through the 1970s), no specific "neurologic" abnormalities could be systematically related to hyperactivity. In 1980, the American Psychiatric Association addressed this problem and created the first uniform guidelines for establishing the diagnosis of Attention Deficit Disorder (see Table 13.1). The guidelines were subsequently revised in 1985, and the current nomenclature for this disorder is Attention Deficit–Hyperactivity Disorder or ADHD (see Table 13.1).

New technological advances have brought about a more refined understanding of the neurobiological mechanisms underlying ADHD and how these mechanisms may affect emotional regulation. For example, Lou, Henriksen, Bruhn, Borner, and

Diagnostic Criteria for Dysthymia-Neurotic Depression

A. Depressed mood (or can be irritable mood in children and adolescents) for most of the day, more days than not, as indicated either by subjective account or observation by others, for at least 2 years (1 year for children and adolescents).

B. Presence, while depressed, of at least two of the following:
   (1) poor appetite or overeating
   (2) insomnia or hypersomnia
   (3) low energy or fatigue
   (4) low self-esteem
   (5) poor concentration or difficulty making decisions
   (6) feelings of hopelessness

C. During a 2-year period (1-year for children and adolescents) of the disturbance, never without the symptoms in A for more than 2 months at a time.

D. No evidence of an unequivocal Major Depressive Episode during the first 2 years (1 year for children and adolescents) of the disturbance.

   NOTE: There may have been a previous Major Depressive Episode, provided there was a full remission (no significant signs or symptoms for 6 months) before development of the Dysthymia. In addition, after these 2 years (1 year in children or adolescents) of Dysthymia, there may be super-imposed episosdes of Major Depression, in which case both diagnoses are given.

E. Has never had a Manic Episode or an unequivocal Hypomanic Episode.

F. Not superimposed on a chronic psychotic disorder, such as Schizophrenia or Delusional Disorder.

G. It cannot be established that an organic factor initiated and maintained the disturbance (e.g., prolonged administration of an antihypertensive medication).

Diagnostic Criteria for Major Depression

A. At least five of the following symptoms have been present during the same 2-week period and represent a change from previous functioning; at least one of the symptoms is either (1) depressed mood or (2) loss of interest or pleasure. (Do not include symptoms that are clearly due to a physical condition, mood-incongruent delusions or hallucinations, incoherence, or marked loosening of associations.)
   (1) depressed mood (or can be irritable mood in children and adolescents) most of the day, nearly every day, as indicated either by subjective account or observation by others
   (2) markedly diminished interest or pleasure in all, or almost all, activities most of the day, nearly every day (as indicated either by subjective account or observation by others of apathy most of the time)
   (3) significant weight loss or weight gain when not dieting (e.g., more than 5% of body weight in a month), or decrease or increase in appetite nearly every day (in children, consider failure to make expected weight gains)
   (4) insomnia or hypersomnia nearly every day
   (5) psychomotor agitation or retardation nearly every day (observable by others, not merely subjective feelings of restlessness or being slowed down)

FIGURE 13.3. DSM III-R criteria for depression.

FIGURE 13.3. *(Continued)*

(6) fatigue or loss of energy nearly every day

(7) feelings of worthlessness or excessive or inappropriate guilt (which may be delusional) nearly every day (not merely self-reproach or guilt about being sick)

(8) diminished ability to think or concentrate, or indecisiveness, nearly every day (either by subjective account or as observed by others)

(9) recurrent thoughts of death (not just fear of dying), recurrent suicidal ideation without a specific plan, or a suicide attempt or a specific plan for committing suicide

B. (1) It cannot be established that an organic factor initiated and maintained the disturbance.

(2) The disturbance is not a normal reaction to the death of a loved one (Uncomplicated Bereavement).

NOTE: Morbid preoccupation with worthlessness, suicidal ideation, marked functional impairment or psychomotor retardation, or prolonged duration suggest bereavement complicated by Major Depression.

C. At no time during the disturbance have there been delusions or hallucinations for as long as 2 weeks in the absence of prominent mood symptoms (i.e., before the mood symptoms developed or after they have remitted).

D. Not superimposed on Schizophrenia, Schizophreniform Disorder, Delusional Disorder, or Psychotic Disorder not otherwise specified.

Nielsen (1989) have recently examined a group of ADHD children with cerebral blood flow emission tomography scanning techniques. Such methods permit the study of brain metabolism in a variety of regions by measuring changes in regional blood flow. In comparison to non-ADHD children, the ADHD subjects displayed hypoperfusion (reduced) regional blood flow in frontal-striatal regions of the brain (refer to Figure 13.1 for location of these structures). This suggests that there is reduced activity in those regions. When given methylphenidate (Ritalin), a stimulant medication known to reduce the symptoms of hyperactivity and increase attention span, these regions were activated. The methylphenidate also increased regional cerebral blood flow in a variety of nonspecific areas and in primary sensory regions of the brains of these ADHD children.

Recently, Gillberg, Gillberg, and Groth (1989) reported the first longitudinal study of neurodevelopmental problems in children with ADHD and a separate group with perceptual-motor deficits. They found that by 7 to 10 years of age, 55% of the ADHD children still demonstrated developmental lag. By age 13 this was reduced to 30%. These findings do support a neurodevelopmental lag in brain maturation in at least some children with ADHD and/or perceptual-motor learning disabilities.

Gillberg et al. (1989) also addressed the very important problem of symptom overlap between perceptual-motor dysfunction and ADHD. They found that 65% of the children in this study with perceptual-motor deficits had ADHD and 50% of the

TABLE 13.1. Comparison of Classification Criteria for ADD (DSM III) and ADHD (DSM III-R)

DSM III: Attention Deficit Disorders (ADD)	**DSM III-R: Attention Deficit–Hyperactivity Disorders (ADHD)**

A. Inattention. At least three of the following:
  1. often fails to finish things he or she starts
  2. often doesn't seem to listen
  3. easily distracted
  4. has difficulty concentrating on schoolwork or other tasks requiring sustained attention
  5. has difficulty sticking to a play activity
 	
B. Impulsivity. At least three of the following:
  1. often acts before thinking
  2. shifts excessively from one activity to another
  3. has difficulty organizing work (this is not due to cognitive impairment)
  4. needs a lot of supervision
  5. frequently calls out in class
  6. has difficulty awaiting turn in games or situations
 	
C. Hyperactivity. At least two of the following:
  1. runs about or climbs on things excessively
  2. has difficulty sitting still or fidgets excessively
  3. has difficulty staying seated
  4. moves about excessively during sleep
  5. is always "on the go" or acts as if "driven by a motor"
 	
D. Onset before the age of 7.
 	
E. Duration of at least 6 months.
 	
F. Not due to schizophrenia, affective disorder, or severe or profound mental retardation
	A. A disturbance of at least 6 months during which at least eight of the following are present:
	  1. often fidgets with hands or feet or squirms in seat (in adolescents, may be limited to subjective feelings of restlessness)
	  2. has difficulty remaining seated when required to do so
	  3. is easily distracted by extraneous stimuli
	  4. has difficulty awaiting turn in games or group situations
	  5. often blurts out answers to questions before they have been completed
	  6. has difficulty following through on instructions from others (not due to oppositional behavior or failure of comprehension), e.g., fails to finish chores
	  7. has difficulty sustaining attention in tasks or play
	  8. often shifts from one uncompleted activity to another
	  9. has difficulty playing quietly
	  10. often talks excessively
	  11. often interrupts or intrudes on others (e.g., butts into other children's games)
	  12. often does not seem to listen to what is being said to him or her
	  13. often loses things necessary for tasks or activities at school or home (e.g., toys, pencils, books, assignments)
	  14. often engages in physically dangerous activities without considering possible consequences (not for the purpose of thrill-seeking), e.g., runs into street without looking
	
	Note: The above items are listed in descending order of discriminating power based on data from a national field trial of the DSM III-R criteria for Disruptive Behavior Disorders.

(Continued)

TABLE 13.1. *(Continued)*

DSM III: Attention Deficit Disorders (ADD)	DSM III-R: Attention Deficit–Hyperactivity Disorders (ADHD)
	B. Onset before the age of 7. C. Does not meet the criteria for a Pervasive Developmental Disorder. Criteria for severity of Attention Deficit–Hyperactivity Disorder: Mild: Few, if any, symptoms in excess of those required to make the diagnoses and only minimal or no impairment in school and social functioning. Moderate: Symptoms or functional impairment between "mild" and "severe." Severe: Many symptoms in excess of those required to make the diagnosis and significant and pervasive impairment in functioning at home and school and with peers.

ADHD children in their study had perceptual-motor dysfunction. Such findings suggest significant coexistence of ADHD and perceptual-motor dysfunction, and such deficits may have a common basis in frontal-striatal dysfunction, as discussed above.

ADHD often coexists with learning disabilities, with either the ADHD or learning disability being the primary disorder but both likely interacting each with another in a negative fashion. Lou, Henriksen, and Bruhn (1984) and Lou et al. (1989) have examined, with the same regional blood flow techniques described above, a group of children with cognitive and motor disturbances in addition to ADHD (so-called ADHD+). They found similar results between these two groups of children, but the ADHD+ group displayed greater reduction in cerebral blood flow and it was more extensive than that seen in the ADHD group. Also in the ADHD group, there was a nearly significant decrease in metabolic activity in the left posterior central region of the brain, a region that may relate directly to verbal learning deficits.

This line of research does have implications for underlying aberrant neural systems in ADHD children. It also is of interest to note that there is some overlap in brain regions implicated in ADHD and reading disabilities (and it can be assumed that this likely applies to other learning disorders as well). Additionally, it is important to note the involvement of the striatal system in these disorders. The striatum consists of the caudate nucleus and putamen (see Figure 13.1), both critical structures in maintaining postural background, integrative aspects of movement, and pertinence of movement (creating a neural image of body motion and synthesizing central movements; Angevine & Cotman, 1981). It may be that involvement of these motor systems in ADHD and learning disability, in general, has some relationship to the minor motor abnormalities associated with these disorders.

Integrating this information suggests that shared neurologic systems may impact attention, motor activity level, perceptual-motor functioning, and emotional regulation. In that ADHD children display no consistent gross abnormalities on CT or MRI brain scans (Bigler, Yeo, & Turkheimer, 1989; Roberts, Varney, Reinarz, & Parkins, 1988), the neurologic deficit is probably at the cellular level, as a defect in neural regulation (i.e., neurotransmitter) and/or neural interconnection. Such defects would disrupt normal functioning and interfere with the complex mechanisms of balancing internal emotional states with the external environment.

Behavior Problems Associated with ADHD

As indicated earlier, it was not until 1980 that the American Psychiatric Association established specific guidelines for diagnosis of Attention Deficit Disorder with or without Hyperactivity, with this subsequently refined in 1985 to reflect what is currently called ADHD. Because these diagnostic classifications are so recent, there has not been sufficient time to undertake the type of research necessary to explore fully behavior problems associated with ADHD. Thus, we have to depend on past research under the MBD (Berry & Cook, 1980) label and extrapolate from those findings as they may apply to ADHD.

Emotional Lability. In a large group of so-called MBD children, Gross and Wilson (1974) found that almost 20% had temper outbursts, and with the next most common problems being displays of moodiness, depression, and frequent crying. These types of problems in ADHD children are often erratically displayed, either without provocation or out of proportion to the incident/stress level present. These changes in mood and behavior may take the form of wide variations in emotional expression and vary on a day-to-day or sometimes hour-to-hour basis. Because of this unpredictable variability in emotional regulation and expression, many ADHD children are considered emotionally labile.

Self-Control. ADHD children tend to be impulsive; they respond impulsively to both external and internal stimuli. Thus, a momentary mental impulse may be acted upon without consideration of the consequences. Likewise, any environmental stimulus that impacts one of the senses, in particular sight and/or hearing, may be responded to impulsively. For example, the little girl who has a pretty bow in her ponytail may walk in front of an ADHD boy who, without consideration of the implications of his acting, will yank at the ponytail. Accordingly, ADHD children are not reflective over their behaviors, self-regulate poorly, and act impulsively.

Aggressive Behavior. In the previously mentioned report by Gross and Wilson (1974), inappropriate aggressiveness was found to be the second most common parental complaint in a study of 817 MBD children. Under the heading of aggressiveness ADHD children often are characterized as being destructive, rude, boisterous, lacking in a sense of fair play, or excessively rough. It is not uncommon for parents to describe their ADHD child as "not being a bad kid," and it is often incomprehensible to them that aggressive behaviors are present in their child. The explanation for this is that these "aggressive" behaviors are usually secondary to impulse problems and poor social monitoring and, hence, are not malicious acts of aggression per se.

Poor Relating. Bryan (1974, 1976), utilizing a sociometric technique, studied the social attraction and rejection of learning disabled children (some of whom were undoubtedly ADHD by today's standards). Learning disabled children were found to have poorer peer relations and greater peer rejection than non–learning disabled children. Similarly, Conners (1970) found that hyperactive children had significantly more difficulty in maintaining friendships with peers. Massman, Nussbaum, and Bigler (1988) demonstrated that greater degrees of emotional immaturity exist in ADHD children and that this persisted into later childhood.

Social Perception. Poor social perception has been noted frequently in studies of hyperactive children (Barkley, 1981). Sulzbacher (1975) demonstrated that learning disabled children often have difficulty in accurate self-perception, especially when irritated or frustrated. They also have difficulty expressing emotions appropriately, with inappropriate emotional gestures and behavioral outbursts commonplace.

Underachievement. In the Gross and Wilson (1974) study previously mentioned, the number one parental complaint in MBD children was found to be underachievement. As the above list attests, the behavioral problems of the ADHD child represent the antithesis of necessary behaviors for effective academic achievement. Accordingly, it is no surprise that these children are often considered "underachievers"!

Intervention/Treatment

A number of studies (see review by Nussbaum & Bigler, 1990) have demonstrated the effectiveness of stimulant medication in the treatment of ADHD. As discussed previously there may be an underactivity or hypoarousal of certain neural systems in the ADHD child, and in those children where the stimulant medication is effective, it is probably stabilizing brain arousal mechanisms.

Methods for Management of ADHD Children. Many behavioral techniques work with these children. The common feature of all of these behavioral treatments is that the environment be strictly controlled and extraneous stimuli or distractors be eliminated. Immediate concrete feedback to the child about appropriate and inappropriate behaviors is essential. Another key ingredient of these treatment programs is that they work within the limits of the child's attention span. For most ADHD children that means reducing tasks to be accomplished in 5- to 15-minute segments. Methods for behavioral and effective instructional management of ADHD children as presented by Schmitt (1977) follow.

1. *Accept your child's limitations.* Teachers and parents must accept the fact that ADHD children are intrinsically active and energetic and possibly always will be. The hyperactivity is not intentional. A teacher or parent should not expect to eliminate totally the hyperactivity but just to keep it under reasonable control. Any undue criticism or attempts to change the energetic child into a quiet child or "model child" will cause more harm than good. As much as possible the parents and teachers should be tolerant, patient, and low key in their interaction with the ADHD child.

2. *Provide outlets for the release of excess energy.* The ADHD child's energy cannot be bottled up and stored. These children need daily outside activities such as running, sports, or long walks. A fenced playground and yard helps. At home, in bad weather they need a recreational room where they can do as they please without criticisms. If no large room is available, a garage will sometimes suffice. Although the expression of hyperactivity is allowed in these ways, it should not be needlessly encouraged. Adults should not encourage roughhousing with these children. Other children at school or siblings should be forbidden to say, "Chase me, chase me," or instigate other noisy play. Rewarding hyperactive behavior leads to its becoming these children's main style of interacting with people.

3. *Keep the classroom and home existence structured.* Classroom and household routines help the ADHD child accept order at home. Mealtimes, chores, and bedtime should be kept as consistent as possible. Predictable responses by the parents to daily events help the child become more predictable. At school daily routines and schedules should be followed.

4. *Avoid formal gatherings.* This is difficult to accomplish in school, but large, unstructured gatherings are overstimulating to the ADHD child and should be avoided when possible. Settings where hyperactivity would be extremely inappropriate and embarrassing should be completely avoided. This is just setting up the child for failure. Examples of this would be church, restaurants, and so on. Of lesser importance, the child can forgo some trips to stores and supermarkets to reduce unnecessary friction between the child and parent. After the child develops adequate self-control at home, these situations can gradually be introduced.

5. *Maintain firm discipline.* These children are unquestionably difficult to manage. They need more careful, planned discipline than the average child. Rules should be formulated mainly to prevent harm to themselves or others. Aggressive behavior and attention-getting behavior should not be more accepted in the hyperactive

child than in the normal child. Unlike the expression of hyperactivity, aggressive behavior should be eliminated. Unnecessary rules should be avoided; these children tolerate fewer rules than the normal child. The family needs a few clear, consistent, important rules, with other rules added at the child's own pace. Parents must avoid persistent negative comments such as, "Don't do this" and "Stop that."

6. *Enforce discipline with nonphysical punishment.* In the school setting a "time-out" behavioral procedure is essential. For the family a similar "isolation room" or "time-out place" to back up their attempts to enforce rules is essential also, if a show of disapproval does not work. When possible this room should not be the child's bedroom. A laundry room is often ideal. Do *not* use a closet. Children should be sent there to "regain control" and allowed out as soon as they have changed their behavior.

7. *Stretch his/her attention span.* For the preschool child, rewarding nonhyperactive behavior is the key to preparing for school. Increased attention span and persistence with tasks can be taught to these children at home. Children can be shown pictures in a book, and if they are attentive, they can be rewarded with praise and a hug. Next the parent can read stories to the child. Coloring of pictures can be encouraged and rewarded. Games of increasing difficulty can gradually be taught to the child, starting with building blocks and progressing eventually to dominoes, card games, and dice games. Matching pictures is an excellent way to build a child's memory and concentration span. The child's toys should not be excessive in number, for this can accentuate the child's distractibility. The toys should also be safe and relatively unbreakable. For older school-aged ADHD children, various games and activities listed later in this section would be appropriate.

8. *Buffer the child against overreaction by neighbors and extended family members.* If the child receives a reputation for being a "bad kid," it is important that this does not carry over into all aspects of his or her school or home life. At home the attitude that must prevail is that he or she is a "good child with excess energy." It is extremely important that parents don't give up on the child. The child must always feel accepted by his or her family. As long as children have this, their self-esteem and self-confidence will survive.

Instructional Methods for ADHD Children. Following is another list of effective instructional methods in the school setting for ADHD children.

1. ADHD children typically learn better with a hands-on type of approach rather than through class lecture alone.

2. Try not to take away recess as a punishment for misbehavior. The ADHD child needs time to discharge pent-up energy and socialize with other children.

3. For ADHD children with severe distractibility, surrounding environmental stimulation will have to be controlled. Create an "office" for the ADHD child using

the sides of a large shipping carton, so that he or she has a quiet place to work with fewer distractions. Never use this area as a punishment but rather as a special place for the child to get his or her work done.

4. Try to schedule some active time into the daily classroom routine.

5. Help the ADHD child organize his or her environment (e.g., use boxes and cardboard dividers to help organize the child's desk; organize subjects and assignments with color-coded folders). The ADHD child may also need more help in learning to use and maintain an organizational system.

6. Provide frequent structured breaks (e.g., 5 minutes of stretching, coloring, songs, etc.).

7. Establish a regular routine in the classroom. Begin the day with the same routine or task. Also, begin new tasks with some readiness signal (e.g., stand up and touch your toes, close your eyes, and settle down and begin working).

8. Try to use short instructional periods. For example, instead of working on math problems for 30 minutes, break the task into three 10-minute periods or two 15-minute periods.

9. Teach the child how to review his or her assignments to check for errors.

10. Achievement testing may need to be administered either individually or in a resource classroom.

11. The ADHD child will require increased external structure in the classroom, particularly when confronted with tasks that involve working independently. You may need to help direct and focus the child's attention at the beginning of a task, and you may need to help monitor attention throughout the task.

12. Instructions should be kept very short and simple. It may be helpful to have the child repeat instructions aloud before a new task is begun. This should be done as inconspicuously as possible to avoid embarrassing the child.

13. ADHD children can be taught a "stop, think, say, do" strategy to control impulsivity. In this approach, children are taught to *stop* before acting; *think* about what they are going to do; *say* aloud what they are going to do; and then *do* what they have said.

14. Teach children to "talk" themselves through rote tasks, such as solving math problems or writing letters.

15. In educational programming, it would generally be best to avoid excessive time pressure and highly competitive classroom situations, as this will make it even more difficult for ADHD children to control themselves.

16. ADHD children's behavior tends to worsen with repetitive, routine activities. The more novelty one can introduce into the learning situation, the better will be

their attention. Also, perhaps more emphasis could be placed on the quality and accuracy of the children's work rather than on the amount of work completed. For example, have children work 10 math problems and check their work, rather than having the children work an entire page of problems or try to work for 30 minutes on a list of problems. Keep the task broken up into segments of time of 10 to 15 minutes duration and vary the tasks.

17. ADHD children may benefit from a concrete tracking system to monitor their completion of assignments. For example, they could receive a star or a poker chip for each assignment completed. After obtaining a certain number of stars, children would be able to trade them in for some small toy or privilege. Don't expect perfect performance for the child to get a reinforcement.

18. Let the child give you some input on both positive and negative reinforcers.

19. "Catch" children behaving appropriately or paying attention and praise them.

20. Clearly identify appropriate and inappropriate behaviors.

21. Clearly communicate expectations and consequences for desirable and undesirable behaviors.

22. Apply behavioral consequences swiftly and consistently.

23. Change positive reinforcers often so that they maintain their effectiveness.

24. Use a time-out corner or area for inappropriate behavior. Try to make this place as unstimulating as possible, and make termination of time out contingent on good behavior rather than on a certain amount of time.

25. Teachers need a lot of support in dealing with ADHD children. If you get stuck or overwhelmed call in another professional for a consultation (e.g., another teacher, school psychologist, principal).

Game Suggestions. Games that help improve attention span include the following:

1. *Simon Says game.* Start with one or two instructions and gradually add more as the child's skills improve.

2. *Concentration game.* This is a board game by Milton Bradley.

3. *Treasure Hunt.* Give a map with a series of locations marked. Have the child find each location with instructions on what to do at each location (e.g., Go to Dad's closet and find a brown shoe with a note inside"). Have a "pirate's treasure" at the final location.

4. *Flashcards.* These will improve visual memory for words and train attention. Make this a game with a prize for a certain number of correct responses. Have the child help you make the cards. Throw in funny pictures and math problems as well as words.

5. *Rhymes*. Teach the child fun rhymes to improve listening skills, attention, and memory.

6. *Riddles*. Ask children to interpret/explain fun riddles and have them try to make up some of their own. This will help improve listening and thinking skills.

7. *Card and dice games, dominoes*. These games can help develop counting skill and concentration.

8. *Computer games*. Arcade-type computer games that require visual hand-eye coordination may help increase attention span along with perceptual-motor integration.

Other Activities for ADHD Children. Other activities that can help the ADHD child include the following:

1. *Social organizations*. Girl Scouts, Boy Scouts, church groups, and so on, can be good places for the ADHD child to interact with peers and develop better social skills. It is very important to talk with the group leader to let him or her know what your child's special needs are (i.e., structure, firmness, and support).

2. *Sports*. Generally, sports that are not highly competitive and are very active are the best for ADHD children (e.g., gymnastics, dance, soccer, swimming). Again, talk with the coach to be sure he or she has the appropriate skills to manage an ADHD child.

3. *Martial arts*. Martial arts training can be helpful in developing self-confidence, concentration, and self-control. The group leader should emphasize nonviolent, nonaggressive techniques of movement and exercise.

Harris, (1983) has reviewed various behavior therapy methods in treating ADHD. These include specific behavior modification programs, cognitive-behavioral approaches, and biofeedback. Specific behavior modification (e.g., token systems) programs can be quite effective in a home or classroom setting, but it is difficult to implement such programs outside of home or school, and often there will be no generalization. Essentially the same can be said about cognitive-behavioral therapy approaches where the child is instructed on how to self-monitor and to provide internal feedback to slow down response rate and improve attention. The ADHD child may learn to use such techniques in a structured setting, but such control often does not generalize to less structured settings. Biofeedback, where an actual physiological sensor provides direct feedback to the child concerning motor activity, may assist the child in improved self-monitoring, but has identical limitations of all the behavioral therapy methods—lack of generalizability.

The combination of medication and structured environment is often the optimal treatment situation for most ADHD children, yet some 20% may not fully respond to either treatment approach or their combination. For these children a highly structured behavioral approach is essential, and since medication is not effective, they should not be medicated.

IMPULSIVITY AND BRAIN DYSFUNCTION

Impulsive behaviors are often observed in learning disabled children. In some learning disordered children, impulse control may be one of the most prominent behavioral symptoms displayed. As is the focus of this chapter, the common basis between disorders of impulse control and learning disabilities may reside at the neurologic level. Some of this was discussed in the previous section on ADHD. This current section first provides some additional background on the relationship between brain dysfunction and impulsivity. This is followed by a discussion of potential treatment and intervention for neurologically based impulsivity.

Overview

A considerable body of clinical and experimental research has demonstrated that damage to frontal and frontal-temporal regions of the brain impact impulsive behaviors the most, whereas damage to occipital and occipital-parietal regions impact the least (Teuber, 1975). The frontal lobe is the largest of all lobes of the brain and has considerable diversity of function with elaborate interconnections to all other brain regions. It is very well suited to be a final integrator of information and an executor of responses. Both the frontal and temporal lobes contain structures from the primitive "emotional" brain—the limbic system. The limbic system appears to be intimately involved in emotional regulation, and its interaction with frontal cortex likely determines outward emotional responses.

Figure 13.4 depicts MRI scans in a 20-year-old male who sustained a very serious traumatic brain injury when 18 years of age. Note the marked damage to frontal regions. This damage did not change the patient's intellect (WAIS-R VIQ score = 110, PIQ score = 100, FSIQ score = 106) but did result in marked alterations in social behavior, judgment, and impaired attention/concentration. Subsequent to this frontal damage, this individual displayed an inability to sustain attention, was extremely impulsive, and had great difficulty in maintaining effective social relations due in large part to socially inappropriate (childish, impulsive) behaviors. Figure 13.5 depicts the EEG abnormalities in frontal regions in a 13-year-old boy with similar behavior problems. His CT and MRI studies were normal, but the EEG demonstrated definite frontal abnormalities, suggesting impaired neural transmission in the frontal regulatory areas. These deficit areas in the frontal lobes are likely responsible, in some fashion, for the impulsive, and socially inappropriate, behaviors exhibited by the child.

As previously discussed, many of the learning and/or attention disorders may have frontal and temporal lobe abnormalities. With this in mind, it is not unexpected

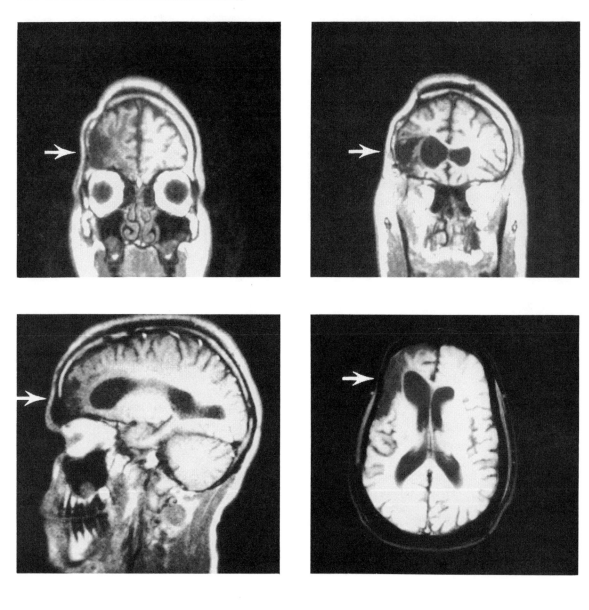

FIGURE 13.4. MRI scans depicting areas of structural brain damage (arrows are pointing to the regions of damaged tissue) in the frontal region of the brain in a 20-year-old traumatic brain injured individual with impulse control problems. The top two scans are as if looking at the person. The bottom left scan is from the side and the bottom right scan is from the top looking down.

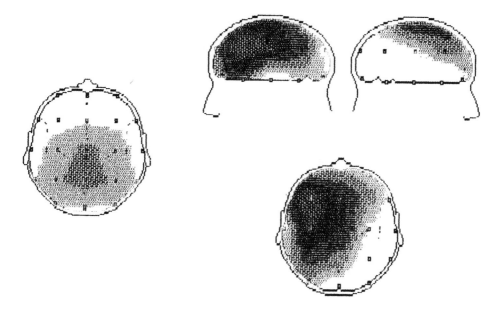

FIGURE 13.5. Brain EEG topography mapping in a 13-year-old with a severe impulse disorder (three views on the right—top left: left hemisphere; top right: right hemisphere; bottom central: left and right hemisphere as if looking from the top). The view on the left is a normal brain map (as if looking down from the top) depicting the normal activation pattern. This child's EEG map demonstrates abnormal activity (dark area) in the left frontal region.

that some learning disabled individuals may exhibit problems with impulse control and social judgment.

Intervention/Treatment

If the impulsivity is due to structural brain damage, as was the case in the examples given in Figure 13.4, then a medication approach may be effective in reducing some of the impulsive behaviors. For example, the 13-year-old boy mentioned above displayed a dramatic reduction, but not elimination, in aggressive and impulsive behavior when placed on the anticonvulsant Tegretol (carbemazepine). Some individuals with organically based impulsivity may respond to other types of medications including major tranquilizers, antidepressants, and lithium. For such cases psychiatric and neurologic consultation is essential.

From the behavioral standpoint, the techniques discussed in the preceding section for the ADHD child also would apply here. Again, the problem with impulsivity is that the child does not possess internal regulatory mechanisms sufficient to override environmental influences. Thus, structuring the environment will help reduce impulsivity.

VISUAL-SPATIAL DEFICITS AND LEARNING DISABILITIES

As pointed out earlier, it is probably unwarranted to conclude that verbal learning disabilities be conceptualized as a left hemisphere dysfunction. But as research focused on such verbal learning disorders, attention also was directed at learning deficits that might attend "right hemisphere" syndromes (Weintraub & Mesulam, 1983). In adults, damage to the right cerebral hemisphere often spares language function, but produces significant deficits in visuomotor, spatial-perceptual, and visual memory function (Bigler, 1988). Similarly, from the neuropsychological perspective, deficits on such tasks imply right hemisphere dysfunction. If significant perceptual deficits exist in a child, it follows that such a child may experience difficulty in distinguishing certain social and emotional situations. However, the problem may have been more extensive neurologic underpinnings than just a perceptual disturbance. The topic of visual-spatial deficits, behavioral/disturbance, and learning disabilities is first overviewed, followed by a discussion of treatment and intervention.

Overview

Myklebust (1975) was the first to refer to visual-spatial deficits as "non verbal learning disabilities," but it probably is more appropriate to characterize them as nonverbal *correlates* of learning disabilities. Several authors have equated right hemisphere dysfunction with such nonverbal correlates (e.g., Tranel, Hall, Olson, & Tranel, 1987; Weintraub & Mesulam, 1983). In such cases, the deficits in learning appear not to be related to verbal or language deficits per se, but to be prominent impairments in perceptual-motor, visual-spatial, and/or visual memory functioning with preserved verbal abilities (e.g., reading, spelling, and verbal intellectual functions). The research of Brumback, Staton, and Wilson (1984), Brumback and Staton (1982), and Nass and Koch (1987) has suggested that emotional dysfunction is frequently associated with the right hemisphere–mediated nonverbal learning disorders. Two factors appear important: (a) the role of the right hemisphere in mediating emotion, particularly certain aspects of mood, affective control of language, and processing nonverbal emotional stimuli (Bruder et al., 1989; Cullum & Bigler, 1988; Hier, Mondlock, & Caplan, 1983; Ross, 1985) and (b) impaired visual-spatial abilities that may predispose the child to impaired social perception and development (Tranel et al., 1987).

Much social and interpersonal interchange takes place at a nonverbal level (e.g., understanding facial expressions, hand/body gestures, social distance between individuals and groups, nonverbal cues of acceptance-rejection, etc.), and many of these activities are mediated by the right hemisphere. As such, individuals with right hemisphere damage/dysfunction may have limitations in a host of nonverbal abilities such as these, and this has a particular negative impact on the development of social skills. This in turn places individuals at a disadvantage in social situations because of their social awkwardness or socially inappropriate behaviors. Such children are often ostracized by other children, further exacerbating the negative feedback they receive. The lack of positive situations in which to learn adaptive social skills will further hinder their social skills development.

Such children also are perceived in a negative fashion by teachers. Badian (1986), in a study of school-aged boys with "nonverbal" learning disability, demonstrated that the teachers perceived these children as "irritating." The so-called irritating behaviors consisted of poor study/work habits (e.g., problems with initiation, poor attention span, failure to complete assignments, etc.), poor motivation, lack of organizational skills, impaired peer interaction, and difficulty accepting criticisms.

Rourke (1989) broadens this concept and suggests that within the framework of his central processing deficiency model of learning disability, nonverbal correlates of learning disabilities may be related to deficits at the level of white (myelinated) matter pathways in the brain. In such a model, the deficits are not restricted to right hemisphere, although a right hemisphere bias may be present. Rourke (1987) suggests that nine common features are present in these children with nonverbal correlates of learning disabilities to make the nonverbal learning disability (NLD) diagnosis. These characteristics are presented below.

1. Bilateral tactile perceptual deficits, usually more marked on the left side of the body.

2. Bilateral psychomotor coordination deficiencies, often more marked on the left side of the body.

3. Outstanding deficiencies in visual-spatial-organizational abilities.

4. Marked deficits in nonverbal problem solving, concept formation, hypothesis testing, and the capacity to benefit from positive and negative informational feedback in novel or otherwise complex situations. (Cause-effect relationships, appreciation of incongruities as in humor).

5. Well-developed rote verbal capacities, including well-developed rote memory skills.

6. Extreme difficulty in adapting to novel and otherwise complex situations.

7. Relative deficiencies in mechanical arithmetic as compared to proficiencies in reading (word recognition) and spelling.

8. Much verbosity of a repetitive, straightforward, rote nature. Content disorders of language characterized by very poor psycholinguistic pragmatics. Misspelling almost exclusively of a phonetically accurate variety. Little or no speech prosody. Reliance upon language as a principal means for social relating, information gathering, and relief from anxiety.

9. Significant deficits in social perception, judgment, and social interaction skills. Tendency toward withdrawal and isolation as age increases.

Rourke, Young, and Leenaars (1989) further contend that the nonverbal learning syndrome predisposes the individual toward a greater likelihood of depression and suicide (see also Bigler, 1989; Fletcher, 1989). As mentioned previously, the frontal lobes are the largest of the brain and hence contain the greatest concentration of white matter. Again, a relationship may exist between delayed or abnormal myelination and abnormal emotional development.

As of this writing, no prevalence studies have been done. So, we know neither the frequency with which these disorders are expressed nor the exact nature of emotional and learning factors that exist in children with visual-spatial deficits in comparison to those with more verbal-language–mediated learning disorders.

Intervention/Treatment

Gresham and Elliott (1989) indicate that only recently social skills deficiencies in learning disabled children have been the focus of research. In fact, they indicate that 75% of all published articles dealing with the topic of social skills deficits/training in learning disabled children were published in the past 5 years. Thus, only limited information on treatment effectiveness is available at this time.

The child with nonverbal deficits that impair social and emotional function may require psychotherapy. Treatment should focus on enhancing nonverbal perception and processing social cues and similar information. For example, videotaping and role playing may be instructive to the nonverbal learning disabled child so that the therapist can assist the child in processing such social information. The guidelines previously given for dealing with depression, stress, and self-esteem problems would be appropriate for the NLD child as well.

The more severely depressed child may respond to antidepressant medication (Brumback & Staton, 1982), but the effectiveness of this has not been examined systematically in the NLD individual. The child displaying suicide risk needs to be seen by mental health specialists.

CONCLUSIONS

The brain is a marvelously complex organ that subserves all of behavior. Embryologically, the brain progresses through a remarkable series of developmental stages at an incredible pace (at some times reaching a rate of 250,000 new cells a minute) on its way to maturity. As a result of such complexity, there is an inherent potential for abnormal development that may disrupt the neural substrates for learning, behavioral regulation, and emotional control. Likewise, the brain is sensitive to injury from a variety of external factors that may similarly affect brain function and development. Such underlying neurologic involvement is likely responsible for many of the deficits in disorders of learning, attention, perceptual-motor functioning, and emotional regulation.

Deficits in frontal and frontal-temporal lobe functioning appear to relate more to problems with attention span, impulse control, and a variety of problems with emotional control and regulation. Left hemisphere dysfunction in some children may be associated with depression; however, right hemisphere dysfunction also disrupts emotional regulation. Treatment for these various problems in emotional control, self-regulation, and social perception in learning disordered individuals will often require the integration of behavioral (e.g., structured and supportive environment, psychotherapy) and medical (e.g., medication) approaches.

14

DEVELOPING PSYCHOLINGUISTIC CORRELATES

The training systems discussed in this chapter are based on various theories originally generated to explain language function in aphasic children and adults. These theories, especially those of Osgood and Wepman, have been integrated by Kirk and his colleagues into a rationale that they used to develop the *Illinois Test of Psycholinguistic Abilities* (ITPA) and its related training activities. Their approach to language disability is decidedly "process-oriented," as evidenced by the fact that basic mental abilities, such as memory status, modality preference, and closure proficiency, play a prominent role in their prescriptions for diagnosis training and academic instruction.

In this chapter, three major aspects of psycholinguistic process training are dealt with. First, Kirk's rationale and the principles he believes should be involved in psycholinguistic-based instruction are discussed. Second, the intervention programs designed by Bush and Giles and Minskoff, Wiseman, and Minskoff are described as representative of the kinds of programs that are currently available. Third, research that has evaluated the effectiveness of the psycholinguistic process approach is reviewed in detail.

KIRK: PSYCHOLINGUISTIC ASSUMPTIONS AND THE ITPA

For all practical purposes the movement toward psycholinguistic process training in the schools began with the development of the *Illinois Test of Psycholinguistic Abilities* (ITPA) (Sievers, 1955; Kirk & McCarthy, 1961; Kirk, McCarthy, & Kirk, 1968, current edition). With this instrument it became possible to profile the performance of children on measures of different psycholinguistic abilities. As a result, it appeared that potentially useful information pertaining to communication behavior could then be used to plan individual remedial programs for the children who evidenced difficulties.

All of the professionals who are reviewed in this chapter have employed the rationale underlying the ITPA as the basis for designing their particular remedial training activities and have used the test either as their primary assessment instrument or as a research tool for investigating the effectiveness of their approaches. Therefore, the teacher who would implement any of the training systems should be thoroughly familiar with (a) the rationale used by Kirk, McCarthy, and Kirk to construct the ITPA; (b) the characteristics, uses, and research base of the test; and (c) the guidelines that govern psycholinguistic instruction.

Rationale Underlying the ITPA

The rationale used by Samuel A. Kirk and his co-workers in constructing the ITPA is based on an interwoven network of assumptions about language, assessment, and training. In particular, Kirk's concepts about the importance of "individual differences" in language learning, Osgood's (1957) ideas about the role of mediating processes and levels of abstraction, and Wepman's (1960) exploratory paradigm of memory and feedback form the theoretical foundation for the ITPA.

To Kirk (Kirk & Gallagher, 1979; Kirk & Kirk, 1971), the term *individual difference* has two distinct meanings. First, it can refer to the comparative differences between one child and another on such variables as intelligence quotients, socioeconomic status, and school achievement scores. Such "interindividual" differences have been useful tools for classifying or labeling children. Second, the term can refer to differential ability patterns existing within a single child, such as relative assets (or deficits) in different facets of linguistic, social, or academic behavior. These "intraindividual" differences are of utmost importance to teachers, since knowledge of them leads directly to the preparation of individualized instructional programs.

Kirk observed that most of the testing being done in the schools seemed to be of the interindividual variety, for the purpose of differentiating one group of children from another. Typical of the labels applied to children because of such evaluations were terms such as "brain-injured," "dyslexic," "aphasic," "retarded," and so on. Kirk suggested that these efforts were of limited instructional value to teachers in that they provided little information about either the specific aspects of deficient performance or the child's preferred learning style or modality. It was for this reason that he sought to develop a test that would measure differences in learning style and ability *within* the individual child being tested.

The utility of intraindividual testing has long been recognized in the field of reading; a number of suitable diagnostic tests, such as the *Durrell Analysis of Reading Difficulty* (Durrell, 1955), Spache's (1981) *Diagnostic Reading Scales*, Brown, Hammill, and Wiederholt's (1986) *Test of Reading Comprehension*, and various informal reading inventories, have been designed. The intraindividual approach has also been used in the areas of cognition [*Wechsler Intelligence Scale for Children* (Wechsler, 1974), *Detroit Tests of Learning Aptitude* (Hammill, 1990), *Kaufman Assessment Battery for Children* (Kaufman & Kaufman, 1983), *Woodcock-Johnson Psycho-Educational Battery* (Woodcock, 1978)]; language [*Test of Language Development* (Newcomer & Hammill, 1988), *Clinical Evaluation of Language Functions* (Wiig, 1987)]; arithmetic [*KeyMath* (Connolly, 1988), *Test of Early Mathematics Ability* (Ginsburg & Baroody, 1990)]; and writing [*Test of Written Language* (Hammill & Larsen, 1988)].

What makes the ITPA unique is that it seeks to tap selected psychological and linguistic abilities that are assumed to underlie, relate to, or contribute to academic achievement. In format and subtest content it bears considerable similarity to the Wechsler Scales, the major difference being that the latter is interpreted within a cognitive-intellectual rather than in a psycholinguistic frame of reference. Kirk does not intend that the ITPA be used as a test of specific intellectual or academic achievement, though some of its scores may correlate well with such tests. Neither is the ITPA, strictly speaking, exclusively a test of language, for only four of the 12 subtests (Grammatic Closure, Auditory Reception, Auditory Association, and Verbal Expression) are even remotely consistent with current linguistic theory. Rather, the ITPA was developed to pinpoint certain psycholinguistic "correlates" of learning disability. Thus some of the subtests measure familiar psychological constructs such as memory and closure, while other subtests assess linguistic constructs such as those mentioned earlier in this paragraph.

Thus it was to provide the field with another psycholinguistically oriented measure of intraindividual differences that Kirk developed the ITPA. Illustrative of this point is the statement of Kirk, McCarthy, and Kirk (1968) that the 12 subtests of the ITPA can be used to

> isolate defects in (a) three processes of communication (b) two levels of language organization, and/or (c) two channels of language input and output. Performance on specific subtests of this battery should pinpoint specific psycholinguistic abilities and disabilities. The identification of specific deficiencies in psycholinguistic functions leads to the crucial task of remediation directed to the specific areas of defective functioning. This is the *sine qua non* of diagnosis. (p. 13)

The precise manner in which the concepts of Osgood and Wepman were utilized in generating subtests is shown in the Clinical Model of the 1968 ITPA presented in Figure 14.1. This model encompasses three dimensions: psycholinguistic processes, levels of organization, and channels of communication (Kirk et al., 1968).

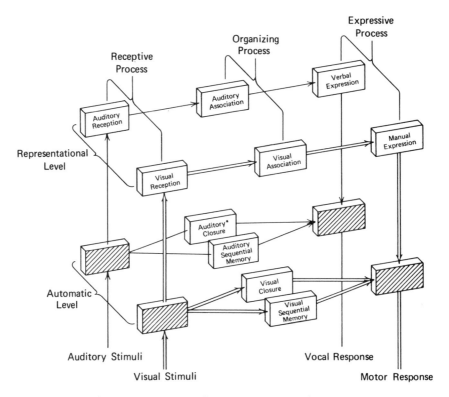

*Auditory Closure, Grammatic Closure, and Sound Blending.

FIGURE 14.1. Three-dimensional model of the ITPA. *Note.* From *Illinois Test of Psycholinguistic Abilities* (p. 8) by S. A. Kirk, J. J. McCarthy, and W. D. Kirk, 1968, Urbana: University of Illinois Press. Reprinted by permission.

Psycholinguistic Processes. The first dimension in the ITPA test model encompasses three sets of abilities involved in transmitting (processing) information efficiently. These sets of abilities relate to the reception (understanding), organization (mediating), and expression (using) of psycholinguistic abilities. Kirk et al. (1968) define reception as the ability to obtain meaning from symbols, expression as the ability to convey meaning either vocally or through gestures, and organization as the ability to associate and manipulate symbols in a meaningful fashion.

Levels of Organization. The ITPA model also includes a dimension that accounts for two levels of language complexity. The main difference between the levels lies in the degree of symbolic meaning involved in each. The first or automatic level mediates activities requiring the retention of nonmeaningful symbol sequences, the execution of automatic habit chains, and both grammatical and visual closure. For example, children in the echo-babble stage of speech development can be said to function at the automatic level, in that they are able to imitate vocalizations but lack firmly established meanings for what they are vocalizing.

The second and more complex level of organization is the representational, which mediates activities that require the individual to grasp the meaning of symbols. When children learn the meaning of signals and use them in meaningful ways, they are operating at the representational level. Reading with comprehension and purposeful conversation are examples of representational abilities.

Channels of Language Input and Output.   The third dimension of the ITPA refers to the sensorimotor pathway through which language is transmitted. This dimension is divided into the modes of input (auditory and visual), the modes of output (vocal and motor), and two combinations of input and output (auditory-vocal and visual-motor). No provisions have been made for testing other combinations of input and output, such as auditory-motor, visual-vocal, or tactile-motor.

The reader will note that several boxes in the test model (Figure 14.1) are marked with diagonal lines and are not labeled. These boxes represent psycholinguistic constructs that are not measured by the ITPA. For example, auditory and visual reception and verbal and manual expression at the automatic level are not tested by the ITPA. This fact should serve as a reminder that there are more constructs in Kirk's psycholinguistic process theory than are accounted for by the ITPA. Also, one must keep in mind that a single construct can be measured in many different ways and that the ITPA subtest is but one way of doing so. Therefore, when teacher-clinicians adopt the test model as a guide to assessment and remediation, they must recognize that the test (as is the case with all standardized measures) is an imperfect approximation of its underlying constructs. While the ITPA can form the bedrock of a psycholinguistically oriented teacher's evaluation efforts, it must be supplemented with additional observations to measure the untapped constructs.

The ITPA and the rationale behind it have been so influential that the constructs measured by the test have become for many school professionals the operational definition of psycholinguistics. Thus learning centers have been set up in the classrooms, and remedial programs have been developed that correspond with the ITPA constructs manifested in the subtests. Key to this approach are the assumptions that these functions are identifiable in individual children, that deficits can be remediated through a planned program, and that the constructs are meaningfully related to academic success.

Before continuing the discussion of Kirk's contribution to psycholinguistic process training, some comment about the term *psycholinguistics* would probably be useful. Psycholinguistics refers to

the study of the mental processes which underlie the acquisition and use of language. As such, it is clearly the progeny of a rather unruly marriage between psychology, the study of behavior, and linguistics, the study of language structure. (Newcomer & Hammill, 1976, p. 1)

Kirk's basic work in this area was done during a time when psychologists were predominant in the field, a time before the advent of Chomsky and his theories of transformational grammar brought linguists to preeminence. As a result, Kirk's constructs relating to assessment and training are far more reflective of psychological than linguistic theory. For example, on the ITPA are many tests of short-term sequential memory, closure, and association abilities (time-honored constructs in psychology); but only a few tests measure constructs that are clearly of linguistic origin. Indeed, there are no tests at all involving current linguistic constructs such as pragmatics, transformational grammar, vocabulary classes, syntactic structure, contextual meaning, and phonology. Even Osgood, the man who formulated the ideas on which Kirk built much of the ITPA, has long since revised his psycholinguistic theories to accommodate these new linguistic hypotheses.

The readers should note that although many people whose work is reviewed in this book use the term *psycholinguistics*, the meaning of the term varies according to the person using it. When advocates of the ITPA and its constructs use the term, they do so in its pre-1960 context. When others, such as Laura Lee, Coughran and Liles, Gray and Ryan, and Fokes, use the term, they do so in a context more reflective of the recent contributions of the linguists.

Description and Purpose of the ITPA

In this section the 12 subtests that make up the ITPA are described in detail, the manner in which the test results are to be used in practice is discussed, and the consensus of accumulated research findings on the ITPA is reviewed.

Descriptions of the ITPA Subtests. Each of the ITPA subtests is described below. Table 14.1 was prepared to help the reader relate the subtests to the constructs of the Clinical Model.

1. *Auditory Reception.* This is a test of children's ability to understand simple spoken sentences presented in question form. For example, children are asked questions such as, "Do dogs eat?" "Do people marry?" "Do penguins waddle?" to which they are asked to respond yes or no. Since the response requirements of the test are minimal, the test authors feel that the expressive factor is insignificant. The vocabulary of the items becomes more and more difficult, but the expressive requirements on this subtest remain minimal.

2. *Visual Reception.* This test is the visual counterpart of Auditory Reception. It is purported to measure the child's ability to understand the meaning of visual symbols. The child is shown a single picture for 3 seconds and is asked to select

TABLE 14.1. ITPA Subtests Coded in Terms of the Test Model

Subtest	Level	Process	Channel
1. Auditory Reception	Representational	Reception	Auditory
2. Visual Reception	Representational	Reception	Visual
3. Auditory Association	Representational	Organizing	Auditory
4. Visual Association	Representational	Organizing	Visual
5. Verbal Expression	Representational	Expression	Verbal
6. Manual Expression	Representational	Expression	Manual
7. Visual Sequential Memory	Automatic	Organizing	Visual
8. Auditory Sequential Memory	Automatic	Organizing	Auditory-Verbal
9. Grammatic Closure	Automatic	Organizing	Auditory-Verbal
10. Visual Closure	Automatic	Organizing	Visual
11. Auditory Closure	Automatic	Organizing	Auditory-Verbal
12. Sound Blending	Automatic	Organizing	Auditory-Verbal

from four pictures on a second page the item that is conceptually similar to the first. For example, the first picture might be of a child running and on the second page would be four pictures of children, only one of whom is running. Thus the "correct" choice is to be made on a conceptual, rather than a perceptual or "look-alike," basis.

3. *Auditory Association.* On this test the auditory and vocal requirements of the test are minimal, but the associative requirements become greater with each item. A sentence completion format is used, in which a statement such as, "A rabbit is fast, a turtle is _____," is presented by the examiner. The child is to complete the statement with responses such as, "slow," "slower," or "slowpoke."

4. *Visual Association.* In the visual channel the organizing process is assessed by presenting a stimulus picture surrounded by four other pictures and then asking the child to select the one that is associated with it. This technique is supposed to provide the examiner with an estimate of a child's ability to relate visually presented concepts. For example, a picture of a dog would "go" with a picture of a bone, because dogs chew on bones.

5. *Verbal Expression.* This test evaluates children's ability to express ideas through spoken language. Subjects are shown a familiar object and required to tell everything they can about it. Scoring on this measure depends on the quantity of different relevant concepts that are produced.

6. *Manual Expression.* The purpose of this test is to determine children's ability to express ideas through the use of gestures. They are shown pictures of objects and asked to show the examiner "what we do" with particular objects. Thus

children are to pantomime the use of such common objects as knife and fork, pencil sharpener, binoculars, and so on.

7. *Grammatic Closure.* This test assesses the ability to make use of oral language habits in acquiring syntax and grammatic inflections. Children are presented with incomplete statements accompanied by pictorial representations and asked questions such as, "Here is a bed, here are two _____." The child should respond with the plural form of *bed*. Also tested are verb tenses, prepositions, possessives, pronouns, and so on. The assumption is made that these linguistic forms have occurred so frequently in the child's experience and that recognition and use of them is so thoroughly overlearned that they have become automatic.

8. *Auditory Closure.* This test is recommended for children who appear to have difficulties in the auditory-vocal channel at the automatic level. The items measure the ability to complete an incomplete auditory stimulus. For example, children are asked, "What am I talking about—bo/ /le?" The medial sound of /t/ is omitted, and it is assumed that the children will be so familiar with the word that they will automatically "fill in" the missing part of the stimulus.

9. *Sound Blending.* This test assesses the organizing process in the auditory-vocal channel and requires the child to recognize a common word spoken in sounds presented at half-second intervals. For example, the examiner presents such stimuli as "b-oa-t," "l-i-tt-le," and "ā-f-ē," separating the sound by half seconds, and the child is expected to respond with the word or nonsense syllable.

10. *Visual Closure.* This test measures the child's ability to recognize a picture of a common object when presented with only portions of the picture. Instead of using a single pictorial representation of the object, scenes are presented with 14 or 15 examples of the object concealed to varying degrees in them. For example, the demonstration item *dogs* is presented to the child as the examiner says, "See these dogs?" and points to the portion of the folded paper strip showing several discrete dogs. The strip is opened, revealing a scene, and the examiner says, "I want you to see how quickly you can find all the dogs in here." The child must then search for the hidden dogs or portions of dogs.

11. *Auditory Sequential Memory.* This is a digit span test similar to the subtest on the Wechlser scales, differing primarily in the speed at which the digits are presented and the number of presentations. The examiner presents increasingly lengthy strings of digits to the child, giving them at the rate of two per second, and the child is expected to repeat the string verbatim.

12. *Visual Sequential Memory.* This test assesses the ability to recall a series of non-meaningful visual symbols and to reproduce the series. Children are shown a sequence of symbols for 5 seconds and are asked to reproduce the sequence using corresponding chips that they place in the proper order.

Analysis of ITPA Scores. The ITPA yields two types of scores: (a) a language age, expresed in years and months; and (b) a standard score expressed on a scale that has a mean of 36 and a standard deviation of 6. The examiner can interpret these scores in several different ways.

First the examiner may look at the global scores: the composite psycholinguistic language age (PLA), the psycholinguistic quotient, the mean or median scaled score, and the Stanford-Binet mental age (MA) or intelligence quotient (IQ). These scores give some idea of the child's overall performance. They can be used to make comparisons between chronological age (CA) and psycholinguistic age, between psycholinguistic age and grade placement, and so on. Such scores have limited value for any purpose other than interindividual comparisons among children, although they may be somewhat useful in determining whether a child is eligible for special education services.

Of greater value to the diagnostician are the individual subtest scores, which yield information about the child's ability to perform the various tasks set by the test. In addition, scores can be obtained for representational and automatic level performance across the entire test for auditory-vocal or visual-motor performance, and for receptive, associative, and expressive process abilities.

The Profile of Abilities. The child's ITPA scores are summarized on the Profile of Abilities. A sample profile of ITPA scores obtained by an individual child is shown in Figure 14.2. When interpreting the profile, the examiner looks first at the section where the developmental ages are recorded. In this example these scores indicate some degree of developmental delay in that the child's MA and PLA lag behind the CA. On the profile the discrepancy between MA and PLA is negligible; therefore, one might decide that the child is experiencing no psycholinguistic difficulties. However, such a conclusion is not necessarily accurate, because it is often the subtest scores rather than the developmental scores that indicate the presence of a problem. The profile presented in Figure 14.2 is a case in point, as subtest analysis shows that performance in Visual Association and Visual Sequential Memory is significantly lower than would be expected in view of the child's MA and PLA.

Next the examiner computes the level, channel, and process composite scores, which is done simply by summing the scores under consideration and dividing by the number of appropriate subtests. For example, one might compute the composite receptive score by summing the scaled scores of Auditory Reception and Visual Reception and dividing by two.

To evaluate the significance of differences between individual subtests and composite scaled scores, Kirk and Kirk (1971) provide guidelines for determining when a discrepancy is meaningful. A difference of ± 6 points between a subtest scaled score and the mean or median scaled scores is not considered significant. Differences of ± 7 to 9 points are considered to be of "borderline" significance, while a difference of ± 10 points or greater is considered to be a substantial discrepancy. In general, the differences between subtest scaled scores are significant when ranges of standard area of measurement for the subtests do not overlap.

When a "borderline" or "substantial" deficit is indicated from a child's test performance, the teacher should verify such an indication through diagnostic teaching

PROFILE OF ABILITIES

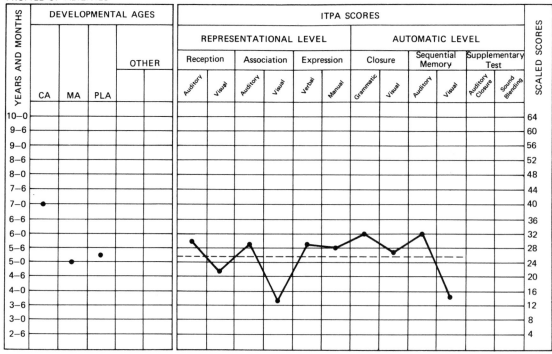

FIGURE 14.2. ITPA profile of abilities.

or direct observation. For example, if a child has done poorly on the Auditory Reception subtest (where children are asked yes/no questions like "Does a bird fly?"), the teacher can present other listening comprehension tasks that measure the construct. Other assessment tasks might include asking the child questions like, "Which one of these do you always find in the forest: snow, trees, hunters, houses?" In another assessment task the teacher might say a word and ask the child to point to the one of four pictures that best fits the stimulus word. Few professionals who adopt the Kirk rationale for psycholinguistic process training accept the ITPA as the sole criterion for psycholinguistic deficiency; thus these additional assessment modes should be the rule rather than the exception when doing diagnoses.

Our discussion of the analysis of ITPA scores is not an attempt to instruct the examiner in the art or science of interpreting the ITPA; rather, it is intended as an overview of ITPA interpretation. Obviously, persons who wish to become proficient in the administration and interpretation of the ITPA have to invest a fair amount of time in familiarizing themselves with the ITPA Examiner's Manual, the manuals by Kirk and Kirk (1971), W. Kirk (1974), and Lombardi and Lombardi (1977), and the statistical text by Paraskevopoulos and Kirk (1969).

ITPA Related Research. Because of the influential role that has been played by the ITPA in diagnosing and programming for children, the status of the test's statistical characteristics assumes critical importance. The degree of a standardized test's usefulness rests ultimately upon the level of its reliability and validity as demonstrated through research. On both points the ITPA has been attacked heavily and continually. After reviewing the existent factor analytic research up to 1972, Sedlak and Weener concluded that "the tentative factors that have been identified offer scant support for the channel-level mode on which the ITPA is based" (1973, p. 124). On the basis of an extensive review of the relevant studies accumulated up to 1975 and their own extensive research, Newcomer and Hammill (1976) concluded that the reliabilities of the subtests were too low to justify profile analysis, the intended purpose of the ITPA, and that the subtests were of questionable validity in that they did not correlate closely with academic performance. In Buros's *Mental Measurements Yearbook* the research on the ITPA is reviewed three times. The authors of all three reviews (Lumsden, 1978; Waugh, 1978; Wiederholt, 1978b) conclude that the ITPA has questionable reliability, equivocal validity, and no educational usefulness. Waugh probably speaks for most researchers who have studied the test when he states regretfully that the ITPA "has been added to the long history of failure to find practical uses for measures of specific abilities" (1978, p. 432). The ITPA fares no better in Salvia and Ysseldyke's review: "The ITPA seems to have inadequate norms, poor reliability, and questionable validity" (1988, p. 273).

Guidelines for Psycholinguistic Instruction

In addition to developing the ITPA as a prime instrument to pinpoint intraindividual psycholinguistic differences in children, Kirk and Kirk (1971) have compiled their suggestions for remediation into the volume *Psycholinguistic Learning Disabilities: Diagnosis and Remediation*. The initial two-thirds of the book deals with the ITPA—its development, its proper use, its validity as a clinical tool, and its limitations. In the remainder of the work they offer nine general principles for teachers to follow when attempting to remediate psycholinguistic learning disabilities. Also presented are examples of activities designed to teach the abilities tapped by the ITPA subtests. The teacher who is planning to initiate a program will find that the nine principles are useful guidelines to follow. Although the activities presented are too few for building a program, they can be useful supplements to those suggested by Bush and Giles and by Minskoff et al., which are described later in this chapter.

1. *Differentiate testing from teaching.* Testing and teaching are two different types of educational functions, though success in the latter ultimately is dependent on

proficiency in the former. Kirk and Kirk (1971) state that testing involves much more than simply the administration of standardized measures to children. They point out that every time teachers monitor a child's school performance, they are testing the child and presumably planning instructional alternatives as a result of their observations. The implication here is that even though the ITPA may be helpful, it cannot be used alone, nor should the knowledgeable teacher depend on it to the exclusion of his or her own professional judgment.

2. *Train the deficient areas.* Kirk and Kirk (1971) maintain that some improvement is to be expected in all deficient areas, even those that are highly resistant to amelioration. Thus one goal of the training program must be to remediate deficiencies, not merely to compensate for them.

3. *Utilize areas of strength.* In the effort to remediate deficits the teacher should not overlook a child's psycholinguistic assets. Teaching tasks that couple strong and weak areas should be designed, thereby facilitating the remedial effort.

4. *Use multisensory presentations appropriately.* After discussion concerning the merits and hazards of both multisensory and unisensory instruction, Kirk and Kirk (1971) recommend the judicious use of multisensory media.

5. *Remediate prerequisite deficits first.* In psycholinguistic remediation the teacher's attention is called to certain teaching patterns, such as teaching receptive before expressive processes and lower level processes before higher level ones. Thus one should teach children to understand the speech of others before expecting them to converse well themselves. Further, children who are poor in speech comprehension might first require remediation for a lower level problem like speech sound discrimination.

6. *Make provisions for utilizing feedback.* The child should engage in as many tasks as possible that involve feedback or self-monitoring. This can be accomplished in two ways: by having the teacher discuss with the child either the task itself or the child's performance on the task itself or the child's performance on the task (external feedback) or by using tasks in which the feedback is "built in," such as in the Fernald (1943, 1988) VAKT reading method, where the child sees a word, writes it from memory, checks his or her work against a model, and recycles if it is done in error.

7. *Develop abilities functionally.* Put simply, train the skills the child has the most immediate need to learn in order to perform normally at home or at school.

8. *Start remedial programs early.* The best time to identify and remediate learning problems in children is before they enter first grade. It is needless and grossly inefficient to allow children to fail for years in school and to attempt remediation only after their difficulties have "blossomed" into serious academic and behavioral problems.

9. *Individualized instruction.* This principle is desirable in a regular elementary class; in a remedial situation it is essential. Learning disabled children truly are unique. They may be grouped briefly with other children with whom they share a learning level in a particular skill at a point in time, but their programs must be planned continually on a one-to-one basis.

BUSH AND GILES: AIDS TO PSYCHOLINGUISTIC TEACHING

Though no longer available, the manual by Wilma Jo Bush and Marian T. Giles (1977), *Aids to Psycholinguistic Teaching,* was an important source of activities for teachers who were interested in remediating psycholinguistic deficits in children and younger adolescents using the ITPA as a theoretical model. The contents of this manual were popular during the late 1970s and are described here because they exemplify so well the manner in which ITPA-based training was done.

The manual is organized into chapters that correspond with the subtests of the ITPA. The ITPA-based chapters are clustered into three major sections: Auditory Modality, Visual Modality, and Expression. Chapters entitled Auditory Reception, Auditory Association, Grammatic and Auditory Closure, and Auditory Memory are grouped into the Auditory Modality section. Chapters dealing with the ITPA subtests that involve visual-motor abilities are allotted to the Visual Modality section. The chapters dealing with verbal and manual communicative abilities are assigned to the Expression section.

Each of the major sections is introduced with a discussion in which the construct used as the basis for grouping the chapters is defined and supported with references to selected research studies. For example, in the introduction to the Auditory Modality section, Bush and Giles (1977) stress the importance of the auditory channel in learning and embrace the assumption that the process-oriented construct has some relevance for teaching. While they mention a few studies that refute their position, they dismiss these studies by giving possible reasons why their negative findings should be disregarded.

Each chapter begins with a brief introduction defining the ITPA construct that is dealt with. This is followed by a series of training activities that are consistent with that definition. These activities are sequenced for children in kindergarten through eighth grade. As *Aids to Psycholinguistic Teaching* was designed for remedial purposes, one can assume that the activities are primarily intended for use with those children who evidence specific deficits in psycholinguistic functioning. Therefore, particular activities are to be selected for individual children on the basis of their specific needs.

Each ITPA construct that was used as the basis of a chapter is described in the following paragraphs, along with sample activities. For brevity, only activities that are offered for use in the third grade are described.

Auditory reception is defined as the ability to recognize and/or to understand what is heard. Activities recommended for use with third graders include (a) asking questions about the content of stories read aloud, (b) playing games and activities such as "Simon Says" in which children have to follow verbal directions, and (c) verbally describing objects or animals and asking children to identify what was described (e.g., "It is an animal. It gives milk. It says moo.").

Auditory association, the ability to associate spoken words in a meaningful way, deals with the auditory process of interpreting relationships. The instructional activities include any task that involves verbal abstraction, classification, or problem solving. Suitable activities include asking children questions such as, "Which of these has legs but cannot walk: a table, a chair, a dog?"; helping them to see the incongruities in spoken sentences such as, "Do people use glasses to eat meat?"; and having them tell how a series of words (*hammer, ax, saw*) are alike.

Grammatic and auditory closure are abilities that allow children to predict future linguistic events from past experience. In training these abilities, Bush and Giles suggest the use of cloze techniques, in which children supply letters or words that are omitted in stories; rhyming activities; and sound-blending exercises.

Auditory memory is the ability to remember words, sounds, or sentences one has heard. At the third-grade level it is trained by giving the child practice in repeating series of related (*turkey, duck, chicken, pigeon*) and unrelated (*cowboy, blue, booth, animal*) words and in repeating sentences verbatim. In another activity the teacher reads a story aloud to a child and has the child either answer specific content questions or retell the story in his or her own words.

Visual reception is the ability to understand or interpret what is seen; that is, to comprehend the meaning of symbols, written words, or pictures. One training activity requires the child to make "pictionaries," compendia of pictures that correspond to written words. These can be indexed in alphabetical order or by specific classifications (pets, foods, clothing, etc.). The use of Cuisenaire rods, which combine color and number concepts, is another way of teaching the ability.

Visual association is the ability to associate visual symbols in a meaningful way; thus it deals with the visual process of interpreting relationships. Training activities include having children tell what they see in examples of abstract art, using visually oriented games like dominoes, and asking children to find the object in a picture that does not "belong" with other elements in the picture.

Visual closure is the ability to recognize by sight an object when only a part of it is shown. A suggested activity has the child place tracing paper over a map, make dots on the tracing paper at half-inch intervals over the boundaries printed on the map, remove the tracing paper, and complete the dots drawing freehand.

Visual memory is the ability to remember objects, events, or words that have been seen. Activities include connecting dots to form pictures where the dots are accompanied by numbers or letters of the alphabet. In another exercise the teacher flashes a printed word to the students, who then reproduce the word on their desks using individual letter cards.

Verbal expression is the ability to express ideas in spoken language. Teaching activities include telling children part of a story and asking them to finish it, having them tell experience stories to the class, and providing them with comic strips that have had the words in the "balloons" blocked out and letting them tell what they think the characters are saying.

Manual expression is the ability to express ideas by gesturing. The game "Charades" and its variations are perhaps the best examples of a training activity for this ability, although all types of pantomiming would be appropriate.

The activities in the Bush and Giles (1977) book are numerous, clearly described, and roughly sequenced. This makes them highly attractive to teachers. The final chapters on perceptual-motor, recreation, and motor activities represent secondary areas of interest and can be used to supplement the programs described in Chapter 15 of this book on perceptual-motor process systems.

Our concerns with this approach deal more with the rationale underlying the use of the activities than with the intrinsic value of the activities themselves. For instance, one is never sure what Bush and Giles believe is really being trained by the use of their activities. Are their exercises intended to enhance something called a basic ability, such as the Auditory Modality, or to improve only those particular tasks being taught, for example, the ability to say yes or no to questions such as, "Do dogs fly?" Nor do Bush and Giles attempt to explain or differentiate the relationship between meaningful (conceptual) and nonmeaningful (perceptual) tasks in their traditional training activities. The mixing of these two levels of tasks in training leads one to assume that Bush and Giles believe that the tasks have some useful, if undefined, relationship to each other. On this point it would be interesting for Bush and Giles to explain the educational relevance of some of the tasks they recommend, such as having children tap out nonsense rhythm patterns or repeat series of unrelated words or digits. Are such tasks taught to strengthen the child's "Auditory Modality"; to make him or her more educable in reading, writing, spelling, or talking; or to master only those singular—and in themselves quite useless—activities?

To maintain that basic abilities like the Auditory Modality or Auditory Memory can be trained by prescribed activities is dangerously close to the long-discredited "faculty psychology" ideas that were so prevalent during the 1800s. On the other hand, if the purpose of training is to teach specific tasks, why not do so directly without employing the ITPA rationale as the means of organizing the tasks to be taught? More of this point is made later in the appraisal section which concludes this chapter.

MINSKOFF, WISEMAN, AND MINSKOFF: THE MWM PROGRAM FOR DEVELOPING LANGUAGE ABILITIES

Using the ITPA rationale as a foundation, Esther H. Minskoff, Douglas E. Wiseman, and J. Gerald Minskoff have developed *The MWM Program for Developing Language Abilities* (1972). Remediation is attempted in 12 psycholinguistic areas, including auditory reception, visual reception, auditory association, visual association, verbal expression, manual expression, auditory sequential memory, visual sequential memory, grammatic closure, visual closure, auditory closure, and sound blending.

The program is the culmination of the authors' long-standing interest in the area of teaching psycholinguistic abilities. The interest was evidenced first in Wiseman's (1965a) doctoral dissertation and in his subsequent article in *Mental Retardation* (1965b). This was followed by J. Minskoff's (1967) doctoral dissertation, which dealt with the effectiveness of individual planned programs in overcoming learning disabilities in mentally retarded and emotionally disturbed children. Their work was supplemented by Minskoff (1967), who studied methods for training the association areas, notably those related to verbal interaction.

Although the MWM Program could be used with all youngsters, the authors' primary intention was to build a remedial program for young children who have specific psycholinguistic problems. The MWM kit has four parts: a teacher's guide, an Inventory of Language Abilities, six remedial manuals, and supplemental remedial materials.

Teacher's Guide

No instruction should be attempted until the teacher is thoroughly familiar with the teacher's guide. This book is an important source of necessary information about the program and how it can be most effectively implemented. In addition to a discussion of the program's purposes and a description of its format, the guide includes useful sections dealing with administration, assessment, and definitions of those psycholinguistic areas that are the concern of the program. Particularly valuable is the final section, which suggests guidelines that the teacher can use to create additional teaching activities and learning materials.

Inventory of Language Abilities

When identifying children in need of training, the teacher can do the initial screening using the Inventory of Language Abilities. This measure is actually an observational checklist of items. The items are divided into sections. There is a section of items for each of the ITPA constructs with the exception of "auditory closure" and "sound blending," which have been combined into a single section. The child who does not pass one-half of the items in a particular section is scheduled for additional assessment. Usually, this involves an administration of the ITPA. If this is not possible, the authors suggest that the teacher should select the training manual associated with the deficit identified by the initial screening and begin remediation.

While approving of the authors' attempt to provide the teacher with an informal assessment device via the Inventory of Language Abilities, we believe that additional information about the inventory is essential. For example, is the procedure reliable? Also, what is the relationship between the subsections of the inventory and the subtests of the ITPA? If the inventory is actually to be used to identify children with psycholinguistic deficits, to approximate the ITPA and its subtests, or to measure intraindividual differences in children, some research evidence should be made available to teachers to show that the inventory can be used effectively for such purposes. In short, careful research dealing with the inventory's reliability and validity should now be undertaken.

Teaching Manuals

Six training manuals are provided: Reception (Auditory and Visual), Association (Auditory and Visual), Expression (Verbal and Manual), Memory (Auditory and Visual), Closure (Grammatic and Visual), and Auditory Closure–Sound Blending. In each of these the construct and its subareas are named and defined. Then follows a discussion of basic remedial strategies and specific activities. The latter are presented sequentially according to level of difficulty and corresponding language age for each subarea. Each activity is accompanied by instructions for restructuring the task in the event of an incorrect response.

The auditory part of the Reception Manual can serve as an example of the program's format. *Auditory reception* is defined as the ability to understand the meaning of what is heard. Five subareas of auditory reception are presented and defined, including auditory discrimination of environmental noises, auditory discrimination of speech sounds, understanding single words, and understanding sentences. Following is a brief statement concerning useful ways for teaching the construct. For example, it is suggested that the children might close their eyes from time to time to shut out distracting visual stimuli; or that the teacher should occasionally alternate from a loud voice to a whisper to attract and hold the children's attention. The remainder of this section of the manual is devoted to listing activities grouped according to the subareas. The following outline is presented to give the reader an idea of the kinds of auditory skills that are taught.

1. Auditory discrimination of environmental sounds
   a. Discrimination among environmental (i.e., nonphonemic) sounds
   b. Recognition of environmental noises

2. Auditory discrimination of speech sounds
   a. Discrimination of speech (i.e., phonemic) sounds
   b. Discrimination of beginning sounds
   c. Discrimination of rhymes

3. Understanding emotional content of spoken material

4. Understanding the meaning of single words
   a. Understanding nouns
   b. Understanding verbs
   c. Understanding descriptive words
   d. Understanding prepositions

5. Understanding the meaning of sentences
   a. Understanding definitions of words
   b. Following directions
   c. Understanding stories

To exemplify the program's format, the first section, which deals with teaching children to discriminate among environmental noises, is described in detail. The initial teaching activities require the child to differentiate between such nonphonemic sounds as snapping fingers, clapping hands, closing doors, ticking clocks, sneezes, crying, coughing, and laughing. The authors suggest that a tape recording of the actual noises in the classroom be made and used in teaching. For all these tasks it is imperative that the child know or be taught the concepts *same* and *different*.

Next, children are taught to recognize the names of these sounds. The procedure here is to start by letting the child hear a series of sounds and saying after each, "That's a door closing," "That's a boy coughing," and so on. Next the teacher says, "You're going to hear sounds. Raise your hand when you hear . . ." (a door closing, a clock ticking, etc.). Variations of this procedure are provided. Finally, the focus on training shifts to expressive language, as the child responds verbally to what makes particular sounds such as "moo" and "honk."

Supplementary Teaching Materials

The training manuals just described are the central element in the program and are supplemented by a judicious number of manipulative and stimulus materials, such as flash cards, a phonograph record, a story book, and a word book. The manuals tell which of these materials are to be employed and when they are to be used to supplement the stimulation of a particular psycholinguistic ability. A series of pupil workbooks that correspond to the manuals are also available. Actually, the number of auxiliary materials in the program package is quite modest. Presumably, the teachers are to augment these with materials that are usually already in their classrooms (e.g., blocks, puzzles, and tape recordings) and to construct their own supplemental materials.

Since the activities in this program are highly sequenced, the procedures governing its use are clearly stated, and an associated assessment instrument is available, the program is ready-made for experimental validation. To date two studies have evaluated the program's effectiveness. Logan (1978) reported that the program was effective in increasing selected aspects of expressive language but that it seemed to have little or no effect on either receptive language or overall language ability. In another controlled study, Sowell et al. (1979) found the MWM Program to be completely ineffective in stimulating any of the language abilities that were studied. As yet, the authors of the MWM kits have offered no experimental research showing that their activities work.

APPRAISAL OF ITPA-RELATED APPROACHES

Hammill and Larsen (1974a) have reviewed the results of 39 studies in which the researchers have attempted to teach the psycholinguistic constructs measured by the ITPA. The findings of the 39 studies are provided in Table 14.2. A plus indicates that the author reported that the trained subjects did considerably better than the nontrained subjects on a particular ITPA subtest. A zero indicates that the control subjects were equal to or better than the experimental subjects on a subtest analysis. Blanks occur in the table when researchers were interested in only selected subtests and/or when they did not report subtest findings. These researchers made 280 different analyses; this is the combined number of pluses and zeros in Table 14.2.

The collective results of these studies are reported in Table 14.3. They indicate the degree to which the programs were successful in training the constructs measured by the ITPA. For example, from reading the table, one learns that of all the analyses that evaluated the effects of training the auditory-vocal modality subtests, only 37% significantly favored the experimental (trained) subjects.

Considered as a group, the results of the studies reviewed suggest that the idea that psycholinguistic process constructs, as measured by the ITPA, can be trained by existing techniques remains nonvalidated. This means simply that the value of ITPA-based training has not yet been clearly established by controlled experimental research. Comparatively speaking, the most encouraging findings pertain to training at the representational level, especially the expressive process. The most discouraging results were associated with training the automatic level abilities, the receptive and organizing processes, and both the auditory-vocal and visual-motor modalities.

Since the publication of the Hammill and Larsen (1974a) review, at least two additional intervention studies have been published. The works of Sowell et al. (1979) and Logan (1978) have both investigated the effectiveness of the MWM Program. Their conclusions were discussed previously and basically confirm the findings of the Hammill and Larsen review.

The advocates of ITPA-related approaches have not been slow in responding to the Hammill and Larsen data and conclusions. Minskoff (1975, 1976), McLeod (1976), Bush (1976), Lund, Foster, and Perez-McCall (1978), and Kavale (1981) have all challenged the findings of the review on various grounds. In turn, each of these challenges has been answered (Hammill & Larsen, 1978; Newcomer & Hammill, 1976; Newcomer, Larsen, & Hammill, 1975; Parker, Larsen, & Hammill, 1982). The reader who desires a full airing of the controversy surrounding the ITPA-related training can profit from studying the original review article, the responses from the ITPA advocates, and the rebuttals to the responses. Collectively, these articles make interesting, often lively, and potentially enlightening reading.

Not all of the concern about ITPA–psycholinguistic process training is based on its lack of experimental research support. A number of professionals are suspicious

TABLE 14.2. Results of Studies that Attempted to Train Psycholinguistic Processes

Researcher	AR	VR	AA	VA	VE	ME	GC	VC	ASM	VSM	AC	SB	Total
Blessing					+								
Blue													0
Bradley et al.	+	+	0	+	+	+	+		0	0			+
Carter	+	+	+	+	+	+	+		+	+			+
Clasen et al.	0	+	0	+	0	0	0		0	0			0
Crutchfield	+	0	0	0	0	0	0		0	+			0
Dickie			0		0								
Dunn and Mueller	0	0	+	+	+	0	0		0	0			+
Ensminger	0	0	+	0	+	0	0		0	0			0
Forgnone													0
Gazdic													0
Gibson	0	0	0	0	0	0	0		0	0			0
Gray and Klaus	+	+	+	+	+	0	+		+	+			+
Guess et al.													0
Hart	0	0	+	+	+	+	0		+	+			+
Hartman	0	0	0	0	0	0	0		0	0			0
Hodges and Spicker													0
Jones	+	0	0	0	+	+	0	0	0	0			0
Karnes et al.	0	+	+	0	0	0	+		0	0			+
Lavin	0	0	0	0	0	0	0	0	0	0			0
Leiss	0	0	0	0	0	0	0	0	0	0			0
McConnell et al.	+	0	+	+	+	+	+		+	+			+
Minskoff				+	0	+			0	0			0
Mitchell	0	0	0	0	0	0	0		+	0			0
Morgan	0	0	+	+	+	0	0	+	0	0			+
Morris		+			+		0						+
Mueller and Dunn	0		0				0			0			+
Painter	0	0	+	0	0	+	0		0	0			
Runyon													+
Sapir		0	+	0	+	+			+	0			+
Saudargas et al.	0	0	0	0	0	0	0	0	0	0	0	0	+
Schifani	0	0	0	0	0	0	0	0	+	0			+
Siders	0		0		0		0						
Smith	+	+	+	+	+	+	+		0	+			+
Spollen and Ballif													0
Stearns	0	0	+	+	+	0	0		0	0			0
Strickland		+							+				0
Wiseman	0	0	0	0	+	+	0		+	0			+

Code:
+ means experimental subjects did considerably better than control subjects.
0 means control subjects were equal to or better than experimental subjects.

ITPA Subtests: AR = Auditory Reception, VR = Visual Reception, AA = Auditory Association, VA = Visual Association, VE = Verbal Expression, ME = Manual Expression, GC = Grammatic Closure, VC = Visual Closure, ASM = Auditory Sequential Memory, VSM = Visual Sequential Memory, AC = Auditory Closure, SB = Sound Blending, Total = Total Language Age

Note. From "The Efficacy of Psycholinguistic Training" by D. D. Hammill and S. C. Larsen, 1974, *Exceptional Children, 41,* pp. 8–9. Reprinted by permission of The Council for Exceptional Children.

TABLE 14.3. Psycholinguistic Constructs, the ITPA Subtests that Comprise Them, and the Percentage of Positive Analyses

Language Dimensions	Constructs	ITPA Subtests*	Percentages of Positive Analyses
Levels	Representational	AR, VR, AA, VA, VE, ME	40
	Automatic	GC, VC, ASM, VSM, AC, SB	25
Processes	Reception	AR, VR	27
	Organization	AA, VA, GC, VC, ASM, VSM, AC, SB	33
	Expression	VE, ME	46
Modalities	Auditory-Vocal	AR, AA, VE, GC, ASM, AC, SB	37
	Visual-Motor	VR, VA, ME, VC, VSM	32

*For subtest code, see Table 14.2.

Note. From "The Efficacy of Psycholinguistic Training" by D. D. Hammill and S. C. Larsen, 1974, *Exceptional Children, 41,* p. 11. Reprinted by permission of The Council for Exceptional Children.

of these programs on theoretical and philosophic grounds (Bateman & Schiefelbusch, 1969; Hartman & Hartman, 1973; Mann & Phillips, 1967; Masland, 1969; Rosenberg, 1970). They fear that such approaches (a) "fractionalize" children, that is, view each of them as a collection of isolated malfunctions rather than as a unitary, complex, and interrelated individual; (b) encourage "off-task" teaching, for example, by training children in "visual sequential memory" in the hope that it will generalize to reading or at least make them more ready for reading; and (c) are based on inadequate or unsubtantiated theoretical assumptions.

In this treatise "Psychometric Phrenology and the New Faculty Psychology," Lester Mann (1971) summarizes the philosophic case against ability training in general and the ITPA-related approaches in particular. He points out that these programs bear more than a little similarity to the long-discredited "faculty psychology" ideas so prevalent during the 1800s and suggests that as applied in schools and clinics, the approach may increase the danger in fractionalizing both the child and the way in which the child's problem is conceptualized. His assertions are strongly challenged in rebuttals by Raymond Barsch, Jack Bardon, Archie Silver, Rosa Hagin, Edward Scagliotta, David Sabatino, and Morton Bortner, all of whom have formulated occasionally powerful apologies for current attempts to train basic abilities. Mann's article and the responses directed to it appear in the Winter-Spring 1971 issue of *The Journal of Special Education.* This is a prime reference for readers who have an interest in the topic, and it should not be overlooked. The more ambitious reader who would like a thorough understanding of the philosophic bases for correlate training will find Mann's (1979) *On the Trail of Process* most rewarding.

Our own opinions on the subject concerning the current status of the ITPA–psycholinguistic process approach are best exemplified by the comments of Newcomer and Hammill:

> We recognize that the results of future research, hopefully utilizing improved designs, may eventually validate the assumptions which are fundamental to psycholinguistic assessment and remediation. Conceivably, old programs and tests along with newly developed ones might be demonstrated, by research not yet completed or undertaken, to be instructionally useful. Should this prove to be the case, none will be more delighted than we. If such a happy event should occur, we would like to believe that our efforts, as exemplified by this book, had in some way served as a catalyst or stimulant to the initiation of the subsequent investigations. Awaiting the accumulation of future findings, however, we . . . (1976, p. 162)

15

DEVELOPING PERCEPTUAL-MOTOR CORRELATES

Perceptually oriented professionals have been most prominent in the field of learning disabilities, contributing a variety of theories, assessment measures, and training programs. All of the professionals whose work is described in this chapter seem to adhere to three basic principles: (a) that discrete perceptual-motor abilities are measurable and therefore a person's specific perceptual weaknesses can be differentially diagnosed, (b) that deficits in perceptual-motor areas can be related directly to children's difficulties in school in that they either cause the failure or make it more resistant to remediation, and (c) that once identified, perceptual-motor problems can usually be corrected through the application of their prescribed techniques.

The writers included in this chapter appear to arrive at their particular viewpoint by different routes; for example, Barsch postulates a biological survival basis for his rationale, while Kephart adheres to a strictly psychophysiological frame of reference. In the end, however, the basic sensory-perceptual-motor orientation and the suggested remedial activities are very much the same. Barsch, Frostig, and Getman emphasize the visual-motor processes of the learner, while Kephart, Ayres, Delacato, and Cratty are concerned mostly with basic motor learning. We find that their suggestions for treating the child with a learning disability are quite similar, and we wonder whether their differing rationales are merely variations on a theme.

Who are the children for whom the procedures reviewed in this chapter might be recommended? What are their strengths and weaknesses? How do they learn, or what have they failed to learn? In general, there seems to be some agreement among the advocates of perceptual-motor training concerning several guidelines to be observed in prescribing any of their approaches. First, they believe that for the most part, children younger than 8 or 9 years of age profit from these systems more than older children and that, generally, the younger the children, the more they profit. Second, they believe that the child whose major deficits are in the visual-motor areas will make greater progress under a perceptual-motor program of training than the child with other types of learning disabilities.

To describe the type of child for whom one of the perceptual-motor programs is usually recommended, a case history approach seems most efficient and illustrative. The following report describes a preschool child with motor, perceptual, and behavioral problems who made substantial progress while enrolled in a remedial program emphasizing perceptual-motor development.

J. L., a 5-year-old girl, was referred for evaluation and treatment on the advice of her pediatrician. Seven months prior to the referral she had experienced a series of convulsions; although the neurological examination and EEG tracing were negative, she had been placed on a drug control program. According to J. L.'s kindergarten teacher, the child's behavior in school had been disruptive, and various signs of a learning disability had been noted.

The results of the speech and hearing evaluations indicated a mild articulation problem, normal function of the speech mechanism, and normal hearing. The language and psychological testing revealed that J. L. was functioning within the low average range of intelligence and that her visual-motor abilities were significantly impaired. She obtained poor scores on drawing tests and the visual, motor, and visual-motor subtests of the ITPA. Her Bender protocol was not scorable, nor was her Draw-a-Man. Tests of gross and fine motor coordination also indicated serious problems.

J. L.'s strengths were revealed by such scores as the following: Peabody Picture Vocabulary Test—IQ 103; sentence length and syntax—adequate; vocal, auditory, and auditory-vocal subtests of the ITPA—average to above average.

Because J. L. had been in kindergarten for a year, some limited academic testing was done. The results revealed numerous letter and number reversals and a fixed, although incorrect, order of letters when writing her name.

J. L.'s behavior during the testing sessions was marked by incessant chattering, impulsivity, and mild hyperactivity. The psychiatric report noted some oppositional and provocative behavior on J. L.'s part when she was with her mother, but no signs of a psychotic or neurotic disorder were evident.

Following evaluation, J. L. was enrolled in the training program, where she remained for 11 months. During that time, techniques suggested by Kephart and Getman were used to improve her motor skills and her visual-motor abilities. Her progress was slow but consistent, and when she was dismissed from the program, her teacher felt that she would have little difficulty in the first grade. J. L. was enrolled in a special education class for children with learning disabilities the following year but has since successfully completed the second grade in a regular class.

J. L. exemplifies the type of child who often is credited with making substantial progress in programs devoted to training perceptual-motor abilities. It is doubtful whether her progress would have been as great in a less intensive program; she attended class 5 days a week for 3 hours daily over a period of 11 months. Even at the end of this lengthy time her teacher felt that she should not attend a regular class but instead needed the more protective atmosphere of a special education class for children with learning disabilities. Other children with similar but less severe problems have made more rapid progress than J. L. and have been enrolled in regular classes after less intensive therapy.

With the exception of Cratty, the authors discussed in this chapter consider visual-motor problems to be examples of specific learning disabilities rather than merely correlates of learning disabilities. They also consider adequate visual-motor channel abilities to be very important if not essential to the development of academic skills, conceptualizing ability, and abstract thinking. The reader should note, however, that most professionals (including Cratty) dispute their stated or inferred hypothesis that problems in visual-motor skills, especially those measured by most currently available tests, adversely affect the acquisition of academic and other abilities. For example, Bateman has observed that "there are children who manifest severe spatial orientation, body image, perceptual, coordination, etc., problems and who are not dyslexic" (1964, p. 11). This point has been underscored by the work of Hynd and Cohen (1983); Larsen, Rogers, and Sowell (1976); Vellutino et al. (1977); Vellutino (1979); and Larsen and Hammill (1975). Of course, a small body of research does exist that appears to support the claims of the perceptual trainers on this matter. For the most part this supportive research consists of uncontrolled investigations and clinical reports.

Of the authors whose work is discussed in this chapter, only Cratty, Delacato, Ayres, and Getman maintain an appreciable following today. By this, we mean (a) that a significant number of professionals in schools and clinics adhere to their theories and implement their procedures; (b) that these authors continue to aggressively promote their ideas about learning disabilities and answer the challenges of critics; and (c) that many college students are taught to use these systems as a part of their professional training. The fact that the merits of the systems continue to be debated hotly in the professional literature indicates that the systems and their authors are very much alive.

In contrast, the systems developed by Kephart, Barsch, and Frostig are extinct for all practical purposes. By extinct, we mean that their authors are dead or no longer advocating their approach actively in articles, speeches, and books; that their seminal works are out of print or difficult to come by; and that professionals no longer identify a particular remedial regimen with them.

While Kephart, Barsch, and Frostig had a great influence on the field of learning disabilities, especially during the years 1950 through 1970, they are not well known by today's professionals. Their work is included in this volume for its historical value and in the hope that their contributions will not be forgotten.

CRATTY: TEACHING MOVEMENT THROUGH DEVELOPMENTAL SEQUENCES

Bryant J. Cratty is a professor of kinesiology at the University of California at Los Angeles. Though largely associated with movement education, Cratty (1986a) accurately refers to himself as a cognitive theorist who uses movement as a tool rather than as a perceptual-motor theorist. Unlike others discussed in this chapter, he does not single out movement (or perception) as the foundation ability from which intelligence and academic skill emerge. Instead, he asserts that intelligence, rather than movement, is the basis of intelligence! Though he discusses perception from time to time, his primary interest is in the motor development of children. Within this category he specializes in the evaluation and teaching of handicapped children with motor problems, especially those with mental retardation and neurological impairments.

The reviews of the motor training literature that are found in Cratty's books are comprehensive, and it is apparent that he has resisted the temptation to "cull" the literature to locate only research that supports a preconceived belief. As a result, he is refreshingly circumspect when discussing the significance of motor processes to language, reading, and thinking; the transfer and generalizability of motor learning; and the effects of motor training on brain organization.

A strong advocate of physical education, Cratty expresses the opinion that it is in a child's best interest to have a well-developed body; to be able to move with speed, agility, balance, and grace; and to have both strength and endurance. To him, these are desirable outcomes of training and need not be justified in terms of their direct influence on academic performance. However, he does point out that motor training can improve children's capacity to play games and sports and consequently change for the better their opinions of themselves and the attitudes of other children toward them, reduce anxiety, and enhance motivation. Such changes can contribute to a more positive school climate, which may in turn result in higher academic attainment. Thus the relationship of motor proficiency to academic learning is presumed to be at best an indirect one, with the exception of those subjects like penmanship that are essentially motor skills.

The reader who desires a candid account of the uses and misuses of motor-perceptual training written by a proponent of such instruction will find the work of Cratty (1969, 1980, 1981, 1986a) to be most informative. In particular, he believes that the assertions of many advocates of perceptual or motor training that the establishment of hemispheric dominance is essential to learning, that movement is the basis of the intellectual development, that improvement in perceptual-motor skill generalizes widely to more cognitive abilities, and so on, are not consistent with the existent research literature.

This point is made most clear in *Perceptual and Motor Development in Infants and Children* (1986a). In this work, the cognitive, verbal, perceptual, and motor channels are depicted as being relatively distinct in their development. From perusing Figure 15.1, one sees that random activity leads to perfected trunk movement and not to the substitution of symbols for thought. Thus early motor behaviors stimulate the development of more mature motor behaviors; early cognitive behaviors lead to more mature cognitive behaviors; and so on. Obviously, Cratty does not follow the commonly held belief of some developmentalists that high level cognitive abilities find their roots in low level motor skills (e.g., random reflexive activity).

Cratty, however, does provide the educator with a list of statements about motor learning that he feels are well rooted in the literature. Knowledge of these should help teachers to formulate realistic goals for their programs of instruction.

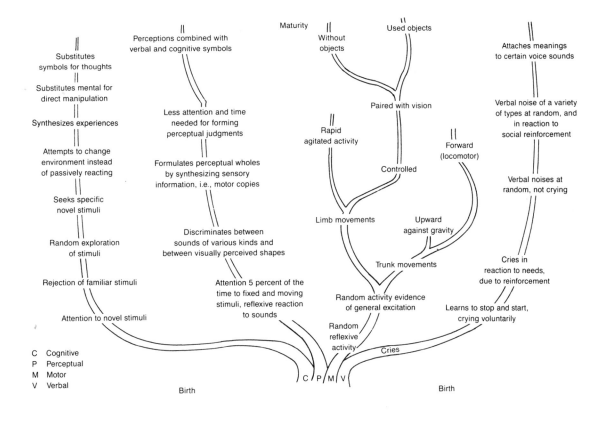

FIGURE 15.1. Four attribute channels illustrating examples of behaviors each contains, as well as the manner in which each tends to branch as a function of age. *Note.* From *Perceptual and Motor Development in Infants and Children* (3rd ed., p. 15) by B. J. Cratty, 1986, Englewood Cliffs, NJ: Prentice-Hall. Reprinted by permission.

1. Movement is one of several important components of the child's emerging personality, not a central core from which all social, intellectual, perceptual and academic skills must invariably spring.

2. Clumsiness in children, whether academically gifted or those with learning difficulties, poses special obstacles which must be overcome. With exposure to a broadly based program of movement experiences, it is likely to elicit some improvement in movement abilities.

3. A comprehensive program containing a wide variety of sensory-motor experiences has been shown to exert positive changes in some severely and profoundly retarded children. Due to individual differences in neuromotor make-up among these children, as well as among all children, the changes are likely to vary from child to child, exposed to the same program experiences.

4. Adequate hand-eye coordination is a necessary component of classroom functioning, enabling a child, whether gifted, average or below average academically, to answer questions and problems in written form and to express himself intellectually. Hand-eye coordinations involved in printing and writing tasks can often be improved by exposure to properly sequenced exercises.

5. Such academic operations as reading consist of numerous subprocesses, any one or combination of which if not intact, will likely impede progress. While most reading processes *may* be translated to movement experiences, they need not necessarily be so translated.

6. A wide variety and combination of peripheral processes may be intact and/or deficit in various ways, while basic intellectual functioning may be relatively unimpaired. The way to change central intellectual processes is not by mindlessly applied peripheral movement and sensory experiences, but by involving the central processes directly . . . by encouraging the child to engage in all dimensions of intellectual behavior within a motivating program of movement experiences.

7. To an increased degree it has been found that when a program of movement experiences is filled with academic content and/or *requires a child to think*, to make decisions about the learning process, and to engage in various intellectual operations, it is likely that such a program will exert a positive influence upon both academic competencies, as well as intellectual functioning. Programs of this nature should proceed along two main dimensions: On one hand, they should afford the child increased freedom to make at least some of the decisions about what he is undertaking, and secondly situations and movement and action problems should be presented which contain increased difficulty, as the child evidences the ability to engage in the simpler intellectual operations. (Cratty, 1969, pp. 3–4)

Three elements of Cratty's approach to motor learning are particularly useful to teachers. First, the model he postulated to account for motor behavior provides the teacher with a rationale with which to formulate a program in movement education. Second, the Screening Test for Evaluating Perceptual-Motor Attributes equips the teacher with an informal assessment procedure for identifying children who need remedial help. Third, the activities and exercises he recommends can be used to ameliorate the deficits identified.

A Three-Level Theory of Perceptual-Motor Learning

Cratty (1969) discusses the long-enduring argument in physical education between those who believe that motor ability is a generalized phenomenon in an individual and those who maintain that it is specific to a particular skill. This dispute is somewhat analogous to that which is continuing in psychology among proponents of Spearman's "g" (general) and proponents of Guilford's fractional approach (specific). To some extent these positions are reflected in the learning disabilities area in the debate between some educators who attempt to pinpoint and train specific process deficits in children (specific) and others who consider such efforts to fractionalize the child and suggest instead a more integrated program (general). Cratty has proposed his three-level model to resolve this problem, at least in the area of movement education, and states that it does not conflict with existing experimental evidence.

The theory assumes that motor performance is influenced by factors found at each of three levels: (a) general behavioral supports (level one), (b) perceptual-motor ability traits (level two), and (c) task specifics (level three). The factors associated with the General Behavioral Support level are basic not only to motor learning, but to language and cognitive behavior as well. They are therefore general qualities and are not specific to motor skills. These include a child's level of aspiration, arousal potential, and persistence.

The second level, Perceptual-Motor Ability Traits, is composed of those constructs that emerged from factorial studies dealing with perceptual-motor variables. These are general constructs in the area of motor learning and include such qualities as static strength, finger-wrist speed, and extent flexibility. The third level, Task Specifics, includes those factors that are specific to particular tasks and situations.

The teaching of handwriting can be used to exemplify the model. First, the child must be interested in mastering the skill (arousal), be psychologically ready to cope with the practice demands required (persistence), believe that he or she can accomplish the skill (aspiration), and so on. Second, the task itself makes certain ability demands such as an optimal amount of strength, coordination, and balance. Given acceptable levels of general supports and abilities, there still exist motor skills that are unique to handwriting and that can only be taught through practice in handwriting. Thus in school practice the teacher should consider both general and specific training if the best results are to be obtained.

The Screening Test for Evaluating Perceptual-Motor Attributes

The purpose of the screening test (Cratty, 1969) is to provide teachers with an objective way of identifying children who require special help in basic motor skills. After administering the measure the teacher will also know some of the particular areas of motor learning that are in need of training. Six categories of functioning are evaluated: body perception, gross agility, balance, locomotor agility, throwing skill, and ball-tracking skill. Each of these is assessed at two levels. The first level is intended for use with children whose movement difficulties are rather obvious; the second level is for children with mild perceptual-motor problems.

Though normative information is available for several types of "retarded" populations, none is offered for typical school-aged children. This omission is of no concern to teachers, however, because Cratty suggests that children who successfully complete all the tests at the second level may be expected to perform effectively with their age-mates. Those children who do not could probably profit from special help. Based on a sample of 83 pupils, the test-retest reliability of the device is reported to be .91, a respectable figure.

In assessing *body perception*, the ability to locate oneself relative to objects in space, the examiner lies on his or her stomach, gets up, and asks the child to imitate the position. The sequence is repeated with the examiner taking various positions and providing verbal cues relating to body parts, for example, "Please lie down on the mat like this on your front or stomach, with your legs nearest me" or "Raise your right arm in the air." *Gross agility* is evaluated by determining the speed with which a child can accurately move his or her total body. For example, a pupil is timed to see how long it takes to rise from a prone to a standing position.

The ability to maintain an upright position in space, that is, *balance*, is estimated by having the child stand on one foot in a timed situation and by variations of this procedure. *Locomotor agility* is assessed by observing the efficiency with which a child can move his or her body over a specified distance; variations include hopping, jumping, running, walking, and crawling. *Ball throwing* is self-explanatory; the criterion is the ability to throw a ball to the examiner or at a target. *Ball tracking* is simply catching or intercepting moving objects, for example, a swinging ball suspended on a string.

Teachers will find that Cratty has clearly specified the criteria for passing each area, and they should be able to use the screening device with no difficulty. They will also appreciate the fact that few materials are necessary. Several balls, a stop watch, a mat, and adequate space are all that is required.

Developmental Teaching Sequences

Cratty's educational ideas are best presented in three books, *Adaptive Physical Education for Handicapped Children and Youth* (1980), *Motor Activity and the Education of Retardates* (1973), and *Development Sequences of Perceptual-Motor Tasks: Movement Activities for Neurologically Handicapped and Retarded Children and Youth* (1967). The reader who is interested in learning disabled children should recognize that even though the activities were originally designed for retarded children, they can also be used effectively with any child who needs motor training. This is demonstrated in the following quote, in which the word *children* has been substituted for "retarded children." In this passage, Cratty is giving advice to persons who are interested in teaching motor skills to retardates; but his suggestions are apparently equally appropriate for teaching typical, disturbed, learning disabled, or any other type of children who have motor problems.

- The presence of distracting stimuli, the size of the area in which the teaching takes place, as well as the number of children in a group are all important considerations when teaching motor skills to children. In general, the younger and less capable children should be dealt with in smaller groups, in controlled environments, and in relatively small areas.

- Initial efforts in the learning situation should concentrate on gaining the attention of the children, on encouraging self-control or teacher control if necessary, and on adjusting their levels of arousal and excitability to those appropriate to the tasks to be learned.

- The quickest learning occurs if a skill is taught as a whole, or as much of the entire skill as the learner is capable of acquiring. Complex skills should be broken down into parts for easier assimilation.

- Transfer of training between various skills will occur to the extent to which it is taught by building cognitive bridges between tasks. Common principles should be emphasized when teaching skills which are in any way similar.

- Transfer to a percept or concept through motor activity or from skill to skill will take place to the extent to which a number of sub-skills or tasks contribute to the acquisition of the concept.

- Transfer occurs because of similar response elements in two tasks, because of common principles and work methods common to the two tasks.

- Teachers of motor skills should be aware of the general order of difficulty of related motor tasks, and of approximate developmental norms appropriate to normal children, so that realistic tasks and expectations are presented to children.

- Visual demonstration, practice, and manual guidance are generally more appropriate than extensive verbal explanations when attempting to teach skills to children. Demonstrations and other instructions are usually more helpful during the initial stages of learning.

- When teaching children motor skills, it is important to engender proper work methods, to aid them with their "motor planning," to help them acquire movement patterns involved. Many children perform motor tasks poorly because they do not decide upon a proper plan of execution, and not because of basic motor ineptitude.

- When teaching for transfer to perceptual or conceptual materials, it is helpful if several sensory modalities are utilized. A triangle may be described, looked at, touched, and walked around.

- Basic learnings of children may be helpfully shaped with simple, immediate, and obvious rewards. As the children become more capable, rewards inherent in the nature of the task, its novelty and complexity, as well as social approval assume increasingly important rules.

- The child should be continually supplied by the teacher with information informing him of his general improvement in physical fitness and skill, as well as with immediate information relative to a single improvement in a given task.

- Retention will be best in skills which are rhythmic and integrated in nature, and in skills which have been overlearned.

- Retention will be best in skills, when previous to practice, the children have been informed that they must .etain the skill, and how the skill is to be used. (1973, pp. 57–58)

Cratty's instructional procedures for preschoolers or children with rather pronounced motor training needs are best presented in his 1967 volume. The bulk of these are devoted to training the six motor constructs that make up the screening device. Even though this section deals exclusively with these activities, the teacher will also wish to be familiar with Cratty's (1969) suggestions for stimulating arousal and maintaining attention and for teaching scribbling, drawing, and writing.

1. *Body Perception.* Rather than presenting lists of specific activities that could be used to develop a child's perceptions about his or her body in space, Cratty gives the teacher descriptions of the kinds of activities that would be appropriate. These include techniques in which body parts come into physical contact with surfaces in the environment (e.g., the child is asked to roll to the side, back, front, etc.); activities in which the child responds motorically to commands (e.g., "Simon Says" games); and activities involving drawing and subsequent visual inspection (e.g., the child lies on newsprint while the teacher outlines the child's form with crayon; the child later looks at it and makes comments).

    The activities are to be used to teach 16 developmental steps in the formation of body image and position in space. The steps can be grouped into five categories: (a) the perception of body planes and their relationship to objects in space, (b) the perception and movement of body parts, (c) left-right awareness, (d) the determination of the left-right dimension of objects in reference to one's self, and (e) the determination of the left-right dimensions of objects and persons in terms of their reference systems.

2. *Balance.* Since it has been documented that there are several different kinds of balance, a breadth of activities must be used when attempting to train this construct. Cratty's activities are designed to develop four types of balance: (a) static balance on a mat, (b) static balance while standing, (c) dynamic balance with task modification, and (d) dynamic balance with visual stress.

    In teaching static (i.e., inactive or passive) balance on a mat, the child learns to balance while seated, lying on his or her side, in a motionless creeping position, upright kneeling position, and so on. Static balance while standing is taught through the use of a variety of exercises where the child stands on one foot with various combinations of arms folded, eyes open, and eyes closed, among other positions.

    Balance beams of varying widths are used to perfect dynamic balance with task modifications. To modify the task further, obstacles are placed on the beam. The child walks the beam forward, backward, and sideways. By specifying certain eye positions while the child engages in walking the beam, dynamic balance with visual stress can be taught. In this instance the child is requested to walk the board while visually fixating on a point in front of him or her. Variations involve walking while moving the eyes from left to right, up to down, or in a circular motion.

3. *Locomotion.* Any activity involving crawling, knee crawling, skipping, hopping, walking, jumping, and the like is appropriate for developing adequate locomotion abilities. Particularly suggested are movement exercises where the child follows a pattern of hand- or footprints painted on the floor. A cross-extension pattern should be encouraged in every activity, that is, the arm movement on one side should be similar to the leg movement on the opposite side.

4. *Agility.* The agility exercises are divided into four groups. In the first of these, Controlled Ascending and Descending, the child is to get up and down following a sequence of steps. For example, the child may be taught to drop one knee to the mat, then the second knee, then one hand back to the mat, then the second hand, and so on. The second group of activities involves teaching Rapid Ascending and Descending Movements. These require that the child move from standing to sitting or prone positions quickly. In the third type, Moving Agility with the Body Near the Mat, the child engages in a variety of mat exercises such as "log rolling," snakelike movements (stomach in contact with the mat), "ball rolling" in a tuck position, somersaults, and so on. Locomotor Agility Exercises, the fourth group, are taught by having the child "jump one-quarter and one-half turns in place using the arms to lift and to turn the body" (1969, p. 49). Numerous variations on this activity are provided.

5. *Throwing.* When teaching a child to throw, two points should be kept in mind—form and accuracy. Form is the integrated use of arms, legs, and body, while accuracy refers to "hitting the target." Using another child or an adult as a model is a useful technique for teaching proper form to children; practice before a mirror is also beneficial, as the child can monitor his or her own movements. In perfecting accuracy the child can throw at large targets that are decreased in size as the child becomes more proficient. Throwing at moving targets is a profitable variation.

6. *Catching.* This skill is considered more difficult than throwing, and initially the teacher may simply have the child watch (i.e., visually track) a ball swinging from a string. Next the child may be encouraged to intercept the ball by touching it while it is in flight. Eventually, if the child becomes efficient in this ability, games like tennis, baseball, and ping-pong would be appropriate.

For school-aged children, Cratty (1985) has prepared a collection of 149 motor-oriented games that can be used to enhance academic abilities. The basic idea underlying these games is that movement should be integrated into teaching (1) "to produce more relaxed and joyful children, and (2) to release children's tensions that might inhibit their efforts to learn" (p. 1). With these reasons, no one can quarrel.

The games themselves are carefully built to conform with the theories of current cognitive psychologists. In most instances, the games require the child to develop academic skills as well as motoric skills. Three examples are provided in Figure 15.2 to illustrate how instruction involving numbers, consonant sounds, and communication can be integrated with movement activity.

DELACATO: A NEUROLOGICAL ORGANIZATION/PATTERNING APPROACH

Carl H. Delacato and G. Doman codirect the Institutes for the Achievement of Human Potential in Chestnut Hill, Pennsylvania, where they work with children diagnosed as brain injured. The training program at the institutes is based upon a theoretical principle referred to as "neurological organization" and is an outgrowth of their dissatisfaction with the results achieved by the methods of speech and physical therapy generally applied to brain damaged children (Doman, Spitz, Zucman, Delacato, & Doman, 1960). The influence of Temple Fay, a noted Philadelphia neurologist, enabled Delacato to form his rationale for the treatment and prevention of reading and language retardation (Delacato, 1959, pp. 10–12). Delacato's principle of neurological organization, diagnostic procedures, and treatment techniques are discussed next. This section concludes with a critical analysis of the approach.

Principle of Neurological Organization

The concept of neurological organization, the cornerstone of the Delacato approach, is based on the theory that neurological development follows the biogenetic postulate that "ontogeny recapitulates phylogeny" (Delacato, 1959, 1963); that is, that individual human development repeats the pattern of humanity's evolutionary development. Delacato concludes:

> Neurological organization is that physiologically optimum condition which exists uniquely and most completely in man and is the result of a total and uninterrupted ontogenetic neural development. The development recapitulates the phylogenetic neural development of man. (1959, p. 19)

Subsequently, Delacato's basic premise is that a human who does *not* follow the sequential continuum of neurological development will exhibit problems of mobility and/or communication.

Delacato (1959, 1963) traces the phylogenetic development of the brain from the lowest level of living vertebrates (e.g., sharks and rays, whose function and movements are controlled by the spinal cord and medulla), through amphibians, which have developed a larger pons and more dominant midbrain, to the primates (monkeys and apes), who have developed a larger and more dominant cortex.

GAME 65   Addition Relays

Equipment: Grids containing squares with numbers and mathematical signs.

Method: One member at a time from each of two teams jumps out a problem in his grid. The second member from each team jumps out the answer. A checker from the opposite team determines the accuracy of the response. This procedure continues, problem alternated with answer, until all members of the team are finished and the winning team is determined by speed and accuracy. Inaccurate answers must be rejumped by the child after being corrected.

FIGURE 15.2. Examples of motor-oriented games for enhancing academic skills. *Note.* From *Active Learning* (pp. 81–82, 107, 128–129) by B. J. Cratty, 1985, Englewood Cliffs, NJ: Prentice-Hall. Reprinted by permission.

FIGURE 15.2. *(Continued)*

GAME 99   Consonant Sounds

Equipment: Blackboard, letter squares containing consonants whose sounds are relatively consistent (as shown).

W	J	V	Z
B	M	N	F
V	Y	Z	S
D	F	T	R

Method: The child tells the sound and finds it in the grid by jumping, etc. Conversely, he may jump in the grid and pronounce the sound on arriving there.

FIGURE 15.2. *(Continued)*

GAME 132 Do What I Say

Equipment: Large floor or matted area, on which the outlines of a house or barn are drawn or taped (see illustration). Barn may contain windows, doors, and the like together with animals' pictures. Implements such as, a bucket to feed the cow, or perhaps a watering can to water the "flowers" drawn near the house may also be included.

Method: This game, which involves receptive language, may start with teacher/parent instructions to go and/or to do something around the house or barn. These can include "Go out the door," "Water the flowers," "Look out the window," etc. As children progress, more complicated directions involving more than one action may be given. Other children evaluate "correctness" of the listener's responses.

Relative to humans, Delacato (1963, pp. 47–67) suggests that the development of the human brain follows a fairly consistent pattern. Beginning before birth and ending around the eighth year of life, neurological functions gradually develop vertically from spinal cord to cortex as myelination takes place. During gestation and up to the time of birth, the spinal cord and medulla oblongata are the upper reaches of neurological organization. Within this organization are found muscle tone, reflex movement, and other reflexes necessary for life. At this level of organization the infant has movement, but no mobility. Movements are trunkal in nature and are not directed toward any object; the infant's reflex activities such as sucking and crying are of a survival nature. Movements at this level resemble those of a fish.

The next developmental stage begins when the infant is about 4 months old. At this time, the child is on an amphibianlike level, which is the responsibility of the pons. The infant's mobility is homolateral crawling; vision is bi-ocular; and hearing is bi-aural. Movements resemble those of a reptile.

The next stage of neurological development is called the midbrain level. The child at this level is about 10 months old. Mobility is marked by cross-pattern creeping; vision is binocular, and eye yoking has begun. Hearing is binaural.

Neurologically, the 1-year-old child has entered the level of the early cortex. Movements resemble those of a primate. The child is able to walk crudely. There is an early fusion of the eyes taking place, and hearing is stereophonic.

The normal 8-year-old has developed cortical hemispheric dominance. He or she has a cross-pattern walk; a predominant eye, hand, and foot; and stereophonic hearing, with a predominant ear. He or she can read and write well. The comparison of phylogenetic neurological development and human neurological development as presented by Delacato (1963) is given in Table 15.1.

Human neurological growth continues considerably beyond that of primates, and humans alone develop the use of symbolic language. Of particular significance for Delacato is the fact that the human is the only creature that has developed hemispheric dominance in neurological function. Delacato has prepared tables showing the duration and sequence of the various stages of growth through which a normal child moves in the course of mobility and language development (Tables 15.2 and 15.3). With the completion of these developmental processes, usually by the age of 8 years, a child is said to have achieved a state of neurological organization. If injury to the brain occurs at any level or if environmental factors restrict the natural progression of the child's development, the child will show evidence of neurological dysfunction or disorganization in either language or mobility. Children who have problems in language, particularly in reading, almost always demonstrate incomplete attainment of cortical hemispheric dominance. Children who do not establish this dominance usually also evidence incomplete development at one or more preceding stages of brain development.

According to the theory of neurological organization, never are all the cells of the brain damaged; those that remain intact can be trained to take over the functions of the ones that have been destroyed. Such a supposition leads naturally to optimism regarding the benefits of treatment.

TABLE 15.1. Comparison of Phylogenetic Neurological Development with Human Neurological Development

	Highest Neurological Level	Mobility	Vision	Audition
Newborn infant	Medulla	Trunkal movement	Reflex	Reflex
Fish	Medulla	Trunkal movement	Reflex	Reflex
4-month-old infant	Pons	Homolateral crawling	Bi-ocular	Bi-aural
Amphibian	Pons	Homolateral crawling	Bi-ocular	Bi-aural
10-month-old infant	Midbrain	Cross-pattern creeping	Binocular yoking	Binaural
Reptile	Midbrain	Cross-pattern creeping	Binocular yoking	Binaural
1-year-old infant	Early cortex	Crude walking	Early fusion	Early stereophonic
Primate	Early cortex	Crude walking	Early fusion	Early stereophonic
8-year-old (who speaks, reads, and writes)	Cortical hemispheric dominance	Cross-pattern walking	Stereopsis with predominant eye	Stereophonic hearing with predominant ear

Note. From *The Diagnosis and Treatment of Speech and Reading Problems* (pp. 66–67) by C. H. Delacato, 1963, Springfield, IL: Thomas. Reprinted by permission.

Diagnostic Procedures

Children with suspected brain damage or neurological dysfunction are first seen at the institutes for a 3-day complete diagnostic evaluation. A detailed history of the child's development is taken, including prenatal and perinatal factors, childhood diseases and injuries, motor and speech development, sleep patterns, and tonality (Delacato, 1963). The child then undergoes clinical examination proceeding from sub-cortical to cortical levels and then to laterality.

TABLE 15.2. The Doman-Delacato Development Language Scale

Stage	Level	Basic Characteristic	Age Range	Brain Stage
I Crying	1. Crying—a reflex creation of sound which, in itself, conveys no meaning other than to indicate the existence of life	Reflex—nonvolitional	Birth	Medulla and spinal cord
II Alarm crying	2. Crying of a nature which seeks to protect life	Vital—to protect the mechanism from threat	3 to 20 weeks	Pons
III Gnostic sound	3. The ability to create meaningful sounds which indicate mood without words	Gnostic—meaningful goal directed	16 to 60 weeks	Midbrain
IV Symbolic sound language	4. The ability to initiate and say two meaningful and understandable words	Depth of meaning	36 to 80 weeks	Human cortex
	5. The ability to use two words in combination plus a 10- to 25-word vocabulary	Depth of meaning exclusive to man	50 to 120 weeks	Human cortex
	6. The ability to form meaningful sentences which are grammatically incorrect or incomplete plus a vocabulary of more than 200 words		75 to 200 weeks	
	7. The ability to create meaningful sentences which are complete and grammatically correct plus an innumerable vocabulary		150 to 350 weeks	

Note. From *The Doman-Delacato Developmental Profile* by G. Doman, C. H. Delacato, and R. Doman, 1964, Philadelphia: Institutes for the Achievement of Human Potential. Reprinted by permission.

TABLE 15.3. The Doman-Delacato Developmental Mobility Scale

Stage	Level	Age Range	Brain Level
I Movement without mobility	1. (Rolling over) 2. (Moving in a circle or backward)	4 to 20 weeks	Medulla and spinal cord
II Crawling	3. (Crawling without pattern) 4. (Crawling homologously) 5. (Crawling homolaterally) 6. (Crawling cross-pattern)	6 to 40 weeks	Pons
III Creeping	7. (Creeping without pattern) 8. (Creeping homologously) 9. (Creeping homolaterally) 10. (Creeping cross-pattern)	16 to 60 weeks	Midbrain
IV Walking	11. (Cruising—walking holding onto objects) 12. (Walking—without help and without pattern) 13. (Walking cross-pattern)	40 to 100 weeks	Cortex

Note. From *The Doman-Delacato Developmental Profile* by G. Doman, C. H. Delacato, and R. Doman, 1964, Philadelphia: Institutes for the Achievement of Human Potential. Reprinted by permission.

The Developmental History.   The parental questionnaire often suggests the etiological factors that can lead to greater diagnostic validity. Conditions during pregnancy are considered of great importance. In addition to traumatic incidences and the Rh factors, the presence of spotting, measles, great weight gain, or illness on the part of the mother are of utmost importance in making a diagnosis. Many aspects of the birth process are taken into consideration. The length and severity of labor, the type and amount of anesthesia used, and the type of presentation are important. Often the birth cry and the time it takes place are overlooked, but they are also important.

Information relative to early childhood development and diseases is collected. Delacato is concerned particularly about feeding, sleep, and elimination patterns during the first 6 months of life. A history of febrile infections is always noted. The opportunity for and the amount of mobility of the child during the early months are considered. Constant motion or not enough movement may be a factor in a child's faulty neurological organization. The modes of crawling, creeping, and walking as well as the ages of onset are noted. Frequently, the age and mode of crawling cannot be accurately determined unless a baby book or pediatric records are available.

Case history information concerning the child's mode of moving is generally obtained from the mother. Detailed information is gathered about the child's behavior in climbing, since climbing is often an indication of the amount of creeping a child has done. Information as to the age of walking as well as the age of talking ideally should come from records.

The Clinical Examination. Delacato's diagnostic approach proceeds from evaluation of subcortical to the cortical levels—then to laterality, since this procedure retraces the course of neurological organization and is representative of the sequence of treatment involved. Tests such as the *Wechsler Intelligence Scale for Children* (Wechsler, 1974) are given, as are measures of language, reading, and math. As a result of this testing, the intelligence quotient is known, and the potential for performance can be estimated. In addition to standardized tests, evaluation procedures associated with Delacato-Doman follow.

PONS LEVEL. It is imperative that the child be observed during sleep. A child who is well developed at the pons level sleeps correctly. Delacato states that as the head is turned while the child sleeps, one of the following behaviors should occur:

1. As the head is turned, the body configuration should reverse itself and the child should remain asleep.
2. As the head is turned, the child should resist its turning and should return to the original position and remain asleep.
3. The child should awaken. (1963 p. 83)

If the child allows the head to be turned, does not awaken, and does not change body configuration, it is assumed that the child is not well organized at the level of the pons. Children who are not organized at the pontine and medullar level are usually quite severely disabled.

MIDBRAIN LEVEL. The next stage of evaluation is the midbrain level. When a child is unable to cross-pattern creep correctly, the eyes are not yoked yet, and he or she is unable to produce the sound components that make up the native language, organization at the midbrain level has not been completely established.

EARLY CORTEX LEVEL. The early cortex level is evaluated next. A child who is well organized at this level is able to cross-pattern walk correctly and smoothly. He or she can oppose the thumb and forefinger of each hand easily with no significant difference between the hands.

The child's overall performance in the areas of general physical activity and play is evaluated next. The child should be able to play with the toys and playground equipment found in the average nursery school and be cautious of the dangers in the physical environment.

At this level of evaluation the child should be given a thorough vision test that involves tests for muscle imbalance, both lateral and vertical at far and near points, fusion, fusion ranges, accommodations, and convergence. The eyes are tested separately, but while the tested eye is perceiving the target, the eye not being tested is seeing the same background. The child who is organized at the level of the cortex should be able to succeed on these tests unless there is some pathological deterrent.

CORTICAL HEMISPHERIC DOMINANCE. Delacato next evaluates the area of cortical hemispheric dominance, an evaluation accomplished by ascertaining the dominant hand, eye, and foot. To find the dominant eye is not as simple as one may think. However, the dominant eye must be determined because an eye-hand relationship is considered a prerequisite to language development.

The evaluation of cortical hemispheric organization consists of tasks such as throwing a ball, using scissors, tracing a circle, and picking up various objects to see which is the dominant hand. Parents are asked to observe the child eating, writing, and brushing teeth. To determine the dominant foot, the child kicks a ball, steps onto a chair, walks forward and backward, walks up steps, picks up small objects with the toes, and occasionally traces a circle with a pencil held between the toes. The assumption behind these tasks is that the child tends to use his or her preferred hand or foot.

Data acquired from the evaluation are recorded on *The Doman-Delacato Developmental Profile* (Doman et al., 1964), a copy of which is included as Table 15.4. The profile permits a child's performance in six areas of expressive and receptive behavior to be displayed conveniently. The areas are mobility, language, manual competence, visual competence, auditory competence, and tactile competence. The profile is presented to demonstrate the dimensions and extent of the institutes' evaluation process; *use of the profile in educational or clinical settings is not recommended where personnel do not have specific training in the use of this particular profile.*

Treatment Techniques

Establishment of the level of dysfunction, using the developmental profile, is followed by therapy that is based on the assumption that a specific therapeutic experience will affect the development of a specific brain level. Treatment begins at which the child fails. The child must master each successive level before moving on to the next level; the test for crawling, therefore, is the mastery of crawling.

The principles of treatment consist of

a. Permitting the child normal developmental opportunities in areas in which the responsible brain level was undamaged;

TABLE 15.4. Doman-Delacato Neurological Developmental Profile

Brain Stage	TERM FRAME	(Writing) Expressive or Motor			(Reading) Receptive or Sensory		
		COLUMN A MOBILITY	COLUMN B LANGUAGE	COLUMN C MANUAL COMPETENCE	COLUMN D VISUAL COMPETENCE	COLUMN E AUDITORY COMPETENCE	COLUMN F TACTILE COMPETENCE
VII	Superior 36 Mo. Average 72 Mo. Slow 96 Mo.	Using a leg in a skilled role which is consistent with the dominant hemisphere	Complete vocabulary and proper sentence structure	Using a hand to write which is consistent with the dominant hemisphere	Reading words using a dominant eye consistent with the dominant hemisphere	Understanding of complete vocabulary and proper sentences with proper ear	Tactile identification of objects using a hand consistent with hemispheric dominance
VI (CORTEX)	Superior 22 Mo. Average 46 Mo. Slow 67 Mo.	Walking and running in complete cross-pattern	2,000 words of language and short sentences	Bimanual function with one hand in a dominant role	Identification of visual symbols and letters within experience	Understanding of 2,000 words and simple sentences	Description of objects by tactile means
V (CORTEX)	Superior 13 Mo. Average 28 Mo. Slow 45 Mo.	Walking with arms freed from the primary balance role	10 to 25 words of language and two-word couplets	Cortical opposition bilaterally and simultaneously	Differentiation of similar but unlike simple visual symbols (STEREOPSIS)	Understanding of 10 to 25 words and two-word couplets (STEREOPHONICS)	Tactile differentiation of similar but unlike objects (STEREOGNOSIS)
IV (CORTEX)	Superior 8 Mo. Average 16 Mo. Slow 26 Mo.	Walking with arms used in a primary balance role most frequently at or above shoulder height	Two words of speech used spontaneously and meaningfully	Cortical opposition in either hand	Convergence of vision resulting in simple depth perception	Understanding of two words of speech	Tactile understanding of the third dimension in objects which appear to be flat
III (MIDBRAIN)	Superior 4 Mo. Average 8 Mo. Slow 13 Mo.	Creeping on hands and knees, culminating in cross-pattern creeping	Creation of meaningful sounds	Prehensile grasp	Appreciation of detail within a configuration	Appreciation of meaningful sounds	Appreciation of gnostic sensation
II (PONS)	Superior 1 Mo. Average 2.5 Mo. Slow 4.5 Mo.	Crawling in the prone position culminating in cross-pattern crawling	Vital crying in response to threats to life	Vital release	Outline perception	Vital response to threatening sounds	Perception of vital sensation
I (MEDULLA and CORD)	Birth	Movement of arms and legs without bodily movement	Birth cry and crying	Grasp reflex	Light reflex	Startle reflex	Babinski reflex

Note. From The Doman-Delacato Developmental Profile by G. Doman, C. H. Delacato, and R. Doman, 1964, Philadelphia: Institutes for the Achievement of Human Potential. Reprinted by permission.

b. Externally imposing the bodily patterns of activity which were the responsibility of damaged brain levels; and

c. Utilizing additional factors to enhance neurological organization. (Doman et al., 1960, p. 257)

The method of treating the brain itself instead of the results of the brain injury was developed at the institutes and is called *patterning*. A group of patterning movements was devised to manipulate the limbs of brain injured children to produce movements that are the responsibility of the damaged level. The levels considered are medulla, pons, midbrain, and cortex. Patterning (the manipulation of arms, legs, and head) is based on the theory that all cells in an area of the brain are not usually affected by injury and that activation of live cells is possible. Intensity, duration, and frequency of the exercises will enable the brain to receive the sensory messages. This method is supposed to treat a central problem where it exists, in the central nervous system, not in the peripheral areas. According to Doman et al. (1960), the movements used in patterning are modifications of the developmental patterns of A. L. Gesell and T. Fay. The patterning process is illustrated in Figure 15.3.

Preremedial Level. MEDULLA LEVEL. At the preremedial level the principles of treatment are applied to the specific levels of neurological development as follows (Delacato, 1963). For the child whose mobility is severely impaired and who is disorganized at spinal cord and medulla level, opportunity is provided to use the basic reflex movements available by placing the child on the floor for most of the day. In addition, undulating, fishlike movements are imposed on the prescribed periods during the day.

PONS LEVEL. The same procedures are used at the level of pons with homolateral patterning being administered; this consists of having several adults work the child's limbs rhythmically while the child lies face down on a table. One person turns the child's head from side to side, while another flexes the arm and leg on the side to which the head has been turned, and a third person extends the limbs on the opposite side. Proper sleeping patterns are prescribed at this level also. The development of bi-ocular vision is aided by having the child follow a self-directed visual stimulus, with each eye occluded, for three or four 1-minute periods a day for 2 or 3 weeks.

MIDBRAIN LEVEL. At the midbrain level the aim of treatment is the mastery of bilateral activity. A summary of useful activities follows. Cross-pattern creeping is taught; practice time for this activity varies from 10 minutes to 1 hour per day. Training for visual yoking of the eyes is facilitated when the child follows a visual stimulus that the child or someone else is moving. Music, tonal discrimination and memory, and sound games are used with children who have articulation problems and difficulty with phonetic elements.

START—in UP position at (1) and DOWN position at (3)

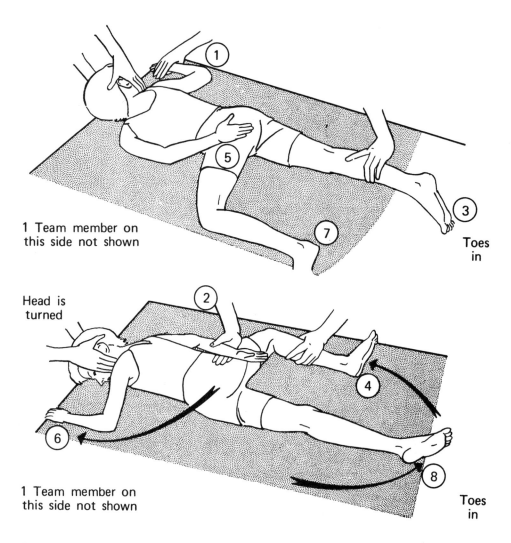

Head faces
UP arm

1 Team member on
this side not shown

Toes
in

Head is
turned

1 Team member on
this side not shown

Toes
in

Team members move, as follows: 1 + 3 to 2 + 4 5 + 7 to 6 + 8

FIGURE 15.3. (a) Cross-pattern—three-person team. (b) Homolateral pattern—five-person team.

FIGURE 15.3. *(Continued)*

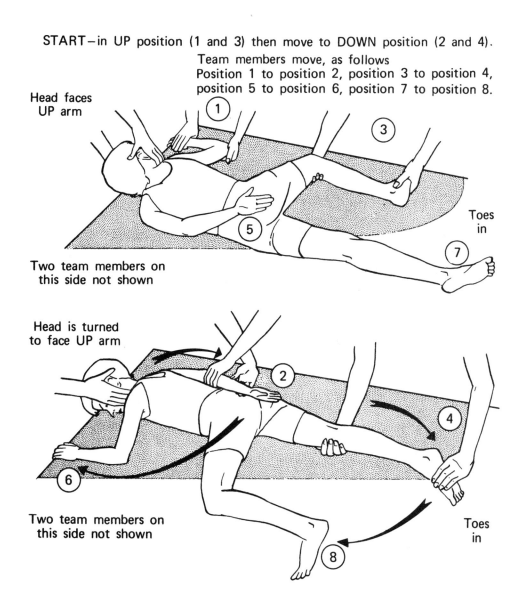

START – in UP position (1 and 3) then move to DOWN position (2 and 4).
Team members move, as follows
Position 1 to position 2, position 3 to position 4,
position 5 to position 6, position 7 to position 8.

Head faces
UP arm

Toes
in

Two team members on
this side not shown

Head is turned
to face UP arm

Toes
in

Two team members on
this side not shown

Perform _____ Sessions per day for _____ Minutes per session.

EARLY CORTICAL LEVEL.   At the cortical level, patterning consists of daily 10-minute or more practice periods in cross-pattern walking, depending upon the diagnosis. Visually, the child should be developing stereopsis through playground games that require learning about spatial relations. The child also must develop comfortable near-point vision if he or she is to become ready to read, and simple table activities such as crayoning are suggested.

CORTICAL HEMISPHERIC DOMINANCE.   The final stage of neurological development is attained when cortical hemispheric dominance is established. At this level, patterns of sleep consistent with sidedness are emphasized. Activities such as kicking, stepping off, and hurdling are used to help develop a dominant foot. Skills such as throwing, cutting, using tools, and picking up objects are used to develop handedness. Eye dominance is taught through the use of games involving telescopes for far-point vision and microscopes for near-point vision. Delacato also favors the use of a device called a Stereo-Reader manufactured by the Keystone View Company. It has the effect of occlusion while giving the illusion that both eyes are seeing the training material. This material consists of exercise cards of visual-motor activities, word families, visual discrimination, phrase reading, reading for interest, and speed reading. Two 20-minute periods per day are usually prescribed.

Remedial Level.   The foregoing procedures make up the preremedial period. In theory, when the neurological organization is complete, the problem is overcome. The only function of the remedial teacher is to bring the child as quickly as possible up to a level that will enable him or her to go into the regular class.

Delacato (1963) recommends specific rules for remedial teaching. In both speech and reading, a child should be introduced first to whole words that arise out of his or her experience. The next step is to help the child recognize words by their relationship to other words and to the meaning of the sentence, that is, from context clues. Following this step, the child moves on to analyzing the smaller components that make up a word and last, to phonetic analysis. Thus reading instruction should proceed from concepts and whole words down to its finer elements. When a child reaches a plateau, the teacher should go back to the conceptual whole and begin the process again. As it is repeated, the cycle should become longer until the child is ready to handle the work of the regular classroom.

Critical Analysis of the Delacato Approach

Both the theoretical base and the treatment techniques employed by Doman and Delacato have stimulated considerable interest and controversy in the professional and popular press. Freeman (1967) has offered a distillation of objections to the institutes' methods that are expressed frequently by professional individuals and groups. These objections, published in the *Journal of the American Medical Associa-*

tion, are listed below; the teacher is referred to Freeman's article for a detailed discussion of each item.

1. A tendency on the institutes' part to ignore the natural clinical course of some patients with brain injuries

2. Assumption that their methods treat the brain itself, whereas other methods are "symptomatic"

3. Assumption that because the "full potential of the brain" is not known, one can conclude that each child not "genetically defective" may have above average intellectual potential

4. The policy that makes parents therapists

5. The forceful prevention of self-motivated activities of the child

6. Assertions that may increase parental anxiety and concern, such as:
   a. The threat of the child's death
   b. The implication that a variety of almost universal child-rearing practices may damage a child's potential
   c. The implication that there is a need for absolutely rigid performance of "patterning" to obtain successful results

7. Assumption that improvements are due to specific factors

8. The test instrument (the Doman-Delacato profile)

9. Statistical defects in the reported studies

Because of the controversy engendered by the objections listed, the institutes have become increasingly alienated from medical, psychological, educational, and parental national organizations. During the spring of 1968 an "official statement" that was critical of the institutes was approved by the American Academy for Cerebral Palsy, American Academy of Physical Medicine and Rehabilitation, American Congress of Rehabilitation Medicine, Canadian Association for Children with Learning Disabilities, Canadian Association for Retarded Children, Canadian Rehabilitation Council for the Disabled, National Association for Retarded Children, American Academy of Pediatrics, American Academy of Neurology, and American Association on Mental Deficiency (Drake, 1968). The institutes' official reply to the "official statement" and to criticisms by Freeman (1967) and by Robbins and Glass (1968) is presented in a series of articles published in *Human Potential* (1968a, 1968b, 1968c, 1969), a publication of the institutes.

In spite of the almost universal opposition of professionals to Doman-Delacato techniques, they continue to be used widely in the United States and in other countries. Attacks on the techniques and the theories behind them have also continued at a consistent and relentless pace. A few of these critics are Cummins (1988) and Hyne and Cohen (1983).

This book is limited to discussion of methods; a detailed review of the research that is pertinent to this method's evaluation can be found in the original studies and the cited critiques. A reading of these primary sources is necessary for personal evaluation of the system's efficacy. That professional opinions as well as research findings differ regarding the value of a particular remedial technique is a common occurrence in education. Studies that do not support the work of others who train at the perceptual-motor level also exist. Since these workers have not made the all-encompassing claims for cures maintained by the institutes, they remain firmly associated with the professional community. Conclusive evidence of this method's value, however, will be established by the patient accumulation of future research findings. Fortunately, the nature of the interest in this subject is such that additional studies are assured.

AYRES: A SENSORY-INTEGRATED APPROACH

The recent proliferation of programs purporting to treat learning disabilities through the enhancement of sensory integration attests to the influence of the work of A. Jean Ayres. Ayres's early training and experience were in the field of occupational therapy rather than in education. From 1946 to 1953 she served as an occupational therapist in several settings in Southern California and received her MA degree in occupational therapy from the University of Southern California (USC) in 1954. While a therapist at the United Cerebral Palsy Pre-Nursery School and Vocational Training Center in Los Angeles, Ayres began to shift her attention in the direction of education. She became especially interested in the role of neurological-developmental factors in early learning disorders. She continued her studies at USC, studying with her mentor Margaret Rood. In 1961 she received a PhD in educational psychology. From 1964 to 1966 she was a postdoctoral trainee in a National Institute of Mental Health training program at the Brain Research Institute and Division of Child Development at the Center for the Health Sciences, affiliated with the University of California at Los Angeles (UCLA). At the time of her death in 1988, she was adjunct associate professor, emeritus, of occupational therapy at USC. The influence of her experience as an occupational therapist is reflected in her theory of learning disabilities, according to which the integrative neural mechanisms linking sensory input with motor output are hypothesized as the fundamental substrate for learning.

Background and Rationale

A comprehensive treatment of Ayres's theory is found in her books *Sensory Integration and Learning Disorders* (1972a) and *Sensory Integration and the Child* (1979). The first of these books is written with the professional in mind; the second is directed to parents. While neither work can be reviewed in detail, an overview of major points will help the reader to understand the origins of Ayres's theory and the rationale underlying her recommended therapeutic techniques. The cornerstone of the theory was described by Ayres as follows:

> Learning is a function of the brain; learning disorders as assumed to reflect some deviation in neural function. . . . Essentially, the theory holds that disordered sensory integration accounts for some aspects of learning disorders and that enhancing sensory integration will make academic learning easier for those children whose problem lies in that domain. Sensory integration, or the ability to organize sensory information for use, can be improved through controlling its input to activate brain mechanisms. (1972a, p. 1)

Ayres goes on to note that the sensory integrative approach "differs from many other procedures in that it does not teach specific skills. . . . Rather, the objective is to enhance the brain's ability to learn how to do these things" (1972a, p. 2). While not claiming that such therapy eliminates the underlying causes of neural disorganization, Ayres sees the therapy as "mitigating some of the conditions, usually arising from unknown causes, that directly interfere with learning" (p. 2). And while the therapy does not necessarily obviate the need for a "symptom-specific" approach to learning problems, it does assume that normalization of these neurological preconditions "comes closer to altering the underlying neurological dysfunction (regardless of cause) than do typical academic procedures" (p. 2). Put more simply, Ayres holds that the root of learning disorders—or at least of "some aspects" thereof—lies in neural dysfunction and that the proper role of therapeutic intervention lies in treating the neurological roots.

The fundamental premise of Ayres's theory, which holds that the human brain "is designed to follow an orderly, predictable, interrelated sequence of development" (1972a, p. 4), is derived from her interpretations of the earlier work of developmental psychologists such as Piaget and Ames and Ilg (1946). A corollary to this premise is that the sequence of these developmental steps is determined by a sort of evolutionary "preprogramming." Like Herrick (1956), Ayres holds that the higher intellectual functions are a product of human evolutionary development.

Therapy thus consists of a variety of sensory experiences and motor activities that are presumed to recapitulate and enhance normal neural development. While Ayres stresses that "it is *not* assumed that each child recapitulates his own evolutionary history" (1972a, p. 6), nonetheless much of her therapy—not unlike that of Delacato—reflects the dictum that ontogeny recapitulates phylogeny. In her words, "the course of therapy follows a similar (evolutionary/phylogenetic) progression. Enhancing maturation at the lower, less complex levels of environmental-response function enables a child to become more competent at the higher, more complex levels" (p. 12).

Familiarity with certain general principles of brain function is an essential, if difficult, step toward understanding Ayres's approach. In brief, these principles include (a) functional interdependency of brain structures, (b) plasticity of neural function, (c) neural synapses, (d) sensory stimulation, and (e) organism-environment interaction. First, it is the principle of *functional interdependence* that underlies the hypothesized neural link between "lower" sensorimotor activities and higher cognitive functions such as thinking, academics, and language. The *plasticity principle* makes it theoretically possible to recapitulate a normal sequence of neural development through a predetermined sequence of sensory inputs and motor activities. Particularly with young children the brain is considered to be sufficiently flexible or "plastic" that its function can be retained along normal lines of neural development. *Neural synapses* constitute the structural and functional basis for neural connections; this in turn suggests the critical role of *sensory stimulation* in activating such synapses. The principle of *organism-environment* interaction is central to the notion of the brain as the mediating link between sensation and action.

The key question of Ayres concerns the processes by which these brain functions are integrated. Citing the pioneering work of Sherrington (1906, 1955), who was among the first to stress the importance of CNS mechanisms for sensory integration, Ayres asserts that such integration is "a primordial experience, a constant experience through the ages, and a critical experience" (1972a, p. 26). Perhaps the most basic type of integration consists of intermodality association, which Ayres finds to be frequently deficient in learning disabled children. A second type she refers to as "centrifugal influences—i.e., influences operating in a direction away from the cerebral cortex and toward the periphery" (p. 31). She hypothesizes that inadequate functioning of these "depressant centrifugal regulators" (p. 32) may account for the hyperactive behavior of some learning disabled children. A closely related concept is that of "inhibitory processes," in that "suppression of input is fully as important as enhancement of input in the integrative process" (p. 34). Finally, and perhaps most important, she cites the role of sensory feedback and movement in the integrative process. She assumes that accurate sensory feedback in transformations from sensory input into motor output is of critical importance. Adaptive motor responses, conversely, are considered to be among the most powerful organizers of sensory input. Ayres's position reflects familiarity with the work of Kephart (1968) on the integrative function of adaptive motor responses and with the clinical work of Fay (1954), who made therapeutic use of subcortical evolutionary motor patterns.

A closely related principle in Ayres's conceptualization of brain function concerns differentiated levels of function of the central nervous system. Basic to this is the idea that any major neural structure that receives sensory input is likely to exert widespread influence over other parts of the brain. Thus stimuli that activate subcortical processes are hypothesized to influence higher level cortical processes, and "therapy aimed at influencing the cortex must consider reaching it through the lower structures" (Ayres, 1972a, p. 53). Ayres further hypothesizes that the lower the level of sensory organization, "the greater the emphasis on sensory integration as opposed to sensory analysis" (p. 53). She concludes as follows:

> These principles clearly point to the necessity for involving the brain stem and thalamus in any therapeutic efforts toward sensory integration. Such an involvement can have widespread influence on the rest of the brain. (p. 54)

Ayres identifies six major modalities through which sensory integration is accomplished: vestibular, tactile, proprioceptive, auditory, olfactory, and visual. The three modalities that are assigned a uniquely important role in the formulation of her approach are the vestibular, tactile, and proprioceptive.

The Vestibular System.   This modality enables the organism to detect motion, whether of deceleration or acceleration; in particular motion related to the earth's gravitational pull. It further helps the organism to distinguish between sensory input associated with movement of the body and input stemming from the external environment. The prominent role of the vestibular system in Ayres's approach strongly reflects the work of Schilder (1933), who conceived of the vestibular system as the fundamental coordinator of all sensory functions.

The Tactile System.   As was mentioned earlier, Ayres's emphasis on the tactile modality owes much to the work of Harlow (1958) and especially to that of Rood (1954). She considers the maturational sequence of tactile functions to be related closely to overall neural development; thus she views poor integration of tactile stimuli as precluding normal integration at higher neural levels.

The Proprioceptive System.   Proprioception refers to sensory input from within the body, particularly from muscles, joints, ligaments, and bone receptors. Ayres considers the transformation of sensory patterns into patterns of motor coordination to be a primary function of the brain and adequate proprioceptive integration to be a prerequisite for such transformation.

In addition to these modalities, posture is another major concern in Ayres's model. This is clear in the following definition.

> Posture is that motor response which reflects an individual's relationship to the earth's surface and gravitational force. . . . Man's response to gravity, as it is expressed in his antigravity reactions to it, is one of the phyletically oldest sensorimotor responses. It serves as a substrate for much of the later sensorimotor and sensory integrative development. (1972a, p. 75)

Ayres's discussion of basic elements of postural development—among them the tonic neck reflex, the tonic labyrinthine reflex, phasic and tonic muscle contraction, and extraocular muscle control—is beyond the scope of the present review. It is important however, to note the close link theorized between posture and the vestibular, proprioceptive, and tactile systems, since all constitute major features of sensory integrative therapy.

Diagnostic Procedures

As a result of her factor analytic studies, Ayres (1965, 1969, 1971a, 1971b, 1972a) developed a theoretical model as a basis for differential evaluation and treatment of sensory integrative-related learning disorders. Her work in this regard acknowledges indebtedness to the earlier attempts of researchers such as Gerstmann (1940) and Halstead (1947) to categorize various "clusters" of brain and perceptual-motor dysfunctions. Ayres's own categorization of symptomatic "syndromes" evolved from factor analyses of scores on perceptual, motor, cognitive, auditory, language, and neuromuscular tests that were administered to "several different sample populations of learning disabled children" (1972a, p. 89). The exact criteria by which members of the sampling population were selected are unclear; but on the basis of her analyses, Ayres postulated five relatively discrete "syndromes" or "neural systems" manifested by the learning disordered children she studied: (a) form and space perception; (b) praxis, or the capacity for effective motor planning and execution; (c) postural and bilateral integration, involving postural and ocular mechanisms presumed to underlie cerebral interhemispheric integration as well as integration of motor function on both sides of the body; (d) tactile defensiveness, or unusually defensive reactions to various tactile stimuli; and (e) auditory-language disorders.

Ayres's (1972c) *Southern California Sensory Integration Tests* (SCSIT) represents her chief diagnostic tool. The SCSIT consists of 17 subtests, which are briefly described below.

> *Space Visualization:* Form boards are utilized to involve visual perception of form and space and mental manipulation of objects in space.
>
> *Figure-ground Perception:* Stimulus figures are superimposed and imbedded to require selection of a foreground figure from a rival background.
>
> *Position in Space:* Simple geometric forms are presented for recognition in different orientations and sequences.
>
> *Design Copying:* The visual-motor task involves duplicating a design on a dot grid.
>
> *Motor Accuracy:* The visual-motor task requires that the child draw a line over a printed line. The motor coordination component is much more demanding than the visual component.
>
> *Kinesthesia:* With vision occluded, the child attempts to place his finger on a point at which his finger previously had been placed by the examiner.
>
> *Manual Form Perception:* The test requires matching the visual counterpart of a geometric form held in the hand.
>
> *Finger Identification:* The child points to the finger on his hand which was previously touched by the examiner without the child's watching.
>
> *Graphesthesia:* The child draws a simple design on the back of his hand, attempting to copy the design previously drawn by the examiner at the same place.
>
> *Localization of Tactile Stimuli:* The child is expected to place his finger on a spot on his hand or arm previously touched by the examiner.
>
> *Double Tactile Stimuli Perception:* Two tactile stimuli are applied simultaneously to either or both the cheek and the hand of the child who then identifies where he was touched.
>
> *Imitation of Postures:* The child is required to assume a series of positions or postures demonstrated by the examiner, a process that requires motor planning.
>
> *Crossing the Mid-line of the Body:* The child imitates the examiner as the latter points either to one of the examiner's eyes or ears.

Bilateral Motor Coordination: Performing this test requires smoothly executed movements of and interaction between both upper extremities.

Right-left Discrimination: The child is asked to discriminate right from left on himself, on the examiner and relative to the location of an object. The only verbal responses required on the entire SCSIT are on two items of this test.

Standing Balance: Eyes Open: The test measures the ability of the child to balance himself while standing on one foot with his eyes open.

Standing Balance: Eyes Closed: Standing balance on one foot is measured with the eyes closed. (Ayres, 1972a, pp. 97–98)

Though the SCSIT subtests constitute the most widely used diagnostic procedures in Ayres's approach, she is careful to suggest that such standardized testing should be supplemented by carefully structured clinical observations, focusing on a number of factors deemed important in Ayres's theorization of learning disorders. These factors include primitive postural reflexes, such as the tonic neck and tonic labyrinthine reflexes; cocontraction of antagonistic muscles; muscle tone; control of extraocular (skeletal) muscles; vestibular system functioning or "equilibrium reactions" (Ayres, 1972a, p. 111); integration of function of the two sides of the body; and choreoathetoid (involuntary) movement patterns.

Ayres (1989) recently completed another test, the *Sensory Integration and Praxis Test* (SIP). This instrument is so new that we did not have time to review it before sending our manuscript to the printer. We do know, however, that the SIT is more than merely a revision of the SCSIT. Readers who are interested in Ayres's work should seek out this new test to learn just what her final views on assessment were.

Treatment Methodology

Ayres's approach calls for differential methods of treatment, based on the "syndrome" or cluster of symptoms deduced from SCSIT results and/or clinical observations. Her 1972 book (1972a) includes a chapter on five of the major syndromes, providing a detailed discussion of typical symptoms of each syndrome and a recommended program of therapeutic activities and materials. There are, however, several general principles that underlie treatment methods for all the hypothesized syndromes. These major features of treatment methodology include the following:

Influencing Sensation and Response. In Ayres's words, "The central principle in sensory integrative therapy is providing planned and controlled sensory input with usually—but not invariably—the eliciting of a related adaptive response in order to enhance the organization of brain mechanisms" (1972a, p. 114). She points out that the graduated sequence of motor activities reflecting this principle is remedial treatment rather than simply exercise, though "the difference is not always evident to the casual observer" (p. 114). Such treatment might take the form of performing balancing tasks, developing skill in games such as accurate ball tossing, or assuming a variety of hypothetically therapeutic postural positions. Some of the positions assumed during treatment are illustrated in Figure 15.4. Ayres also stresses that therapy should not ask the child to plan or execute more complicated motor patterns until and unless simpler, "ontogenetically earlier" ones have been mastered. Unfortunately, her criteria for ontogenetic primacy of motor tasks, as well as for mastery of such tasks, are not made very clear.

Tactile Stimulation.   Ayres calls tactile stimuli "a primal source of input to the reticular formation, one of the oldest and most powerful central integrating systems" (1972a, p. 115). She recommends initiating a therapy session with such tactile stimulation. This can include simple touching, either by the therapist or by the child, rubbing with a cloth or brush, application of lotions or unguents, or use of a camel's hair brush mounted on a battery-driven rotating shaft, a device invented by her mentor, Rood. The length of time such stimulation is applied is left largely up to the discretion and convenience of the therapist, as is determination of the body areas to be stimulated; Ayres does, however, recommend that "the ventral surface of the trunk should be avoided unless the child elects to rub it himself" (p. 218).

Vestibular Stimulation.   Ayres considers vestibular stimulation to be "one of the most powerful tools available for therapeutic use in the remediation of sensory integrative dysfunction" (1972a, p. 119). Along with tactile stimulation, it is introduced early in therapy because of the subserving role both types of stimulation are felt to play in relation to more complex types of sensory integration. Perhaps the most commonly used activity in this component of therapy consists of swinging or spinning the child as she or he is sitting or lying in a net hammock; a child who appears threatened by such passive vestibular stimulation can be given an active role in postural or balancing activities. Ayres noted from clinical observations that many learning disabled children tend to show no or diminished nystagmus (eye-righting) responses and have a tendency not to become dizzy easily after being spun around in such activities. "The gradual appearance of nystagmus and dizziness from vestibular stimulation is assumed to be an indication that dormant pathways are beginning to be used and may then be available for other sensory integrative processes" (p. 119). Another common activity consists of the child's lying prone on a large (36-inch-diameter) "therapy ball" and being rolled slowly back and forth by the therapist. Quadrupedic postural activities, that is, activities performed on hands and knees, are also recommended; the rationale being that with regard to both phylogenetic and ontogenetic evolution, "the quadruped posture was predominant and determined the position of the gravity receptors" (p. 121). For children who are presumed to have had insufficient vestibular stimulation in their development, "therapy should probably provide a bombardment of stimulation through the many different vestibular receptors" (p. 120).

Other Proprioceptive Stimuli.   A number of other activities are suggested by Ayres as promoting proprioceptive sensory integration. These include scooter board

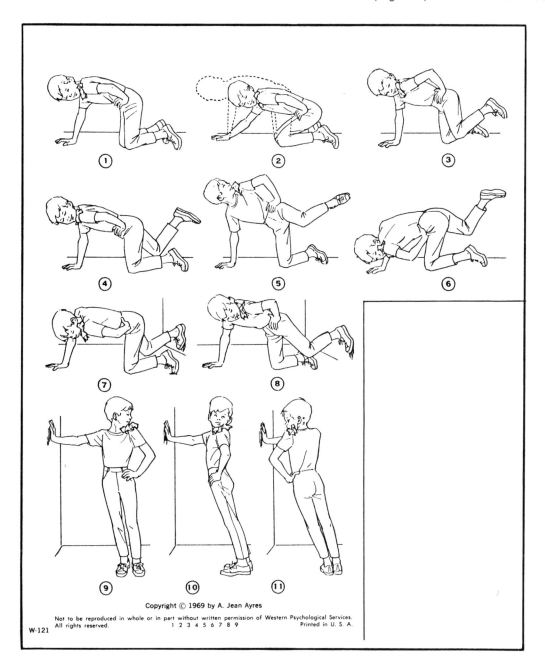

Copyright © 1969 by A. Jean Ayres

Not to be reproduced in whole or in part without written permission of Western Psychological Services.
All rights reserved. 　　　　　1 2 3 4 5 6 7 8 9 　　　　　Printed in U. S. A.

W-121

FIGURE 15.4. Positions for inhibition of the tonic neck reflex. *Note.* From *Sensory Integration and Learning Disorders* (p. 106) by A. J. Ayres, 1972, Los Angeles: Western Psychological Services. Reprinted by permission.

activities; muscle contraction, especially against resistance provided by the therapist; vibration; and activation of righting and equilibrium responses by rolling the child in a cloth-lined barrel or a tube made of five large inner tubes tied or taped together. In her 1972 book, Ayres (1972a) describes 30 different activities for the scooter board alone. One sample scooter board activity is described as follows.

> Push off from wall with feet and "crash" into a tower of cartons. Use helmet to protect head and be sure neck muscles can contract enough to stabilize head. Push off from wall with hands and hit tower with feet. Try either task with eyes closed. (p. 182)

Adaptive Responses.   Given Ayres's definition of an adaptive response as one that "adds functional meaning to motion" (1972a, p. 128), the number of activities that can be presumed to facilitate adaptive responses is virtually limitless. In addition to activities described above, procedures include the use of a platform swing, a one-legged stool, and an equilibrium board (see Figure 15.5). In these as in other activities the guiding principle is to begin with simpler activities before requiring more complex adaptive responses. Ayres also notes that the younger the child—and hence the greater the plasticity of the brain—the greater the likelihood that therapy will be successful. In any event it should be stressed that the success or failure of therapy is not judged by changes in academic task performance. Indeed, adaptive academic responses are virtually absent from the therapeutic repertoire, largely because in Ayres's concept, "sensory integrative therapy should precede academic work ontogenetically" (p. 129).

Precautions.   Ayres admonishes practitioners of her approach to exercise considerable caution in employing it. She cites potential dangers of both overexcitation and overinhibition of children's response pattern through inappropriate choice or poor timing of activities. In addition, she herself concedes that many of the procedures and positions required by therapy "are not appealing to children" (1972a, p. 152). Thus the therapist must be careful not to exacerbate whatever emotional lability the child might have brought to therapy. Even pleasant and successful therapeutic activities are seen to entail some degree of risk, as early successes can bring about premature and fragile notions of progress on the part of the child, the child's parents, and the therapist. However, the nature and sequencing of activities seem to be left mainly to the discretion of the therapist, so it is difficult to know precisely how the therapist is to avoid these pitfalls.

Ayres (1968) maintains strongly that her ideas about neural functions and her activities for training those functions have relevance for the teaching of academic skills, especially reading. It is on the issue of the importance of the sensory integration approach to academic learning that Ayres is the most vulnerable to criticism.

Ayres bases many of her claims about the efficacy of her approach in improving academic performance on her 1972 study (Ayres 1972b) of the effects of sensory integrative therapy on a selected sample of 68 learning disabled children. While there is some precedent for this sort of study in the work of Denhoff, Hainsworth, and

A sitting equilibrium board.

One use of the platform swing. This and some of the other equipment illustrated is available from Western Psychological Services, 12031 Wilshire Blvd.,
Los Angeles, California 90025.

Use of a one leg stool.

FIGURE 15.5. Sample equipment and activities in sensory integrative therapy. *Note.* From *Sensory Integration and Learning Disorders* (pp. 157, 159, 160) by A. J. Ayres, 1972, Los Angeles: Western Psychological Services. Reprinted by permission.

Siqueland (1968), who found that 79% of the children they tested who failed more than 7 items of a 36-item test of motor proficiency also failed to pass first or second grade, Ayres's hypothesized link between sensory integration and academics has failed to enlist much support in subsequent research done in this area. Indeed, both the methodology and the conclusions of her 1972 study have been called into question by a number of researchers, among them Kanter, Clark, Allen, and Chase (1976) and Cratty (1986a). Nor has confirmation been found for Ayres's assumption that enhancing balance through vestibular stimulation will have an effect on either academic achievement (Ismail & Gruber, 1967) or hyperkinesis (Bhatara, Clark, & Arnold, 1978). A doctoral study by D. Johnson (1973), in addition, found no significant relationship between postural and bilateral integration and reading achievement.

A particularly discouraging paper concerning the merits of sensory integrative therapy was published by Densem, Nuthall, Bushnell, and Horn (1989). They summarize the results of 14 investigations that studied the effects of this approach. They concluded that "the majority of studies that can be considered well designed—show no significant differences between treatment and control groups, while the remainder are equally divided between mixed and positive results" (p. 222). In addition, Densem et al. reported the results of a study that they had conducted to test the effects of sensory integrative therapy. They found that such therapy was ineffective in developing language, perceptual-motor skills, or handwriting.

Silver (1987) reviewed the research literature dealing with the relationship of children's vestibular functioning and academic learning. In particular, he focused on the theories expressed by Ayres and by Levinson (1980, 1984). He concluded that at present no evidence supports the vestibular theories or the treatment approaches based on such theories.

In short, the assumptions underlying both the theoretical rationale and the practical efficacy of Ayres's sensory integrative approach remain unconfirmed. With the exception of the 1972 study, Ayres has failed to substantiate the effectiveness of her model with anything more than anecdotal clinical observations. Her own words confirm the wisdom of remembering that the assumptions underlying her approach are at this point still only assumptions, and that the remedial activities she recommends may be irrelevant to the etiology and treatment of learning problems.

> Someday the accurate guesses will be separated from the nonaccurate. In the meantime, hypotheses will be considered as suggestions for exploring therapeutic procedures or as providing tentative explanation for their apparent effectiveness. (1972a, p. 55)

Until Ayres's explanation of learning disorders is more than "tentative" and the effectiveness of her therapy more than "apparent," perhaps the soundest conclusion to be drawn about the sensory integrative approach is caveat emptor, a classic adage that could well be applied to all the programs discussed in this chapter.

GETMAN: AN ACTION PROGRAM FOR DEVELOPING VISUAL PERCEPTION

Gerald N. Getman, who emphasizes a developmental approach to visual perception, holds doctoral degrees in both optometry and ocular science. In the 1940s he served the original Clinic of Child Development at Yale University as visiting staff optometrist and worked with Gesell. Later, he studied the relationships between basic perceptual abilities and reading skills with Betts at Temple University. For several years, Getman was the director of child development at the Pathway School in Norristown, Pennsylvania, a facility dedicated exclusively to brain injured children who manifest learning and/or behavioral difficulties. In October of 1986, Getman retired. Presently he is living in Waldorph, Maryland.

In *How to Develop Your Child's Intelligence*, Getman (1984) has (a) advanced his basic theory, (b) presented six stages of visual-motor development, and (c) suggested a collection of activities to train at each stage. Both the theory and stages of development and the activities are discussed in the following section.

Rationale

Four concepts that seem characteristic of Getman's remedial approach are repeatedly emphasized throughout his work:

1. Educational success depends heavily upon visual adequacy.

2. Direct experience enhances perceptual development.

3. The child learns to perceive and learns to learn as well.

4. Perceptual success follows a logical, systematic sequence of development.

To Getman, a child's growth, behavior, and intellectual achievement conform to a basic sequence of visually related developments, regardless of the diagnostic category into which the child might be placed. Distinction is made between sight and vision. Sight is considered to be nothing much more than the basic biological response of the eye to light. Vision, by contrast, is the interpretation of what is seen. Sight is a passing ray of light striking the retina. Vision is a lifetime brought to bear upon the optical clue of the moment, which triggers every possible associated and interrelated cognitive response. The importance attached to visual perception by Getman is repeatedly underscored by such statements as the following:

1. "Vision is intelligence" (Getman, 1984, p. 21).

2. "It has been estimated that approximately 80% of everything we learn is learned visually" (Getman & Kane, 1968, p. III).

3. ". . . recall that children grow up to live in a visual world" (Getman, 1984, p. 21).

4. "Visual success is reading success" (Getman, 1961, p. 1).

The idea that no knowledge can be as useful as that gained from one's own experience is accentuated in Getman's writings; and consequently, the importance of participation and involvement in one's own development is stressed strongly. A frequently emphasized point is that children learn best when they are most actively involved; that is, learning is intensified when children not only perform a task but also observe themselves in the performance.

To Getman, infants have the basic machinery for learning through which they learn all they know; children must even learn how to learn with this machinery. Although it is generally accepted that children learn to walk and to talk, Getman (1984) points out that they also learn to see, feel, smell, and taste and therefore suggests a training program designed to provide experiences for helping children learn how to learn.

The foundation of Getman's training program is the basic sequence of growth and development associated with the first 5 years of life. This sequence is organized into six sequential and interrelated developmental areas or stages (Getman, 1984, pp. 24–31).

1. *General Movement Patterns.* When children move, they learn; without movement, learning does not take place. The body learns to explore—the eyes become the steering mechanism, the bone frame becomes the supporting structure, the nervous system becomes the start-control-stop circuit, and the muscles become the anatomical parts for action.

2. *Special Movement Patterns.* General movement skills are extended to include synchronized use of body parts and manipulation. Eye-hand coordination is achieved early and sets the pattern for subsequent integrations within the body's perceptual system.

3. *Eye Movement Patterns* (to reduce action). Vision replaces general and/or special movements, and the hands are freed for more economical uses. The less manipulation the hands must exercise, the more available they are to produce shapes, forms, and symbols with greater and greater steering from the visual system. Subsequently, the acquisition of information involves less and less manipulation.

4. *Communication Patterns* (to replace action). For the mastery of speech, considerable control of lip, mouth, tongue, and throat muscles must be acquired. According to Getman, nonverbal communication (i.e., meaningful gesturing) is related to eye movement patterns and other special movement patterns. He suggests that children with inadequate eye movement development have much difficulty with words of distance, direction, and position. Examples of such words include *up, down, right, left, near,* and *far.* Language communication gives children the opportunity to verify visual discriminations.

5. *Visualization Patterns.* Sometimes called visual memory, visualization involves (a) the recall of previous learnings, (b) the matching of new learnings against those already known, and (c) the inspection and interpretation of new learnings. Therefore, visualization patterns substitute for action, speech, and time.

6. *Visual Integrations.* This level of development makes it possible for an individual to interchange body mechanisms when interpreting the environment. By touching an object, for example, certain reliable inferences can be made regarding its appearance without sight input. Vision remains most important in interpretation, however, since it characteristically provides more accurate distance reception than audition and yields information on texture, size, shape, direction, and color as well.

A Training Program for the Development of Visual Perception

In outlining a program for the development of visual perception and closely related skills, Getman (1984, pp. 37–111) has organized the activities to correspond to five of the six development stages discussed previously (in the section on rationale):

1. General movement patterns

2. Special movement patterns

3. Eye movement patterns

4. Vision-language patterns

5. Visualization patterns

No activities are suggested specifically for the visual integration stage, because Getman is convinced that these patterns emerge when adequate perceptual organization exists at the other four levels.

Examples of activities associated with each stage are listed in Table 15.5. The table, however, does not provide all the information concerning the individual tasks needed for initiation of the program. For example, consultation with Getman's work is necessary to understand what is meant by "angels-in-the-snow" or how the trampoline is intended to be used. Although Getman's training procedures are presented only very briefly in Table 15.5, they illustrate his basic principle that learning takes place best when the child's experience "involves *movement use* of the neuromuscular system (general movement patterns), practice and repetition for the combination of parts and body mechanisms (special movement patterns), and the resulting interpretations of all information thus received and integrated by all body mechanisms" (Getman, 1984, p. 30).

Specific activities designed to develop perceptual skills are grouped into six categories. In theory, these categories form a developmental sequence corresponding to a considerable degree with the developmental stages described in the earlier section on rationale.

TABLE 15.5. Example of Activities for Each Stage of Getman's Program for Development of Visual Perception

General Movement Patterns	Special Movement Patterns	Eye Movement Patterns	Vision-Language Patterns	Visualization Patterns
1. Basic movements	1. Percolator for toy	1. Fixation practice	1. Verb games	1. Simple jigsaw
a. Angels-in-the-snow	2. Cupboard or drawer for child	a. Identifying game	2. Encourage talking about interests and activities	2. Sorting real objects
b. Stomach roll	3. Blockcraft and construction blocks (single-color set)	b. Making child *look* or *reach*		3. Visual comparison—size, shape, weight, texture, check with touch or lift
c. Rolling sit-ups		c. Making child *look* and *listen*	3. Adverb games	
d. Sit-ups	4. Hammer and nails	d. Have child look, point, speak	4. Preposition games	4. Object identification, eyes closed—tactual
e. Bent-knee sit-ups	5. Permission for use of preferred hand	2. Pursuit—golf ball	5. Adjective games	
f. Feet lift	6. Activities requiring bilateral and reciprocal inter-weaving of the two halves of the body	a. to and fro	6. Naming and classifying	5. Matching old labels to new cans
g. Roll from back to hands and knees		b. side to side	7. Picture description	
h. Roll from back to hands and feet		c. circular	8. Imitation of sounds	6. Visual comparison outdoors
i. Toe touch		3. Plane spotter and pilot (pursuit and fixation)	9. Storytelling, main points	7. Coloring books
2. Obstacle course	a. Jacks	4. Skill of seeing clearly at various distances. Rhythmic fixation. Ability to shift from near to far	10. Opposites	8. Tracing visualizing of a word
3. Jump board	b. Lincoln Logs		11. Slow, then fast articulation	
4. Walking beam	c. Swings			9. Visual memory
5. Trampoline	d. Wheelbarrow		12. Different types of voices; imagination visualization	a. Recalling familiar objects
6. Rhythmic work with music	e. Tricyles and bicycles	a. Finger to finger		b. Telling which is missing
7. Running and throw-ing games	7. Tracing blocks or cutouts	b. Pencil to wall calendar	13. Let child "rattle on" occasionally	c. Recalling items in pictures
	8. Catching and throwing	5. Chalkboard practice and play	14. Have child retell short stories	d. Reproducing erased forms
	a. Large, light balloon	a. Bimanual circles	15. Varied tapping for numbers, rhythm	e. Reproduce parts from memory
	b. Smaller balloons	(1) R-clockwise L-counter-clockwise	16. Nursery rhymes, unison	f. Label familiar objects: Let child copy
	c. Heavier beach balls	(2) L-clockwise R-counter-clockwise	17. Identification and location of noises	10. Visual projection
	d. Softballs and baseballs	(3) Both clockwise	18. Have child watch for meaning in mouth and facial expression	a. "I am thinking of . . ." Visualize from description
	9. Cutting out pictures	(4) Both counter-clockwise	19. Initial consonant discrimination	b. Identify family or friend from description
	10. Fit objects together	b. Bimanual straight lines	20. Encourage repeti-tion of radio and TV commercials	c. Identify a place in town from description
	11. Peg board pictures	(1) All horizontal	21. Provide phone for repetitive listening	
	12. Tracing and copying	(2) Both horizontal and vertical	22. Use action/sound records	d. Have child describe trip to store, etc.
		(3) Diagonal	23. Voice, identification	
		(4) All possible combinations	24. Oral directions, increasing number	
		6. Follow the dots		

1. *Practice in General Coordination.* Tasks presented in the first section are designed to develop coordination of the torso, head, and limbs. At this level of training, visually directed gross motor behavior is emphasized; "angels-in-the-snow" is a characteristic activity. In the accomplishment of this task the child is placed in the Starting Position, that is, on his or her back in a relaxed state with eyes fixed on a spot on the ceiling. The child is instructed to clap his or her hands overhead while his or her legs extend to a wide position at the same time. Next the arms return to the sides and the heels are brought back to touch in the center. Arms and legs are relaxed but straight throughout the exercise.

2. *Practice in Balance.* These activities develop balance through visually directed movement, that is, visually interpreted, steered, appraised, and corrected movement. The Walking Board, a 2-inch by 4-inch board at least 8 feet in length resting upon supports placed under each end, is fundamental to all tasks in this section. The child is taught to walk the board forward and backward with suitable variations.

3. *Practice in Eye-Hand Coordinations.* Tasks included in this section assist children to develop integration of the visual-tactual systems. Getman asserts that these systems are basic to all symbolic interpretations and manipulations. By the use of chalkboard exercises, the child experiences and learns the concepts of the circle and horizontal, vertical, and diagonal lines. Success in these tasks should result in greater speed and accuracy when the child uses workbooks and textbooks in school.

4. *Practice in Eye Movements.* Activities presented in this section develop control and accuracy of eye movements. Successful performance results in the acquisition of ocular fixation and pursuit abilities, movements necessary for reading. Included are exercises that require the child to shift focus from one fixed point to another (ocular fixation) and to follow with the eye his or her finger moving across a table top (pursuit).

5. *Practice in Form Perception.* Mastery of form perception develops continuity and rhythm of hand movements and permits visual inspection of resulting patterns. The child is given templates (patterns) for the circle, the square, the triangle, the rectangle, and the diamond and draws each form on the chalkboard. The direction of movements is reinforced by having the child walk out the chalkboard pattern in an open floor space. Transition from the chalkboard to the desk is made, and templates are correspondingly reduced in size.

6. *Practice in Visual Memory.* The final group of activities is designed to develop skill in visual memory through the acquisition of (a) greater awareness of size and form relationships, (b) increased speed in visual recognition, (c) increased span of visual form recognition, and (d) more adequate retention of visual images. Practice necessitates the use of a tachistoscope, a projection instrument that flashes a pattern on a screen at regular time intervals. A series of slides is presented to which the child responds in varying ways. For example, the child may be required to

name the form (oral), trace it in the air (kinesthetic), circle it on a worksheet (matching), trace over it on a worksheet (tactile), or reproduce it (visual memory).

Appraisal of Getman's Techniques

Concern has been expressed regarding various aspects of Getman's position. Most of the criticism centers on (a) the strong emphasis placed by him upon visual perception and (b) the lack of research-established validity.

Hagin (1965) has stated that Getman overemphasizes the role of visual perception in the classroom and has pointed out that classroom learning actually involves a considerable amount of talking and listening (auditory-vocal skills). In fact, the value of auditory training and the contribution of auditory skills to school success are scarcely mentioned in Getman's writings, even though most writers in remedial education would probably agree that auditory processes are most important to adequate language (including reading) development. If this is so, then Getman's unqualified remarks relative to vision and intelligence, some of which were listed previously, would seem to be exaggerated.

Although many clinicians have successfully used the Getman techniques or modifications of these techniques to develop visual adequacy, the validity of neither the whole program nor the individual tasks has been established by carefully designed research. Silver (1965) even questions a basic premise of the approach, saying, "The training of gross motor functional patterns, such as balancing on a rail has not been proven to improve perception and learning" (p. 20). In his discussion of Getman's teaching suggestions, Hagin (1965) concluded, "I am concerned that his training procedures have not been tested through careful sampling and controlled research. I'm concerned about oversimplification and lack of specificity" (p. 25).

In general, most of the questions concerning the validity of Getman's techniques could be, or have been, directed toward the procedures of Delacato, Kephart, and others who train at the perceptual-motor level. Although similarities do exist among these systems, Getman (1967) draws several distinctions between his approach and those advocated by these workers.

1. Neither Kephart nor Delacato has a functional, performance-centered concept of child development.

2. Neither sees vision as a dynamic process of cumulative and emerging cognitive performance that involves the entire organism and is merely triggered by light.

3. Neither demands use of the visual system as the ultimate guidance and appraisal system to control and correct the action system.

4. Both see movement as significant unto itself.

5. Both insist that an organism that has lived for years may be returned to actions and experiences of a much earlier developmental period and function as if it were in tune with that period.

Relative to research support for these techniques, it must be pointed out that Getman views himself as a clinician and as such is not personally interested in undertaking a series of validity studies. To Getman, the accumulated clinical evidence derived from his experience is sufficient validation for the suggested approach. Getman readily agrees, however, that formal investigations into the efficacy of his techniques would be desirable, and he encourages interested persons to research this area.

Getman (e.g., 1985) frequently pens emotional apologies for vision training. Generally, these pieces follow a similar format. A rational, though rhetorical, conceptual foundation is laid down first. Next, a supportive research base is alluded to but not cited. Finally, the accusation is made or inferred that researchers and clinicians who hold contrary opinions are biased and ill informed. While Getman's writings make lively reading, they are no substitute for controlled research.

KEPHART: A DEVELOPMENTAL APPROACH TO TEACHING MOTOR GENERALIZATIONS

Newell Carlyle Kephart was born in Parker, Kansas. He received the PhD degree in child welfare from the University of Iowa and worked as a mental hygienist with the Wayne County Training School for several years. During World War II he served in the U.S. Navy. In 1946 he joined the faculty of Purdue University, where he served as professor of psychology and education and conducted the Achievement Center for Children, a research and treatment center for handicapped children.

Kephart made major contributions to both the theory and practice of special education. His neuropsychological approach to the diagnosis and treatment of learning difficulties greatly influenced the thinking in the field. Since his classroom applications were presented in a manner readily understood by teachers, they were widely employed throughout the United States during the perceptual-motor training movement of the 1960s, to which Kephart was a leading contributor.

Kephart's contributions to the literature include *The Slow Learner in the Classroom* (1971), widely used by teachers; *Psychopathology and Education of the Brain-Injured Child* (Strauss & Kephart, 1955), which he co-authored with A. A. Strauss; and numerous articles and papers. Retiring from Purdue University in 1968, Kephart served until his death in 1973 as director of the Glen Haven Achievement Center in Fort Collins, Colorado, a school devoted to the education of handicapped children and their parents.

Kephart's theory of perceptual-motor learning development, based on clinical experience as well as developmental psychology, is perhaps more systematic than his remedial "method," which is actually a collection of techniques rather than a method. In fact, puzzles, pegboards, finger painting, and dot-to-dot pictures, all recommended by Kephart, have been used for some time by kindergarten and special education teachers, although not for the reasons provided by Kephart.

The uniqueness of Kephart's approach lies in his strong emphasis on the sensorimotor basis of all learning, which consists of certain generalizations rather than highly specific skills. He notes that reading, writing, and arithmetic involve many perceptual and motor skills; even a so-called basic skill such as drawing a square requires the integrity of even more basic skills, such as gross motor abilities, eye-hand coordination, laterality, directionality, ocular control, dexterity, temporal-spatial translation, and form perception. Therefore, rather than basing remediation upon skills such as drawing a square, Kephart believes that greater success in developing readiness accrues from breaking down simple activities into more basic skills and teaching those skills. Further, he states that no training technique should be considered a goal in itself, but that the technique is merely the vehicle by means of which a child can be taught certain generalized skills and abilities. This attitude toward remediation represents a major shift in emphasis from task-oriented to process-oriented teaching. For example, many authors suggest treating children with reading disabilities by teaching them to read, but Kephart suggests treating them by remediating impairments of the basic skills and generalizations upon which the reading act is dependent.

The Stages of Learning Development

Kephart illustrates his emphasis in his theory, which is organized into three stages of learning development (practical, subjective, and objective), all stages based upon four motor generalizations (posture and the maintenance of balance, contact, locomotor, and receipt and propulsion).

The Practical Stage. The first stage of development is marked by the infant's physical manipulation of objects without any evidence that the infant perceives the objects as being separate and distinct from his or her own activity. Infants at this motor learning stage of development are unaware of themselves as separate from their environment or of objects in the environment as separate from their handling of them; the major task is to produce a movement of the various movable parts of the body, a movement combining parts, and to control the movement. This early stage lays the foundation for future learning, and Kephart assumes that all behavior is basically motor, that is, prerequisites for any kind of behavior are muscular and motor responses.

The basic motor generalization upon which the practical stage is based is posture and the maintenance of balance. The only stable environmental condition around which children may build their postural model of themselves is gravity, which they react to in two ways:

1. They resist the force of gravity, thus calling upon their righting reflexes to prevent falling.

2. They learn to maintain a constant balance between antagonistic sets of muscles, thereby keeping themselves in the erect position in various settings.

This maintenance of balance requires awareness of the center of gravity and muscular flexibility.

Out of the kinesthetic information of posture and balance arises the balancing generalization, which allows children to explore space without worrying about gravity. They are able to get from one place to another, changing their movements to meet the changing demands of the situation without direct regard for the movement pattern but with concern only for the purpose of the movement. They need not worry about alterations to be made in specific movements; the movement pattern takes care of the changes.

Kephart notes that specific motor skills, such as walking, may be taught with relative ease but that the teaching of movement patterns presents a much more difficult task. Children taught a specific skill may perform adequately as long as the series of movements they have learned is appropriate, but if the situation changes and alteration in the series of movements must be made, the children have no pattern of movement upon which to depend. Their motor performances are therefore often awkward and stilted with infrequent variation.

Motor exploration and the resulting feedback data, facilitated by the balancing generalization, result in motor awareness and lead to the emergence of a second generalization—the concept of body schema. Body schema, according to Kephart, is a "learned concept resulting from observation of the movements of parts of the body and relationships of different parts of the body to each other and to external objects" (1971, p. 51). It is an internal conceptualization of self, fluid and dynamic, and depends on kinesthetic input relating any new posture to the ones preceding it. Once children have established their body image, they are able to develop practical directionality or awareness of dimension along body axes.

Directionality consists of verticality, or awareness of the up-and-down axis, and laterality, or awareness of the relative position of one side of the body versus the other. Directionality, in its vertical and lateral aspects, develops with respect always to the body's center of gravity. Awareness of a point in space, that is, practical directionality, is complemented in the child by a growing awareness of a point in time—synchrony. Synchrony, or precise timing, allows control of starting and stopping an activity and is based upon a sense of "nowness" in time. Other aspects of the practical stage of development are

1. practical succession—the beginning of directional ordering of objects and temporal ordering of events, which is experienced directly by the child at this stage; and

2. practical continuity—the beginning of figure-ground orientation through exploration of continuous surfaces and related movements.

The Subjective Stage.   The second stage of learning development is the subjective or perceptual-motor stage, in which perceptual knowledge as well as motor knowledge must be referred always to the self. This stage is based on the motor generalizations of contact and of locomotion. Contact generalizations, employing patterns of reach, grasp, and release, enable children to manipulate and to explore objects, shapes, and relationships in terms of movement patterns and body schema. Locomotor generalizations enable children to explore space and its relationships in the same fashion, employing, however, movement patterns pertinent to moving the body from one place to another. Form perception is based on contact generalizations; spatial perception is based on locomotor generalizations, and the two together prepare the way motorically for the perceptual-motor match.

Before discussing Kephart's focal principle, the perceptual-motor match, early motor and early perceptual activity must be clarified. Dunsing and Kephart (1965) define "movement" as observable response and "motor" as an internalized neurophysiological event relating to the output system. Thus a covert motor generalization is built upon many movement patterns and frees children from direct attention to the movement so that they may move unhampered about their environment in a purposeful and exploratory fashion. Motor generalizations are built in two ways:

1. by increasing differentiation of hitherto gross, undifferentiated movement, followed by integration of the movements into total patterns; and

2. by integration of reflexes into patterns so that muscles act as part of a total, purposive activity.

While these motor generalizations are developing, perceptual activity, which begins later, follows much the same sequence—that is, from gross generalizations to differentiation to integration into meaningful patterns. For example, form perception begins with an innate awareness of globular, undifferentiated masses, which probably differ only in intensity, extension, and color. Such a mass gradually becomes differentiated by the child into its signal qualities, or characteristic details, which are then integrated into a constructive form having a new quality that is characteristic of only this form.

Although one may speak of perception and motor as two different processes, they actually must always be related, according to Kephart (1971), who subscribes to a servomechanistic model of the perceptual process, as illustrated in Figure 15.6.

In the servo system, part of the output pattern is fed back into the input side of the model in a continuous cycling fashion until input matches output. This process may explain covert activities such as problem solving in which the greater part of the output pattern is fed back to input instead of to a muscular or overt response. Thus Kephart cannot sanction the "textbook" separation of perceptual and motor activity and believes that such a dichotomy can lead only to error. Learning experiences, then, should be designed in terms of the total perceptual-motor process.

Thus to be meaningful, perceptual information must be matched to basic motor generalizations through the body schema. Since motor generalizations develop first, perception must always be matched to motor activity; never is motor activity matched to perception. Kephart speaks of two worlds, perception and motor, which must be combined for the child to function objectively and consistently in the environment.

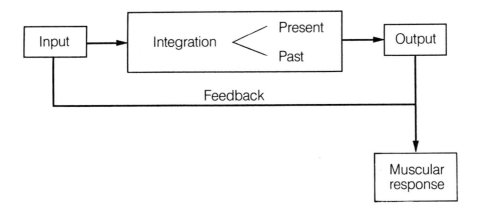

FIGURE 15.6. Diagram of feedback mechanisms in perception. *Note.* From *The Slow Learner in the Classroom* (p. 56) by N. C. Kephart, 1971, Columbus, OH: Merrill. Reprinted by permission.

The perceptual-motor match is necessary for verification of spatial information and for further development of continuity, or figure-ground orientation. Concerning the development of continuity, the child's visual exploration of continuous surfaces must be matched to his or her motor awareness of them. Objective laterality, or the projection of laterality into space, cannot take place without an intermediary step of perceptual-motor matching, in this case, visual perceptions matched with haptic-motor activity. This step of spatial localization is a difficult one; the child must match the two worlds simultaneously, having no direct knowledge of space.

The Objective Stage. Subjective continuity, subjective succession, and signal qualities can be used to describe an object, but the awareness of the total configuration is lacking and is not fully developed until the end of the objective or perceptual stage of learning development. In this stage, Kephart feels that perception, particularly vision, assumes primary importance in receiving information. The objective stage is based upon the advanced motor generalizations of receipt and propulsion, patterns that involve dynamic relationships between a moving child and objects that are moving or are about to be moved. In receipt patterns, children interfere with a moving object; in propulsion patterns, they impart movement to an object. In their objective spatial structure, children perceive relationships among a number of different objects. For knowledge of direction they can utilize information not only about Euclidean coordinates, but about diagonals, slants, and curves. They have developed temporal percepts of rhythm and sequence. Time and space are now seen as different dimensions of the same objective reality and can be translated from one to the other. Finally, children make the ultimate projection, that is, they project beyond the range of their visual and temporal fields and are able to learn conceptually as well as perceptually.

Kephart notes that one of the many problems faced by children in the objective stage of development is that of dealing with activities that require crossing the body midline. Children must learn that an object, when crossing the midline, changes in pattern from outside-in to inside-out but does not change in constancy of movement or of shape.

The highest level of generalization, according to Kephart (1963), is that of the concept based upon similarities between objects or situations. The basic point Kephart makes in discussing conceptual development is that the concept can be no better than the perception upon which it is based. "If perceptions lack in generalization, concepts will likely be weak, restricted, or bizarre" (Kephart, 1963, p. 18).

Treatment for Specific Learning Disabilities

Treatment procedures suggested by Kephart are derived through the administration of the Perceptual Motor Rating Scale, which emphasizes the assessment of sensorimotor learning, ocular control, and form perception. Results of the evaluation indicate the developmental stages of learning that are inadequate and must be treated. Sensorimotor training equipment and activities include walking boards, balance boards, trampolines, games such as "angels-in-the snow," scribbling, finger painting, midline-crossing exercises, dot-to-dot drawing, and bilateral and unilateral exercises. Ocular control is developed in a sequential fashion through the use of monocular training, rotary pursuit, and Marsden ball activities. Form perception training is achieved through chalkboard activities, puzzles, matchstick figures, and pegboard designs.

Part III of Kephart's (1971) manual for the classroom teacher is devoted to training activities and is divided into four major sections: (a) chalkboard training, (b) sensorimotor training, (c) training ocular control, and (d) training form perception.

Chalkboard Training. The activities in this section are primarily visual-motor in nature, beginning with random scribbling and progressing through directionality exercises, including those that require the child to cross the midline, to orientation exercises in which the child copies forms, reproduces them from memory, and varies the reproductions with respect to size, speed, direction, and so on. Throughout these activities the child is taught to attach the verbal symbol to the productions. In general, however, the child is experimenting with movement patterns and observing closely the pattern left on the chalkboard that results from his or her activity; both activities constitute the essentials of visual-motor perception. Specific activities recommended are

1. Scribbling

2. Finger painting

3. The clock game—a device to teach the child to use various combinations of bilateral movements, namely, movements toward and away from the center, parallel movements, and crossed movements

4. Drawing circles and other geometric forms

Sensorimotor Training. Activities discussed under sensorimotor training generally include exercises requiring the use of the large muscles or groups of muscles. Emphasis first is placed on the development of balance but progresses through the development of body image and bilaterality and unilaterality. The child is taught balance through a number of activities requiring a walking board; walking forward, backward, and sideways, and turning and bouncing on the board are typical exercises. In addition to the walking board, and usually after proficiency on it has been attained, the child is introduced to the balance board and taught many of the same skills learned on the walking board. The trampoline is used in this phase of training as well as the walking and balance boards. Other activities included in the sensorimotor training program include

1. Angels-in-the-snow—used in teaching bilateral, unilateral, and cross-lateral movements and in teaching the child to change the time and position of movements

2. Stunts and games—for example, the duck walk, rabbit hop, crab walk, measuring worm, and elephant walk; all aimed at teaching variations in movements patterns and providing the child with opportunities to elaborate movement patterns which he or she has learned.

3. Rhythmical activities—both bilateral and unilateral

Ocular Control Training. The third section dealing with remedial techniques is devoted to activities in the area of control of the eyes. Kephart emphasizes the point that information obtained only through the eyes does not provide adequate data regarding location and orientation in space, and therefore visual control must be matched to the general motor and kinesthetic patterns that the child has learned. As Kephart states, it is apparent from the foregoing that the child must achieve a measure of competency in motor patterning before ocular control can be expected.

Kephart outlines five stages in ocular-pursuit training that serve as a basis for remediation.

1. *Stage one.* The child is taught to follow with the eyes an object, such as a pencil, while it is moved first laterally and vertically and then moved diagonally and in rotary fashion. The latter movements are the more difficult and are not employed until the child is able to follow lateral and vertical movements of the target.

2. *Stage two.* The second stage of training differs from the first in that the target used is a small pen-shaped flashlight, thereby increasing the intensity of the visual stimulus. The same type of target movements are used in training.

3. *Stage three.* The penlight is the target in the third stage, and the same type of movements are used; but the child follows the moving target with a finger while simultaneously following with the eyes. In this stage, kinesthetic information from extraocular muscles is matched to kinesthetic information from the ocular muscles.

4. *Stage four.* The fourth stage differs from the previous stage only in that the child is asked to put a finger on the light from the penlight and move the finger as the target light moves. In this fashion, kinesthetic and tactile stimulation is increased just as in stage two visual stimulation was increased. In stage four, however, the intensity of the stimulus not only is increased but is still correlated with other stimuli, that is, the intensified kinesthetic stimulus is associated with the visual stimulus.

5. *Stage five.* The fifth stage of ocular training requires the use of a ball—first large, such as a beach ball, then smaller, such as a baseball. In this stage the teacher places both hands, palms flat, on one side of the ball, and the child places his or her hands on the opposite side. The teacher moves the ball in lateral, vertical, diagonal, and rotary patterns, carrying the child's hands along and encouraging the child to keep the ball in sight as it is moved. Kephart makes several points in reference to the fifth stage of training: that kinesthetic and tactual information is increased; that both hands are used; and that since the teacher is guiding the ball, resistance may be created, thereby increasing tactual stimulation, by the teacher's pressing against the ball.

Kephart recommends that ocular training begin at the level on which the child is able to perform and that all phases of training in the various stages should be completed. Other ancillary techniques suggested by Kephart include the following.

1. Special practice aimed at increasing the extent or range of the child's eye movements if it becomes apparent that his or her movement range is restricted.

2. Binocular and monocular training.

3. The Marsden ball—a soft rubber ball suspended by a string from the ceiling so that when the ball is moved, it will swing like a pendulum. Basically, the technique for using the swinging ball consists of having the child touch the ball just as it passes in front of him or her, which means that the child must follow the moving target with the eyes and respond in terms of the position of the ball, an activity requiring accurate time and correlation of visual and motor systems. Other variations and elaborations of the basic technique are provided by Kephart.

Training Form Perception. In training the child with poor constructive form perception, Kephart discusses several activities, such as puzzles, stick figures, and pegboards. The tasks, by and large, require the child to match and reproduce various forms and patterns. Several general principles are laid down with respect to the materials and activities.

1. The form or the picture should be more striking than the shape of the individual pieces; puzzles depicting a single human figure are probably best for beginning a training program. Particularly, overlapping figures should not be used on puzzles, nor should pictures poorly differentiated from the background be given to the children. Kephart also suggests that the cutout pieces of the puzzle should conform to the outline of the picture rather than being randomly cut.

2. The teacher should prepare a series of forms made of matchsticks glued to a piece of cardboard or wood. From a supply of separate matchsticks (without heads) the child must reproduce the constructive aspects of the forms. The coordination necessary for copying or drawing is not needed, nor are the elements of the forms so emphasized as in drawing.

3. The pegboard tasks suggested by Kephart are modifications of the Strauss Marble Board (Strauss & Kephart, 1955; Strauss & Lehtinen, 1947, 1989). The pegs should be of fairly large size—for example, golf tees—to provide ease in handling. The pegboard should be about 12 inches square with ⅛-inch diameter holes half an inch apart. The tasks set for the children involve their copying patterns boards with model figures on them.

4. Two types of activities may be used with both the stick figures and the pegboards. The children either may copy directly from the model or may be asked to construct the forms after having seen the model for only a brief period.

The children for whom the Kephart techniques might be beneficial may be found among groups classified as "minimally brain injured," "language disordered," "learning disabled," or "perceptually damaged." The classification—the label—is not the important factor in determining whether to use Kephart procedures; rather, the developmental level of the child in sensory-perceptual-motor areas is crucial. If a child is found to be deficient in any of the developmental aspects discussed by Kephart, one may assume that the child can profit to a lesser or greater degree from the techniques described by Kephart. The secondary factor in deciding whether to use Kephart's techniques should be the diagnostic classification of the child. Teachers of various groups of children—mentally retarded, learning disordered, and developmentally delayed—have reported positive results from the use of the materials and activities recommended by Kephart.

BARSCH: MOVIGENICS

Ray Barsch is a man entranced with the world of space and movement within that space. In his frame of reference, even language, that highly auditory and temporal accomplishment, is reduced to a visuospatial phenomenon. He states,

Man is a visual spatial being. At birth he is surrounded by space and "makes his living" in space from one end of life's cycle to the other. . . . Man is a symbolically oriented being. Symbols become his system for logging his journey through space. (Barsch, 1965a, p. 3)

Barsch further asserts that "movement efficiency is symbolically communicated through the visual-spatial phenomenon called language" (1976, p. 87).

In his earlier writing, Barsch was concerned primarily with the brain damaged child, and he discussed parent counseling (1961), the concept of regression (1960), and a method of evaluation and classification (1962). Barsch has now abandoned the concept of minimal brain damage in children, and his efforts have been directed toward developing a conceptual schema that describes the child as a learner and provides an approach to education designated by Barsch as the "physiologic approach," in contradistinction to the more traditional "intellectual" and "psychiatric" approaches (1965b). The implementation of the physiologic approach resulted in an experimental curriculum based on 12 dimensions of learning derived from what Barsch terms "movigenics." He defines movigenics as "the study of the origin and development of movement patterns leading to learning efficiency" (1965b, p. 5).

Rationale and Basic Postulates

Barsch's (1967) theory of movement—movigenics—rests on 10 postulates synthesized from the work of numerous theorists and researchers in many disciplines. Without exception, all of the postulates deal with humans as moving beings within a spatial world. The basic principle underlying the human species is "movement efficiency," which develops in a sequential fashion throughout its forward thrust toward maturity and which is characterized by a striving for equilibrium or homeostasis. Survival in a spatial world is the prime objective of movement efficiency, which develops in a climate of physical and psychological stress. The ability to process information by means of the "preceptocognitive system" is necessary to the emergence of movement efficiency. This system is composed of the six sense channels—auditory, visual, kinesthetic, tactual, olfactory, and gustatory—as well as a "cognitive sequence," which includes discrimination, categorization, and generalization. Barsch notes that the adequacy of feedback is essential to the development of movement efficiency. Movement and communication are viewed in an antecedent-consequent relationship; that is, communication depends upon the ability to process information from the various portions of the perceptocognitive system, an ability that, in turn, is dependent upon efficient movement patterns.

The Dimensions of Learning

From the postulates, Barsch (1967) derives 12 dimensions pertaining to human learning that serve as the areas constituting the educational curriculum.

Postural-Transport Orientations. The first four dimensions of learning deal with control of the body and movement through space. *Muscular strength*, the first dimension, provides support of the body and the initial impetus for such activities as rolling, crawling, sitting, and standing. Adequate muscular strength implies appropriate muscle tonus, power, and endurance, which, naturally, are expected to vary according to the individual's size and age. Given adequate muscular strength, the second dimension, *dynamic balance*, is necessary for overcoming the pull of gravity; a person may maintain posture by facilitating and inhibiting muscular contractions. The adjustments made in achieving dynamic balance are bilateral in nature because both sides of the body are brought into play, but bilaterality is considered a separate dimension and is only incidental to dynamic balance. The developing child who has acquired appropriate muscular strength and balance is "ready to move," but before the child can interact with the environment in a meaningful way he or she must arrive at the third dimension, *body awareness*, that distinction between self and not-self. As Barsch explains, the child must answer the question, "Who am I?" before he or she can answer the next question, "Where am I?" This leads to the fourth dimension, *spatial awareness*. The child integrates muscular strength with information regarding self, places, and positions, thereby moving both self and objects in accordance with his or her needs and environmental demands.

Perceptocognitive Modes. As children are learning to transport themselves in space, they are learning simultaneously to process information from the four primary modalities, the tactual, kinesthetic, auditory, and visual modes. Barsch (1967) states that the modes are not considered senses but are functional channels of reception and expression, although each mode has a sensory component. The fifth dimension, *tactual dynamics*, is defined as the ability of children to process information gained from the cutaneous surface of their bodies. According to Barsch, tactual dynamics implies a process, not the simple sense of touch; but his discussion of the dimension appears to be confined to tactile stimulation and discrimination. All parts of the body are involved, and all kinds of tactile stimulation such as heat, texture, and pressure are discussed. Touch is divided into two types: active touch, in which the child reaches out for contact, and passive touch, in which the child receives contact. It is somewhat difficult, however, to distinguish the types of touch on physiological or developmental bases.

Kinesthesia, which constitutes the sixth dimension, refers to the ability to feel movement, to remember movement patterns, and to integrate the perceptual and cognitive elements of movement sequences. Barsch views kinesthesia as a "function of tactuality and proprioception with the added ingredient of a specific perception of movement to bring the action of the body to a full state of meaning" (Barsch, 1965b, p. 24). Tactual dynamics and kinesthesia thus complement one another; kinesthesia may be necessary to bring the body into contact with another surface, but the perception of contact is primary, and kinesthesia only facilitates the act.

The seventh dimension of learning is *auditory dynamics*, composed of the perception of sound and the expression of a communication system. The dimension is defined as the ability to process information from the world of sound, that is, to receive and to express. Other than dividing audition into receptive and expressive components and noting the absence of hearing loss in most learning disabled children, Barsch devotes little time to the auditory process. In essence, he says that the "individual must find some way of gaining meaning from the acoustic energy that impinges on his tympanic membrane and passes through the auditory neurologic system" (Barsch, 1965b, p. 23).

Barsch's discussion of auditory dynamics is sparse, but the eighth dimension, *visual dynamics*, is described in great detail (1967). This dimension encompasses far more than vision or sight alone. It includes visual tracking and steering, the visual definition of the limits of surroundings, the discrimination of the details of a task, and the interpretation of the relationship between details of more than one task. Vision describes distance and the relationship of objects in space. "Vision defines distance, color, relationships, textures—and becomes the *true integrating agent* for touch, kinesthesia and audition" (Barsch, 1965b, p. 7; our italics). No single statement could better exemplify the emphasis that Barsch places on the visual processes. Neither Kephart nor Frostig considers vision to be of such primary importance in learning and development, although they do not discuss the auditory processes in detail.

Degrees of Freedom. The last four dimensions of learning set forth by Barsch "represent those factors which enlarge, enrich, expand, and explicate the performance efficiency of all others" (1965b, p. 8). The ninth dimension is *bilaterality*, the ability to perform efficient, reciprocal movement patterns on both sides of the body midline. In contrast to the findings of Orton (1937), Kephart (1971), and Delacato (1959), Barsch states that most of the children he saw were firmly one-sided and could not perform adequately when using the nonpreferred side of the body. The dimension of bilaterality is included to ensure smooth, coordinated movement of the body as a whole. The 10th dimension, *rhythm*, is the ability to coordinate and synchronize movements of the body to achieve harmony and grace. Patterns of movement are labeled arhythmic, dysrhythmic, and rhythmic; the underlying factor is apparently temporal sequencing of movements. Arhythmic movements are random and diffuse, while dysrhythmic movement is jerky and spasmodic. Rhythmic movement is graceful and occurs in a well-defined temporal sequence.

Flexibility, the ability to modify or shift patterns of movement in an appropriate fashion, constitutes the 11th dimension. In order to facilitate the modification or shifting of movement patterns, children must have at their command a repertoire of responses that enable them to change as the situation dictates. The modifications discussed by Barsch are speed, direction, force, and time, all of which must be available to the children as alternative choices when they are faced with the necessity for changing a movement pattern. The 12th and final dimension is *motor planning*, which "requires a knowledge of one's own movement repertoire and some spatial estimate of the presented demand"; this is concerned primarily with planning rather than execution of the movement. Such planning necessitates forethought as preparation for movement and, according to Barsch, may be thought of as cognitive rehearsal.

The dimensions in the category degrees of freedom are those leading to outstanding performance in motor areas and are exemplified in professional athletes.

The 12 dimensions were employed by Barsch (1965b) in constructing a curriculum for children with learning disabilities that was sponsored by the Wisconsin State Department of Public Instruction and was used experimentally at Longfellow School in Madison.

The Movigenic Curriculum

The curriculum devised by Barsch is based directly upon the 12 dimensions of development and learning discussed above. No provision is made in the curriculum for differential treatment of individual children; instead, the program assumes that each child will receive instruction in each dimension and that no other program will be included. Each dimension is now defined in Barsch's words, and the activities he suggests are given.

Dimension I—Muscular Strength. Muscular strength is "the capacity of the organism to maintain an adequate state of muscle tonus, power and stamina to meet the daily demands appropriate to his body size and chronological age" (Barsch, 1965b, p. 15). The activities suggested for improvement of muscular strength are those that would be included in most physical education programs for young children. A variety of exercises is recommended along with specific instruction in positioning the body for jumping, lifting, pushing, balancing, and so forth.

Dimension II—Dynamic Balance. Barsch states that "dynamic balance is the capacity of the organism to activate antigravity muscles in proper relationship to one another against the force of gravitational pull to maintain alignment, sustain his transport pattern and aid in recovery" (1965b, p. 16). To aid in recovery of balance, the child may use balance boards, imitate animal gaits, and learn to move about a darkened room avoiding obstacles. Walking rails are recommended to teach the maintenance of alignment; also used are twisting, turning, and spinning activities. The child learns to sustain a transport pattern by walking, hopping, tiptoeing, and so on, to the beat of a metronome or tom-tom, by performing these same activities on the walking rail and by maneuvering on a scooter board, or on abdomen or knees, or while sitting.

Dimension III—Spatial Awareness. According to Barsch, "spatial awareness is the capacity of the organism to identify his own position in space relative to his surround with constant orientation to surface, elevation, periphery, back and front" (1965b, p. 18). The activities for training in spatial awareness are arranged in eight categories:

1. *Rotation in space.* The children turn in the direction they are commanded: left, right, toward various objects in the room while imitating the teacher, later without watching the teacher.

2. *Labeling directions in space.* The children follow the teacher's directions to point up, down, to the side, and so on, in relation to parts of their own bodies.

3. *Basic lateral patterning in space.* The children are taught to imitate the tonic neck reflex pattern.

4. *Visualization of space.* Activities consist of describing objects when blindfolded and recalling the identity and position of objects.

5. *Reorganization of space.* The children are taught to form new designs from materials arranged in patterns by the teacher. Activities progress from rearranging furniture in the classroom to creating designs using geometric forms, word lists, or parquetry blocks.

6. *Reproduction of designs in space.* Designs formed in a great variety of materials are copied by the children.

7. *Rolling in space.* The synchronization of the four-count roll is taught, that is, on the count of one, two, three, four the child lifts the head, turns the shoulder, raises the hips, and rolls over.

8. *Variable transport in space.* The children walk, run, jump, and perform other transport activities in many different directions in the room.

Dimension IV—Body Awareness. "Body awareness is the capacity of the organism to achieve a conscious appreciation of the relationship of all body segments to movement, to be able to label body parts and to appreciate the functional properties of various body parts" (Barsch, 1965b, p. 19). One series of activities is intended to develop body image and consists of games like "Simon Says," finger games, figure drawings, and identification of body parts. Another series of exercises used in training body awareness is designed to teach the children how various parts of the body function. Exercises are devoted to teaching relaxation and the movement of discrete body parts in isolation as well as an explanation of function taught didactically through questions such as, "What do you see with?" and "What do you walk with?"

Dimension V—Visual Dynamics

Visual dynamics is the capacity of the organism to fixate accurately on a target at near, mid and far points in space, to scan a surround for meaning in the vertical and horizontal planes, to converge and accommodate, to equalize the use of both visual circuits in a binocular pattern to achieve fusion and to steer the body in proper alignment for movements through space. (Barsch, 1965b, p. 20)

The activities for training in visual dynamics suggested by Barsch are grouped in five sections: steering, tracking, attention, shifting, and memory.

1. *Visual steering.* Although visual steering is included in many of the activities given in following sections, a few are recommended as being specifically related to steering, for example, using visual targets when walking, rolling, or walking the rail and when throwing bean bags.

2. *Visual tracking.* Any activities that require children to follow a moving target with their eyes are suitable for training in this area.

3. *Sustained attention.* While in a darkened room, the children focus their attention on a light beam and keep their eyes on that spot as long as the light remains.

4. *Visual shifting.* The activities recommended in this area are similar to those described for visual tracking, the primary difference being that the children must shift their eyes from one visual target to another as quickly and as smoothly as possible.

5. *Visual memory.* Tachistoscopic slides, also used for visual shifting, are recommended to train visual memory. Other activities included are the recall of a number of objects previously seen and the answering of such questions as, "What color is a lemon?" and "Can you tell me something that is red?"

Dimension VI—Auditory Dynamics. Barsch (1965b) defines auditory dynamics as "the capacity of the organism to process information on a receiving and a sending basis from the world of sound and to attach appropriate relationships to the world of sound" (p. 22). Activities suggested in this area are aimed at improving receptive and expressive audition through imitation, discrimination, and comprehension tasks. The exercises are not presented in a developmental fashion; instead they seem appropriate to a language enrichment program.

Dimension VII—Kinesthesia. "Kinesthesia is the capacity of the organism to maintain an awareness of position in space and to recall patterns of movement from previous experience for utility in resolving continuing demands" (Barsch, 1965b, p. 23). Exercises for improving kinesthesia are related to gross and fine movement patterning. Activities for gross motor patterning include rolling; homologous, homolateral, and cross-diagonal crawling; angels-in-the-snow; and writing in the air with hands, elbows, or feet. To improve fine movement patterning, some suggestions are using pegboards, cutting with scissors, and blowing and catching bubbles. Several exercises described in the sections devoted to spatial awareness and body awareness are also appropriate.

Dimension VIII—Tactual Dynamics. Barsch says "tactual dynamics encompass the capacity of the organism to gain information from the cutaneous contact of active or passive touching" (1965b, p. 25). All activities described in this dimension are related to teaching children to discriminate and identify tactual stimuli whether they are touching or being touched. They are taught to identify by touch alone geometric shapes, scraps of material (texture), temperature, and whole objects. Many of the activities require that children identify stimuli with their bare feet.

Dimension IX—Bilaterality.   Barsch describes bilaterality as "the capacity of the organism to reciprocally interweave two sides in a balanced relationship of thrusting and counterthrusting patterns around the three coordinates of vertical, horizontal and depth in proper alignment from initiation to completion of a task" (1965b, p. 27). All of the activities that Barsch suggests in this dimension require bilateral movements: The child writes or draws with both hands, imitates bilateral movements of the teacher, and performs a variety of exercises with alternating sides of the body and then with both sides simultaneously.

Dimension X—Rhythm.   "Rhythm is the capacity of the organism to synchronize patterns of movements according to situational demands, thus achieving harmony, grace and use of movement" (Barsch, 1965b, p. 28). Any rhythmic activity utilizing metronomes, tom-toms, clapping, tapping, and the like, and manifested in walking, running, singing, choral speaking, and so on, would be appropriate for improving performance in the dimension of rhythm.

Dimension XI—Flexibility.   According to Barsch, "flexibility is the capacity of the organism to modify or shift patterns of movement appropriate to the situational demand" (1965b, p. 29). The exercises to improve flexibility are the same as those described in the other dimensions, the only difference being the shifting of patterns as dictated by the teacher. Therefore, no specific suggestions are described.

Dimension XII—Motor Planning.   "Motor planning is the capacity of the organism to plan a movement pattern prior to execution in order to meet the demands of a task" (Barsch, 1965b, p. 29). Again, no specific descriptions of activities to improve motor planning are given because the exercises are the same as those recommended in other dimensions of the program. To facilitate motor planning while performing the various exercises, the teacher reminds the children to plan their movement and then to check their plans against what happened when they moved.

Like the approaches of authors discussed previously in this chapter, Barsch's orientation remains essentially nonlanguage, the primary emphasis being upon perceptual-motor learning. The child who exhibits delays in motor and/or visual-perception development may benefit from these programs, but the child with a severe auditory receptive language disorder can profit most from the language development systems of Barry, McGinnis, and Myklebust.

FROSTIG: A LEARNING THROUGH MOVEMENT APPROACH

Marianne Frostig was born in Austria in 1906. She and her family came to the United States in 1939 just after the outbreak of World War II. She taught school in the daytime and continued her education at night. She received a master's degree from Claremont Graduate School (1949) and a PhD in educational psychology from the University of Southern California (1955). She founded the Marianne Frostig Center of Educational Therapy in Los Angeles in the early 1950s and served as its executive director until she retired in 1972. The center was set up to provide professional training and treatment of children with learning disabilities. Marianne Frostig died on June 21, 1985, in West Germany after suffering a stroke while on a lecture trip. Readers who desire more details about Dr. Frostig are referred to a tribute to her written by Phyllis Maslow (1985), a long-time colleague.

Frostig's work in visual perception gained national recognition. The recognition was based in part on the fact that she, with others, had designed a widely used test of visual perception and a training program to accompany this measure. One should not assume, however, that Frostig's interest in visual perception results in a remedial approach that emphasizes that process to the exclusion of others. On the contrary, Frostig's writings (1966, 1967a, 1967b, 1968, 1972a, 1972b, 1973, 1976; Frostig & Maslow, 1968, 1973) show increased concern for the treatment of auditory, language, cognitive, and academic problems. Her concern with motor learning in particular has led to the publication of an activities manual (Frostig, 1970) and some materials (Frostig, 1969) in the area of movement education.

Recognizing that perceptual adequacy may be fundamental to academic success, Frostig's main interest centers on the development of perceptual skills rather than on providing instruction specifically in reading, spelling, and writing. Even when academic subjects are taught, their perceptual aspects are emphasized.

Although Frostig (1967a) maintains that knowledge of subject matter is important, she does not think this knowledge alone provides enough information to formulate optimal educational programs for learning disabled children. A detailed analysis of the learner cannot be neglected; styles of learning, preferred sensory channels, and areas of perceptual and cognitive deficits or strengths must be determined if the child is to be taught effectively. Once sufficient information about the learner has been acquired, curricula may be adapted, selected, or developed that are appropriate to the child.

The Developmental Test of Visual Perception

According to Frostig and Horne, perception is one of the prime psychological functions without which "all but the simplest body functions, such as breathing and elimination, would stop and survival would be impossible" (1964, p. 7). In short, perception is the ability to recognize stimuli, and it includes not only reception from outside the body but also the capacity to interpret and identify sensory impressions by correlating them with other experiences. Perception takes place not in the receiving organ (the eye, ear, etc.) but in the brain itself. Although no specific causative factor for inadequate perceptual development has been identified, Frostig and Horne have pointed out that a disability in visual perception may be the result of either delayed maturation, actual cerebral injury, or genetic and environmental factors.

Unlike some writers, Frostig as well as Getman and Barsch maintains that most learning is acquired through the visual channel; and if development in visual perception, which occurs between the ages of 3½ and 7½ years, is hindered, some cognitive deficits will result. Examples of possible handicaps include difficulty in recognizing objects and their relationship to each other in space as well as the development of distortions that make the world appear unstable and unpredictable. The acquisition of these and other perceptual problems increases the probability that the child will experience some degree of emotional disturbance and eventual academic failure

The test's development was a natural outgrowth of Frostig's expressed concern with the need for acquiring more detailed information about children with learning problems. The *Developmental Test of Visual Perception* (DTVP) (Frostig et al., 1964) was formulated to facilitate the early detection of visual perception impairments and addresses attention to both the degree and kind of deviation. The present discussion of the test includes (a) a description of the instrument itself and (b) an overview of standardization information.

Description of the Instrument. The measure, published originally in 1961, has had two revisions. Test items were constructed to interest children in the 3- to 9-year age range. Item analyses were used to sequence the items along an easy-to-difficult continuum. Administration time is less than an hour for either individuals or small groups of children.

Five subtests were developed in an attempt to measure a variety of visual perception skills. Criteria for inclusion of these particular perceptual abilities are the following:

1. They are critical for the acquisition of school learning.
2. They affect the total organism to a much greater degree than some other functions, such as color vision or pure tone discrimination.
3. They develop relatively early in life.
4. They are frequently disturbed in children diagnosed as neurologically handicapped.
5. They are suitable for group testing.
6. And, we have observed that training in these areas is very frequently successful. (Frostig, Lefever, & Whittlesey, 1961, p. 384)

The five relatively independent areas of visual perception that constitute the subtests of the current form of the Frostig test are (a) eye-motor coordination, (b) figure-ground, (c) form constancy, (d) position in space, and (e) spatial relations.

1. *Eye-Motor or Visual-Motor Coordination.* The ability to integrate vision with movements of the body, particularly with the fine visual-motor skills necessary for success with pencil-and-paper activities, is involved in this subtest. Continuous

straight, curved, or angled lines are drawn between boundaries of various widths or from point to point without guidelines. One example of these tasks requires the child to draw a continuous pencil line between two pictures of houses without violating specified boundaries (Figure 15.7, part I). In Frostig's opinion, adequate visual-motor coordination is an important prerequisite for reading and is essential for writing.

2. *Figure-Ground.* This subtest is offered as a measure of the ability to select from a mass of stimuli a particular center of attention (the figure) and to disregard the rest of the stimuli (the ground). One task included in the test requires that the child outline in colored pencil the stars in a figure composed of superimposed stars and circles (Figure 15.7, part II). Confusion of the lines of the two forms may be indicative of a figure-ground difficulty. Frostig suggests that the ability to distinguish figure from ground is essential for the analysis and synthesis of written words, phrases, and paragraphs.

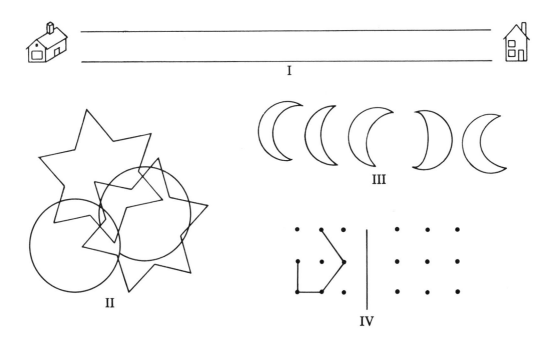

FIGURE 15.7. Selected items from the *Developmental Test of Visual Perception*. *Note*. From *The Marianne Frostig Developmental Test of Visual Perception* by M. Frostig, P. Maslow, D. W. Lefever, and J. R. B. Whittlesey, 1964, Palo Alto, CA: Consulting Psychologist Press. Reprinted by permission.

3. *Form Constancy.* The ability measured is that of recognizing that a figure may vary in size, texture, or position without altering its basic form. For example, a circle may have a half-inch or a one-inch diameter, but it remains a circle. In this instance the child is presented with a page on which a collection of forms is printed. One task requires that the child locate and outline as many circles as he or she can find. The circles, however, vary in size and texture and must be distinguished from other geometric forms. According to Frostig, adequate shape and size constancy is necessary for the recognition of familiar words seen in an unfamiliar context, color, size, or style of print.

4. *Position in Space.* Involved in this subtest is the ability to distinguish a particular form from other figures as it is presented in an identical, rotated, or reversed position. One task presents a series of printed quarter moons to the child, who is asked to specify the one that faces a direction different from the others (Figure 15.7, part III). Frostig maintains that mastery of position in space is needed to differentiate letters that have the same form but different positions—such as *b* and *d*.

5. *Spatial Relations.* The ability to perceive the position of two or more objects in relation to oneself and to each other is measured by this subtest. In one item the child is provided with an example in which lines have been drawn among nine points in such a way as to form a pattern. The task requires that the child duplicate the pattern (Figure 15.7, part IV). Spatial adequacy is assumed by Frostig to be necessary for the recognition of letters in a word and words in a sentence.

The DTVP yields two kinds of scaled scores: the Perceptual Quotient (PQ) and the Perceptual Age (PA). In addition, raw scores on the subtests may be converted to scaled scores. The PQ is indicative of the child's level of visual ability when compared with that of age-mates. A PQ of 90 is the suggested cutoff score below which a kindergarten child should receive special training. The distinction can be made, therefore, between children who may require training in visual perception and those who do not need special training. The PA, on the other hand, estimates the developmental level of the child. Since age equivalents are not related to chronological age, the PA in itself neither predicts the child's ability to profit from training nor indicates the need for training (Frostig et al., 1964). Thus the test is constructed to provide the educator with useful information that includes (a) an estimation of the overall visual perception adequacy of the child and (b) a delimination of the distinct perceptual areas in need of training.

Test Evaluation.   The DTVP was evaluated in *A Consumer's Guide to Tests in Print* (Hammill, Brown, & Bryant, 1989). In this source, the normative, reliability, and validity information included in a test's manual is rated by several experts in assessment. The DTVP total and subtests scores were all rated "F" by the raters. This means that the test is not recommended because its norms are old and not representative, its reliability is low, and its validity is poor.

Thorough reviews of the research that has accumulated over the years relative to the DTVP are available in Hammill and Wiederholt (1973), Larsen and Hammill (1975), and Hammill and Wiederholt (1971). In total, the conclusions of these reviews substantiate the "F" ratings found in the *Consumer's Guide*.

Frostig-Horne Program in Visual Perception

The following section contains a description of the Frostig-Horne training program and a discussion of its uses.

Description of the Training Program. While the Frostig test contributed to the diagnosis of the child's perceptual assets and disabilities, Frostig and Horne's (1964) materials provide a well-structured developmental program aimed at remediation of specific areas of perceptual weakness. The materials are recommended by Frostig for use with children in kindergarten and first grade as preparation for reading and other more complex visual activities as well as for use with children who have problems in perception. Modifications of the program are included in the manual for most types of exceptional children, and the procedure is set forth in explicit, carefully worded directions.

The program may be used remedially as well as developmentally. Remediation should begin immediately after evaluation of the visual perception areas, for early identification is necessary to prevent academic failure and concomitant emotional disturbance.

Not only does the program provide training in each of the five areas of measured visual perception, but it also suggests techniques for developing gross and fine muscle coordination, training eye movements, and enhancing body image and concept— skills that are basic to adequate perceptual functioning. In the Teacher's Guide (Frostig & Horne, 1964), these latter activities are arranged in order of difficulty under the five areas and are to be used to prepare the child for the fine motor paper-and-pencil worksheets or as supplemental techniques.

EYE-MOTOR. Children who have eye-motor problems experience difficulty when they reach for items, dress themselves, or attempt movements that depend heavily upon visual adequacy. The supplemental procedures, which involve eye movement training, are followed up by 90 Frostig worksheets. The exercises include coloring, tracing, and the drawing of straight, curved, or broken lines between boundaries that become increasingly more narrow and are ultimately eliminated by the end of this section.

FIGURE-GROUND. Problems in this area may cause the child to be disorganized and inattentive because of inability to screen out superfluous environmental stimuli. Numerous worksheets are provided that require the child to trace lines and to identify figures printed on increasingly complex backgrounds. Recognition of intersecting and hidden figures as well as figure completion and assembly activities are used in the training program.

PERCEPTUAL CONSTANCY. Inability of the child to perceive constancy of shapes and sizes can make the environment seem unstable and inconsistent. A familiar symbol may not be recognized when presented in a different color, size, form, or context. Worksheets provide exercise in the matching, discrimination, and categorizing of various forms and animals.

POSITION IN SPACE. Reversal problems such as the confusion of *b* and *d*, *42* and *24*, *on* and *no* frequently result from an inability to interpret position. Training in body image, body schema, and body concepts precedes the use of worksheets. In Frostig's program, awareness of the body's position in relation to objects is promoted by encouraging the child to crawl correctly under, over, and around various pieces of classroom furniture. Additional exercises are suggested that help develop the sense of directions in space, such as *right, left, before, behind, over,* and *under.* After the child can perform these activities successfully, worksheets are introduced.

SPATIAL RELATIONS. Disabilities in this area can make it impossible to sequence sufficient perceptual information for word writing, arithmetic, and map reading. Worksheets are provided that afford practice in visually oriented sequential problems such as figure completion, recall of sequence, assembly of parts, and figure copying. Exercises concerned with spatial relations are complex and to an extent involve the perceptual abilities of the other areas.

Evaluation of the Program. The positive tone and creative presentation of the worksheets elicit teacher enthusiasm, and the "games" that foster high motivation and help maintain success furnish step-by-step progression in terms of difficulty and flexibility. These techniques make it possible for the child to progress at his or her own rate. In accordance with the present authors' experience, the work periods are sufficiently short to maintain the attention and tolerance of young children.

Use of the program is possible with a variety of groups of children who possess social-cultural, emotional, sensory, or neurological handicaps; it is useful also with groups who are heterogenous in terms of mental ability. When limitations of the program are considered, acknowledgment is made that although perceptual training helps prepare a child for higher cognitive development, such training does not ensure successful performance in higher cognitive processes. Seldom is a program comprehensive enough to meet the many needs of the developing child; instead, it must be used in combination with other programs and activities for maximum growth and development. However, Frostig's program is one of the few organized approaches to the assessment and remediation of these difficulties, and many educators faced with the assessment and remediation of perceptual disorders use it. Readers who require a detailed discussion concerning the Frostig test and the efficacy of Frostig and Horne's visual perceptual materials are referred to the reviews of Mann (1972) and Hammill and Wiederholt (1973).

Throughout the 1960s and 1970s, Frostig's opinions about the role of visual perception and movement in learning disability assessment and training were very popular. Unfortunately, they were so prominent that Frostig's less controversial ideas about education were overshadowed. In time, her concepts about the importance of teaching the whole child in an individualized curriculum went unnoticed as she increasingly became associated in the public's mind with advocating unilateral perceptual-motor training as a precursor to academic objectives (Smith, 1985).

Over the years, interest in Frostig's perceptual-motor theories has diminished considerably. Both her test and the Frostig-Horne program are rarely used today. In addition, Bennett Ross (1988), executive director of the Frostig School which was founded by Frostig, asserts that while the program at the school remains committed to Frostig's positions relative to individualized whole child–centered instruction, it is no longer tied to her visual-motor model of special education.

AN APPRAISAL OF PERCEPTUAL-MOTOR TRAINING

Of all the instructional systems reviewed in this book, those associated with perceptual-motor training have stimulated by far the most research. In particular, the theories and techniques of Delacato, of Ayres, of Kephart, and of Frostig have been thoroughly investigated. While many experiments have been designed and executed to test the validity of the theoretical assumptions that underlie these systems—for example, that visual discrimination, eye-hand coordination, and motor efficiency, among other abilities, are significant correlates of school success—an impressive number of investigations have studied the effectiveness of the training activities themselves. As this latter research has an obvious relevance for teachers and clinicians, it will be reviewed in some depth.

Our search of the literature located more than 200 studies that were concerned with the effects of perceptual-motor training of children's various abilities. From these we eliminated the ones that used a case history approach, that employed fewer than 10 experimental subjects, and that included neither a control nor a contrast group. We recognize that the case history approach and the noncontrolled investigation have many uses in educational and psychological research. They are excellent procedures for the generation of hypotheses about children's learning and training, but they are totally unsuitable for testing the efficacy of treatments because they fail to account adequately for maturation. For example, as a group, kindergarten children will improve significantly in perception ability during the school year whether or not they receive special improvement exercises. The question is: How much improvement is due to the special program and how much is due to maturation? The use of a control group is the most expeditious way to answer this question.

In all, 109 suitable studies, that is, studies that used control groups and more than 10 experimental subjects, were found. Of these, 85 dealt with the activities recommended by authors reviewed in this chapter. These latter studies are reviewed in this section. The remaining studies evaluated programs that had been designed by individual researchers expressly for use in their experiments and therefore could not be used in our review.

Though there are notable exceptions, for the most part this research is poorly designed and probably poorly executed as well. We are therefore tempted to list the sources of experimental invalidity in each study as Robbins and Glass (1968) have done for many studies relating to Delacato's techniques, or at least to indicate to the reader those studies in which there exist sources or possible sources of significant error as Hallahan and Cruickshank (1973) have done in their review of 42 perceptual training studies. The shortcomings of each study could be duly noted. Instances could be indicated

1. where subjects were not randomly assigned to treatment groups;

2. where in fact the treatment groups were not even equivalent at the time of the pretest on the variables being studied;

3. where the researchers concluded that the experimental subjects had outperformed their controls when the difference between them was due entirely to the regression of the control subjects rather than to the improvement of the trained subjects;

4. where Hawthorne, that is, novelty, effect was not adequately accounted for;

5. where the number of subjects was too few and the duration of the program was too short;

6. where improvements were noted in reading or IQ and not in the perceptual and/or motor skills being trained;

7. where the teacher-pupil ratio differed drastically between groups, which resulted in the experimental pupils getting more individualized attention and support than their "match" controls;

8. where it was impossible to tell just how many hours of training each child received;

9. where individuals who were already committed to, that is, believed in, the merits of the experimental program provided the training;

10. where the data were analyzed in such a manner that the success of the program was indicated when the selection of a different analysis would result in a contrary conclusion (e.g., $E_{pre} - E_{post}$ comparison is significant; $C_{pre} - C_{post}$ comparison is not significant; while $E_{post} - C_{post}$ comparison is not significant); and

11. where as many as 20% or more of the subjects simply "disappeared" during the experimental period without any explanation.

Instead of discussing the shortcomings of each study and thereby discrediting its results, we chose to accept the findings of all these studies at face value, at least for the purposes of this evaluation. In so doing, we recognize that we have biased our analyses *in favor of* the experimental programs; we therefore caution the reader that our conclusions are likely to represent *overestimations* of the programs' value. Evidence supporting our position on this matter is available in the work of Hallahan and Cruickshank (1973). They designated which of the 42 studies that they reviewed were free from possible sources of methodological error. It was therefore possible to arrange a 2 × 2 chi-square matrix depicting the presence or absence of potential errors on one axis and positive or negative findings on the other. Our analysis yielded a highly significant chi-square, which means that the better designed research, as defined by Hallahan and Cruickshank, is more likely to produce negative findings than the poorly designed research (only 23% of the comparisons associated with the "better" research indicated that training was beneficial, while 76% of the "poor" research supported training).

Also, instead of selecting several of the best studies and describing their procedures and findings in detail, an approach that would necessitate our justifying why this or that study was selected for review, we have decided to analyze collectively a considerable number of research studies relating to the efficacy of the systems advocated by those professionals whose work is the subject of this chapter. While we recognize that there are many studies that have inadvertently escaped our search and some studies that were not readily available to us—for example, unpublished reports and master's theses—we do believe that a representative sample of the literature has been located.

The characteristics of these investigations have been condensed and presented in tabular form in Table 15.6. An example of how the table should be read follows. "In 1973, Klanderman studied the effects of a composite Kephart-Barsch-Cratty program on the sensorimotor, readiness, academic, and cognitive abilities of normal kindergarten-aged children. No significant differences were found between trained and control children in any ability area studied."

The reader will note the frequent use of the abbreviation "UTE." This stands for "unable to estimate." It is used in those cases when it was difficult or impossible to determine the type of children used or their grade levels. Understandably, these omissions were especially common in research that was reported in brief notes or in *Dissertation Abstracts*.

While literally dozens of tests, checklists, and observational devices were used as criterion measures in these studies, we have grouped them into five categories: sensorimotor, visual-motor, readiness, academics, and cognitive-language. All criterion measures that related to gross motor development, directionality, laterality, body image, or "neurological organization" were assigned to the sensorimotor category (e.g., the *Purdue Perceptual-Motor Survey*, the *Lincoln-Oseretsky Motor Development Scale*, and the *Benton Left-Right Discrimination Test*). Tests that tapped visual discrimination, memory, and spatial relations were assigned to the Visual-Motor category (e.g., *Developmental Test of Visual-Motor Integration*, the *Developmental Test*

TABLE 15.6. Characteristics of Visual Perception Training Studies

Researcher	Type of Subjects	Grade Level	Approach	Categories				
				Sensori-motor	Visual-Motor	Readiness	Academics	Cognitive-Language
Alcuin (1966)	Poor Readers	Elementary-Jr. High	Delacato				+	
Allen et al. (1966)	Educables	UTE	Frostig	0	0			
Alley (1968)	Educables	Elementary	Frostig	0	0		0	0
Alley and Carr (1968)	Educables	Elementary	Kephart		0		0	0
Alley et al. (1968)	Disadvantaged	Kindergarten	Frostig		0	+/0		
Anderson (1965)	Learning Prob.	Elementary	Delacato				0	
Anderson (1965)	Normal	Kindergarten	Delacato			0		
Anderson & Stern (1972)	Poor Readers/Poor in Visual Perception	Elementary	Frostig		0			
Arciszewski (1968)	Normals	Elementary	Frostig		0		0	
Armbruster (1973)	Normals	Kindergarten	Getman-Kephart Delacato			0		
Ayres (1968)	BI/Low Achievers	Elementary	Ayres	0	0		0	0
Ayres (1972c)	Poor Percep.-Motor	Elementary	Ayres	+	+		+/0	+
Ayres (1972c)	Aud.-Lang. Dis.	Elementary	Ayres	+	+		+/0	+
Ball and Edgar (1967)	Normals	Kindergarten	Kephart	0	+			0
Beck and Talkington (1970)	Disadvantaged	Kindergarten	Frostig		0			0
Bennett (1968)	Normals	Elementary	Frostig		+		0	+
Bosworth (1968)	Normals	Kindergarten	Kephart-like		+	0		
Buckland and Balow (1973)	Low in Readiness	Elementary	Frostig		0	0	0	
Burke et al. (1974)	Normals	Elementary	Getman		0	0	0	
Cohen (1966)	Poor Readers/Poor in Vis. Perception	Elementary	Kephart-like		+		0	
Cowles (1968)	Normals	Elementary	Frostig			+		
Cratty and Martin (1971)	Low in Achievement	Elementary	Cratty	0	0		0	0
Eason (1973)	Normals	Kindergarten	Kephart	0				0
Edgar et al. (1969)	Retarded	Preschool/Elementary	Kephart-like					+
Elmore (1973)	Poor in Vis. and Aud. Percep.	Kindergarten	Frostig		0			
Emmons (1968)	Disadvantaged	Elementary	Kephart			0		0

(Continued)

TABLE 15.6. *(Continued)*

Researcher	Type of Subjects	Grade Level	Approach	Sensori-motor	Visual-Motor	Readiness	Academics	Cognitive-Language
Emmons (1968)	Disadvantaged	Elementary	Getman			0	0	0
Falik (1969)	Low in Readiness	Kindergarten	Kephart-like		0	0	0	
Faustman (1967)	Normals	Kindergarten	Kephart-Frostig		0		+	
Fisher (1971)	Educables	Elementary	Kephart	0			0	0
Forgnone (1966)	Educables	Elementary	Frostig		+		0	0
Fortenberry (1968)	Disadvantaged	Elementary	Frostig		0		0	0
Foster (1966)	Mixed Dominance Boys	Elementary	Delacato				0	0
Gamsky and Lloyd (1971)	Normals	Kindergarten	Frostig		+	+	+	
Garrison (1965)	Normals	Elementary	Kephart			0	0	
Geis (1968)	Poor Readers/Poor in Vis. Perception	Kindergarten	Kephart-Cratty, Frostig-like			0	+	
Getman and Kane (1964)	Normals	Elementary	Getman				+	
Glaeser et al. (1966)	Poor Readers	UTE	Delacato				+/0	+
Goodman (1973)	Orthopedics	Preschool	Kephart-Getman	0	0			
Hall and Deacon (1970)	Trainables	Elementary	Frostig		+/0		0	+/0
Halliwell and Solan (1972)	Normals	Elementary	Kephart-like			0	0	
Jacobs (1968)	Disadvantaged	Preschool/Kindergarten/Elementary	Frostig		+/0	0		
Kabot (1966)	Poor Readers	Elementary	Delacato					
Keim (1970)	Poor in Vis. Perception	Kindergarten	Kephart-like		0	0	0	0
Kershner (1968)	Trainables	Elementary	Delacato				+	+
Klanderman (1973)	Normals	Kindergarten	Kephart-Barsch-Cratty	0		0	0	0
Klein and Marsh (1969)	Poor Readers/Poor in Vis. Perception	Elementary	Frostig		0		0	
Lavin (1971)	Disadvantaged	Preschool	Delacato					0
Linn (1967)	Normals	Kindergarten	Frostig		+			
Litchfield (1970)	Poor Readers/Poor in Vis. Perception	Elementary	Kephart-Getman		0		0	0

(Continued)

TABLE 15.6. *(Continued)*

Researcher	Type of Subjects	Grade Level	Approach	Categories				
				Sensori-motor	Visual-Motor	Readi-ness	Aca-demics	Cognitive-Language
Maloney et al. (1970)	Trainables	Jr. High	Kephart	0				
Maslow et al. (1964)	Poor in Vis. Perception	Kindergarten	Frostig		+			
Masterman (1966)	Normals	Elementary	Delacato				0	
McBeath (1966)	Poor in Vis. Perception	Kindergarten	Kephart			0		
McBeath (1966)	Poor in Vis. Perception	Kindergarten	Frostig			0		
McBeath (1966)	Poor in Vis. Perception	Kindergarten	Kephart-Frostig			0		
McClanahan (1967)	Slow Learners	Elementary	Frostig		+		+	0
McClanahan (1967)	Educables	Elementary	Frostig		0		0	0
McCormick et al. (1969)	Normals/Poor	Elementary	Kephart-Delacato				0	
McCormick et al. (1969)	Poor Readers	Elementary	Kephart-Delacato				+	
Meyerson (1967)	Poor in Vis. Perception	Kindergarten	Kephart		0	0		
Miracle (1966)	Poor Readers	Elementary	Delacato				+	
Mould (1965)	Poor Readers/Poor in Vis. Perception	UTE	Frostig		+		+/0	
O'Connor (1969)	Normals	Elementary	Kephart	+/0	0	0	0	
O'Donnell and Eisenson (1969)	Trainables	Elementary	Delacato		0		0	
Painter (1966)	Normals	Kindergarten	Kephart-Barsch		+			
Pryzwanksi (1972)	Normals	Kindergarten	Kephart			0		
Pryzwanksi (1972)	Normals	Kindergarten	Frostig			0		
Raven and Strubing (1968)	Normals	Elementary	Frostig				+/0	0
Rice (1967)	Retarded-Orthopedic	UTE	Frostig		+		0	
Ritz (1970)	Normals	Kindergarten	Frostig		+	0		
Roach (1966)	Slow Learners	Elementary	Kephart	0			0	0
Robbins (1966)	Normals	Elementary	Delacato				0	0

(Continued)

TABLE 15.6. (Continued)

				Categories				
Researcher	Type of Subjects	Grade Level	Approach	Sensori-motor	Visual-Motor	Readi-ness	Aca-demics	Cognitive-Language
Rosen (1966)	Normals	Elementary	Frostig		+	0	0	
Rutherford (1964)	Normals	Kindergarten	Kephart			+/0		
Ryan (1973)	Poor in Read/Perc.	Elementary	Kephart-Getman	0	+/0		+/0	
Ryan (1973)	Poor in Read/Perc.	Elementary	Kephart-Getman	0	0		+/0	+/0
Sherk (1968)	Poor Readers	UTE	Frostig		0		0	
Simpkins (1970)	Normals	Kindergarten	Frostig			0		
Stone and Pielstick (1969)	Normals	Kindergarten	Delacato		+	0		0
Sullivan (1972)	Poor Readers	Elementary/Sr. High	Kephart				0	
Talkington (1968)	Trainables	Jr. High	Frostig		+			
Turner and Fisher (1970)	Disadvantaged	Kindergarten	Kephart	0	0	+		0
Vivian (1966)	Normals	Elementary	Delacato				+	
Wiederholt and Hammill (1971)	Disadvantaged/Poor in Vis. Perception	Kindergarten/Elementary	Frostig		0	0	0	
Wimsatt (1967)	Normals	Kindergarten/Elementary	Kephart				+/0	0

of Visual Perception, the *Perceptual Forms Test*, the *Bender Visual-Motor Gestalt Test*, the *Southern California Figure-Ground Test*, and the *Seguin Form Board Test*). All tests of school readiness, such as the Metropolitan, Gates-MacGinitie, and Brenner, and of school achievement, such as the Stanford, Iowa, Metropolitan, and Durrell, were assigned to the Readiness and the Academics categories, respectively. The Cognitive-Language category was composed of tests like the *Peabody Picture Vocabulary Test*, the *Wechsler Intelligence Scale for Children*, the *Revised Stanford-Binet Intelligence Test*, the *Slosson Intelligence Test*, and the *Illinois Test of Psycholinguistic Abilities*, which measures various aspects of intelligence and language.

The researchers who implemented the 85 studies actually computed at least 500 different statistical comparisons between the performance of perceptually trained and nontrained subjects on the tests listed in the previous paragraphs. Where the differences were significant at the .05 level of confidence, we accepted them as evidence supporting the positive effects of training; where differences were not significant or where they favored the control group, they were taken as evidence that training was not beneficial.

It was possible, therefore, to classify each of the 85 studies in terms of its supportiveness of perceptual training in relation to the five categories of performance (e.g., sensorimotor, visual-motor, readiness, etc.). This has been done in Table 15.6 in the section titled Categories A: + means that the study's findings support the value of training; 0 indicates the contrary; +/0 means that the results are inconclusive, that is, mixed; blank spaces denote areas that were not investigated. For example, Forgnone (1966) reported that after training with the Frostig-Horne materials, his retarded subjects were significantly better in the visual-motor area than his non-trained subjects, but that no differences were found in the academics or cognitive-language areas. He did not investigate the effects of training on sensorimotor or readiness performance.

The findings of the 31 studies that evaluated the Frostig and Horne worksheets are summarized in Table 15.7. This approach has been studied more than any other single perceptual-motor training program. This interest is in part because the sequenced materials are easy to use in research projects and in part because Frostig has provided a convenient research tool in her *Developmental Test of Visual Perception*, a test that is conceptually related to the program. Approximately two-thirds of the results (i.e., analysis of the +'s, 0's and +/0's) recorded in Table 15.6 indicate that such training is ineffective; another 7% provided only mixed support for the program. The results are overwhelming regarding the lack of influence that the approach has had on readiness, academics, and cognitive growth. Inexplicably, only one study was concerned with the program's effects on sensorimotor performance.

Because the systems share many similarities, the 35 studies that utilized the programs of Kephart, Barsch, Cratty, Ayres, and Getman were combined for evaluation; and the results are presented in Table 15.8. As can be seen readily, 71% of the study's results failed to validate these approaches, and another 10% offered only scant support. As Delacato's techniques have been evaluated in only 17 studies, we thought that a special table to depict the overall results was not necessary. In light

TABLE 15.7. **Percentage of Positive, Mixed, or Negative Results Relative to Five Areas of Performance Reported for Studies that Evaluated the Frostig Approach (N = 31 Studies)**

Performance Area	Results			
	Positive "+"	Mixed "+/0"	Negative "0"	Total
Sensorimotor	—	—	—	1%
Visual-Motor	40%	8%	52%	43%
Readiness	20%	0%	80%	17%
Academics	13%	13%	74%	27%
Cognitive-Language	0%	13%	77%	14%
Total	25%	7%	68%	100%

TABLE 15.8. **Percentage of Positive, Mixed, or Negative Results Relative to Five Areas of Performance Reported for Studies that Evaluated the Kephart, Getman, Cratty, Ayres, and Barsch Approaches (N = 35 Studies)**

Performance Area	Results			
	Positive "+"	Mixed "+/0"	Negative "0"	Total
Sensorimotor	12%	6%	81%	18%
Visual-Motor	32%	5%	63%	21%
Readiness	7%	7%	86%	16%
Academics	18%	23%	59%	24%
Cognitive-Language	21%	5%	74%	21%
Total	19%	10%	71%	100%

of the previous paragraphs, one should not be surprised to learn that only a third of the findings supported the use of this system.

In reviewing the research, however, one *is* surprised to learn that while researchers have devoted much time and effort to testing Delacato's claims about the effect of neurological organization training on academics—especially reading—and intelligence, they have left relatively unexplored his contention that basic motor and perceptual-motor abilities can be successfully perfected through patterning exercises. In short, more research should investigate the effects of Delacato's motor training on the development of sensorimotor and visual-motor abilities. It is particularly unfortunate that additional work has not been done using this system. As it is, almost all of the positive research that is available comes from a single source, Delacato's book *Neurological Organization and Reading* (1966), in which five or six intervention studies are presented. As was mentioned earlier, Robbins and Glass (1968) have rather convincingly challenged the validity of all of these studies on methodological grounds. Research drawn from other sources is decidedly negative concerning the program's merits.

The results of four studies (Faustman, 1967; Geis, 1968; McBeath, 1966; McCormick, Schnobrinch, & Footlik, 1969) were not included in the evaluation because they used composite programs including relatively dissimilar elements, for example, selected activities from Frostig, Cratty, Delacato, and Kephart.

Let us be the first to point out that our evaluation, as presented here, is decidedly actuarial and should be taken with certain reservations. Admittedly, we have combined the results of studies that in many cases are quite dissimilar regarding characteristics of subjects, duration and hours of training, and so on. We have done this in order to "grossly" indicate to the reader the situation regarding perceptual training in the currently available research literature. If the reader objects in any way to the manner in which we have handled these research reports, we encourage him or her to take the individual studies listed in Table 15.6 and apply to them any methods of inquiry that seem appropriate. (We do imagine that the general conclusions will be similar to our own, however.)

As a consequence of our reviews of these systems, we would recommend that perceptual-motor training in the schools be carefully reevaluated. Unlike 25 years ago, when research on the topic was sparse, one can no longer assume that these kinds of activities will be beneficial to the children who engage in them. In fact, in the long run they may even be somewhat harmful because (a) they may waste valuable time and money and (b) they may provide a child with a placebo program when the child's problems require a real remedial effort. We would suggest that when these programs are implemented in the schools, they be considered as highly experimental, nonvalidated services that require very careful scrutiny and monitoring.

Our conclusions are reinforced by the work of Kavale and Mattson (1983), who meta-analyzed 180 studies that investigated the efficacy of perceptual-motor training. They found that, regardless of the subjects' characteristics, the types of programs used, the grade levels trained, or the statistical designs employed, the collective results were the same. That is, perceptual-motor training did not result in improvement of any of the academic, cognitive, or perceptual-motor variables studied. It appeared to them that existing research has demonstrated that "perceptual-motor training is not effective and should be questioned as a feasible intervention technique for exceptional children" (p. 165).

The positive findings reported in a few well-designed studies should not be brusquely disregarded, however. Such results suggest that under some presently unidentified conditions, perceptual-motor training might be effective. Future research studies using innovative, improved techniques may one day conclusively validate the existing training programs. Therefore, we recommend that further research efforts be undertaken and suggest that these be directed toward the following:

1. identifying the characteristics of children for whom training has been demonstrated to be beneficial;

2. determining the optimal amount and type of training necessary to produce real perceptual and/or motor growth; and

3. demonstrating that perceptual-motor processes can actually be improved as a result of training.

Until the merits of the activities have been clearly shown by carefully designed research, we maintain that these approaches must be viewed as highly experimental, non–data-based intervention strategies. In short, at this time we second the ideas expressed officially by The American Academy of Pediatrics, The American Academy of Ophthalmology, and The American Association of Ophthalmology and Strabismus. In *Pediatrics* (1972, *49*, pp. 454–455), they concluded:

> No known scientific evidence supports claims for improving the academic abilities of learning-disabled or dyslexic children with treatment based solely on:
> a. visual training (muscle exercises, ocular pursuit, glasses).
> b. neurologic organizational training (laterality training, balance board, perceptual training).
>
> Furthermore, such training may result in a false sense of security, which may delay or prevent proper instruction or remediation. The expense of such procedures is unwarranted.

In 1984, these organizations restated their strong position on the merits of visual-perceptual training in a policy statement titled "Learning Disabilities, Dyslexia, and Vision." A copy of this updated document is available in the appendix of this book.

PART IV

ADJUNCTIVE THERAPIES THAT INFLUENCE INSTRUCTION

This last section of the book presents three approaches to the amelioration of learning disabilities that for various reasons do not fit comfortably into the other sections. These are strategy training, behavioral approaches, and biomedical treatment. Previous chapters dealt with pedagogical approaches to the remediation of specific learning disabilities in the academic, linguistic, or correlate areas. The adjunctive therapies deal with generalized strategies that may be used in conjunction with the previously discussed methods or, as in the case of biomedical treatments, are not part of the instructional program.

The most recent approach to teaching students with learning disabilities is generally called strategy training. A good bit of the training is based upon sets of principles and a few techniques that have been developed in the past few years in the Institutes for Research on Learning Disabilities at the universities of Kansas and Virginia. Teachers will not find that these are formalized systems that they can readily implement, such as those of Gillingham or Fernald, but many helpful suggestions are given and a comprehensive bibliography is provided.

The behavioral systems discussed in Part IV are those of Thomas Lovitt and Frank Hewett. Neither of these provides a scope and sequence of content to be taught, but instead deals with levels of learning competence, stages of instruction, modification of behavior, ongoing assessment, physical arrangement of the classroom, and daily schedules. Many of these same principles are used by Gray and Ryan in their Programmed Conditioning for Language (PCL), but the major difference is that PCL also presents a detailed scope and sequence for the curriculum, and therefore that program is included in the chapter on remediation of listening and speaking disabilities.

The biomedical treatments discussed are not under the control of the teacher, although he or she may be asked to ensure that medication is administered appropriately or that a recommended diet is observed. Teachers must cooperate in implementing the treatment, observing the effects of medication or dietary regimens, and reporting to parents and/or physicians the results of their observations. Negative as well as positive results are important, and teachers should request that they be told about medications, changes in medication, unusual diets, or other biomedical treatments so that they can become informed observers and reporters.

16

COGNITIVE STRATEGY TRAINING WITH LEARNING DISABLED STUDENTS

Laurie U. deBettencourt

"There is absolutely no doubt that strategy instruction is a 'hot' topic in both regular and special education" (Pressley, Symons, Snyder, & Cariglia-Bull, 1989). Research examining the extent to which learning disabled students can be trained to use cognitive strategies to improve their performances has increased dramatically in the last 10 years (Swanson, 1989). Several lines of research concerning cognitive behaviors of children (e.g., metacognition, memory, and selective attention) have provided the impetus for cognitive strategy training with the learning disabled population.

Each perspective describes and defines cognitive strategy training in unique ways, thereby causing much confusion as to what constitutes strategy intervention. "It appears that strategy-training programs suffer from many of the same problems that have continued to plague the field of learning disabilities—problems of definition of terms, methodological issues, and subject selection" (deBettencourt, 1987, p. 29). Regardless of the confusion, most strategy research has converged on several issues.

What strategies improve LD students' academic learning? How should cognitive strategies be taught? Can learning strategies be taught so they generalize across academic settings? These questions embody issues that are being addressed by researchers in the field. In partial response to these issues, several cognitive strategy training models are reviewed in this chapter.

The strategy procedures addressed can be viewed as specific approaches for facilitating the use of acquisition, storage, or expression skills. The similarities between these strategy training procedures and study skills training methods often lead to confusion. Basically, cognitive strategy training is a form of study skills instruction. However, strategy training approaches may also be appropriately identified as subsets of cognitive skill instruction, a feature that does not necessarily apply to study skills. Essentially, study skills is a broad term under which learning strategy procedures are subsumed (Ellis & Lenz, 1987). We provide an overview of the impetus leading to the development of such cognitive strategy training procedures and discuss several such training model programs currently documented in the field.

AREAS OF RESEARCH UNDERLYING STRATEGY TRAINING

During the past 10 years, research in cognition provided the impetus for the development of specific teaching strategies for the instruction of learning disabled students. The following section does not provide a comprehensive review of the research but instead highlights research in metacognition, memory, and selective attention that is particularly pertinent to the development of strategy training.

Metacognition

Metacognition refers to individuals' awareness of their own cognitive performance and their use of this awareness in altering their own behavior (Flavell, 1970, 1979). Metacognition involves knowing about and controlling one's own thinking and learning. Metacognitive skills include self-monitoring, predicting, reality testing, and coordinating the processes of studying and learning. Learning disabled students' deficiency in applying strategies may be caused by their lack of awareness of when and how to use strategies (deBettencourt, 1987). As Loper (1982) suggested, the critical metacognitive variable may not be simply learning disabled children's cognitive abilities, but their application of such information.

Memory

Torgesen and his colleagues have conducted several investigations in the area of memory that suggest that learning disabled children's poor performance may, in part, be due to inefficient use of cognitive strategies (e.g., Torgesen & Goldman, 1977; Torgesen & Houck, 1980; Torgesen, Murphy, & Ivey, 1979). Results of these investigations support the hypothesis that many of the performance problems of disabled children may not stem from limited memory or learning capacity, but rather from a failure to apply efficient task strategies. When learning disabled children are instructed to use a strategy such as verbal rehearsal, they do approach tasks in an active manner (e.g., Torgesen et al., 1979).

Selective Attention

Inattention is a characteristic frequently attributed to learning disabled (LD) children. Hallahan and his colleagues at the University of Virginia (Virginia Learning Disabilities Research Institute) have extensively studied attention processes in children. The results of Virginia LDRI's investigations suggest that LD children exhibit a developmental lag in their selective attention abilities relative to their normal peers. Although learning disabled children do not routinely apply efficient strategies such as verbal rehearsal and chunking spontaneously, when trained to apply a cognitive strategy, they perform similarly to normal children (Dawson, Hallahan, Reeve, & Ball, 1980; Hallahan, Tarver, Kauffman, & Graybeal, 1978; Tarver, Hallahan, & Kauffman, 1976). Positive reinforcement also was shown to increase selective attention in learning disabled children (Hallahan et al., 1978). Thus, as with the metacognitive and memory research, the investigations in the area of selective attention suggest that LD children's poor performance may be due, in part, to inefficient use of cognitive strategies.

AN OVERVIEW OF COGNITIVE STRATEGY TRAINING

The three areas of research (i.e., metacognition, memory, and selective attention) discussed in the preceding section have provided an impetus for development of several cognitive strategy approaches. Many researchers have examined the importance of cognitive and metacognitive strategy training for increasing learning disabled students' academic learning potential. However, a precise understanding of what "cognitive strategy training" involves is rarely defined clearly. Each researcher/author defines his or her strategy training approach uniquely.

Paris and Oka (1989) define cognitive strategies as "enabling skills that promote effective reading because they are mental resources for students to use" (p. 40). Swanson (1989) conceptualizes strategy instruction within a broad instructional continuum. At one end of the instructional continuum, the teacher acts as the model and engineer of the instructional activity. As one moves along the continuum, the teacher's level of participation diminishes (e.g., Palincsar & Brown, 1987) and the learner's self-regulatory controls become more internalized. Alley and Deshler (1979) define learning strategies as "techniques, principles or rules that will facilitate the acquisition, manipulation, integration, storage and retrieval of information across situations and settings" (p. 13).

Learning strategies is most often a generic term used to describe a series of task-specific strategies that incorporate features of cognitive and metacognitive training (Ellis, Lenz, & Sabornie, 1987a). Often a learning strategy is composed of a set of self-instructional steps the student proceeds through to solve a problem. The steps cue students to use specific cognitive strategies (e.g., paraphrasing) or to employ metacognitive strategies (e.g., self-monitoring) (Ellis et al., 1987a). A mnemonic device is often employed to help the student remember the steps (see Figure 16.1).

Many learning strategies are designed to improve a student's academic performance by teaching how to acquire, manipulate, store, or retrieve knowledge. Some cognitive strategies overlap these areas. For example, a study skills strategy may instruct a student to identify the relevant information from the text and then to organize it in some way to facilitate memory. Although learning disabled students have been shown to have difficulty with such executive functions, studies (e.g., Warner, Schumaker, Alley, & Deshler, 1980) have shown that these students can learn to use cognitive strategies in controlled situations.

Swanson (1989) summarizes several universal principles characterizing effective cognitive strategy interventions. Following are a few of Swanson's principles that describe effective cognitive strategy instruction with learning disabled students.

Strategies serve different purposes. There are a number of ways in which different strategies can effect different cognitive outcomes. There is not necessarily a single best strategy.

Strategy instruction must operate on the law of parsimony. There are in the field a number of multiple-component strategy training packages. However, as Pressley (1986) suggested, good strategies are composed of only the *absolutely* necessary processes for accomplishing their intended goal.

Good strategies for non-LD students are not necessarily good strategies for LD students. Strategies that are appropriate for non-LD students may, in fact, be less effective for LD students.

RATIONALE FOR USE OF STRATEGY TRAINING PROCEDURES

Researchers have suggested that LD students appear to reach a learning plateau in high school that is equivalent to about a fourth- or fifth-grade achievement level (Deshler, Schumaker, Alley, Warner, & Clark, 1982). This achievement level is the point at which basic skills instruction generally stops and students move on to apply those skills to inferential reading comprehension, math applications, expository writing, and extensive use of content textbooks for learning science and social studies (Deshler, Warner, Schumaker, Alley, & Clark, 1984). Academic learning at this level requires that students know *how* to learn rather than just *what* to learn. Such strategic learning is essential for successful, efficient functioning in the regular classroom (Sheinker, Sheinker, & Stevens, 1988).

Teachers have long been aware of learning disabled students' lack of success in efficiently applying what they are taught in the resource room to tasks they

C = Create a list of items to be learned.
A = Ask self if the list is complete.
N = Note the main ideas from details using a tree diagram.
D = Describe each component and how components relate.
O = Overlearn the main parts first, supporting details last.

E = Elicit questions to identify important information.
A = Ask self questions to identify important information.
S = Study the easy parts first, hard parts last.
Y = Yes to self-reinforcement following each batch.

FIGURE 16.1. CAN-DO and EASY: Two strategies for learning content information. *Note.* From "Generalization and Adaptation of Learning Strategies to Natural Environments: Part 1: Critical Agents" by E. S. Ellis, B. K. Lenz, & E. J. Sabornie, 1987, *Remedial and Special Education 8*(1), p. 7. Reprinted by permission.

encounter in the regular classroom and in generalizing those skills from one task to another (Schumaker, Deshler, Alley, & Warner, 1983). Teachers and researchers alike have characterized the learning disabled student as a student with average intelligence yet who is an inefficient learner, that is, one who either lacks certain strategies or chooses inappropriate ones and, therefore, is unable to meet his or her academic potential (Torgesen, 1977).

Yet a number of researchers in learning disabilities agree that when learning disabled students are explicitly prompted to use strategies such as organizing a list of words or rehearsing a code to remember a step-by-step procedure, their performances improve (e.g., Palincsar & Brown, 1984; Torgesen, 1977). A number of training programs over the past few years indicate that cognitive strategies instruction can be an effective tool to help students become more efficient learners and to help students achieve beyond the basic skills level (e.g., Palincsar & Brown, 1984; Schumaker, Deshler, & Ellis, 1986; Wong, 1985). Learning disabled students are not necessarily strategy deficient, but rather are strategy inefficient or strategy inflexible.

The advantages of strategy training approaches for improving learning disabled students' academic performances are numerous. Primarily, they focus on instructional principles rather than internal processing deficiencies. Second, instructional procedures are based on effective instruction (Bickel & Bickel, 1986; Rosenshine, 1983) (see Figure 16.2). Third, strategy training approaches encourage the student to become actively involved in his or her learning activities. Fourth, strategy training approaches that include metacognitive training have provided learning disabled students with a motivational aspect to learning (Paris, Lipson, & Wixson, 1983; Paris & Oka, 1989). Finally, cognitive strategies may hold the greatest promise for spanning the distance between settings.

1. reviewing, checking previous day's work

2. presenting new content/skills

3. initial student practice (and checking for understanding)

4. feedback and corrections (and reteaching if necessary)

5. student independent practice

6. weekly and monthly reviews

FIGURE 16.2. Effective instructional components. *Note.* From "Teaching Functions in Instructional Programs" by B. V. Rosenshine, 1983, *Elementary School Journal, 83,* p. 337. Reprinted by permission.

STRATEGY TRAINING APPROACHES

A variety of new models of strategy training approaches have been proposed in recent years. Attention has focused on teaching cognitive strategies, metacognition about those strategies, and motivation to use such strategies (Pressley et al., 1989).

The following section discusses several strategy training models that have shown to be effective in improving learning disabled students' performances. By no means should the following section be considered an exhaustive review of relevant research; rather, we have selected recent approaches that represent promising practices with documented effectiveness that appear to have relevance for the practitioner.

Deshler's Strategies Intervention Model

One strategy training approach that meets the needs of many learning disabled adolescents is the learning strategies model Deshler and his colleagues have developed at the University of Kansas Institute for Research in Learning Disabilities (KU–IRLD) (see Alley & Deshler, 1979; Deshler, Schumaker, & Lenz, 1984; Deshler, Schumaker, Lenz, & Ellis, 1984). Deshler and his associates advocate instruction of a core group of strategies that promote the academic and social skills important for effective school functioning at the secondary level. The basis for their strategy model is the philosophy that secondary students who have learning disabilities should be provided with interventions based on cognitive psychology and learning theory (Deshler, Alley, & Carlson, 1980).

Deshler and his colleagues suggest that the traditional curriculum models offered to learning disabled students entering the elementary level are inadequate for secondary students because the administrative structure and curriculum demands of secondary schools are radically different. The KU–IRLD learning strategies are based on an intense analysis of high school requirements and demands, for example, self-questioning, error monitoring, visual imagery, test-taking skills, and paraphrasing (Lenz, Schumaker, Deshler, & Beals, 1984; Nagel, Schumaker, & Deshler, 1986; Schumaker, Denton, & Deshler, 1984).

Procedures. In a learning strategies intervention program, rather than teaching specific content, teachers teach students how to learn that content. Students are taught both how to learn and how to effectively use skills that are already in their repertoire (Schumaker et al., 1986). For example, students are taught test-taking skills that would apply to a test in social studies as well as a test in science. Studies conducted by the Kansas Institute for Research in LD have shown that an effective acquisition program for learning disabled adolescents consisted of a 10-step programming procedure (see Figure 16.3) (Alley & Deshler, 1979; Deshler et al., 1982).

A specific example of a learning strategy is Multipass. Multipass is a learning strategy designed to enable students to gain information from textbook chapters. In the Multipass strategy, students pass through a content chapter three times to familiarize themselves with the main ideas and organization of the passage, to gain specific information, and to test themselves on the chapter material. Schumaker, Deshler, Alley, Warner, and Denton (1982) investigated the use of the Multipass strategy with secondary learning disabled students, and their results suggest that after training in the use of the Multipass strategy the students could apply the strategy in ability-level textbooks used in their regular classes.

1. testing the student's current level of functioning

2. describing the steps of the strategy and providing a rationale for each step

3. modeling the strategy so the student could observe all of the processes involved in the strategy

4. verbal rehearsal of the steps of the strategy to 100% criterion

5. practice in controlled materials written at the student's reading ability level

6. positive and corrective feedback

7. testing in materials written at the student's reading ability level

8. practice in content materials from the students' grade placement level

9. positive and corrective feedback

10. posttest

FIGURE 16.3. Learning strategies 10-step procedure. *Note.* Adapted from "Learning Strategies: An Instructional Alternative for Low-Achieving Adolescents" by D. D. Deshler and J. B. Schumaker, 1986, *Exceptional Children, 52,* pp. 583–590.

Researchers at the KU–IRLD have developed several other strategies that train LD secondary students to increase their academic skills—for example, a self-questioning strategy that trains a student to read a passage and form visual images representing passage content. The student forms questions about the passage during reading in order to maintain interest and improve recall (Clark, Deshler, Schumaker, Alley, & Warner, 1984). Another example is the paraphrasing strategy in which the student is trained to paraphrase the main idea and important details of each paragraph.

Advantages. Two major advantages of the KU–IRLD learning strategies model are that (a) it allows students to use a strategy to attack situations not previously encountered (Ellis, Lenz, & Sabornie, 1987a, 1987b) and (b) it also places students in an interactive role with the content to be learned. The main strength of this model lies in its effect on generalized use (Ellis et al., 1987a, 1987b). Generalization is promoted through presentation of multiple exemplars at every phase of instruction. For example, students are repeatedly reminded where strategies can be used, and they are given guided practice at generalizing strategies to in-class assignments.

Also, throughout the instructional procedures, motivation plays a critical role. Students are made aware of the important role of the strategic skills they are acquiring, and the students play a role in choosing what strategies to acquire and which educational goals to target. In essence, the Kansas approach provides explicit, extensive, and intensive strategy instruction (Pressley et al., 1989).

Lloyd's Attack Strategy Training

Another strategy training approach that has been validated is an approach called academic or attack strategy training (Lloyd, 1980). Lloyd defined attack strategy training as teaching students a limited set of prerequisite skills and a system for using these skills in working through an academic problem to its solution. Lloyd's academic strategy emphasizes the use of curriculum analyses, task analyses, and instructional designs by teachers. Such strategies consist of steps through which students move to solve related academic problems.

Procedures. The procedures that one would follow to implement Lloyd's academic strategy training program are dependent on the curriculum in which the strategy would be used. For example, a student may be taught a system for solving single-digit division problems. Prior to the teaching of this system, the student would be taught multiplication facts, recognition of the division symbol, and other pertinent prerequisite skills. Such prerequisite skills (e.g., $8 \times 4 = 32$, $4 \times 4 = 16$), other component skills (e.g., divide the divisor into current dividend), and finally, the strategy for putting the skills together are taught (see Figure 16.4). Implementation of the strategy training is accomplished by the teacher modeling the procedure, providing corrective practice, and rewarding correct performances (see Lloyd & deBettencourt, 1982).

STRATEGY: (Using 3 + __ = 9 as an example)

Steps in Strategy	**Example**
1. Read the problem;	3 plus what equals 9?
2. Decide whether the missing addend strategy will work; IF not, select correct strategy: IF it will, continue;	yes, it will
3. Point to present addend and name it at beginning of counting;	3 . . .
4. a. Count, making marks for each count and b. Stop counting at the sum;	4, 5, 6, 7, 8 . . . 9;
5. Count number of marks;	1, 2, 3, 4, 5, 6 . . .
6. Write numeral for number of marks in answer space.	write 6.

ANALYSIS: The student would have to know:
        Number-numeral relationships;
        How to write numerals;
        How to count from a given number;
        How to stop counting at a given number;
        Names for signs (i.e., +, =);
        Decision rule for discriminating when to use simple and missing-addends strategies.

FIGURE 16.4. A missing-addends strategy and its analysis. *Note.* From *Academic Strategy Training: A Manual for Teachers* (p. 19) by J. Lloyd and L. U. deBettencourt, 1982, Charlottesville: University of Virginia Learning Disabilities Research Institute.

In this academic strategy approach, specific strategies are taught for use with specific types of academic problems. Major components required for effective implementation of any academic strategy training program include effective instructional techniques such as modeling, corrective feedback, and reinforcement.

Advantages. The following conclusions have been suggested by the research on the academic strategy training approach: (a) LD students can learn to use various strategies for attacking numerous academic tasks; (b) not only can strategies be taught in very short periods of time, but also students will continue to apply them correctly without further training; (c) it does not appear necessary for students to verbalize the steps in strategies; and (d) students can learn closely related strategies without confusing them (Lloyd, Cameron, Cullinan, Kauffman, & Kneedler, 1981; Lloyd, Kneedler, & Cameron, 1982; Lloyd, Saltzman, & Kauffman, 1981). The work of Lloyd et al. speaks clearly for the need to explicitly teach the prerequisite skills as well as the strategy for applying those skills to promote generalization. For a detailed explanation and description of procedures, one would need to implement academic strategy training programs in the classroom (see Lloyd & deBettencourt, 1982).

Hallahan's Self-Monitoring

Hallahan and his colleagues have studied the effects of self-monitoring on the attentional behavior and academic productivity of inattentive learning disabled children (see Hallahan & Sapona, 1983). Although this self-monitoring approach is not a direct academic strategy training procedure, it is a strategy intervention that promotes academic learning. If students are taught to effectively self-monitor their on-task behavior, the chances are good that their academic productivity will increase.

Procedures. The self-monitoring procedure consists of the following steps:

• the teacher operationally defines what is meant by on-task behavior and provides examples;

• the teacher models the procedures the student is to follow to self-assess and self-record if he or she is on-task;

• the student is cued by a signal (supplied by a tape-recorded sound at random intervals) and asks himself or herself, "Was I paying attention?" and records his or her evaluation on a special recording sheet (see Figure 16.5);

• the self-recording and cuing signals are faded as on-task behavior becomes established (see Hallahan, Lloyd, & Stoller, 1982).

This procedure is often put into practice during a student's independent seatwork period. Yet this self-recording procedure has been shown to be effective in group instruction settings (see Hallahan, Marshall, & Lloyd, 1981).

Such self-monitoring of on-task behavior by learning disabled elementary school-aged students with attentional problems has resulted in increased on-task behavior and, in some cases, improved academic productivity (Hallahan, Lloyd, Kosiewicz, Kauffman, & Graves, 1979; Hallahan, Marshall, & Lloyd, 1981). Self-monitoring procedures also were taught successfully to LD and non-LD students in a second-grade classroom (Rooney, Hallahan, & Lloyd, 1984).

Advantages. Although the self-monitoring strategy procedure involves training students to be on-task and is not a "direct" academic strategy training procedure, it is included in this chapter because of the advantages of such a procedure for increasing learning disabled students' academic productivity. Prior to academic learning taking place, learning disabled students must learn to attend to the academic task on hand.

Also as Rooney and Hallahan (1988) suggest, direct instruction in self-monitoring procedures may be a potential intervention to prepare academically ready learning disabled students for successful transitions to mainstream settings. Self-monitoring enables learning disabled students to perform acceptably with minimal adult assistance or interaction and thus may supply an essential component necessary for successful mainstreaming of some LD students.

DATE _____

WAS I PAYING ATTENTION?

	YES	NO
1		
2		
3		
4		
5		
6		
7		
8		
9		
10		
11		
12		
13		
14		
15		
16		
17		
18		
19		
20		

	YES	NO
21		
22		
23		
24		
25		
26		
27		
28		
29		
30		
31		
32		
33		
34		
35		
36		
37		
38		
39		
40		

FIGURE 16.5. Self-monitoring sheet. *Note.* From *Improving Attention with Self-Monitoring: A Manual for Teachers* (Appendix) by D. P. Hallahan, J. W. Lloyd, and L. Stoller, 1982, Charlottesville: University of Virginia Learning Disabilities Research Institute. Reprinted by permission.

Palincsar and Brown's Reciprocal Teaching Strategy Training

Another effective strategy training procedure enlists peers as tutors. Palincsar and Brown's reciprocal teaching approach involves teaching students to coach each other in applying effective reading strategies (Palincsar & Brown, 1984). Students are trained to pose questions, ask for clarification, make predictions, and construct summaries of text while reading. These four activities were selected because they provide a dual function, that of enhancing comprehension and at the same time affording an opportunity for the student to check whether it is occurring (Palincsar & Brown, 1984).

Procedures. Brown and Palincsar (1982) developed the reciprocal teaching procedure, where a teacher and student take turns leading a dialogue concerning sections of a text. The procedure involves the following steps:

1. *Locate the information.* Students read a passage and answer comprehension questions.

2. *Define the strategies.* Students are informed about the strategies they will use.

3. *Teach reciprocally.* Teacher and students discuss the story to be read and predict passage content, decide who will act as teacher, and read a portion of the passage.

4. *Explicate the need and means for generalization.* Students are informed of the rationale for the use of these strategies and are given explanations of how paraphrasing text and anticipating questions that might be asked can be helpful in understanding what is read.

Initially, the adult teacher models the activities, but gradually the students with feedback from the teacher become more capable of assuming their role as dialogue leader. Basically, the reciprocal strategy training procedure involves extensive modeling of comprehension activities that are usually difficult to detect in the expert reader because they are executed covertly (Palincsar & Brown, 1984). The reciprocal training procedure provides a model of what readers do when they try to understand and remember texts.

Advantages. The reciprocal strategy training procedure forces students to respond and gives teachers an opportunity to appraise the students' competence and provide appropriate feedback. Teachers are engaged in "on-line diagnosis," a level of participation that is finely tuned to the students' changing cognitive status (Palincsar & Brown, 1984).

In addition to the advantages in terms of instructional issues, there are also advantages in terms of student motivational issues and generalization of the strategy training procedures. When students act as teachers, it appears their understanding of the strategies increases as well as their motivation to use them (Palincsar, Brown,

& Martin, 1987). Results of interventions using reciprocal strategy training procedures suggest that significant improvements in comprehension skills can be made by students using the procedures, and these improvements are not only maintained over time, but also generalized to overall improved classroom performances (see Palincsar & Brown, 1987).

CAUTIONS AND CONCLUSIONS

With growing documentation of the effectiveness of cognitive strategy training procedures and the pressing need for the academic progress these strategies may foster, teachers are beginning to incorporate strategy training procedures indiscriminately into their teaching repertoire (Sheinker et al., 1988). Educators should be asking very hard questions and demanding research illustrating the training procedure's effectiveness before accepting any strategy program into their teaching repertoire.

Some cautions that Sheinker et al. (1988) suggest should be considered in the implementation of strategy training procedures are as follows:

- Don't abandon methods already in use that have proven effective for improving the academic performance of mildly handicapped students. For example, the cognitive strategies approach is not a substitute for direct instruction.
- Don't use cognitive strategy techniques as merely an add-on to what you are already doing (Palincsar & Brown, 1984). Cognitive strategies should be a distinct, well-organized integral part of the instructional sequence.
- Before attempting to implement cognitive strategy training in a classroom, be thoroughly versed in the aspects found by research to be effective.
- Use cognitive teaching strategies appropriately; these strategies are not substitutes for basic instruction. (p. 196)

A critical aspect of cognitive strategy intervention is the degree to which the strategies taught under controlled conditions are generalized across settings and maintained over time (Schumaker et al., 1983). To assure promotion of generalization, Ellis et al. (1987b) suggest the following tips for packaging of strategies:

(a) the learning strategy should contain a set of steps that lead to a specific outcome;
(b) the learning strategy should be designed to cue use of cognitive strategies and metacognitive processes;
(c) the strategy should contain no more than seven steps;
(d) each step should begin with a verb or other word that directly relates to the action being cued;
(e) a remembering system should be attached to the strategy to facilitate recall;
(f) the learning strategy should be task specific rather than situation specific or content specific. (p. 8)

Critical to generalization is that the student is provided with the expectation for generalization and is provided feedback during the strategy training process. Students need to be convinced of the importance or necessity of using strategies following demonstrations or directions on how to use particular procedures. When students understand which strategies are appropriate to use, how they are to be used, and why they are necessary, they are more motivated to use them (Paris et al., 1983) and more likely to generalize their use across settings.

As Swanson (1989) concludes, "there is no single best strategy for LD students within or across domains" (p. 7). The abundance of investigations studying strategy training illustrates that researchers are pursuing the best strategies for teaching learning disabled students. If further investigations continue to validate the effectiveness of cognitive strategy training with learning disabled students, this training may add a vital component to the generalization of the instruction process.

BEHAVIORAL APPROACHES TO MANAGING LEARNING DISABILITIES

Given the powerful impact of behaviorism on the fields of psychology and education, the development in recent years of behavioral approaches to the remediation of learning disorders should come as no surprise. While it would perhaps be inaccurate to speak in global terms of a behavioral "system" per se, the approaches that have been developed for use with learning disabled youngsters share a common grounding in basic principles of operant learning theory—most notably those elucidated in the work of B. F. Skinner. This chapter begins with an examination of the central features of the Skinnerian functional learning model and then moves on to a description of two of the best-known and systematic operationalizations of that model in the field of learning disorders: the Applied Behavior Analysis approach of Thomas C. Lovitt and Frank M. Hewett's "engineered classroom."

SKINNER: A FUNCTIONAL MODEL OF LEARNING

Skinner refuses to label his ideas concerning learning as a theory and, in fact, claims to be "atheoretical." In truth, he does not supply theoretical explanations, only observable, behavioral ones. No matter how much Skinner decries theory, most people consider him one of this country's outstanding learning theorists, and his book *Verbal Behavior* (1957) has had a tremendous impact on the teaching of language and reading.

Skinner's Theory

Skinner speaks of two types of behavior: respondent and operant. Before Skinner, Pavlovian or classical conditioning psychologists believed that without a stimulus, no response would occur. They maintained this stance even if no single stimulus could be identified when a response occurred; in such instances they would assert that the observer merely was unable or not equipped to discover the stimulus. What makes operant conditioning separate and distinct from classical conditioning are Skinner's rejection of this position and his efforts to make theorists face facts rather than fitting facts to their established theories. His explanation of operant behavior, as opposed to respondent, enables us to deal with those responses that do not appear to be elicited by single, known stimuli. In general, we do know the antecedents of respondent behaviors. For example, if food powder is placed in the mouth of a dog, the dog will begin to salivate. Salivation is the respondent behavior; food powder is the stimulus. On the other hand, operant behaviors are emitted, not elicited, and we do not know what the stimuli may be. For example, the dog who suddenly gets up from a comfortable chair and goes to sit at its owner's feet is demonstrating operant behavior; the stimulus is not identifiable. According to Skinner, the most notable example of operant behavior is verbal behavior.

Anyone who stops for a moment and considers the extent and variety of human behavior will soon come to the conclusion that by far the greater part could be classified, in Skinner's terms, as operant. It is the most important and most human type of behavior, and it is learned, or not learned, as a result of the consequences that the behavior brings about. Those consequences can be "pleasant" and rewarding or can be aversive and punishing. In general, we can say that operant behavior comes under the control of positive or negative reinforcement. A response that is followed by a reward is said to be positively reinforced. However, a response that causes an aversive stimulus to cease is said to be negatively reinforced. In both cases the likelihood of the response or behavior recurring is increased. Behavior that is followed by no consequence or reinforcement will be extinguished; that is, over a period of time the likelihood of the behavior's recurring will decrease. Teachers and parents should keep in mind that punishment per se can be reinforcing because the attention that the child receives as the consequence for bad behavior may be what he or she is seeking.

In *Verbal Behavior*, Skinner (1957) presented a model that he believes can account for the most significant elements of speech and language behavior. Often, the model is referred to as a "single-stage" model because Skinner posits only stimulus and response events; no intervening or covert variables are considered. No assumptions about neural or "mental" events are made; we might say that the "black box" is never peeked into, much less opened. The task when dealing with speech and language behavior is to observe the verbal behavior, the conditions under which it is emitted, and the conditions under which it is reinforced; and after doing so to hypothesize purely functional relationships between verbal operants and their consequences. Skinner says,

> Our first responsibility is simple *description*: what is the topography of this subdivision of human behavior? Once that question has been answered in at least a preliminary fashion we may advance to the stage called *explanation*: what conditions are relevant to the occurrence of the behavior—what are the variables of which it is a function? (1957, p. 10)

Skinner spent a great deal of time describing the verbal behavior and searching for the stimuli or, better, the conditions that control it. The following are the types of verbal operants he identified along with the variables controlling them.

Mands. A mand is a verbal operant that is under the control of drive states, such as thirst or hunger, and that bears, in name, a close resemblance to words like *demand* and *command*. If a child is hungry and utters the word *cookie*, we may say that the child has produced a mand in response to a drive state. The utterance will serve to alleviate the child's hunger by means of securing food. Mands are generally quite easy to identify in verbal behavior. Statements like, "Come here!" "Pass the butter," "Water, please," specify both the behavior of the listener and, in the latter two, the reinforcement that is expected. The specification of listener behavior and ultimate reinforcement is typical of mands.

Tacts. Verbal operants that serve as labeling responses are termed *tacts*, suggesting behavior that "makes con*tact*" with the nonverbal world. In the presence of some physical object or event, for example, a table, the likelihood of emitting the verbal operant *table* is increased. Obviously, tacting can be increased greatly by structuring the verbal situation so that the listener asks the name of specific objects. This is a common procedure in teaching situations where, as a result, children engage in much tacting behavior. Mands and tacts both are considered to be under the control of nonverbal elements, drive states for the former and physical objects for the latter. The remaining verbal operants that Skinner discusses are controlled by verbal stimuli. These are echoic, textual, and intraverbal operants.

Echoic Operants. Echoic operants are under the control of speech that has been heard by the listener. In general, it is an imitative or "echoing" type of response that is observed frequently in young children's speech. Other occurrences of echoic operants would be found in the pathological condition termed *echolalia*, in which the individual, usually a child, consistently produces imitative responses to all heard speech.

Textual Operants. Nonauditory verbal stimuli, most commonly written symbols, control textual operants. The "text" could consist of any type of orthographic symbol—hieroglyphs, phonetic symbols, letters, and so on. Obviously, reading is an example of textual behavior. Several distinctions between echoic and textual behavior have been noted by DeVito (1970), as follows:

1. In echoic behavior the same modality, the auditory, is used for both the stimulus and the response; however, different modalities, the visual and auditory, are used in textual behavior.

2. Feedback is immediate and fairly precise in echoic behavior. The speaker can compare the stimulus and response with relatively good accuracy. In textual behavior the feedback is limited; the speaker may see a word and say it without ever knowing whether the response was accurate.

Intraverbal Operants. The cliché is the prime example of intraverbal behavior. When someone greets a person with "How are you?" and that person responds with "Fine, thank you," both are probably engaging in intraverbal behavior. Responses on word association tests and on other verbal analogies tests may be of the intraverbal type. As the reader can see, intraverbal operants are under the control of verbal behavior but in a distinctly different way than is the case with echoic and textual operants. Stimulus and response may differ in modality; that is, a written response may be given to either an oral or written stimulus, and an oral response may be given to a written or oral response.

Audience. Skinner includes the speaker's audience as a factor that influences and controls both the form and content of verbal operants. The native language, the profession, and the educational level of the audience will influence the verbal behavior of the speaker as will the purpose for which the audience has gathered. In other words, we say different things to different people or groups of people. A sophisticated discussion of the etiology of learning disabilities will not be presented to a neighborhood rally for your favorite political candidate.

Given the explanations of verbal operants as described by Skinner, we can provide examples of how verbal behavior is learned and controlled. Let us suppose that a person engages in manding behavior with the response, "Give me water." The listener positively reinforces the response by providing the speaker with water, and as a result, the speaker when under the same drive state of thirst will again use manding behavior. However, the listener could ignore the speaker and, in time, manding behavior would be extinguished (at least this particular type would be). The critical point to keep in mind is that any verbal operant will increase in frequency if reinforced and decrease if not reinforced.

Skinner's paradigm for verbal behavior is the best representation of an effort to deal with the complexities of language on the basis of only what is observable without making reference to or assumptions about nonobservable, covert activities.

It appears that some aspects of language development can be explained quite par-
simoniously by application of Skinnerian principles; in fact, those principles are highly
useful in teaching language to children. If one wishes to teach vocabulary items to
a child, the elicitation of labeling responses through echoic and tact behavior, reinforcing desired responses and extinguishing inappropriate ones is a common approach
used by many teachers and clinicians. To teach such linguistic units, it is unnecessary
to draw elaborate models of the learning process and speak at great length about
covert, mediating responses. Just do it! When the teacher begins dealing with other,
more complicated activities—such as the production of grammatically correct
sentences—there may be some problems in using a Skinnerian approach.

Instructional Applications: The Technology of Teaching

It was probably Skinner's dissatisfaction with some of the features of his own
daughter's public school curriculum that led him to "respond" by developing some
practical classroom applications of the basic tenets of his learning model. While the
methods he developed were not aimed specifically at satisfying the needs of learning disabled children, it can be reasonably assumed that he considered the methods
appropriate to virtually any type of learning situation. Many of Skinner's suggestions
for classroom application of behavioral theory are presented in *The Technology of
Teaching* (1968), the very title of which indicates his commitment to a structured,
systematic approach to instruction.

Two of the most widely adopted features of Skinner's instructional "technology"
are those of programmed instruction and teaching machines. Just as Skinner had
"shaped" pigeons in a famous experiment toward an improbable degree of facility
in ping-pong, he felt that the learning behaviors of students could likewise be shaped
by presenting instructional materials or "stimuli" in a predetermined sequence of
steps leading toward the ultimate goal or "terminal behavior." Skinner described the
two basic features of programmed learning as follows:

> ... the gradual elaboration of extremely complex patterns of behavior and the
> maintenance of behavior in strength at each stage. The whole process of becoming
> competent in any field must be divided into a very large number of very small steps,
> and reinforcement must be contingent upon the accomplishment of each step. . . .
> By making each step as small as possible, the frequency of reinforcement can be raised
> to a maximum, while the possibly aversive consequences of being wrong are reduced
> to a minimum. (1968, p. 21)

Programmed learning, then, proceeds in a manner not unlike that in which
Skinner's pigeons became proficient in ping-pong. The student is led in small, gradually
more complex steps toward the terminal goal of proficiency and is reinforced at each
step along the way. It is vitally important that the steps in this process not be too
difficult, for the absence of success will mean the absence of reinforcement—hence,

in Skinner's conceptualization, the absence of learning. In arranging the sequence of learning steps, teachers (or "programmers") can use either a *linear* or a *branching* program. The former tries to ensure that every response on the path to the terminal behavior will be correct. An example of such a program is presented in Figure 17.1. A branching program allows a bit more leeway for incorrect responses, since it provides for "branches" to provide further instruction in areas where mistakes are made. In both cases, however, the basic sequence of success-reinforcement-learning is preserved.

Learning, according to Skinner, is basically a function of direct and immediate reinforcement. One of his major criticisms of the typical classroom is that the teacher is often unable and/or unwilling to provide reinforcement for learning as often and effectively as is needed. It was for this reason that Skinner proposed the utilization of teaching machines in the classroom.

> The important features of the device are these: reinforcement for the right answer is immediate. The mere manipulation of the device will probably be reinforcing enough to keep the average pupil at work for a suitable period each day, provided traces of earlier aversive control can be wiped out. A teacher may supervise an entire class at work on such devices at the same time, yet each child may progress at his own rate, completing as many problems as possible within the class period. If forced to be away from school, he may return to pick up where he left off. . . .
>
> The device makes it possible to present carefully designed material in which one problem can depend upon the answer to the preceding problem and where, therefore, the most efficient progress to an eventually complex repertoire can be made. (1968, p. 24)

Despite criticisms that such an approach turns the teacher into little more than a "teaching machine," Skinner's proposals met a wide and appreciative audience in many quarters. Two particularly appreciative figures in the field of special education were Thomas C. Lovitt and Frank M. Hewett, who borrowed heavily from Skinner in developing their own approaches to the remediation of learning difficulties. Whatever their differences, both methodologies reflect adherence to the basic maxim that "what you reinforce is what you get."

LOVITT: APPLIED BEHAVIORAL ANALYSIS

In learning disabilities, perhaps the best-known theoretician-practitioner of an instructional methodology based on the Skinnerian model is Thomas C. Lovitt. Indeed, in the minds of many professionals his name is nearly synonymous with the classroom application of Applied Behavior Analysis (ABA). Lovitt is unique in several respects. For one thing, while the behavioristic model has been repeatedly applied to remediating *behavioral* problems, relatively few behaviorists have employed the technique in treating problems of school subject learning. For another, Lovitt's early

1. **Manufacture** means to make or build. *Chair factories manufacture chairs.* Copy the word here:

    □ □ □ □ □ □ □ □ □ □

2. Part of the word is like part of the word **factory**. Both parts come from an old word meaning *make* or *build*.

    m   **a**   **n**   **u**   □ □ □ □   **u**   **r**   **e**

3. Part of the word is like part of the word **manual**. Both parts come from an old word for *hand*. Many things used to be made by hand.

    □ □ □ □   **f**   **a**   **c**   **t**   **u**   **r**   **e**

4. The same letter goes in both spaces.

    m   □   **n**   **u**   **f**   □   **c**   **t**   **u**   **r**   **e**

5. The same letter goes in both spaces.

    m   **a**   **n**   □   **f**   **a**   **c**   **t**   □   **r**   **e**

6. **Chair factories**   □ □ □ □ □ □ □ □ □ □   chairs

FIGURE 17.1. Part of a program in elementary grade spelling. *Note.* From "Teaching Machines" by B. F. Skinner, October 24, 1956, *Science, 128,* pp. 969–977, figs. 1 and 2. Reprinted by permission of the American Association for the Advancement of Science and B. F. Skinner.

training was in neither education nor psychology, but in music. He received both undergraduate and graduate degrees in music education, and for a number of years he pursued a career as a professional musician. Lovitt (1976) points out in an auto-biographical sketch that a number of "behaviors" acquired from his musical experi-ence have "generalized" to his present field. The professional musician and the applied behavior analyst, he recounts, hold in common several basic tenets. These include a recognition of the importance of "doing-it-every-day" (1976, p. 275); of clear, immediate feedback on performance; of natural (as distinct from artificial) con-sequences; of continuous measurement; and of the strategy of one-on-one teaching. Finally, and perhaps most important, the musician and the behaviorist share a fealty to the notion of *directness*; that is, that the best way to learn to play the flute (or read) is to . . . play the flute (or read).

These commonalities suggest that Lovitt's shift from a musical to an educational occupation was itself something of a natural consequence. He began his career as a special education teacher in 1962, and by 1966 he had earned his EdD in special education from the University of Kansas. From 1966 to 1968, Lovitt was coordinator of the learning disabilities program at the University of Washington, where he was appointed professor of special education. From 1967 to the present he has also served as coordinator of the Curriculum Research Classroom at Washington's Experimental Education Unit. His affiliation with this experimental classroom has allowed him to practice—as well as preach—the application of behavioral theory to the actual classroom.

Rationale and Assessment Procedures

The basic rationale behind the ABA methodology was set forth by Lovitt (1967) in a widely read article in *Exceptional Children* entitled "Assessment of Children with Learning Disabilities." In that article he notes a number of problems inherent in conventional assessment practices. Chief among these problems were the fruitless and impractical search for a global definition of the learning disabled population, the overdependence on standardized measures such as the ITPA for assessment and remediation, and the potential for misuse (and/or nonuse) of the findings from such measures. Lovitt maintains that at best, information derived from norm-referenced measures is "at least one step removed from the direct programming tasks of the referring agent" (1967, p. 233). There is always the possibility, moreover, that the teacher might seek "diagnostic solace" (p. 234) in test results.

> As a result, when the child does not adequately perform, the teacher need only draw out her file and read the diagnosis to reassure herself that the student's poor performance is unalterably determined by some medical or psychological malady. Then, no teaching obligation follows for altering the stimulus or consequence conditions of the program, nor is there any necessity for an assessment of possible errors within the teacher's management techniques. (p. 234)

As an alternative to the frequently instructionally irrelevant practice of superimposing a set of population characteristics on individual children, Lovitt proposes an outline for a four-step assessment methodology in which "time is spent in treatment of explicit behaviors rather than in what is frequently a fruitless search for correlate but often unrelated behaviors" (p. 234). The four steps are as follows: (a) baseline assessment, (b) assessment of behavioral components, (c) assessment based on referral, and (d) generalization of assessment.

Baseline Assessment. This initial phase is characterized by direct, continuous, carefully documented (usually via charts or graphs) assessment of student performance in the problem area(s). No intervention is attempted in this phase, as the goal is to determine the student's level of performance under "natural" conditions. This phase is to continue until an accurate, relatively stable picture of the student's task-specific performance has emerged. Lovitt avers that this diagnostic procedure is both more reliable and more valid than standardized measures, in that it is not based on a "one-shot" sampling of student performance and focuses directly and objectively on individual areas of difficulty.

Assessment of Behavioral Components. This second aspect focuses on a number of variables that serve to either maintain or modify behavior: antecedent (or stimulus) events, movement (or response) behaviors, contingency arrangements, and subsequent (or consequent) events. *Antecedent events* that can affect individual performance include such stimulus preference variables as the rate at which material is read and the gender or other characteristics of the teacher presenting the material. As Lovitt notes, the performance of individual children can and does vary as a function of manipulating such variables. Next, *movement (response) behaviors* need to be evaluated with reference to both topography (mean sentence length, psycholinguistic processes, manding or tacting behaviors, etc.) *and* function (i.e., the effect of such behaviors on the environment). Topographic assessment alone is not enough, since it presents an essentially static picture of behavioral characteristics under consideration. Functional assessment, on the other hand, is dynamic; it affords a "situational analysis" (Lovitt, 1967, p. 236) of behaviors in the contexts in which they are (or are not) occurring. Both *contingency arrangements* and *subsequent (consequent) events* refer to the determination of optimal reinforcement modes for the individual child. This determination requires attention to both the temporal sequencing of reinforcement (i.e., how often does the child need to be reinforced in order to modify behavior?) and the choice of "high-payoff" consequent events or activities that are particularly effective for particular children. While Lovitt does not proscribe the use of a token (e.g., stars or candy) in planning reinforcement, we have already noted his belief that the positive consequences that ensue from positive performance should be as natural and non-"token" as possible.

Assessment Based on Referral. Lovitt observes, somewhat ruefully, that too often what looks like a learning disability may in fact be more accurately characterized as a teaching disability, in which case what is needed is a "program for adults with programming disabilities, rather than one for children with learning disabilities" (1967, p. 237). In any event, whether the major "blame" lies with the student or the teacher, it is vitally important for the assessment agent to work closely with the teacher/ referral agent and to take the latter's opinions and goals into account in formulating a diagnosis and prescription.

Generalization of Assessment. Generalization refers to the commonsensical but oft forgotten proposition that "the end product of an evaluation should be to present to the referring agent information that can be immediately transmitted into programming procedures" (Lovitt, 1967, p. 238). Again, such transmittal is far less likely when the only guidelines given the teacher are standardized test data and clinical jargon. What is needed, rather, is a coordinated two-dimensional assessment procedure in which both topographic (product) and functional (process) data form the basis for generalization to instructional planning.

Major Features of the ABA Instructional Methodology

Lovitt's early article on assessment was perhaps the germinal work in his development of an instructional methodology based on the principles of applied behavior analysis. We say "perhaps" because Lovitt recently confessed that upon rereading the article, it struck him as "incredibly naive" (1976, p. 285), primarily by dint of its lack of concrete, practical suggestions for classroom teachers. To his credit, Lovitt has devoted a considerable amount of time since 1967 to the task of making his suggestions less "naive" and more practical. Nonetheless, his present explication of the major characteristics of the ABA approach is not inconsistent with his earlier position. In a more recent article, Lovitt (1975a) delineates five major characteristics of the approach: (a) direct measurement, (b) daily measurement, (c) replicatable teaching procedures, (d) individual analysis, and (e) experimental control. Now as before, the emphasis is on specific, ongoing, individualized assessment and analysis of problematic learning behaviors. Likewise familiar is the stress on replicatable (i.e., generalizable) teaching procedures, which would be impossible without careful specification of the "what" and "how" of the instructional intervention. Experimental control finally is necessary in order to determine that it was the instructional intervention, rather than some other "contaminating" variable(s), that was responsible for whatever improvements in performance were observed.

Lovitt's affiliation with the Curriculum Research classroom at the University of Washington has provided him with an ideal opportunity to emphasize the "applied" in Applied Behavior Analysis. He and his colleagues have conducted research utilizing the approach in a number of different academic areas: reading, math, spelling, penmanship, composition, and pupil management. On the basis of this research Lovitt (1978) recommends a fivefold task for the teacher who would employ the ABA approach:

1. to *pinpoint* the behaviors to be modified in some accurately quantifiable fashion;

2. to *chart* or graph those behaviors on a daily or at least frequent basis;

3. to *evaluate* what needs to be done on the basis of the information gathered;

4. to *decide* whether and when a particular instructional mode should be altered or discontinued; and

5. to *individualize,* for the purposes of instruction as well as for assessment.

Given these general guidelines, let us examine in a step-by-step manner how the ABA approach would appear in practice. Readers who wish a more fully detailed description of the approach are referred to two articles by Lovitt (1975b, 1978), which provide a helpful and relatively concise "do-it-yourself" resource for those who wish to employ the ABA approach. For the purposes of simplification, these steps will be discussed with reference to four major stages or phases: baseline stage, instructional stage, decision stage, and generalization stage. In practice, of course, such neat categorization is difficult to attain, and some degree of overlap between stages could—and perhaps should—be expected.

1. *Baseline Stage.* In this stage a number of preliminary steps are taken for purposes of assessment and planning:

a. Identify the precise behavior to be taught. Whether the behavior to be taught is naming letters, spelling *ie* words, or adding two-digit numbers, the key word here is *precise.*

b. Determine the level to which the behavior should be taught; that is, establish a performance goal or criterion for success. Again, the goal should be precisely stated. It can be specified in either or both of the following ways: percentages (i.e., the proportion of correct responses in the identified skill area over a specified period of lessons and/or days) or frequency counts (i.e., the desired rate of correct vs. incorrect responses). During the earliest stages of "acquisition," where accuracy rather than speed is the major goal, Lovitt suggests that these performance objectives be set in terms of percentage of correct responses. Later, the teacher can specify performance goals in terms of desired rates or frequencies, thereby assessing speed of response as well as accuracy.

c. Arrange a situation in which the identified behavior is to occur. As before, the teacher (or "manager") needs to be specific about *when* and *how long* this "sampling" period is to run and *how much* material will be covered. In arithmetic, for example, one method of arranging the instructional situation is to prepare worksheets containing problems of a particular class or subclass. An example of such a worksheet is presented in Figure 17.2. The basic rule of thumb in planning and preparing worksheets or other assessment modes to be used for the purpose of placement is to work from the general to the specific—that is, from "Johnny is poor at addition" to "Johnny is poor at addition problems involving carrying from the 10s place." As part of the scheduling task, the teacher should determine whether the baseline data are to be gathered in terms of time and/or amount.

d. Obtain several days' baseline data. During this period the teacher must decide what kind of instructions should be provided the student and how much feedback on performance should be given. As was noted earlier, the goal at this point is to assess the student's "normal" performance level, so extensive instruction, feedback, or other forms of assistance should generally be avoided. These data can be summarized on a raw data sheet (see Figure 17.3) and used for assessment and planning.

e. Study the student's error patterns. The previous steps help to ensure accurate placement and a realistic choice of performance goals. This step helps (or forces) the teacher to determine *where* the problem areas are and, possibly, *why* they came into being.

2. *Instructional Stage.* Next, the data gathered during the baseline stage are used for the planning and implementation of instruction.

a. Determine whether instruction is necessary. Analysis of the percentage, frequency rates, and patterns of errors may indicate that a problem exists. However, an important question still needs to be asked: Is there a problem because the child *cannot* do the work or because the child *will not*? This question recalls the importance of a "functional" as well as "topographic" assessment of stu-

Name _____ # Correct _____ Correct rate _____

Date _____ # Incorrect _____ Incorrect rate _____

Time begun _____ Time ended _____ Total time _____

25	71	51	31	91
− 8	− 6	− 8	− 5	− 3
54	71	22	31	63
− 9	− 4	− 5	− 5	− 4
52	41	31	67	23
− 3	− 8	− 3	− 8	− 4
41	32	52	41	31
− 5	− 5	− 8	− 9	− 8
81	25	92	81	42
− 5	− 9	− 8	− 6	− 3
23	62	95	21	54
− 5	− 5	− 9	− 9	− 9

FIGURE 17.2. Sample arithmetic sheet. *Note.* From "Arithmetic" by T. C. Lovitt, 1978, in N. G. Haring, T. C. Lovitt, M. D. Eaton, and C. L. Hansen (Eds.), *The Fourth R: Research in the Classroom* (p. 135), Columbus, OH: Merrill. Reprinted by permission.

dent performance. If the problem is more one of motivation than of ability, it may be that new modes of reinforcement rather than new modes of instruction are called for.

b. Select a teaching design. If baseline data indicate that special instruction is in fact necessary, Lovitt (1978) suggests several possible instructional designs. The first and most basic design, described as "the bread and butter pattern of teaching" (p. 135), is a four-phase A¹BA²M design. The first (A¹) phase is, of course, the baseline stage, which should run a minimum of 2 or 3 days. The second (B) phase is the instructional phase, which should continue until the preestablished performance objectives have been attained. During the third (A²) phase the instructional component is removed, and performance is

Day	Date	Minutes	Number	#C	CR	#E	ER	%	Comments

FIGURE 17.3. Sample raw data sheet. *Note.* From "Arithmetic" by T. C. Lovitt, 1978, in N. G. Haring, T. C. Lovitt, M. D. Eaton, and C. L. Hansen (Eds.), *The Fourth R: Research in the Classroom* (p. 136), Columbus, OH: Merrill. Reprinted by permission.

observed for a specified period of time. This would indicate, for example, whether a child who had used an abacus to master a particular type of arithmetic problem would retain mastery without the assistance of the abacus. The fourth (M) phase is very similar to the previous phase except that sessions are scheduled intermittently rather than daily, thereby allowing assessment of whether the child is able to retain mastery over an extended period of time.

A second and related design—A^1BA^2GM—allows the teacher to test for generalization effects. In the fourth (G) phase of this model the child is presented with problems requiring generalization from material presented previously. Thus a child who had been working on problems such as $22 - 15 = ?$ might be asked to subtract 115 from 222. Yet another design—$A^{w1}B^{p1}B^{p2}A^{w1}M$—is a bit too complex to describe in detail here, but it in essence allows the teacher to break down a problem area into subsets of skills to be taught, subsets characterized here as B^{p1} and B^{p2}.

c. Select contingent and/or noncontingent events to modify behavior. Put simply, contingent events are those that have a direct cause-and-effect relationship with the behavior being measured. For example, extra recess time could be granted "contingent" upon 80% or greater accuracy on, say, the daily spelling lesson. Of course, some trial and error can be expected in the search for effective (i.e., reinforcing) contingent events. Noncontingent events, on the other hand, occur regardless of whether and how well the measured behavior is performed. The most commonly employed types of noncontingent events include modeling (demonstrating how the behavior or skill is performed correctly); informing (simply telling the student how to do something); cuing or prompting (telling the child in advance—and in part—what is to be done); and using mnemonic devices and other teaching aids such as Cuisenaire rods.

d. Assess and monitor the student's learning stage. Lovitt (1978) postulates several different learning stages, each of which might call for different instructional strategies. The first stage in his schema is that of "initial acquisition," in which the child's correct percentage and frequency rates are nearly zero, and in which the child "needs to be shown or told how to do something" (p. 140). The next stage postulated by Lovitt is that of "advanced acquisition," a middle learning stage in which approximately 50% of the child's responses are correct. In the next, "initial proficiency" stage, the student's percentage of correct responses is nearly 100%, but the desired rate of correct responses has not been achieved. We can presume that when the rate as well as the percentage of correct responses meets the criterion level established, the child has attained "total proficiency," although Lovitt is less than clear on this point. Lovitt (1975b) also suggests that during the acquisition stage it would "perhaps" be better to use a noncontingent technique and that it "might be preferable" to use a contingent technique when the child is in the proficiency stage and thus has some familiarity with the material (p. 516). Unfortunately, it is not made clear exactly why different techniques "might" be more effective in different stages.

e. Keep instructional techniques as natural and simple as possible. Whether the teacher is using contingent or noncontingent events, this principle should be kept firmly in mind. Lovitt describes it as follows: "A natural event is one which is indigenous to a particular environment. A simple technique is one that is readily available, easy and quick to administer, and inexpensive" (1975b, p. 516). There are at least two important, and obvious, reasons for selecting natural and simple events. For one thing, the simpler a technique, the faster and more effective it is likely to be. For another, the ultimate goal is for the student to be able to perform without the aid of special techniques. "Ordinarily, behaviors maintain better after the techniques have been withdrawn when those techniques are natural and simple" (Lovitt, 1975b, p. 517).

f. Keep the instructional technique(s) in effect for at least a few days. The rationale for this stipulation should be self-evident, particularly in view of Lovitt's critique of the "one-shot" approach. Just as during the baseline stage, decisions should not be made until adequate and accurate information has been gathered.

3. *Decision Stage.* This is essentially a one-step stage, in which data from the baseline and instructional stages are compared with reference to the preestablished performance objectives. Lovitt (1978) notes, however, that there are at least two kinds of decisions that can be made. The first is whether to continue using the instructional technique originally selected or to modify this technique in favor of another. The second type of decision is about whether to discontinue instruction in a particular skill and begin teaching another. In either case, data gathered during the prior two stages should serve as the basis for the decision.

4. *Generalization Stage.* Lovitt denotes at least four types of generalization: maintenance, retention, response, and stimulus. These can be assessed by means of the steps described below.

    a. Remove the instructional technique when the criterion performance level has been attained. When this is done, one or two consequences can ensue. The level of performance can be maintained, either on a short-term (maintenance) or a long-term (retention) basis. Should this occur, the teacher is justified in moving on to instruction in another skill area. If, on the other hand, performance declines when the instructional technique is removed, the teacher can reestablish the technique, modify it, or replace it with another.

    b. Test for response and stimulus generalization. Response generalization occurs when a pupil learns a certain problem or skill even though teaching had not been specifically directed toward that skill. For example, a student who had been taught to add 46 and 14 might be asked to "generalize" this "response" to a problem such as 54 + 16 = ? Stimulus (or situation) generalization occurs when the student can solve problems when a presentation mode other than—though generally similar or related to—the original instructional mode is used. For example, a student who had learned to respond orally to certain addition facts might be asked to exhibit similar mastery in writing his or her responses.

    c. Teach self-management behaviors as much as possible. Contrary to the popular view of the behaviorist-as-manipulator, Lovitt believes in involving the student directly in the planning, implementation, and monitoring of the instructional program. Not only does such direct student involvement assist the teacher, it also generates greater motivation on the part of the student. In fact, Lovitt (1975b) proposes that self-management instruction be given as much "curricular status" as reading and math. He takes quite seriously the mandate of the schools to produce independent, self-directed citizens and feels that this task "should not be left up to the capriciousness of Mother Nature" (p. 515). He summarizes his philosophy on this point as follows:

    > People must know what steps to take in order to change themselves. It is not enough simply to want to change; an individual must be able to analyze what he is currently doing that pleases him and assists others; he must be able to pinpoint those events that irritate him and the circumstances that are bringing on those events. He must be able to rearrange his life to decrease the irritants and increase the pleasures so that he may then assist himself and others.

He must be able to evaluate his life constantly (once a year at New Year's is not enough) and be able to make the necessary adjustments in order that he and those he is trying to teach independence (not those dependent on him) can enjoy a consistently rich and productive life. (1975b, p. 515)

Appraisal of the ABA Method

At least intuitively, the use of the Applied Behavior Analysis approach in the remediation of learning disorders has considerable appeal. Reinforcement and other techniques such as modeling and cuing have been shown to be effective in many other areas; so it stands to reason that they might likewise be effective in modifying academic behaviors. Certainly, Lovitt is persuaded of the efficacy of the approach. He has written,

In the situation where I have worked in Washington, we have taken children labeled as "learning disabled," primarily because of reading problems. With these children we have arranged brief, one-on-one teaching situations throughout the year. Generally, these children have gained from two to three years in reading during a twelve-month period. (Lovitt, 1976, p. 277)

However, Lovitt would probably be among the first to admit that this sort of testimony can scarcely be considered definitive "proof" of the superior efficacy of the ABA methodology. For one thing the situation at the Curriculum Research Classroom, at which Lovitt has conducted most of his research, can hardly be thought of as being typical of most classrooms for the learning disabled. The number of students enrolled is small (seven children in each class), the financial and personnel resources are considerable, and the children studied are predominantly middle class. Moreover, the precise nature of the disabilities of the student population and of the criteria by which they have been determined are not clearly specified, so that it is difficult to know how—and perhaps whether—these children are in fact learning disabled at all. Lovitt himself questions whether the gains he has noted can be attributed to the efficacy of the ABA approach per se.

I am convinced that these gains were not due to the super techniques we used, for as I will explain later, our procedures are very simple. I believe the primary reason the pupils have thrived is that they were in situations where they could interact individually with a teacher. . . . We did not give them a quickie "blitz" treatment. (Lovitt, 1976, p. 277)

We share Lovitt's doubt that the ABA methodology represents a "super technique" for the remediation of learning disorders, as well as his belief that close, individualized teaching will enhance the effectiveness of the ABA—or any other—approach. Until and unless controlled studies are performed on a scale much larger than that of his experimental classroom, the jury will have to remain "out" on the practical utility of the approach advocated by Lovitt.

In the meantime, certain limitations of the ABA approach ought to be mentioned. Some of these limitations have been pointed out by Lovitt himself (1975a). One is the difficulty often encountered in developing a sufficiently simple and workable data-gathering system. While Lovitt is second to none in his view of simplicity as a consummation devoutly to be wished, some of his data-gathering instruments (see Figure 17.4) would strike the average classroom or resource teacher as bedazzling in their complexity. Another limitation is what Lovitt called the "programming rigidity" (1975a, p. 441) of the approach. As he notes, this "rigidity" can cause problems on

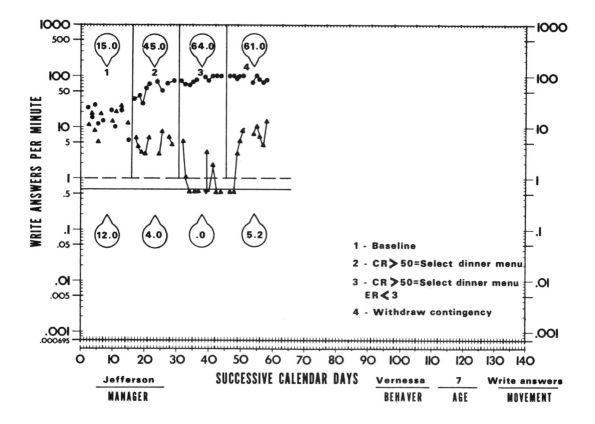

FIGURE 17.4. Data showing that a meal-planning contingency was effective during the advanced acquisition stage. *Note.* From "Arithmetic" by T. C. Lovitt, 1978, in N. G. Haring, T. C. Lovitt, M. D. Eaton, and C. L. Hansen (Eds.), *The Fourth R: Research in the Classroom* (p. 146), Columbus, OH: Merrill. Reprinted by permission.

a number of fronts. In most actual classrooms it might be difficult if not impossible to isolate the "critical" variable in instruction; that is, tight experimental control is far easier to maintain in the laboratory than in the classroom, where it is a formidable task to hold all the students, much less the variables, "constant." Likewise, the one-task-at-a-time orientation may be more workable in theory than in practice. To paraphrase John Donne, "No skill is an island, entire of itself," and to isolate a particular skill for purposes of instruction necessitates "controlling" (i.e., overlooking) the important interrelationships it may have with other skills. Nor is there any guarantee that skills acquired during special instruction will generalize in other, "uncontrolled" situations.

To Lovitt's credit, he has acknowledged these limitations and made no extravagant claims about ABA as a "super technique." However, if the approach is to be adopted to the extent he would like it to be, more extensive and rigorous research will have to be conducted in order to mitigate the limitations and establish the efficacy of Applied Behavior Analysis in the classroom. It would also be desirable to conduct at least a few studies using ABA with children clearly identified as learning disabled who have extreme to moderate problems in spoken and written language.

In preparing this second edition of our book, we asked Dr. Lovitt to share with us any philosophical or methodological changes that he has made during the past several years. His reply, which is quoted below, serves as a fitting conclusion to this section.

> Although I still adhere to the basic tenets of Applied Behavior Analysis—direct and frequent measurement and contingency management—I'm not as task analytic or sequence bound as I once was. I don't believe either that I'm what others would call "holistic": That's a bit trendy. But I do tend to look more at forests and less at trees than I used to. This is particularly indicated in my current beliefs about reading instruction. Although I still maintain that it is necessary to have a solid phonics and structural analysis base, I believe it is important to go about the business of actually reading as soon as possible.
>
> I have also backed off quite a bit when it comes to gathering data. I suppose a lot of this has to do with the fact that I have been working more in schools than in laboratory situations and I'm working more with large classes taught by regular teachers. Now, I will settle for data of many types. Obviously, the more the better, and the more directly related to the curriculum the better. (A somewhat interesting aside is that the people who now advocate "curriculum-based instruction" don't recognize or pay much homage to the applied behavior analysts who have directly measured curriculum for 25 years. Another interesting and similar aside is that many of us in the ABA business have for some time investigated the effects of self-management. Now it's called metacognition!)
>
> Generally, I've become less incestuous, methodologically speaking. In the last 5 years I have read and studied much more in non-ABA areas than I have in my identified area. I'm more comfortable now about trying to assimilate information from other disciplines and methodologies than I once was, and I see more clearly the myopia of professional tricks. (Lovitt, 1986)

HEWETT: THE ENGINEERED CLASSROOM AND THE ORCHESTRATION OF SUCCESS

Frank M. Hewett's work on the "engineered classroom," supplemented by his ideas about the "orchestration of success," represents one of the most systematic and ambitious attempts to translate behavioral theory into educational practice in the instruction of exceptional learners. Hewett, a professor of education and psychiatry at the University of California at Los Angeles, has had a long-standing interest in special education by dint of his affiliation with UCLA's Neuropsychiatric Institute School. Though originally interested in the education of emotionally disturbed children, Hewett has developed a model that purports to be appropriate to the needs of virtually any exceptional learner, regardless of diagnostic label. Three aspects of Hewett's approach are addressed in this section: (a) the conceptual principles underlying the orchestration-of-success approach, (b) the role of assessment in instructional planning, and (c) specific curricular recommendations.

Conceptual Underpinnings of the Orchestration-of-Success Approach

Hewett's dissatisfaction with the labeling practices used in the field of emotional disturbance led him to devise his own approach. In an early article (1967) introducing the basic tenets of "educational engineering," he discussed three then-prevalent models of emotional disturbance: the psychotherapeutic model, which conceives of the disturbed learner in terms of psychodynamic interpersonal influences; the pathological or medical model, with its emphasis on observed or inferred cerebral process dysfunction; and the pedagogical model, which focuses most directly on remedial techniques for intellectual and academic development. While Hewett disavowed none of these models, neither did he embrace them. What was needed, he felt, was a model that is more easily understandable and generally applicable to the classroom teacher; one that focuses on the learning capacities, rather than on the disabilities, of children who have been labeled exceptional. Hewett further contended that behavior modification provided such a model.

> Recently, a model called behavior modification has demonstrated usefulness with exceptional children. Rather than view the emotionally disturbed child as a victim of psychic conflicts, cerebral dysfunction, or merely academic deficits, this approach concentrates on bringing the overt behavior of the child into line with standards required for learning. Such standards may include development of an adequate attention span; orderly response in the classroom; the ability to follow directions; tolerance for limits of time, space, and activity; accurate exploration of the environment; and appreciation of these standards as well as self care and intellectual skills through assignment of carefully graded tasks in a learning environment which provides both rewards

and structure for the child in accord with principles of empirical learning theory are the basic goals of the behavior modification model. (1967, p. 459)

More recently, Hewett (Hewett & Taylor, 1980) has presented a broader and more eclectic view of approaches to emotional disturbance and other categories of exceptionality. In addition to the psychodynamic (teacher-as-therapist), medical/neurological (teacher-as-diagnostician/trainer), pedagogical (teacher-as-teacher), and behavioral (teacher-as-behavior modifier) models, he has acknowledged an ecological model, which views the teacher (and child) as cohabitants of the same educational ecosystem or life-space. Basically, however, his orientation over the years has remained consistent. He retains his distaste for labeling practices that "can alter our expectations regarding a child's potential for learning, affect the child's self-concept directly, and become self-fulfilling prophecies allowing us to explain lack of learning as the result of a child failure rather than as the result of a teacher failure" (Hewett & Taylor, 1980, p. 49). Consistent, too, is his impatience with assessment practices—be they medical and psychiatric diagnoses or standardization test scores—which may pinpoint the shortcomings of the child most plausibly but which have little functional relevance to actual classroom practice. Finally and most important, Hewett retains his fundamental view of the child-as-learner. While Hewett's perspective is basically behavioral, he considers his approach to be easily adapted to these other theoretical models of exceptionalness.

> It is an orientation completely compatible with all the ideas of the teacher as a diagnostician-trainer, as a therapist, as a behavior modifier, or as a part of the child's ecosystem. It is compatible with all the views of children as neurologically impaired, as emotionally disturbed, as maladaptive behavers, or as individuals who are experiencing discordance in their ecosystems. We are proposing an eclectic approach based on the behavioral perspective. Considering all children—normal and exceptional— first and foremost as learners may seem obvious and simplistic. However, it is the cornerstone upon which an effective educational program can be built. Furthermore, it is one answer to the effects-of-labeling dilemma special educators have suffered with for so long.
>
> The term *learner* is exciting and dynamic. It is optimistic. It overshadows the negative and sidetracking aspects of the term *handicapped.* It suggests change. It directs us to look at what children can do, not at what some ominous label says they can't do. Teachers can *teach* learners, while they may have second thoughts about being able to teach autistic, psychotic, sociopathic, schizophrenic, or neurotic children. (Hewett & Taylor, 1980, p. 94)

Two basic concepts are fundamental to both the understanding and the implementation of Hewett's approach: (a) levels of learning competence and (b) the learning triangle. Each of these concepts is considered in turn, followed by an examination of how they are applied to the classroom.

Levels of Learning Competence. Hewett's initial premise of child-as-learner suggests an immediate and important question, namely, at what level is the child a learner? The search for the answer to this question has led Hewett to adopt a developmental framework for describing student competencies in educationally functional terms, whereby student progress can be charted along a sequence of competency levels. Originally, these levels were called a "hierarchy of educational tasks" (Hewett, 1964); somewhat later, they were referred to as a "developmental sequence of educational goals" (Hewett, 1968). More recently, however, Hewett has come to see these levels less as hierarchical than as an overlapping sequence of behaviors and has adopted the term "levels of learning competence" (Hewett & Forness, 1977; Hewett & Taylor, 1980). Six basic levels are identified in this sequence:

Attention

Response

Order

Exploratory

Social

Mastery

The first five steps in this sequence—attention, response, order, exploratory, and social—are, in a sense, *pre*-educational. In other words, there are certain basic competencies that children must possess *before* they can be expected to perform academic tasks in the classroom. First of all, they must be willing and able to attend to the educational "somethings" presented to them by the teacher. Second, they must do something with or to those "somethings," that is, respond to them. Third, they must learn (and/or be taught) to develop orderly, appropriate patterns of attending and responding to the stimuli presented them. Fourth, they must explore their environments to become familiar with a wider and wider field of stimuli ("somethings") to which they can attend and respond in an orderly fashion. Up to this point, children are conceived of as individual learners. At the fifth, or social, stage they must notice and respect the fact that there are other learners going through the same developmental sequence as they. It is at this point that the child—attentive, responsive, orderly, curious, and socially adjusted—is optimally prepared for mastery of educational and vocational tasks.

Hewett and Taylor (1980) note that each of these levels provides general guidelines for educational planning.

> The *attention* level is concerned with children making contact with the environment; the *response* level with getting them to actively participate motorically and verbally; the *order* level with teaching them to follow routines; the *exploratory* level with helping them become accurate and thorough explorers of their environments; the *social* level with aiding them in gaining the approval and avoiding the disapproval of others; and finally the *mastery* level with helping them learn skills related to self-care, academics, and vocational pursuits. (p. 97)

For Hewett, as for Shakespeare, "The readiness is all." Thus it is not until the mastery level that the child is expected to perform tasks characteristic of the "normal" school curriculum. The mastery task level

> all but completes the learning process in school for the child. This level is concerned with the mastering of basic intellectual and adaptive skills and acquisition of a fund of information about the environment which will enable the child to function independently and successfully within the limits of his abilities. (Hewett, 1968, p. 53)

At the highest achievement level the child becomes self-motivated and undertakes in-depth development of intellectual and adaptive skills.

Hewett maintains with some justification that many of the problems of exceptional learners stem from the failure to determine where they are "at" in terms of this developmental sequence. Too often, children are expected to perform at the mastery level when they are developmentally unprepared for doing so. Thus if a child would rather look at pictures than do math problems, Hewett would find it senseless to label the child "dyscalculic" or to swamp him or her with remedial math work. Rather, Hewett would begin from and build upon what the child *is* doing, an activity that in his model would not be called "off-task behavior," but rather attending behavior.

These six levels of learning competence provide the basis for development of what Hewett terms a "functional-descriptive approach" to instruction. It is functional in that it builds on the competencies that do exist, rather than simply confirming the absence of those that do not; thus it constitutes a direct link to setting curriculum goals. It is descriptive in that it provides for—indeed, it demands—behavioral specificity. Such description utilizes a "bipolar" approach whereby behavior can be described along a "too much/too little" continuum at every level. Thus, for example, hyperactivity would be redefined as "too much" competence at the response level, and listlessness redefined as "too little" competence at the level. The key point is that such definitions devolve from an emphasis on what the child *can* do at the various competency levels.

The Learning Triangle. The second basic concept underlying Hewett's approach is that of the learning triangle. As Figure 17.5 suggests, the success of the child-as-learner is conceptualized as a function of the integration of the interrelated factors of curriculum, conditions, and consequences.

To Hewett (Hewett & Taylor, 1980), "Curriculum can be defined as any activity, lesson, or assignment given to the child which is directed toward assisting him or her in achieving competence on one or more of the levels of learning competence" (p. 108). Originally referred to as the "task" component (Hewett, 1968), this side of the learning triangle involves decisions about what the child is to do in the classroom—which, of course, requires determination of the level(s) of learning competence at which the child is operating.

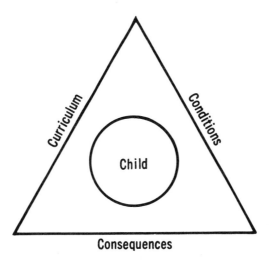

FIGURE 17.5. The learning triangle. *Note.* From *The Educationally Disturbed Child in the Classroom* (p. 109) by F. M. Hewett and F. D. Taylor, 1980, Boston: Allyn & Bacon. Reprinted by permission.

     The conditions component involves decisions about *when, where,* and *how* a particular task is to be done; *how long* it is to be performed; *how much* will be accomplished; and *how well* it will have to be performed in order to satisfy preestablished performance criteria. The key elements in all of these curriculum decisions about the scheduling, setting, methodology, duration, extent, and success criteria of classroom tasks are structure and predictability, which serve to maximize the child's sense of confidence and chances for success at whatever competence level.

     Consequences are contingent events that occur following the child's task performance. Six types of positive consequences have been identified as possible contingencies for successful task performance (Hewett & Forness, 1977):

1. Acquisition of knowledge and skill

2. Knowledge of results

3. Social approval

4. Multisensory stimulation and activity

5. Task completion

6. Tangible rewards

Like other behaviorally oriented practitioners, Hewett has been criticized for over-reliance on tangible rewards. Yet he sees such rewards not as "bribery," but as useful and temporary means for preparing the child for more intrinsically motivating consequences. Hewett's approach is strongly positive and success oriented, but he recognizes the need for aversive consequences in cases when a task is *not* performed. These include such strategies as overcorrection, response cost, and time-out. Nor does he rule out the use of old-fashioned punishment on occasion, but in all cases he maintains steadfastly that the more positive the consequence component is, the more effective it is likely to be.

The levels of competence and the components on the learning triangle constitute the basic concepts that the teacher can use to orchestrate each child's success.

> The process of assigning a task the child needs to learn, is ready to learn, and can be successful learning; selecting conditions which are appropriate; and providing meaningful consequences can be conceived of as the orchestration of success leading to harmony in the classroom. . . . Harmony is not achieved through inconsistency, randomness, or lack of knowledge of expectations. It is accomplished through structure. (Hewett & Taylor, 1980, pp. 122–123)

Conceptualizing instruction through this framework of competence levels and the learning triangle would, at least theoretically, allow the teacher to devise an appropriate educational program for any learner at any level of the sequence. While the content of the consequences might vary from level to level, the vital implication of this framework is that the child is always doing something and thus that there is always something more for the child to do.

Assessment Procedures

Given the key role of the development sequence in Hewett's approach, accurate and ongoing assessment is obviously a cornerstone of his model. As indicated earlier, Hewett considers many conventional assessment procedures to be excessively prone to using labels that focus more on what the student cannot (or does not) do than on what he or she *does* do. In *Education of Exceptional Learners* (Hewett & Forness, 1977), he discusses a number of the currently prevalent diagnostic categories of exceptionality: behavior disorders, learning disabilities, cultural/economic disadvantage, speech disorders, sight and hearing handicaps, emotional disturbance, mental retardation, and giftedness. His emphasis in this discussion is on the commonalities rather than the differences among children thus labeled. This stress on commonalities reflects two basic assumptions behind the orchestration of success:

1. All exceptional children are first and foremost learners, and many can be combined into a single special educational program.

2. Most exceptional children can profit from some integration in a regular class program, provided they are properly scheduled and are provided with appropriate supportive services. (p. 608)

In practice, as well as in theory, Hewett remains faithful to these assumptions. In the engineered classrooms developed under the Santa Monica Madison School Plan, children from every diagnostic category except severely retarded and deaf were represented. This reflects Hewett's belief that the proper business of assessment should be the determination of developmental competencies, rather than the labeling of inadequacies.

Thus assessment procedures in his approach are derived directly from the conceptual framework discussed previously. The key question about the child being assessed is not whether he or she is "emotionally disturbed" or "learning disabled" or "disadvantaged," but rather the developmental level on which the child is operating and the curriculum tasks, instructional conditions, and performance consequences appropriate to that level.

> Assessment of a child is made by first considering whether or not he has attained the goals at each level, next by selecting the rewards which are appropriate to him, and, finally by deciding on the structure or degree of teacher control which will assure successful learning. (Hewett, 1968, p. 80)

In response to the requirement under Public Law 94-142 that an Individualized Education Program (IEP) be developed for every handicapped child, Hewett has developed a strategy called "the ABCs of the IEP," which provides a useful model for instructional planning as well as for assessment. In this approach, basic skill areas are identified and targeted at each of the six levels of learning competence (see Figure 17.6). In the "A" stage these skill areas are described in very general terms; the "B"

I. ATTENTION LEVEL
    A. Vision and Visual Perceptual Skills
    A. Hearing and Auditory Perceptual Skills
    A. Task Attention Skills

II. RESPONSE LEVEL
    A. Motor Coordination Skills
    A. Verbal Language Skills
    A. Nonverbal Language Skills
    A. Task Response Skills

III. ORDER LEVEL
    A. Direction-following Skills
    A. School Adjustment Skills

IV. EXPLORATORY LEVEL
    A. Degree of Active Participation
    A. Knowledge of Environment

V. SOCIAL LEVEL
    A. Relationships with Others
    A. Self-concept

VI. MASTERY LEVEL
    A. Self-help Skills
    A. Health and Hygiene Skills
    A. Reading Skills
    A. Written Language Skills
    A. Computation Skills
    A. Vocational and Career Development Skills

FIGURE 17.6. Competency assessment format for the IEP. *Note.* From *The Educationally Disturbed Child in the Classroom* (pp. 134–135) by F. M. Hewett and F. D. Taylor, 1980, Boston: Allyn & Bacon. Reprinted by permission.

stage delineates subcomponents of these skills; and the "C" stage identifies specific short-term objectives pertaining to mastery of these skill subcomponents. Thus at the attention level, for example, "Vision and Visual Perceptual Skills" is an "A" stage skills category; "Visual Discrimination Skills" is a "B" stage subcomponent of that category; and within this subcomponent are "C" stage objectives such as "follows moving objects with eyes," "matches like objects," and "identifies look-alike words."

Such a procedure provides a feasible, individualized, and ongoing mode of assessment for every exceptional student. The resulting data can be used to ascertain patterns of progress at the various levels and as the basis for adopting different types of curriculum tasks, conditions, and consequences. Provisions are likewise made for the inclusion of additional information, as well as for instructional implications of the data presented. It is perhaps no accident that very little attention is paid to the reporting of standardized achievement test data, since normative comparisons are mostly incompatible with Hewett's individualized, mastery-oriented approach to assessment and instruction. Interested readers are referred to Hewett and Taylor's 1980 book for a detailed description of this assessment procedure.

Methodology of the Engineered Classroom

Beginning in 1965, the engineered classroom model has been operationalized in a number of different settings including the Tulare (California) County Schools, UCLA's Neuropsychiatric Institute School, the University Elementary School of the University of Hawaii, and, perhaps most extensively, the Santa Monica (California) Unified School District. Whatever their differences, the "orchestration of success" in these settings devolves from a common set of general guidelines or principles for the establishment of a harmonious learning climate. These principles are summarized as follows:

1. *Every Child Is a Learner.* Despite the seeming unreadiness of some children to learn, there is never a child who is not ready to learn something. Children who learn nothing in school are clearly teaching failures, not child-failures.

2. *Give the Child the Dignity of Being Expected to Learn.* If all children are learners, we must expect them to learn. Allowing them to continuously wallow in the confusion of self-directed learning is a questionable approach. How many disturbed children are going to "discover their way" out of their learning and behavior problems without our careful and thoughtful guidance?

3. *Don't Ask if the Child Is Ready to Learn, Ask if the Classroom Is Ready to Teach.* The classroom environment should be ready to spring to life at a moment's notice in order to engage the child in a successful learning experience. Don't rummage through cupboards and drawers to find alternative tasks when problems arise; have an instant intervention-oriented classroom set up well in advance.

4. *Recognize that Time Is Often Our Enemy.* While some disturbed children "grow out" of their problems during the elementary years, a substantial number do not.

Autistic children who have not acquired communicative speech by age five usually never learn to talk. The second grade hellion who never settles down to learn to read is in serious trouble in the upper elementary grades and a disaster in junior high school if we aren't effective in teaching him or her.

5. *Think Thimblefuls.* We may fail with children if we conceive of learning in bucketful amounts. No task is too small to be considered legitimate if it moves the child even slightly ahead on the learning track. Try to have a specific set of A-B-C goals with each child. If we don't plan our strategy in advance and prioritize, we may miss our chance to truly help the child.

6. *Think Sequentially.* There is a building-block logic in the use of shaping techniques. Identify the bottom block and build your learning tower step by step. Be willing to use smaller or even larger blocks if it seems appropriate. Be prepared to back up and dismantle your tower block by block if necessary. But start building again as soon as possible.

7. *Consider Conditions.* Don't let children fail because they are asked to work too long or to do too much in the wrong place or at the wrong time. And don't let concern for correctness or accuracy eliminate the child as a candidate for some level of success. Be flexible. Move quickly to alter when, where, how, how long, how much, or how well.

8. *Consider Consequences.* Don't be squeamish about rewards. They are a fact of life. Be sure there is something that makes it worth the child's while to try in the program. Don't use candy if the child is rewarded by praise or multisensory stimulation and activities. But don't not use candy if it offers a quick and efficient means of rewarding the child. Punishment is a risky business. While it may be effective at times, exhaust all positive possibilities before considering it. Withholding rewards is probably the most appropriate negative consequence for use in the classroom.

9. *Keep the White Rabbit of Schoolness Moving.* Try to establish each child's tolerance level for handling demands, schedules, competition, rules, tests, assignments, and directions. Expect the child to function toward his or her highest tolerance level by moving the rabbit closer. But when bad news develops, gracefully and imaginatively move the rabbit back until a reassignment or alteration reduces the child's discomfort. (Hewett & Taylor, 1980, pp. 214–215)

Within these general principles the orchestration of success is conducted with reference to the three basic components of the learning triangle, each of which is discussed in turn.

Curriculum. As was noted, curriculum decisions in the "engineered classroom" flow from determination of the level(s) of learning competence at which students are operating. Archetypal floorplans for such classrooms at the elementary and secondary levels are presented in Figures 17.7 and 17.8, respectively. As can be seen, the room is arranged so that specific areas are available for work at each of the six levels, although the secondary-level floorplan devotes relatively more space and emphasis to mastery-level tasks. The communication center features activities that

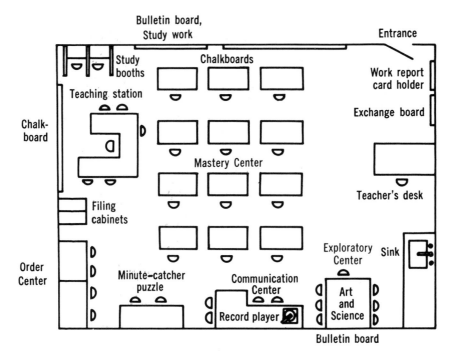

FIGURE 17.7. The floorplan of an elementary-level special day classroom. *Note.* From *The Educationally Disturbed Child in the Classroom* (p. 216) by F. M. Hewett and F. D. Taylor, 1980, Boston: Allyn & Bacon. Reprinted by permission.

minimize competition and encourage cooperation and waiting one's turn, while the exploratory center utilizes a number of activities in art and science designed to engage students' curiosity. In the order center are activities emphasizing active participation, direction following, and task completion, which also involve tasks at the attention and response levels. As a complement to the mastery center, finally, are individual study booths for students who become too easily distracted. Ordinarily, the classroom is populated with 10 to 12 students and is "conducted" by a teacher and a teacher's aide.

Hewett and Taylor (1980) provide general guidelines for enhancing a success-oriented curriculum at each of the levels of learning competence. At the attention level, four such guidelines are identified: (a) removal of distracting stimuli, (b) presentation of small, discrete units of work, (c) heightening the vividness and impact of instructional stimuli, and (d) use of concrete rather than abstract tasks.

Almost invariably, such attention tasks involve some sort of responding as well, and Hewett puts particular emphasis on two characteristics of tasks at the response

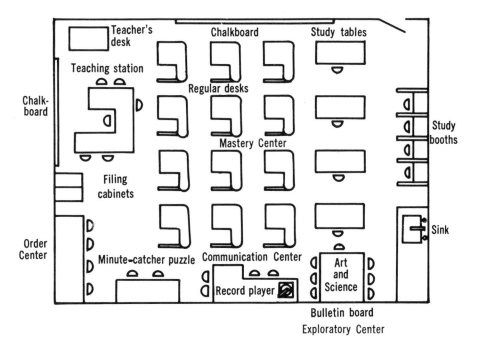

FIGURE 17.8. The floorplan of a secondary-level special day classroom. *Note.* From *The Educationally Disturbed Child in the Classroom* (p. 217) by F. M. Hewett and F. D. Taylor, 1980, Boston: Allyn & Bacon. Reprinted by permission.

level: (a) reduction of the criteria for success and (b) guaranteeing the child success in learning. As he notes, "Response tasks should emphasize involvement and 'trying' rather than accuracy and quality. The effort itself is the focal point, not the quality of the behavior or product" (Hewett & Taylor, 1980, p. 188).

Tasks at the order level are intended to help children learn to adapt to routines, follow directions, complete assignments, and gain control over their behavior. A common characteristic of such tasks (see Figure 17.9 for an example) is defining a specific starting point and a series of steps leading to a conclusion that can be scored as complete or incomplete. At the exploratory level, emphasis is placed on providing (a) a wide range of multisensory experiences, (b) an emphasis on reality, and (c) activities leading to predictable outcomes. As was noted earlier, art and science activities are particularly appropriate in this regard.

At the social level, children are introduced to characteristics of the "student role." These include communicating with the teacher or one or more peers, maintaining appropriate social behavior, and learning to cooperate with others and tolerate periods of delay by waiting one's turn. Listening and social communication tasks such as the

Name_____ Date_____

Order Task   No. 6

324975	_24 _ _5	3_ _9_5	_ _497_
832931	8_29_ _	_3_9_1	8_2_3_
471649	47_6_ _	_716_9	_ _1_4_
831027	8_10_7	_310_7	8_ _02_

FIGURE 17.9. A sample order task. *Note.* From *The Educationally Disturbed Child in the Classroom* (p. 248) by F. M. Hewett and F. D. Taylor, 1980, Boston: Allyn & Bacon. Reprinted by permission.

Morse code activity depicted in Figure 17.10 are employed at this level, as are such strategies as group projects, modeling, role taking, and planned positive peer interaction. Theoretically, at least, success at these five levels culminates in student readiness to perform tasks at the mastery level. The stress at this level is on mastery of basic "three Rs" skills, for which a variety of commercially available materials and programs are recommended (see Hewett & Forness, 1977; Hewett & Taylor, 1980).

Conditions. Conditions, as we indicated earlier, involve decisions about when, where, how, how long, how much, and how well curricular tasks are to be performed. A typical daily elementary schedule expressive of how these conditions are arranged is presented in Figure 17.11. While such a schedule suggests a high degree of order, Hewett would not only allow but encourage flexibility in its implementation, in order to "keep the white rabbit of schoolness moving."

Conditions also include certain expectations about appropriate behavior implicit in the role of "being a student." The key word in such appropriateness is respect— for the working rights of others, for the limits associated with time, working space, and curricular tasks, and for classroom rules. Unfortunately but inevitably, students

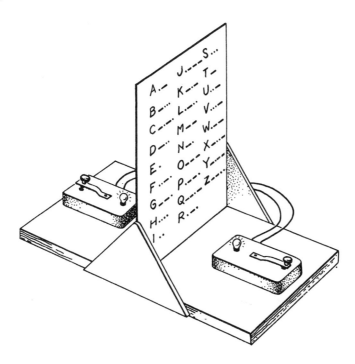

FIGURE 17.10. The apparatus used in the Morse code communication task. *Note.* From *The Educationally Disturbed Child in the Classroom* (p. 203) by F. M. Hewett and F. D. Taylor, 1980, Boston: Allyn & Bacon. Reprinted by permission.

Elementary Daily Schedule

	Mon/Wed/Fri		Tues/Thurs	
8:45	Order task			
9:00	Individual reading	⎫	Motivation for story writing	⎫ Story
	Word study	⎬ Reading	Story writing	⎬ writing
	Skill development	⎭	Sharing	⎭
10:10	Recess			
10:25	Practice in basic facts	⎫		
	Arithmetic instruction	⎬ Arithmetic		
	Skill development	⎭		
11:25	Language instruction (phonics, spelling, handwriting, language development)			
11:50	Lunch			
12:40	Listening (teacher reads to class)			
1:00	Art tasks	⎫		
	Science tasks	⎬ Exploratory		
	Communication tasks	⎬		
	Order tasks	⎭		
	(Two exploratory tasks are selected daily. The students are divided into two groups, the teacher supervising one, the aide, the other. Both groups spend 25 minutes on each task.)			
1:50	Recess			
2:00	Physical education			
2:20	Group and individual activities (music, current events, sharing, group discussion, individual tutoring)			
3:00	End of school day			

FIGURE 17.11. Typical daily schedules for elementary special day classrooms. *Note.* From *The Educationally Disturbed Child in the Classroom* (p. 246) by F. M. Hewett and F. D. Taylor, 1980, Boston: Allyn & Bacon. Reprinted by permission.

do not always demonstrate such respect, and they either retreat from or rebel against "the white rabbit of schoolness." In such cases, Hewett suggests a graduated sequence of interventions based on behavioral principles. These are described as follows:

STUDENT INTERVENTIONS

1. *Send Student to Study Booth (Mastery Level).* The first intervention involves sending the child to work on an assigned mastery task in one of the study booths or "offices." These booths are presented to the children in a positive manner; as a result, they are desirable working areas. Merely allowing the child to change position and move around in the room often effectively interrupts a period of boredom or resistance.

2. *Modify Assignment (Mastery Level).* The next intervention is to change the mastery task given to the child, making it easier, different, or perhaps more difficult in an effort to get him or her involved. Sending the student to the study booth with modified assignment may also be used at this time.

3. *Restructure Verbally (Social Level).* When the mastery interventions just described are not successful or appear inappropriate, an intervention at the social level should be considered next. This intervention involves verbal restructuring on the part of the teacher, using social approval or disapproval as leverage. The child is reminded of the teacher's expectations in relation to the assigned task and behavior. The interactions between teacher and child may initially be largely task-oriented because of the poor relationships with adults previously experienced by many disturbed children. Nevertheless, with some students a reminder by the teacher regarding what is expected may be all that is necessary to help them improve their behavior. This intervention is perhaps most often used by teachers in regular classrooms with children who display problem behavior. It often reinforces the child's negative concept of school and teachers. Therefore, it should be used only after careful consideration, and it is often left out of the intervention process.

4. *Send Student to Exploratory Center (Exploratory Level).* The next intervention reassigns the child to another task center in the room. The teacher selects a previously demonstrated science, art, or craft task and assigns it to the child, making sure all the materials are available and that the child understands what to do. Assignments at the Exploratory Center are always teacher-selected. In practice, the teacher should always have one or two exploratory tasks set up in advance for instant use as interventions.

5. *Send Student to Order Center (Order Level).* Since the Exploratory Center involves a high degree of stimulation, it may not be as appropriate for some disturbed children at a given time as the Order Center. At this center, the child is given a simple direction-following task such as making a puzzle, copying a pegboard design, stringing beads, deciphering a secret code with the aid of a key, or constructing a model of plastic or metal components.

6. *Take Student Outside Classroom and Agree on a Task (Response Level).* In an effort to maintain contact with the student, an intervention at the response level may be undertaken outside the room. Both student and teacher (or aide) go out of the classroom and agree on some task the child will undertake, such as turning somersaults on the lawn, swinging on a swing for fifteen minutes, punching a punching bag, or even resting in the nurse's office for a period of time. Following a response intervention, the teacher attempts to select some assignment in the classroom to ensure the student's success.

7. *Provide Individual Tutoring (Attention Level).* The intervention corresponding to the lowest level of learning competence involves the teacher or aide devoting full time to individual instruction with the student. Such individual tutoring is not always possible for extended periods of time because of the needs of the other students, but it is the next logical step to take in order to help the child.

NONSTUDENT INTERVENTIONS

8. *Send Student Outside Classroom for Specified Time-out.*

9. *Send Student Home.* (Hewett & Taylor, 1980, pp. 221–222)

The first seven interventions are termed "student interventions" because they are generally of a positive nature and allow the child to remain in the classroom and continue to earn check marks. The major advantage of such a system, according to Hewett, is that it provides a systematic, predictable, and fair method for dealing with classroom discordance and enables the teacher to deal with rowdyness in a proactive and logical manner.

Consequences. The third side of the learning triangle is typically characterized by utilization of a check mark system, whereby students are awarded a certain number of check marks on a fixed interval basis (every 15 minutes) during the course of the school day. For each 15-minute marking period, students can earn up to 10 points: 2 for starting a task, 3 for working on it, and 5 "bonus" points for "being a student." These check marks are transcribed by the teacher or aide onto the student's daily work record card (see Figure 17.12), which in turn is entered into the student's cumulative work record sheet. At periodic intervals during the course of the year these cumulative points can then be "cashed in" for a variety of tangible rewards.

Hewett acknowledges that there is no magic in the 15-minute interval, but he does feel that reinforcement should be frequent, immediate, and systematic. He also acknowledges criticisms that such a system turns the teacher into little more than a check-dispensing "robot," but he feels that such a task-oriented relationship is more productive with exceptional children than one based on excessive and frequently counterproductive teacher verbalization.

> Without dwelling on why this occurs, the fact remains that such verbal excess is probably one of the most prominent characteristics of schools and classrooms that negatively orient children toward learning. . . . In this regard, the teacher may be viewed as a "working partner" who credits workers for actual accomplishments and yet is also a worker in the school setting. Check marks are presented as objective consequences of the child's efforts and, literally, as part of a reality system over which the teacher has little subjective control. The teacher's message to the child is, in essence: "That's just the way it is. I work here, too." (Hewett & Taylor, 1980, p. 230)

This system is not without its drawbacks. For one thing, as Hewett notes, the process of having children exchange their completed work record cards for tangible rewards can become unnecessarily elaborate. For another, the check-giving process itself consumes fully 15 minutes of each hour of instructional time. Also, it is not clear how this activity serves to promote acceptance of more intrinsic types of positive consequences, such as acquisition of knowledge and skill or knowledge of results. Perhaps it was with these critiques in mind that Hewett admonishes that his method "is only effective if the teacher believes in it and takes such routines as the check-mark giving process seriously" (Hewett & Taylor, 1980, p. 231).

Appraisal of the Engineered Classroom

Just how effective is the method? Clearly, a major strength of Hewett's approach is his provision of clear and comprehensive guidelines to those who would adopt

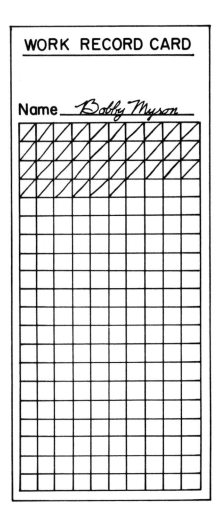

FIGURE 17.12. The work record card. *Note.* From *The Educationally Disturbed Child in the Classroom* (p. 227) by F. M. Hewett and F. D. Taylor, 1980, Boston: Allyn & Bacon. Reprinted by permission.

it. Unfortunately, very little research has been done on the efficacy of the engineered classroom, and that which has been done is somewhat equivocal. The pioneering program at the Tulare County Schools in 1965 was evaluated by pre/post ratings provided by parents and teachers (Hewett, 1968). On the parent ratings, significant differences were reported on the variables of attitudes toward school and learning; teachers reported significant improvement in learning and classroom behavior.

However, rating scales alone are at best imperfect indices of program impact, and the absence of a control group makes the results even less conclusive.

Hewett, Taylor, and Artuso (1969) performed a more extensive and comprehensive evaluation on the Santa Monica Project during 1966–1967. In this study, statistically significant differences were found between experimental and control children on the variables of task attention and arithmetic fundamentals as measured by the *California Achievement Test* (CAT). No significant differences were reported on the reading subtest of the CAT. In a more recent study the Madison School Plan (Hewett & Forness, 1977), an extension and elaboration of the Santa Monica model, was found to have produced more favorable attitudes about the handicapped among teachers who received inservice training. Unfortunately, we could locate no other controlled research on the Santa Monica Project or related programs. Therefore, any conclusions about the effectiveness of the "orchestration of success" in the engineered classroom are necessarily tentative. At present it appears that the primary usefulness of the approach may lie in helping the exceptional child get ready for schoolwork, rather than in the remediation of specific learning disorders. In short,

> the engineered classroom design as evaluated in the Santa Monica Project appears basically a launching approach. Its provision for increasing the teacher's effectiveness as a social reinforcer through systematic association with student success and primary rewards and for building fundamental learning competencies often forgotten about in education past the primary grades may greatly aid the disturbed child in taking the first step toward achieving success in school. (Hewett et al., 1969, p. 529)

18

BIOCHEMICAL TREATMENTS OF HYPERACTIVITY: PILLS AND DIETS

During the past 15 years a number of biochemical theories and treatment methodologies have arisen in the field of learning disorders. As a result, new "villains" have been postulated as causes of learning and/or behavior problems. Food additives, allergies, vitamin deficiencies, hypoglycemia, lead and other trace minerals, alpha-wave dysfunction, and even fluorescent lighting have all been posited, with varying degrees of proof, as causing deficient learning. New treatment methods derived from such theories have likewise begun to make their way into the schools. These new "methods" include megavitamin therapy, allergic immunology, the use of full-spectrum fluorescent tubes with lead foil shields to block X rays, biofeedback training, and relaxation tapes.

Doubtless the two most extensively known and widely employed of the new approaches are drug therapy (particularly stimulant drug therapy) and dietary interventions, of which the best known is perhaps Benjamin Feingold's K-P (Kaiser-Permanente) diet. The teacher who works with learning disabled children on a regular basis would be justified in wondering where all these biomedically oriented theories come from and whether the methods based on them are as effective as they are purported to be. Such questions are addressed in this chapter, a reading of which should help minimize, if not dispel, much of the confusion that exists about the nature and impact of these new approaches.

THE HYPERKINETIC BEHAVIOR SYNDROME: TARGET OF THE NEW THERAPIES

Before discussing pharmacological and dietary interventions, it is probably useful to describe the kinds of children for whom the new approaches are intended. A typical case is described in a pamphlet, "Caring About Kids: Helping the Hyperactive Child," published by the National Institute of Mental Health (1978):

Mark cannot sit still. At school he frequently does not complete his assignments, is often running around the classroom and disrupting other students with his incessant talking and clowning around. Mark acts impulsively—he often leaves the room without the teacher's permission. His impatience and frequent temper tantrums make it difficult for him to keep friends. Although he has above-average intelligence, Mark has trouble with his reading and writing, often reversing letters (b = p) and words (cat = tac).

At home, Mark has similar problems. He constantly fights with his younger sister, rides his bicycle recklessly, has difficulty catching a ball, and has trouble sitting through a television program. Because Mark has experienced few successes—academically as well as socially—he has begun to develop a very poor opinion of himself. (pp. 1–2)

Children like Mark are said to be suffering from the *hyperkinetic behavior syndrome*, more commonly referred to as *hyperkinesis* or *hyperactivity*. An earlier term for the condition, and one that is still considered by many to be synonymous with hyperactivity, is *minimal brain dysfunction*. While some question exists as to whether the two terms can or should be used interchangeably, the fact that they often are reflects a common belief in the biochemical/neurological etiology of the syndrome. This assumption of an organic basis for the hyperkinetic behavior syndrome has been increasingly questioned by research (Axelrod & Bailey, 1979), but the assumption persists nonetheless. Critics of that assumption, such as Dubey (1976), have noted some of the potentially undesirable implications that can follow from a belief in organic etiology. These include a medical orientation to treatment; a diminished emphasis on preventive measures; the potential tendency for parents, teachers, and children themselves to absolve themselves of responsibility for behavior problems; and the risk of overlooking or underestimating educational, psychological, and environmental factors in the problem behavior(s).

Given these implications, it is important to know as clearly as possible what is meant by the term *hyperkinetic behavior syndrome*. Regrettably, there is far more consensus about the characteristics or "symptoms" of the syndrome than about the precise definition or etiology of the syndrome itself. Of course, one of the symptoms is a level of activity that is (or at least is perceived as) excessive. The behavior of hyperactive children tends to be seen not only as excessive, but as excessively inappropriate. Such children appear to have difficulty in controlling their actions and in learning *how* to control their actions. They characteristically have short attention spans and are easily frustrated and distracted (Bremer & Stern, 1976). Their behavior is often described by teachers and parents as fidgety, restless, impulsive, and quarrelsome. Clearly, there is considerable room for subjectivity—and perhaps even bias—in the ascription of such characteristics; what is considered "excessive" or "inappropriate" might well rest as much in the mind of the observer as in the behavior of the observed. While attempts have been made to control for such observational subjectivity—most notably in the development of rating scales such as the Conners Abbreviated Symptom Questionnaire (Conners, 1976b)—serious questions still remain about the reliability and validity with which the existence of the condition can be determined, and indeed about whether the condition exists at all.

Regardless of whether hyperactivity might simply be a cluster of symptoms in search of a "disease," many professionals and parents believe that the condition does exist and can be assessed. Recent estimates of its frequency among school-aged children in the United States range from 4% to 10%, the majority of whom are males in their early school years (Brundage-Aguar, Forehand, & Ciminero, 1976). Some estimates, in particular that of Feingold (1975), run as high as 25% or more. In fact, Feingold (1976) has spoken of a hyperactivity "epidemic" affecting over 5 million children.

Whatever the precise nature, cause, and prevalence of the condition, questions of how it can be "cured" remain largely unresolved. Unresolved as well is the question of the extent to which hyperactivity and learning disabilities can be considered concomitant parts of the same syndrome. In the minds of proponents of pharmacological and dietary interventions, the two problems are closely interrelated. There is some basis for this assumption, in that many children deemed hyperactive *do* evidence learning problems as well; in addition, the notion that reducing inattentive and distractive behaviors will bring about an increase in learning behaviors is at least theoretically persuasive. On the other hand, a factorial analysis by Lahey, Stempnick, Robinson, and Tyroler has identified hyperactivity and learning disabilities as two separate and largely independent dimensions. This study warns that "the unknowing confounding of these apparently independent factors will almost certainly lead to confusion" (1978, p. 95).

The current situation certainly seems to bear out the prediction of Lahey and his colleagues. The sense of confusion and irresolution about the definition, assessment, etiology, remediation, and educational relevance of the hyperactive behavior syndrome has been used advantageously by both proponents and detractors of the newer biochemically based approaches. Proponents cite biochemical interpretations as an antidote to the current confusion, while critics see them as emblematic of misguided conceptualizations of diagnosis and treatment. The remainder of this chapter is devoted to an examination of both sides of the issue, after which, it is hoped, readers will be better able to decide on which side of the debate they stand.

PHARMACOLOGICAL INTERVENTIONS

That drugs affect behavior is, of course, hardly a new idea. That they can and should be used to modify school-related behavior, on the other hand, is a somewhat more novel and controversial proposition. The origins of the proposition can be traced to the pioneering research of Charles Bradley (1937/1938), who noted that the amphetamine Benzedrine brought about dramatic reductions in the hyperactivity of children who manifested disturbed behavior in school. Bradley ascribed the results achieved with his 30 subjects to the "paradoxical effects" of stimulant drugs when administered to hyperactive children. The mechanisms underlying this paradox were not very clearly explained, nor did Bradley employ a control group to determine whether the effects of stimulant drugs on normal children might not be equally "paradoxical." Nonetheless, and for whatever reason, Bradley's subjects did show a reduction in activity level.

Since then, more and more people have adopted, uncritically and enthusiastically, the idea of psychopharmacological management of hyperactivity. Grinspoon and Singer (1973) report that today it is by far the most often used and firmly established treatment method for hyperactivity. While precise figures are lacking, a 1971 survey reported that between 150,000 and 200,000 children were receiving medication to reduce their hyperactive behavior; a subsequent estimate by Offir (1974) put the number of school children receiving drugs at between 500,000 and 2 million. Krager and Safer (1974) reported a 62% increase in the usage of drug treatment between 1971 and 1973; and a survey by Rogers (1971) indicated that from 5% to 10% of elementary-aged school children were prescribed drugs to control their classroom behavior. Among children with learning problems, moreover, the rate is reported to be much higher; McIntosh and Dunn (1973) stated that well over half of all students classified as having specific learning disabilities received medication to control their behavior. Cruickshank (1977) told of one institution for the learning disabled in which 90% of the population was on some sort of medication. In short, and whatever the precise number, drugs have become a staple of the educational diet for a very great number of children.

By far the most commonly used drugs in the treatment of hyperactivity are stimulants. These include amphetamine (Benzedrine), dextroamphetamine (Dexedrine), magnesium pemoline (Cylert), and—currently the most widely prescribed of all—methylphenidate or Ritalin. Less frequently used to control behavior are major tranquilizers (e.g., phenothiazines) and antidepressants, primarily because their usage involves a higher probability of negative side effects and impairment of academic ability. Readers who are interested in a discussion of the major drugs prescribed to school-aged learning disabled children and their effects are referred to Forness and Kavale (1988).

According to a review by Brundage-Aguar et al. (1976), the effects of stimulant drugs appear to include not only a reduction in hyperactivity but also improved performance on tasks requiring sustained attention, a lower incidence of disruptive behavior, and a higher degree of cooperation with others. While these and other effects differ as a function of individual characteristics, age, dosage level, and so on, one report cites positive changes as a result of drug administration in from 80% to 90% of the children receiving stimulant drug treatment (Katz, Savat, Gittelman-Klein, & Klein, 1975). We now turn to a more detailed investigation of the evidence supporting the positive changes brought about by such treatment.

The vast amount of research into the effects of drug treatment has focused essentially on two basic questions: (a) Do stimulant drugs reduce hyperactivity? and (b) Do they promote learning? Recent reviews of the research into those questions include those conducted by Barkley (1976), Dimond (1976), Conners (1976a), Alabiso and Hansen (1977), and Kavale (1982). With regard to the control of hyperactivity, the collective conclusion suggested by the reviews is unsurprising. Apparently, stimulant drugs *do* bring about a decrement in hyperactive behaviors in most cases. As to the effects on learning, the results are equivocal. Those supporting the value of drug therapy could point to research suggesting the positive impact of stimulant drug therapy on a number of factors assumed to be related to school learning: motor learning (Wade, 1976), Bender Gestalt Test performance (Lerer & Lerer, 1977), and IQ test performance (Bradford & Rapaport, 1974). A doctoral study by Conley (1973) investigated the effects of psychostimulants on visual-motor functioning, short-term auditory and visual memory, auditory and visual attention span, work recognition, and retention skills. The sample of hyperactive children that were treated with psychostimulants showed significant improvement in all these abilities. As will be seen shortly, however, there are a number of solid reasons why the results of studies such as Conley's should be interpreted with more than the usual caution.

In sum, the evidence for the existence of a "smart pill" is at best suggestive. Even proponents such as Conners (1976a) note that stimulant effectiveness is confined largely to learning problems related to deficits in selective attention or inhibition. Nonetheless, many educators seem willing to take up the suggestion. A recent article by Murray (1976) poses the question, "Is there a role for the teacher in the use of medication for hyperkinetics?" He answers affirmatively, concluding that "while amphetamines, stimulants, and other types of drugs are not cure-alls for everyone, they do, apparently, help some, and in some cases the classroom teacher may be the best person to initiate action leading toward this type of intervention" (p. 46). While there are doubtless many who would agree with Murray's position, it is important that teachers and others be aware that serious questions still remain about the appropriateness and effectiveness of drug therapy for learning problems. We shall now consider the research that has addressed these questions.

The proliferation of stimulant drug treatment for learning and behavior problems has been accompanied by a concomitant increase in the criticism of such treatment. Critics of pharmacological interventions in the school have focused their criticisms on one or more of the following broad issues: (a) the methodological flaws, and hence the questionable validity, of much of the pharmacological research; (b) the questionable benefits and potential risks of stimulant drug effects; (c) the relationship of drug-related changes to actual learning; and (d) the possible abdication of educational responsibility implied by considering drugs as "treatment." Let us consider each of these issues in turn.

Methodological Problems in Stimulant Drug Research

The first question raised by critics of stimulant drug research deals with the construct validity of the condition purportedly treated by such drugs. In *Myth of the Hyperactive Child*, Schrag and Divoky (1975) charge that terms such as *hyperkinetic behavior syndrome* are symptomatic of a "growing fashion for giving ordinary children ill-defined or meaningless pseudo-scientific labels" and of "an ideology of 'early intervention' which regards almost every form of undesirable behavior, however benign, as a medical ailment requiring treatment" (p. xi). While there may be good reason to wonder whether the behavior of many children currently termed hyperactive is "benign," Schrag and Divoky nonetheless have a point. A similar, if somewhat less polemical, critique has been made by Rie, Rice, Stewart, and Ambuel (1976), who note there are neither norms nor well-standardized measures of activity levels in children and that the frequent coincidence of high activity levels and poor school performance has led to a common but questionable interchangeability of terms like hyperkinesis, minimal brain dysfunction, and learning disabilities. They conclude:

> The sometimes vaguely defined "syndromes" of minimal brain dysfunction and learning disability may or may not be characterized by hyperactivity. The confusion then leads to the use of stimulant medication to contend with problems on which it may not have the same demonstrable effects as it does on activity level. (p. 64)

In short, while studies investigating the effects of stimulant drugs on hyperactivity are numerous, questions continue to exist as to whether the term *hyperactivity* means the same thing to different researchers and, by implication, whether it means anything at all.

In addition to the construct validity of the hyperkinetic syndrome, questions have been raised about methodological flaws in much of the research purporting to investigate the syndrome. Axelrod and Bailey (1979) have indicated three basic areas of methodological concern: (a) placebo effects, (b) double blinding, and (c) evaluation techniques. For the findings of a drug research study to be considered reliable and valid, those conducting the study must demonstrate that they have controlled for positive (or negative) bias by using placebo and double-blind controls and have employed trained observers and reliable measures for the objective evaluation of behavior changes. Unfortunately, the vast majority of drug research has failed to meet some or all of these basic conditions. A comprehensive study by Sulzbacher (1973) reviewed all the studies of the effects of psychotropic medication on children that had been published between 1937 and 1971. Of the 756 studies reviewed, 548 were considered uncontrolled and hence procedurally biased owing to lack of placebo and double-blind conditions. When the third precondition of objective measurement devices was added, fewer than 10% of the 756 studies could be considered proce-durally unbiased. Of the remaining 75 studies, only 20 reported significant findings in favor of drugs. Sulzbacher concluded, "Neither the current diagnostic categories nor the global rating scales often used to assess improvement are sufficiently precise to permit any valid conclusions to be reached regarding which patients might bene-fit in what ways from one or another dose of any given psychotropic medication" (p. 62).

While the development of standard behavior rating scales such as Conners's (1976b) ASQ reflects an attempt to remediate some of the methodological deficien-cies criticized by Sulzbacher, serious methodological problems still remain. It would be difficult if not impossible to control for the myriad variables that could affect (and confound) the findings of drug studies, among them such variables as dosage levels, age, body weight, and previous experience with drugs. In addition, a recent study by Whalen, Henker, Collins, Finck, and Dotemoto (1979) indicates that medica-tion effects vary as a function of situational variables such as ambient noise level and type of activity. Thus, although we may one day be able to reliably predict result x in child y with drug z, that day is not yet here.

Effects of Stimulant Drugs

The second major area of criticism deals with the effects of stimulant drugs, antici-pated and otherwise. While the "paradoxical effect" of stimulants on hyperactive children is a notion that has long been accepted, it has recently begun to be ques-tioned. Axelrod and Bailey (1979) note both the lack of consistent findings with regard to this "paradoxical effect" and the paucity of research dealing with the reaction of normal children to stimulant drugs. Paradoxical or not, the effect of such drugs is commonly seen as a reduction in hyperactive and inappropriate behavior; but even here, the research findings have not been entirely consistent.

Research (Eaton, Sells, & Lucas, 1977; Grinspoon & Singer, 1973; Offir, 1974) has also reflected a growing concern about the potentially harmful side effects of stimulant drugs. These effects include reports of inhibition of normal growth, depressed caloric intake, irritability, nausea, insomnia, dizziness, tremors, gastro-intestinal distress, and increased blood pressure. In addition, there is increasing con-cern about the emotional and psychological side effects of stimulants, an area in which remarkably little research has been done. A recent study by Rie et al. (1976) dealt with 28 children between 6 and 9 years of age who were undergoing stimulant drug treatment. Clinical observations in this study revealed not only many of the physio-logical side effects cited above, but a marked decrement in emotional "responsivity" as well. These emotional side effects were described as follows:

> Children who were retrospectively confirmed to have been on active drug treatment appeared at the times of evaluation, distinctly more bland or "flat" emotionally, lack-ing both the age-typical variety and frequency of emotional expression. They responded

less, exhibited little or no initiative or spontaneity, offered little indication of either interest or aversion, showed virtually no curiosity, surprise, or pleasure, and seemed devoid of humor. (p. 72)

In sum, the effects of stimulant drug "therapy" for curing learning disorders may not be as therapeutic as is commonly assumed. Research into the physiological and emotional side effects of such drugs raises disturbing questions—questions that have yet to be explored adequately.

Do Stimulant Drugs Stimulate Learning?

The third major criticism of drug therapy pertains to questions about the effects of drugs on learning and on behaviors assumed to be related to learning. For one thing, as Lahey et al. (1978) point out, there is strong evidence that activity level and learning are independent dimensions. For another, there is a need to study the a priori assumption that stimulant drug therapy affects the hyperactive child's general cognitive style (van Duyne, 1976). For still another, even the findings of studies that *do* report improvement on measures of academic aptitude and/or achievement can hardly be considered definitive. The caveat attached to Alabiso and Hansen's (1977) review of such studies is typical: "The results of these studies must be interpreted with caution. There are probably as many studies which show no improvement in either IQ or learning as a result of drug treatment. . . . At this point none of the schools of thought regarding the relationship between learning and drug treatment have provided conclusive evidence to support their tenants [sic]" (p. 54). A similar conclusion is reached by Rie et al. (1976):

> The reactions of the children strongly suggest a reduction in commitment of the sort that would seem to be critical for learning. There would then appear to be improved, not only a reduction of the disapproved behaviors that interfere with learning, but also of the desirable behaviors that facilitate it. The net effect on learning would presumably be nil, or precisely the findings of the present study. (p. 73)

Thus there appear to be good reasons for questioning the assumption that the reduction of such factors as distractibility and impulsiveness via stimulant drugs will thereby enhance learning ability. Indeed, to the extent that the observations of Rie and others are typical, such drugs may well impede some of the psychoemotional components of a positive learning experience.

Drugs: An "Easy Way Out"?

The fourth major area of criticism raises ethical as well as instructional issues. For even if stimulant drugs can be said to "work," there still remain the questions of whether such effectiveness is worth the price of its apparent risks and of whether less risky, more educationally relevant interventions might not be just as effective. These issues have been raised by more and more critics, among them Krippner, Silverman, Cavallo, and Healy (1973), who write, "If it is correct that the diagnosis of hyperkinesis is used excessively, it appears that some schools, instead of trying to help overly active children through special educational techniques, may be attempting to calm them by the easiest method available" (p. 268). We are reminded of what Coles (1978) called the current penchant for providing "biological explanations for problems that require social solutions" (p. 332). Biological explanations and pharmacological "solutions" may provide parents and educators with an "easy way out," but doubtless there are other ways.

The most commonly explored alternative to stimulants for the control of hyperactive behavior involves the employment of behavioral intervention strategies. A number of studies have compared the relative effectiveness of stimulant medication and behavioral techniques such as social reinforcement (Weissenburger & Loney, 1977); token reinforcement (Ayllon, Layman, & Kandel, 1975); contingency management (Wulbert & Dries, 1977); behavior therapy (Gittleman-Klein, Klein, Katz, Gloisten, & Kates, 1976; O'Leary, Pelham, Rosenbaum, & Price, 1976); and programmed teacher intervention (Shafto & Sulzbacher, 1977). Taken together, such studies demonstrate that behavioral interventions can be as effective as stimulants in reducing the incidence of hyperactive behavior. The findings of the study by Ayllon and his colleagues are particularly suggestive. They showed not only that reinforcement was as effective as Ritalin in controlling hyperactivity, but also that it led to far superior performance on measures of math and reading ability.

We conclude this section on drug therapy by pointing out that there *are* viable alternatives to the pharmacological "method" for treating hyperactivity and learning disorders. Stimulant drugs may represent the easiest means for handling (or at least postponing) these problems, but the price for such convenience is high—perhaps too high. We have already noted in some detail the questionable benefits and real risks of drug treatment. There are additional costs as well—now largely hidden—that could one day make the "easy way out" the hard way back. For if current trends continue, our nation will be peopled with millions of young citizens who have learned at a very early age to approach the tasks of learning and living with a fundamental and insidious question: namely, "Where's my pill?"

DIETARY INTERVENTIONS: THE FEINGOLD HYPOTHESIS

In 1965, Benjamin Feingold, former chief of the Department of Allergy at the Kaiser-Permanente Medical Center in San Francisco, treated an adult female patient who was suffering from an acute case of hives. He placed her on an elimination diet that removed all salicylates—naturally occurring compounds found in a number of fruits and vegetables and some herbs and spices—from her diet. The surprising result was that in less than 2 weeks he observed not only that the hives had cleared up but also that the patient reported improvement in previously unreported psychiatric symptoms of aggression and hostility (Feingold, 1975). This was the first of many clinical reports by Feingold dealing with the salubrious effect of such an elimination diet on psychobehavioral disturbances. What makes Feingold's hypothesis of current interest to educators is that he began to use his dietary intervention as a means of treating hyperactive behavior disorders in schoolchildren.

In the spring of 1974 the California State Department of Education sponsored what was called a "demonstration study" for which Feingold acted as a consultant. The unpublished study of 25 hyperactive children from the Santa Cruz City Schools reported that 16 of the 25 children responded favorably to treatment with Feingold's Kaiser-Permanente (K-P) elimination diet, which forbade all salicylates and artificial food coloring and flavors. On the basis of this and several other uncontrolled dietary studies with which he was associated (see Feingold, 1975), Feingold arranged a joint news conference with Wilson Riles, California State Superintendent of Public Instruction, and announced that

> hyperactivity in children can be significantly reduced by the elimination of artificial food coloring and flavoring from their diets, according to the results of a study conducted by the California State Department of Education. (Spring & Sandoval, 1976, p. 564)

They went on to state that the diet "brings hope to thousands of parents who have been distressed by the need to cope with the problems of hyperactivity by giving their children prescribed drugs" (p. 564).

There followed in the wake of this announcement "TV talk shows, press conferences, nationally distributed news reports, magazine articles, a popular book, and even legislative hearings at the State and federal levels" (Spring & Sandoval, 1976, p. 561). So strong was the public response to the Feingold diet that there now exists a national Feingold Association in the United States, with a total membership of over 10,000 families in 120 local affiliates. Clearly, then, the diet has "caught on." Many people see the diet as the "cure" not only for hyperactivity but for learning disorders as well. In the November 1976 issue of the *Journal of Learning Disabilities*, Feingold states his conclusion unequivocally:

> Artificial food colors and flavors have the capacity to induce adverse reactions affecting every system of the body. Of all these adverse reactions, the nervous system involvement, as evidenced by behavioral disturbances and learning disabilities, is the most frequently encountered and most critical, affecting millions of individuals in this country alone.
>
> The K-P diet, which eliminates all artificial food colors and flavors as well as foods with a natural salicylate radical, will control the behavioral disturbance in 30 to 50% (depending on the sample) of both normal and neurologically damaged children. (p. 558)

In view of the drawbacks of stimulant drug treatment delineated in the previous section of this chapter, it is understandable that Feingold's claim to have discovered an effective nonpharmacological intervention for hyperactivity and learning disorders would find a receptive audience among many concerned parents and teachers. As Divoky (1978) notes, "Along comes Feingold. Not only is he going to get hyperactive kids off drugs, but he's going to do it with a wonderfully appealing treatment: additive-free, healthful food" (p. 56). Other factors in addition to concern about side effects of stimulants served to make the timing for promotion of Feingold's approach particularly auspicious. One was the increasing attention that was and is being paid in academic journals to the relationship between learning and such factors as metabolism (Buckley, 1977), nutrition (Kelin & Pertz, 1978), diet (Powers, 1973), and allergy (Mayron, 1979). Even beyond the relatively narrow range of readers of such journals, observed Spring and Sandoval (1976), there is a widespread and growing public acceptance of the notion popularized by authors like the late Adelle Davis that "you are what you eat," as well as a growing public concern about contaminants in our air, water, and food. Clearly, then, there are a number of reasons why people would *want* to believe that the Feingold diet works. But, as Divoky and a number of other critics have observed, there is considerably more evidence of the popularity of the diet than of its effectiveness. Thus it is vital for educators to examine closely a number of very basic questions: What is the Feingold hypothesis? What evidence exists to substantiate it? What is the substance of criticisms leveled against it?

Feingold (1975) contends that an "explosion" of hyperactivity has occurred in this country since 1945. As a possible explanation for this, he poses the rhetorical question:

> Was it possible that the artificial flavorings and colorings were causing the behavioral disturbances? The time factor favored it. The additives, particularly the flavorings, had not been used in any great quantity until after World War II. Most of the synthetic additives, aside from colors, were less than thirty-five years old. Could the mass of convenience foods, the great tangle of additives, have anything to do with the recent alarming incidence of H-LD? (p. 21)

Feingold's answer to the question, of course, is an emphatic yes. He maintains that largely as a result of this mushrooming "tangle of additives" in our food, hyperkinesis has likewise mushroomed into "a prevalence of epidemic proportions affecting approximately 5,000,000 children in this country" (1976, p. 551).

As we shall see, Feingold's belief in the existence of such an "epidemic" has been questioned. Nonetheless, it forms the fundamental premise for his hypothesis. The major elements of his hypothesis are as follows:

- The hyperactive disturbance is "nonimmunologic." Unlike allergic reactions, he feels, "there is no natural body defense against it."
- Those children who react to synthetic additives have genetic variations—not abnormalities—which predispose them to such adverse responses.
- An "innate releasing mechanism" is closely involved in the disturbance. (Nutrition Foundation, 1976, p. 2)

Feingold's recommended treatment for the disturbance is the K-P "exclusion diet" (see Figure 18.1). As is evident from the figure, the extent of "exclusion" in the diet is substantial. Not only are a vast number of common features in the everyday diet "verboten," but a wide variety of nonfood items such as mouthwashes, toothpastes, and cough drops are likewise excluded. Gone from the diet are hot dogs, catsup, tomatoes, oranges, apples, and commercially baked products: "In short, almost everything in the daily diets of many if not most children" (Divoky, 1978, p. 57). Nor is there necessarily a limit to the time during which the diet must be observed. According to Feingold (1975), people who are sensitive to artificial colors and flavors should avoid them throughout their lives.

In addition, Feingold recommends that the rationale underlying his hypothesis be used to bring about several changes in public policy relating to food distribution:

1. full disclosure on food labels of the use of flavors and colors in all food products;

2. a broad educational program by the U.S. Food and Drug Administration to inform the public on the "inherent potentials" of these chemicals; and

3. the use of a special symbol on food packages to indicate the absence of synthetic colors and flavors. (Nutrition Foundation, 1976)

Feingold considers his hypothesis valid enough and his diet effective enough that they can be used to justify dramatic changes both in individual lives (in fact, he recommends that entire families be involved in the diet) and in public policy. Much of the evidence he cites to substantiate the hypothesis is drawn from clinical impressions and anecdotes, such as one describing a young boy who prior to the diet was a "small, terrifying Mr. Hyde" (Feingold, 1975). Other than the 1974 demonstration study mentioned earlier, Spring and Sandoval (1976) cite but three studies that could be interpreted as supporting Feingold's 1976 estimate of a 30% to 50% success rate for the diet. More recent research by Rose (1978) and Rapp (1978) also constitutes statements of support for the Feingold hypothesis. In addition, the large number of "Feingold Families" (Feingold, 1976) might also be considered as evidence that the diet is sensible and effective. By and large, however, the major source of support for the Feingold hypothesis is found in anecdotal reports rather than in controlled, large-scale studies.

Not surprisingly, the growing popularity of the Feingold diet has been accompanied by increasing scrutiny of the claims being made about it. In 1975 the Nutrition Foundation assembled a National Advisory Committee on Hyperkinesis and Food Additives, consisting of 14 experts in food, medicine, and behavioral science. The committee was charged with the task of critically and objectively evaluating the evidence supporting Feingold's hypothesis and the recommendations stemming from it. Its conclusion read as follows:

- No controlled studies have demonstrated that hyperkinesis is related to the ingestion of food additives.

- The claim that hyperactive children improve significantly on a diet that is free of salicylates and food additives has not been confirmed.

Omit the following, as indicated:

1. Foods containing natural salicylates

Almonds	Mint flavors
Apples (cider and cider vinegars)	Nectarines
Apricots	Oranges
Blackberries	Peaches
Cherries	Plums or prunes
Cloves	Raspberries
Cucumbers and pickles	Strawberries
Currants	All tea
Gooseberries	Tomatoes
Grapes or raisins (wine and wine vinegars)	Oil of wintergreen

The salicylate-containing foods may be restored following 4 to 6 weeks of favorable response provided no history of aspirin sensitivity exists in the family.

II. All foods that contain artificial colors and flavors

III. Miscellaneous items

All aspirin-containing compounds
All medications with artificial colors and flavors
Toothpaste and toothpowder (substitute salt and soda or unscented Neutrogena® soap)
All perfumes

Note: Check all labels of food items and drugs for artificial coloring and flavoring. Since permissible foods without artificial colors and flavors vary from region to region, it is not practical to compile a list of permissible foods. Each individual must learn to read the ingredients on the label. When added colors and flavors are specified, the item is prohibited. If in doubt, the food should not be used. Instead, it is advisable to prepare the substitute at home from scratch.

FIGURE 18.1. The Kaiser-Permanente (K-P) diet. *Note.* From "Hyperkinesis and Learning Disabilities Linked to the Ingestion of Artificial Food Colors and Flavors" by B. Feingold, 1976, *Journal of Learning Disabilities, 9,* p. 554. Reprinted by special permission.

- The nutritional qualities of the Feingold diet have not been evaluated, and it may not meet the long-term nutrient needs of children.

- The diet should not be used without competent medical supervision. (Nutrition Foundation, 1975, p. 3)

In the wake of the committee's report, the Institute of Food Technologists' Expert Panel on Food Safety and Nutrition and the Committee on Public Information produced a Scientific Status Summary of evidence on the hypothesized relationship between diet and hyperactivity (Nutrition Foundation, 1976). The panel cited a number of reasons why the Feingold hypothesis had come under criticism:

1. *More than diet changed.* Although Feingold considers the diet the critical variable in whatever changes are brought about by undergoing it, the panel noted that diet is only one of the several critical variables of the child's life that are changed. Other family members are directly involved in the child's treatment, and drastic changes in the manner of food preparation and attitudes about food and behavior are involved. Thus the possibility exists that such alterations in family dynamics may be related to any reported improvement in the child. Spring and Sandoval likewise note that "in such an altered environment, it seems likely that the hyperactive child will experience strong social demands as well as social support for improved behavior" (1976, p. 32). A related point is raised in the Nutrition Foundation report:

   > Behavioral change is the deciding factor in all of this research, and behavior and its measurement is so dependent upon psychological influences in the home and school that it is difficult to isolate the single variable of food additives. (1976, p. 8)

2. *Suggestibility.* It has long been demonstrated that positive expectations about an intervention can bring about positive changes, regardless of the nature of the intervention. Current public attitudes about nutrition, Feingold's "charismatic personality," the wide publicity received by the diet, public uneasiness about drugs, the opportunity to "blame" hyperactivity on food rather than on practices in the home and/or school, and the considerable time and effort involved in following the diet are all factors that can contribute to self-fulfillment of the Feingold "prophecy."

3. *Subjectivity of observations.* The panel notes that knowledge by parents and/or teachers that the child is on the diet can bias their behavior ratings in a positive direction, particularly in view of the highly general improvement ratings suggested by Feingold. Spring and Sandoval likewise note "the subjectivity and flexibility in reporting and interpreting data which *permits* a placebo effect" (1976, p. 32).

4. *Chemical basis undefined.* Feingold does not—and very likely cannot—specify which are the particular chemicals whose omission is critical to whatever changes are brought about by the diet. Indeed, the panel notes that Feingold himself has recently lessened emphasis on the suspected role of salicylates in favor of other food ingredients. In view of the vast number of forbidden foods, and the even vaster number of chemical combinations within them, the list of "suspects" is virtually limitless; and the task of isolating the critical chemical variables is well-nigh impossible.

5. *Results similar to other approaches.* Even if Feingold's claims of success rates are true, the diet has not been shown to be more effective than alternative approaches, pharmacological or otherwise.

Feingold's hypothesis has been criticized on other fronts as well. The review of Spring and Sandoval (1976) has cast serious doubt on Feingold's premise of an "explosion" in the incidence of hyperactivity since World War II. Further, even if there were such an "explosion," the assumption of its causal link to food additives is at best inferential. There is likewise the same problem that hinders evaluation of stimulant drug research: namely, the difficulty of accurately defining and measuring the construct of hyperactivity. One can also imagine the difficulty of ensuring that a child on the diet never encounters—or succumbs to—the temptation to ingest delicacies forbidden by the diet.

Two major studies have been undertaken recently in an attempt to avoid some or all of the methodological problems plaguing earlier studies (i.e., the use of non-validated rating instruments, the lack of placebo and experimental controls, and the lack of objective evidence of behavior change) and to address questions raised by the Nutrition Foundation and Institute of Food Technologists' reports. The first was undertaken by Harley et al. (1976) at the University of Wisconsin, consisting of a controlled study of 36 hyperactive youngsters in two age groups (CA 3–6 and 8–12), extended over an 8-month period. Their basic conclusion was as follows:

> With the possible exception of the youngest age sample, the preliminary analyses completed to date in the Wisconsin study do not appear to offer strong support for the efficacy of the experimental diet. . . . The frequency with which positive diet effects were judged to be present was highest in the parent ratings, declined sharply in the teacher rating data, and essentially disappeared in the objective classroom and grid room observational data. (Harley et al, 1976)

It should be noted, however, that the Wisconsin group stated the preliminary nature of their findings and indicated that there were a sufficient number of reports of improvement to merit further investigation.

A second major controlled study was conducted by Conners, Goyette, Southwick, Lees, and Andrulonis (1976) at the University of Pittsburgh's Department of Psychiatry. The 3-month study investigated the responses of 15 hyperactive school-aged children, both male and female, on both the K-P and a control diet. Of the 15 subjects, 4 were rated by parents and/or teachers as showing improved behavior while on the additive-free diet. Conners and Goyette are quoted in a special publication of the Nutrition Foundation (1976) as stating that the findings of the Pittsburgh study lend some support to the Feingold hypothesis, but they also add this note of caution:

> Although the results favor the Feingold hypothesis, methodological limitations warrant caution as well as concern regarding possible long-term negative consequences of unmonitored diet fads among parents of hyperkinetic children looking for simple solutions to a complex group of disorders. (p. 5)

After reviewing the research available at the time, Baker (1980) concludes that the improvements seen in children by Feingold and parents may be nothing more than placebo effects. He concludes with the statement that "serious questions must be raised concerning the advisability of prescribing the Feingold diet as a viable method of treating hyperkinesis" (p. 34). In a review of more current research, Silver (1987) seconds Baker's conclusions.

We echo the calls for caution and concern that are often made by researchers with reference to "diet fads" and to drugs and other biomedical "fancies" that are being promoted as methodological solutions to educational problems. Their widespread usage threatens simply to perpetuate further procrastination in the task of developing more appropriate and effective instructional and behavioral strategies for children with learning disorders. Readers who would like a more detailed discussion of the effects of the Feingold diet, megavitamins, drug therapy, biofeedback, radiation, and allergens on the treatment of the learning disabled are referred to Reid and Hresko's (1981) chapter, "Hyperactivity."

CONCLUSIONS

Whatever their differences, these biochemical treatments have at least two things in common: (a) They all adhere to a "medical model" of learning disabilities; and (b) they all are controversial. Fealty to the medical model is evident in the background and training of the leading proponents of these approaches, most of whom have little or no experience in classroom teaching. Acceptance of the medical model is also evident in the perspective they have toward both the etiology and the treatment of learning problems. The "disease" in this case is inferred from "symptoms" evident in classroom performance; and the subsequent "cure" is felt to lie in *treating* the "patient" (i.e., the student) rather than in modifying the socioacademic ecology of the school environment. Such a cure might take the form of a special diet, a special pill, special lighting fixtures, or a special form of biofeedback training. In any case the focus is more on effecting biochemically related changes in the child than on modifying his or her behavior through instructional means.

This point is one reason for the considerable controversy generated by these new approaches. Approaching the treatment of instructionally related problems from a basically noninstructional perspective is bound to seem alien, if not alienating, to many classroom teachers. But the infiltration of pharmacologists, dietitians, allergists, physicians, and neurometricians into the classroom would in any case be expected to create at least some degree of "culture shock" among teachers; and it is clear that the controversy is more than just a matter of strange faces in unlikely places.

Both in and out of the field of education a number of serious questions have been raised: What is it that is being "treated"? What is the relation, if any, between the condition being treated and actual classroom learning? Do the benefits of treatment outweigh the risks? Are the new approaches effective, and if so, why? At this point, as we have seen, definitive answers to such questions are in painfully short supply. Nonetheless, such approaches continue to be more and more widely employed, adding more and more fuel to the fires of debate.

However it may be resolved, two contributions to the debate reflect our own concerns about the injudicious use of biochemical treatments for learning and behavior problems. Interestingly enough, both critiques come from physicians, an indication that reservations about the appropriateness of the medical model in the classroom are not confined to educators alone. The first is taken from an article by Coles (1978) in the *Harvard Educational Review,* in which he criticizes the attempt by many professionals to provide "biological explanations for problems that require social solutions" (p. 332). Coles concludes:

> It is my firm impression that educators, consciously or not, have attempted to enhance their profession, which otherwise has only moderate social status. They have sought affiliation with the medical world not only because multidisciplinary work is valued but also because it provides them with an aura of greater knowledge, authority, and importance. And who can blame them? How mundane to tell someone you teach remedial reading. How awesome to announce that you do clinical work with minimally brain dysfunctional children, more dyslexic than dyscalculic, who are benefitting from methylphenidate. (p. 335)

A similar conclusion is reached by Sieben (1977) in a critique of the increasingly popular medical treatments recommended by many of his fellow physicians:

> It is unfortunate that the understandable desire of both parents and teachers to find a quick and easy cure has encouraged a widespread acceptance of very dubious medical treatments. There is no such ready cure. The treatment of these problems is largely a laborious educational and social one. (p. 146)

Despite such criticisms, the search for a "ready cure" continues.

While the search for simply biochemical "solutions" to complex educational problems may be tempting, succumbing to the temptation may be an abdication of our professional responsibility as educators. We must keep our conceptions about learning and behavior problems—and our methods of dealing with such problems—close to the concrete and compelling realities of the classroom. There lie the problems. There, too, in the final analysis, lie the solutions.

APPENDIX

LEARNING DISABILITIES, DYSLEXIA, AND VISION*

Policy:

The American Academy of Pediatrics, the American Academy of Ophthalmology, and the American Association for Pediatric Ophthalmology and Strabismus support the position that a child or adult with dyslexia or a related learning disability should receive:

(1) Early medical, educational, and/or psychological evaluation and diagnosis

(2) Remediation with educational procedures of proven value, demonstrated by valid research

Background:

The problems of the dyslexias and related learning disabilities have become matters of increasing public attention. A child's or adult's inability to read with understanding is a major obstacle to school learning and may have far-reaching social and economic implications. The normal and appropriate concern of parents for the welfare of their children and of societyfor its disadvantaged has fostered a proliferation of purportedly diagnostic and remedial procedures, many of which are controversial. Research shows that deficient visual perception

---

*Policy Statement of the American Academy of Ophthalmology

of letters or words accounts for inability to read in only a small minority of children, the majority suffering from a variety of linguistic defects (16,17). Therefore, the diagnosis and treatment of dyslexia and associated learning disabilities have recently been reviewed with the following conclusions endorsed by the American Academy of Pediatrics, the American Academy of Ophthalmology, and the American Association for Pediatric Ophthalmology and Strabismus.

Evaluation and Conclusions:

1. Learning disabilities, including the dyslexias, as well as other forms of learning underachievement, often may require a multidisciplinary approach from medicine, education, and psychology in evaluation, diagnosis, and treatment. Certain problems may be detected during early childhood through the use of screening techniques by educational specialists. Children with potential problems include those with language defects, emotional problems, or a family history of learning disability. These individuals should be assessed by educational and psychological specialists as early as possible to identify individuals at risk for learning disabilities.

2. Eye care should never be instituted in isolation when a person does have dyslexia or a related learning disability. Children identified as having such problems should be evaluated for general medical, neurologic, psychologic, visual, and hearing defects. If any problems of this nature are found, corrective and/or remedial steps should be applied as early as possible.

3. Since the decoding of written language involves transmission of visual signals from the eyes to the brain, it has, unfortunately, become common practice to attribute reading difficulties to subtle ocular abnormalities, presumed to cause faulty perception. Although eyes are necessary for vision, "visual perception" depends on the interpretation of visual symbols by the brain. Remediation directed to the eyes cannot be expected to alter the brain's processing of visual stimuli. Indeed, children with dyslexia or related learning disability have the same incidence of ocular abnormalities, e.g., refractive errors and muscle imbalances (including near point of convergence and binocular fusion deficiencies), as children without (1–3). There is no peripheral eye defect which produces dyslexia and associated learning disabilities (4). Eye defects do not cause reversal of letters, words, or numbers. Indeed, recent studies suggest dyslexia and associated learning disabilities may be related to genetic (5), biochemical (6), and/or structural brain changes. Further controlled research is warranted.

4. Correctable ocular defects should be treated appropriately. However, no known scientific evidence supports claims for improving the academic abilities of dyslexic or learning disabled children with treatment based on: (a) visual training, including muscle exercises, ocular pursuit or tracking exercises, or glasses (with or without bifocals or prisms) (8–14); (b) neurologic organizational training (laterality training, balance board, perceptual training) (2–4, 8–14, 15). Furthermore, such training may result in a false sense of security, which may delay or prevent proper instruction or remediation. The expense of such procedures is unwarranted. They cannot be substituted for appropriate remedial education measures. Improvement claimed for visual training or neurologic organizational training typically results from those remedial educational techniques with which they are combined.

5. The teaching of dyslexic and learning disabled children and adults is a problem for educational science. Proper proven, expert educational and psychological testing should be per-

formed to identify the type of learning disability. Since remediation may be more effective during the early years (10), especially prior to the development of a pattern of failure, early diagnosis is paramount. Since deficient ability to learn to read can be the result of a variety of factors, including different neurophysiologic deficiencies, cognitive deficits, or psychological factors, no single educational approach is applicable to all children. A change in any variable may result in improved performance and reduced frustration (including placebo benefits).

The American Academy of Ophthalmology, the American Association for Pediatric Ophthalmology and Strabismus, and the American Academy of Pediatrics strongly support the early diagnosis and appropriate treatment of persons with dyslexia and related learning disabilities. We commit ourselves to these efforts and to scientifically valid research on the cause, diagnosis, and remediation of these conditions or defects.

Approved by: American Academy of Pediatrics
January 5, 1984

American Association for Pediatric
Ophthalmology and Strabismus
February 27, 1984

American Academy of Ophthalmology
February 18, 1984

Footnotes:

1. E. M. Helveston, F. D. Ellis, J. C. Weber, K. Miller, K. Robertson, R. Estes, G. Hohberger, N. Pick, and B. H. Helveston, "Visual Function and Academic Performance," read before the American Association for Pediatric Ophthalmology and Strabismus Annual Meeting, Vail, February 27, 1984.

2. J. W. Bettman, Jr., E. L. Stern, L. J. Whitsell, and H. F. Gofman, "Cerebral Dominance in Developmental Dyslexia: Role of Ophthalmology," *Arch. Ophthalmol.*, 78:722–730, December, 1967.

3. M. D. Norn, Rindziunsky, and Skydsgaard, "Ophthalmologic and Orthopitic Examinations of Dyslectics," *Acta Ophthalmologica*, 47:147, 1969.

4. H. K. Goldberg and P. W. Drash, "The Disabled Reader," *J. Ped. Ophthalmol.*, 5:11–24, 1968.

5. Univ. of Miami, "Chromosome 15 May Cause Dyslexia," *Medical World News*, p. 24, December 22, 1980.

6. S. E. Shaywitz, D. J. Cohen, and B. A. Shaywitz, "The Biochemical Basis of Minimal Brain Dysfunction," *J. Pediatrics*, 92/2:179/187, February, 1978.

7. A. M. Galaburda and T. L. Kemper, "Cytoarchitectonic Abnormalities in Development Dyslexia," *Ann. Neurol.*, 6/2:96–100, August, 1979.

8. H. J. Cohen, H. G. Birch, and L. T. Taft, "Some Considerations for Evaluating the Doman-Delacato Patterning Method," *Pediatrics*, 45:302–314, 1970.

9. American Academy of Pediatrics, "The Doman-Delacato Treatment of Neurologically Handicapped Children. A Policy Statement," *Pediatrics*, 70:5, 1982.

10. H. K. Goldberg and W. Arnott, "Ocular Motility in Learning Disabilities," *J. Learning Disabilities*, 3:160, March, 1970.

11. W. F. Cygan, "Research in Visual-Perceptual-Motor Activities Related to Reading Achievement," *Optometric Weekly*, pp. 796–803, August 29, 1974.

12. B. Keogh, "Optometric Vision Training Programs for Learning Disability Children: Review of Issues and Research," presented, in part, at the 10th Annual Meeting of the Association for Children with Learning Disabilities, Detroit, Michigan, March 15, 1973.

13. J. F. Kavanagh and G. Yeni-Komshian, "Developmental Dyslexia and Related Reading Disorders," NIH Publication No. 80–92, January, 1980.

14. GAO Report, "Perceptual and Visual Training as a CHAMPUS Benefit," Report to Congress, May 31, 1979.

15. H. M. Smith, "Motor Activity and Perceptual Development," *J. Health-Physical-Recreation*, February, 1968.

16. S. Mattis, J. H. French, and I. Pepin, "Dyslexia in Children and Young Adults: Three Independent Neurological Syndromes," *Dev. Ped. Child Neurol.*, 17:150–163, 1975.

17. S. Mattis, "Dyslexia Syndromes: A Working Hypothesis That Works," *Dx. Dyslexia: An Appraisal of Current Knowledge*, A. Benton and D. Pearl, editors, pp. 45–58, Oxford University Press, New York, 1978.

GLOSSARY

Acalculia. See *Dyscalculia.*

Agnosia. Loss of or impairment of the ability to recognize objects or events presented through the various modalities when the sense organ is not significantly defective.

    Auditory. Inability to recognize sounds or combinations of sounds without regard to their meaning.

    Tactile (Astereognosis). Disorder of body orientations; characterized by inability to recognize stimuli through the sense of touch.

    Visual. Inability to recognize objects by sight.

Agraphia. See *Dysgraphia.*

Alexia. See *Dyslexia.*

Anomia. Inability to appropriately name objects, persons, activities; classically refers to difficulty in recalling nouns.

Anoxia. Deficient amount of oxygen in the tissues of a part of the body or in the bloodstream supplying such part.

Aphasia. See *Dysphasia.*

Apraxia. See *Dyspraxia.*

Articulation. The production of speech sounds by modifying the breath stream through movements of the lips, tongue, and velum.

Astereognosis. See *Agnosia.*

Astigmatism. A defect in the curvature of the lens causing distorted images.

Auditory agnosia. See *Agnosia.*

Auditory memory span. The number of items that can be recalled from oral stimulation; includes immediate and delayed recall of digits, words, sentences, and paragraphs or free and controlled recall (latter entails questions pertaining to content).

Autotopagnosis. See *Agnosia.*

Aversive stimulus. A negative stimulus, the removal or cessation of which is reinforcing.

Bilateral. Involving both sides.

Body concept. See *Body image.*

Body image. The concept and awareness of one's own body as it relates to orientation, movement, and other behavior.

Body schema. See *Body image.*

Branching. A programming technique that allows a person who fails an item on the program to be exposed to a series of items not usually used in the program but leading up to the failed item.

Central nervous system. The neural tissue that comprises the brain and spinal cord.

Cerebral cortex. The gray matter composing the external layer of the brain that is responsible for the integration of stimuli received and responses made.

Cerebral dominance. The state in which one hemisphere of the brain is more involved in the mediation of various functions than the other hemisphere; a theory expostulated largely by Orton, Delacato, and Travis that one hemisphere is a dominant controller; right-hemisphere dominant and ambidextrous people show mixed dominance.

Cerebrum. The extensive portion of the brain that comprises the cerebral hemispheres. That part of the brain other than the brain stem and cerebellum.

Channels of communication. The sensorimotor pathways through which language is transmitted, for example, auditory-vocal, visual-motor, among other possible combinations.

Circumlocution. Literally, to speak around the point; inability to present ideas in a concise and clear manner.

Classical Conditioning. A type of learning in which a stimulus presented simultaneously with a reflexive behavior comes to elicit the behavior.

Closure. A behavior that signifies pattern completion; the mechanism responsible for the automatic completion of familiar events.

Cognition. Intellectual activities as distinguished from feeling or willing.

Color coding. A teaching technique that uses colors to facilitate learning, for example, designating each of the sounds in English with a different color or using particular colors for the various parts of speech.

Conceptualization. The ability to infer from what is observable.

Conditioning. A term often used synonymously with learning but usually including both classical and instrumental conditioning.

Congenital. Present at birth; usually a defect of either familial or exogenous origin that exists at the time of birth.

Consonant. The speech sounds formed by altering, modifying, obstructing the stream of vocal sound with the organs of speech, that is, teeth, tongue, etc. Represented by all the letters of the alphabet except vowels.

Contralateral. On the opposite side.

Convulsive disorder. A clinical syndrome, the central feature of which is recurrent seizures or convulsions; recurrent disturbances of consciousness, with or without muscular components, and accompanied by changes in the electrical potentials of the brain.

Cortex. See *Cerebral cortex.*

Crawling. A means of locomotion in which the trunk is in contact with the surface.

Creeping. A means of locomotion on hands and knees with the trunk free of the surface.

Criterion test. A test, either standardized or nonstandardized, that measures precisely the criterion behavior that is to be learned.

Cross-pattern. A highly integrated movement in which arms and legs operate in an alternating fashion, for example, in walking, as the right leg extends, the right arm swings back while comparable body parts on the left side are in reverse position.

Cursive. A type of writing with the strokes of successive characters joined and the angles rounded.

Cutaneous. Pertaining to the skin.

Decoding. The receptive habits in the language process, for example, sensory acuity, awareness, discrimination, vocabulary comprehension.

Deep structure. That which determines the meaning of a sentence, for example, "John is easy to please" and "John is eager to please" have the same surface structure, but because the agent or actor in each is different, they have differing deep structures.

Directionality. Awareness of the up-and-down axis (verticality) and awareness of the relative position of one side of the body versus the other (laterality).

Discrimination. The act of distinguishing differences among stimuli.

Dissociation. Inability to synthesize separate elements into integrated meaningful wholes.

Distractibility. Forced responsiveness to extraneous stimuli.

Dyscalculia. Loss of or inability to calculate, to manipulate number symbols, or to do simple arithmetic.

Dysfunction. Abnormal or imperfect behavior of an organ.

Dysgraphia. Impairment in spontaneous writing, the ability to copy being intact.

Dyslexia. Impairment in the ability to read; generally believed to be the result of cerebral lesions.

Dysphasia. Disorders of linguistic symbolization; the partial or complete loss of ability to speak (expressive dysphasia) or to comprehend the spoken word (receptive dysphasia); generally believed to be the result of injury, disease, or maldevelopment of the brain.

Dyspraxia. Partial loss of the ability to perform purposeful movements in a coordinated manner in the absence of paralysis, cerebral palsy, or sensory loss.

Echoic. A speech utterance that is merely a repetition of a previously heard utterance.

Echolalia. Senseless repetition of words or sounds.

EEG. See *Electroencephalogy.*

Electroencephalogy. Technique of recording brain waves for the purpose of detecting pathological conditions.

Emotional lability. Unstable feelings, emotions, and moods characterized by rapid shifts from one extreme to the other.

Encoding. The expressive habits in the language process, that is, response formation including word selection, syntax, grammar, and the actual motor production of the response.

Engram. A memory trace or pattern supposedly left in the brain cells following a mental stimulus.

Epilepsy. See *Convulsive disorder*.

Etiology. The cause of an abnormal condition.

Evocative mechanism. Habits formed when external or response events occur with high frequency or temporal contiguity; closure function is apparent, and once initiated, these activities tend to complete themselves in a fairly predictive fashion, for example, the completion of the sentence "The boy ran up the _____" is probably included in the following set: *hill, alley, road, path*, and so on.

Expressive dysphasia. See *Dysphasia*.

External feedback. See *Feedback*.

Feedback. The process of monitoring and modifying one's own responses; a cybernetic system; includes both an internal form where part of the response pattern is fed back into the system prior to effecting the response and an external form where the overt response is monitored.

Figure-ground. Tendency of one part of a perceptual configuration to stand out clearly while the remainder forms a background.

Grammar. The study of language as a system of rules governing the regularity of any specific language.

Graphic. Pertaining to writing.

Gustatory. Pertaining to taste.

Handedness. Refers to hand preference of an individual.

Hard signs. Behaviors or test results that are strongly indicative of brain dysfunction, for example, convulsions, athetosis, and so on.

Hemorrhage. Bleeding.

Homolateral. Pertaining to one side.

Homologous. Pertaining to body structures that have the same origin in a different species, for example, the arm of a man and the wing of a bird.

Hyperactivity. Disorganized, disruptive, and unpredictable behavior; overreaction to stimuli.

Hyperkinetic. See *Hyperactivity*.

Hypoactivity. Insufficient motor activity characterized by lethargy.

Hypokinetic. See *Hypoactivity*.

Ideation. Reflective thought; the organization of concepts into meaningful relationships.

Imagery. Representation of images.

Impulsivity. The initiation of sudden action without sufficient forethought or prudence.

Initial teaching alphabet. An alphabet of 44 characters, each of which represents a single English phoneme.

Inner language. Develops prior to receptive and expressive language; initially concerned with the formation of simple concepts as evidenced in the child's play activities; later, more complex relationships evolve, and the child plays with toys in a meaningful fashion.

Instrumental Conditioning. A type of learning in which a stimulus, having elicited a behavior that is accompanied by a rewarding stimulus, thereafter is more likely to elicit that same behavior or response. See also *Operant Behavior*.

Integration. (1) The second level of organization postulated by Osgood, which organizes and sequences both incoming and outgoing neural events. (2) In the composite model (chapter II), imitative behaviors are included along with Osgood's predictive and evocative activities. (3) To Wepman, the mediating processes of the CNS including the memory bank.

Internal feedback. See *Feedback.*

Intraverbal. A speech utterance under the control of the verbal behavior with which it is closely associated but separate from, for example, the completion response as in "Roses are red; violets are _____."

i.t.a. See *Initial teaching alphabet.*

Kinesthesia. The sense by which muscular movements are perceived.

Language. An arbitrary system of vocal symbols by which ideas are conveyed.

Language acquisition device (LAD). According to some psycholinguists, an innate property of the "mind" that permits developing children to acquire the rules of their language.

Language processes. The habits associated with decoding, association, and encoding of symbolic information.

Laterality. Sidedness. See also *Directionality.*

Lesion. Any hurt, wound, or local degeneration.

Lexical. Referring to single words; vocabulary items.

Linguistic approaches to reading. Emphasis on the relationship between the words as printed and the sounds for which the letters are conventional signs; goal is to develop automatic association between letters and sounds.

Linguistic competence. The speaker's intuitive knowledge of the rules governing his or her native language.

Linguistic performance. The speaker's production of his or her native language in both receptive and expressive aspects that reflects underlying competence.

Linguistics. The science of languages; the study of human speech including the units, structure, and modification of language or languages.

Localization. The discovery of the locality of a disease; the hypothesis that assigns specific actions or functions to particular areas of the brain; establishing separate and individual centers in the brain for controlling speech, vision, audition, and so on.

Locomotion. Movement from one place to another.

Mand. A speech utterance that makes a demand on the listener and brings a reward to the speaker, for example, the request, "I want a drink."

Manuscript. A type of writing using only straight lines and circular movements; frequently called "printing."

Marker. In linguistics, anything that marks or distinguishes one phoneme, morpheme, or semantic unit from another, for example, the inflection *ed* used to denote past tense when added to a regular verb is a morphemic marker or tense marker.

Medulla oblongata. The portion of the brain directly above the spinal cord.

Memory. The function of reviving past experience related to objects, places, people, events, and so on. Short-term or immediate memory refers to memory of what has been presented within the preceding few seconds.

Midbrain. Also *mesencephalon*; the portion of the brain directly above the pons.

Modality. An avenue of acquiring sensation; visual, auditory, tactile, kinesthetic, olfactory, and gustatory are the most common sense modalities.

Model. A diagrammatic representation of a concept.

Morphology. The aspect of linguistics that deals with meaningful units in the language code.

Motility. The range and speed of motion.

Motor. Pertaining to the origin or execution of muscular activity.

Movigenics. The motor-based curriculum developed by Barsch for children with specific learning disorders.

Multisensory. Generally applied to training procedures that simultaneously utilize more than one sense modality.

Myelinization. The production of the soft material surrounding the axon of a nerve fiber.

Neuron. A unit of the nervous system consisting of the cell body, nucleus, and cell membrane.

Noun phrase. A noun and its modifiers; one of the constituents of language, for example, "the small box."

Nucleus sentence. In its most elemental form, a subject plus a verb.

Nystagmus. A continuous rolling movement of the eyeball.

Ocular. Pertaining to the eye.

Olfactory. Pertaining to the sensation of smell.

Ontogeny. The developmental history of an individual organism.

Operant Behavior. See *Instrumental Conditioning.*

Organicity. Dysfunction due to structural changes in the central nervous system.

Paradigm. A model, pattern, or example that exhibits all the variable forms of something.

Paroxysmal. Pertaining to a spasm or convulsion.

Partitive. In grammar, a word or form such as *few, some, any.*

Pathology. A diseased, disordered, or abnormal condition of the organism or of any of its parts.

Patterning. The regimen of development exercises proposed by Delacato for the treatment of motor and learning disorders.

Pavlovian Conditioning. See *Classical Conditioning.*

Perception. Recognition of a quality without distinguishing meaning, which is the result of a complex set of reactions including sensory stimulation, organization within the nervous system, and memory; an immediate or intuitive judgment involving subtle discriminations.

Perinatal. The period of life from the 21st week of gestation to the second month after birth.

Perseveration. The tendency for a specific act or behavior to continue after it is no longer appropriate; related to difficulty in shifting from one task to another.

Phonation. The production of vocalization, distinguished from articulation.

Phone. A single, discrete speech sound represented usually by a single symbol in a phonetic system.

Phoneme. A group of closely related speech sounds, all of which are generally regarded as the same sound; for example, /t/ in *top* and in *stop* is one phoneme, although it is produced differently in the two words.

Phonetics. The study of the production of vocal sounds, especially in relation to language.

Phonics. The system of relating speech sounds to specific letters or letter combinations.

Phonogram. A letter symbol that represents a speech sound.

Phylogeny. The origin and development of a species, distinguished from ontogeny.

Pons. The portion of the brain directly above the medulla oblongata.

Predictive mechanisms. Mechanisms formed at the integration level of language that, according to Osgood, account for the learning of automatic and serial behavior.

Prenatal. Pertaining to the period preceding birth.

Process-oriented methods. Those methods emphasizing the processes of language, such as decoding, encoding, and memory; distinguished from task-oriented methods.

Projection level. According to Osgood, the lowest level of language organization; represents the simple, reflexive, sensory response to a stimulus.

Propositional speech. The production of meaningful units of speech, usually sentences, which are used to communicate a specific idea.

Proprioception. The reception of stimuli arising within the body; sensation is received by nerve endings in muscles, tendons, and joints, which are sensitive to alterations in muscular tension.

Protocol. The original records of the results of testing.

Prototype. An early, if not the earliest, form of a response pattern that is regarded as evolving.

Psycholinguistics. The study of mental processes that underlie the acquisition and use of language.

Psychomotor. Pertaining to the motor effects of psychological processes. Psychomotor tests are tests of motor skill that depends upon sensory or perceptual motor coordination.

Reauditorization. A term used by Myklebust to denote the retrieval of auditory images.

Rebus. A method of expressing words or phrases by pictures or objects whose names resemble these words, for example, a picture of a bird substituted for the written word *bird* in a sentence.

Reinforcement. The presentation of a stimulus that rewards an organism and that increases the likelihood of recurrence of the response to which it is attached.

Representational level. According to Osgood, the highest level of language organization; imparts meaning to what is received by the senses.

Representational mediation process. The process whereby the incoming stimulus is invested with meaning; a process that eventuates in encoding.

Resource room. Any instructional setting to which a child goes for specified periods of time, usually on a regularly scheduled basis.

Respondent Behavior. See *Classical Conditioning.*

Response. The overt reaction to a stimulus.

Response mode. The form of the response—oral, motor, graphic, and so on.

Revisualization. A term used by Myklebust to denote the retrieval of visual images.

Schema. See *Model.*

Self-concept. A person's idea of himself; the person's feeling about the way he views himself is included; comparable to Myklebust's concept of self-perception.

Semantics. In linguistics, the science of meanings of words or other signs; includes the rules that describe how signs relate to objects.

Sensorimotor (sensory-motor). Pertaining to the combined functioning of sense modalities and motor mechanisms; distinguished from *psychomotor.*

Sensory acuity. The ability to respond to sensation at normal levels of intensity.

Sensory signal. A pattern of stimuli to which the organism responds.

Servomechanism or *servosystem.* A control system that includes input, feedback, and output; the response of the servomechanism to the signals received regulates the input so that the output may also be regulated.

Soft signs. Behaviors or test results that are reported by many professionals to be associated occasionally with brain dysfunction, for example, distractibility, awkwardness, and short attention span. Equivocal signs of brain dysfunction.

Spatial orientation. Awareness of space around the person in terms of distance, form, direction, and position.

Special class. An instructional setting in which a child spends the major part of every day; children are assigned on the basis that they satisfy the criteria for one of the fundable categories of the handicap, for example, mental retardation, emotional disturbance, or learning disability.

Speech. Audible communication through a system of arbitrary vocal symbols.

Stereopsis. The perception of objects in three dimensions.

Stimulability. The ability to respond appropriately after stimulation; imitation.

Stimulus. An external event that causes physiological change in the sense organ.

Stimulus mode. The form of the stimulus—auditory, visual, tactile, kinesthetic, and so on.

Strauss syndrome. The cluster of symptoms characterizing the "brain injured" child; includes hyperactivity, distractibility, and impulsivity.

Strephosymbolia. Literally, "twisted symbols"; used as a synonym for dyslexia.

Structural reading. A reading method devised by Catherine Stern, based upon the child's own spoken vocabulary.

Substantive. In grammar, a word that denotes existence, such as the verb *to be*; a noun or group of words used as a noun.

Surface structure. In linguistics, the set of constituents, or sets of words, and how they are combined grammatically, for example, "The big dog stole a bone" and "The old man saw a boy" have the same surface structure. See *Deep structure.*

Symbol. Something that represents or stands for something else; restricted to association of symbol and concept or idea; distinguished from sign.

Symptom. A manifestation of disordered functioning; applied to both physiological and psychological aspects.

Symptomatology. Pertaining to the symptoms presented by the individual.

Syndrome. The cluster or pattern of symptoms that characterizes a specific disorder.

Synergy. The combining of elementary motor processes into a complex coordinated movement.

Syntax. The way in which words are ordered, relative to one another, to form phrases, clauses, or sentences.

Tachistoscope. A mechanical device that provides brief, timed exposure of visual material.

Tact. A speech utterance that serves the function of naming or labeling, for example, "That is a ball."

Tactile or *tactual.* Pertaining to the sense of touch.

Task-oriented methods. Teaching methods that emphasize the content of material to be learned, such as reading and arithmetic; distinguished from process-oriented methods.

Textual operant. A speech utterance under the control of nonauditory verbal stimuli, for example, pictographs, phonetic symbols, or any other nonverbal stimuli.

Thought. A covert activity involving symbols.

Transformational grammar. The study of language initiated by Chomsky and his colleagues; distinctive from descriptive grammar and marked by an emphasis on syntax as opposed to word classes.

Trauma. Any wound or injury, especially an organic injury.

Unilaterial. On one side; usually applied to the body.

Unvoiced. See *Voiced.*

VAKT. A multisensory teaching method involving visual, auditory, kinesthetic, and tactile sense modalities; the Fernald "hand-kinesthetic" method.

Verb phrase. A verb and its modifiers; usually the predicate of a sentence; may be broken into a verb plus a noun phrase as in "ran a mile."

Vertical. Pertaining to the axis from head to foot of the human body.

Vestibular. Pertaining to the sensory mechanism for the perception of the organism's relation to gravity.

Visual-motor. The ability to relate visual stimuli to motor responses in an appropriate way.

Voiced. The production of a speech sound that is accompanied by vibration of the vocal cords.

Vowel. The speech sounds produced in the resonance chamber formed by the stream of air passing through the oral cavity. Represented by the alphabet letters, *a, e, o, i, u,* and sometimes *y.*

Word blindness. An inability to recognize or recall letters and words.

Word deafness. An inability to recall or recognize auditory equivalents of spoken words.

REFERENCES

Abt Associates. (1976). *Education as experimentation: A planned variation model* (Vol. 3A). Cambridge, MA: Author.

Adair, M. (1976). Archaic linguistic symbols and cortico-hemispheric specialization. *Dissertation Abstracts International, 36,* 5241–5242.

Adamson, W. C. (1979). Psychosocial, medical, and neurological assessments. In W. C. Adamson & K. K. Adamson (Eds.), *A handbook for specific learning disabilities* (pp. 23–62). New York: Gardner.

Adelman, H. S. (1979). Diagnostic classification of LD: Research and ethical perspectives as related to practice. *Learning Disability Quarterly, 2,* 5–16.

Adelman, H. S. (1989). Beyond the learning mystique: An interactional perspective on learning disabilities. *Journal of Learning Disabilities, 22,* 301–304, 328.

Alabiso, F. P., & Hansen, J. L. (1977). *The hyperactive child in the classroom.* Springfield, IL: Thomas.

Alcuin, M. (1966). The effect of neurological training on disabled readers. In C. H. Delacato (Ed.), *Neurological organization and reading* (pp. 150–155). Springfield, IL: Thomas.

Allen, R. M., Dickman, I., & Haupt, T. A. (1966). A pilot study of the immediate effectiveness of the Frostig-Horne training program with educable retardates. *Exceptional Children, 33,* 41–42.

Alley, G. (1968). Perceptual-motor performance of mentally retarded children after systematic visual-perceptual training. *American Journal of Mental Deficiency, 73,* 247–250.

Alley, G., & Carr, D. L. (1968). Effects of systematic sensory-motor training on sensory-motor, visual perception, and concept formation performance of mentally retarded children. *Perceptual and Motor Skills, 27,* 451–456.

Alley, G., & Deshler, D. (1979). *Teaching the learning disabled adolescent: Strategies and methods.* Denver: Love.

Alley, G., Snider, W., Spencer, J., & Angell, R. (1968). Reading readiness and the Frostig-Horne training program. *Exceptional Children, 35,* 68.

American Psychiatric Association. (1980). *Diagnostic and statistical manual of mental disorders* (3rd ed.). Washington, DC: Author.

Ames, L. B., & Ilg, F. L. (1946). The developmental point of view with special reference to the principle of reciprocal neuromotor interweaving. *Journal of Genetic Psychology, 105,* 195–209.

Anderson, R. W. (1965). *Effects of neuro-psychological techniques on reading achievement.* Unpublished doctoral dissertation, University of Northern Colorado.

Anderson, W. F., & Stern, D. (1972). The relative effects of the Frostig program, corrective reading instruction, and attention upon the reading skills of corrective readers with visual perceptual deficiencies. *Journal of School Psychology, 10,* 387–395.

Angevine, J. B., & Cotman, C. W. (1981). *Principles of neuroanatomy.* New York: Oxford University Press.

Angler, L. F., Hannah, E. P., & Longhurst, T. M. (1973). Linguistic analysis of speech samples: A practical guide for clinicians. *Journal of Speech and Hearing Disorders, 38,* 192–204.

Arciszewski, R. A. (1968). The effects of visual perception training on perceptual ability and reading achievement of first grade students. *Dissertation Abstracts, 29,* 4174-A.

Arena, J. (1982). *Diagnostic Spelling Potential Test.* Novato, CA: Academic Therapy Publications.

Armbruster, R. H. (1973). Perceptual-motor, gross-motor, and sensory-motor skills training: The effect upon school readiness and self-concept development of kindergarten children. *Dissertation Abstracts International, 33A,* 6644.

Arter, J. A., & Jenkins, J. R. (1977). Examining the benefits and prevalance of modality considerations in special education. *The Journal of Special Education, 11,* 281–298.

Ashlock, P., & Stephen, A. (1966). *Educational therapy in the elementary school.* Springfield, IL: Thomas.

Ashlock, R. (1986). *Error patterns in computation: A semi-programed approach.* Columbus, OH: Merrill.

Association for Children and Adults with Learning Disabilities. (1986). ACLD description: Specific learning disabilities. *Newsbrief,* September–October, pp. 15–16.

Aukerman, R. C. (1971). *Approaches to beginning reading.* New York: Wiley.

Auxter, D. (1971). Learning disabilities among deaf populations. *Exceptional Children, 37,* 573–578.

Axelrod, S., & Bailey, S. (1979). Drug treatment for hyperactivity: Controversies, alternatives, and guidelines. *Exceptional Children, 45,* 544–552.

Ayllon, T., Layman, D., & Kandel, L. (1975). A behavioral-educational alternative to drug control of hyperactive children. *Journal of Applied Behavior Analysis, 8,* 137–147.

Ayres, A. J. (1964). Tactile functions, their relation to hyperactive and perceptual-motor behavior. *American Journal of Occupational Therapy, 6,* 6–11.

Ayres, A. J. (1965). Patterns of perceptual-motor dysfunction in children: A factor analytic study. *Perceptual and Motor Skills, 20,* 335–368.

Ayres, A. J. (1968a, September). *Effect of sensorimotor activity of perception and learning in the neurologically handicapped child*. Office of Education. Final Progress Report. Project Number H-126.

Ayres, A. J. (1968b). Reading—A product of sensory integrative process. In H. K. Smith (Ed.), *Proceedings of the 12th Annual Convention (Vol. 12, Part 4). Perception and reading*. Newark, DE: International Reading Association.

Ayres, A. J. (1969). Deficits in sensory integration in educationally handicapped children. *Journal of Learning Disabilities, 2*, 160–168.

Ayres, A. J. (1971a). Characteristics of types of sensory integrative dysfunction. *American Journal of Occupational Therapy, 25*, 329–334.

Ayres, A. J. (1971b). *Sensory integrative processes and learning disorders*. Project No. H-126-1. Rockville, MD: Department of Health, Education, and Welfare, Maternal and Child Health Services.

Ayres, A. J. (1972a). *Sensory integration and learning disorders*. Los Angeles: Western Psychological Services.

Ayres, A. J. (1972b). Improving academic scores through sensory integration. *Journal of Learning Disabilities, 5*, 338–343.

Ayres, A. J. (1972c). *Southern California Sensory Integration Tests*. Los Angeles: Western Psychological Services.

Ayres, A. J. (1979). *Sensory integration and the child*. Los Angeles: Western Psychological Services.

Ayres, A. J. (1989). *Sensory Integration and Praxis Test*. Los Angeles: Western Psychological Services.

Badian, N. A. (1986). Nonverbal disorders of learning: The reverse of dyslexia. *Annals of Dyslexia, 36*, 253–269.

Baker, A. M. (1980). The efficacy of the Feingold K-P diet: A review of pertinent empirical investigations. *Behavior Disorders, 6*, 32–35.

Bakker, D. (1973). Hemispheric specialization and stages of the learning-to-read process. *Bulletin of the Orton Society, 23*, 15–27.

Ball, T. S., & Edgar, C. L. (1967). The effectiveness of sensory-motor training in promoting generalized body image development. *The Journal of Special Education, 4*, 387–395.

Bangs, T. E. (1977). *Vocabulary Comprehension Scale*. New York: Teaching Resources.

Bankson, N. W. (1989). *Bankson Language Screening Test*. Austin, TX: PRO-ED.

Bannatyne, A. D. (1966). *Psycholinguistic color system*. Urbana: University of Illinois Press.

Barkley, R. A. (1976). Predicting the response of hyperkinetic children to stimulant drugs: A review. *Journal of Consulting and Clinical Psychology, 44*, 250–260.

Barkley, R. A. (1981). *Hyperactive children*. New York: Guilford.

Barry, H. (1955a). Classes for aphasics. In M. E. Frampton & E. D. Gall (Eds.), *Special education for the exceptional* (Vol. II). Boston: Sargent.

Barry, H. (1955b). Classes for aphasics. In M. E. Frampton & E. D. Gall (Eds.), *The physically handicapped and special health problems* (Vol. II, pp. 362–367). Boston: Sargent.

Barry, H. (1960). Training the young aphasic child. *Volta Review, 7*, 326–328.

Barry, H. (1961). *The young aphasic child: Evaluation and training*. Washington, DC: Volta Bureau.

Barry, H. (1988). The aphasic child: Evaluation and training. In H. Barry & M. McGinnis, *Teaching aphasic children* (pp. 3–60). Austin, TX: PRO-ED.

Barsch, R. (1960). The concept of regression in the brain-injured child. *Exceptional Children, 27*, 84–90.

Barsch, R. (1961). Counseling the parent of the brain-damaged child. *Journal of Rehabilitation, 3,* 1–3.

Barsch, R. (1962). Evaluating the organic child: The Functional Organizational Scale. *Journal of Genetic Psychology, 100,* 345–354.

Barsch, R. (1965a). The concept of language as a visuo-spatial phenomenon. *Academic Therapy Quarterly, 1,* 2–11.

Barsch, R. (1965b). *A movigenic curriculum.* Madison, WI: State Department of Public Instruction.

Barsch, R. (1967). *Achieving perceptual-motor efficiency: A space-oriented approach to learning.* Seattle, WA: Special Child Publications.

Barsch, R. (1971). On the trail of the shark. *The Journal of Special Education, 5,* 45–52.

Barsch, R. (1976). Ray H. Barsch. In J. M. Kauffman & D. P. Hallahan (Eds.), *Teaching children with learning disabilities: Personal perspective* (pp. 58–93). Columbus, OH: Merrill.

Bartel, N. R. (1990a). Teaching students who have reading problems. In D. Hammill & N. R. Bartel (Eds.), *Teaching students with learning and behavior problems.* Boston: Allyn & Bacon.

Bartel, N. R. (1990b). Problems in mathematics achievement. In D. Hammill & N. R. Bartel (Eds.), *Teaching students with learning and behavior problems.* Boston: Allyn & Bacon.

Bateman, B. (1964). Learning disabilities—Yesterday, today, and tomorrow. *Exceptional Children, 31,* 167–176.

Bateman, B., & Schiefelbusch, R. L. (1969). In S. D. Clements (Ed.), *Minimal brain dysfunction in children, phase II.* No. 2015. Washington, DC: U.S. Department of Health, Education, and Welfare.

Bates, E. (1976). *Language and context: The acquisition of pragmatics.* New York: Academic Press.

Beatty, L. S., Madden, R., Gardner, E. F., & Karlsen, B. (1976). *Stanford Diagnostic Mathematics Test.* New York: Harcourt Brace Jovanovich.

Beck, R., & Talkington, L. W. (1970). Frostig training with Headstart children. *Perceptual and Motor Skills, 30,* 521–522.

Becker, M. G., Isaac, W., & Hynd, G. W. (1987). Neuropsychological development of nonverbal behaviors attributed to "frontal lobe" functioning. *Developmental Neuropsychology, 3,* 275–298.

Belmont, L., & Birch, H. (1965). Lateral dominance, lateral awareness, and reading disability. *Child Development, 36,* 57–71.

Bennett, R. M. (1968). A study of the effects of a visual perception program upon school achievement, IQ and visual perception. *Dissertation Abstracts, 69,* 2864-A.

Benton, A. (1965). The problem of cerebral dominance. *The Canadian Psychologist, 6,* 38–51.

Benton, C., McCann, J., & Larsen, R. (1965). Dyslexia and dominance. *Journal of Pediatric Ophthalmology, 53,* 50–57.

Bentzen, F. A., & Petersen, W. (1962). Educational procedures with the brain-damaged child. In W. T. Daley (Ed.), *Speech and language therapy with the brain-damaged child.* Washington, DC: Catholic University of America Press.

Berko, J. (1958). The child's learning of morphology. *Word, 14,* 150–177.

Berman, A. (1930). The influence of the kinesthetic factor in the perception of symbols in partial reading disability. *Journal of Education Psychology, 30,* 187–198.

Berry, K., & Cook, V. J. (1980). Personality and behavior. In H. E. Rie & E. D. Rie (Eds.), *Handbook of minimal brain dysfunctions* (pp. 324–344). New York: Wiley Interscience.

Best, C. H., & Taylor, N. B. (1939). *The physiological basis of medical practice.* Baltimore: Williams & Wilkins.

Bhatara, V., Clark, D. L., & Arnold, L. E. (1978). Behavioral and nystagmus response of a hyperkinetic child to vestibular stimulation. *American Journal of Occupational Therapy, 32,* 311–316.

Bickel, W. E., & Bickel, D. D (1986). Effective schools, classrooms, and instruction: Implications for special education. *Exceptional Children, 52,* 489–500.

Bigler, E. D. (1988). *Diagnostic clinical neuropsychology,* Austin: University of Texas Press.

Bigler, E. D. (1989). On the neuropsychology of suicide. *Journal of Learning Disabilities, 22,* 180–185.

Bigler, E. D. (1990). *Traumatic brain injury.* Austin, TX: PRO-ED.

Bigler, E. D., Yeo, R. A., & Turkheimer, E. (1989). *Neuropsychological function and brain imaging.* New York: Plenum.

Blankenship, C. S., & Lilly, M. S. (1981). *Mainstreaming students with learning problems: Techniques for the classroom teacher.* New York: Holt, Rinehart, & Winston.

Bley, N. S., & Thornton, C. A. (1989). *Teaching mathematics to the learning disabled.* Austin, TX: PRO-ED.

Bloom, B. (1954). *A taxonomy of educational objectives in the cognitive domain.* New York: David McKay.

Bloom, B. (Ed.). (1956). *Taxonomy of educational objectives, the classification of educational goals: Handbook 1, Cognitive domain.* New York: Longman, Green.

Bloom, L. (1970). *Language development: Form and function in emerging grammars.* Cambridge, MA: MIT Press.

Bloom, L., & Lahey, M. (1977). *Language development and language disorders.* New York: Wiley.

Bogen, J. (1969). The other side of the brain: Parts I, II, and III. *Bulletin of the Los Angeles Neurological Society, 73–203.*

Bortner, M. (1971). Phrenology, localization, and learning disabilities. *The Journal of Special Education, 5,* 23–31.

Bosworth, M. H. (1968). Pre-reading improvement of visual-motor skills. *Dissertation Abstracts, 28,* 3545-A.

Bradford, G., & Rapaport, J. (1974). Imipramine and methylphenidate: Treatment of hyperactive boys. *Archives of General Psychiatry, 30,* 789–793.

Bradley, C. (1937/1938). The behavior of children receiving Benzedrine. *American Journal of Psychiatry, 94,* 577–585.

Braine, M. (1963). The ontogeny of English phrase structure: The first phase. *Language, 39,* 1–13.

Bremer, D., & Stern, J. (1976). Attention and distractibility during reading in hyperactive boys. *Journal of Abnormal Child Psychology, 4,* 323–334.

Brown, A. L., & Palincsar, A. S. (1982). Inducing strategic learning from texts by means of informed, self-control training. *Topics in Learning and Learning Disabilities, 2,* 1–17.

Brown, R. (1973). *A first language: The early stages.* Cambridge, MA: Harvard University Press.

Brown, V. (1975). Learning about mathematics instruction. *Journal of Learning Disabilities, 8,* 476–485.

Brown, V., Hammill, D. D., & Wiederholt, J. L. (1986). *Test of Reading Comprehension.* Austin, TX: PRO-ED.

Brown, V., & McEntire, E. (1990). *Test of Mathematical Abilities.* Austin, TX: PRO-ED.

Brownell, W. R. (1935). Psychological considerations in the teaching of arithmetic. In *The teaching of arithmetic*. NCTM, The 10th Yearbook. New York: Bureau of Publications, Teachers College, Columbia University.

Bruder, G. E., Quitkin, F. M., Stewart, J. W., Martin, C., Voglmaier, M. M., & Harrison, W. M. (1989). Cerebral laterality and depression: Differences in perceptual asymmetry among diagnostic subtypes. *Journal of Abnormal Psychology, 98*, 177–186.

Brumback, R. A., & Staton, R. D. (1982). An hypothesis regarding the communality of right-hemisphere involvement in learning disability, attentional disorder, and childhood major depressive disorder. *Perceptual and Motor Skills, 55*, 1091–1097.

Brumback, R. A., Staton, R. D., & Wilson, H. L. (1984). Right cerebral hemispheric dysfunction. *Archives of Neurology, 41*, 248–250.

Brundage-Aguar, D., Forehand, R., & Ciminero, A. (1976). A review of treatment approaches for hyperactive behavior. *Journal of Clinical Psychology, 6*, 3–10.

Bruner, J. (1963). *Towards a theory of instruction*. Cambridge MA: Harvard University Press.

Bryan, T. H. (1974). Peer popularity of learning disabled children. *Journal of Learning Disabilities, 10*, 621–625.

Bryan, T. H. (1976). Peer popularity of learning-disabled children: A replication. *Journal of Learning Disabilities, 9*, 307–311.

Bryan, T. H., & Bryan, J. H. (1986). *Understanding learning disabilities*. Palo Alto, CA: Mayfield.

Bryant, N. D. (1972). *Final report, Vols. 1 & 2, USOE contract, Leadership training institute in learning disabilities*. Sponsored by the Department of Special Education, University of Arizona, Tucson, and the Program Development Branch, Division of Educational Service, Bureau of Education for the Handicapped.

Bryant, N. D., & McLoughlin, J. A. (1972). Subject variables: Definition, incidence, characteristics, and correlates. In N. D. Bryant & C. E. Kass (Eds.), *Final report, Vol. I, USOE contract, Leadership training institute in learning disabilities* (pp. 5–158). Sponsored by the Department of Special Education, University of Arizona, Tucson, and Program Development Branch, Division of Educational Service, Bureau of Education for the Handicapped, USOE, Grant No. OEO-0-71-4425 604, Project No. 127145.

Buckland, P., & Balow, B. (1973). Effect of visual perceptual training on reading achievement. *Exceptional Children, 38*, 299–304.

Buckley, R. (1977). Nutrition, metabolism, brain function, and learning. *Academic Therapy, 12*, 321–324.

Burke, J., Peterson, W., Brekke, B., Harlow, S. D., Lewy, R., & Williams, J. D. (1974). *The effects of a visual motor program and two other experimental programs on reading readiness*. Unpublished manuscript, East Grand Forks, MN.

Burnette, E. (1962). *Influences of classroom environment on word learning of retarded with high and low activity levels*. Unpublished doctoral dissertation, Peabody College, Nashville, TN.

Bursuck, W. D., Rose, E., Cowen, S., & Yahaya, M. A. (1989). Nationwide survey of postsecondary education services for students with learning disabilities. *Exceptional Children, 56*, 236–245.

Burt, C., & Lewis, R. B. (1946). Teaching backward readers. *British Journal of Educational Psychology, 16*, 116–132.

Bush, W. J. (1976). Psycholinguistic remediation in the schools. In P. Newcomer & D. Hammill (Eds.), *Psycholinguistics in the schools* (pp. 85–100). Columbus, OH: Merrill.

Bush, W. J., & Giles, M. T. (1977). *Aids to psycholinguistic teaching*. Columbus, OH: Merrill.

Bzoch, K. E., & League, R. (1978). *Receptive-Expressive Emergent Language Scale.* Austin, TX: PRO-ED.

Caramazza, A., Gordon, J., Zurif, E., & DeLuca, D. (1976). Right-hemispheric damage and verbal problem-solving. *Brain and Language, 3,* 41–46.

Carnine, D. (1987). A response to the "false standards, a distorting and disintegrating effect on education, turning away from useful purposes, being inevitably unfulfilled, and remaining unrealistic and irrelevant." *Remedial and Special Education, 8,* 42–43.

Carrow-Woolfolk, E. (1985). *Test for Auditory Comprehension of Language.* Allen, TX: DLM/ Teaching Resources.

Carrow-Woolfolk, E. (1974). *Carrow Elicited Language Inventory.* Allen, TX: DLM/Teaching Resources.

Cawley, J. (1976). *Learning disabilities in mathematics: A curriculum design for upper grades.* U.S. Office of Education Grant No. G007605223, Project No. 443CH60166. Storrs: University of Connecticut.

Cawley, J., Fitzmaurice, A., Shaw, R., Kahn, H., & Bates, H. (1978a). Mathematics and LD youth: The upper grade levels. *Learning Disability Quarterly, 1,* 37–52.

Cawley, J., Fitzmaurice, A., Shaw, R., Kahn, H., & Bates, H. (1978b). Math word problems: Suggestions for learning disabled students. *Learning Disability Quarterly, 2*(1), 25–41.

Cawley, J., Fitzmaurice, A., Shaw, R., Kahn, H., & Bates, H. (1979). LD youth and mathematics: A review of characteristics. *Learning Disability Quarterly, 2,* 29–44.

Cawley, J., Goodstein, H., Fitzmaurice, A., Sedlak, R., & Althans, V. (1976). *Project math: A program of the mainstream series.* Wallingford, CT: Educational Services.

Cawley, J., & Vitello, S. (1972). A model for arithmetical programming for handicapped children. *Exceptional Children, 38,* 101–110.

Cazden, C. (1972). *Child language and education.* New York: Holt, Rinehart, & Winston.

Chalfant, J. C. (1989). Learning disabilities: Policy issues and promising approaches. *American Psychologist, 44,* 392–398.

Chalfant, J. C., & Scheffelin, M. A. (1969). *Central processing dysfunctions in children: A review of research.* NINDS Monographs, No. 9. Bethesda, MD: U.S. Department of Health, Education, and Welfare.

Chomsky, N. (1957). *Syntactic structures.* The Hague, Netherlands: Mouton.

Chomsky, N. (1965). *Aspects of the theory of syntax.* Cambridge, MA: MIT Press.

Chomsky, N. (1967). The general properties of language. In F. Darley (Ed.), *Brain mechanisms underlying speech and language.* New York: Grune & Stratton.

Clark, F. L., Deshler, D. D., Schumaker, J. B., Alley, G. R., & Warner, M. M. (1984). Visual imagery and self-questioning: Strategies to improve comprehension of written material. *Journal of Learning Disabilities, 17,* 145–149.

Clark, J. B., & Madison, C. L. (1986). *Clark-Madison Test of Oral Language.* Austin, TX: PRO-ED.

Clements, S. D. (1966). *Minimal brain dysfunction in children: Terminology and identification.* Washington, DC: Cosponsored by the Easter Seal Research Foundation of the National Society for Crippled Children and Adults and the National Institute of Neurological Diseases and Blindness Public Health Service.

Cohen, J. (1982). *Handbook of resource room teaching.* Austin, TX: PRO-ED.

Cohen, R. I. (1966). Remedial training of first-grade children with visual perceptual retardation. *Educational Horizons, 45,* 60–63.

Coleman, R., & Deutsch, C. (1964). Lateral dominance and right-left discrimination: A comparison of normal and retarded readers. *Perceptual and Motor Skills, 19,* 43–50.

Coles, C. S. (1978). The learning-disabilities test battery: Empirical and social issues. *Harvard Educational Review, 48*, 313–341.

Conley, D. (1973). Effect of Ritalin on hyperactive children attending the Glendale elementary schools. Doctoral dissertation, Arizona State University. *Dissertation Abstracts International, 34*, 1072A–1073A.

Conners, C. K. (1970). Symptom patterns in hyperkinetic, neurotic, and normal children. *Child Development, 41*, 667–682.

Conners, C. K. (1976a). Learning disabilities and stimulant drugs in children: Theoretical implications. In R. Knights & D. Bakker (Eds.), *The neuropsychology of learning disorders* (pp. 389–401). Baltimore: University Park Press.

Conners, C. K. (1976b). Rating scales for use with children. In W. Guy (Ed.), *ECDEU assessment manual for psychoparmacology* (rev. ed.) (Department of Health, Education, and Welfare Publication No. ADM 76-338). Washington, DC: U.S. Department of Health, Education, and Welfare.

Conners, C. K., Goyette, C., Southwick, D., Lees, J., & Andrulonis, P. (1976). Food additives and hyperkinesis: A controlled double-blind study. *Pediatrics, 58*, 154–166.

Connolly, A. J. (1988). *KeyMath–Revised.* Circle Pines, MN: American Guidance Service.

Connolly, C. (1971). Social and emotional factors in learning disabilities. In H. R. Myklebust (Ed.), *Progress in learning disabilities* (Vol. 2, pp. 151–178). New York: Grune & Stratton.

Copeland, R. W. (1974). *How children learn mathematics: Teaching implications of Piaget's research.* New York: Macmillan.

Coughran, L., & Liles, B. (1979). *Developmental syntax program.* Allen, TX: DLM/Teaching Resources.

Cowan, W. M. (1979). The development of the brain. *Scientific American, 241*, 112–133.

Cratty, B. J. (1967). *Development sequences of perceptual-motor tasks: Movement activities for neurologically handicapped and retarded children and youth.* Freeport, NY: Educational Activities.

Cratty, B. J. (1969). *Perceptual-motor behavior and educational processes.* Springfield, IL: Thomas.

Cratty, B. J. (1973). *Motor activity and education of retardates.* Philadelphia: Lea & Febiger.

Cratty, B. J. (1980). *Adaptive physical education for handicapped children and youth.* Denver: Love.

Cratty, B. J. (1981). Sensory motor theories and practices. In R. Walk & H. Pick (Eds.), *Intersensory perception and sensory integration* (pp. 345–369). New York: Plenum.

Cratty, B. J. (1985). *Active learning.* Englewood Cliffs, NJ: Prentice-Hall.

Cratty, B. J. (1986a). *Perceptual and motor development in infants and children* (3rd ed.). Englewood Cliffs, NJ: Prentice-Hall.

Cratty, B. J. (1986b, January 30). Personal communication.

Cratty, B. J., & Martin, M. M. (1971). *The effects of a program of learning games upon selected academic abilities in children with learning difficulties.* Evaluation of USOE Program Grant No. 0-0142710-032.

Cravioto, J. (1973). Nutritional deprivation and psychobiological development in children. In S. Sapir & A. C. Nitzburg (Eds.), *Children with learning problems* (pp. 218–240). New York: Bruner/Mazel.

Critchley, McD. (1970). *The dyslexic child.* Springfield, IL: Thomas.

Cruickshank, W. M. (1972). Some issues facing the field of learning disability. *Journal of Learning Disabilities, 5*, 380–388.

Cruickshank, W. M. (1976). William M. Cruickshank. In J. M. Kauffman & D. P. Hallahan (Eds.), *Teaching children with learning disabilities: Personal perspectives* (pp. 94–127). Columbus, OH: Merrill.

Cruickshank, W. M. (1977). Myths and realities in learning disabilities. *Journal of Learning Disabilities, 10,* 51–58.

Cruickshank, W. M. (1983). Straight is the bamboo tree. *Journal of Learning Disabilities, 16,* 191–197.

Cruickshank, W. M. (1985). The search for excellence: An encore. *Journal of Learning Disabilities, 18,* 574–580.

Cruickshank, W. M., Bentzen, F. A., Ratzeburg, F. H., & Tannhauser, T. (1961). *A teaching method for brain-injured and hyperactive children.* Syracuse, NY: Syracuse University Press.

Cullum, C. M., & Bigler, E. D. (1988). Short form MMPI findings in patients with predominantly lateralized cerebral dysfunction: Neuropsychological and CT-derived parameters. *Journal of Nervous and Mental Disease, 176,* 332–342.

Cummins, R. A. (1988). *The neurologically impaired child: Doman-Delacato techniques reappraised.* New York: Croom Helm.

Dale, P. S. (1976). *Language development: Structure and function* (2nd ed.) New York: Holt, Rinehart, & Winston.

Daley, W. T. (1962). *Speech and language therapy with the brain-damaged child.* Washington, DC: Catholic University of America Press.

Dawson, M. M., Hallahan, D. P., Reeve, R. E., & Ball, D. W. (1980). The effect of reinforcement and verbal rehearsal on selective attention in learning disabled children. *Journal of Abnormal Child Psychology, 8,* 133–144.

deBettencourt, L. U. (1987). Strategy training: A need for clarification. *Exceptional Children, 54,* 24–30.

Dechant, E. V. (1964). *Inproving the teaching of reading.* Englewood Cliffs, NJ: Prentice-Hall.

Delacato, C. H. (1959). *The treatment and prevention of reading problems.* Springfield, IL: Thomas.

Delacato, C. H. (1963). *The diagnosis and treatment of speech and reading problems.* Springfield, IL: Thomas.

Delacato, C. H. (1966). *Neurological organization and reading.* Springfield, IL: Thomas.

Denhoff, E., Hainsworth, P. K., & Siqueland, M. L. (1968). The measurement of psychoneurological factors contributing to learning efficiency. *Journal of Learning Disorders, 1,* 636–644.

Densem, J. F., Nuthall, G. A., Bushnell, J., & Horn, J. (1989). Effectiveness of a sensory integrative therapy program for children with perceptual-motor deficits. *Journal of Learning Disabilities, 22,* 221–229.

Deshler, D. D., Alley, G. R., & Carlson, S. C. (1980). Learning strategies: An approach to mainstreaming secondary students with learning disabilities. *Education Unlimited, 2,* 6–11.

Deshler, D. D., Schumaker, J. B., Alley, G. R., Warner, M. M., & Clark, F. L. (1982). Learning disabilities in adolescent and young adult populations: Research implications. *Focus on Exceptional Children, 15*(1), 1–12.

Deshler, D. D., Schumaker, J. B., & Lenz, B. K. (1984). Academic and cognitive interventions for LD adolescents: Part I. *Journal of Learning Disabilities, 17,* 108–117.

Deshler, D. D., Schumaker, J. B., Lenz, B. K., & Ellis, E. S. (1984). Academic and cognitive interventions for LD adolescents: Part II. *Journal of Learning Disabilities, 17,* 170–187.

Deshler, D. D., Warner, M. M., Schumaker, J. B., Alley, G. R., & Clark, F. L. (1984). The learning strategies intervention model: Key components and current status. In J. D. McKinney & L. Feagans (Eds.), *Current topics in learning disabilities* (pp. 245–284). Norwood, NJ: Ablex.

DeVito, J. A. (1970). *The psychology of speech and language: An introduction to psycholinguistics.* New York: Random House.

Dimond, S. (1976). Drugs to improve learning in man: Implications and neuropsychological analysis. In R. Knights & D. Bakker (Eds.), *The neuropsychology of learning disorders* (pp. 367–379). Baltimore: University Park Press.

Dimond, S., & Beaumont, J. (Eds.). (1974). *Hemispheric function in the human brain.* London: Paul Elek.

Directory of Facilities and Services for the Learning Disabled (13th ed.). (1989). Novato, CA: Academic Therapy Publications.

Divoky, D. (1978). Can diet cure the LD child? *Learning, 3,* 56–57.

Doman, G., Delacato, C. H., & Doman, R. (1964). *The Doman-Delacato Developmental Profile.* Philadelphia: Institutes for the Achievement of Human Potential.

Doman, R., Spitz, E. B., Zucman, E., Delacato, C. H., & Doman, G. (1960). Children with severe brain injuries. *Journal of the American Medical Association, 174,* 257–262.

Drake, C. D. (1968). Ten agencies rap institute for retarded. *The Philadelphia Inquirer,* May 7.

Duane, D. D. (1989). Commentary on dyslexia and neurodevelopmental pathology. *Journal of Learning Disabilities, 22,* 219–220.

Dubey, D. (1976). Organic factors in hyperkinesis: A critical evaluation. *American Journal of Orthopsychiatry, 46,* 353–366.

Duckworth, E. (1967). Piaget rediscovered. In E. Victor & M. Learner (Eds.), *Readings in science for the elementary school.* New York: Macmillan.

Duffy, F. H. (1980). Dyslexia: Automated diagnosis by computerized classification of brain electrical activity. *Annals of Neurology, 7,* 421–428.

Duffy, F. H., & McAnulty, G. B. (1985). Brain electrical activity mapping (BEAM): The search for a physiological signature of dyslexia. In F. H. Duffy & N. Geschwind (Eds.), *Dyslexia: A neuroscientific approach to clinical evaluation* (pp. 105–122). Boston: Little, Brown.

Dunn, L. M. (1967). Minimal brain dysfunction: A dilemma for educators. In E. C. Frierson & W. B. Barbe (Eds.), *Educating children with learning disabilities* (pp. 117–132). New York: Appleton-Century-Crofts.

Dunn, L. M., & Dunn, L. (1981). *Peabody Picture Vocabulary Test.* Circle Pines, MN: American Guidance Service.

Dunn, L. M., Dunn, L., & Smith, J. O. (1981). *The Peabody Language Development Kit: Level 2 revised.* Circle Pines, MN: American Guidance Service.

Dunn, L. M., Horton, K. B., & Smith, J. O. (1981). *The Peabody Language Development Kit: Level P revised.* Circle Pines, MN: American Guidance Service.

Dunn, L. M., & Markwardt, F. C. (1970). *Peabody Individual Achievement Test.* Circle Pines, MN: American Guidance Service.

Dunn, L. M., & Mueller, M. W. (1966). *The efficacy of the Initial Teaching Alphabet and the Peabody Language Development Kit with grade one disadvantaged children: After one year.* IMRID papers and reports. Institute on Mental Retardation and Intellectual Development. George Peabody College, Nashville, TN.

Dunn, L. M., & Mueller, M. W. (1967). *Differential effects on the ITPA profile of the experimental version of level #1 of the Peabody Language Development Kits with disadvantaged first grade children.* IMRID papers and reports. Institute on Mental Retardation and Intellectual Development. George Peabody College, Nashville, TN.

Dunn, L. M., Nitzman, M., Pochanart, P., & Bransky, M. (1968). Effectiveness of PLDK with educable mentally retarded children. A report after 2.5 years. *Institute on Mental and Intellectual Development Papers and Reports, 5,* 1–36.

Dunn, L. M., Smith, J. O., & Dunn, L. (1981). *The Peabody Language Development Kit: Level 1 revised,* Circle Pines, MN: American Guidance Service.

Dunn, L. M., Smith, J. O., Smith, D. D., & Dunn, L. (1982). *The Peabody Language Development Kits: Level 3 revised.* Circle Pines, MN: American Guidance Service.

Dunsing, J. D., & Kephart, N. C. (1965). Motor generalizations in space and time. In J. Hellmuth (Ed.), *Learning disorders* (Vol. I). Seattle, WA: Special Child Publications.

Durrell, D. D. (1955). *Durrell Analysis of Reading Difficulty.* New York: Harcourt Brace Jovanovich.

Dwyer, J. (1976). Contextual inferences and the right cerebral hemisphere: Listening with the left ear. *Dissertation Abstracts International, 36,* 5862.

Eason, J. E. (1973). The comparison of the effects of two programs of physical activity on perceptual-motor development and primary mental abilities of preschool aged children. *Dissertation Abstracts, 33,* 2147-A.

Eastman, N. J. (1959). The brain-damaged child: Why does he happen? *The Dallas Medical Journal.* Special Edition, March 3–7.

Eaton, M., Sells, C., & Lucas, B. (1977). Psychoactive medication and learning disabilities. *Journal of Learning Disabilities, 10,* 403–410.

Edgar, C. L., Ball, T. S., McIntyre, R. B., & Shotwell, A. M. (1969). Effects of sensory-motor training on adaptive behavior. *American Journal of Mental Deficiency, 73,* 713–720.

Eisenson, J. J. (1954). *Examining for aphasia.* San Antonio, TX: Psychological Corp.

Ellis, E. S., & Lenz, B. K. (1987). A component analysis of effective learning strategies for LD students. *Learning Disabilities Focus, 2*(2), 94–107.

Ellis, E. S., Lenz, B. K., & Sabornie, E. J. (1987a). Generalization and adaptation of learning strategies to natural environments: Part 1: Critical agents. *Remedial and Special Education, 8,* 6–20.

Ellis, E. S., Lenz, B. K., Sabornie, E. J. (1987b). Generalization and adaptation of learning strategies to natural environments: Part 2: Research into practice. *Remedial and Special Education, 8,* 6–23.

Elmore, W. R. (1973). Effects of training procedures on visual perceptual skills of disadvantaged youngsters. *Dissertation Abstracts, 33,* 4979-A.

Emmons, C. A. (1968). A comparison of selected gross-motor activities of the Getman-Kane and the Kephart perceptual-motor training programs and their effect upon certain readiness skills of first-grade Negro children. *Dissertation Abstracts, 29,* 3442-A.

Englemann, S. (1969). *Preventing failure in the primary grades.* Chicago: Science Research Associates.

Englemann, S., & Bruner, E. C. (1988). *Reading mastery program.* Chicago: Science Research Associates.

Englemann, S., & Carnine, D. (1972). *DISTAR: Arithmetic level III.* Chicago: Science Research Associates.

Englemann, S., & Carnine, D. (1976). *DISTAR: Arithmetic level II.* Chicago: Science Research Associates.

Englemann, S., & Carnine, D. (1990). *DISTAR: Arithmetic level I.* Chicago: Science Research Associates.

Englemann, S., & Osborn, J. (1976, 1977, 1973). *DISTAR: An instruction system: Language I, II, and III.* Chicago: Science Research Associates.

Englemann, S., & Silbert, J. (1983). *Expressive writing 1 & 2.* Chicago: Science Research Associates.

Ervin-Tripp, S. (1975). Discourse agreement: How children answer questions. In J. R. Hayes (Ed.), *Cognition and the development of language.* New York: Wiley.

Falik, L. H. (1969). The effects of special training in kindergarten with second grade reading. *Journal of Learning Disabilities, 2,* 325–329.

Faustman. M. N. (1967). *Some effects of perception training in kindergarten on first grade success in reading.* International Reading Association Conference (Seattle, May 1967). ERIC Document Reproduction Service No. ED 017 397)

Fay, T. (1954). The use of pathological and unlocking reflexes in the rehabilitation of spastics. *American Journal of Physical Medicine, 33,* 347–352.

Federal Register. (1977). Definition and criteria for defining students as learning disabled, *42:* 250, 65083. Washington DC: U.S. Government Printing Office.

Federal Register. (1977). Vol. 42, No. 163 (Tuesday, August 23).

Feingold, B. (1975). *Why your child is hyperactive.* New York: Random House.

Feingold, B. (1976). Hyperkinesis and learning disabilities linked to the ingestion of artificial food colors and flavors. *Journal of Learning Disabilities, 9,* 551–559.

Fernald, G. M. (1943). *Remedial techniques in basic school subjects:* New York: McGraw-Hill.

Fernald, G. M. (1988). *Remedial techniques in basic school subjects.* Austin, TX: PRO-ED.

Fisher, K. L. (1971). Effects of perceptual-motor training on the educable mentally retarded. *Exceptional Children, 38,* 264–266.

Fitzgerald, E. (1912). Manual spelling and English. *American Annals of the Deaf, 57,* 197–203.

Fitzgerald, E. (1918). Language building in the primary grades. *American Annals of the Deaf, 63,* 342–353.

Fitzgerald, E. (1966). *Straight language for the deaf.* Washington, DC: Volta Bureau.

Flavell, J. (1970). Developmental studies of mediated memory. In H. Reese & L. Lipsitt (Eds.), *Advances in child development and behavior* (Vol. 5, pp. 181–211). New York: Academic Press.

Flavell, J. (1979). Metacognition and cognitive monitoring: A new area of cognitive-developmental inquiry. *American Psychologist, 34,* 906–911.

Flavell, J., & Wohlwill, J. F. (1969). Formal and functional aspects of cognitive development. In D. Elkind & J. H. Flavell (Eds.), *Studies in cognitive development* (pp. 67–120). New York: Oxford University Press.

Flesch, R. (1955). *Why Johnny can't read.* New York: Harper & Row.

Fletcher, J. M. (1989). Nonverbal learning disabilities and suicide: Classification leads to prevention. *Journal of Learning Disabilities, 22,* 176–179.

Fokes, J. (1976). *Fokes sentence builder.* Allen, TX: DLM/Teaching Resources.

Forgnone, C. (1966). Effects of visual perception and language training upon certain abilities of retarded children. *Dissertation Abstracts, 27,* 1197-A.

Forness, S. R. (1988). Reductionism, paradigm shifts, and learning disabilities. *Journal of Learning Disabilities, 21,* 421–424.

Forness, S. R., & Kavale, K. A. (1987). Holistic inquiry and the scientific challenge in special education: A reply to Iano. *Remedial and Special Education, 8,* 47–51.

Forness, S. R., & Kavale, K. A. (1988). Psychopharmacologic treatment: A note on classroom effects. *Journal of Learning Disabilities, 21,* 144–147.

Fortenberry, W. D. (1968). Effectiveness of a special program for development of word recognition by culturally disadvantaged first grade pupils. (ERIC Document Reproduction Service No. ED 027 368)

Foster, J. M. (1966). Effect of mobility training upon reading achievement and intelligence. *Dissertation Abstracts, 26,* 3779-A.

Fountain Valley Teacher Support System in Mathematics. (1976). Huntington Beach, CA: Zweig.

Fowler, W. (1971). Cognitive baselines in early childhood: Development learning and differentiation of competence rule systems. In J. Hellmuth (Ed.), *Cognitive studies, Vol. 2: Deficits in cognition* (pp. 231–280). New York: Bruner/Mazel.

Frankenburg, W., Dodds, J., Fandal, A., Kazuk, E., & Cohrs, M. (1975). *Denver Developmental Screening Test.* Denver: LADOCA Project and Publishing Foundation.

Freeman, M. A., & Becker, R. L. (1979). Competencies for professionals in LD: An analysis of teacher perceptions. *Learning Disability Quarterly, 2,* 70–79.

Freeman, R. D. (1967). Controversy over "patterning" as a treatment for brain damage in children. *Journal of the American Medical Association, 202,* 385–388.

Frey, R. M. (1960). *Reading behavior of brain-injured children of average and retarded mental development.* Unpublished doctoral dissertation, University of Illinois.

Frostig, M. (1966). The needs of teachers for specialized information on reading. In W. Cruickshank (Ed.), *The teacher of brain-injured children* (pp. 87–109). Syracuse, NY: Syracuse University Press.

Frostig, M. (1967a). Testing as a basis for educational therapy. *The Journal of Special Education, 2,* 12–34.

Frostig, M. (1967b). Education of children with learning disabilities. In E. C. Frierson and W. B. Barbe (Eds.), *Educating children with learning disabilities* (pp. 387–398). New York: Appleton-Century-Crofts.

Frostig, M. (1968). Education for children with learning disabilities. In H. Myklebust (Ed.), *Progress in learning disabilities* (Vol. I, pp. 234–266). New York: Grune & Stratton.

Frostig, M. (1969). *Frostig MGL. Move-grow-learn. Movement education activities by Marianne Frostig.* Chicago: Follett.

Frostig, M. (1970). *Movement education: Theory and practice.* Chicago: Follett.

Frostig, M. (1972a). Disabilities and remediation in reading. *Academic Therapy, 4,* 373–391.

Frostig, M. (1972b). Visual perception, integrative function and academic learning. *Journal of Learning Disabilities, 5,* 1–15.

Frostig, M. (1973). *Selection and adaptation of reading methods.* San Rafael, CA: Academic Therapy Publications.

Frostig, M. (1976). *Education for dignity.* New York: Grune & Stratton.

Frostig, M., & Horne, D. (1964). *The Frostig program for the development of visual perception* (Teacher's guide). Chicago: Follett.

Frostig, M., Lefever, D. W., & Whittlesey, J. R. B. (1961). A developmental test of visual perception for evaluating normal and neurologically handicapped children. *Perception and Motor Skills, 12,* 383–394.

Frostig, M., Lefever, W., & Whittlesey, J. (1963). Disturbance in visual perception. *Journal of Educational Research, 57,* 160–162.

Frostig, M., & Maslow, P. (1968). Language training: A form of ability training. *Journal of Learning Disabilities, 1,* 105–114.

Frostig, M., & Maslow, P. (1973). *Learning problems in the classroom.* New York: Grune & Stratton.

Frostig, M., Maslow, P., Lefever, D. W., & Whittlesey, J. R. B. (1964). *The Marianne Frostig Developmental Test of Visual Perception* (1963 standardization). Palo Alto, CA: Consulting Psychologists' Press.

Fuchs, D., & Fuchs, L. S. (1988). Evaluation of the adaptive learning environments. *Exceptional Children, 55,* 115–127.

Fuchs, D., & Fuchs, L. S. (1988). Response to Wang and Walberg. *Exceptional Children, 55,* 138–146.

Gagne, R. (1970). *The conditions of learning.* New York: Holt, Rinehart, & Winston.

Galaburda, A. M. (1985a). Developmental dyslexia: Four consecutive patients with congenital anomalies. *Annals of Neurology, 13,* 222–233.

Galaburda, A. M. (1985b). Developmental dyslexia: A review of biological interactions. *Annals of Dyslexia, 35,* 21–32.

Galaburda, A. M. (1989). Learning disability: Biological, societal, or both? A response to Gerald Coles. *Journal of Learning Disabilities, 22,* 278–282.

Galaburda, A. M., & Kemper, T. L. (1979). Cytoarchitectonic abnormalities in developmental dyslexia: A case study. *Annals of Neurology, 6,* 94.

Galaburda, A. M., Sherman, G. F., Rosen, G. D., Aboitiz, F., & Geschwind, N. (1985). Developmental dyslexia: Four consecutive patients with cortical anomalies. *Annals of Neurology, 18,* 222–233.

Gallagher, J. J. (1966). Children with developmental imbalances: A psychoeducational definition. In W. M. Cruickshank (Ed.), *The teacher of brain-injured children.* Syracuse, NY: Syracuse University Press.

Gamsky, N. R., & Lloyd, F. W. (1971). A longitudinal study of visual perceptual training and reading achievement. *Journal of Educational Research, 64,* 451–454.

Gardner, M. F. (1979). *Expressive One-Word Picture Vocabulary Test.* Novato, CA: Academic Therapy Publications.

Gardner, W. I., Cromwell, R. L., & Foshee, J. G. (1959). Studies in activity level. II. Visual. *American Journal of Mental Deficiency, 63,* 1028–1033.

Garofalo, J., & Lester, F. K. (1985). Metacognition, cognitive monitoring, and mathematical performance. *Journal for Research in Mathematics Education, 16,* 163–176.

Garrett, E. (1969). *Automated stimulus control for articulation therapy.* Albuquerque: University of New Mexico.

Garrison, E. B. (1965). *A study in visual-motor perception training in first grade.* (ERIC Document Reproduction Service No. ED 031 292)

Gates, A. I. (1947). *The improvement of reading* (3rd ed.). New York: Macmillan.

Gattegno, C. (1962). Words in color. In J. Money (Ed.), *The disabled reader.* Baltimore: Johns Hopkins Press.

Gazzaniga, M. (1970). *The bisected brain.* New York: Appleton-Century-Crofts.

Gearheart, B. R., & Gearheart, C. J. (1989). *Learning disabilities: Educational strategies.* Columbus, OH: Merrill.

Geis, R. A. (1968). A preventive summer program for kindergarten children likely to fail in first grade reading. (ERIC Document Reproduction Service No. ED 030 495)

German, D. G. (1986). *Test of Word Finding.* Allen, TX: DLM/Teaching Resources.

Gerstmann, J. (1940). Syndrome of finger agnosia, disorientation for right, left, agraphia, and acalculia. *Archives of Neurology & Psychiatry, 44,* 398–440.

Geschwind, N. (1962). The anatomy of acquired disorders of reading. In J. Money (Ed.), *Reading disability* (pp. 115–130). Baltimore: Johns Hopkins Press.

Geschwind, N. (1970). The organization of language and the brain. *Science, 170,* 940–944.

Geschwind, N., & Galaburda, A. M. (1987). *Cerebral lateralization: Biological mechanisms, associations, and pathology.* Cambridge, MA: MIT Press.

Getman, G. N. (1961). Visual success in reading success. *Journal of the California Optometric Association, 29,* 1–4.

Getman, G. N. (1967). Personal communication.

Getman, G. N. (1984). *How to develop your child's intelligence.* Irvine, CA: Research Publications.

Getman, G. N. (1985). A commentary on vision training. *Journal of Learning Disabilities, 18,* 505–512.

Getman, G. N., & Kane, E. R. (1964, 1968). *The physiology of readiness: An action program for the development of perception for children.* Minneapolis, MN: Programs to Accelerate School Success, 1964. (Revised and retitled. Getman, G. N., Kane, E. R., Halgren, M. R., & McKee, G. W. *Developing learning readiness.* Manchester, MO: Webster Division, McGraw-Hill.)

Gillberg, I. C., Gillberg, C., & Groth, J. (1989). Children with preschool minor neurodevelopmental disorders. V. Neurodevelopmental profiles at age 13. *Developmental Medicine and Child Neurology, 31,* 14–24.

Gillingham, A., & Stillman, B. (1965, 1970). *Remedial training for children with specific disability in reading, spelling and penmanship* (7th ed.). Cambridge, MA: Educators Publishing Service.

Ginsburg, H. (1987). Assessing arithmetic. In D. D. Hammill (Ed.), *Assessing the abilities and instructional needs of students* (pp. 412–503). Austin, TX: PRO-ED.

Ginsburg, H., & Baroody, A. J. (1990). *Test of Early Mathematics Ability.* Austin, TX: PRO-ED.

Ginsburg, H., & Mathews, S. (1984). *Diagnostic Test of Arithmetic Strategies.* Austin, TX: PRO-ED.

Gittleman-Klein, R., Klein, D., Katz, H., Gloisten, A., & Kates, W. (1976). Relative efficacy of methylphenidate and behavior modification in children: An interim report. *Journal of Abnormal Child Psychology, 4,* 361–379.

Glaeser, G., DeWaide, S., & Levi, R. (1966). Reading improvement program at Miguel High School Reading Clinic. In C. H. Delacato (Ed.), *Neurological organization and reading* (pp. 131–142). Springfield, IL: Thomas.

Glennon, V., & Wilson, J. (1972). Diagnostic prescriptive teaching. In *The slow learner in mathematics: 35th annual yearbook.* Reston, VA: National Council of Teachers of Mathematics.

Goldman, S. R. (1989). Strategy instruction in mathematics. *Learning Disability Quarterly, 12,* 43–57.

Goldstein, K. (1939). *The organism.* New York: American Book Co.

Goldstein, K. (1948a). *Aftereffects of brain injuries in war.* New York: Grune & Stratton.

Goldstein, K. (1948b). *Language and language disturbances.* New York: Grune & Stratton.

Goodman, L. (1978). The efficacy of visual-motor training for orthopedically handicapped children. *Rehabilitation Literature, 34,* 299–304.

Goodman, L., & Hammill, D. D. (1973). The effectiveness of the Kephart-Getman training activities. *Focus on Exceptional Children, 40,* 1–9.

Goodman, Y., & Burke, C. L. (1972). *Reading Miscue Inventory: Manual, and procedures for diagnosis and evaluation.* New York: Macmillan.

Goodstein, H. (1975). Assessment and programming in mathematics for the handicapped. *Focus on Exceptional Children, 1,* 7.

Gray, B. B., & Fygetakis, L. (1968). Mediating language acquisition for dysphasic children. *Behavior Research and Therapy, 6,* 263–280.

Gray, B. B., & Ryan, B. (1973). *A language program for the nonlanguage child.* Champaign, IL: Research Press.

Green, O. C., & Perlman, S. M. (1971). Endocrinology and disorders of learning. In H. Myklebust (Ed.), *Progress in learning disabilities* (Vol. II). New York: Grune & Stratton.

Greenbaum, C. (1987). *Spellmaster Assessment and Teaching System.* Austin, TX: PRO-ED.

Gresham, F. M., & Elliott, S. N. (1989). Social skills deficits as a primary learning disability. *Journal of Learning Disabilities, 22,* 120–124.

Grinspoon, L., & Singer, S. (1973). Amphetamines in the treatment of hyperactive children. *Harvard Educational Press, 43,* 515–555.

Gross, M. D., & Wilson, W. C. (1974). *Minimal brain dysfunction.* New York: Bruner/Mazel.

Hagin, R. I. (1965). In *Perceptual training for children with learning difficulties.* Symposium of the New Jersey Association for Brain Injured Children et al.

Hagin, R. I., & Silver, A. (1971). Ability assessment and training. *The Journal of Special Education, 5,* 35–40.

Hall, R. V., & Van Houten, R. (1983). *The measurement of behavior.* Austin, TX: PRO-ED.

Hall, S. L., & Deacon, K. F. (1970). Effects noted from the use of the Frostig training program with trainable retardates. *The Training School Bulletin, 67,* 20–24.

Hallahan, D. P. (1973). University of Virginia learning disabilities institute. *Learning Disability Quarterly, 1,* 74–76.

Hallahan, D. P., & Cruickshank, W. M. (1973). *Psychoeducational foundations of learning disabilities.* Englewood Cliffs, NJ: Prentice-Hall.

Hallahan, D. P., Kauffman, J., & Lloyd, J. (1985). *Introduction to learning disabilities.* Englewood Cliffs, NJ: Prentice-Hall.

Hallahan, D. P., Lloyd, J., Kosiewicz, M. M., Kauffman, J. M., & Graves, A. W. (1979). Self-monitoring of attention as a treatment for a learning disabled boy's off-task behavior. *Learning Disability Quarterly, 2,* 24–32.

Hallahan, D. P., Lloyd, J. W., & Stoller, L. (1982). *Improving attention with self-monitoring: A manual for teachers.* Charlottesville: University of Virginia Learning Disabilities Research Institute.

Hallahan, D. P., Marshall, K. J., & Lloyd, J. W. (1981). Self-recording during group instruction: Effects on attention to task. *Learning Disability Quarterly, 4,* 407–413.

Hallahan, D. P., & Sapona, R. (1983). Self-monitoring of attention with learning disabled children: Past research and current issues. *Journal of Learning Disabilities, 16,* 616–620.

Hallahan, D. P., Tarver, S. G., Kauffman, J. M., & Graybeal, N. L. (1978). A comparison of the effects of reinforcement and response cost in the selective attention of learning disabled children. *Journal of Learning Disabilities, 11,* 430–438.

Hallgren, B. (1950). Specific dyslexia: A clinical and genetic study. *Acta Psychiatrica et Neurologica,* Supplement 65. Copenhagen, Munksgaard.

Halliwell, J. W., & Solan, H. A. (1972). The effects of a supplemental perceptual training program on reading achievement. *Exceptional Children, 38,* 613–621.

Halstead, W. C. (1947). *Brain and intelligence: A quantitative study of the frontal lobes.* Chicago: University of Chicago Press.

Hammill, D. D. (1972). The resource room model in special education. *The Journal of Special Education, 6,* 349–354.

Hammill, D. D. (1972). Training visual perceptual processes. *Journal of Learning Disabilities, 5,* 552–559.

Hammill, D. D. (1976). Defining "learning disabilities" for programmatic purposes. *Academic Therapy, 12,* 26–37.

Hammill, D. D. (1987). *Assessing the abilities and instructional needs of students.* Austin, TX: PRO-ED.

Hammill, D. D. (1990). *Detroit Tests of Learning Aptitude–3 School Edition.* Austin, TX: PRO-ED.

Hammill, D. D. (1990). Defining learning disabilities: The emerging consensus. *Journal of Learning Disabilities, 23,* 74–84.

Hammill, D. D., & Bartel, N. (1990). *Teaching students with learning and behavior problems* (5th ed.). Boston: Allyn & Bacon.

Hammill, D. D., Brown, L., & Bryant, B. R. (1989). *A consumer's guide to tests in print.* Austin, TX: PRO-ED.

Hammill, D. D., Brown, V., Larsen, S., & Wiederholt, J. L. (1987). *Test of Adolescent Language–2.* Austin, TX: PRO-ED.

Hammill, D. D., Goodman, L., & Wiederholt, J. L. (1974). Visual-motor processes: What success have we had in training them? *The Reading Teacher, 27,* 469–478.

Hammill, D. D., & Larsen, S. C. (1974a). The efficacy of psycholinguistic training. *Exceptional Children, 41,* 5–14.

Hammill, D. D., & Larsen, S. C. (1974b). The relationship of selected auditory perceptual skills and reading ability. *Journal of Learning Disabilities, 7,* 429–436.

Hammill, D. D., & Larsen, S. C. (1978). The effectiveness of psycholinguistic training: A reaffirmation of position. *Exceptional Children, 6,* 402–417.

Hammill, D. D., & Larsen, S. C. (1988). *Test of Written Language–2.* Austin, TX: PRO-ED.

Hammill, D. D., Larsen, S. C., & McNutt, G. (1977). The effects of spelling instruction. *The Elementary School, 78,* 67–72.

Hammill, D. D., Leigh, J., McNutt, G., & Larsen, S. C. (1981). A new definition of learning disabilities. *Learning Disability Quarterly, 4,* 336–342.

Hammill, D. D., & Newcomer, P. (1988). *Test of Language Development–2: Intermediate.* Austin, TX: PRO-ED.

Hammill, D. D., Parker, R., & Newcomer, P. (1975). Psycholinguistic correlates of academic abilities. *Journal of School Psychology, 13,* 248–254.

Hammill, D. D., & Wiederholt, J. L. (1971). Appropriateness of the Developmental Test of Visual Perception when used with economically disadvantaged children. *Journal of School Psychology, 9,* 480.

Hammill, D. D., & Wiederholt, J. L. (1973). Review of the Frostig Visual Perception Test and the Related Training Program. In L. Mann & D. A. Sabatino (Eds.), *The first review of special education* (Vol. 1, pp. 33–48). Austin, TX: PRO-ED.

Hansen, E. (1963). Reading and writing difficulties in children with cerebral palsy. In M. Bax & R. MacKeith (Eds.), *Minimal cerebral dysfunction.* London: William Heinemann Medical Books, Little Club Clinics in Developmental Medicine, No. 10.

Haring, N. G., & Miller, C. A. (Eds.). (1969). *Minimal brain dysfunction in children: Educational, medical, and health related services.* Public Health Publication, No. 2015. Washington, DC: U.S. Department of Health, Education, and Welfare.

Harley, J., Chun, R., Cleeland, C., Eichman, P., Matthews, C., Ray, R., & Tomasi, L. (1976, January 29). *Hyperkinesis: Food additives and hyperactivity in children.* Paper presented to Food and Nutrition Liaison Committee, Nutrition Foundation, Naples, FL.

Harlow, H. (1958). The nature of love. *American Psychologist, 13,* 673–685.

Harris, S. L. (1983). Behavior therapy with children. In M. Harsen, A. E. Kazdin, & A. S. Ballack (Eds.), *The clinical psychology handbook* (pp. 525–535). New York: Pergamon.

Hartman, N. C., & Hartman, R. K. (1973). Perceptual handicap or reading disability? *The Reading Teacher,* April, 684–695.

Hawisher, M. F., & Calhoun, M. L. (1978). *The resource room: An educational asset for children with special needs.* Columbus, OH: Merrill.

Head, H. (1926). *Aphasia and kindred disorders of speech* (Vols. I & II). London: Cambridge University Press.

Hebb, D. O. (1949). *The organization of behavior.* New York: Wiley.

Hegge, T. G., Kirk, S. A., & Kirk, W. D. (1970). *Remedial reading drills.* Ann Arbor, MI: George Wahr.

Heilman, K. M., Bowers, D., & Valenstein, E. (1985). Emotional disorders associated with neurological diseases. In K. M. Heilman & E. Valenstein (Eds.), *Clinical neuropsychology* (2nd ed., pp. 377–402). New York: Oxford University Press.

Heron, T., & Harris, K. C. (1987). *The educational consultant.* Austin, TX: PRO-ED.

Herrick, C. J. (1956). *The evolution of human nature.* Austin: University of Texas Press.

Hewett, F. (1964). A hierarchy of educational tasks for children with learning disorders. *Exceptional Children, 34,* 107–116.

Hewett, F. M. (1967). Educational engineering with emotionally disturbed children. *Exceptional Children, 33,* 459–467.

Hewett, F. M. (1968). *The emotionally disturbed child in the classroom.* Boston: Allyn & Bacon.

Hewett, F. M., & Forness, S. R. (1977). *Education of exceptional learners.* Boston: Allyn & Bacon.

Hewett, F. M., & Taylor, F. D. (1980). *The educationally disturbed child in the classroom: The orchestration of success.* Boston: Allyn & Bacon.

Hewett, F. M., Taylor, F. D., & Artuso, A. A. (1969). The Santa Monica Project: Evaluation of an engineered classroom design with emotionally disturbed children. *Exceptional Children, 35,* 523–529.

Hier, D. B., Mondlock, J., & Caplan, L. R. (1983). Behavioral deficits after right hemisphere stroke. *Neurology, 33,* 337–344.

Hill, A. A. (1958). *Introduction to linguistic structures: From sound to sentence in English.* New York: Harcourt, Brace.

Hinshelwood, J. (1917). *Congenital word blindness.* London: H. K. Lewis.

Howell, K. W., & Kaplan, J. S. (1980). *Diagnosing basic skills.* Columbus, OH: Merrill.

Hresko, W. (1988). *Test of Early Written Language.* Austin, TX: PRO-ED.

Hresko, W., Reid, K., & Hammill, D. (1981). *Test of Early Language Development.* Austin, TX: PRO-ED.

Hudson, F., & Colson, S. E. (1989). *Hudson Education Skills Inventory–Mathematics.* Austin, TX: PRO-ED.

Hudson, F., Colson, S. E., Banikowski, A. K., & Mehring, T. A. (1989). *Hudson Education Skills Inventory–Writing.* Austin, TX: PRO-ED.

Hudson, F., Colson, S. E., & Welch, D. L. H. (1989). *Hudson Education Skills Inventory–Reading.* Austin, TX: PRO-ED.

Hudson, P. J., Morsink, C. V., Branscum, G., & Boone, R. (1987). Competencies for teachers of students with learning disabilities. *Journal of Learning Disabilities, 20,* 232–236.

Human Potential. (1968a). Institutes' official reply, *1,* 301–306.

Human Potential. (1968b). Institutes' official statement, *1,* 307–310.

Human Potential. (1968c). Letters to and about the Institutes, *1,* 311–331.

Human Potential. (1969). Editorial statement, *1,* 332–333.

Hunt, R. D., & Cohen, D. J. (1984). Psychiatric aspects of learning difficulties. *Pediatric Clinics of North America, 31,* 471–497.

Hunter, M. (1984). *Mastery teaching.* El Segundo, CA: TIP Publications.

Hynd, G. W., & Cohen, M. (1983). *Dyslexia: Neuropsychological theory research, and clinical differentiation.* New York: Grune & Stratton.

Hynd, G. W., & Semrud-Clikeman, M. (1989). Dyslexia and neurodevelopmental pathology: Relationships to cognition, intelligence, and reading skill acquisition. *Journal of Learning Disabilities, 22,* 204–216.

Iano, R. P. (1986). The study and development of teaching. *Remedial and Special Education, 7,* 50–61.

Iano, R. P. (1987). Neither the absolute certainty of prescriptive law nor a surrender to mysticism. *Remedial and Special Education, 8,* 52–61.

Idol, L. (1983). *Special educator's consultation handbook.* Austin, TX: PRO-ED.

Idol, L. (1988). Foreword. In G. Fernald, *Remedial techniques in basic school subjects.* Austin, TX: PRO-ED.

Interagency Committee on Learning Disabilities. (1989). *Learning disabilities: A report to the U.S. Congress.* Bethesda, MD: National Institutes of Health.

International DCLD Board of Trustees. (1980). A reply from the board of trustees for DCLD: A factual response to April's fiction. *Journal of Learning Disabilities, 13,* 412–419.

Ismail, A. A., & Gruber, J. J. (1967). *Integrated development, motor aptitude, and intellectual performance.* Columbus, OH: Merrill.

Jacobs, J. J. (1968). An evaluation of the Frostig visual-perceptual training program. *Journal of the Association for Supervision and Curriculum Development, 25,* 332–340.

Jedrysek, E., Klapper, Z., Pope, L., & Wortis, J. (1972). *Psycho-educational evaluation of the preschool child: A manual utilizing the Haeusserman approach.* New York: Grune & Stratton.

Johnson, D. J., & Myklebust, H. R. (1967). *Learning disabilities: Educational principles and practices.* Boston: Allyn & Bacon.

Johnson, D. W. (1973). *Neural basis for reading: The relationship of sensorimotor integration to reading achievement in third grade youngsters.* Doctoral dissertation, Temple University, Philadelphia.

Johnson, W., Darley, F., & Spriestersbach, D. (1963). *Diagnostic methods in speech pathology.* New York: Harper & Row.

Jorgensen, C., Barrett, M., Huisingh, R., & Zachman, L. (1981). *The Word Test.* Moline, IL: LinguiSystems.

Kabot, R. R. (1966). A study of improvement in reading through improvement of neurological organization. In C. H. Delacato (Ed.), *Neurological organization and reading* (pp. 118–121). Springfield, IL: Thomas.

Kagan, J., & Kogan, N. (1970). Individual variation in cognitive processes. In P. H. Mussen (Ed.), *Manual of child psychology* (Vol. I, 3rd ed., pp. 1273–1365). New York: Wiley.

Kanter, R., Clark, D., Allen, L. M., & Chase, M. (1976). Effects of vestibular stimulation on nystagmus response and motor performance in the developmentally delayed infant. *Physical Therapy, 56,* 414–421.

Kappelman, M. M., Kaplan, E., & Ganter, R. L. (1969). A study of learning disorders among disadvantaged children. *Journal of Learning Disabilities, 2,* 261–268.

Karlsen, B., Madden, R., & Gardner, E. F. (1978). *Stanford Diagnostic Reading Test.* San Antonio, TX: Psychological Corp.

Karnes, M. (1968). *Helping young children develop language skills.* Arlington, VA: Council for Exceptional Children.

Kass, C. F. (1970). *Final Report.* USOE contract, Advanced institute for leadership personnel in learning disabilities. Sponsored by the Department of Special Education, University of Arizona, Unit on Learning Disabilities, Division of Training Programs, Bureau of Education for the Handicapped.

Katz, S., Savat, K., Gittelman-Klein, R., & Klein, D. (1975). Clinical pharmacological management of hyperkinetic children. *International Journal of Mental Health, 4,* 175–181.

Kaufman, A. S., & Kaufman, N. L. (1983). *Kaufman Assessment Battery for Children.* Circle Pines, MN: American Guidance Service.

Kauffman, J. M. (1977). *Characteristics of children's behavior disorders.* Columbus, OH: Merrill.

Kauffman, J. M. (1989). The Regular Education Initiative as Reagan-Bush education policy: A trickle-down theory of education of the hard-to-teach. *The Journal of Special Education, 23,* 256–278.

Kavale, K. (1981). Functions of the Illinois Test of Psycholinguistic Abilities (ITPA): Are they trainable? *Exceptional Children, 47,* 496–513.

Kavale, K. (1982). The efficacy of stimulant drug treatment for hyperactivity: A meta-analysis. *Journal of Learning Disabilities, 15,* 280–289.

Kavale, K., & Mattson, P. D. (1983). One jumped off the balance beam: Meta-analysis of perceptual-motor training. *Journal of Learning Disabilities, 16,* 165–173.

Kavale, K., & Forness, S. (1985). *The science of learning disabilities.* San Diego: College-Hill.

Keim, R. P. (1970). Visual-motor training, readiness, and intelligence of kindergarten children. *Journal of Learning Disabilities, 3,* 265–269.

Kelin, R., & Pertz, D. (1978). Nutrition and learning. *Academic Therapy, 13,* 527–535.

Kephart, N. C. (1963). *The brain injured child in the classroom.* Chicago: National Society for Crippled Children and Adults.

Kephart, N. C. (1968). *Learning disability: An educational adventure.* Danville, IL: Interstate.

Kephart, N. C. (1971). *The slow learner in the classroom.* Columbus, OH: Merrill.

Kershner, J. (1968). Doman-Delacato's theory of neurological organization applied with retarded children. *Exceptional Children, 34,* 441–452.

Kershner, J. (1975). Reading and laterality revisited. *The Journal of Special Education, 9,* 269–279.

Kimball, W. H., & Heron, T. E. (1988). A behavioral commentary on Poplin's discussion of reductionist fallacy and holistic/constructivist principles. *Journal of Learning Disabilities, 21,* 425–428.

Kinsbourne, M., & Smith, W. (Eds.). (1974). *Hemispheric disconnection and cerebral function.* Springfield, IL: Thomas.

Kirk, S. A. (1936). *A manual of directions for use with the Hegge-Kirk remedial reading drills.* Mimeographed paper. Distributed by George Wahr, Ann Arbor, MI.

Kirk, S. A. (1962). *Educating exceptional children.* Boston: Houghton-Mifflin.

Kirk, S. A. (1963). *Behavioral diagnosis and remediation of learning disabilities.* In Proceedings of the Annual Meeting of the Conference on Exploration into the Problems of the Perceptually Handicapped Child (Vol. 1).

Kirk, S. A., & Bateman, B. (1962). Diagnosis and remediation of learning disabilities. *Exceptional Children, 29,* 73–78.

Kirk, S. A., & Chalfant, J. (1984). *Academic and developmental learning disabilities.* Denver: Love.

Kirk, S. A., & Elkins, J. (1975). Characteristics of children enrolled in the Child Service Demonstration Center. *Journal of Learning Disabilities, 8,* 31–38.

Kirk, S. A., & Gallagher, J. J. (1989). *Educating exceptional children.* Boston: Houghton-Mifflin.

Kirk, S. A., & Kirk, W. D. (1956). How Johnny learns to read. *Exceptional Children, 22,* 158–160.

Kirk, S. A., & Kirk, W. D. (1971). *Psycholinguistic learning disabilities: Diagnosis and remediation.* Urbana: University of Illinois Press.

Kirk, S. A., Kirk, W. D., & Minskoff, E. H. (1985). *Phonic remedial reading drills.* Novato, CA: Academic Therapy.

Kirk, S. A., Klieban, J., & Lerner, J. (1978). *Teaching reading to slow and disabled learners.* Boston: Houghton-Mifflin.

Kirk, S. A., & McCarthy, J. J. (1961). *Illinois Test of Psycholinguistic Abilities.* Experimental Edition. Urbana: University of Illinois Press.

Kirk, S. A., McCarthy, J. J., & Kirk, W. D. (1968). *Illinois Test of Psycholinguistic Abilities* (rev. ed.). Urbana: University of Illinois Press.

Kirk, W. D. (1974). *Aids and precautions in administering the Illinois Test of Psycholinguistic Abilities.* Urbana: University of Illinois Press.

Klanderman, J. W. (1973). A study of the effects of a kindergarten perceptual-motor development program. *Dissertation Abstracts, 33,* 1023-A.

Klein, I., & Marsh, H. R. (1969). *Identification and remediation of perceptual handicaps in learning to read.* (ERIC Document Reproduction Service No. ED 029 773)

Kohn, B., & Dennis, M. (1974). Selective impairments of visuo-spatial abilities in infantile hemiplegics and right hemidecortication. *Neuropsychologia, 12,* 505–512.

Kolligian, J., & Sternberg, R. J. (1987). Intelligence, information processing, and specific learning disabilities: A triarchic synthesis. *Journal of Learning Disabilities, 20,* 8–17.

Kottmeyer, W. (1970). *Teacher's guide for remedial reading.* New York: McGraw-Hill.

Kottmeyer, W., & Claus, A. (1988). *Basic goals in spelling.* New York: McGraw-Hill.

Krager, J., & Safer, D. (1974). Type and prevalence of medication used in the treatment of hyperactive children. *New England Journal of Medicine, 291,* 1118–1120.

Krippner, S., Silverman, R., Cavallo, M., & Healy, M. (1973). A study of 'hyperkinetic' children receiving stimulant drugs. *Academic Therapy, 8,* 261–269.

Kuhn, T. S. (1970). *The structure of scientific revolutions.* Chicago: University of Chicago Press.

Laberge, D., & Samuels, S. J. (1974). Toward a theory of automatic information processing in reading. *Cognitive Psychology, 6,* 293–323.

Lahey, B., Stempnick, M., Robinson, E., & Tyroler, M. (1978). Hyperactivity and learning disabilities as independent dimensions of child behavior problems. *Journal of Abnormal Child Psychology, 87,* 333–340.

Larsen, S. C. (1976). The learning disabilities specialist: Role and responsibilities. *Journal of Learning Disabilities, 9,* 498–508.

Larsen, S. C. (1978). Learning disabilities and the professional educator. *Learning Disability Quarterly, 1,* 5–12.

Larsen, S. C., & Hammill, D. D. (1975). The relationship of selected visual perceptual abilities to school learning. *The Journal of Special Education, 9,* 281–291.

Larsen, S. C., & Hammill, D. D. (1986). *Test of Written Spelling–2.* Austin, TX: PRO-ED.

Larsen, S. C., & Hammill, D. D. (1989). *Test of Legible Handwriting.* Austin, TX: PRO-ED.

Larsen, S. C., Rogers, D., & Sowell, V. (1976). The use of selected perceptual tests in differentiating between normal and learning disabled children. *Journal of Learning Disabilities, 9,* 85–90.

Lavin, C. M. (1971). The effects of a structured sensory-motor training program on selected cognitive and psycholinguistic abilities of preschool children. *Dissertation Abstracts, 32,* 1984-A.

Laycock, M., & Watson, G. (1975). *The fabric of mathematics: A resource book for teachers.* Hayward, CA: Activity Resources.

Lee, L. (1966). Developmental sentence types: A method for comparing normal and deviant syntactical development. *Journal of Speech and Hearing Disorders, 31,* 311–330.

Lee, L. (1971a). *Northwestern Syntax Screening Test.* Evanston, IL: Northwestern University Press.

Lee, L. (1971b). Developmental sentence scoring: A clinical procedure for estimating syntactic development in children's spontaneous speech. *Journal of Speech and Hearing Disorders, 36,* 315–331.

Lee, L. (1974). *Developmental Sentence Analysis.* Evanston, IL: Northwestern University Press.

Lee, L., Koenigsknecht, R. A., & Mulhern, S. T. (1975). *Interactive language development teaching.* Evanston, IL: Northwestern University Press.

Leigh, J., & Patton, J. (1986). State certification standards of learning disabled students. *Learning Disability Quarterly, 9,* 259–267.

Lenz, B. K., Schumaker, J. B., Deshler, D. D., & Beals, V. L. (1984). *The word identification strategy.* Lawrence: The University of Kansas Institute for Research in Learning Disabilities.

Lerer, R., & Lerer, M. (1977). Response of adolescents with minimal brain dysfunction to methylphenidate. *Journal of Learning Disabilities, 10,* 223–227.

Levinson, H. N. (1980). *A solution to the riddle dyslexia.* New York: Springer-Verlag.

Levinson, H. N. (1984). *Smart but feeling dumb.* New York: Warner.

Levy, J. (1969). Possible basis for the evolution of lateral specialization of the human brain. *Nature, 224,* 614–615.

Lieberman, L. M. (1980). Territoriality—Who does what to whom? *Journal of Learning Disabilities, 13,* 124–128.

Liederman, J., Merola, J. L., & Hoffman, C. (1986). Longitudinal data indicate that hemispheric independence increases during early adolescence. *Developmental Neuropsychology, 2,* 183–201.

Lilly, M. S. (Ed.). (1979). *Children with exceptional needs: A survey of special education.* New York: Holt, Rinehart, & Winston.

Linn, S. H. (1967). From the classroom: Visual perceptual training for kindergarten children. *Academic Therapy Quarterly, 4,* 255–258.

Litchfield, T. B. (1970). *A program of visual-motor perceptual training to determine its effect upon primary level children with reading and learning deficiencies.* (ERIC Document Reproduction Service No. ED 043 994)

Lloyd, J. (1980). Academic instruction and cognitive behavior modification: The need for attack strategy training. *Exceptional Education Quarterly, 1,* 53–63.

Lloyd, J. (1987). The art and science of research on teaching. *Remedial and Special Education, 8,* 44–46.

Lloyd, J., Cameron, N., Cullinan, D., Kauffman, J., & Kneedler, R. (1981). *Addition strategy training with learning disabled children* (Tech. Rep. No. 40). Charlottesville: University of Virginia Learning Disabilities Research Institute.

Lloyd, J., & deBettencourt, L. (1982). *Academic strategy training: A manual for teachers.* Charlottesville: University of Virginia Learning Disabilities Research Institute.

Lloyd, J., Kneedler, R., & Cameron, N. (1982). Effects of verbal self-guidance on word reading accuracy. *Reading Improvement, 19,* 84–89.

Lloyd, J., Saltzman, N. J., & Kauffman, J. M. (1981). Predictable generalization in academic learning as a result of preskills and strategy training. *Learning Disability Quarterly, 4,* 203–216.

Logan, R. L. (1978). The effects of structured language programs on linguistic skills of culturally different children. *Dissertation Abstracts International, 38A,* 4096.

Lombardi, T. P., & Lombardi, E. J. (1977). *ITPA: Clinican Interpretation and remediation.* Seattle, WA: Special Child Publications.

Loper, A. B. (1982). Metacognitive training to correct academic deficiency. *Topics in Learning and Learning Disabilities, 2,* 61–68.

Lou, H. C., Henriksen, L., & Bruhn, P. (1984). Focal cerebral hyperfusion in children with dysplasia and/or attention deficit disorder. *Archives of Neurology, 41,* 825–829.

Lou, H. C., Henriksen, L., Bruhn, P., Borner, H., & Nielsen, J. B. (1989). Striatal dysfunction in attention-deficit and hyperkinetic disorder. *Archives of Neurology, 46,* 48–52.

Loudon, B., & Arthur, G. (1940). An application of the Fernald method to an extreme case of reading disability. *Elementary School Journal, 40,* 599–606.

Lovitt, T. C. (1967). Assessment of children with learning disabilities. *Exceptional Children, 34,* 233–238.

Lovitt, T. C. (1975a). Characteristics of ABA, general recommendations, and methodological limitations (Part 1). *Journal of Learning Disabilities, 8,* 432–443.

Lovitt, T. C. (1975b). Applied behavior analysis and learning disabilities (Part 2): Specific research recommendations and suggestions for practitioners. *Journal of Learning Disabilities, 8,* 504–517.

Lovitt, T. C. (1976). Thomas C. Lovitt. In J. M. Kauffman & D. P. Hallahan (Eds.), *Teaching children with learning disabilities: Personal perspectives.* Columbus, OH: Merrill.

Lovitt, T. C. (1978). Arithmetic. In N. G. Haring, T. C. Lovitt, M. D. Eaton, & C. L. Hansen (Eds.), *The fourth r: Research in the classroom* (pp. 127–166). Columbus, OH: Merrill.

Lovitt, T. C. (1986). Personal communication.

Lovitt, T. C. (1989). *Introduction to learning disabilities.* Boston: Allyn & Bacon.

Lumsden, J. (1978). Review of ITPA. In O. K. Buros (Ed.), *The eighth mental measurements yearbook* (Vol. 1, p. 431). Highland Park, NJ: Gryphon.

Lund, K., Foster, G., & Perez-McCall, F. (1978). The effectiveness of psycholinguistic training: A revaluation. *Exceptional Children, 44,* 310–321.

Luria, A. R. (1966). *Higher cortical functions in man.* New York: Basic Books.

Maloney, M. P., Ball, T. S., & Edgar, C. L. (1970). Analysis of the generalizability of sensory-motor training. *American Journal of Mental Deficiency, 74,* 458–469.

Mangrum, C. T., & Strichart, S. S. (1988). *College and the learning disabled student* (2nd ed.). Philadelphia: Grune & Stratton.

Mann, L. (1971). Psychometric phrenology and the new faculty psychology: The case against ability assessment and training. *The Journal of Special Education, 5,* 3–14.

Mann, L. (1972). Marianne Frostig Developmental Test of Visual Perception. In O. K. Buros (Ed.), *The seventh yearbook of mental measurements.* Highland Park, NJ: Gryphon.

Mann, L. (1979). *On the trail of process.* New York: Grune & Stratton.

Mann, L., & Phillips, W. A. (1967). Fractional practices in special education: A critique. *Exceptional Children, 33,* 311–317.

Masland, R. L. (1969). Children with minimal brain dysfunction—A national problem. In L. Tarnpol (Ed.), *Learning disabilities: Introduction to educational and medical management.* Springfield, IL: Thomas.

Maslow, P. (1985). In memoriam: Marianne Frostig. *Journal of Learning Disabilities, 18,* 570–573.

Maslow, P., Frostig, M., Lefever, D. W., & Whittlesey, J. R. B. (1964). The Marianne Frostig Developmental Test of Visual Perception: 1963 standardization. *Perceptual and Motor Skills, 19,* 463–499.

Massman, P. J., Nussbaum, N. L., & Bigler, E. (1988). The mediating effect of age on the relationship between child behavior check list, hyperactivity scores, and neuropsychological test performance. *Journal of Abnormal Child Psychology, 16,* 89–95.

Masterman, J. (1966). The effect of neurological training on reading retardation. In C. H. Delacato (Ed.), *Neurological organization and reading* (pp. 109–114). Springfield, IL: Thomas.

Mayron, L. (1979). Allergy, learning, and behavior problems. *Journal of Learning Disabilities, 12,* 32–42.

Mazurkiewicz, A. J., & Tanzer, H. J. (1966). *The i/t/a handbook for writing and spelling: Early-to-read i/t/a program.* New York: Initial Teaching Alphabet Publications.

McBeath, P. M. (1966). The effectiveness of three reading preparedness programs for perceptually handicapped kindergarteners. *Dissertation Abstracts, 27,* 115-A.

McClanahan, L. J. (1967). The effectiveness of perceptual training for slow learners. *Dissertation Abstracts, 28,* 2560-A.

McCormick, C. C., Schnobrinch, J. N., & Footlik, S. W. (1969). The effect of perceptual-motor training on reading achievement. *Academic Therapy, 4,* 171–176.

McDonald, C. W. (1967, January). *Problems concerning the classification and education of children with learning disabilities.* Report presented to Southern Regional Education Board, Atlanta.

McGinnis, M. A. (1963). *Aphasic children.* Washington, DC: Volta Bureau.

McGinnis, M. A. (1964). In S. Rappaport, *Childhood aphasia and brain damage.* Narberth, PA: Livingston.

McGinnis, M. A. (1988). Aphasic children: Identification and education by the Association Method. In H. Barry & M. McGinnis, *Teaching aphasic children* (pp. 61–225). Austin, TX: PRO-ED.

McGinnis, M. A., Kleffner, F. R., & Goldstein, P. (1956). Teaching aphasic children. *Volta Review, 58,* 239–244.

McGuire, T. L., & Sylvester, C. E. (1989). Neuropsychiatric evaluation and treatment of traumatic brain injury. In E. D. Bigler (Ed.), *Traumatic brain injury.* Austin, TX: PRO-ED.

McIntosh, D. K., & Dunn, L. M. (1973). Children and major specific learning disabilities. In L. M. Dunn (Ed.), *Exceptional children in the schools* (2nd ed.). New York: Holt, Rinehart, & Winston.

McLeod, J. (1976). A reaction to Psycholinguistics in the Schools. In P. Newcomer & D. Hammill (Eds.), *Psycholinguistics in the schools* (pp. 128–143). Columbus, OH: Merrill.

McCloughlin, J. A., & Lewis, R. B. (1986). *Assessing special students.* Columbus, OH: Merrill.

McNeill, D. (1970). *The acquisition of language: The study of developmental psycholinguistics.* New York: Harper & Row.

Mecham, M. J. (1989). *Utah Test of Language Development–3.* Austin, TX: PRO-ED.

Meier, J. (1971). Prevalence and characteristics of learning disabilities found in second grade children. *Journal of Learning Disabilities, 4,* 6–21.

Menyuk, P. (1974). *The acquisition and development of language.* Englewood Cliffs, NJ: Prentice-Hall.

Mercer, C. D. (1987). *Students with learning disabilities.* Columbus, OH: Merrill.

Mercer, C., & Mercer, A. R. (1989). *Teaching students with learning problems.* Columbus, OH: Merrill.

Merrill, M. D., & Goodman, R. I. (1972). *Selecting instructional strategies and media: A place to begin.* East Lansing: National Special Media Institutes, Michigan State University.

Meyerson, D. W. (1967). *A reading readiness training program for perceptually handicapped kindergarten pupils of normal vision.* (ERIC Document Reproduction Service No. ED 013 119)

Milner, B. (1971). Interhemispheric differences and psychological processes. *British Medical Bulletin, 27,* 272–277.

Minskoff, E. H. (1967). *An analysis of the teacher-pupil verbal interaction in special classes for the mentally retarded.* Unpublished doctoral dissertation, Yeshiva University. (Also: Final report, Project No. 6-8092, Grant No. 32-42-1700-6008, U.S. Department of Health, Education, and Welfare, Office of Education, Bureau of Research.)

Minskoff, E. (1975). Research on psycholinguistic training: Critique and guidelines. *Exceptional Children, 42,* 136–143.

Minskoff, E. (1976). Research on the efficacy of remediating psycholinguistic disabilities: Critique and recommendations. In P. Newcomer & D. Hammill (Eds.), *Psycholinguistics in the schools* (pp. 103–121). Columbus, OH: Merrill.

Minskoff, E., Wiseman, D. E., & Minskoff, J. G. (1972). *The MWM program for developing language abilities.* Ridgefield, NJ: Educational Performance Associates.

Minskoff, J. G. (1967). *The effectiveness of a specific program based on language diagnosis in overcoming learning disabilities of mentally retarded–emotionally disturbed children.* USOE Project No. 6-8375, Grant No. OEG-1-6-068375-1550, May. (See also: A psycholinguistic approach to remediation with retarded-disturbed children. Unpublished doctoral dissertation, Yeshiva University, New York, 1967. *International Dissertation Abstracts, 28,* 1625-A.)

Miracle, B. F. (1966). The linguistic effects of neurological techniques in treating a selected group of retarded readers. In C. H. Delacato (Ed.), *Neurological organization in reading* (pp. 156–179). Springfield, IL: Thomas.

Mokros, H. B., Poznanski, E. O., & Merrick, W. A. (1989). Depression and learning disabilities in children: A test of an hypothesis. *Journal of Learning Disabilities, 22,* 230–233.

Morgan, D. L., & Guilford, A. M. (1984). *Adolescent Language Screening Test.* Austin, TX: PRO-ED.

Mori, K., Murata, T., & Hashimoto, N. (1980). Clinical analysis of arteriovenous malformations in children. *Child's Brain, 6,* 13–25.

Mould, R. E. (1965). An evaluation of the effectiveness of a special program for retarded readers manifesting disturbed visual perception. (Doctoral dissertation, Washington State University). *International Dissertation Abstracts, 26,* 228.

Mueller, M. W., & Dunn, L. M. (1967). *Effects of level #1 of the Peabody Language Development Kits with educable mentally retarded children—An interim report after 4½ months.* IMRID papers and reports. Institute on Mental Retardation and Intellectual Development. George Peabody College, Nashville, TN.

Murray, J. (1976). Is there a role for the teacher in the use of medication for hyperkinetics? *Journal of Learning Disabilities, 9,* 130–135.

Myers, P., & Hammill, D. D. (1969). *Methods for learning disorders* (1st ed.). New York: Wiley.

Myklebust, H. R. (1947). Remedial reading children with impaired hearing. *Training School Bulletin, 43,* 170–176.

Myklebust, H. R. (1952). Aphasia in childhood. *Journal of Exceptional Children, 19,* 9–14.

Myklebust, H. R. (1954). *Auditory disorders in children.* New York: Grune & Stratton.

Myklebust, H. R. (1955). Training aphasic children. *Volta Review, 57,* 149–157.

Myklebust, H. R. (1957a). Aphasia in children. In L. Travis (Ed.), *Handbook of speech pathology* (pp. 503–530). New York: Appleton-Century-Crofts.

Myklebust, H. R. (1957b). Babbling and echolalia in language theory. *Journal of Speech and Hearing Disorders, 22,* 356–360.

Myklebust, H. R. (1963). Psychoneurological learning disorders in children. In S. A. Kirk & W. Becker (Eds.), *Conference on children with minimal brain impairment.* Urbana: University of Illinois Press.

Myklebust, H. R. (1964a). *The psychology of deafness.* New York: Grune & Stratton.

Myklebust, H. R. (1964b). Learning disorders: Psychoneurological disturbances in childhood. *Rehabilitation Literature, 25,* 354–359.

Myklebust, H. R. (1965). *Development and disorders of written language.* New York: Grune & Stratton.

Myklebust, H. R. (1968). Learning disabilities: Definition and overview. In H. R. Myklebust (Ed.), *Progress in learning disabilities* (Vol. I, pp. 1–15). New York: Grune & Stratton.

Myklebust, H. R. (1975). Nonverbal learning disabilities: Assessment and intervention. In H. R. Myklebust (Ed.), *Progress in learning disabilities* (Vol. III). New York: Grune & Stratton.

Myklebust, H. R., & Boshes, B. (1960). Psychoneurological learning disorders in children. *Archives of Pediatrics, 77,* 247–256.

Myklebust, H. R., & Boshes, B. (1969). *Minimal brain damage in children.* U.S. Public Health Service Contract 108-65-142. U.S. Department of Health, Education, and Welfare. Evanston, IL: Northwestern University Publication.

Nagel, D. R., Schumaker, J. B., & Deshler, D. D. (1986). *The FIRST letter mnemonic strategy.* Lawrence: University of Kansas Institute for Research in Learning Disabilities.

Nass, R., & Koch, D. (1987). Temperament differences in toddlers with early unilateral right- and left-brain damage. *Developmental Neuropsychology, 3,* 93–99.

National Advisory Committee on Handicapped Children. (1968). *First Annual Report, Special Education for Handicapped Children.* Washington, DC: U.S. Office of Education, Department of Health, Education, and Welfare.

National Institute of Mental Health (NIMH). (1978). *Caring about kids: helping the hyperactive child.* Rockville, MD: Author.

National Joint Committee on Learning Disabilities. (1981). *Learning disabilities: Issues on definition.* Unpublished manuscript. (Reprinted in *Journal of Learning Disabilities, 20,* 107–108, 1987.)

National Joint Committee on Learning Disabilities. (1989, September 18). *Letter from NJCLD to member organizations.* Topic: Modifications to the NJCLD definition of learning disabilities.

Nebes, R. (1975). Man's so-called "minor" hemisphere. *Educator, 2,* 13–16.

Nelson, N. W. (1979). *Planning individualized speech and language intervention programs.* Tucson, AZ: Communication Skill Builders.

Nelson, R., & Lignugaris/Kraft, B. (1989). Postsecondary education for students with learning disabilities. *Exceptional Children, 56,* 246–265.

Newcomer, P. L. (1978). Competencies for professionals in learning disabilities. *Learning Disability Quarterly, 1,* 69–77.

Newcomer, P. L. (1986). *Standardized Reading Inventory.* Austin, TX: PRO-ED.

Newcomer, P. L. (1989). The new, improved Holy Grail. *Learning Disability Quarterly, 12,* 154–155.

Newcomer, P. L., & Curtis, D. (1984). *Diagnostic Achievement Battery.* Austin, TX: PRO-ED.

Newcomer, P. L., & Hammill, D. D. (1975). ITPA and academic achievement. *The Reading Teacher, 28,* 731–741.

Newcomer, P. L., & Hammill, D. D. (1976). *Psycholinguistics in the schools.* Columbus, OH: Merrill.

Newcomer, P. L., & Hammill, D. D. (1988). *Test of Language Development–2: Primary.* Austin, TX: PRO-ED.

Newcomer, P. L., Larsen, S., & Hammill, D. D. (1975). A response to Esther Minskoff. *Exceptional Children, 42,* 144–148.

Nussbaum, N. L., & Bigler, E. D. (1986). Subgroups of learning disabled children derived from the cluster analysis of neuropsychological data: Neuropsychological profiles and personality/behavioral characteristics. *International Journal of Clinical Neuropsychology, 8,* 82–89.

Nussbaum, N. L., & Bigler, E. D. (1990). *Identification and treatment of attention deficit disorder.* Austin, TX: PRO-ED.

Nussbaum, N. L., Bigler, E. D., & Kocke, W. (1987). Neuropsychologically derived subgroups of learning disabled children: Personality/behavioral dimensions. *Journal of Research and Development in Education, 19,* 57–67.

Nutrition Foundation, National Advisory Committee on Hyperkinesis and Food Additives. (1975). *Report to the Nutrition Foundation.* New York.

Nutrition Foundation. (1976). Diet and hyperactivity: Any connection? *Nutrition Reviews, 34,* 151–158.

O'Connor, C. (1969). Effects of selected physical activities upon motor performance, perceptual performance and academic achievement of first graders. *Perceptual Motor Skills, 29,* 703–709.

O'Donnell, P. A., & Eisenson, J. (1969). Delacato training for reading achievement and visual-motor integration. *Journal of Learning Disabilities, 2,* 441–450.

Offir, C. A. (1974). A slavish reliance on drugs: Are we pushers for our own children? *Psychology Today, 8,* 49.

Ofman, W., & Shaevitz, M. (1963). The kinesthetic method in remedial reading. *Journal of Experimental Education, 31,* 317–320.

O'Leary, K., Pelham, W., Rosenbaum, A., & Price, G. (1976). Behavioral treatment of hyperkinetic children. *Clinical Pediatrics, 15,* 510–515.

Orton, J. (1966). The Orton-Gillingham approach. In J. Money (Ed.), *The disabled reader* (pp. 119–145). Baltimore: Johns Hopkins Press.

Orton, S. (1928). Specific reading disability: Strephosymbolia. *Journal of the American Medical Association, 90,* 1095–1099.

Orton, S. (1937). *Reading, writing and speech problems in children.* New York: Norton.

Orton, S. (1943). Visual functions in strephosymbolia. *Archives of Ophthalmology, 30,* 707–713.

Orton, S. (1989). *Reading, writing, and speech problems in children and selected papers.* Austin, TX: PRO-ED.

Osgood, C. E. (1957). Motivational dynamics of language behavior. In M. Jones (Ed.), *Nebraska symposium on motivation* (pp. 348–424). Lincoln: University of Nebraska Press.

Painter, G. (1966). The effect of a rhythmic and sensory-motor activity program on perceptual motor spatial abilities of kindergarten children. *Exceptional Children, 33,* 113–116.

Palincsar, A. S., & Brown, A. L. (1984). Reciprocal teaching of comprehension-fostering and comprehension-monitoring activities. *Cognition and Instruction, 1,* 117–175.

Palincsar, A. S., Brown, A. L., & Martin, S. M. (1987). Peer interaction in reading comprehension instruction. *Educational Psychologist, 22,* 231–253.

Palincsar, A. S., & Brown, D. A. (1987). Enhancing instructional time through attention to metacognition. *Journal of Learning Disabilities, 20,* 66–75.

Paraskevopoulos, J., & Kirk, S. A. (1969). *The development and psychometric characteristics of the revised Illinois Test of Psycholinguistic Abilities.* Urbana: University of Illinois Press.

Paris, S. G., Lipson, M. Y., & Wixson, K. K. (1983). Becoming a strategic reader. *Contemporary Educational Psychology, 8,* 293–316.

Paris, S. G., & Oka, E. R. (1989). Strategies for comprehending text and coping with reading difficulties. *Learning Disability Quarterly, 12,* 32–42.

Parker, R., Larsen, S., & Hammill, D. D. (1982). The effectiveness of psycholinguistic training: A response to Kavale. *Exceptional Children, 48,* 60–66.

Parks, A. W., Antonoff, S., Drake, C., Skiba, W. F., & Soberman, J. (1987). A survey of programs and services for students with learning disabilities in graduate and professional schools. *Journal of Learning Disabilities, 20,* 181–188.

Passler, M. A., Isaac, W., & Hynd, G. W. (1985). Neuropsychological development of behavior attributed to frontal lobe functioning in children. *Developmental Neuropsychology, 1,* 349–370.

Penfield, W., & Roberts, L. (1959). *Speech and brain mechanims.* Princeton, NJ: Princeton University Press.

Piaget, J. (1952). *The origins of intelligence in children.* New York: Norton.

Piaget, J. (1953). How children form mathematical concepts. *Scientific American, 185,* 74–79.

Pirozzolo, F. J., & Wittrock, M. C. (1982). *Neuropsychological and cognitive processes in reading.* New York: Academic Press.

Polloway, E. A., Patton, J. R., Payne, J. S., & Payne, R. A. (1989). *Strategies for teaching learners with special needs.* Columbus, OH: Merrill.

Poplin, M. S. (1988a). The reductionist fallacy in learning disabilities: Replicating the past by reducing the present. *Journal of Learning Disabilities, 21,* 389–400.

Poplin, M. S. (1988b). Holistic/constructivist principles of the teaching/learning process: Implications for the field of learning disabilities. *Journal of Learning Disabilities, 21,* 401–416.

Poplin, M. S. (1989). Reply to Vaughn [Letter to the editor]. *Journal of Learning Disabilities, 22,* 202–203.

Powers, H. (1973). Dietary measures to improve behavior and achievement. *Academic Therapy, 9,* 201–215.

Prall, R. C. (1964). In S. Rappaport, *Childhood aphasia and brain damage.* Narberth, PA: Livingston.

Pressley, M. (1986). The relevance of the good strategy user model to the teaching of mathematics. *Educational Psychologist, 21,* 139–161.

Pressley, M., Symons, S., Snyder, B. L., & Cariglia-Bull, T. (1989). Strategy instruction research comes of age. *Learning Disability Quarterly, 12,* 16–30.

Pryzwanski, W. W. (1972). Effects of perceptual-motor training and manuscript writing on reading readiness skills in kindergarten. *Journal of Educational Psychology, 63,* 110–115.

Pugh, B. (1947). *Steps in language development.* Washington, DC: Volta Bureau.

Public Law 94-142. (1975). (The Education of All Handicapped Children Act of 1975).

Pulliam, R. A., & Clinical Assistants. (1945). Delta State Teachers College, Cleveland, MS. Indented word cards as a sensori-motor aid in vocabulary development. *Peabody Journal of Education, 23,* 38–42.

Rapp, D. J. (1978). Does diet affect hyperactivity? *Journal of Learning Disorders, 11,* 383–389.

Rappaport, S. R. (1966). Personality factors teachers need for relationship structure. In W. M. Cruickshank (Ed.), *The teacher of brain-injured children.* Syracuse, NY: Syracuse University Press.

Raven, R., & Strubing, H. (1968). The effect of visual perception units on achievement in a science unit. *American Educational Research Journal, 5,* 333–342.

Reid, D. K. (1988). Reflections on the pragmatics of a paradigm shift. *Journal of Learning Disabilities, 21,* 417–420.

Reid, D. K., & Hresko, W. (1981). *A cognitive approach to learning disabilities.* Austin, TX: PRO-ED.

Reid, D. K., Hresko, W., & Hammill, D. D. (1989). *Test of Early Reading Ability–2.* Austin, TX: PRO-ED.

Reisman, F. K. (1977). *Diagnostic teaching of elementary school mathematics: Methods and content.* Chicago: Rand McNally College Publishing.

Reisman, F. K. (1978). *A guide to diagnostic teaching of arithmetic.* Columbus, OH: Merrill.

Reisman, F. K., & Kauffman, S. H. (1980). *Teaching mathematics to children with special needs.* Columbus, OH: Merrill.

Reitan, R. (1964). Relationships between neurological and psychological variables and their implications for reading instruction. In H. Robinson (Ed.), *Meeting individual differences in reading.* Chicago: University of Chicago Press.

Reynolds, M. C. (1988). A reaction to the JLD special series on the Regular Education Initiative. *Journal of Learning Disabilities, 21,* 352–356.

Rice, D. M. (1967). The effects of visual perception techniques with cerebral palsied individuals functioning at a mentally retarded level. *Dissertation Abstracts, 27,* 3732-A.

Rie, H., Rice, E., Stewart, S., & Ambuel, J. (1976). Effects of methylphenidate on underachieving children. *Journal of Consulting and Clinical Psychology, 44,* 250–260.

Rie, H., & Rie, E. D. (1980). *Handbook of minimal brain dysfunctions.* New York: Wiley-Interscience.

Ritz, W. C., (1970). The effect of two instructional programs on the attainment of reading readiness, visual perception, and science skills of kindergarten children. *Dissertation Abstracts, 30,* 1082-A.

Roach, E. G. (1966). Evaluation of an experimental program of perceptual-motor training with slow readers. In J. A. Figurel (Ed.), *Vistas in reading,* IRA, Conference Proceedings II, 446–450.

Robbins, M. P. (1966). A study of the validity of Delacato's theory of neurological organization. *Exceptional Children, 32,* 517–523.

Robbins, M. P., & Glass, G. V. (1968). The Doman-Delacato rationale: A critical analysis. In J. Hellmuth (Ed.), *Educational therapy* (Vol. II). Seattle, WA: Special Child.

Roberts, R. W., & Coleman, J. C. (1958). An investigation of the role of visual and kinesthetic factors in reading failures. *Journal of Educational Research, 51,* 445–451.

Roberts, R. J., Varney, N. R., Reinarz, S. J., & Parkins, R. A. (1988). CT asymmetrics in developmentally dyslexic adults. *Developmental Neuropsychology, 4,* 231–237.

Robinson, R. G., Kubos, K. L., Starr, L. B., Rao, K., & Price, T. R. (1984). Mood disorders in stroke patients: Importance of location of lesion. *Brain, 107,* 81–93.

Robinson, R. G., & Szetela, B. (1981). Mood change following left hemispheric brain injury. *Annals of Neurology, 9,* 447–453.

Rogers, J. (1971). Drug abuse: Just what the doctor ordered. *Psychology Today, 5,* 16–24.

Rood, M. S. (1954). Neurophysiologic reactions as a basis for physical therapy. *The Physical Therapy Review, 34,* 444–449.

Rood, M. S. (1962). The use of sensory receptors to activate, facilitate, and inhibit motor response, autonomic and somatic, in developmental sequence. In C. Sattley (Ed.), *Approaches to the treatment of patients with neuromuscular dysfunction.* Dubuque, IA: Brown.

Rooney, K. J., & Hallahan, D. P. (1988). The effects of self-monitoring on adult behavior and student independence. *Learning Disabilities Research, 3,* 88–93.

Rooney, K. J., Hallahan, D. P., & Lloyd, J. W. (1984). Self-recording of attention by learning disabled students in the regular classroom. *Journal of Learning Disabilities, 17,* 360–364.

Rose, T. (1978). The functional relationship between artificial food colors and hyperactivity. *Journal of Applied Behavior Analysis, 11,* 439–446.

Rosen, C. L. (1966). An experimental study of visual perceptual training and reading achievement in first grade. *Perceptual and Motor Skills, 22,* 979–986.

Rosenberg, S. (1970). Problems of language development in the retarded. In H. C. Haywood (Ed.), *Socio-cultural aspects of mental retardation* (pp. 203–216). New York: Appleton-Century-Crofts.

Rosenshine, B. V. (1983). Teaching functions in instructional programs. *Elementary School Journal, 83,* 335–352.

Ross, B. (1988). Executive Director of The Frostig School. (Personal communication, March 3).

Ross, E. D. (1985). Modulation of affect and nonverbal communication by the right hemisphere. In M. M. Mesulam (Ed.), *Principles of behavioral neurology* (pp. 239–257). Philadelphia: F. A. Davis.

Rossi, A. O. (1972). Genetics of learning disabilities. *Journal of Learning Disabilities, 5,* 489–496.

Rost, K. J. (1967). Academic achievement of brain injured and hyperactive children in isolation. *Exceptional Children, 34,* 125–126.

Rourke, B. P. (1987). Syndrome of nonverbal learning disabilities: The final common pathway of white-matter disease/dysfunction. *The Clinical Neuropsychologist, 1,* 209–234.

Rourke, B. P. (1989). *Nonverbal learning disabilities.* New York: Guilford.

Rourke, B. P., Bakker, D. J., Fisk, J. L., & Strang, J. D. (1983). *Child neuropsychology.* New York: Guilford.

Rourke, B. P., Young, G. C., & Leenaars, A. A. (1989). A childhood learning disability that predisposes those afflicted to adolescent and adult depression and suicide risk. *Journal of Learning Disabilities, 22,* 169–175.

Rumelhart, D. E. (1977). Understanding and summarizing brief stories. In D. Laberge & S. J. Samuels (Eds.), *Basic processes in reading: Perception and comprehension* (pp. 265–304). Hilldale, NJ: Lawrence Erlbaum.

Rutherford, W. L. (1964). The effects of a perceptual-motor training program on the performance of kindergarten pupils on Metropolitan Reading Tests. *Dissertation Abstracts, 25,* 4583–4584.

Rutter, M. (1982). Syndromes attributed to "minimal brain dysfunction" in childhood. *American Journal of Psychiatry, 139,* 21–33.

Rutter, M. (1983). *Developmental neuropsychiatry.* New York: Guilford.

Ryan, P. J. (1973). *An experiment in the remediation of reading retardation of first-through-sixth graders by means of auditory, visual, and/or motoric perceptual therapy.* Final report for Project No. 43-69384-35-26424. Bureau of Professional Development, Division for Compensatory Education, California State Department of Education.

Sachar, E. J. (1981). Psychobiology of affective disorders. In E. R. Kandel & J. H. Schwartz (Eds.), *Principles of neural science* (pp. 611–619). New York: Elsevier.

Salvia, J., & Ysseldyke, J. E. (1988). *Assessment in special and remedial education.* Boston: Houghton-Mifflin.

Samuels, S. J. (1987). Information processing abilities and reading. *Journal of Learning Disabilities, 20,* 18–22.

Sartain, H. W. (1976). Instruction of disabled learners: A reading perspective. *Journal of Learning Disabilities, 9,* 489–497.

Satz, P. (1976). Cerebral dominance and reading disability: An old problem revisited. In R. Knights & D. Bakker (Eds.), *The neuropsychology of learning disorders.* Baltimore: University Park Press.

Scheiber, B., & Talpers, J. (1987). *Unlocking potential: College and other choices for learning disabled people.* Bethesda, MD: Adler & Adler.

Schilder, P. (1933). The vestibular apparatus in neurosis and psychosis. *Journal of Nervous and Mental Disease, 78,* 139–164.

Schmitt, B. D. (1977). Letter to the editor. *Pediatrics, 60,* 387–394.

Schrag, P., & Divoky, D. (1975). *The myth of the hyperactive child.* New York: Random House.

Schuell, H. (1970). Aphasia in adults. In *Human communication and its disorders: An overview.* A report of the Subcommittee on Human Communication and Its Disorders, National Institute of Neurological Diseases and Stroke, U.S. Department of Health, Education, and Welfare, Bethesda, MD.

Schuell, H., Jenkins, J. J., & Jimenez-Pabon, E. (1964). *Aphasia in adults.* New York: Haeber Medical Division, Harper.

Schumaker, J. B., Denton, P. H., & Deshler, D. D. (1984). *The paraphrasing strategy.* Lawrence: The University of Kansas Institute for Research in Learning Disabilities.

Schumaker, J. B., Deshler, D. D., Alley, G. R., & Warner, M. M. (1983). Toward the development of an intervention model for learning disabled adolescents. The University of Kansas Institute. *Exceptional Education Quarterly, 4,* 45–74.

Schumaker, J., Deshler, D., Alley, G., Warner, M., & Denton, P. (1982). Multipass: A learning strategy for improving reading comprehension. *Learning Disability Quarterly, 5,* 295–304.

Schumaker, J. B., Deshler, D. D., & Ellis, E. S. (1986). Intervention issues related to the education of LD adolescents. In B. Y. L. Wong & J. K. Torgesen (Eds.), *Psychological and educational perspectives and learning disabilities* (pp. 329–365). New York: Academic Press.

Sedlak, R. A., & Weener, P. (1973). Review of research on the Illinois Test of Psycholinguistic Abilities. In L. Mann & D. A. Sabatino (Eds.), *The first review of special education* (pp. 113–164). New York: Grune & Stratton, JSE Press Division.

Semmel, M. I. (1960). Comparison of teacher ratings of brain-injured and mongoloid severely retarded (trainable) children attending community day-school classes. *American Journal of Mental Deficiency, 64,* 963–971.

Semmel, M. I. (1980). Comparison of teacher ratings of brain-injured and mongoloid severely retarded (trainable) children attending community day-school classes. *American Journal of Mental Deficiency, 64,* 963–971.

Shafto, F., & Sulzbacher, S. (1977). Comparing treatment tactics with a hyperactive preschool child: Stimulant medication and programmed teacher intervention. *Journal of Applied Behavior Analysis, 10,* 13–20.

Shaywitz, S. E., & Shaywitz, B. A. (1988). Attention deficit disorder: Current perspectives. In J. F. Kavanaugh & T. J. Truss (Eds.), *Learning disabilities: Proceedings of the national conference.* Parkton, MD: York Press.

Sheinker, A., Sheinker, J. M., & Stevens, L. J. (1988). Cognitive strategies for teaching the mildly handicapped. In E. L. Meyen, G. A. Vergason, & R. J. Whelan (Eds.), *Effective instructional strategies for exceptional children* (pp. 194–215). Denver: Love.

Sherk, J. K. (1968). A study of the effects of a program of visual perception on the progress of retarded readers. *Dissertation Abstracts, 28,* 4392-A.

Sherrington, C. S. (1906). *The integrative action of the nervous system.* New Haven: Yale University Press.

Sherrington, C. S. (1955). *Man on his nature.* Garden City, NY: Doubleday.

Sieben, R. L. (1977). Controversial medical treatments of learning disabilities. *Academic Therapy, 13,* 133–148.

Sievers, D. J. (1955). *Development and standardization of a test of psycholinguistic growth in preschool children.* Doctoral dissertation, University of Illinois.

Silberberg, N., Iverson, I., & Goins, J. (1973). Which remedial method works best? *Journal of Learning Disabilities, 6,* 547–556.

Silbert, J., Carnine, D., & Stein, M. (1990). *Direct instruction mathematics.* Columbus, OH: Merrill.

Silvaroli, N. J. (1976). *Classroom Reading Inventory.* New York: Barnes & Noble.

Silver, A. A. (1965). In *Symposium: Perceptual training for children with learning difficulties.* New Jersey Association for Brain Injured Children et al.

Silver, L. B. (1971). Familial patterns in children with neurologically-based learning disabilities. *Journal of Learning Disabilities, 4,* 349–358.

Silver, L. B. (1987). The "magic cure": A review of the current controversial approaches for treating learning disabilities. *Journal of Learning Disabilities, 20,* 498–504.

Silver Burdett Spelling. (1986). Morristown, NJ: Silver Burdett. (Series unauthored.)

Silverman, S. R. (1967, Spring). Editorial in *News Notes.* Central Institute for the Deaf, Saint Louis, MO. (School newspaper obtained from Central Institute in Saint Louis, MO.)

Simpkins, K. W. (1970). Effect of the Frostig program for the development of visual perception on the readiness of kindergarten children. *Dissertation Abstracts, 30,* 4286-A.

Siperstein, G. N. (1988). Students with learning disabilities in college: The need for a programmatic approach to critical transitions. *Journal of Learning Disabilities, 21,* 431–436.

Skinner, B. F. (1957). *Verbal behavior.* New York: Appleton-Century-Crofts.

Skinner, B. F. (1958). Teaching machines. *Science, 128,* 969–977.

Skinner, B. F. (1968). *The technology of teaching.* Englewood Cliffs, NJ: Prentice-Hall.

Slobin, D. I., & Welsh, C. A. (1973). Elicited imitation as a research tool in developmental psycholinguistics. In C. A. Ferguson & D. I. Slobin (Eds.), *Child language: A book of readings* (pp. 235–246). Englewood Cliffs, NJ: Prentice-Hall.

Smith, C. R. (1985). Learning disabilities: Past and present. *Journal of Learning Disabilities, 18,* 513–517.

Smith, D. E., & Carrigan, P. M. (1959). *The nature of reading disability.* New York: Harcourt, Brace, & World.

Smith, F. (1979). *Reading without nonsense.* New York: Teachers College Press, Columbia University.

Smith, J. O. (1962). Group language development for educable mental retardates. *Exceptional Children, 29,* 95–101.

Sowell, V., Parker, R., Poplin, M., & Larsen, S. (1979). Effects of psycholinguistic training on improving psycholinguistic skills. *Learning Disability Quarterly, 2,* 69–77.

Spache, G. D. (1981). *Diagnostic Reading Scales.* Monterey, CA: California Test Bureau.

Spalding, R. B., & Spalding, W. T. (1986). *The writing road to reading.* New York: Morrow.

Spradlin, J. E., Cromwell, R. L., & Foshee, J. G. (1960). Studies in activity level III—Auditory stimulation. *American Journal of Mental Deficiency, 64,* 754–757.

Spreen, O. (1989). The relationship between learning disability, emotional disorders, and neuropsychology: Some results and observations. *Journal of Clinical and Experimental Neuropsychology, 11,* 117–140.

Spring, C., & Sandoval, J. (1976). Food additives and hyperkinesis: A critical evaluation of the evidence. *Journal of Learning Disabilities, 9,* 560–569.

Starkstein, S. E., & Robinson, R. G. (1989). Affective disorders and cerebral vascular disease. *British Journal of Psychiatry, 154,* 170–182.

Stern, C., & Stern, M. B. (1971). *Children discover arithmetic.* New York: Harper & Row.

Stick, S. (1976). The speech pathologist and handicapped learners. *Journal of Learning Disabilities, 9,* 509–519.

Stone, M., & Pielstick, N. L. (1969). Effectiveness of Delacato treatment with kindergarten children. *Psychology in the Schools, 6,* 63–68.

Strang, R., McCullough, C., & Traxler, A. (1967). *The improvement of reading.* New York: McGraw-Hill.

Straughn, C., & Colby, M. (1984). *Lovejoy's college guide for the learning disabled.* New York: Monarch.

Strauss, A. A., & Kephart, N. C. (1955). *Psychopathology and education of the brain-injured child* (Vol. II). New York: Grune & Stratton.

Strauss, A. A. & Kephart, N. C. (1989). Progress in theory and clinic. In A. A. Strauss, L. E. Lehtinen, & N. C. Kephart, *Psychopathology and education of the brain-injured child.* Austin, TX: PRO-ED.

Strauss, A. A., & Lehtinen, L. (1947). *Psychopathology and education of the brain-injured child* (Vol. I). New York: Grune & Stratton.

Strauss, A. A., & Lehtinen, L. E. (1989). Fundamentals and treatment of brain-injured children. In A. A. Strauss, L. E. Lehtinen, & N. C. Kephart, *Psychopathology and education of the brain-injured child.* Austin, TX: PRO-ED.

Strong, J. M. C. (1983). *Language facilitation: A complete cognitive therapy program.* Austin, TX: PRO-ED.

Sullivan, J. (1972). The effects of Kephart's perceptual motor-training on a reading clinic sample. *Journal of Learning Disabilities, 5,* 545–551.

Sulzbacher, S. (1973). Psychotropic medication with children: An evaluation of procedural biases in results of reported studies. *Pediatrics, 51,* 315–317.

Sulzbacher, S. I. (1975). The learning-disabled or hyperactive child: Diagnosis and treatment. *Journal of the American Medical Association, 234,* 841–938.

Suydam, M. N., & Osborne, A. (1977). *The status of pre-college science, mathematics, and social science education: 1955–1975. Vol II: Mathematics education.* Columbus: Ohio State University Center for Science and Mathematics Education.

Swanson, H. L. (1987). Information processing theory and learning disabilities: An overview. *Journal of Learning Disabilities, 20,* 3–7.

Swanson, H. L. (1989). Strategy instruction: Overview of principles and procedures for effective use. *Learning Disability Quarterly, 12,* 3–14.

Talkington, L. W. (1968). Frostig visual perceptual training with low-ability-level retarded. *Perceptual and Motor Skills, 27,* 505–506.

Tarver, S. G., Hallahan, D. P., & Kauffman, J. M. (1976). Verbal rehearsal and selective attention in children with learning disabilities: A developmental lag. *Journal of Experimental Child Psychology, 22,* 375–385.

Tarver, S., & Maggiore, R. (1979). Cognitive development in learning disabled boys. *Learning Disability Quarterly, 2,* 78–84.

Taylor, H. G. (1987). Childhood sequelae of early neurological disorders: A contemporary perspective. *Developmental Neuropsychology, 3,* 153–164.

Texas Education Agency. (1985). *A manual for instructional leadership training.*

Torgesen, J. K. (1977). Memorization processes in reading-disabled children, *Journal of Educational Psychology, 69,* 571–578.

Torgesen, J. K. (1986). Learning disabilities theory: Its current state and future prospects. *Journal of Learning Disabilities, 19,* 399–407.

Torgesen, J. K., & Goldman, T. (1977). Verbal rehearsal and short-term memory in reading-disabled children. *Child Development, 48,* 56–60.

Torgesen, J. K., & Houck, D. G. (1980). Processing deficiencies of learning disabled children who perform poorly on the digit span test. *Journal of Educational Psychology, 72,* 141–160.

Torgesen, J. K., Murphy, H. A., & Ivey, C. (1979). The influence of an orienting task on the memory performance of children with reading problems. *Journal of Learning Disabilities, 12,* 396–401.

Toronto, A. S. (1973). *Screening Test of Spanish Grammar.* Evanston, IL: Northwestern University Press.

Toubin, A. (1960). *The pathology of cerebral palsy.* Springfield, IL: Thomas.

Towbin, A. (1978). Cerebral dysfunctions related to perinatal organic damage. Clinical neuropathologic correlations. *Journal of Abnormal Psychology, 87,* 617–635.

Tranel, D., Hall, L. E., Olson, S., & Tranel, N. N. (1987). Evidence for a right-hemisphere developmental learning disability. *Developmental Neuropsychology, 3,* 113–127.

Turner, R. V., & Fisher, M. D. (1970). The effects of a perceptual-motor training program upon the readiness and perceptual development of culturally disadvantaged kindergarten children. (ERIC Document Reproduction Service No. ED 041 663)

U.S. Office of Education (1977). Procedures for evaluating specific learning disabilities. *Federal Register, 42,* 65082–65085.

van Duyne, H. J. (1976). Effects of stimulant drug therapy on learning behaviors in hyperactive/minimal brain damaged children. In R. Knights & D. Bakker (Eds.), *The neuropsychology of learning disorders* (pp. 381–387). Baltimore: University Park Press.

Vellutino, F. R. (1979). *Dyslexia: Theory and research.* Cambridge, MA: MIT Press.

Vellutino, F. R., Steger, B. M., Moyer, S. C., Harding, C. J., & Niles, J. A. (1977). Has the perceptual deficit hypothesis led us astray? *Journal of Learning Disabilities, 10,* 375–385.

Vernon, M. (1971). *Reading and its difficulties.* London: Cambridge University Press.

Vidaurri, O., Cano, E., & Schmidt, B. (1973). *An individualized curriculum.* From a report to the Bureau of Education for the Handicapped on Early Childhood Education Program for the Handicapped in Edgewood Independent School District, San Antonio, TX.

Vivian, M. (1966). An experiment with the concept of neurological organization. In C. H. Delacato (Ed.), *Neurological organization and reading* (pp. 122–130). Springfield, IL: Thomas.

Vogel, S. A. (1975). *Syntactic abilities in normal and dyslexic children.* Baltimore: University Park Press.

Wade, M. G. (1976). Effect of methylphenidate on motor skill acquisition of hyperactive children. *Journal of Learning Disabilities, 9,* 443–447.

Wallace, E. E., Taylor, W. D., Fay, L., Kucera, H., & Gonzalez, G. (1988). *Riverside spelling.* Chicago: Riverside.

Wallace, G. (1976). Interdisciplinary efforts in learning disabilities: Issues and recommendations. *Journal of Learning Disabilities, 9,* 520–525.

Wallace, G., Cohen, S., & Polloway, E. A. (1987). *Language arts: Teaching exceptional students.* Austin, TX: PRO-ED.

Wallace, G., & Kauffman, J. (1986). *Teaching students with learning and behavior problems.* Columbus, OH: Merrill.

Wallace, G., & Larsen, S. C. (1978). *Educational assessment of learning problems.* Boston: Allyn & Bacon.

Wang, M. C., Reynolds, M. C., & Walberg, H. J. (1986). Rethinking special education. *Educational Leadership, 44*(1), 26–31.

Wang, M. C., & Walberg, H. J. (1988). Four fallacies of segregationism. *Exceptional Children, 55,* 128–137.

Warner, M. M., Schumaker, J. B., Alley, G. R., & Deshler, D. D. (1980). Learning disabled adolescents in public schools: Are they different from low achievers? *Exceptional Education Quarterly, 1,* 27–56.

Waugh, R. P. (1978). Review of ITPA. In O. K. Buros (Ed.), *The eighth mental measurements yearbook* (Vol. I, p. 432). Highland Park, NJ: Gryphon.

Wechsler, D. (1974). *Wechsler Intelligence Scale for Children.* San Antonio, TX: Psychological Corp.

Weinberg, W. A., Rutman, J., Sullivan, L., Penick, E. C., & Dietz, S. G. (1973). Depression in children referred to an educational diagnostic center: Diagnosis and treatment. *Behavioral Pediatrics, 83,* 1065–1072.

Weintraub, S., & Mesulam, M.-M. (1983). Developmental learning disabilities of the right hemisphere: Emotional, interpersonal, and cognitive components. *Archives of Neurology, 40,* 463–468.

Weissenburger, F., & Loney, J. (1977). Hyperkinesis in the classroom: If cerebral stimulants are the last resort, what is the first resort? *Journal of Learning Disabilities, 10,* 339–348.

Welsh, M. C., & Pennington, B. F. (1988). Assessing frontal lobe functioning in children: Views from developmental psychology. *Developmental Neuropsychology, 4,* 199–230.

Wepman, J. M. (1960). Auditory discrimination, speech and reading. *Elementary School Journal, 60,* 245–247.

Wepman, J. M. (1973). *Auditory Discrimination Test.* Los Angeles: Western Psychological Services.

Wepman, J. M., Jones, L. V., Bock, R. D., & Van Pelt, D. (1960). Studies in aphasia: Background and theoretical formulations. *Journal of Speech and Hearing Disorders, 25,* 323–332.

West, F., Idol, L., & Cannon, G. (1989). *Collaboration in the schools.* Austin, TX: PRO-ED.

Whalen, C., Henker, B., Collins, B., Finck, D., & Dotemoto, S. (1979). A social ecology of hyperactive boys: Medication effects in structured classroom environments. *Journal of Applied Behavior Analysis, 12,* 65–81.

Wiederholt, J. L. (1974). Historical perspectives on the education of the learning disabled. In L. Mann & D. A. Sabatino (Eds.), *The second review of special education* (pp. 103–152). Austin, TX: PRO-ED.

Wiederholt, J. L. (1978a). Adolescents with learning disabilities: The problem in perspective. In L. Mann, L. Goodman, & J. L. Wiederholt (Eds.), *Teaching the learning-disabled adolescent.* Boston: Houghton-Mifflin.

Wiederholt, J. L. (1978b). Review of ITPA. In O. K. Buros (Ed.), *The eighth mental measurements yearbook* (Vol. I, pp. 431–432). Highland Park, NJ: Gryphon.

Wiederholt, J. L. (1985). *Formal Reading Inventory.* Austin, TX: PRO-ED.

Wiederholt, J. L. (1989). Restructuring special education services. The past, the present, the future. *Learning Disability Quarterly, 12,* 181–191.

Wiederholt, J. L., & Bryant, B. (1986). *Gray Oral Reading Test.* Austin, TX: PRO-ED.

Wiederholt, J. L., & Bryant, B. (1987). *Assessing the reading abilities and instructional needs of students.* Austin, TX: PRO-ED.

Wiederholt, J. L., & Hammill, D. D. (1971). Use of the Frostig-Horne visual perceptual program in the urban school. *Psychology in the Schools, 8,* 268–274.

Wiederholt, J. L., Hammill, D. D., & Brown, V. (1983). *The resource teacher* (2nd ed.). Boston: Allyn & Bacon.

Wiig, E. M. (1987). *Clinical Evaluation of Language Functions.* San Antonio, TX: Psychological Corp.

Will, M. (1986). Educating children with learning problems: A shared responsibility. *Exceptional Children, 52,* 411–415.

Williams, E. & Shuard, N. (1970). *Primary mathematics today.* London: Longman Group.

Wimsatt, W. R. (1967). The effects of sensory-motor training on the learning abilities of grade school children. *Dissertation Abstracts, 68,* 347-A.

Wiseman, D. E. (1965a). The effects of an individualized remedial program on mentally retarded children with psycholinguistic disabilities. Unpublished doctoral dissertation, University of Illinois, Urbana. *Dissertation Abstracts International, 26,* 5143.

Wiseman, D. E. (1965b). A classroom procedure for identifying and remediating language problems. *Mental Retardation, 3,* 20–24.

Wissink, J. F. (1972). *A procedure for the identification of children with learning disabilities.* Unpublished doctoral dissertation, University of Arizona, Tucson.

Witelson, S. F. (1985). On hemispheric specialization and cerebral plasticity from birth: Mark II. In C. Best (Ed.), *Hemispheric function and collaboration in the child.* New York: Academic Press.

Wong, B. Y. L. (1985). Metacognition and learning disabilities. In T. G. Waller, D. Forrest, & E. MacKinnon (Eds.), *Metacognition, cognition, and human performance: Vol 2: Instructional practices* (pp. 137–180). New York: Academic Press.

Wong, B. Y. L. (1986). Problems and issues in the definition of learning disabilities. In J. K. Torgesen & B. Y. L. Wong (Eds.), *Psychological and educational perspectives on learning disabilities* (pp. 1–22). Orlando, FL: Academic Press.

Woodcock, R. W. (1978). *Woodcock-Johnson Psycho-Educational Battery.* Allen, TX: DLM/Teaching Resources.

Woodcock, R. W. (1984). A response to some questions raised about the Woodcock-Johnson: II. Efficacy of the aptitude clusters. *School Psychology Review, 13,* 355–362.

Woodcock, R. W. (1988). *Woodcock Reading Mastery Tests.* Circle Pines, MN: American Guidance Service.

Woodcock, R. W., & Clark, C. (1969). *Peabody rebus reading program.* Circle Pines, MN: American Guidance Service.

Wulbert, M., & Dries, R. (1977). The relative efficacy of methylphenidate (Ritalin) and behavior modification techniques in the treatment of a hyperactive child. *Journal of Applied Behavior Analysis, 10,* 21–31.

Yeni-Komshian, G. H., Isenberg, D., & Goldberg, H. (1975). Cerebral dominance and reading disability: Left visual field deficit in poor readers. *Neuropsychologia, 13,* 83–94.

Ysseldyke, J. E. (1973). Diagnostic-prescriptive teaching: The search for aptitude-treatment interactions. In L. Mann & D. Sabatino (Eds.), *The first review of special education (Vol. I).* Austin, TX: PRO-ED.

Ysseldyke, J. E., Algozzine, B., Shinn, M. R., & McGue, M. (1982). Similarities and differences between low achievers and students classified learning disabled. *The Journal of Special Education, 16,* 73–86.

Ysseldyke, J. E., O'Sullivan, P. J., Thurlow, M. L., & Christenson, S. L. (1989). Qualitative differences in reading and math instruction received by handicapped students. *Remedial and Special Education, 10,* 14–20.

Zigler, E. (1962). Social deprivation in familial and organic retardates. *Psychological Reports, 10,* 370.

AUTHOR INDEX

SUBJECT INDEX

About the Authors

Donald D. Hammill worked in the Texas Public Schools for 5 years as a teacher and a speech therapist before earning his doctorate degree from The University of Texas. Dr. Hammill has served on the teaching staffs of Wichita State University and Temple University. In 1976–77, he was president of the Council for Learning Disabilities. He is author of 60 articles published in journals having peer review. He has written eight textbooks and monographs. In addition, he has participated in the development of 16 diagnostic, norm-referenced assessment tests, including the *Detroit Tests of Learning Aptitude* (DTLA-2), *Test of Language Development* (TOLD), and the *Test of Written Language* (TOWL). Presently his time is split between two positions. He is president of PRO-ED, Inc., a company that specializes in psychoeducational testing instruments, curricular materials, and professional books in the area of special and remedial education. He is also a trustee of the Donald D. Hammill Foundation, a nonprofit agency that funds fellowships, research, and symposia in all areas pertaining to handicapped individuals.

Patricia I. Myers was born in Goodland, Kansas, and reared in Georgia and Texas. She graduated from Gonzales High School in Gonzales, Texas, and received her baccalaureate degree in speech and drama from Texas College of Arts and Industries. A master's in speech pathology and a doctorate in educational psychology (special education) were awarded to her by The University of Texas at Austin. She has worked as a public school speech pathologist and has taught at Louisiana State University in New Orleans and Our Lady of the Lake College in San Antonio. After serving 3 years as the chair of the Department of Communication Disorders at Our Lady of the Lake, Dr. Myers spent 15 years at Education Service Center, Region 20, as director of special education. Although presently retired, she teaches speech pathology courses part-time at Our Lady of the Lake. In addition to various community endeavors, Dr. Myers's major professional interests lie in the areas of children's and adults' language disorders, motor speech disorders, and communication-based learning disabilities.

Laurie U. deBettencourt is assistant professor, Department of Counseling and Specialized Educational Development, School of Education at the University of North Carolina at Greensboro. She has a background in teaching mentally retarded, learning disabled, and emotionally disturbed students in public and private schools. Dr. deBettencourt received her PhD at the University of Virginia and worked several years at the University of Pittsburgh. Her research interests include strategy training, curriculum-based measurement procedures, and secondary special education. Her work with exceptional individuals has been published extensively.

Erin D. Bigler is an adjunct professor of psychology at The University of Texas at Austin and in private practice at the Austin Neurological Clinic. He received his PhD in psychology from Brigham Young University in 1974. Dr. Bigler is a diplomate in clinical neuropsychology from the American Board of Professional Psychology and the current president (1989–90) of the National Academy of Neuropsychology. He is the author of *Diagnostic Clinical Neuropsychology* (University of Texas Press), which is in its second edition, and has also edited two texts: *Traumatic Brain Injury* (PRO-ED, 1989) and *Neuropsychological Function and Brain Imaging* (Plenum Press). He has authored over 150 research articles in the area of neuropsychology. He is the associate editor of *Archives of Clinical Psychology* and on the editorial board of the *Journal of Learning Disabilities, International Journal of Clinical Neuropsychology,* and *Neuropsychological Review.*

YORK COLLEGE OF PENNSYLVANIA 17403

0 2003 0030871 1

LC 4704 .M93 1990
Myers, Patricia I., 1929-
Learning disabilities